Cloud Data Centers and Cost Modeling

Cloud Data Centers and Cost Modeling

A Complete Guide To Planning, Designing and Building a Cloud Data Center

Caesar Wu

Rajkumar Buyya

AMSTERDAM • BOSTON • HEIDELBERG • LONDON
NEW YORK • OXFORD • PARIS • SAN DIEGO
SAN FRANCISCO • SINGAPORE • SYDNEY • TOKYO

Morgan Kaufmann is an imprint of Elsevier

Acquiring Editor: Todd Green
Editorial Project Manager: Lindsay Lawrence
Project Manager: Punithavathy Govindaradjane
Designer: Matthew Limbert

Morgan Kaufmann is an imprint of Elsevier
225 Wyman Street, Waltham, MA 02451, USA

ISBN: 978-0-12-801413-4

British Library Cataloguing-in-Publication Data
A catalogue record for this book is available from the British Library

Library of Congress Cataloging-in-Publication Data
A catalog record for this book is available from the Library of Congress

For information on all Morgan Kaufmann publications
visit our website at www.mkp.com

Working together
to grow libraries in
developing countries

www.elsevier.com • www.bookaid.org

Contents

PART I   CLOUD COMPUTING FOUNDATIONS AND BUSINESS REQUIREMENTS

PART III   CLOUD INFRASTRUCTURE AND MANAGEMENT

PART IV   CLOUD COMPUTING COST MODELS AND FRAMEWORK

PART V   CLOUD STRATEGY AND CRITICAL DECISION MAKING

Preface

How can we measure the sky? This question sometimes refers to how to measure the cost of cloud computing. For many people, it is a very challenging and tough question. And yet, many C-class senior executives (CEO, CFO, and CIO), stakeholders, and cloud investors would not only want to know "how" (cost model assumptions and calculations), but also want to know "why" (logic behind these assumptions).

Why is this so important? The simple answer is it is too big to be ignored. We have heard many stories about how some decision makers just throw big money into cloud projects without proper understanding of cloud technology and expect to catch up to the "wind" (win). This book will lay out the basic concepts and foundation of cloud computing and data center facilities and then provide tools and practical approaches for decision makers to make the right strategic investment decisions. It will help the decision maker to not only rely on "gut feelings" or previous experiences but also count on the scientific method.

One of the goals of this book is to establish a practical framework to enable IT executives to make a rational choice when they are facing a multimillion-dollar investment decision for a cloud project, which is to determine whether IT workloads should stay local or fly to a cloud. (inhouse or cloud computing).

Almost five years ago, this challenging task was assigned to us because a senior IT executive wanted to justify a multimillion investment decision that he had already made but he was not sure whether the decision was a rational choice or not. The original idea of this exercise was to check his intuition, estimate the strategic value, communicate with all the stakeholders, and change the scope of the cloud investment project if necessary.

At that time, many trial projects of cloud computing, server virtualization, and software multitenancy had just taken off. Various companies made different investment decisions in order to test the water or get a foothold on the cloud market.

With these intentions in our mind plus many years' practical experience in cost modeling of utilities and grid computing, hosting services management, network design, construction, operation, lifecycles, and service delivery, we elicited eight basic questions about this cost modeling exercise:

- What is the ultimate goal of measuring the sky?
- How many cost models are there?
- How can we make a logical and rational comparison with different models?
- Why is the TCO/ROI model is so popular? If we use TCO/ROI, would it be the right choice?
- What are the assumptions of these models?
- How can I select the right model to fit a particular business need?
- How can we establish both revenue- and nonrevenue-based cost models?
- What are the risks of keeping the IT workload in house versus migrating to the cloud?

We believe that most people, whether they are cloud service providers or cloud service consumers, will also face similar questions if they are asked to measure "the sky" or to prepare a business case for a cloud investment project. From this perspective, this book is also targeted for IT business analysts and MBA students as reference material.

In essence, the core objective of this book is to demonstrate how to build a cloud cost model. It will illustrate the process of establishing the cost framework and calculating the costs. One of the main reasons to address the cloud cost modeling issue is that many ordinary people have two popular misconceptions:

1. The cloud is free.
2. My data is stored anyway up in the air.

If this is so, why should we bother to measure the sky? The answer is dependent on who you are. If you are just an individual consumer and require very limited cloud resources, it is quite clear that you can obtain nearly free cloud resources. However, if you are a business consumer, especially for medium- and large-scale businesses, there will be no free lunch. You have to pay for what you have consumed. This leads to the issue of how to make the rational investment decision for the usage of IT resources.

For most small or medium size companies, the investment decision would be relatively simple. The decision criteria could be mainly based on financial or economic returns plus a decision maker's intuition or personal satisfaction. However, for a large enterprise, the strategic investment decision (very often involving millions of dollars) is not a simple intellectual exercise but rather than process of negotiation and compromise among different Line of Business (LoB) units.

However, to some degree, all models are subjective because cost modeling involves many subjective assumptions and selection of raw data and material. It would be impossible to avoid subjective assumptions and personal opinions. Strictly speaking, any data selected and assumption made are subjective. It is based on personal experiences and intuition or perhaps, a gut feeling.

Many people think a gut feeling is negative or nonscientific. As a matter of fact, a gut feeling is kind of a super-logic or sixth sense or recognition of a subconscious pattern. It gives us a shortcut to quickly reach a solution. Sometimes, this shortcut serves us quite well, especially if we do not have enough time to analyze the circumstances surrounding us or do not have enough information available. In this case, the sixth sense would be the only choice for us to reach a self-satisfactory conclusion. It is not purely arbitrary or an illogical guess but rather meta–knowledge built upon the subconscious mind. Actually, people's minds are always searching for a recognised pattern based on available information, knowledge, experiences and most importantly, wisdom. Perhaps that is why a gut feeling is very often called an "educated guess," self-learning, working experience, or armchair thinking.

Many strategic investment decisions made by IT legends such as Steve Jobs and Marc R. Benioff [1] led to great success for their companies. Why did they achieve what most people cannot achieve? Is it because they not only have years of working experiences and cumulative knowledge, but also have "gut feelings" or wisdom? People speculate that they may have absorbed wisdom from Eastern philosophy and religion because they both went to India for enlightenment. In Steve Jobs' own words, "Trust in destiny" and "Follow your heart." Walter Isaacson, the exclusive biographer of Steve Jobs, wrote it this way:

> Jobs's interest in Eastern spirituality, Hinduism (Krishna/God Consciousness), Zen Buddhism, and the search for enlightenment was not merely the passing phase of a nineteen-year-old. Throughout his life he would seek to follow many of the basic precepts of Eastern religions, such as the emphasis on experiential prajñā, wisdom or cognitive understanding that is intuitively experienced through concentration of the mind. Years later, sitting in his Palo Alto garden, he reflected on the lasting influence of his trip to India [2].

For the East, it is the soul. The soul did not come with body nor die with the body. The body is just a temporary home for the soul. The soul can be enlightened by many sophisticated methodologies and practices that have been developed by Eastern philosophy, religion, and culture for many thousands of years or by messages delivered by the Supreme God personally (e.g., Lord Krishna's teachings compiled as Bhagavad Gita) or his incarnations.

For the West, it is subconsciousness. In Sigmund Freud's teachings, it is the unconscious mind beneath consciousness and awareness. It is a repository of idea, desire, memories, and emotion. It consists of any information and data the mind collects from five senses but cannot consciously process to make meaningful sense of. However, it can be retrieved or recalled to consciousness by the simple direction of attention.

In order to make the right decision at the right time, the spiritual mind constantly needs not only information and knowledge but also wisdom. Without that, a strategic decision may just be a tactical one. Long-term success would be dependent on pure luck rather than a strategy. Here, wisdom means abstract pattern recognition at hierarchical level. It is the experience of cumulative knowledge. Cumulative knowledge has four different levels:

- Level 1: You do not know what you do not know (ignorance).
- Level 2: You know what you do not know (know unknowns).
- Level 3: You know what you know and what you do not know (know your boundaries).
- Level 4: You know all — knowledge of knowledge or meta-knowledge, wisdom (wizard).

For many people and under many circumstances, they are just wandering around at knowledge level 1. If we borrow the Indian philosophy term, it is so-called "ignorance." There are two different scenarios when people face the unknown. One is either leaving to chance or pretending to know. The other is to wonder about the unknown and continuously search for knowledge and wisdom. That is why people often say wondering is the beginning of wisdom.

Unfortunately, we have witnessed many IT strategic decisions made by some wayward people subject to purely static analysis, shallow observation, personal opinion, preference, taste and prejudice and, above all, ignorance. The results of these decisions often led to great fiascos or disaster.

Certainly, this book does not intend to tell readers how to make a particular decision or to enlighten readers on how to search for wisdom, but rather to share some common experiences that we have learned from previous lessons of cloud investment projects. By Buddhist philosophy, enlightenment depends only on oneself. Wisdom cannot be taught or demonstrated but one can only be shown the path to be followed.

This book will provide analytic tools and some practical processes of decision making for people to follow. It will not only provide readers with knowledge and analytic methods to establish a cost framework for strategic decision making but also will help readers to understand the logic behind the strategic decision making for cloud computing investment in practice.

We think it is important because not all decisions can be made by "gutfeelings," especially for a multimillion-dollar strategic investment decision that is made in a complex and dynamically changing environment. It requires hard mental work and comprehensive analysis. Gut feelings and educated guesses may add some value but not enough. Perhaps we can summarize the main point by altering the old English proverb "Look before you jump" as "Analyze before you decide."

ORGANISATION OF THE BOOK

This book is organized into five major parts:

I. Cloud Computing Foundations and Business Requirements (Introduction)
II. Cloud Data Center Facility (Below the Floor)
III. Cloud Infrastructure and Management (Above the Floor)
IV. Cloud Computing Cost Models and Framework (Framework)
V. Cloud Strategy and Critical Decisions with Real Option Theory (Example)

The structure of this book is similar to a five-paragraph essay. Actually, the structure of the entire book can be loosely considered a recursive five-paragraph essay.

Part I is made up of three chapters (Chapter 1−3) that offer an introduction to cloud computing, define related computing paradigms such as parallel computing, identify business requirements through a five-phase process for defining business needs, and conclude with a case study.

Part II consists of seven chapters (Chapters 4−10) that cover issues related to data center architecture and key components and elements of data centers including space, power, cooling, fire suppression, and physical security.

Part III consists of three chapters (Chapter 11−13) that focus on cloud physical infrastructure elements namely servers, storage, and networking.

Part IV is made up of three chapters (Chapters 14−16). They cover topics related to the cost modeling framework and associated challenges. They also offer a detailed review of literature on cost modeling and key classifications, and how these concepts are put into practice in the real world.

Part V consists of two chapters (Chapters 17 and 18), which discuss the application of cost modeling to a real-life case scenario and present real option theory as one of the effective strategic methodologies for a decision maker to steer the business based on three basic elements: planning, opportunities, and decision making.

Caesar Wu and Rajkumar Buyya
Melbourne, Australia, 2014

Acknowledgments

First and foremost, we are grateful to all the researchers, industrial developers, and organizations worldwide for their contributions to the various concepts and technologies discussed in the book. Special thanks to all of our colleagues at Telstra and the CLOUDS (Cloud Computing and Distributed Systems) Lab at the University of Melbourne who have influenced our experience.

We thank all of our colleagues at the University of Melbourne, especially Professors Rao Kotagiri, Iven Mareels, and Glyn Davis for their mentorship and positive support for our research and knowledge transfer efforts.

We thank the members of the CLOUDS Lab for proofreading one or more chapters. They include Rodrigo Calheiros, Nikolay Grozev, Amir Vahid, Maria Rodriguez, Adel Toosi, Atefeh Khosravi, Yaser Mansouri, and Jungmin Jay Son.

We thank our colleagues Guoqi Qian, Kerry James Hinton, Peter Hormann, Joe Disisto, Sascha Suesssspeck, Tao Lin, and Arash Tayebi for their support.

We thank our family members, including Summa Wu, Smrithi Buyya, Soumya Buyya, and Radha Buyya, for their love and understanding during the preparation of the book.

We sincerely thank external reviewers commissioned by the publisher for their critical comments and suggestions on enhancing the presentation and organization of many chapters to a finer level. This has greatly helped us in improving the quality of the book.

Finally, we would like to thank the staff at Elsevier Inc. for their enthusiastic support and guidance during the preparation of the book. In particular, we thank Todd Green for inspiring us to take up this project and set the process of publication in motion. They were wonderful to work with!

CLOUD COMPUTING FOUNDATIONS AND BUSINESS REQUIREMENTS

Today "cloud computing" may be one of the most popular buzzwords in nearly every IT professional's vocabulary, but not many people deeply understand the term. What are the differences between traditional computing and cloud computing? Why do we need cloud computing? What does it mean to my business? If the cloud is as good as many consulting firms claim, why do some companies still stick to traditional computing? How can I apply it to my business? How significant is it to my business? Why now?

All these questions will be answered in Part I of this book. It consists of three chapters. In the first chapter, we will first focus on the term "cloud computing" from three historic phases: build, buy, and lease. Before we unveil our definition of cloud computing, we will review four other types of computing that are closely related to cloud computing, namely grid, parallel, distributed, and utility computing. Then we will introduce some widely adopted terms, such as NIST's cloud definition. In order to serve the purposes of this book, we define cloud computing using a functional definition. Of course, it doesn't matter how we define the term "cloud computing," the real purpose of our definition is to set up the groundwork for us to establish the cloud cost model or framework.

Why do we need a cost model of cloud computing? It is because we want the cloud to serve our business needs. In Chapter 2, we will describe how to define the business needs via three aspects (volume, variation, and variety) and how to implement a business analysis from a professional business analyst perspective. With respect to the five-phase process for business problem solving, we will only focus on the first three phases, namely problem definition, requirement gathering, and solution definition. In order to achieve the best problem solving results, we briefly discuss the topic of expectation management.

Chapter 3 puts the theory into practice. It contains a real business case of a leading telco company. In order to solve the real business problem of saving a significant amount on opex, we propose a cloud solution, which this book will unveil in all its details in other parts (II to V).

CLOUD COMPUTING

This chapter aims at laying out the groundwork of cloud cost modeling. We will use a functional definition to define the term "cloud computing" to establish a cost framework for supporting strategic investment decision making.

The chapter will review the evolution of different computing paradigms and how they relate to cloud computing. From a business perspective, the ultimate goal of cloud computing is to drive cost reduction or to increase utilization and reduce provisioning time. The significance of cloud computing is for a business to gain a competitive edge in a marketplace.

In order to illustrate this significant point, we will first introduce some popular terms related to the cloud and then discuss four different types of traditional computing that are closely associated with the cloud. Finally, we will give our functional definition of cloud computing and describe the relationship between cloud and traditional types of computing.

1.1 INTRODUCTION

The time was late 2008. The world had just experienced the shock of the global financial crisis. One of the senior business directors of a large organization asked his IT (Information Technology) people to rationalize the cost for many IT services. These IT services were mainly dedicated to hosting, web contents, managing services, utility computing, data storage, and Ethernet network connectivity for many enterprise customers. The reason for this exercise was very simple—the sales revenue could not keep up with the pace of the capital expenditure (capex) and operation expenditure (opex) growth of IT infrastructure. From a business perspective, the profit margin was shrinking due to the growing IT expenditure. Unfortunately, when IT staff tried to identify some cost items for cost reduction, it appeared none of them could be eliminated. Does this sound familiar to you? If so, you are not alone.

1.1.1 OPERATION COST RATIONALIZATION

Actually, this issue is quite common for many IT professionals of large enterprises and government agencies, which are constantly battling with this issue due to cost pressures. If we dive into the details, we can find a few fundamental issues behind this symptom:

• Although many IT cost items have no direct sales revenue contribution, they are an essential part of business because they are either critical to maintain the current business operation, such as data storage, corporation email, company web pages, customer databases, Enterprise Resource Planning (ERP), Human Resource Management (HRM) and Supply Chain Management (SCM), or are necessary to create future business growth such as research and development (R&D).

- Many IT platforms or applications are shared by different Line of Business (LoB) units due to IT horizontal integration. There will be no cost advantages even if one application has been abandoned by one LoB unit but is still adopted by other LoB units.

- The IT cost is not transparent. There is no one-to-one relationship between IT cost item and revenue contribution for many large enterprises. One of the common approaches to resolve this issue is to adopt "benchmarking," which was introduced by Xerox in early 1980s. Based on the Xerox definition, benchmarking means "a continuous systematic process of evaluating companies recognized as industry leaders, to determine business and work process that represent 'Best practice' and establish rational performance goals" [3]. The issue is that benchmarking is just like a rule. It has a disappointing way of being too general. Each company will have its own special environment. It would be impossible to find two companies that are perfectly identical. A benchmark can only be approximated rather than precisely defined. Consequently, it is quite challenging to decide which IT cost should be cut and by how much. Very often, IT staff will face the dilemma of either overshooting or undershooting. We will discuss the benchmark issue in later chapters.

- It would be wrong to assume that IT service vendors are always part of the solution, but they also are a part of problem. In many large enterprises or government agencies, the common practice is that certain or a large proportion of IT functions have been outsourced to third parties or service vendors. Timothy Chou in his book [4] defined this outsourcing model very clearly. He called it "model three." The issue is if the vendor's goal can be aligned with yours, you can find a win-win solution. However, this is not always the case. External vendors are always looking for revenue growth or at least keeping the existing revenue pie. No vendor would like to cut itself out of revenue. But you as a customer would continuously ask a vendor to do more for less. It is a zero sum game. In many circumstances, the vendor would not tell you there is a better and more cost-effective solution until you find it yourself, because this would potentially jeopardize the vendor's revenue bottom line. Sometimes, the valuable information may be intentionally filtered out. The customers of IT services may become the victim of "unknown of unknown." All these issues are still with us even if we move IT functions into the cloud.

- In general, the organizational structure of many large corporations still remains the same as 100 years ago. Basically, it is a military dictatorship with excessive control. One famous slogans made by a high profile CEO (of Telstra in 2005) was "catch the vision or catch the bus." This is another way to say that I'll not tolerate different options. The culture of "doing what I (the boss) say" is still pervasive in many large organizations. This may be good for the scale of production but it would be less advantageous for a company that intends to generate innovative and creative thinking. The dictatorship leadership style will suppress many talented employees from generating innovative ideas and smart solutions for business problems. This often leads to the phenomenon of the so-called "Market for Lemons" [5] because only people who are less talented and lack their own opinions can survive in this kind of environment. Of course, other reasons may be behind this phenomenon but the dictatorship way of management is one of major driving forces behind this symptom. It will cause the issue of "status quo." People who are not only in the management team but also the ordinary staff are happy to keep the status quo. However, the Internet has already provided a level playing field. If you do not advance, your competitors will, especially in the IT industry. The mentality of keeping the status quo is not a good survival or competitive strategy for any IT company or group.

All these issues are very challenging but not new. The question is how can we find an effective solution to resolve these issues? The answer leads to one of the main topics of this book: cloud computing. Would the cloud be an effective solution for cost rationalization? The answer will be "it depends." It sounds quite diplomatic, but it is a fact. Based on much research, estimated savings for cloud solutions can vary from -144% to $+500\%$. The gap is 644%. You may wonder why this is so. This is actually the starting point of our journey for cloud cost modeling.

If all the above issues mainly focus on IT service consumers, then the following example shows that the cloud solution can also bring possible benefits to many IT service providers.

At the end of 2008, one of the key decision makers of an IT service company decided to launch cloud products and services in order to leverage the sales of managing services for many medium-size companies or customers. Instead of addressing the issue of internal cost rationalization, the goal of this case was to focus on the business revenue forecasting from a cloud service provider's perspective.

1.1.2 REVENUE ESTIMATION FOR EMERGING PRODUCTS

The strategic goal of the cloud business was emphasizing emerging market growth or getting a foothold in an emerging market. The cost model of the cloud is quite different than traditional IT hosting service due to its strategic value. It is quite challenging to estimate this strategic value because there are so many variables and uncertainties for emerging markets. Very often, when many people estimate business revenue, they will overshoot during the initial phase of the cloud project but undershoot when the market conditions become tough. Gartner has special terms for these stages, namely "peak of inflated expectation" and "through of disillusionment." Gartner publishes a "Hype Cycle for Emerging Technologies" every July or August.

In July 2008, Gartner published its first Hype Cycle for Emerging Technologies that included cloud computing. It was the first time the cloud computing was on the horizon (see Figure 1.1).

The main issue with Gartner's hype cycle is that it does not have clearly quantitive measurements for both visibility and time. It might be easier to understand and visualize for many emerging technologies for certain periods if you knew what the exact length of time is. For example, consider the period of the "Trough of Disillusionment." Is it 2 years or 5 years or even 7 years? Perhaps, this is why Gartner uses the term of "Hype," which means emotional or overexcited or exaggerated. It has more subjective sense than objective. It means there is a sentiment.

Talking about sentiment, Nicholas Carr's book, "The Big Switch" [7], generated sentiment toward the cloud and really caught many people's attention, especially many high-flying executives. He argued that computing will be eventually like electricity, and will become one of the household utilities or a commodity service. Although his book was very popular, his claim was sometimes considered controversial similar to his other claims about IT in "IT doesn't matter" [10] or "Does IT matter?" [11]. Many people think that the fundamental issue of his work is lack of detailed analysis in term of business applications, cloud ideas, cloud alternatives, cloud opportunities, and cloud risks. However, his work has predicted a certain path of transformation for future IT consumption.

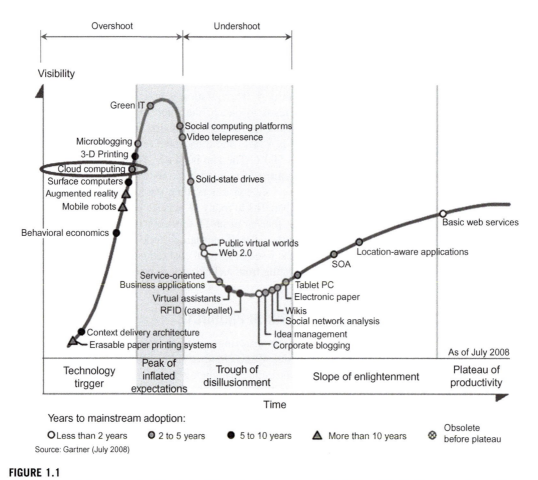

FIGURE 1.1

Gartner's Hype Cycle for Emerging Technologies in 2008 [7].

Whether it is a big or small, gentle or hard, big bang or gradual switch, one thing is certain: we are facing the eve of an IT transformation from the "buy" mode of IT consumption to a "lease" one. But we have to be very careful with how we handle cloud investments. The dot-com boom showed that during the peak of the inflated period, many investors or companies might not care whether the cloud would make a profit or not; they just want to get the foothold in this emerging market. However, when the market becomes gloomy and staggering, many people will become quite pessimistic. It is what Geoffrey Moore called the "chasm" [12]. In other words, an emotional and hype-cycle approach to business analysis is not a smart way to decide on the quantitative and strategic value of the emerging market. It may lead us to either overestimation or underestimation of the cloud market. As a result, a decision maker may make the incorrect investment decision for cloud business.

What this book is trying to focus on is how to establish an objective cost model or framework so that a decision maker can make a realistic investment decision for cloud computing. It addresses the cloud cost model from two perspectives:

1. Cloud cost model from an internal IT consumption perspective (IT cost rationalization)
2. Cloud cost model from a cloud or IT service provider perspective (business strategic value)

In essence, this book will propose two basic cloud cost models. One is a revenue-based cost model from a cloud service provider's perspective and the other is a nonrevenue-based cost model from an IT cost rationalization perspective.

Before building a cloud cost model, you may wonder, is the cloud the right solution for IT cost rationalization or not? How can you make sure the "cloud" is not just another illusion like the dot-com boom? To answer these questions, we should first understand, "What is cloud computing?" There have been so many answers for this question, but none of them is quite compelling. Why is this so? Let's begin our cost-modeling journey from this question.

1.2 CLOUD COMPUTING AT A GLANCE

Today, cloud computing has quickly become a buzzword not only in the IT industry but also in other sectors, such as banking, finance, education, health, utilities, airlines, retail, real estate, and telecom. Actually, many e-commerce activities have been utilizing many cloud applications one way or the other. However, when people encounter the definition of "cloud computing," they are often puzzled or confused because there are so many different definitions. According to the research of Luis M. Vaquero et al. [13], there were over 22 different definitions in 2008 alone. People often ask, "What does cloud computing really mean?" The common answer is again very tactful: "It is really dependent on what you mean." The answer actually indicates the subjectiveness of the cloud definition and the broad spectrum of meanings for the cloud.

When people talk about the cloud-computing paradigm, they often have different purposes in mind. Thus, the term "cloud" inevitably covers so many aspects of computing. It signifies that the entire IT industry is transforming from a physical world towards a virtual world. It is not just an incremental change. It is the latest profound transformation for the IT industry. We can list the following six common definitions many people use for cloud computing:

- "Just another molecule of the cloud" [7].
- Running one's computing processes in someone else's physical infrastructure [16].
- Cloud computing means four pillars: applications, platforms, infrastructure and enabling services [17].
- The fifth utility (water, electricity, gas, telecommunication, and cloud computing) [18]
- Cloud computing is a style of computing where computing resources are easy to obtain and access, simple to use, cheap, and just work [19].
- "Cloud Computing is an approach to computing that leverages the *efficient pooling* of an *on-demand, self-managed, virtual infrastructure*" [VMware's definition] [20].

The most widely cited definition is, however, the one is published by the US Department of Commerce, National Institute of Standard and Technology or NIST [21], which we will discuss later in the chapter. It covers almost all technical aspects of the cloud. It is essential for us to have the right definition out there. It will assist us in understanding, classifying, and applying different definitions of our goal. The bottom line is that the right definition will lay out a solid foundation for us to establish an adequate cost model and framework. Let's explore how to define the term "cloud."

1.3 RIGHT APPROACH TO DEFINITION

Having read through many academic articles, conference papers, Wikipedia pages, vendors' white-papers, and recently published cloud books, although there have been many different definitions made by many authors from different perspectives, it appears none of the definitions is quite compelling or irrefutable.

Some people have drawn a conclusion: if we cannot find an satisfactory irrefutable definition, the term "cloud computing" might not be really definable. However, others believe although there are many definitions that cannot be satisfied, it does not mean the term cannot be defined. It actually means the term "cloud" can be defined in many different ways. The question is, what do we do with the many different definitions? One of the approaches is to look at the term from a historical perspective.

A definition is a paradigm to guide us to further thought. In general, if we have already been familiar with one of definitions, it may color our way of thinking about an object. For instance, what aspects of the object should be taken consideration and what should not be counted; what should be paid attention to and what should be left off. Theoretically speaking, the certain approach of definition may influence our way of thinking to investigate and analyze the object before a conclusion has been made. In other words, it may restrict our capability of creativity and innovation.

In order to set up the cloud paradigm for cost modeling, we need a right definition of "cloud computing" to guide our diversified considerations and innovative thinking about cost modeling. One of practical approaches is to ask three basic questions:

- Why do we define the term of "cloud"?
- How can a definition of the cloud help us?
- Can we have more than we think?

As a result of this approach of inquiry, we have four different types of definitions that will help us to categorize many aspects of cloud computing:

- An essential-intuitive definition (EID) is actually leaving it alone or not defining a term, but rather taking an attitude of "I know it when I see it," the famous comment made by US Supreme Court Justice, Potter Stewart, about pornography in 1964.[1] This is an open-ended definition.

---

[1]"I shall not today attempt further to define the kinds of material I understand to be embraced within that shorthand description ["hard-core pornography"]; and perhaps I could never succeed in intelligibly doing so. But I know it when I see it, and the motion picture involved in this case is not that. [Emphasis added.]"

- Lexical definitions (LD) describe how terms have been used historically; this is what dictionaries provide. They only recover historic meanings. The issue is that some words have more than one historic meaning. For example, the word "set" has 464 different meanings, the highest number in the Oxford English Dictionary (OED). The second highest word is "run" (396 definitions). The word "cloud" has six different meanings.
- Functional definitions (FD) allow the authority to provide his/her own definition for a finite context. Usually, an author may use one of the lexical definitions and emphasize it for purposes of argument or discussion with a particular meaning.
- Real definitions (RD) attempt to capture the essence of a reality, and are deployed mostly for debate purposes. By real definition, Plato means a set of necessary and sufficient conditions that exactly determine the entities to which a given concept applies. For a real definition, an author does not seek your agreement for a word or term, but rather asks you to jump on his/her bandwagon.

Once we understand the different types of definitions, it is quite easier for us to categorize different types of cloud computing definitions presented above. For example, NIST's definition about cloud computing is a lexical definition.

In order to serve the main purpose of this book, many of the words, terms, ideas, and thoughts in this book will be classified with functional definitions to help guide the reader's understanding. In other words, the cloud definition of this book will extend additional meanings based on a standard lexical definition, such as the NIST definition, in order to build the cost model or a framework.

1.4 A BRIEF HISTORY OF CLOUD COMPUTING DEFINITIONS

The first academic term of cloud computing was casted by Ramnath K. Chellappa [22] in 1997. In his paper of "Intermediaries in cloud computing: A new computing paradigm," Ramnath claimed that a computing paradigm will not be restricted within a technical boundary but will be defined by economic rationality. During the 1990s, the term "cloud" meant large Asynchronous Transfer Mode (ATM) networks because the packet switches formed a virtual private network (VPN), which can balance data traffic and utilize the network bandwidth very effectively.

Strictly speaking, the term "cloud computing" is still evolving because it is supported by several emerging technologies, such as server virtualisation (hardware), multitenancy (software) and auto-orchestration (operational process). It is less than two decades old. If we look back at the history of computing, in the 1960s, cloud computing might have just meant "sharing." In the 1970s, it might have meant the advanced function of a mainframe computer, such as virtual memory. In the1980s, it would refer to parallel computing. In the earlier 1990s, the meaning might have extended to grid computing from High-Performance Computing (HPC). In the later 1990s, the meaning of cloud computing might have shifted into "virtualization." During this period, VMware launched its VMware workstation 1.0. It has a similar meaning of a term used today Infrastructure as a Service (IaaS). At the same time, Marc Benioff [1] established his own business, Salesforce.com, to sell subscription-based Customer Relationship Management (CRM) software or applications, which competed head-to-head with Thomas Siebel's Siebel Systems or license-based software. Marc's software delivery model is what now we call Software as a Service (SaaS).

Actually, service on-demand, utility computing, and multitenant service models have been widespread since then. In 2002, Amazon Web Service (AWS) launched two IaaS products, namely Elastic Compute Cloud (EC2) and Simple Storage Service (S3). These are representative of the contemporary meaning of cloud computing or more precisely, the public cloud. Very often, the terms server virtualisation, IaaS, SaaS, and cloud computing become interchangeable.

All these definitions not only provide the evolutionary meaning of the new business concept that we are trying to investigate here, but also make us think beyond these definitions. Behind the cloud definition, we can see that the real benefits that the cloud can bring are infrastructure sharing, increasing utilization rate, auto-provisioning, speed to market, and minimizing up-front capex. In essence, it can create cost efficiency.

After more than one decade of evolution, the term "cloud computing" has become popular in the information technology (IT) world, especially among many medium and large organizations. This is the result of the combination effects of the Internet, web browsers, new hypervisor technologies, parallel computing (multicore processors), open source software, auto-orchestration, and server virtualization. These cloud technology advances have not only made the new business model (cloud computing) possible, but also very attractive to many companies' decision makers because this new way of IT resource consumption has three very irresistible features or characteristics for the business:

- Pay as you go (PAYG)
- Elastic or scalable and unlimited computer resources pool
- No up-front capex

These new characteristics are perfectly aligned with the requirements of a competitive advantage business model, which has to possess the following:

- Speed to market
- Significant reduction of provisioning time (auto-provisioning)
- Shift of the business focus from technology to service orientation
- Gain in return on investment (ROI)
- Focus on core business or competence
- Improvement of customer experience of the services
- Advancement of company's competitiveness in the market

Focus Consulting Group [23] made a very good comparison between technology (blade servers and hypervisors) evolution and business value propositions. We extended the timeline from 2007 to 2016. Since 2007, many hardware and software vendors have joined the cloud race (see Figure 1.2 for hardware vendors; Cisco, Huawei, and Oracle/Sun have joined in the x86 server market). This has made one of the key cloud elements (server) a commodity product. This is one of the influential factors that impacts cloud evolution. We will give more details in Part III of this book.

If we have a further extension of the time span, we can find a macro trend of a computing cost model that has actually shifted from a "make" orientation of consuming IT resources (or "self-make," especially for software) to "buy" and from a "buy" orientation to today's "lease." If we look from an operational perspective, the macro trend of computing has been moving from a "centralization" model to "decentralization" and from "decentralization" to "re-centralization" (see Figure 1.3).

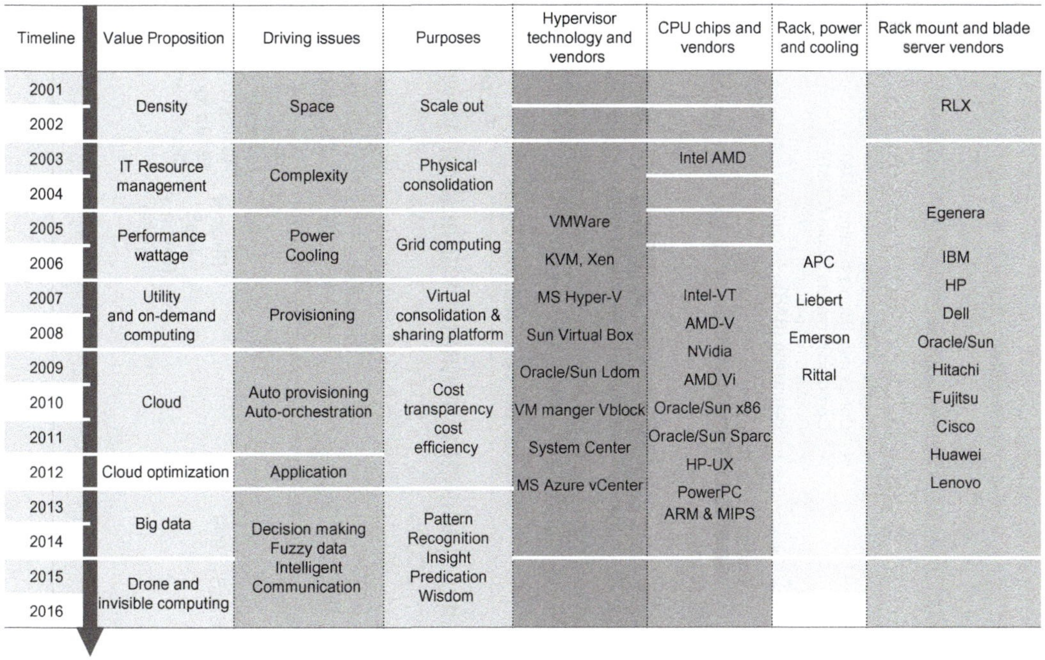

Timeline	Value Proposition	Driving issues	Purposes	Hypervisor technology and vendors	CPU chips and vendors	Rack, power and cooling	Rack mount and blade server vendors
2001	Density	Space	Scale out				RLX
2002							
2003	IT Resource management	Complexity	Physical consolidation		Intel AMD		
2004							Egenera
2005	Performance wattage	Power Cooling	Grid computing	VMWare			
2006				KVM, Xen		APC	IBM
2007	Utility and on-demand computing	Provisioning	Virtual consolidation & sharing platform	MS Hyper-V	Intel-VT	Liebert	HP / Dell
2008				Sun Virtual Box	AMD-V / NVidia	Emerson	Oracle/Sun
2009	Cloud	Auto provisioning Auto-orchestration	Cost transparency cost efficiency	Oracle/Sun Ldom	AMD Vi	Rittal	Hitachi
2010				VM manger Vblock	Oracle/Sun x86		Fujitsu
2011				System Center	Oracle/Sun Sparc		Cisco / Huawei
2012	Cloud optimization	Application		MS Azure vCenter	HP-UX / PowerPC		Lenovo
2013	Big data	Decision making Fuzzy data	Pattern Recognition Insight Predication Wisdom		ARM & MIPS		
2014							
2015	Drone and invisible computing	Intelligent Communication					
2016							

FIGURE 1.2

Technologies, issues, and business value propositions from 2001 to 2016.

Both diagrams have perfectly illustrated that the concept of cloud computing is the result of business requirements and the evolution of various IT technologies. It may potentially drive a business to be much more competitive. The concept of cloud computing is an evolution of many IT paradigms. The fundamental infrastructure to underpin the cloud is actually the integration of the data center resource and Internet capability.

During the "make" or "build" era, an enterprise had to build its own hardware and applications. Normally, it would take years to build a vertical proprietary application, such as Financial Resource Management (FRM), Supply Chain Management (SCM), and other ERP packages. The issue with the homegrown application is that it is not compatible with other applications. You need a team of dedicated IT professionals to maintain it. It is very costly.

The popular solution to resolve this issue of "making" was either outsourcing or "buying" an application licence "off-the-shelf." However, many enterprise customers quickly found their IT budget growth well exceeded its revenue growth and the utilization rate of IT resources was very low. This led to Salesforce.com's "leasing"- or "subscribing"-based IT resource consumption model or SaaS. Since 2000, the "buy" cost model has been slowly shifted to a "lease" model. This gave rise to the birth of cloud computing. From a cloud consumer's perspective, the "lease" model can deliver many business values in term of financial, operational, and infrastructure (see Figure 1.3) benefits. Subsequently, it is inevitable that we have seen more than one kind of definition for cloud

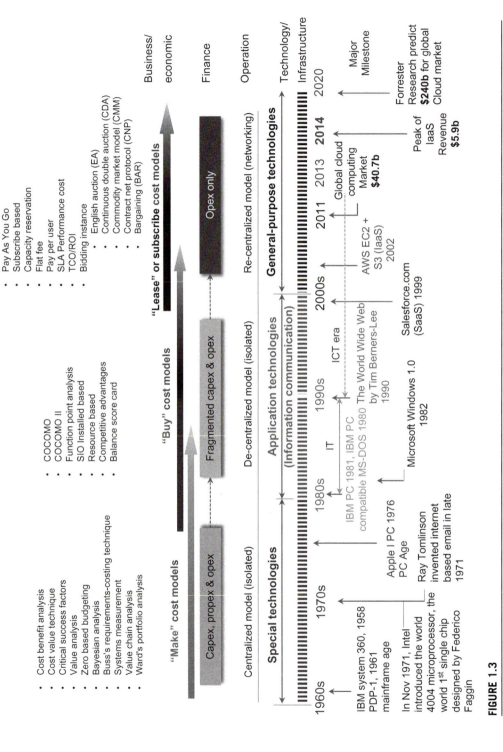

FIGURE 1.3

Computer industry and market: 60-year time span.

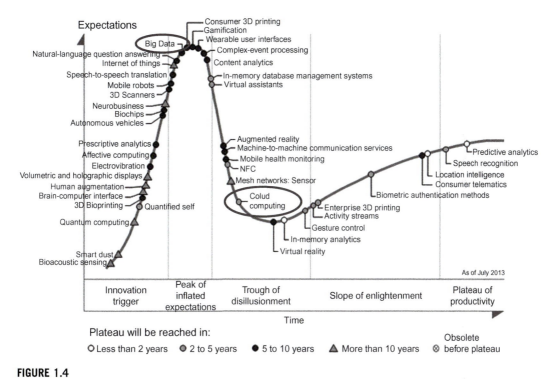

FIGURE 1.4

Gartner's Hype Cycle for Emerging Technologies from August 2013 [8].

computing. However, the bottom line of the cloud for any cloud consumer is to deliver cost efficiency and market competitiveness for its business.

When a cloud service provider defines the cloud, it focuses on the cloud market perspective. As we have illustrated before, Gartner publishes its historical hype cycle of many emerging technologies every year. In 2013, Gartner prophesized that cloud computing was already out of the peak of inflated expectations and expected to dip into so-called plateau of productivity for 2 to 5 years (see Figure 1.4). Big Data, which is one of applications of cloud computing, is now at the peak of inflated expectations in 2013.

If we align Gartner's hype cycle with the Technology Adoption Life Cycle, we can see the cloud is now getting into so called "Chasm" zone in Geoffrey Moore's theory [12] (see Figure 1.5).

If these two cycles can be correlated, we can see there is a "Chasm" period. It will be a tough period for many cloud service providers because the cloud market will become overcrowded and it will difficult to see the results from the many investments that were made in haste before the Chasm era. As a result, the IT assets would be quickly devaluated because of a lower IT asset utilization rate. This would lead to cloud benefits being quickly evaporated in comparison with the traditional dedicated hosting model. People may wonder why we bothered to develop a cloud.

In order to answer this question, we should understand that the "cloud" is not just a single technology, but rather a combination of many complex domains. Gartner has another hype cycle

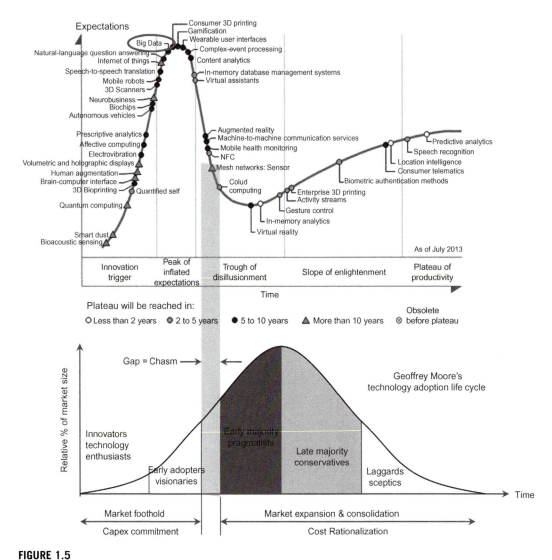

FIGURE 1.5

Combination of Gartner's Hype Cycle and Moore's Technology Adoption Life Cycle.

that is especially designed for cloud computing (see Figure 1.6). From Figure 1.6, we can see that cloud computing consists of many complex domains, such as cloud orchestration (Cloud Management Platforms), IaaS middleware, cloud Business Process Management (BPM), cloud security, and Cloud Service Brokerage. Some of them are just on the horizon in the next 2 to 5 years according to Gartner. In essence, cloud computing is a combination of different emerging cloud technologies during a long period of time. We should consider the cloud a long-term journey and paradigm shift that transforms the method of computing consumption from dedicated infrastructure to a completely shared and elastic domain. Geoffrey Moore suggested that the right way to cross

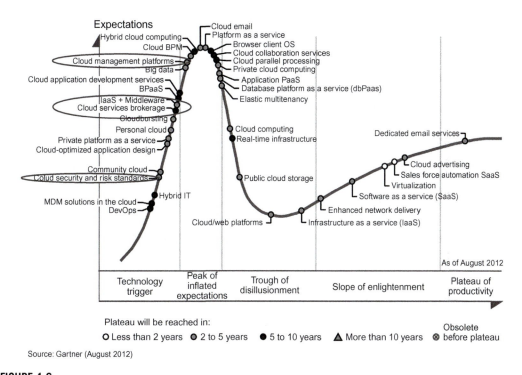

FIGURE 1.6

Gartner's Hype Cycle of Cloud Computing (August 2012).

the Chasm period is to have a proper business plan in the first place in order to fight against any emotional and immature decisions during market fluctuations.

Because the cloud has been leveraging different emerging technologies, we should consider it as a large and complex system that is crossing many different disciplines. (business, decision making, economics, and computer science). Thus, we should define the term "cloud computing" in a unique way.

From a certain viewpoint, Figure 1.6 is a complement of Figure 1.4 and Figure 1.2 is a complement of Figure 1.3. They have demonstrated that cloud computing is one of the rapidly emerging technological paradigms. But it has transformative impact for IT and other service industries.

For the sake of clarifying the logic of this transformation, we review four other computing paradigms that are closely associated with the cloud. They are:

- Parallel computing
- Distributed computing
- Grid computing
- Utility computing

Of course, there are other types of computing that are also associated with the cloud, such as high-performance computing (HPC), ubiquitous computing, pervasive computing, dedicated computing and on-demand computing. We will briefly highlight their important points.

1.5 PARALLEL COMPUTING

Parallel computing is opposed to serial computing. It can perform multiple tasks at the same time. From a hardware perspective, hardware parallelism increases processing speed. In contrast to the "one by one" method of serial computing, parallel computing can implement multiple computational tasks simultaneously or in an overlaping fashion. The hardware-oriented definition is just the intuitive way of describing parallel computing. The comprehensive method [28] of expressing parallel computing actually covers a broad range of topics. It includes program algorithms, applications, programming languages, operating systems, and computer architecture, which includes multicores, multithreaded, multiprocessor, or multisocket (CPU) and multinode hardware. Each of these components underpins parallel computing, and should be implemented harmonically in order to support streaming and highly efficient parallel computational workloads.

During the 1950s, parallel meant to share common memory with multiple processors. Today, parallel computing doesn't only mean hardware parallelism but also software and application parallelism. It has become the mainstream computing architecture from laptops to the top end of computing. What is a new ingredient in today's parallel computing is the extension of it so that it is ubiquitous and available to everyone.

The main driving force behind parallelism is to continuously improve computing performance or speed. Over the last 50 years or so, CPU clock speed has been doubled almost every 18 months based on the famous Moore's law. As a result of rising CPU speeds, the power density has also increased dramatically (see Figure 1.7). For example, if CPU clock speed is increased by 20%, the power consumption of the CPU would rise almost five times or 100%.

If we continue to improve performance or increase CPU clock speed using the serial computation from 1990s, the surface heat of a CPU will eventually reach the sun's temperature [29], which is also called the power wall barrier. Clearly, it is not a sustainable solution to continuously

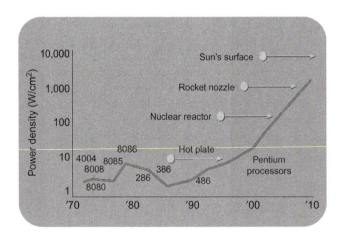

FIGURE 1.7

The power density trend of CPUs [29].

increase CPU clock speed. This physical limitation has presented three issues for consideration for computer hardware engineering:

- How to solve transistor density; in an integrated circuit this limits CPU clock speed.
- How to break the barrier of the speed of light; this limits data transmission time or latency.
- How to reduce the manufacturing cost of hardware; this limits the complexity.

The sufficient way to resolve these issues or overcome these physical limitations is to adopt the parallel computation model. From an overall perspective, the use of parallelism can solve the following computing performance problems:

- Reducing CPU surface heat: This is an alternative solution to improve CPU performance or CPU clock speed further by controlling CPU surface temperature and managing heat dissipation.
- Escaping the serial computation limit: Parallelism can handle large and complex computing problems that serial computation cannot solve.
- Saving computing cost: The parallel approach has made it possible for computing resources to become a cheap commodity product. In contrast to traditional serial computation, with parallel it is possible to have more resource inputs and shorter times for tasks, with potential cost savings.
- Saving time: A serial computation model can only perform one task at a time. Parallel computing can perform multiple tasks simultaneously.
- Using integrated resources: With parallel computation, the computing resource pool has been extended from a local data center to nonlocal computer resources. The concept underpins distributed computing.

In order to solve the above performance problems, people classify the parallel computing into two basic categories: hardware parallelism and software parallelism.

1.5.1 HARDWARE PARALLELISM

Based on the hardware architecture, we can also divide hardware parallelism into two types of parallelism: Processor parallelism and memory parallelism. Again, the main objective of hardware parallelism is to increase the processing speed.

1.5.1.1 Processor parallelism

Process parallelism means that the computer architecture has multiple nodes, N-ways, multiple CPUs or multiple sockets, multiple cores, and multiple threads. Today, multiple processors for a computer are very pervasive from laptops to mainframe computers. It has become a mainstream CPU hardware architecture. We will give a detailed explanation of these terms in Chapter 11.

1.5.1.2 Memory parallelism

Memory parallelism means shared memory, symmetric multiprocessors, distributed memory, hybrid distributed shared memory, multilevel pipelines, etc. Sometimes, it is also called a parallel random access machine (PRAM). "It is an abstract model for parallel computation which assumes that all the processors operate synchronously under a single clock and are able to randomly access a large

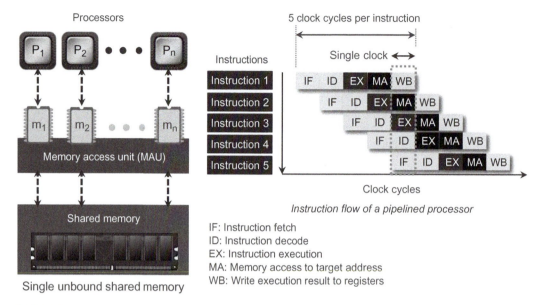

IF: Instruction fetch
ID: Instruction decode
EX: Instruction execution
MA: Memory access to target address
WB: Write execution result to registers

FIGURE 1.8

Parallel random access machines.

shared memory. In particular, a processor can execute an arithmetic, logic, or memory access operation within a single clock cycle" [33] (see Figure 1.8). This is what we call using overlapping or pipelining instructions to achieve parallelism.

1.5.2 SOFTWARE PARALLELISM

Software parallelism can be further classified as algorithm, programming, data size, and architecture balance parallelism. Algorithm parallelism is a process of algorithm implementation for software or an application. The traditional algorithm is based on the concept of sequential processing. Since task execution is linear, the traditional approach will become very counterproductive. In comparison with hardware parallelism, the progress of parallel software development is very slow. It suffers from all the problems inherent in sequential programming.

1.5.2.1 Algorithm parallelism

Algorithm parallelism means the computer implements "a prescribed set of well-defined rules or processes for the solution of a problem in a finite number of steps" at the same time. It means the adopted algorithms must avoid dependence among operations that force one step to follow another, which is a serial method. An example of algorithm parallelism is an interactive program that has many sequential algorithms where each algorithm can be executed independently and simultaneously. Fayez Gebali [30] summarized the details of parallel computing with five layers to

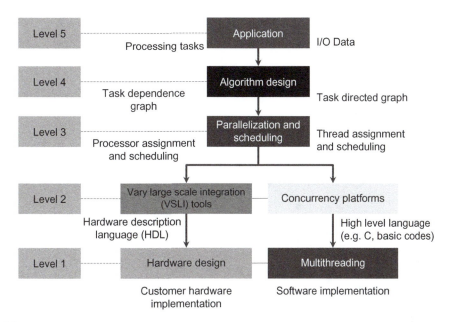

FIGURE 1.9

Phases or layers of implementing an application in software or hardware using parallel computing [30].

illustrate the relationship of algorithm, programming, software and hardware parallelism (see Figure 1.9).

1.5.2.2 Programming parallelism

Programming parallelism is facilitated by what are called concurrency platforms, which are tools that help the programmer manage the threads and the timing of task execution on the processors (see Figure 1.9). The practical aim of programming parallelism is to decompose a large and complex problem into the number of units for parallel execution, which is referred to as a threading arrangement. It can also be considered as one of the six types of parallel models, which we will give further details about in the following section.

1.5.2.3 Data parallelism

Data parallelism represents the number of independent data structures and the size of each one, which are indicators of the degree of available parallelism in a computation. A successful parallel computation requires data locality in that program references stay relatively confined to the data available in each processor—otherwise too much time may be consumed, ruining parallel performance, which is expressed in Amdahl's law (see Figure 1.10).

1.5.2.4 Architecture balance parallelism

In order to achieve better parallel performance, the architecture of parallel computing must have enough processors, and adequate global memory access and interprocessor communication of data

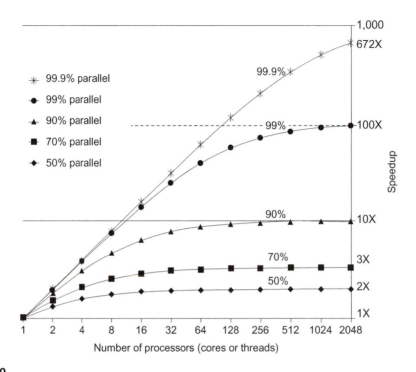

FIGURE 1.10

Amdahl's law of parallel computing [29].

and control information to enable parallel scalability. When the parallel system is scaled up, the memory and communication systems should also be increased by the architecture of the design. This is what we call it Gustafson-Barsis' law (see Figure 1.11).

Both Amdahl's law and Gustafson-Barsis' Law explain the characteristics of parallelism. Amdahl's law emphasizes the fixed workload, but Gustafson-Barsis' law focuses on the fixed time while the workload is scaled up. IT trends indicate that the growth of the workload has increasingly become much larger and complex. From a long-term perspective, Gustafson-Barsis' law is aligned with the historic trend. Nevertheless, Amdahl's law is still held to be true if you would like to speed up for a particular workload.

1.5.3 DIFFERENT TYPES OF PARALLEL MODELS

We can achieve parallelism with six different approaches. These approaches give programmers choices about the kind of parallel model to be implemented in their programming code

Distributed parallelism: This executes application tasks in the boundary of different physical nodes of a cluster of computers. The Message Passing Interface (MPI) is one of the popular parallel environments for creating applications. It supports operations such as "send" and "receive" for messages in order to distribute and manage tasks of the applications.

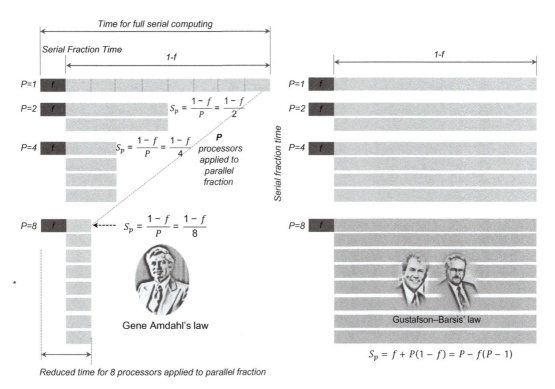

Time for full serial computing

Serial Fraction Time

1-f

1-f

$P=1$ f

$P=2$ f $S_p = \dfrac{1-f}{P} = \dfrac{1-f}{2}$

$P=1$ f

$P=2$ f

$P=4$ f $S_p = \dfrac{1-f}{P} = \dfrac{1-f}{4}$ P processors applied to parallel fraction

$P=4$ f

Serial fraction time

$P=8$ f $S_p = \dfrac{1-f}{P} = \dfrac{1-f}{8}$

$P=8$ f

Gene Amdahl's law

Gustafson–Barsis' law

$$S_p = f + P(1-f) = P - f(P-1)$$

Reduced time for 8 processors applied to parallel fraction

FIGURE 1.11

Amdahl's law vs. Gustafson-Barsis' law.

Virtualization: This method runs a number of operating systems on one machine. This function is closely associated with hardware architecture or multicore CPUs (see Figure 1.12). For example, a four-core socket or CPU can host four virtual machines (VMs). Each core can dedicate resources to one VM and operate one operating system (OS). A hypervisor sits between the OS and hardware and manages VM and hardware resources including I/O, network and switch ports, memory, and storage.

Task-level parallelism: This uses tasks rather than software thread execution. For example, an application may have 10 tasks but only have 3 threads. The parallel mechanism can execute tasks with each task being scheduled by a runtime scheduler. A thread is an independent flow of control that operates within the same address space as other independent flows of control within a process. Traditionally, thread and process characteristics are grouped into a single entity called a process.

Thread-level parallelism: In contrast to the hardware parallelism approach, this achieves parallelism within a program, with each of the parallel parts running on a separate thread. In a multicore environment, each thread can run on a separate core. The Oracle/Sun RISC server uses this approach (see Figure 1.13 and Table 1.1). For example, one machine has four cores

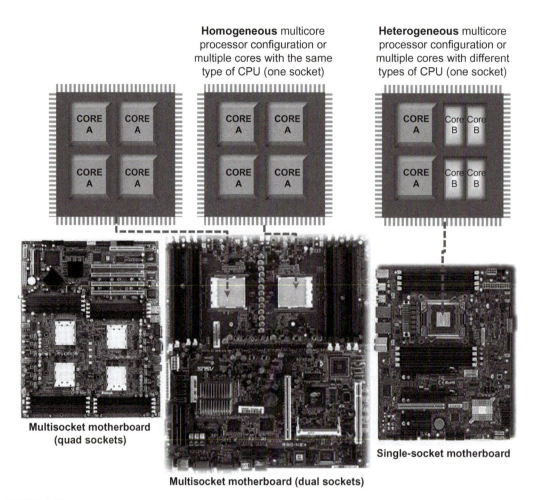

Homogeneous multicore processor configuration or multiple cores with the same type of CPU (one socket)

Heterogeneous multicore processor configuration or multiple cores with different types of CPU (one socket)

Multisocket motherboard (quad sockets)

Single-socket motherboard

Multisocket motherboard (dual sockets)

FIGURE 1.12

Multicore CPU and multisocket motherboard.

but runs two logical threads per core. Table 1.2 shows some details of common Oracle/Sun RISC server hardware.

Instruction-level parallelism: This parallel function is executed at the instruction level of a CPU because most CPUs have several execution units. Very often, the CPU does it automatically, but it can be controlled by the layout of a program's code.

Data-level parallelism: This form of parallelism relies on the CPU supporting single instruction, multiple data (SIMD) operations, such as those that can be found in various streaming SIMD extensions (SSE).

You are not limited to one type of parallel mechanism. Actually, you can use all six of these parallel models together.

RISC CPU   **Chip multithreading (CMT)**

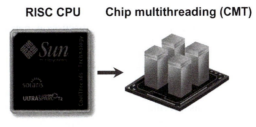

2 threads per core

FIGURE 1.13

SPARC RISC CPU with four cores.

Table 1.1 Configuration Tasks for Oracle SPARC ISC CPU: Two Logical Threads

Physical Core Number	Thread 0	Thread 1
Core 0	CPU 0 (general usage)	CPU 4 (general usage)
Core 1	CPU 1 (general usage)	CPU 5 (general usage)
Core 2	CPU 2 (writer thread)	CPU 6 (reader thread)
Core 3	CPU 3 (engine thread)	CPU 8 (engine thread)

Table 1.2 Oracle/Sun SPARC Server

Hardware Model	Processor (Socket)	Cores	Threads	L2 Cache	Unit Cost*
T-3 (1.65 GHz)	4	64	512	6	$95,000
T2000 (1.0 or 1.2 GHz)	4	6 or 8	48 or 64	3	$27,600
T5220 (1.2 or 1.4 GHz)	1	4, 6, or 8	64 (max)	4	$35,000

Note: Here, the price is just an indication. The real price is a variable of time.

However, based on Amdahl's law, there is a limit to the number of processors to be parallelized. After 1,024 processors, the performance of a computer will be improved very little or trivially and after 2,048 processors, there will be no performance improvement (see Figure 1.10).

The formula for Amdahl's law is the following:

$$S_p = \frac{P}{[f \times P + (1-f)]} = \frac{1}{\left[f + \frac{1-f}{P}\right]}$$

where S_p is the speed and f is the sequential function of a process; this calculates the magnitude of theoretical speed improvement that can be achieved for a given process by having more concurrent processors available (or parallel). In other words, it is percentage of sequential code. P represents the number of processors or cores or threads.

In order for further clarification of network communication parallelism and architecture balance parallelism terms, we have to bring another concept into the discussion, namely, distributed computing.

1.6 DISTRIBUTED COMPUTING

The rise of distributed computing was originally for a totally different reason. As we know, it is very common that many large enterprises have multiple data centers that are located at different sites. When they want to exchange results among different data centers, such as financial or sales or production information for the whole enterprise, they have to leverage distributed computing via an interconnected network (WAN or LAN).

From a decentralization perspective, it is a distributed computing system, but if we look from a centralization perspective, it is a cluster computing system. The key characteristic of a distributed computing system is the synthesis capability through the interconnected network. In comparison with parallel computing, distributed computing often has less communication requirements.

We often see that the meanings of distributed, parallel, cluster, concurrent, and high-performance computing blur. Normally, we can define distributed computing as a type of computation approach to manage computer resources from multiple administrative domains for a common computational purpose.

In short, we can say that distributed computing is about leveraging computing resources from different locations through multiple connected networks for a large and complex computation. The precise phrase for distributed computing is, "A computer system consisting of a multiplicity of processors, each with its own local memory, connected via a network. Loading or store instructions issued by a processor can only address the local memory and different mechanisms are provided for global communication" [33] (see Figure 1.14).

From a system perspective, it is a distributed system with noninteractive workloads involving a large number of files, yet more loosely coupled, heterogeneous, and geographically dispersed as compared to cluster computing. The typical example is "peer-to-peer" (P2P) computing [34], especially for wireless applications. Today distributed computing requires the following essential elements:

- A distributed-memory multiprocessor (DMM) or a server farm with connected nodes
- Shared memory multiprocessors (SMPs) or a connected uniprocessor (see Figure 1.15)
- Interconnection network (IN) and switch
- High-availability (HA) cluster
- Support for dynamic provisioning of computing resources
- Scalability
- Degree of Parallelism

There are a number of distributed computing standards or protocols have been developed, such as Common Object Request Broker (CORBA), Enterprise Java Bean (EJB), Java 2 Enterprise Edition (J2EE), and Microsoft's Distributed Common Object Manager (DCOM). The basic idea of developing these protocols is to specify how objects talk to each other. This idea is also the primary concept for cloud computing.

However, although distributed computing intends to leverage a commodity cluster, the purpose of distributed computing was mainly driven by high-performance computing for academic and laboratory applications rather than commercial interests.

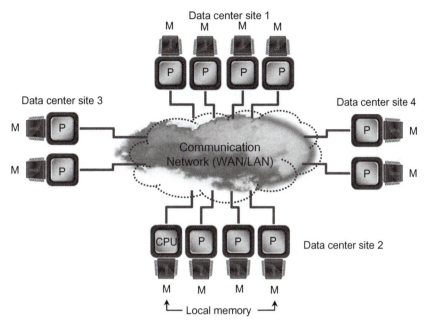

A message-passing multicomputer

FIGURE 1.14

Interconnected distributed computing.

1.7 GRID COMPUTING

Back in 1998, Ian Foster and Carl Kesselman described the term "grid computing" [24] as follows: "a computational grid is a hardware and software infrastructure that provides dependable, consistent, pervasive, and inexpensive access to high-end computational capabilities." They used an electricity grid network as an analogy to explain a computer resourse supply model. In other words, grid computing uses many computers of the same class to form a grid environment as a computing infrastructure to perform a resource-intensive computing task, such as a weather forecast or nuclear fusion simulation.

Rajkumar Buyya defined utility-oriented grid computing as follows [25]: a "grid is a type of parallel and distributed system that enables the sharing, selection, and aggregation of geographically distributed 'autonomous' resources dynamically at runtime depending on their availability, capability, performance, cost, and users' quality-of-service requirements."

We can consider grid computing as one of the roots of cloud computing. Cloud computing is a natural extension of grid computing. By its definition, we can see that grid computing has three distinguishing characteristics:

- Virtual computer capability
- Performing large tasks
- Cooperating with a loosely clustered network

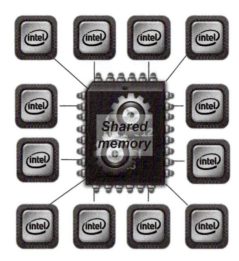

A shared-memory multiprocessor

FIGURE 1.15

Shared-memory multiprocessors (SMPs).

In comparison with cloud computing, grid computing is not a business-oriented model of Internet computing. This is why it was not widely accepted in the business community. Despite its limitations, it has made a lot of progresses in terms of the Open Grid Services Architecture (OGSA), Open Grid Services Infrastructure (OGSI), and Web Services Resource Framework (WSRF). From a technical perspective, grid computing shares some common characteristics with cloud computing, such as web access, the fact that the underlying hardware can be anywhere, a scalable resource pool, on-demand computing, etc.

After more than 10 years development, the grid community established the grid architecture or infrastructure, which allows different third-party vendors to deploy their application services (both software and hardware) so they can be plugged in to grid resources (see Figure 1.16).

This grid model is a layer-based architecture. From this perspective, grid computing is also called "network computing." We can loosely correlate the grid with cloud service delivery models. The original idea of grid architecture model was actually derived from Internet Protocol (IP) architecture. Precisely, we can trace it back to the principle of the hourglass model [27] (see Figure 1.17).

Originally, people thought that the grid would be very applicable for the extension of the parallel computing paradigm because the grid provides a geographically distributed architecture in contrast to parallel computing's tightly coupled clusters. However, in practice, the grid has been utilized more as a platform for the integration of loosely coupled applications.

Fundamentally, the grid has replaced tight synchronization of typically identical components (or the single program, multiple data (SPMD) model) for a domain-decomposed parallel application with heterogeneous components, which the grid can scale to size within distributed systems.

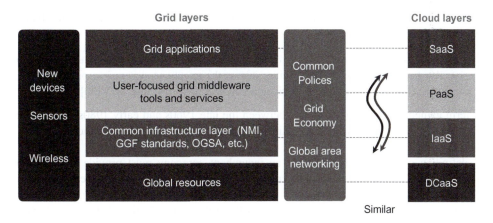

FIGURE 1.16

Layer architecture of the Community Grid Model [26].

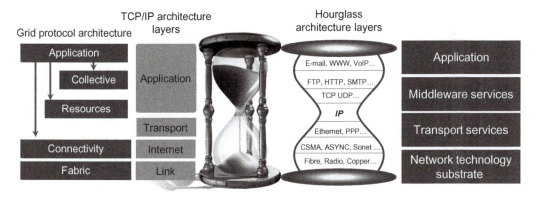

FIGURE 1.17

Comparison of grid protocol architecture and TCP/IP architecture or hourglass architecture layers.

In conclusion, the grid tries to solve the key problems of science and engineering research at a large scale. It is not particularly designed for applications for of small- and medium-size companies or even large enterprises. The grid does not place an emphasis on the issue of cost-effectiveness.

1.8 UTILITY COMPUTING

Utility computing was described by John McCarthy, a professor at MIT in 1961, when he gave his speech to celebrate MIT's centennial. At that time, he regarded the term "utility" as a computer time-sharing solution. He meant that future computing power or resources could be sold through a utility business model that is similar to water, gas, electricity, and telecommunication. His original quote was

> If computers of the kind I have advocated become the computers of the future, then computing may someday be organized as a public utility just as the telephone system is a public utility.... The computer utility could become the basis of a new and important industry" [36].

The term gained much more popularity between the late 1960s and early 1980s until the "client-server" computer because the fashion of mainstream computing and it has resurfaced after the burst of the dot-com bubble.

The definition of public utilities means an incumbent company must provide essential services to society. Normally, the government will create legislation to regulate the business or company to ensure that reliable utility services are widely available at the reasonable rate without discrimination. For example, the Australian government legislated the Telecommunication Act 1997, which fulfills the Universal Service Obligation (USO) of telecommunication utility services for every Australian.

Richard E. Brown [37] indicated that the terms "public utility" and "utility" have become interchangeable for most of people. He considered that utility services have at least following characteristics:

- The services must be an essential part of people's daily life.
- The services require large amount of capital investment in a fixed infrastructure. The return on investment (ROI) of capital may take a long time. For some rural areas, the investment may never be profitable.
- The services are often subject to regulatory oversight when it comes to rates and quality of service. The purpose of regulation is to maintain a competitive market environment for the benefits of entire society.
- The services are standardized in terms of delivery, consumption, metering, and billing.
- The accounting principle is a subscription base or pay as you go.
- The services normally have a large economic scale.

The ownership of a utility company takes different forms. Many utilities are owned and operated by different levels of government entities, such national or federal governments, state governments, cities, or municipal councils. It also can be privately owned or a publicly listed company. Based on the above-described characteristics of utility services, we will consider the following seven services as utilities (see Figure 1.18):

- Water
- Sewage discharge
- Gas
- Electricity
- Telephone
- Public transport and traffic system (including roads, railways, buses, airports, and subways)
- Public parks

For comparison with other utilities, Bunker and Thomson's [38] definition of utility computing includes the following five main points:

- "It must deliver IT as a number of services.
- It provides the right service in the right amount at the right time.

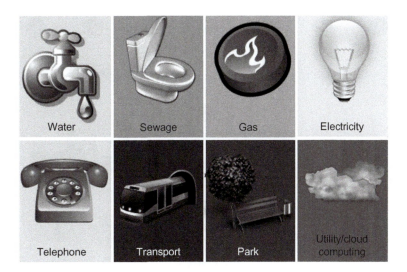

FIGURE 1.18

Utility services.

- It raises accountability for responsible consumption and reliable service delivery.
- It optimizes reliability, performance and total cost of ownership.
- It responds quickly to changing business requirements."

They argued that "utility computing is as much about process and principle as it is about technology." This definition lacks clarity and comprehensiveness. By contrast, Nicholas G. Carr [39] stated the concept or characteristics of utility computing differently; his version of utility computing has the following three basic characteristics (see Figure 1.19).

- Data centers: This will be the core resource for utility computing (large capital investment).
- Service utility: This has a lot of network equipment, along many computing elements, servers, storage disks, operating systems, and applications to use with a single resource pool (standardized resources).
- Distributed network (ultra-high-capacity data communication line) with economic scale.

Chris Almond et al. [41] claimed the history of utility computing showed that earlier utility computing was a result of hosting storage services. The first utility service that Amazon launched in March 2006 was for storage. Amazon named it Simple Storage Solution or S3. Later, Amazon extended its utility service from a storage service to computing, called the Elastic Compute Cloud or EC2.

In conclusion, utility computing can be considered the service or business model for grid or distributed computing. That is why sometimes people call it a utility computing grid. It contrasts with the client-server or PC style of computing. The fundamental technologies of utility computing are virtualized hardware and multitenant software. These technologies can integrate all computing hardware and software elements into a large standardized resource pool. Nicholas Carr predicted

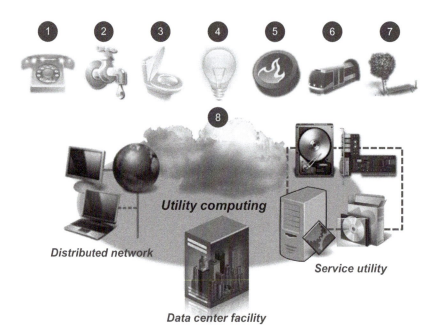

FIGURE 1.19

Utility computing.

that although "it may take many years for the utility computing system to mature...The PC age is giving way to a new era: the utility age" [7].

This usage of utility computing is almost identical to the definition of cloud computing today. Now, let's come back to the main topic of this chapter.

1.9 CLOUD COMPUTING

Since Ramnath K Chellappa first used the term "cloud computing," there have been numerous definitions for it. Many people in both the academic and commercial world are confused by usage of the term "cloud" with other types of computing, such as utility, on-demand, and even grid computing.

In order to clear these confusions, Buyya et al. [18] proposed one of the early definitions of cloud computing: "[the] cloud is a market-oriented distributed computing system consisting of a collection of inter-connected and virtualized computers that are dynamically provisioned and presented as one or more unified computing resource(s) based on service-level agreements established through negotiation between the service provider and consumers." This definition has a similar

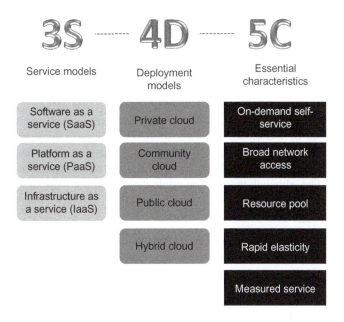

FIGURE 1.20

NIST's "3-4-5" definition of cloud computing.

meaning as the American National Institute of Standards and Technology (NIST) term, which has now been widely adopted. NIST defined the term "cloud" as follows [42]:

> Cloud computing is a model for enabling ubiquitous, convenient, on-demand network access to a shared pool of configurable computing resources (e.g., networks, servers, storage, applications, and services) that can be rapidly provisioned and released with minimal management effort or service provider interaction.

Based on the above description, we can simplify the NIST term of cloud into three service models, four deployment models, and five essential characteristics or "3S-4D-5C" (or simply "3-4-5") cloud definition (see Figure 1.20). This is a comprehensive and concise definition and easier to remember. However, it is not very compelling in term of business sense because it only emphasizes the technical and processing deployment and fails to underscore the business aspects of the cloud, such as:

- No up-front capex
- No contractual obligations
- Pay per use
- Highly abstracted hardware
- Virtual nature
- Fine-grained resource allocation

Moreover, it doesn't include three critical cloud enabling technologies:

• Process auto-orchestration
• Software multitenancy
• Hardware or infrastructure virtualization

Armbrust et al. [43] tried to define the term from a business orientation. Their definition filled in some of the points that NISTmissed, such as no up-front capex, and pay per use but did not cover all characteristics of the cloud. In order to find a comprehensive meaning of the term "cloud," we have done an extensive search crossing a few hundred cloud books, articles, and white-papers that have been published since 2008. Unfortunately, we cannot find a single definition as comprehensive as we like, although there are multiple definitions out there. If we consider the defi-nitions for other types of computing as described above, we may have the same conclusion as Larry Ellison drew on September 26, 2008:

> The interesting thing about Cloud Computing is that we've redefined Cloud Computing to include everything that we already do. … I do not understand what we would do differently in the light of Cloud Computing other than change the wording of some of our ads.[2]

If cloud computing is redefining what we've already done during the last two decades, why should we bother to redefine it again? Is it just a marketing hype campaign? The answer is, "yes and no."

The answer is "yes" because cloud computing can be considered as just the extension of grid, distributed, parallel, pervasive, heterogeneous, ubiquitous, nomadic, and other types of computing. The answer is "no" because cloud computing can also be assigned new meanings based on new ways of computing resource consumption.

Therefore, we should give cloud computing a functional definition. It is not an exclusive or reductionism style of definition, such as x is really nothing but y. Instead, we will define cloud computing as a formula or cumulative equation, $Z = A + B + \ldots + X$.

If Z equals cloud computing, then $A =$ utility computing and $B =$ on-demand computing, and $X =$ other new innovative business models of computing.

In very simple terms, cloud computing is utility-based computing plus on-demand and other new business functions or new ways of resource consumption when they are available and applicable.

If $Z = A$, it is utility computing, and if $Z = B$, it is on-demand computing If $Z = A + B$ or $Z = A + B + X$, it is cloud computing. In summary, the term "cloud computing" is an open-ended definition. It is utility computing with different resource consumption models.

Cloud computing has shifted the paradigm from new technologies to new business models (see Figure 1.21).

Technically, we can consider grid computing as an extension of both parallel and distributed computing; they are derived from high-performance Ccmputing (HPC), and are all within the Internet domain, which is shown on the upper-left side of Figure 1.21. In the wireless and sensor network domain, pervasive computing can be seen as the extension of both ubiquitous (sometime also called ambient computing) and nomadic computing. However, heterogeneous computing is set

---

[2]Larry Ellison's view of the cloud quoted in the *Wall Street Journal*, September 26, 2008.

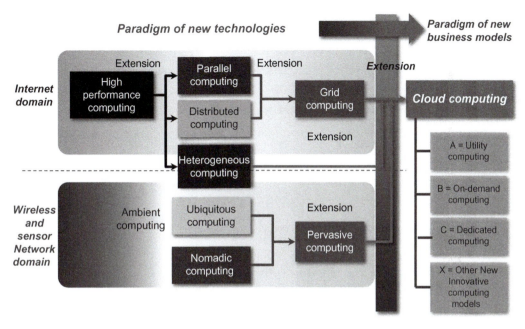

FIGURE 1.21

Paradigm shift from technologies to business models.

between the Internet and wireless domains. All these terms of computing are within the paradigm of new technologies.

On the right side of Figure 1.21, we can consider cloud computing as technically the extension of grid, pervasive, and heterogeneous computing. However, from a business perspective, it is also underpinned by utility, on-demand, dedicated, and other new innovative computing models. All these terms are within the paradigm of new business models. In essence, the innovation of cloud computing has triggered the paradigm shift from new technologies to new business models.

Practically, there is no clear break between utility (or traditional) hosting and the cloud model. Instead, cloud computing is complementary to the traditional utility business model.

The term "cloud computing" may sound very abstract, fuzzy, ambiguous, and illusive to ordinary people. It seems we cannot feel, touch, taste, and grasp it. However, in reality, all virtual infrastructures are built on the physical infrastructure. The physical components should include the data center, distributed network, and service utilities, which include servers and storage.

Based on NIST's cloud definition and considerations of computing technology extension or evolution, we can draw a compelling and functional definition of cloud computing, where we add three key cloud-enabling technologies (see Figure 1.22).

Moreover, if we look at the cloud from a business model perspective, we find that the cloud is similar to an airline business, which delivers transportation services from one place to another. The cloud deployment models are more like different classes of airlines. The private cloud can be considered a private jet, the public cloud as economy class, and the hybrid cloud as business

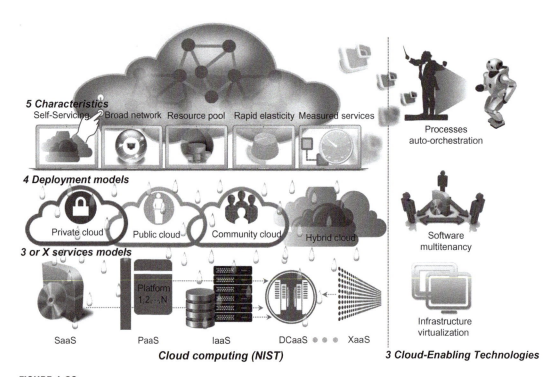

FIGURE 1.22

Overview of cloud computing definition.

class via a commercial airline (see Figure 1.23). An airport is similar to a data center and the goods and passengers are like data or information handled by a data center computing infrastructure. The Internet can be considered the flight network (see Figures 1.24 and 1.25). As a matter of the fact, the recent AWS price model is almost identical toan airline ticket price model (see Figure 1.26).

However, some people have a different view [44]. They believe the following three types of situations or characteristics should not be considered cloud computing:

- "Renting dedicated server hardware in a data center for a single task, such as hosting a website, even if it is on a subscription basis
- Server virtualization (running multiple virtual computers on a single server) in itself, unless servers can be deployed and destroyed in minutes by the consumer themselves rather than the provider
- Connecting to your home PC or office PC from anywhere using remote desktop or VPN (Virtual Private Network) technology"

If the meaning of cloud computing is purely a technical term or restricted within a fixed and static boundary, the first point might appear to be reasonable, but the cloud is neither a purely technical definition nor a closed or fixed boundary term.

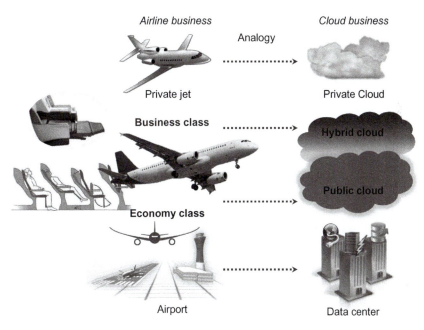

FIGURE 1.23

Analogy of airline and cloud computing businesses.

FIGURE 1.24

Details of international air travel flight network.

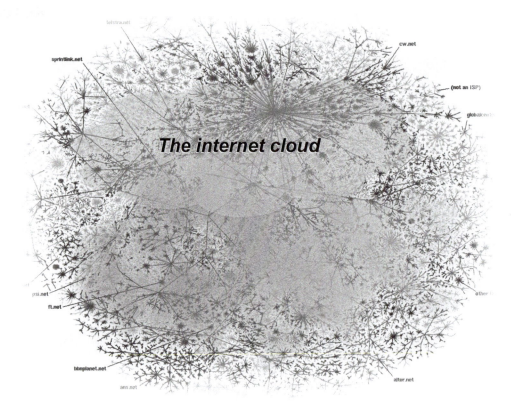

The internet cloud

FIGURE 1.25

The world Internet map [40].

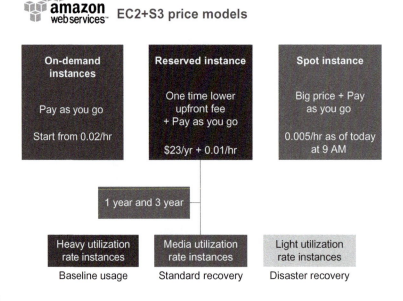

FIGURE 1.26

AWS price models.

We believe the term "cloud computing" has not only evolved but also assigned the new and innovative meaning of different business models. If we consider the cloud as a dynamic computing environment, then "renting dedicated server hardware in a data centre facility for a single task of web hosting" would be a temporary mode. The state of this website hosting can be changed at any time. It is really dependent on the business needs. The beauty of the cloud is that it is a dynamic environment with an ever-changing nature. The dedicated server hardware for a single task is just a special case of the cloud.

When we talk about the cloud, server virtualization always comes with it because it is one of three fundamental technologies that underpin the cloud, especially for IaaS. It is a part of the cloud. Without server virtualization, there would be no cloud. The relationship between server virtualisation and the cloud is not exclusive, but rather complementary. The method of virtual machine (VM) resource consumption, monitoring, and management is really dependent on each individual business or customer. The second characteristic of the noncloud argument has a lack of cogency because the characteristic of a cloud has nothing to do with who should operate the process of provisioning, deploying, cloning, or destroying a VM.

Regarding of the third point of the cloud definition exclusion, it is unnecessary to make the distinction between a remote desktop connection and cloud computing. It doesn't make any sense. To some degree, remote desktops and VPN should be a part of the cloud. A remote desktop or VPN is one of the enabling technologies to deliver the virtualization desk infrastructure (VDI) or application virtualization. It should be part of Desktop as a Service.

There are so many illogical and noncogent cloud definitions around. They do not serve the purposes of our goal and make it confusing for people to understand what the real cloud is. Consequently, they wouldn't be helpful for a decision maker to make a correct and strategic investment decision. Therefore, we believe it is vital to have a clear and logical definition of the cloud out there first.

So far, we have spent a lot of effort to define cloud computing. You may wonder, why is this so? And how is it significant for our cost framework and strategic investment decision making? The answer is in the value proposition of cloud computing. It doesn't matter how you define the cloud. Our main driver behind the above definition exercise is to elicit cloud business values: cost efficiency, time to market, flexibility, high scalability of computing resource pool, auto-provisioning, self-service, self-management, higher utilization rate, and no contractual obligations (see Figure 1.27).

These values will not only shape our cost framework construction but also underpin the foundation of strategic investment decision making. During the last five years or so, there have been so many terms and definitions of cloud computing, and the meaning of cloud computing is always drifting from time to time and person to person. As a result, it can be challenging to discuss the business values and cost efficiency of cloud computing.

By an extensive literature review (academic research papers and whitepapers written by different cloud service providers, hardware and software vendors [45−51]), we have found the estimated cost savings for cloud computing could vary from 24% to the significant amount of 300%−500%. Moreover, the cloud could also deliver negative business value. William Forrest's [52] research found that cloud computing could cost more than traditional computing by as much as 144% with Amazon's EC2 service (see Figure 1.28).

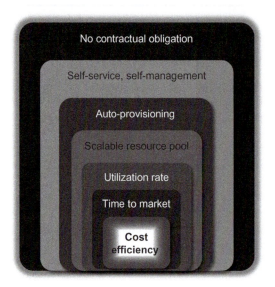

FIGURE 1.27

Driving forces of cloud computing value proposition.

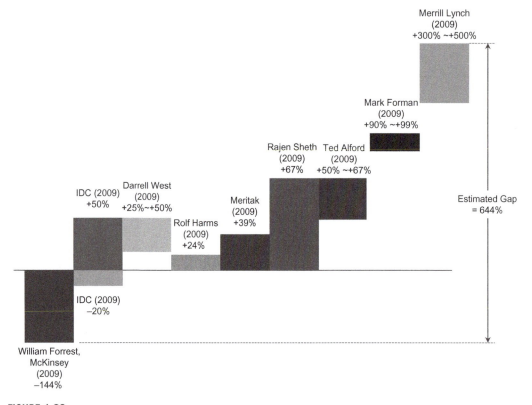

FIGURE 1.28

Estimated cost savings for cloud computing from different authors and sources.

The wide variation of cost savings indicates the following key points are very challenging to decide.

1. People define and understand cloud computing differently.
2. There is no unified standard to estimate cost savings from the cloud.
3. People use different economic metrics and different methods to measure the cloud.
4. People use the cloud differently for different purposes or applications.
5. A cloud consumer may have different legacy IT systems, such as legacy data center infrastructure or computer hardware and software in co-location. or even doesn't have at all if a cloud user may be a startup company.
6. The cloud is still an emerging business model supported by emerging technologies
7. There are considerable uncertainties around cloud technology selection, architecture design, capacity planning, vendor discount ratio, cloud deployment, and migration.
8. There are also many operational influences such as utilization rate, support contract terms, SLA, business impact on downtime cost estimation, life cycle or exit cost, disaster recovery cost, and degree of auto-provisioning and auto-orchestration.
9. Finally, both the user's and operator's skill are critical factors in terms of operation cost.

In addition to these challenges, people often use so called "typical" examples or configurations to estimate the cost savings, but it can be quite hard to have a common setup for the "typical" criteria in the IT industry.

With different understandings, perceptions, expectations, purposes, yardsticks, metrics, methodologies, and utilization rates used when forecasting the future for cloud computing, it is inevitable that we have a wide variation of cost estimates.

That is why we present this book to readers: to provide a broad cost framework that covers all aspects of the cloud computing cost modeling and analysis process. The analysis process will discuss cost estimates, assumption making, and model simulation. The book can ultimately help the decision maker to make smart, transparent, and correct investment decisions in a highly dynamic environment.

1.10 SUMMARY

In this chapter, we discussed different ways of computing before the definition of the cloud. As we noted, cloud computing is mainly driven by cost efficiency rather than new technologies. This is why many cloud experts concluded that the cloud is not about a new technology but rather a new business model. The model drives a transformation from a "buy" mode to a "lease" mode as the way of consuming computing resources. We can look this transformation from two aspects.

1.10.1 SOFTWARE (APPLICATIONS)

From the application perspective, a user doesn't have to purchase the software licence, but rather lease the software or subscribe to it. Ownership of a software licence doesn't add to the business value for the company. Sometime, it only carries a cost burden for the business because the company doesn't only make large initial capex investment, but also has to maintain, patch, and upgrade it. The concept of SaaS is really to shift the focus from software to service, which means the business or application users can divert more resources or energy to core competences rather than software. The significant points of cloud computing are:

- It will make the IT capex fade away from many enterprises' account books.
- Software defines everything. The physical infrastructure will be virtualized. Today's physical server will become a virtual file stored in a database.
- The break-fix service supported by many hardware vendors will become unnecessary because virtualized infrastructure can support v-motion, v-storage, v-switch ports, and other high-availability (HA) functions.

1.10.2 IT INFRASTRUCTURE (HARDWARE)

The second aspect of this transformation is the elastic IT resource or resource pool. In the past or during the "buy" era, the relationship between software and hardware was a one-to-one coupling relationship, which is the so-called client-server architecture. One hardware device was dedicated to one software program or application. As a result, the average utilization rate of hardware was much lower, especially for a physical server. Based on the statistical data, the average utilization rate was around $10-15\%$. Some applications such as a hosting server for mobile content could be less than 1% for many consumer application types, such as a hosting server for retail content that only gets busy during particular seasons, such as Christmas. In other words, the IT resource is just utilized for a particular month. The rest of the year it is sitting in an idle mode. This had led to the Amazon Web Service (AWS) or EC2 + S3 business model, which is about leasing computing power capacity. The key element of this model is time. To borrow the legal term, "time is of the essence."

From the customer perspective, the cost of a cloud computing resource (time) is totally transparent. Like never before, computing resources can be charged on an hourly basis. AWS's EC2 model doesn't only mean time-based charges, but also gives customers great flexibility or scalability without a long term commitment (PAYG). Theoretically speaking, a customer can have unlimited computing resources. The hardware has been moved from a one-to-one relationship to one-to-many or many-to-one or many-to-many relationship.

The elastic way of computing resource consumption can help a customer to minimize IT resource inefficiency due to business fluctuations. It shifts the risks of IT resource inefficiency from a customer to a cloud service provider.

Overall, we can recap the main points of this chapter as follows:

- We should see cloud computing as a paradigm shift from "buy" to "lease" and from a technology paradigm to a business paradigm. This means a mixing of both traditional and innovative ways of consuming resources for computing. Traditional ways of computing include utility, on-demand, dedicated, and pervasive computing. Innovative ways of computing mean PAYG, no contractual obligations, no up-front capex, an unlimited resource pool, cost transparency, auto-portioning, and auto orchestration.
- NIST's "3S-4D-5C" description of cloud computing is the comprehensive technical definition.

- Cloud computing is an extension of grid and other ways of computing. It leverages all other ways of computing for business advantages.
- The universal definition of cloud computing should not only include technical terms but also a business meaning.
- The key driving forces of cloud computing are cost efficiency, time to market, flexibility, high scalability of the resource pool, auto-provisioning, self-service, self-management, higher utilization, high availability, and no contractual obligations.
- Cloud computing is the evolution of different ways of computing. It is not really a new technology but is supported by three emerging technologies, namely, virtualization, multitenancy, and auto-orchestration.
- Because of a variety of cloud definitions and metrics, and the many uncertainties surrounding the cloud, the estimated cost savings for adopting the cloud can vary from -144% to $+500\%$. Obviously, such a large variation is unacceptable when we want to make a strategic investment decision.

The goal of this book is to unveil a comprehensive cost framework and a set of methodologies to reduce this cost variation to an acceptable level. In essence, we try to find a practicable way to estimate the cost for decision makers so they make the right strategic investment decision.

1.11 REVIEW QUESTIONS

1. What are the three new technologies that underpin cloud computing?
2. If I say cloud computing is "just another molecule of the cloud," what kind of definition is that?
3. Is NIST's cloud definition comprehensive? If not, why?
4. What is the best way to describe the cloud?
5. What are the fundamental differences between the grid and the cloud?
6. Why has the cloud become popular in the IT industry?
7. Why do people have such wide range of variation for cloud computing cost estimates?
8. What are the key value propositions of cloud computing?
9. What are the significant points of cloud computing?

BUSINESS NEEDS

Understanding what the business needs is the process of identifying business problems and providing a cost-effective solution to the business owner[1] or customer.[2] Basically, the process of identifying business needs can be considered business analysis. This is one of the essential and critical steps for the IT professional to add IT value to the business. If a cloud service provider or IT professional does not understand what the business wants, then the subsequent solution provided by IT will be hardly satisfactory for the business or customer.

This chapter covers the following basic topics: why we need business analysts, how to understand what the business needs, how to identify business problems, and how to provide effective IT or cloud solutions to solve business problems. We will organize these issues in the following order.

First, we will begin with an introduction to certain business termsa dn definitions and a look at the evolution of the business analysis (BA) role. Then, we will discuss how to elicit different business requirements based on the volume, variation, and velocity of a business. We will particularly focus on some issues concerning business requirements and the cloud infrastructure, not only from a consumer perspective but also from a cloud service provider's point of view. Finally, we will unveil the practical process of identifying business needs, including how to communicate with stakeholders and customers, and how to meet customers and stakeholders' expectations and avoid become a blame attractor (BA).

The primary goal of this chapter is to find out how we can translate the business objective (or a strategic goal) into a language that a cloud service provider can fully understand so that the cloud architecture or solution provider can articulate a number of alternatives or options and recommend the right solutions to the business owner or decision makers so that the right strategic decision can be made. In essence, this chapter focuses on how to use a cloud infrastructure to solve business problems.

2.1 INTRODUCTION

"Analysis is 90% business driven and 10% technically driven" [53, 54]. Although this statement may be slightly overexaggerated, it does emphasize that the bottom line of business analysis is to

---

[1]The term of "the business" means "line of business" (LoB) for a large organization, such as consumer business, enterprise business, media business, etc. For small- or medium-size companies, the term "the business" would be very simple, the company itself.

[2]The term "customer" or "customers" stands for product or service consumers. This can be either an end user or a business that sell its services or products to the end users.

deliver what a business needs (solve a business problem) rather than just achieving an analytic result for IT purposes. As a matter of fact, the purpose of business analysis is to make sure that IT expenditure is aligned with business needs. You may think this is quite obvious and that it is needless to say it. However, when the size of a company is growing larger, the purpose of IT expenditures or IT activities often deviates further away from business reality. In other words, the IT costs will become hard to justify for the needs of the business. This is because some decision makers in many large organizations could just chase fancy and fashionable IT solutions rather than searching for real business value or business needs when they are making IT investment decisions for projects such as cloud investment. Very often, this is because IT expenditures have no direct relationship with the business or IT costs are not transparent to the business.

Consider this scenario: Once a CIO called his IT manager into his office and said, "Here is 5 million dollars. We want to build our cloud infrastructure because many of our competitors have already constructed their cloud infrastructure. If you need further IT capex, please let me know." Is this right or a rational decision? If not, what was wrong?

From a cognitive bias perspective, we can see that this CIO made a classic mistake due to two cognition fallacies:

- Social proof bias
- Action bias

"Social proof" is also sometime called the "herd instinct." It indicates that each individual wants to behave or act the same as others. And the more people act a certain way, the better the justification for people who follow the behavior. This may sound very ridiculous. Logically, "if 50 million people say something foolish, it is still foolish."[3] However, we often see it happen in real estate auction bidding or in the stock market. As Rolf Dobelli [56] indicated, it is quite pervasive across the fashion industry, management techniques, product types, hobbies, and even religions. The reason that we act like this is because being a copycat was a good survival strategy during the Stone Age. The instant response to follow others' behavior is deeply embedded in our genes.

But now, we are in the information or Internet age. "Social proof" may do more harm than good because our new decision environment has become much more complex than it used to be. Nowadays, decision making requires a careful analysis, intelligent thinking, and logical reasoning rather than a gut feeling or instinct response, especially for those decisions that have long-term impact or millions of dollars in consequences.

"Action bias" refers to the scenario where people face uncertainty and believe they should take some intervention or action rather than sit quietly and do nothing. Whether the intervention is good or bad is another matter because if you just wait there, you believe you will not get a reward, although in actuality doing nothing is often the right choice.

We believe doing something is better than nothing when we are suddenly facing unfamiliar and wobbly circumstances as it often makes us feel better even if we have made things worse by acting too quickly or too often. The typical example is that when a person has lost his/her wallet, action bias will lead to the person running around and looking for his/her wallet everywhere rather than thinking about the last time he/she used his/her wallet first. Just as French mathematician, physicist,

---

[3]W. Somerset Maugham's quote.

inventor, theology and philosopher Blaise Pascal said, "All of humanity's problems stem from man's inability to sit quietly in a room alone."[4]

Even if the decision on a cloud investment project is proven to be correct technologically, it might still have a lack of business orientation; the result of the project delivery might not be satisfactory for the business manager or stakeholders.

There have been numerous stories where the business manager complained about IT people that could not deliver what they really wanted or expected. There have also been cases where many IT people muttered that the business leadership do not know what they really want and expect everything or too much. Subsequently, many valuable resources (time, budget, and energy) have been wasted. Here is one of typical stories told by a business manager:

> It is absolutely a mess! I do not know who is in charge of our project. It appears everyone claims they are working on it but no one really takes the responsibility for it.
>
> My team has generated many incredible business initiatives for the cloud market. These initiatives have led to many subsequent IT projects. We expect IT people to deliver the projects on time and within the budget. But, unfortunately, the results of projects were very disappointing. We want "A" but they give "B." There is no clear deliverable result. I do not think IT people have an idea what they were doing. They are hopeless. Now, not only have we lost opportunities to catch up the market leader, but also we are falling far behind other competitors at the peer level. I think the IT people never understand what we really want in the first place. I cannot recall the last time they have delivered a result where we were really satisfied. No one in the business team has any confidence with IT people.
>
> Furthermore, whenever I ask for the project's progress, they always ask for additional resources (headcounts and extra capex). I'm afraid the IT capex budget will be out of control in this financial year. I cannot see a good solution for this mess because I do not know enough about information technology. I think I have been trapped into this deadly spiral that I can never get out of it

This is just one side of story. However, if you talk to an IT manager or professional, you may hear the other side of the story, which is totally different from what the business manager has stated:

> These guys have no idea what they really want and change business requirements and technical specifications almost daily but they still expect us to deliver IT solutions on time and within the budget. They absolutely have no idea how the technology works but they always hold too many unrealistic expectations. They think IT people are supermen. My view is they do not know what they really want in the first place but always expect IT to deliver more than what they required. It is very hard to communicate with them because they are on different wavelengths. These guys are very difficult please and to deal with.

This is a very typical story of IT project delivery. Many business managers and senior executives have the same experiences as the above business manager. The issue has become worse in recent years as IT has been growing from a simple project to a very complex one that crosses the domain of multiple programs (see Figure 2.1). It used to be possible for one man to do it but now

---

[4]Blaise Pascal, Letters Provincials and Pensees (Thoughts).

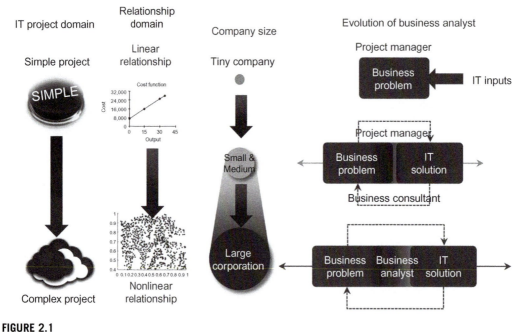

FIGURE 2.1

Evolution of business analyst function.

it has become a collaborative work that should be completed by a team or a group of people who may cross many different organizations.

Based on the Standish Group's biannual reports for 1994 to 2012 [55], the average successful rate of 90,000 IT projects is only around 30% and the approximate standard deviation is 7%. The majority of IT projects had either serious challenges (46% late, over budget, and/or with less than the required features and functions) or failed (24% cancelled prior to completion or delivered and never used) (see Tables 2.1 and 2.2).

In accordance with the Standish Group's statistical data, there have been many other consulting firms, such as Gartner, McKinsey, IDC, and KPMG, as well as surveys such as the Robbin-Gioia Survey, Conference Board Survey, and OASIG Survey, that released reports having the same conclusion. One influential article written by Robert N. Charette [56] and published in a 2005 IEEE Spectrum magazine listed 31 notable disasterous IT projects from 1993 to 2005, which Robert called the "Software Hall of Shame." Nine years later, is the situation getting better or worse? Well, the situation might appear to be slightly better, but the fundamental issues that cause IT project failure or fiascos still have not been resolved. Based on the Software Hall of Shame and "catalogue of catastrophe" [57], we expanded this list and added 79 more IT projects from 2006 to 2013. Altogether, we have the total of 110 failed IT projects. From this list, we can see:

- Over 65% of these projects were sponsored by either federal or state governments. (Many private companies might not report their IT projects catastrophes.)
- The total estimated cost was more than $174 billion.

Table 2.1 The Standish Group International Report on IT Projects

Year	Successful	Challenged	Failed
1994	16%	53%	31%
1996	27%	33%	40%
1998	26%	46%	28%
2000	28%	49%	23%
2002	34%	51%	15%
2004	29%	53%	18%
2006	35%	46%	19%
2008	32%	44%	24%
2010	37%	42%	21%
2012	39%	43%	18%

Table 2.2 Issues within Challenges Category

Year	Time (Late)	Cost (Budget)	Completed Features (Functions)
2004	84%	56%	64%
2006	72%	47%	68%
2008	79%	54%	67%
2010	71%	46%	74%
2012	74%	59%	69%

For over 20 years, "Nothing has changed," "Not a damn thing" [58]. "Trends come and go in the technology industry but some things, such as IT system failures, bloom eternal." Some IT disasters have happened twice, perhaps three times, such as Sydney Water's CISB project (in 2002, 2009 and after overhaul again in 2011). Robert Charette's remark was "Sydney Water doesn't seem to learn prior IT lessons well" [59]. It has now become one of the typical case studies for many universities, including Harvard Business School. You may wonder, "How could it happen once, twice, and perhaps three times?" Why did not they learn their lesson? Do IT people know what the real reasons behind these IT project fiascos are?

Actually, back in 2005, Robert Charette had identified 12 the most common factors that lead to IT project catastrophe:

- Unrealistic or unarticulated project goals
- Inaccurate estimates of needed resources
- Badly defined system requirements

- Poor reporting of the project's status
- Unmanaged risks
- Poor communication among customers, developers, and users
- Use of immature technology
- Inability to handle the project's complexity
- Sloppy development practices
- Poor project management
- Stakeholder politics
- Commercial pressures

In addition to tryind to address these common factors, many methodologies have been developed, such as PRINCE2, waterfall, agile, lean, PMP, critical path management (CPM), benefits realization management, process based management, etc. Many project experts and consultant firms emphasize project processes and useful tools and systems. However, even with these certified methods and useful tools, people still witness many IT projects that fail spectacularly. Referring to Appendix A, we can find a long list of failed projects after 2005.

You may wonder why people do not learn from previous mistakes and why IT project failure doesn't seem to change. It is because people put too much emphasis on project processes and useful tools but fail to mention one of the fundamental reasons behind many IT project disasters, which is the human factor. For any IT project, if it is successful, it is the people's success and if it is failure, it is the people's failure.

2.2 PROJECT CONTENTS AND PROCESSES

Many large-scale projects fail so often because the project process and project content have been driven apart due to the complexity of the project. If people just focus on the project process and forget about the contents behind the process, project failure is likely inevitable. We can possibly draw an analogy between overemphasizing project process and formal logical reasoning, which is deductive in nature. As we know, formal logical reasoning has three characteristic properties:

1. The conclusion follows necessarily from the premise.
2. The conclusion does not contain any new information.
3. Formal logical reasoning does not refer to any external worlds. It does not add any new knowledge to our understanding. It just rearranges content in different orders. It just makes content from implicitly to explicitly.

The basic unit of reasoning in formal logical reasoning is the syllogism, which the structure consists of two premises and a conclusion. For example,"If all project managers are ambitious and all ambitious people are selfish, therefore, all project managers are selfish." Regardless of whether these premises are correct or not, this syllogism is perfectly right in terms of formal logical reasoning. We can replace these premises with symbols A, B, and C and write as "If A is B and B is C, then A must be C." In other words, the process of formal logical reasoning can be totally independent from its contents. The question is, "How often is this the case in reality?" What we would like out of logical reasoning is to start from what we know and move to what we do not know. Unfortunately, the process of the formal logical reasoning only rearranges contents rather than generating new knowledge.

Similarly, many people often separate the content and process of a project and believe if they can follow the standard project process correctly (such as PMP, PRINCE2, lean project management, etc.) they will achieve the project goal or make the project successful. (Here, the project contents mean the business goal). Again, how often this is a case? The answer is not very often.

The conclusion is that it does not matter how complex the project is. You can never divorce the IT project content or the business reality (business goal, technology to support the business, organization politics, etc.) from the IT project process. If you do, project failure is inevitable.

2.3 ALLOCATE THE RIGHT PEOPLE FOR THE RIGHT JOB

We have made the claim that any successful IT project is due to people's success. Why is this so? This is because we often allocate the wrong people for the wrong job. Because many decision makers believe that the project content can be separated from its process, many incapable individuals have been promoted to project manager or program manager positions.

Normally, we can classify many IT project jobs into four categories via a 2×2 matrix (see Figure 2.2) in term of complexity and degree of collaboration:

- Sausage machine works
- Complex works
- Daily operation works
- Innovative and exploring works

Ideally, a large project or program manager should be a universal genius. He/she can not only perform all four types of work but also has a higher IQ and EQ (see Figure 2.2), which means he/she is very smart and works hard, and has a good attitude and high level of communication ability. In short, the person has both the right skill and the right attitude or passion.

Unfortunately, we have seen many people who do not have a passion for IT but are highly motivated promoted to the manager position because many decision makers believe that project contents can be divorced from the process. This will lead to disaster for any project. Remember, a highly motivated and ignorant individual will accelerate the speed of destroying the business value. We should never allocate ignorant, highly motivated, paper-pushing types for the role of a large IT project manager.

Speaking about motivation, people normally have different motivations to participate in a project or join a project team. The most common motivations are:

- Money
- Power

However, some people focus on:

- Self-achievement
- VRecognition
  - Passion

Still others may just want to release their emotions.

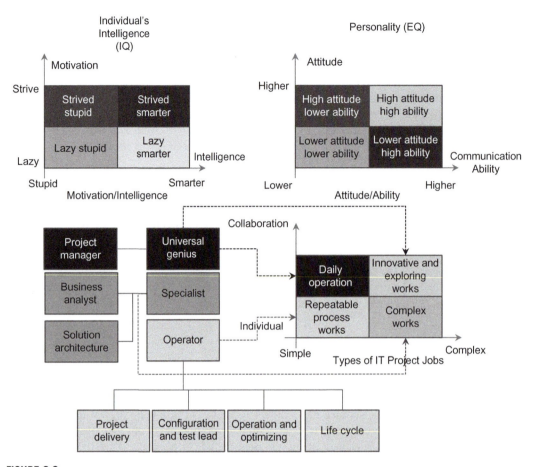

FIGURE 2.2

People's Capabilities and Project Job Allocation.

In order to achieve success for any large-scale project, the project manager should not only have the right skills (or intelligence or IQ) and a good personality (or EQ), but also the right motivation. We have to understand that a person can exceed his/her capability but can never exceed his/her personality. Each individual's personality will decide his/her fate. It is a part of the personal decision pattern. Preferably, the person who has the motivation of passion, recognition, and self-achievement is the right candidate for the management role for large-scale projects. We have seen many IT project catastrophes that are mainly fueled by intense political fights for power or a promotion (salary increase or money) within the organization.

To some degree, a project is similar to a "startup business." A project manager would be the captain who can steer and navigate the project through unfamiliar territory.

Of course, it is impossible and unnecessary to find universal geniuses for all project tasks. This is why a project will need many specialists or different types of human resources. What is a specialist? What is the different between a universal genius and a specialist?

In simple terms, a universal genius is gold. He/she will shine for any project role at any time. In contrast, a specialist is brass. He/she will only flare when he/she is in the right position (or role). If you put him/her in the wrong position, he/she will rust. The typical specialist roles for many projects are the business analyst and solution architect.

In comparison with the universal genius and specialist roles, there is another role that is defined for duplicated tasks or activities within a process, such as delivery, configuration, and testing. We call this role the operator. Many companies will outsource these roles in order to keep costs lower. Of course, some delivery, configuration, and test roles may be considered specialist roles. It would depend on the circumstances of each individual project. Normally, the company should never outsource universal genius and specialist roles to third-party vendors.

To focus on the topic of this chapter, we will concentrate on the details of the business analyst role and its activities.

2.4 **BUSINESS ANALYST ROLE**

After more than a half century's evolution, any sizable IT project is not just a simple or isolated task, but rather a complex and interactive program that consists of activities including networks, security, software, databases, contents, applications development, and web hosting. There are so many layers from an end-to-end perspective. The relationship of input and output is not linear or straightforward. The project has to draw from many different domains of knowledge or toolkits. It is almost impossible for one individual to cope with a complex IT project where he/she will deliver an end-to-end IT solution. You need a group of IT professionals who specialize in different fields or disciplines to complete a complex IT project. This has led to the gap between the business and IT domains. People often ask:

- Who should understand, collaborate, and document the business requirements?
- Who should identify the business problem?
- Who should recommend the right solution for the business problem?
- Who should interpret business terms into IT language?
- Who should communicate with different stakeholders?
- Who should manage the stakeholders' relationship?
- Who should manage the conflicts among different stakeholders?
- Who should manage the business and stakeholders' expectations?

Traditionally, these tasks or functions were scattered across many different roles in an organisation, such as IT project manager, system engineer, business manager, software engineer, product manager, IT architecture, delivery manager, application or solution developer, configuration manager, software test lead, quality assurance analyst, etc. (see Figure 2.3).

Actually in April 1972, when Federico Faggin designed the world's first microprocessor chip, the Intel 4004 for the Busicom project, he did everything from logic and circuit design, layout,

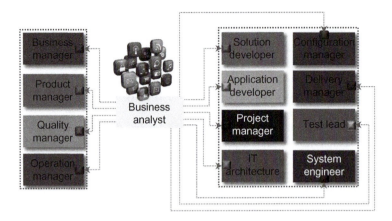

FIGURE 2.3

Business analyst responsibility scattered across all roles.

ruby cutting, mask-making, wafer fabrication, test program development and transfer to production. In addition, he had to communicate and work together with his customer or working partner, Masatoshi Shima from Busicom. He was not only a microprocessor designer or an innovator but also a project manager. In essence, he was playing the universal genius role. Of course, Ted Hoff created the idea of the universal microprocessor and did a sketch of architecture design of the 4001, 4002, 4003 and 4004. Moreover, Ted was a business development manager or liaison officer between Busicom and Intel. We will have a further discussion about the first microprocessor chip in a later part of this book.

Today, we cannot imagine that all these tasks could be assigned to one individual because today's business requirements are not just to produce a simple calculator. They have become much more complex. A more sophisticated microprocessor has been embedded into all aspects of our daily life from a smart phone to an automobile, from a TV set to a washing machine. Subsequently, one individual's job has been segmented into many different professional roles.

Business requirements, problem identification, and effective solution delivery have moved from one person's responsibility to many people's responsibility. Unfortunately, if everyone has the responsibility, it often means no one has the responsibility. The above story has told us exactly what will happen if the responsibility has been scattered across many people. It will result in people finger pointing or blaming each other.

So, if IT has gradually become a "universal" or "pervasive" tool for every business, why can't we have a "universal" person who is responsible for the business requirements and problem solving? As we all understand, the business or end users normally have no interest in knowing how the technology works. What they only want to know is how to use the technology to solve their business problems. This is what we often refer to as "What's in it for me?" (WIIFM).

As IT becomes more complex and the business environment becomes dynamic, the issues will become severe. The consequences of this issue have led to the natural conclusion of a BA role requirement in many large organizations to help C-class executives get their hands dirty and to "attract blame." Very often, you will see that BAs are external consultants or contractors.

Now, you may ask what the context of business analysis is or what do business analysts exactly do? Steven Blais [62] made the following comment regarding the business analyst (BA) role:

> There is a new position in the corporate hierarchy. A purebred technologist or an entirely business-oriented worker cannot fill this position. It is not management level and does not possess authority; however, it is a key contributor to most of the successful IT-related changes in an organization. Those occupying this position are fully versed in how to increase productivity, lower costs, and comply with regulations from both the business and technology perspectives. They can look at any problem from the perspective of the entire organization to determine the impacts, positive and negative, of any proposed change. They are adept at fashioning solutions to business problems, generally using computer technology. This position is the business analyst.

In essence, Blais defined the BA's role from three perspectives:

- It is not a management role because it does not have authority power.
- It is a key contributor to finding business problems (productivity, lower costs, and other issues).
- It has an obligation to find the right technical or IT solution for any business problem.

Actually, the most recognized definition of BA was made by the International Institute of Business Analysis (IIBA). Based on the usage of the term in *A Guide to the Business Analyst Body of Knowledge* (BABOK Guide) [65], the role of business analyst can be summarized by the following four key responsibilities:

- Liaises and communicates with project stakeholders
- Elicits, analyzes, and validates project requirements for changes to business processes, policies, and information systems
- Understands business problems and opportunities in the context of the requirements
- Recommends solutions enabling the organization to achieve its goals

In very simple terms, the BA has four responsibilities among three domains or groups of people.

- Communication
- Requirements
- Problems
- Solutions

Subsequently, the BA has to have a set of skills and knowledge in order to perform this task from three perspectives, which is shown in Figure 2.4.

The skill of "analytical thinking" means BAs should have a logical mind to understand, assess, and evaluate a business situation and problems and then facilitate IT solutions for business problems. The "problem solving" skill refers to using analytical thinking to find one or more potential solutions for business needs, problems, and opportunities. "Business knowledge" means understanding both internal and external business environments, business principles, and the impacts of surrounding IT projects. The purpose of business knowledge is that a BA should point out pros and cons along with recommended solutions.

In order to provide cost-effective solutions, BAs should have full knowledge of IT solutions. It is similar to a worker knowing all tools in his toolbox very well. In other words, he/she knows which tool is the right one under the particular circumstance. Without solid software and hardware

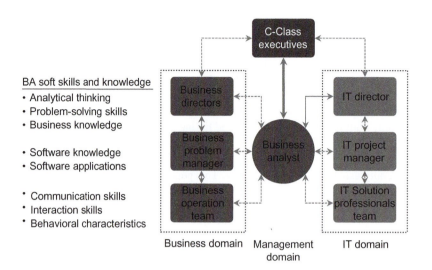

BA soft skills and knowledge
- Analytical thinking
- Problem-solving skills
- Business knowledge

- Software knowledge
- Software applications

- Communication skills
- Interaction skills
- Behavioral characteristics

FIGURE 2.4

New position in the corporate hierarchy.

knowledge, even if a problem has been identified the solution might not be adequate. A BA should also understand the software market very well. In addition, BAs should have enough capability and skills to utilize many common software applications and project management tools for effective communication.

Based on much previous experience on projects, one of major reasons for project failure is poor communication [65]. BAs must have excellent communication skills to resolve business problems effectively. Of course, communication skills do not only mean talking but also listening to others. Interactive skills can be considered a part of the communication skill set. It is the ability to work effectively with other members of both the physical and virtual teams. It requires BAs to have the leadership capability to coordinate both business and IT solution teams and make sure that both teams work together smoothly. Understanding behavioral characteristics are part of the interpersonal relationship skill. It is part of how to deal with different people to resolve or manage problems during the BA process.

In essence, a BA is more like a multiskilled business agent. A BA should have all capabilities and skills that any executive has, except the authority and overall responsibility. However, a BA should have enough practical experience and capability to get things done.

This would require many years of experience. IIBA recommends that a Certification of Competency in Business Analysis (CCBA) needs at least 3,750 hours (or 2.5 years) and a Certified Business Analysis Professional (CBAP) needs at least 7,500 hours (or 5 years) of practice. These hours are distributed into the following six knowledge or practical experience areas:

- Business Analysis Planning and Monitoring (900 hours)
- Elicitation (900 hours)

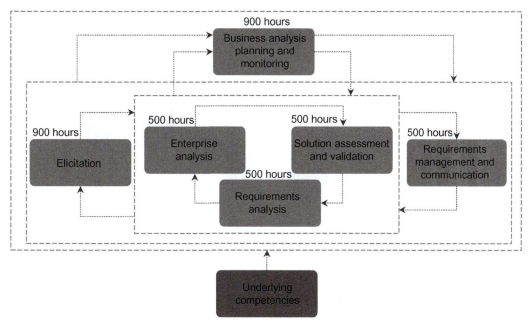

FIGURE 2.5

Relationship of BA's six knowledge areas.

- Requirements Management and Communication (500 hours)
- Enterprise Analysis (500 hours)
- Requirements Analysis (500 hours)
- Solution Assessment and Validation (500 hours)

Of course, the number of hours for any knowledge area can be either 900 or 500 hours as long as the total number of practical hours is equal to 3,750 for the CCBA. The qualification for the CBAP should be double the amount of hours of the CCBA. For example, if "Elicitation" has 500 hours, "Requirements Analysis" can be assigned 900 hours as long as the total number of hours equals 3,750 hours. The relationship of these six knowledge areas is as shown in Figure 2.5.

Whether the above standard is useful or not, the structure of these knowledge areas may be helpful for people who have no experience. In addition, the point of emphasizing the underlying competencies for BA capability is very important. Actually, the key metric to evaluating a BA is the capability of solving real business problems and utilizing underlying competencies rather than just the number of hours that the BA spends on the BA process. As we know, there will be not one BA rather than a group of BAs for a large-scale IT project. Therefore, one individual BA can only contribute one part of the analysis for a business problem. He/she may have 10 years of BA experience but he/she might not resolve a business problem independently from an end-to-end perspective. Having the independent problem-solving skill is particularly important for a BA to resolve cloud

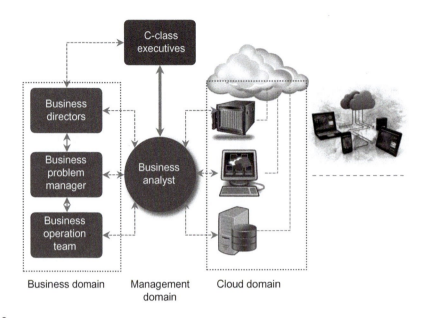

Business domain   Management   Cloud domain
                    domain

FIGURE 2.6

Business analyst in the cloud environment.

business problems because the characteristic of the cloud environment is very dynamic, and thus vol-atile and highly abstract in nature. Resolving some business problems may require innovative ways of thinking. This is why the underlying competencies are so important.

To some degree, a business analyst is similar to a visionary or a strategic decision maker. He/she can help the business decision maker to stand in the future and look back at the present (note it is not "stand in the present and look at the future") A good business analyst can recommend the best option among many possible solutions to achieve the desired business goal. Therefore, a more realistic statement to describe the activities of a business analyst may be the 80/20 rule, that is 80% business communication and 20% technical analysis. Here, we have outlined the key point as to why IT needs business analysts.

Once we have understood the role of business analyst, it is easier for us to explain why we should emphasize business needs. In comparing Figure 2.4 with Figure 2.6, if we replace the IT domain with cloud domain, we find the fundamental role of the BA is the same. The only differ-ence is that we use the cloud domain to resolve the business problem rather than the traditional IT domain (see Figure 2.6). In other words, the business domain remains the same but the IT tool has been replaced with a cloud. The reason of doing so is to provide a cost-effective solution for the business.

So far, you have seen the term "business" in almost every discussion. You may wonder what the term "business" represnets anyway. Before moving to the next topic, let us make clear what the term "business" means in a cloud environment.

2.5 **DEFINING BUSINESS**

We have been using the term "business," but what does it really mean? Surely, there are many definitions for this term. Let us have a look one of very comprehensive one from the *Encyclopaedia of Business Ethics and Society* [82]. It defines business as follows:

> The word business derives from the Middle English terms for "busy" and "ness," and its primary meaning is to engage in purposeful activity. Thus, the notion of the purpose of business is in one sense redundant since in its generic meaning, business means having a purposeful activity. However, there is a secondary meaning of the word business, which denotes activities that involve the production and exchange of goods for economic purposes, primary among which is the generation of profit. Consequently, business is often defined as economic activity engaged in for the sake of profit. For that reason, business engaged in for the profit motive is distinguished from other "busy" activities, such as those carried on by non-profit enterprises such as schools, hospitals, government bodies, and nongovernmental organizations. So those businesses generating profit are a species of organizations unto themselves and are concerned with generating enough profit to continue to exist in a competitive marketplace. Because of this specific difference from other organizations engaged in productive activities, it appears that the profit-making feature is the specific differentiating factor, and consequently, it is thought that the generation of profit is the primary purpose of business. However, despite this account, the question remains as to whether this is the correct way to characterize the purpose of business activity. There are alternative accounts of the purpose of business that can be articulated.

If we use a deductive approach and throw all fancy and theoretical descriptions away and boil down to the very basic meaning of business, we can probably summarize the above defintion into two simple and blunt points:

1. Insert your idea into someone else's brain (propagate)
2. Transfer the money from someone else's pocket into your pocket (making profit) effectively

Actually, these two things are very difficult for any business. The key point of the definition is that a business means having a purposeful activity for the sake of profit.

In essence, the main goal of any business is to make the profit through effective means. Unfortunately, we have seen that many IT project decision makers in some large organisations have completely forgotten this, because the fundamental issue is that the IT cost is not transparent or not explicit. For some IT decision makers, the main focus of IT investment capex is to secure the ongoing capital budget for their group rather than to add the value to business. In short, some IT groups are completely out of touch with the business reality. Cloud computing provides an opportunity not only to refocus on business issues but also to realign IT capex with the business goals.

In order to have a better understanding of the term "business," let us use the above example and walk through the key issues between business and IT people. Can you recall the first example that we mentioned above? Let's compare the term "business" with the complaints that have been made by both thebusiness manager and IT manager and see what the real issue is.

From the business manager's perspective, firstly IT people deliver the wrong result, which is not what the business wants, and the business cannot effectively make profit and compete with other market competitors in the marketplace. If this is so, the IT group has no reason to exist. Secondly, there is a serious communication issue between the business and IT groups. Thirdly, the IT cost or capex is not transparent to the business group.

From the IT manager's perspective, firstly, the business requirements are not captured and documented properly. Secondly, the IT solution does not have enough flexibility to foresee future changes. Thirdly, there is no effective communication channel between the business and IT groups.

In summary, the issues between business and IT groups are:

- Failure to identify business requirements
- Incapable of solving business problems
- Ineffective communication
- IT cost not transparent

As we have already discussed, cloud computing creates a new business model and aims at delivering business needs. The business needs look to solve the business problem effectively. From this perspective, the cloud is not different from other IT tools. The only reason to develop or deploy a cloud solution is to adopt an innovative way to add to the business value (or making profits). Therefore, we should always ask the following fundamental questions when we implement any cloud investment project:

- What does cloud computing really mean to the business?
- What is the relationship between the business and the cloud?
- How can the cloud add value to the business?
- How can I capture the business requirements and identify business problems?
- How can I satisfy the business owner and a cloud user?

To answer the above questions, we can probably build an input and output system or business entity (see Figure 2.7) to see where the cloud is located in this system. From a business analysis perspective, we can easily identify the number of inputs, business variables (assumptions), and outputs. This has actually established a relationship between cloud inputs and business outputs. By doing so, we can eliminate all the issues about which the above business and IT managers complain. Let's put these details in the context of an example using the methodology of BABOK.

However, before moving to the detailed explanation, we first have to clarify some of basic terms for the business system shown above, which are:

- Business entity (system)
- Business strategy (time)
- Business profile (variety)
- Business size (volume)
- Business changes (velocity)
- Business model
- Business database
- Business process

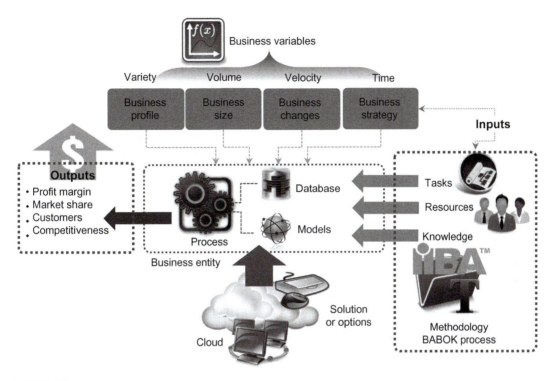

FIGURE 2.7

Relationship of business variables, inputs, outputs, and the cloud.

2.6 BUSINESS VARIABLES

2.6.1 BUSINESS ENTITY

A business entity or system is the appearance or form of the business. It leads to different ways to profit and benefits distribution or sharing. There are many different forms of business entities that exist, such as sole proprietary limited, partnership, limited liability company (LLC), and corporation. The purposes of having different types of business entity are:

- Taxation
- Accounting
- Shareholder dividends

Of course, different types of business will have different types of business entity. The most common type of business entity for small- and medium-size companies is proprietary limited (or Pty Ltd).

The information from business entity analysis will give you a general idea of the hierarchical structure of the company and the way it operates. The key component of this analysis is to find dependent and independent relationships and characteristics among the different business entities if one company has many different business entities.

2.6.2 BUSINESS STRATEGY

Business strategy is the roadmap of a company. It guides the company on how to compete with its competitors in the marketplace. A company's strategy depends on time due to different business owners or CEOs. Normally, a large enterprise will have an overall strategy that is supported by three substrategies:

- Industry strategy (choice of business operation based on profitability)
- Competitive strategy (cost leadership and differentiation)
- Corporate strategy (synergy among different business portfolios)

This is the first variable that should be reviewed for any business analysis because it will set the baseline of many cost model assumptions. Normally, a business analyst should identify all business goals and objectives for the business strategy and make sure that the IT capability or resources can match the defined strategic goals and objectives.

For example, if the business has just launched a new product on the market, its main objective is to reach the breakeven point (BEP) within 12–24 months and the long-term goal is to achieve a 20% average annual growth rate in the next five years because the company's goal or the mission statement is "to be the market leader" in the next five years and the current leading competitor has 15% average annual growth rate.

In order to align with the business strategy, IT professionals should make sure that the cloud infrastructure is scalable and flexible. The IT infrastructure doesn't only have to meet fluctuating demands but also should enhance customer experience and minimize customer churn rate.

Once the business or new product has been stabilized, the business goal is to optimize IT infrastructure resources and improve the profit margin. As IT supports this goal, they should make a strategic realignment along with the business strategy change. This means they should place more effort in process rationalization and automation.

At the final stage, the business strategy is to abandon the legacy products or services because the business is either unsustainable or has been replaced by new products or technologies. The IT people should either decommission and cycle the IT infrastructure or divert available IT resources for other new products or services (see Figure 2.8).

Overall, the strategic analysis is to find where the business is heading to during different business operation phases. A change of strategic direction will trigger IT resource realignment. If IT cannot be aligned with the business strategy, IT will not be relevant to the business. The above example has highlighted the context of business strategy analysis, which is basically to focus on four elements of the business strategy (see Figure 2.9):

- Business goal or mission
- Time frame
- Organizational resources
- The environment

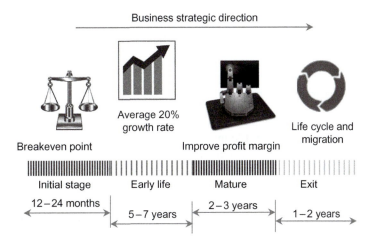

FIGURE 2.8

Example of business strategy analysis.

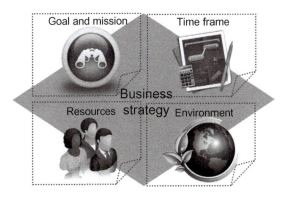

FIGURE 2.9

Four elements of business strategy.

A business goal or mission means a strategic direction, such as to be the market leader or the best company to deliver the services or production in five years.

Time frame refers to long-term goals and shorter time period objectives. For example, the long-term or strategic goal is to be the market leader in terms of profit margin and market share but in order to achieve this long-term goal, the company strategy within the short time period is to lower the profit margin and gain market share.

The organizational resources will not only consist of financial capital but also other tangible and intangible assets, such as people's skill and knowledge, processes, intellectual property, and even the brand name.

Environment analysis figures out all the external factors that may impact on the company's operation. The typical environment analysis may include competitors' analysis, regulation, risk, and overall market conditions.

2.6.3 BUSINESS PROFILE (VARIETY)

The business profile is the second input for business variables. A company may have a number of businesses that make up a business profile in order to maximize profit and minimize business risks.

For example, a cloud service provider might not only provide IaaS but also PaaS, SaaS, and Data Center as a Service to its customers. From a product or service perspective, the business profile means a list of product categories that the company offer to its customers.

Every business category has special characteristics, value chains, markets, major customers, regulations, and processes. Each category will have its own special terms and definitions in term of business operation. Therefore, when we capture business needs or requirements, it is very important to pay special attention to these special characteristics and value chains. For example, the banking business may require more reliable cloud services than an education or consumer type of business because the business regulation requirements are different. From a data center infrastructure perspective, the banking business may require a four 9s SLA and tier III data center infrastructure and active-active disaster recovery (DR). In contrast, the education or consumer type of business may be able to tolerate lower SLA. Many applications are not mission critical. They may not require 24×7 IT support.

Theoretically speaking, a business can have different SLAs for different IT applications based on different business requirements, For example, for a SQL database server that is running a customer billing application, you may need four 9s SLA with DR backup but for a web portal or research and development server, you can downgrade SLA to two or three 9s. In addition, the cloud would allow you to rapidly expand or reduce your IT resource pool.

The bottom line is to fully understand what type of business is and why the business needs IT resources and what if the resources are not able to cope with the business demands in a certain period of time, is it going to impact on the business' revenue or growth? By asking these questions, you, as a BA can have a clear picture of the IT budget profile based on the business profile (see Figure 2.10).

As a result of business profile analysis, you can optimize your IT or cloud resource pool so that IT can support the business very effectively. This is one of the important steps in making IT cost transparent for the business so that the decision maker can make an optimized and wise decision at any given time based on the different circumstances (mainly revenue growth, capex and opex costs, and potential risks). These decisions will include business expansion, deferring, switching, contracting, or abandoning. We will have a detailed discussion of real operation theory in later chapters.

2.6.4 BUSINESS SIZE (VOLUME)

Business size can also be considered business volume. Very often, the size of many businesses is calculated by looking at the number of customers or the amount of revenue. It is quite obvious that different size businesses will have different requirements for cloud resources.

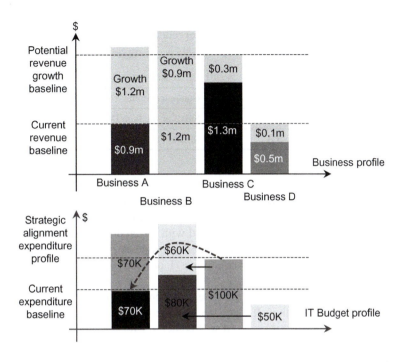

FIGURE 2.10

IT budget profile and business profile alignment.

Table 2.3 Business Size	
Business Size	**No. of Employees**
Micro business	1–4
Small business	5–19
Medium business	20–200
Large business	200

Business size is not fixed or static. It is varied by many other business factors such as general economic climate, market size, production features, technology advances, operation support, market campaigns, and similar products provided by other competitors in the market.

For a rule of thumb, the quickest way to decide the business size is to find out the number of employees, and then review the relationship between business size and the number of employees. According to *Australian Small Business (Key Statistics and Analysis)* provided by the Australian government's Department of Industry [332], the number of employees for a small business is between 5 and 19 and a medium-size business is between 20 and 200. If the number of employees is over 200, it is considered a large business (Table 2.3). The size of a business will be loosely correlated to business revenue and investment capital.

Table 2.4 Business Size and Data Center Scale Correlation

Business Size	No. of Employees	Data Center Size	No. of Racks
Micro business	1−4	Office base	None
Small business	5−19	Computer room	None or 1−5
Medium business	20−200	Small or medium DC	5−20 or 20−100
Large business	More than 200	Medium or large DC	20−100 or >100

From the IT requirements perspective, the business size will give a certain indication of IT resource requirements or cloud resources. For example, if we adopt the traditional client-server architecture, the business size can be loosely coupled with different data center scales (Table 2.4).

Table 2.2 is just an indication to use to allocate IT resources. The actual size of a data center could be based on type or category of business. Some IT or hosting businesses might need more IT resources than other non-IT business.

During the initial phase of gathering business requirements, it is important to pay close attention to this important piece of information. It gives the baseline business requirements for IT resources. If the business or LoB unit has historic data, it will be helpful for the predication of future business size variation.

2.6.5 BUSINESS VARIATION

Variation means any kind of business changes with time. Some changes are regular changes, such as seasonal or yearly changes. The typical example of business variation would be seasonal gas consumption being higher during the winter or the sales of children's toy increasing before Christmas. Others are irregular changes, which is quite challenging to predict. These changes are purely random.

If a company is running a mature business, the historic data might give you some indication or clues of future business trends, such as the variation of standard deviation (see Figure 2.11). These important statistical data will not only help you to establish a compelling business cost model with realistic assumptions but also help the strategic decision maker to understand the risks regarding of the strategic cloud investment. One of the cornerstones for a strategic decision maker is "look forward, reason backward."

In addition, business variation does not just mean volume variation but also profile, strategy, growth, policy, and market variation. By considering business variation, IT professionals can avoid many issues due to unexpected changes requested by business managers, which was an we heard from the IT manger in the above example.

The ultimate goal of finding business variation within a certain time period is to make sure that the cloud resources can match the business demands or needs. Although some cloud service providers allow users to elastically scale their resources, the PAYG or on-demand price model is about 37% more expensive than annually reserved price model (see Figure 1.26).

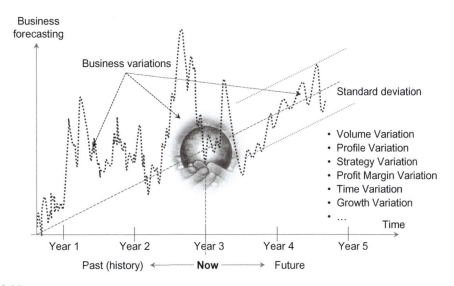

FIGURE 2.11

Predicting future business growth.

Once we understand the above business variables, it is quite easier to follow the business process and quantify or allocate cloud resources for business needs, which we are going to discuss in the following section.

2.7 CLASSIFICATION OF BUSINESS REQUIREMENTS

The goal of identifying business requirements is to understand what the business outputs are. Normally, we do not only have to provide a cloud solution or the number of solution options but also clarify the benefits that a cloud solution delivers for your customers or stakeholders.

From a BA perspective, the meaning of business needs is any requirement made by the business or someone on behalf of the business. The inputs of these business requirements will describe the capabilities that cloud solutions must provide to the business. Therefore, the process of acquiring business requirements is very important. BABOK provides clear guidelines for this process, which we will discuss next.

The process of gathering business requirements can be classified into four or five different levels where a BA systematically acquires or documents the business requirements. Some are essential requirements and others are not essential (see Figure 2.12):

- Business requirements
- Stakeholder requirements
- Solution requirements
- Functional and nonfunctional requirements
- Transitional requirements

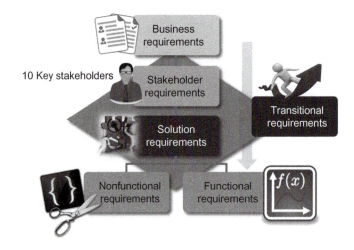

FIGURE 2.12

Classification of business requirements.

2.7.1 BUSINESS REQUIREMENTS

Business requirements are actually the result of the strategic analysis. They are the top level of requirements and should be developed during enterprise analysis activities. These requirements will define the company's strategic goals and the mission statement. They are underpinned by stakeholders' requirements.

2.7.2 STAKEHOLDER REQUIREMENTS

In order to discuss stakeholder requirements, we have to clarify the term "stakeholder." Based on the BABOK guide, the definition of stakeholder covers nearly everyone involved in the IT project. BABOK listed 10 key business stakeholders (see Table 2.5).

The stakeholder requirements define the solution interface among the different stakeholders. The requirements will make sure that all stakeholders or working groups work towards the same goals. They can be considered as the medium to consolidate the high-level business requirements into the tangible and detailed solution requirements that are practicable, measurable, and deliverable. The stakeholders' requirements lead to solution requirements.

2.7.3 SOLUTION REQUIREMENTS

Solution requirements are the detailed requirements. They consist of two subsolution requirements, namely the functional requirements and nonfunctional requirements. The solution requirements should meet both the high level and stakeholders' requirements. They will be rolled into the project tasks.

Table 2.5 Key Business Stakeholder List

Stakeholder	Description	Comments
Customer	Who uses the IT solution, such as the billing staff.	It could be a billing group.
Domain Subject Matter Expert (SME)	This person has detailed, in-depth knowledge of a particular topic or problem area of the solution scope or the business need, such as a doctor in the medicine domain.	Any professional who has the special knowledge or expertise.
End User	Who directly interface with the solution when it has been completed or deployed, such as mobile phone user	Sometimes, the end user is the same as the customer but not always.
Implementation SME	This person is responsible for designing and implementing potential solutions and providing specialist expertise. Subsets of the Implementation SME role include developers, software engineers, organizational change management professionals, system architects, trainers, and usability professionals.	The SME has the knowledge to implement the IT solution.
Operational Support	Helps to keep the solution functioning by providing end user support or day-to-day operational support.	Once the solution is delivered, the project will be handed over to theoperational group.
Project Manager	Manages the work performed to deliver the solution.	This person is responsible for the delivery of the IT project.
Tester	Verifies that the designed and constructed solution meets the requirements and quality criteria for that solution.	This person will verify the solution and make sure it meets the design specification.
Regulator	This person or group defines and enforces standards for developing the solution or for the resulting solution itself, such as the corporation security policy or financial regulations.	It may be a standard that is set up by the government authority.
Sponsor	Authorizes the performance of solution development work and controls the budget, for example a C class executive.	This may be the department director or a company's CFO.
Supplier	This company or person provides products or services to the organization for solution delivery.	It may be the vendor or subcontract or consultant.

The result of capturing solution requirements will be Requirements Definition Documentation (RDD) and a Solution Architecture Document (SAD). This may contain a solution overview, project roles and responsibilities, requirements matrix, release classification, and different user case scenarios or models.

2.7.3.1 Functional requirements

Functional requirements specify the capabilities that the solution must provide to its customers and the final users. It defines the functionality the solution needs to work. For example, a web portal's function is that users can browse its web pages and their contents.

2.7.3.2 Nonfunctional requirements

Nonfunctional requirements are the qualities of the solution. They consist of the solution limitations or implementation constraints, and external factors such as system reliability. Taking the web portal as an example, the nonfunctional requirements of a web portal are 99.99% system availability, 15-minute response time, and 2-hour resolution time. The nonfunctional requirements will underpin the functional requirements.

2.7.4 TRANSITION REQUIREMENTS

Transition requirements describe the capability of the solution to transfer a product or system from the current state to the defined or future state. Once the transition is completed, the transition requirements are no longer required. A typical example is in the case of server virtualization where we want to move the workloads from a physical server to a virtual server, often referred to as P2V. The transition requirements may include live migration if the workload doesn't allow any plan outage. Cycling the resources of a project often necessitates the detailing of "transition requirements." However, launching new production or a new service may also require transition requirements in terms of the transition from the test environment to a production environment.

Once we clear away all these basic ideas and concepts, we should be able to move to the next step, namely the process of business problem solving.

2.8 E2E PROCESS OF BUSINESS PROBLEM SOLVING

If we look the process of business problem solving from an end-to-end (E2E) perspective, we find the overall process has five phases (see Figure 2.13). Moreover, we can divide the business requirement gathering phase into six steps. These activities interact with other phases of problem solving.

The process of gathering business needs is relatively easier than the solution definition phase. It is basically processing three key activities, namely stakeholders' communications, information or requirements gathering, and requirements documentation. The most challenging job or task for the second phase is to review and upgrade business requirements. It could be an iterative process for some projects. When a BA is planning the process of identifying business requirements, he/she should leave enough flexibility for later variations or changes from different stakeholders. This could be a very tedious process, but it is a very important phase. It will decide the scope of the problem and subsequent solution. This is the critical step of managing stakeholders' expectations. In other words, if the BA can correctly elicit the real problem and effectively communicate with all stakeholders and gather all business requirements and update the requirements based on variation from time to time, the BA can manage stakeholders' expectations well.

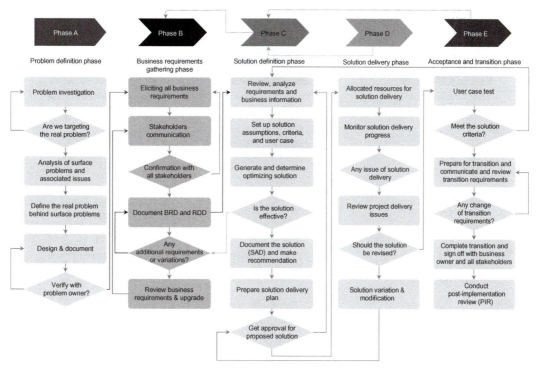

FIGURE 2.13

E2E process of business problem solving.

From a responsibility perspective, the BA is in charge of all three processing phases and activities. The IT project team should be responsible for the processing phase, "D," and the test team should be responsible for the process phase, "E." During the project delivery phase, the BA should work with the project team and make sure that the project can be delivered on time and within the budget. During the testing and acceptance phase, the BA should work with the IT test team and make sure that not only the business requirements are met but also that the transition requirements are also met.

Moreover, if we combine Figure 2.7 with 2.13, we can find the relationship between all the business input variables and processing phases (see Figure 2.14). The five-phase process is to take consideration of all business variables and inputs and come up a solution to solve the real problem. The cloud is just one of the solutions in the solution box.

Michael Hugos et al. [66] argued:

> Technology does not generate revenue for most companies. Business processes powered by technology generate revenue and profits. The management of technology has just been a means to enable the operation of business processes. Cloud computing enables a company to make the shift from managing technology to managing business processes. And in the process of making that shift, companies can reduce their fixed cost structure and redirect their money to activities more directly related to generating revenue.

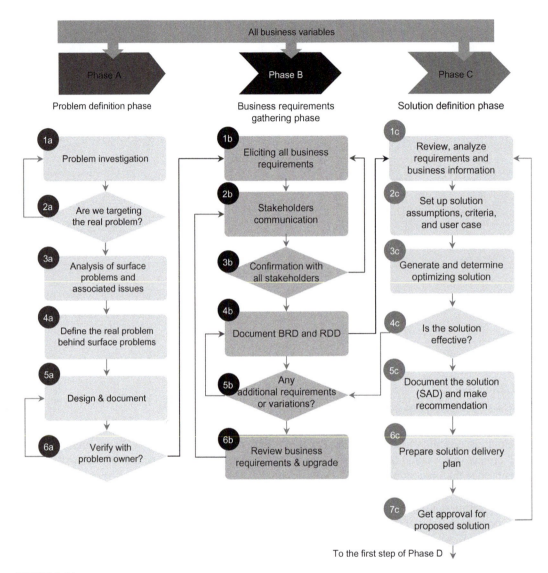

FIGURE 2.14

Detail of first three phases.

In other words, companies and organisations can leverage this new business model, namely cloud computing, to make the right strategic change from technology management to business process management. Perhaps this is most significant meaning of cloud computing for many enterprises.

To put the concept into context, one of the typical examples is the efficiency of data centers. Hugos et al. indicated the following:

> Tens of thousands of companies rely on one or more data centers to power the vast majority of their technology applications and transactions. Planning and constructing these data centers requires a capital expenditure that can reach into hundreds of millions of dollars, which doesn't include the ongoing operating expenses related to staffing, maintaining, and upgrading them.
>
> The world's corporations have collectively built tens of thousands of data centers all replicating some basic functions, all providing the same capabilities, and all of them with considerable excess capacity. Numerous studies show that, in most companies, only about 6% of the total computing power in their data centers is ever in use at any given time The remaining additional power is there to handle occasional surges in demand or is simply there because it accumulated over time and no one did anything to stop it [69].

Our experiences have proved that this observation basically reflects today's IT reality. Actually, this is the main driving force for the paradigm shift from technology to business management. From a physical IT infrastructure perspective, the competition in cloud computing is actually data center efficiency. If most data centers are only using on average 6% of the total computing power, the questions are:

- How can these companies make profits and stay sustainable?
- Why is the utilization of the majority of data centers so low?
- What is the fundamental difference between the cloud and traditional IT?

In the later chapters, we will answer these questions and have a detailed discussion about the data center infrastructure for a cloud but for now, let's focus on our primary issue—defining the business problem clearly.

According to the previous discussion regarding the role of the BA in the business analysis process, we find the ultimate goal of a BA is to provide an effective solution to resolve business problems. Although the process phases have been written separately, we can take a look at how they interact combining process phases A, B, and C together.

2.8.1 BUSINESS PROBLEM DEFINITION

The business problem definition phase consists of six steps. The process itself is quite simple, and consists of three process stages (see Figure 2.15): preliminary definition, elicitation and analysis, and confirmation with documentation.

The final goal of phase A is to reach common ground with the problem owner. In other words, you have to penetrate different appearances to pinpoint the real issue behind many illusions. It is one of key challenges for the E2E process. Therefore, we will not only explain each main processing step in detail but also we will highlight some key challenges during implementation of phase A. Because it is possible that you may find the real issue after you gather all business requirements and interact with all stakeholders or work out a list of solution options, we will highlight these challenges across the boundaries of phases A, B, and C. We will also suggest some techniques to identify the real problem.

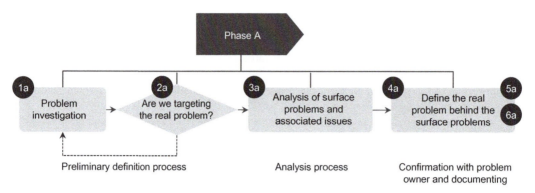

FIGURE 2.15

Business problem eliciting phase.

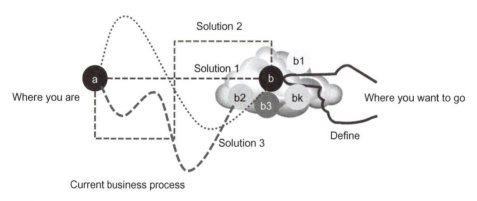

FIGURE 2.16

Define the real business problem.

From a BA perspective, the process of problem definition is to find where you are and where you want to go. If we present this process in very simple terms, it is to define the path from point "a" to point "b." However, it is sometimes not very easy to define the real business problem because there are many surface problems that cloud or cover the real destination point "b," such as points b_1, b_2, b_3... b_k (see Figure 2.16). The question of how to get to point "b" is how to define a problem.

2.8.1.1 Preliminary definition

The preliminary problem definition process is to understand the conditions surrounding the real issue "b." It is extremely important to define the business problem correctly and accurately. If the real problem cannot be defined correctly, the rest of the efforts will be wasted, the so-called "barking up the wrong tree." We will highlight all these challenges including the problem of barking up the wrong tree after the discussion of this phase of processing.

The starting point of the entire process of business problem solving is to gather all information regarding the problem first, but if you do not know the real problem, how can you gather the associated information about the problem? It is a paradoxical situation.

2.8.1.2 Analysis process

Fortunately, what you can do is to collect all symptoms of the problem, which is exactly like when a doctor diagnoses a patient's illness or a detective investigates a homicide case. Based on all the symptoms, you can probably infer or derive the root causes.

The analysis process can help a BA to find the real problem when other simple methodologies (such as interviewing, brainstorm, face-to-face meeting with stakeholders, etc.) cannot determine the real problem. Sometimes, the analysis process is the only way to define the real problem because there are so many reasons that may block a BA from pinpointing the real problem (see Tables 2.6 and 2.7). These reasons can be classified into two big categories:

- Ignorance or lack of capacity to describe the problem
- Politics

Under most of circumstances, the political barriers are the largest roadblock for a BA in identifying the real problem. This is why the BA is very often named the "blames attractor." Identifying the real problem requires very sophisticated political and communication skills.

Table 2.6 Ignorance and Incapacity Barriers [62]

Ignorance and Incapacity Barriers	Reasons
Noise, static (other problems interfering with the real problem or politics)	Solution seems obvious or already exists
System or process already has a solution, but stakeholder does not know it is there or how to use it	Stakeholder cannot express what the problem is—"It just isn't right"
Does not appear to be a problem to the one who you are talking to	The person is not directly involved so does not see the problem
Stakeholder only knows his perspective	Only seeing one facet
Only sees the symptoms	May not really know
May just need something better so does not raise the issue as a problem	Does not know the problem; it just does not feel right
The business presents a solution instead of a problem	The business wants to solve the problem in its way
Know the problem, but cannot describe it accurately	Too close to the problem to see it
Do not really know what the problem is	They may be the cause of the problem
Sometimes business managers conceive problems and require solutions to overcome their inability to manage	The problem is a conglomeration of several things so it cannot be defined as a single problem to be solved
May be looking at surface issues only	Does not care about the problem or solving it
It is opinion not fact	Does not know all the information

Table 2.7 Political Barriers for BA in Identifying the Real Problem

Political Barriers	Reasons
Afraid of change	Solution may not be beneficial
Being afraid to admit what the problem is might indicate incompetence or politics	Afraid of the solution—"Band-Aid the break."
They have other vested interests	Not aware of the real problem.
Conflicting solutions—solution may cause another problem or be perceived to do so	Currently using a workaround so there is no perceived problem
Hide the problem	It could reflect badly on the stakeholders
Deflect the problem to reduce its seriousness	Mitigate the blame or other consequences
Point the finger at or blame another person or department	Do not want to take responsibility
Afraid of getting blamed for the problem whether it is their problem or not	Avoid political war or casualty
Try to hide the problem	Avoid or shift responsibility
Fear of retribution	Fear of firing or penalty
Stakeholder cannot express what the problem is—"it just isn't right."	Too many complaints—too much emotion, too much detail, too many other irrelevant issues for the problem
I do not care. It is not my business	Too much historical baggage

2.8.1.3 Confirmation and documentation of the real problem

Confirming and documenting the real problem is the last part of the process in the first phase. It is coming to agreement on the terms of the issue with the business problem owner. The details of the problem are written in the problem statement. It should be stated very clearly and accurate without any other possible interpretation. Normally, the problem statement may be presented in a negative tone but you can also describe it as a challenging game. To win the game, you have to walk through six steps (see Figure 2.17).

Step 1: The first step of problem confirmation is to gather all descriptions and information about the problem. These descriptions may just be the surface problems and may be a part of the problem description. It does not matter how many descriptions you have. Actually, the more problem descriptions you have, the more chances you will pinpoint the real problem. However, as a BA, you have to differentiate which ones are for the same problem with different descriptions from different views, which ones are for the same problem with just partial descriptions, and which ones are descriptions for different problems altogether.

Step 2: No one will have unlimited resources. A BA should know where the problem's perimeter is. If any request is beyond the BA's current capability or scope, the problem description should be eliminated. For example, your main focus is to solve IT storage capacity but one of the problem descriptions regards eliminating storage vendors for the business; this issue should be disregarded.

Step 3: As a BA, you are being paid to solve specific problems. If you see a problem that is not related to what your company or the problem owner asks for, the problem should be crossed out.

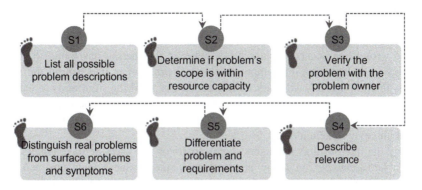

FIGURE 2.17

Confirming the problem statement with problem owner.

If you are barking up the wrong tree, you will not have another chance for the work. In other words, you should always verify the problem statement with your problem owner.

Step 4: Focusing on the problem relevance is another way for you to concentrate limited resources on the real problem. The way of determining relevancy is asking the following two questions: Is the problem or problem's appearance current? Or does the problem exist today? If the answers are "yes," it should be included. Otherwise, it should be excluded.

Step 5: Based on the Oxford dictionary, a problem means something that is regarded as unwelcome or harmful or difficult to achieve and that needs to be dealt with and overcome. On the other hand, a requirement is a thing that is needed or wanted.

In the IT domain, a problem may have a number of solutions (see Figure 2.16). For example, you have a problem that you want walk through from point A to B. There are a number of alternative routes for you to pass through from point A to B. These paths can be referred to as solutions. Requirements are the specified status that should be achieved, such as user requirements, performance requirements, functional requirements, nonfunctional requirements, transitional requirements, etc. We will discuss the different requirements in the discussion of phase B.

Step 6: When we list all possible problems, we should be very careful to differentiate the root causes of the problem and the surface problems or symptoms. If you eliminate the root causes, the problem and the problem's symptoms will go away. If you just remove symptoms, the problem will still be there. For example, a company is losing customers. This is not a problem but rather a surface problem. The real problem is due to the quality of your service. If you focus on this surface problem and spend more money on advertising, you will still lose customers. In order to fix the problem, you have to focus on the customer service quality.

The final goal of this part of process is to confirm the real problem. There are three issues to pinpointing the real problem:

- Gathering all the problem candidates (list possibilities)
- Penetrating all the problem symptoms
- Assembling all aspects of a problem if the problem has different aspects.

In addition to these issues, there are many challenges for problem definition listed below.

2.8.1.4 Challenges of problem definition

2.8.1.4.1 Barking up the wrong tree

Barking up the wrong tree occurs because a BA believes that he/she has found the real issue but actually it is just a surface issue or symptom. The real problem is laid behind the many surface issues. It is possible that the BA will bark up the wrong tree until the solution is tested. Many inexperienced BAs often bark up the wrong tree in many circumstances. If the real problem cannot be identified, all subsequent efforts will be wasted or meaningless. This will lead to an unhappy problem owner and unhappy stakeholders.

You may say that the business managers or customers or end users or stakeholders should know their problems. Unfortunately, in many circumstances, the business managers and stakeholders have no idea what the real issue is. They only know the symptoms, but the symptoms are not equal to the real problem. It is the BA's responsibility to identify the real problem. If you believe the symptom is the problem, then you might never resolve the real problem. This is the challenge of "barking up the wrong tree."

2.8.1.4.2 Solution side effects

Sometimes, the problem is quite obvious but a solution is not so effective because the solution resolves the problem may cause a side effect or many side effects. We have seen many consultants who cannot offer the real and effective solution instead offer a cheaper and dirty solution that causes many serious consequences for the business.

This often occurs when there is time pressure. The BA does not have enough time or resources to find an effective solution for the business instead of a cheaper and quick solution. The consequence of the cheaper solution is many side effects, which may cause the business to spend more resources to undo the changes or otherwise recover.

A typical example involves a telco company that wanted to slash the operation costs for its service delivery unit; it reorganized the service delivery group and slashed the service assurance group. It did save a certain amount in opex but the service delivery performance went into freefall and many big corporate customers were screaming because the poor service performance had impacted the customers' bottom line. The company realized it was a cheaper solution, but it was too late. It had to spend over 18 months and triple the amount of resources to pull the performance back to what it was. A cheaper solution or side effect is always a challenge for many problem owners. The best way to eliminate the side effects is to clearly define the business requirements and make sure these requirements can be translated into solid performance metrics. The performance metrics can be tested and verified.

2.8.1.4.3 Complex problems

Sometime, a complex problem may intertwine with other issues. This is especially true for many shared IT systems or infrastructure, such as security, storage, virtual private networks, and server virtualization. You may be able to resolve it but you have to resolve other issues first. This may lead to the issue of problem scale. Under these circumstances, a BA has to find a solution to work around other issues.

Other problems could be interfering with the real problem or the real problem could be hiding behind other problems. One typical example is that you will be told that certain solutions have already been proposed because different stakeholders have different interests and they want to resolve the problem in their way.

Furthermore, the problem may be so complex they are beyond the problem owner's knowledge. You may hear the comment, "It just isn't right but I do not know how to explain it."

2.8.1.4.4 Hidden or avoided problems

The situation is similar to a complex problem. The problem owner has currently found a way to work around the issue so there is no perceived problem, but the problem will eventually occur under certain circumstances. Many stakeholders will not care to resolve the real problem because it may impact on their bottom line in the short term. Therefore, the problem owner would prefer to hide or avoid the problem rather than resolve it.

2.8.1.4.5 Sensitive problems

This is a very ironic situation, which the problem is caused by the problem owner or his decision but he/she is not aware of this. A typical example is that some business managers only adopt a Band-Aid solution that only fixes surface issues rather than taking a risk to make a radical change and solve the real problem.

Many business mangers do not only have an interest in the business problem but also the political issues associated with the problem. The real problem may be resolved but the working relationship with other stakeholders may also be damaged beyond repair.

2.8.1.4.6 Presenting the wrong information

When a BA is trying to define the business problem, the business owner may present a solution directly rather than problem. It is "my way or the highway." Based on your knowledge and experience, you know that the solution will not work. In other words, the business owner presents the wrong information. He/she has too many opinions, too much baggage, too many allegations, and too much emotion for the problem but lacks key facts or logical or clear thinking.

2.8.1.4.7 No single solution for the problem

Sometimes, there is no an effective single solution for a particular problem or you might have 100% certainty for it. What you can do is only mitigate the problem's phenomenon or partially resolve it, but not cure it completely. If this is a case, a BA should communicate with the problem owner and make the business owner aware of the consequences of the solution.

If it is a multimillion project, you may be able to run a test lab to test not only one solution but a combination of different solutions, of course, if the time permits.

2.8.2 GOALS OF DEFINING BUSINESS PROBLEMS

Surely, we cannot include all the challenges for problem definition, but the above list highlighted some of the most common challenges. In general, it does not matter what the appearance of a problem is, as all business problems can probably be classified into four types:

- Generate more revenue streams (revenue or income problem)
- Reduce opex or overall costs (cost efficiency or profit margin problem)

- Improve customer service (service quality problem)
- Increase market share (competitiveness problem)

If a BA is thinking along these lines, the real problem can be found. Of course, finding the problem is one thing and finding the solution is another thing. Like solving mathematics problems, some business problems may never have an effective solution. If this is the case, we have to find a way to manage them. This is another topic that is beyond the scope of this book. However, many problems do have solution if we apply some common techniques that we use to identify mathematics problems.

2.8.3 TECHNIQUES FOR IDENTIFYING REAL PROBLEMS

Based on some techniques or strategies for identifying mathematics problems [70], we can classify 19 solving techniques into four big categories (see Table 2.8):

- Analysing
- Synthesizing
- Analogizing
- Valuing

It may be too many for some inexperienced BAs. Based on Barry Schwartz's work, we encounter *The Paradox of Choice: Why More Is Less* [71]. The simple way is to select one or two of your favorite techniques from each category and master these techniques.

2.8.4 BUSINESS REQUIREMENTS GATHERING PHASE

The second phase of the business problem solving process is to gather business requirements. As we have indicated above, the business requirements can be divided into four or five different types of requirements (see Figure 2.10). A BA might have to work with up to 10 different stakeholders to gather these different types of requirements. In this process phase, the critical step of business requirement gathering is stakeholder communication. BABOK suggests 16 techniques listed in Table 2.9.

Table 2.8 Problem Solving Strategy Classification

Analyzing	Synthesizing	Analogizing	Valuing
• Finding patterns • Working backwards • Deductive reasoning • Determining characteristics of objects • Specializing • Generalizing	• Adopting a different point of view • Systematically accounting for all possibilities • Sequencing • Using other tools	• Solving a simpler analogous problem • Visual representation • Intelligent guess and testing • Wishful thinking • Approximating	• Consider extreme cases • Determining necessary and sufficient conditions • Organizing data • Specification without loss of generality

Table 2.9 Techniques for Eliciting Requirements from BABOK's Guide			
Communication	**Tactical Analysis**	**Observation**	**Strategic Analysis**
• Brainstorming • Requirement Workshops • Interviews • Focus Groups • Survey /Questionaries	• Data Dictionary and Glossary • Document Analysis • Data Modelling • Process Modeling • Interfacing Analysis • Prototyping	• Acceptance and Evaluation Criteria Definition • Data Flow Diagrams • Scenarios and Use Cases • Observation	• Decision Analysis • Metrics and KPI • Organisation Modeling • Problem Tracking • Business Rule Analysis • Nonfunctional Requirement Analysis

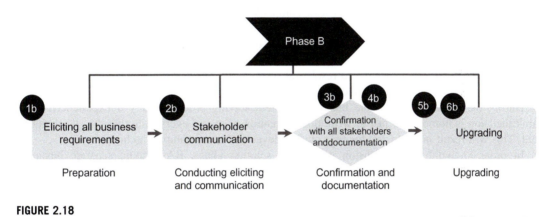

FIGURE 2.18

Key steps of Phase B for gathering business requirements.

In addition, we added five more techniques and divided the 21 techniques into four different categories. Of course, there are other techniques that we have not included in the above table, but the techniques within this table should be sufficient to deal with most situations.

Although the process phase has six detailed steps, the key aspect of the process can be condensed into four (see Figure 2.18).

2.8.4.1 Preparation

The first step is so important. Without sufficient preparation, some of the recommended techniques will not work, just as Benjamin Franklin indicated: "By failing to prepare, you are preparing to fail." For example, the brainstorming technique is only useful when each participant is fully prepared before the brainstorm session starts and each individual is willing to make his/her contribution. From a topic perspective, the brainstorm can be divided into the particular area of interest for different stakeholders and each session should have the specified time frame. Normally, it should be within one hour. The most manageable size of a brainstorm session should be around six or eight people. Before the session is kicked off, the brainstorm host should have a list of questions ready regarding the session topic.

2.8.4.2 Conducting eliciting

The second step is to conduct the information gathering meeting or workshop. It is similar to a business meeting, but this business meeting is not only to report business results but also to make business decisions and resolve business problems. In contrast, the requirement gathering meeting is only to report the business problems to be resolved. The key is how to motivate each participant to actively join the meeting. The meeting must reflect the participants' interests. In other words, the BA should convince the participating stakeholders that the requirements gathering meeting will lead to the business problem solving.

2.8.4.3 Documenting

The third step of this phase is the observation and documentation step. The purpose of including observation is because many documents are useless. Tom DeMarco et al. [68] made these comments regarding documentation: "Voluminous documentation is part of the problem, not part of the solution."

"Observation" means evaluating, selection, and decision making. It is not just documenting everything that the stakeholders have said because in many circumstances, the stakeholders will raise all issues that they would like to resolve at once. Many raised issues during the communication session are ambiguous, fuzzy, unclear, uncertain, too complicated, or even misleading.

During the second phase of the business problem solving process, many unexperienced BAs think their job is nothing but just to write documentation or record everything that the stakeholders said. This will result in confusion for the solution developer or the solution architect.

In order to avoid later confusion during the solution phase, BAs should separate business requirements documentation into two types of documents:

- Persistent
- Transitory

The persistent category represents the permanent document and will be kept after the business solution is delivered. Examples of persistent documents are the Solution Architecture Document (SAD), Requirements Definition Document (RDD), Business Requirements Document (BRD) (See Appendix B for an example of a BRD) and Key Decision Document (KDD). These are important documents that should be written in a company's format. They should be precise, concise, plain, logical, direct, consistent, friendly, and systematic. Above all, they should be easily readable for any person who does not have a strong technical background. One of the issues for a formal document is that it consists of many technical jargons and acronyms without explanations.

A transitory document is the temporary one for recording only. It only serves a purpose for the process rather than for business problem identification and solution. Typical examples of a transitory document would be a project meeting record, meeting agenda, and preparation documents for communication questions.

Moreover, there are some communications and items that should be documented, while others can just be informal and verbal communication. For example, some issues will not cause serious consequences or damages for solution delivery. It is the BA who has to decide or draw the line as to which item should be documented and which one should be excluded. For a rule of thumb, we list the following guidelines for the decision on whether the content should be documented or not (see Table 2.10).

Table 2.10 Guidelines on When to Document	
To Be Documented	**Not Necessary**
• Regulations and policy • Guidelines of operations • Performance metrics and Key Performance Index (KPI) • Service Level Agreement (SLA) • Standard of testing • Change requirements • Auditing procedure	• Once of report or business query • Everyone is involved and will remember • Interim documents • Circumstances where no one is interested in the processing state but just the results • Idea-generating records or documents created during the brainstorm process

However, you should be aware that when we are trying to manage stakeholders' expectations, some kind of verbal communication is necessary for justification, although it may be completely redundant. For example, although you might not have new information for the progress of a project you can still give a very short information briefing to your stakeholders. Writing a requirements document is different from verbal communication. Regular briefing can grease the wheels of stakeholder interaction. It is a good strategy to manage stakeholders' expectations.

2.8.4.4 Updating

The final step is also very important for this processing phase. Any project will require some kind of upgrade or change, especially if the project will last a few years. Some immediate changes will be due to changes from the solution. Others may be from market variation and lead to many changes to project scope and quality.

A good solution should be flexible enough to accommodate all the business variables (variety, volume, and variation) that we have discussed above. If the BRD, RDD, and SAD do not have enough flexibility, it will be quite difficult to manage stakeholders' expectations and the relationship with them.

Although the strategic goals do not change frequently, quite often the strategic decision maker may shift his/her focus (emphasize different objectives) from time to time based on the market environment. For example, when the company has a sharp revenue decline, the revenue growth will become the first priority for the decision maker. When the revenue has been stabilized but many customers are complaining about the service or product quality, the decision maker's focus will shift to the quality issue. However, this does not mean that the revenue target is not important. Actually, improving the quality of the service or product can help lift the company's revenue. In other words, if you can identify the real problem, you can help your stakeholders reach multiple goals.

2.8.5 PROVIDE THE RIGHT SOLUTION

This is the third phase of the problem solving process. If the problem has been defined properly, the solution can be found. The question is, how effective is the solution? Actually, this phase of the process is not an isolated or independent phase. It should interact with both phase A and B. The key successful factors in this phase are:

- Realistic and logical assumptions
- Solution criteria
- Testing the chosen solution

Of course, you may have many solutions for a problem but no matter how many potential solutions you have, there may be only one optimal solution for the problem. It might not be the best solution, but it is the politically correct solution for the problem at the particular time. The criteria to determine the best solution are:

- It resolves the real problem effectively.
- It is the most cost effective solution.
- It is most politically correct and looks after all the stakeholders' interests.
- It is the easiest solution for all stakeholders to accept.
- It has the lowest life cycle cost with minimum risks.

It may sound like mission impossible foror a solution to meet all the above criteria. A BA has to decide what key aspects will matter most to the business and then get approval from the problem owner for the selected solution. The details of the process can be simplified into four stages as follows if we exclude the steps of documentation, implementation planning, and approval (see Figure 2.19):

- Information processing
- Modeling processing
- Solution processing
- Communication processing

2.8.5.1 Information processing

Information processing consists of four basic steps, namely classification, prioritization, activities analysis, and historic story analysis. This is not only to decide the scope and priority of the information and requirements but also to elicit the solution's goal and objectives.

2.8.5.1.1 Information classification

The goal of classification is not just to separate the information and requirements into different categories, but also to clarify information and requirements that have been collected during phase B that are ambiguous, abstract, unclear, fuzzy, and difficult to understand. Moreover, the classification should include the mapping of missing information and identifying inconsistencies between business goals and requirements.

2.8.5.1.2 Information prioritization

Once information has been sorted and classified, business requirements should be prioritized based on different requirement categories, such as functional, nonfunctional, system, performance, user, etc. It will be very helpful for the solution architect to understand how important a particular feature or requirement is to the overall business solution. As a result, the solution delivery team will deliver the final solution based on this prioritization. The typical priority matrix is as shown in Table 2.11.

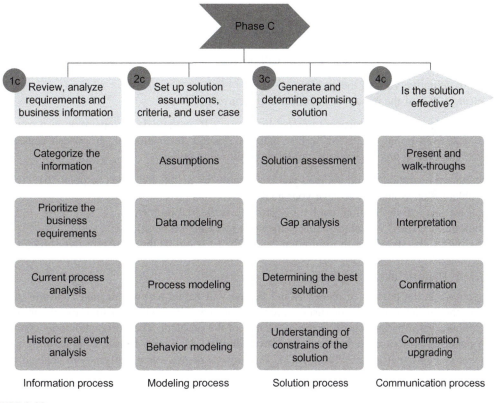

FIGURE 2.19

Detail of steps of phase C process.

Table 2.11 Requirements Priority List		
Priority	**Description**	
1	Mandatory	Legislation and similar requirements that MUST be addressed at all costs (it is a legal issue)
2	Very High	Requirements associated with the competitive market that MUST be incorporated and planned for (but not necessarily at all costs)
3	High	Requirements that SHOULD be incorporated
4	Medium	Requirements that could be incorporated if scope and effort permit.
5	Low	Requirement does not have any external or company-wide drivers

2.8.5.1.3 Current process analysis

The goal of current process analysis is to see the response of the business process via the user's inputs. The business process will start from the initial step and walk through a series of activities and then complete the process. The analysis will provide:

- A more definitive view of the problem
- A clear picture of the impact of activities in the current process

For example, the current business process in Figure 2.16 is the existing operation or a solution. It leads you from point "a" to "b1" rather than the desired destination of "b," which causes the problem. The current process analysis can tell you following points:

1. The current operation would not lead you from point "a" to "b," but rather to point "b1." (b1 is a problem. You would not achieve your goal.)
2. Point b is the real destination, not b1, b2, or b3 (b is the real problem).
3. Solutions 1, 2, and 3 will reach point b (they can solve the problem).
4. Solution 1 is the shortest path from point "a" to "b" (it could be the most effective solution).

2.8.5.1.4 Historic event analysis

When you are in the process of phases A and B, you will gather and record many real life events regarding the business problem or surface problems or symptoms. These historic events or stories have particular information regarding the root cause of the problem. The information may contain a special pattern that you can turn into an effective solution. All events consist of at least eight elements that you can analyze (see Table 2.12). The process of real event analysis will analyze these elements in detail.

2.8.5.2 Modeling process

Modeling processing refers to developing the potential solution for the business problem. It consists of four steps: assumption, data modeling, solution modeling, and process modeling. The process will allow the business analyst to better understand the problem and problem environment.

Table 2.12 Real Event Analysis of Eight Elements

Event Elements	Description
Intention	Which goal or objects were achieved?
Actions	What was done?
Objects	What tools, systems, or techniques were adopted?
Context	What were the details of the environment?
Accident	What unexpected things occured?
Cost	What was the overall cost to carry out the event?
Agent	Who was involved in the event?
Relation	What was the relationship between inputs and outputs?

When we build a model, we can establish a logical relationship between the existing business environment and new requirements because the model can describe the workflow from the inputs to the outputs. The process itself can provide the following benefits when we try to find an optimized solution:

- Simplifies a complex environment and filters out unnecessary details
- Defines many abstract concepts, terms, and structures with visible diagrams
- Facilitates communication among all stakeholders
- Elicits the relationship among many different business variables
- Shows interactive responses between inputs and outputs
- Demonstrates the workflow of a business process
- Provides a platform for all stakeholders to communicate each other
- Presents multiple aspects of the business system
- Shifts from problem definition to solution design
- Spells out the strategic business objectives or goals with appreciated levels for solution development
- Develops a way that the business problem can be practically solvable

This is the solution modeling process. Later in this book, we will discuss cost modeling. They share similar principles but for now, let us have a look at the context of the modeling process to develop the right solution for the business problem in detail.

2.8.5.2.1 Assumptions

Any decision making will need to make multiple assumptions. This is the knowledge that a BA takes for granted. Explicit assumptions are made consciously. Many of them are made based on the prejudgments, perceptions, facts, values, definitions, policy, and knowledge that are well understood and shared by all stakeholders. Implicit assumptions are made unconsciously.

Different assumptions lead to totally different conclusions. Remember that you are dealing with assumptions, not facts. Any assumption needs to be consistently and constantly challenged to reflect the environment changes. Assumptions for a solution model build the perimeter around the solution. For example, we can assume a business system can process on average 300 customers per day. If business hours are from 8 a.m. to 5 p.m., the hourly rate is 37.5 customers per hour. However, during peak times, the business needs to process on average 60 customers per hour. This peak time may be between 80 or 100 minutes. This is an assumption for the solution, which needs to accommodate peak customer demand for the business.

2.8.5.2.2 Data modeling

By BABOK's definition, data modeling is organizing requirements by describing the concepts and relationships between the concepts that are relevant to the defined solution scope. This definition appears to be hard for some to understand. In simple terms, the data model defines the real world information. It has three levels of meaning:

1. It is a representation of requirements for an organization.
2. It is an effective communication tool for discussion.
3. It is a bridge between the real world information and the database.

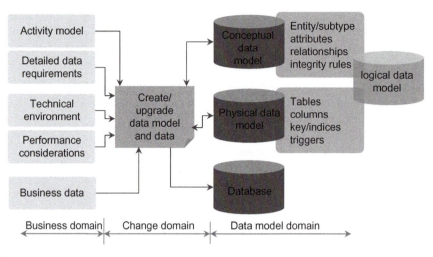

FIGURE 2.20

Three levels of data modeling from ANSI.

Table 2.13 Comparison of Three Data Models			
Feature	**Conceptual**	**Logical**	**Physical**
Characteristics of different data models	• Information content • Human concept of app • Data system	• Details of all info • Reference to DB S/W • No details of H/W	• Details data storage • Specific database • Details of physical implementation
Entity Names/Subtype	√	√	
Relationship	√	√	
Attributes		√	
Primary Keys		√	√
Foreign Keys		√	√
Table Names			√
Column Names			√
Data Types			√

As a part of requirements analysis modeling, it describes the attributes associated with a particular concept or set of related concepts. ANSI defined three kinds of data model instance (see Figure 2.20).

What are the differences among conceptual, logical, and physical data models? Table 2.13 compares the difference among the three.

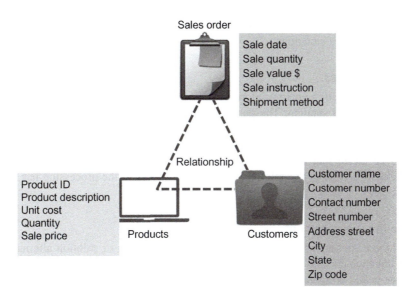

FIGURE 2.21

Data models.

In essence, data models are visually representing things (products), people (customers), and concepts (relationship) that matter to the business (sales) (see Figure 2.21).

The conceptual data model is at the highest level. It contains some general ideas about the contentsu. It describes the contents in the application domain, which end users can understand because this data model represents business objects, constraints, and characteristics. At this level, the data model is the medium between the domain experts and end users.

The logical data model refers to all the abstract information, such as data attribute relationships and concepts associated with business, but it doesn't have detailed information.

In contrast, the physical data model has all the information, such as column names, data types, values, descriptions, etc. It cannot be a tool to communicate with end users because it has too many intricate details. The primary purpose of a data model is to play a role as a blueprint for implementation of a database system.

2.8.5.2.3 Process modeling

The purpose of process models is to make sure the stakeholders can get the job done via a series of steps. In order to achieve the business requirements, you have to create a process from start to finish. Normal process modeling techniques include flow charts, petri nets, UML activity diagrams, data flow diagrams, workflow diagrams, and business process modeling notation. These techniques basically represent the sequential flow and logic of a set of related activities.

2.8.5.2.4 Behavior modeling

Behaviour modeling is used to model user stories. The common tools or techniques for behavior modelling are use cases and scenarios. The purpose of behavior modeling is to simulate the result between an end user and a system. The use case or scenario can test the system to see if achieves the correct result in various situations.

2.8.5.3 Solution process

This part of the process is for preparing information and requirements and assembling a plan to determine the best or optimized solution. The purpose of this part is to make an assessment and validate the solution information. Therefore, it is important to understand the business environment where the solution will be deployed and how the proposed solution will impact the business environment.

We have to be aware that it is not just to assess the solution implementation or deployment phase, but also the life cycle of the solution. Therefore, this part of the processing has four key processing deliverables.

2.8.5.3.1 Solution assessment

The task of solution assessment is to assess your proposed solution or solution alternatives that are related to all stakeholders and business requirements. You have to make sure that all business requirements are ticked or approved by stakeholders. Sometime, one of the solutions meets most of the solution requirements but only one or a few requirements of lower priority are not met. You should highlight these issues and prepare for the next step of the process (communication with stakeholders).

During the solution assessment, we will assess multiple solutions. In order to determine the best and optimized solution, you should prioritize all alternative solutions against the deliverable values and risks. You should come up with comparison pros and cons for each proposed solution. Normally, the process will include the following assessment tasks:

- Solution performance assessment
- Solution validation assessment
- Solution requirements assessment
- Transition requirement assessment
- Organization readiness assessment
- Solution defects, risk mitigation actions assessment

2.8.5.3.2 Gap analysis

Gap analysis identifies the conditions that may cause potential issues or problems between the desired status and the proposed solution for the business problem. What you have to do is to change these conditions and eliminate the potential problems or issues. Actually, there are two types of gap analysis:

- Problem gap
- Solution gap

The problem gap refers to the distance between the desired state and problem state, to which a solution has not been implemented yet. This gap should be the biggest. Problem gap analysis can help you to generate a different alternative solution. Solution gap analysis on the other hand finds the gap between the idea condition and solution states (see Figure 2.22).

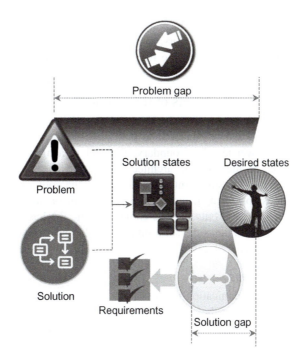

FIGURE 2.22

Gap analysis.

The goal of gap analysis is to minimize the difference between the existing capabilities and the desired future business condition for a company. With different solutions in your hand, you will identify the best or optimized solution for the business problem as discussed in the following.

2.8.5.3.3 Determining the best solution

Determine the best solution is a part of the decision-making process. Ideally, you should avoid politics and prejudgments to select the best solution but in reality, it is not possible to be absolutely objective. One way to determine the best solution is to establish the criteria for the best solutions, which are agreed upon by all or a majority of stakeholders. These criteria for the best solution are:

- It can solve the defined problem effectively.
- It can solve the problem in the most cost effective manner.
- It is the most politically correct.
- It meets all stakeholders' primary requirements.
- It is the easiest and fastest to deploy.
- It is independent of platform or technology.
- It is very simple for all stakeholders to understand.
- The implementation cost is within the specified budget.
- It has the lowest amount of risks and side effects.

These criteria are not equally important. In practice, the solution should be subject to some primary criteria that are specified by stakeholders. You should weight each criterion with different levels. In other words, you do not have absolute freedom to define the best solution. Any solution has some constrains, such as time, budget, and policy.

2.8.5.3.4 Understanding the constraints of the solution

When a BA is implementing the business analysis, which is defining a business problem and the needs or requirements, it is important to understand that a BA is not a solution designer or architect. It would not be wise to overstep that boundary. In order to achieve the best solution, a BA should give enough freedom to the solution architect. Therefore, the BRD and RDD should be specified in a way that can provide sufficient possibilities for the solution architect to design the right solution for the business problem. It would be unintelligent or unwise to force the solution architect to come up with nothing but only the one choice that the BA has already decided upon.

After the solution architect completes the solution process, the next step is to communicate with all stakeholders about the solution.

2.8.5.4 Communication process

The primary purpose of the communication process is to confirm the recommended solution with your stakeholders. It is mainly to test the solution or alternative solutions. It will not be a one-way process, but rather an interactive communication between you and all your stakeholders. You should expect not only confirmation but also critics. You'll likely have to compromise among different stakeholders and make various changes to your recommended solution. This part of the process consists of four steps, namely presenting and walking through the recommendation solution and solution alternatives, interpretation, confirmation, and update. Let us look at these steps in detail.

2.8.5.4.1 Presentation and walking through the solution

This step of the process reviews the accuracy of the information and requirements. It is basically to elicit the problem, problem environment, and agreed upon requirements. It makes sure that the information that you have understood is accurate and you and your stakeholders are on the same page. What you do is give an information briefing and bring every stakeholder up to the speed because not every stakeholder will remember all the details. It is your responsibility to remind everyone about the conditions, environment, and defined problem. Then you should walk through all your assumptions, data, processing, and behavior models. Finally, you should draw your conclusion and confirm it with all stakeholders.

2.8.5.4.2 Interpretation

Interpretation is another important step because your beliefs, perceptions, facts, and assumptions are not necessarily the same as your stakeholders. You should communicate with your stakeholders regularly. Do not wait until the final minutes when the final solution has been generated. A good strategy is keeping in touch with your stakeholders and checking in with them about all your facts, assumptions, perceptions, and beliefs. In other words, you should interpret all this information into your stakeholders' language and make sure they fully understand it. Normally, if people do not understand, they will simply either reject it altogether or assume something based on their perceptions. It does not matter if this is right or wrong or beneficial or nonbeneficial. Therefore, it is important that everyone can interpret your view correctly, accurately, and visually.

2.8.5.4.3 Confirmation

Confirmation is not equal to approval. Only the decision maker can decide on approval. Confirmation is neither unanimity nor reaching the same conclusion. It is rather a consensus. The confirmation process may slow down reaching the final solution, but overall the process can be beneficial for stakeholders' expectation management and the relationship with the stakeholders. It will elicit many hidden issues and problems and uncover misunderstandings. It may appear like you just have to spend more time on the communication process, but the confirmation process can reduce the total business problem solving time because you have eliminated misunderstandings in the first place.

2.8.5.4.4 Confirmation upgrading

As we have discussed above, the confirmation process is an iterative process. The process of confirmation is not only an interactive engagement but also a series of continuous activities between the BA and all stakeholders.

Some previously established confirmations should be upgraded due the new findings, new ideas, new opportunities, or new circumstances. Confirmation and confirmation upgrading is a gradual and incremental process for finding the best solution for the business problem.

2.9 MANAGING EXPECTATIONS

Once management has decided to implement the optimizing solution, the next critical phase is to manage all stakeholders' expectations. It is not an easy task. It is dependent on your communication skills. If you cannot properly manage stakeholders' expectations, the delivered solution may lead to failure or even a disaster.

The common meaning of expectation refers to a strong belief that the problem solution will or should be delivered based on stakeholders' standards or metrics, such as time, solution quality, and cost. Whether this expectation is realistic or not is another matter. For example, stakeholders expect that a cloud solution delivery team should deliver the solution within five working days. If the solution team spent seven working days to deliver the solution, the team has failed to meet the stakeholders' expectation. Remember that expectation is a relative concept. It is closely associated with two other terms: satisfaction rate and stakeholders' measurement.

If the received service has exceeded the expectation level or stakeholders' measurement, the delivered service will satisfactory and if the received service is below the expectation level, it will be unsatisfactory (see Figure 2.23).

Managing stakeholders' expectations is one of the critical elements of successfully solving the business problem and solution delivery. There are many cases where although the solution has been successfully deployed and the business problem has been effectively solved, the stakeholders' attitude was still negative because the solution did not meet stakeholders', especially the business manager's, expectations.

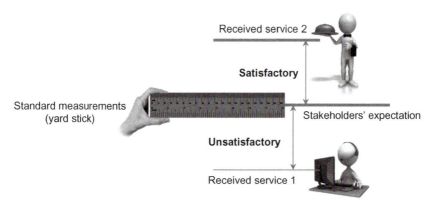

Received service 2

Satisfactory

Standard measurements
(yard stick)

Stakeholders' expectation

Unsatisfactory

Received service 1

FIGURE 2.23

Expectation management.

Professional IT BA should understand that corporate restructures and leadership and team changes happen very frequently for many large organizations. If this kind of change is not a daily event, it will be at least be a monthly or quarterly episode, especially for many IT groups within these large organizations. Of course, it may be dependent on how you see these changes. If you are conservative, you may view these changes as negative. This is why some IT professionals refer to the acronym of CIO as "Career Is Over" rather than "Chief Information Officer."

When these major changes occur, it is inevitable that politics, emotions, perceptions, negative sentiment, incorrect options, and prejudice will replace facts or truth. Projects will come and go or live and die. The results of project delivery may be dependent on management's opinions rather than facts. Sometimes management expectation is far more important than actual effectiveness of the solution for the business problem.

Therefore, to some degree, stakeholders' expectation management and business problem solving are two quite different kettles of fish because many expectations are unstated requirements or assumptions that exist in your stakeholders' minds subconsciously. These subconscious expectations may resurface when something occurs during the project delivery phase. So, the rule of thumb is that you should do your best to write down as much information as possible. The more written expectations that are in the document, the easier you can manage them. Here is some advices for handling stakeholders' expectations:

- Spell out the problem statement up front and state it as simply as possible so stakeholders know what your goal is and what they will get.
- Before the solution delivery process starts, you should determine measurements for all expectations so that you can demonstrate that expectations have been met.
- Make sure all expectations are realistic.
- Never overcommit your capacity for the delivery.
- Constantly confirm the solution results with your stakeholders and eliminate any incorrect perceptions and misunderstandings. Never keep your stakeholders in the dark. If you do, it will simulate your stakeholders' imaginations, which quite turns negative.

- Keep track of every new expectation from regular meetings and informal conversations, and discuss new expectations. If they are realistic and achievable, you should always commit to these new expectations. If not, you should explain why they are not. Although some reasons or explanations might appear to be completely redundant, they are a necessary process to calm your stakeholders down or gain understanding from your stakeholders.
- When you are facing complaints from your stakeholders, you should concentrate on facts rather than the actual result.

Overall, expectation management is highly dependent on your communication skills. This skill does not only mean talking or getting your idea across to stakeholders but also listening, interpreting, understanding, eliciting, and identifying your stakeholders' subconscious or unstated requirements.

Expectation management does not mean to manipulate the truth rather than actively engaging with your stakeholders and identifying those unstated requirements. Active engagement means catching an expectation when you encounter it. It is quite often easy to ignore or dismiss some sentiments, options, or perceptions that are contradictory to your value proposition or written contract or agreements because it seems to be common knowledge that only written statements can have legal precedence and any unstated expectations will eventually fade away. However, this is not always so "because language is imperfect as a medium for conveying knowledge, it also functions as an obstacle to communication" [89]. In other words, even if the requirements have been documented, different people may have different interpretations because when we encounter a proposition or claim, we may have four different interpretations: fact, definition, value, and policy.

Expectation management can eliminate these differences. Normally, we should have two types of expectations:

- Stated expectations
- Unstated expectations

Stated expectations are the explicitly written down statements for business requirements from different stakeholders. Stated expectation management mainly focuses on content interpretation and understanding between you and your stakeholders. Since different people come from different backgrounds, have different knowledge bases, look at things from different angles, and represent different interests, misinterpretation is sometime inevitable.

What we wrote down on the solution document are not only a series of words but also a number of terms. "A term is not a word — at least, not just a word without further qualifications" [72]. If a term and a word were exactly the same, then there would be no room for any misinterpretation. Unfortunately, "a word can have many meanings, especially an important word." Vice versa, one term can be represented by different words. If you documented the word with one meaning in mind but your stakeholder reads it in another way, you and your stakeholder have not come to terms. If this is so, how can we manage the stakeholder's expectation? How can we make sure that the stakeholder's expectation is the same as mine? The traditional approaches are:

- Document the solution in as detailed a manner as possible
- Increase the communication level in term of quantity and quality
- Emphasize the key words for the critical terms of the solution
- Give further qualification of the technical words and special vocabulary

Unstated expectations are those implicit requirements or beliefs or perceptions that exist in your stakeholders' minds. They think you should deliver certain solution values to them by default but you think differently. Unstated expectation management is mainly discovering the stakeholders' expectations or requirements that are not expressed or presented explicitly. Despite this, they think that these requirements are very obvious and should be delivered by default.

2.10 SUMMARY

At the opening of this chapter, we began with two examples and raised some typical issues regarding cloud computing investment and IT project delivery, which are:

- What is the real purpose of cloud investment?
- How can cloud investment be divorced from business needs in many large organizations?
- Why is the successful rate of IT projects so low?
- How can people learn from previous mistakes if they know what went wrong?

The simple answer for the first question is "business needs," which is the main focus of this chapter. The answer of the second question is the "cost transparency" issue. We will discuss in detail in Chapter 16. The answer to the third question is the issue of a disconnection between project contents and project process because people believe if the process is right, the project goal will automatically be achieved. The answer to the fourth question is that the wrong people are often selected for the wrong position.

In order to answer these questions, we first started to clarify some basic terms or concepts. We highlighted the purpose of business is to make profit. Cloud computing is one of the IT tools that can help a business make profit. Unfortunately, because of the complexity and changing velocity of information technology, many people have forgotten about the real purpose of IT. The cost of IT has become opaque for many large organizations or enterprises. Many executives or decision makers believe that IT is more like an isolated realm rather than an integral part of business and many IT project expenditures including cloud computing seem irrelevant to the business.

Second, we argue that a BA role is necessary because today's IT technology is not like what it used to be. It is much more complex than ever before. The BA can not only build the bridge between IT professionals and the business community, but also help IT people to deliver value to the business.

Following a discussion of the term "business," the business analyst role, business strategy, and input variables, we then focused on the meaning of business needs or requirements. We highlighted five different types of requirements and their relationship.

It does not matter how many requirements there are. The ultimate goal of business needs is to solve the business problem. Actually, the real value of IT or cloud computing is helping the business to solve its problems. Therefore, we lay out the entire process of how to solve a business problem from end to end. In order to focus on the BA, we only discussed the first three phases of the process rather than the entire E2E process because the last two phases basically deal with project management.

Last, we discussed how to manage expectations, especially a management team's or decision makers' expectations. Their expectations may hold the critical key for your success in solving the business problem.

Although we did not spend too much time on the topic of the cloud in this chapter, we believe the topic of business needs is the primary focus of any cloud computing project. If we fail to understand the business goal, the investment in cloud computing will become meaningless. In the next chapter, we will use a particular example to prove our propositions.

In short, the goal of any cloud investment is to serve a company's business needs. It should be vigorously examined by business criteria and proved by business managers and key stakeholders.

2.11 REVIEW QUESTIONS

1. What does cloud computing really mean to the business?
2. What is the relationship between the business and the cloud?
3. Why is the success rate of IT projects so low?
4. What can IT people learn from previous lessons?
5. How can we align the strategic goals of business and cloud capabilities?
6. If you are a cloud business analyst or IT professional, how can you identify and capture business requirements?
7. How can we manage my stakeholders' expectations?
8. Why do we need a cloud business analyst?
9. How do we identify the business problems and provide an optimal solution?

IDENTIFYING BUSINESS PROBLEMS: A CASE STUDY

Understanding the theory and principles is one thing. How to apply these theories and principles in practice is another. This chapter presents a case study on applying the step-by-step process discussed in the previous chapter to identify the real business problem.

We will first give a brief outline of the problem that the business manager is facing. Second, we will try to identify the real problem behind the many apparent issues, such as decision motivation, cost transparency, and the decision process. Third, we will lay out the business environment and stakeholders' requirements and then find the possible cloud solution to resolve the business problem. We will use the process discussed in the previous chapter to identify the business problem, gather business requirements, and identify potential business solutions.

Finally, we will highlight some issues and explain how to manage stakeholders' expectations and handle the politics behind some unstated expectations, decision motivations, and requirements during the decision process.

As we stated before in Chapter 1, cloud computing is a new business model and a realization of the utility computing paradigm. Coming up with a cloud cost model is relatively easy if we understand the principles of the cloud infrastructure and basic financial models. The most difficult part is how to apply cloud knowledge to achieving business goals and objectives, which requires the skill of making rational assumptions for the business goals and objectives. It not only requires enough cloud technical knowledge, but also business acumen or savvy as well as sophisticated communication skills.

3.1 CASE INFORMATION BRIEFING

This example business problem is quite simple on the surface at least, with the IT group within a large ICT company having a service contract supported by one of the leading global IT service providers. The service contract is worth about $48 m Australian dollars per annum. The main purpose of this services contract was to fix any IT hardware component out of about 18,400 devices (servers, storage, and network switches) with the specified SLA if any component failed. Therefore, the service contract was also named a break/fix contract. (Please note that the figures shown in this example are hypothetical numbers. We injected a percentage coefficient into the real case.)

By any standard, the cost of $48 million per annum (pa) is not cheap because the average cost per hardware component is over $2600 pa (some components are still within the warranty period) and the service provider has the right to raise the service cost 4% per year in the next five years based on the terms of the service contract. The legitimate argument for raising the price is the standard inflation rate and labor rate increases. This means that although the break/fix contract cost $48 m in the first year, the ICT Company has to pay an average of over $56 million pa for five years.

Clearly, the primary business problem for the IT group is how to reduce the cost of this break/fix service contract. In order to find a good solution for reducing costs, we have to find out what the contract supports or what the business value of this service contract is and how the service provider charges this price for its break/fix service.

At a glance, we can find this service contract supports three types of IT hardware:

- Servers (quantity = 12,000 and cost = $34 m)
- Storage array disks and systems (quantity = 6,000 and cost = $10 m)
- Storage switches (quantity = 400 and cost = $4 m)

The total number of pieces of IT hardware is about 18,400 and the annual cost is worth around $48 million Australian dollars (see Figure 3.1).

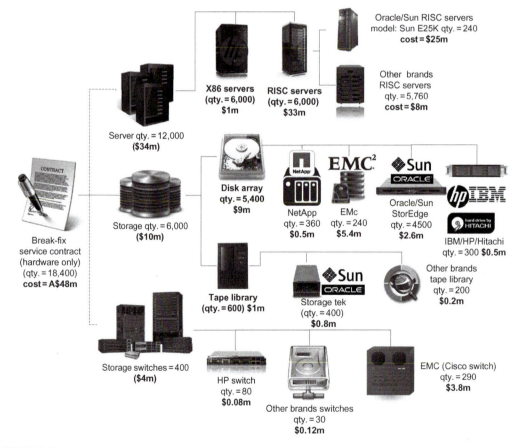

FIGURE 3.1

Overview of break/fix service contract value.

3.1.1 SERVERS

Based on the overview of cost distribution, we can see that the cost for RISC servers takes over 70% or $33 m ($25 m + $8 m). Among these RISC servers, the largest amount of cost occurs due to supporting 240 Oracle /Sun Enterprise 25K (or E25K) RISC servers. In the later chapters of this book, we will discuss the technical differences between RISC and x86 servers. Here, it is quite clear that RISC or E25K servers have become a major challenge to solving this problem. In other words, if we would like to bring the overall break/fix service contract cost down, we have to find a solution to reduce the contract cost for the E25K servers.

3.1.1.1 x86 servers: HP

You may wonder why the cost of maintaining x86 servers is so cheap because in comparison with RISC servers, the support cost for x86 servers is only worth about one million. This is a good question. Actually, the cost of maintaining x86 servers is not cheaper. The reason of the lower cost is because nearly 70% of the HP x86 servers (3,600) are still within the warranty period. HP normally asks its enterprise customers to buy a three-year maintenance and support contract (24×7) almost compulsorily. For any new purchased HP servers, the support cost would be around 10% of the server purchase price. Moreover, the x86 servers will be on the life cycle targeting list after three years of operation based on the ICT Company's policy. In essence, the majority of x86 servers supported by this contract belong to vendors other than HP, such as Dell (420), Sun, IBM (1240), Cisco (108), and others (632).

From a total cost of ownership (TCO) perspective, nearly all major server vendors will charge 10%−15% of the purchasing price or higher for maintenance and support. However, if you virtualize your server infrastructure, it might be unnecessary to purchase the maintenance and support service. We will explain why in the later chapters of this book.

3.1.1.2 RISC servers: Oracle/Sun E25K

Now, let's find out the details of the E25K RISC server and why it is so costly to maintain these 240 RISC servers. As we have indicated above, the principles of RISC will be discussed later. In this chapter, we will only focus on the physical size and architecture of a E25K RISC server. If you cannot differentiate between x86 and RISC servers, you can just think that x86 servers are equipped with the popular Intel or AMD CPUs and RISC servers have different types CPUs, such as IBM PowerPC, HP-UX, ARM, and Intel Itanium. One of most popular RISC servers is the Oracle/Sun SPARC.

3.1.1.2.1 E25K RISC server details

The E25K is a very powerful midrange server. The codename is Amazon 25. Actually, it was one of the top enterprise or Sun Fire serial servers produced by Sun Microsystems. It was first released in Febrary 2004 and superseded by the new SPARC M9000 in 2009.

The E25K can be configured with up to 72 Ultra SPARC IV plus processors (each processor has a dual-core SPARC CPU) per frame or rack. The clock speed of the processor is up to 1.5 GHz for the Ultra SPARC IV + chip and 1.05, 1.2, and 1.35 GHz for the Ultra SPARC IV chip. Each E25K frame consists of up to 18 system boards and each system board can have four processors

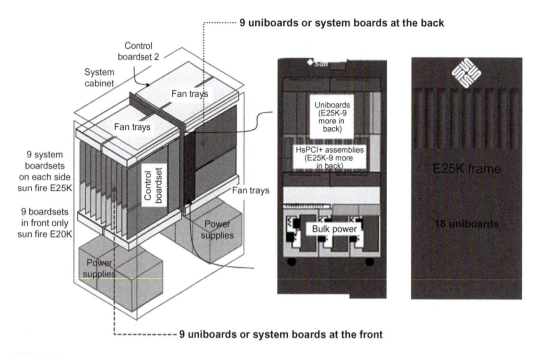

FIGURE 3.2

Maximum Number of uniboards or system boards of each E25K frame (rack).

and up to 32 GB memory per board. In other words, the maximum memory capacity can reach up to 576 GB per frame (see Figure 3.2).

All these E25K frames were bought between 2004 and 2009 by the ICT Company but the majority of frames (or racks) were bought between 2006 and 2007 during the IT transformation program (see Figure 3.3).

However, not all frames were bought with the full capacity of system boards (or 18 system boards). Many system boards might be bought at a later stage when the capital budget allows. In other words, the system boards are not fully populated (all 240 frames equipped, 4,320 boards or 240 × 18), rather approximately 1,600 system boards have been installed based on the latest monthly report supplied by the service provider.

The purchase cost of all frames was approximately $374 million and the total three-year support contract (24 × 7 with 4-hour response time) cost for 220 frames was about $114 million (each frame break/fix service cost ≈ $172k/per frame/per annum, 172k × 220 × 3 ≈ $114 m), which is equivalent to the standard support price or 10% of hardware purchasing price. Although there were 240 frames, 10 frames bought before 2006 were excluded in the initial support contract back in 2007. The last few frames were bought with a discount price because these frames were second-hand hardware and shipped from Europe in 2009.

According to Sun Microsystem's product roadmap, the E25K had reached its end-of-life in January 2009. If this is the case, it is not clear why the ICT Company still purchased a few frames

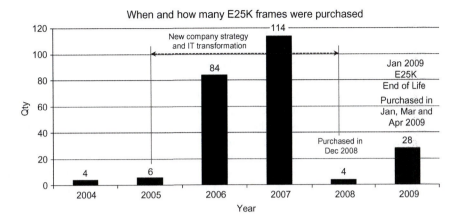

FIGURE 3.3

E25K server quantity over five years.

after the E25K product had been superseded by Oracle/Sun because it did not seem to have a capacity issue even if the number of frames was less than 200.

3.1.1.2.2 Maintenance and support requirements for E25K

You may wonder why we have to spend so much time discussing the details of E25K frames. Given the details of this example, we can clearly understand the business problem and lay out the foundation for a cloud solution. One of the other issues for this contract is that the support price is based on the service level. For example, the price for Gold support would is $147K/per frame/per annum with 4-hour response time (24×7) and Bronze support would cost $62K/per frame/per annum (7 a.m.−7 p.m., 5 days a week excluding public holidays). As you can see, in comparison with Oracle/Sun's price, the current price charged by the existing service provider is still about 15% cheaper than Oracle/Sun's price, which should cost about $34 million dollars per annum to maintain 240 E25K frames. It was the result of a negotiation between the existing service provider and the ICT Company led by the former acting CIO of the ICT Company. It appears to be a good deal but if you dive into the details, you may find this is not a case. Why is this so?

Having a look the new maintenance service that the ICT Company receives, we can find the SLA is different from the original SLA, which means that not all E25K frames would be supported by the Gold SLA and only 118 frames have the Gold SLA. Actually, the former acting CIO was trying to get all frames under the Gold SLA support. Unfortunately, keeping spare parts for these end-of-life servers (E25K) could be very expensive and risky business. The service provider would not give in.

In order to achieve about $14 m dollars in savings (the business goal for the consolidated number of E25K frames = 240), the acting CIO decided to take risks and reduced the service level of 122 frames of the E25K servers from Gold to Bronze. The proposition for this decision was that not every frame would run production applications and only a certain number of frames would load the production applications. Therefore, it would be a good idea to slash the number of frames supported by Gold SLA for nonproduction applications. The question is how many frames can be downgraded from Gold to Bronze and which servers or frames are the right candidates for the downgrade? Surely, the expected number ought to be greater than 122 frames because the opex budget in 2011 required $14 million in cost savings.

Based on the latest business users' complaints, it appears that the decision was made quite recklessly at that time because a recent analysis report shows that there are 200 noncritical application instances that have the Gold SLA support and 160 critical application instances just have Bronze SLA support. It might not sound real but it was true. Fortunately, there had not been so many business complains because most of the E25K frames were quite reliable. However, the risk has always been there since 2011. It will not disappear.

From a commercial perspective, the idea of reducing SLA for more than 50% of frames was not too bad. It did solve part of the problem, but it created risks for the business, which is a so-called side effect solution. Later, many people believed that the acting CIO did not care about any long-term consequences. After all, he would eventually leave the ICT Company soon after the service contract was signed.

However, it is fair to say that the acting CIO did not have enough time to find which SLA of E25K frame could be downgraded and which one could not; the person who manages the service contract should carry out this task. Unfortunately, although this person has been in the position for more than 20 years, he did not have enough knowledge and expertise to manage such a complex service contract. To some degree, he destroyed over $20 or even $40 million of the ICT Company's value and opportunities. We will give more details regarding the politics behind the solving of this business problem later. Actually, when a customer later complained about one of the production applications running on the E25K server supported by Bronze SLA, the same person pointed the finger at the former acting CIO. Surely, this guy used the former acting CIO as a scapegoat. Whatever he did, the real issue is that his manager and the manager's manager (or senior IT executive) did not realize there was a serious risk for many critical applications. A savvy manager or talented executive should always focus on abnormal events rather than normal ones and pay attention to the exceptional rather than the regular. We will have a further discussion on this topic later.

The details on how to deliver over $14 million dollars/per annum savings in the IT opex budget is shown in Table 3.1. As we can see, the original cost for the support contract was $19.5 m pa.

Table 3.1 Irresponsible Operational Cost Reduction

Company	SLA Type	Unit Price per Annum	Qty	Total Value per Annum
Oracle/Sun Price	Gold = 24 × 7, 4-hour response time	$172,000	226	$39 m
The service provider	Gold = 24 × 7, 4-hour Response time	$147,000	118	$17.4 m
The service provider	Bronze = 7 a.m.−7 p.m., 5 days a week, 8-hour response time	$62,000	122	$7.6 m
Subtotal				$25 m
Cost savings for support				$39−$25 = $14 m

After the negotiation, the unit price for Gold SLA support was slashed to $147 k pa rather than $172 k pa. The number of Gold-supported servers was cut from 226 to 118. However, the total number of E25K frames had increased from 226 to 240, which means 14 more frames managed by other service contracts had been consolidated into this service contract. The rest of the 122 frames would be supported by Bronze SLA and the unit price for each frame was $62 k pa. Overall, the new service contract delivered $14 m pa cost savings for IT opex.

If we disregard all the potential risks, it was not a too bad a deal. Unfortunately, this hidden and huge risk is too big to be ignored. The problem is that none of the IT executives in the ICT Company was aware of this. The only person who knew this trick already knew how to point the finger at the former acting CIO or find a scapegoat.

It is one part of the opex story. If you are an experienced IT executive, you may ask, "Are there any additional operational costs on the top of this support cost?" This is a good question. Let's explore further for other cost items, namely power and space.

3.1.1.2.3 Space requirements for E25K frame

The physical size of the E25K frame is not the same as the dimesnions of a standard rack. Based on Oracle/Sun's specification, each frame is 33.3 inches (846 mm) wide $\times$ 64.5 inches (1638 mm) deep and 75 inches (1905 mm) high. In other words, each frame will occupy at least six tiles (or six standard racks) of space (see Figure 3.4).

Furthermore, because we have to access the frame from both the front and back, the actual space requirement for each frame or rack is far more than its physical dimensions (if we consider the clearance space requirements). In addition, if we take into consideration the frame's ventilation requirements plus a dedicated storage rack, each E25K would need at least 15 standard tiles (or standard racks) of space (see Figure 3.5).

From Figure 3.1, we can find 4,320 SE 3120 disk arrays (2,000 disks have Gold SLA support and 2,320 disks have Bronze support) and the total support cost is about $2.6 m pa. These hard drive disks are dedicated to E25K system files. The monthly report shows 240 standard 42RU racks to accommodate 4,320 HDD. Each standard 42RU rack has 18 SE3120 systems (1RU). Each SE3120 pizza box consists of 4 HDDs (each HDD is configured with 73 GB storage capacity). In other words, each storage pizza box has 292 GB system storage capacity. The average cost for each HDD is about $621 pa.

If we adopt the Uptime Institute's assumption of $13,562 per square meter per annum [112] in 2008 to calculate the cost of space, we can find that the space cost for each E25K frame would be $73,234.80 per frame per annum.

Unfortunately, the ICT Company does not have enough data center space to accommodate these E25K racks. Subsequently, the ICT Company has to lease nearly 45% of the space for 108 frames (see Tables 3.2 and 3.3), which are located in the "U" data center.

If the leasing cost of each frame is $75 k pa in 2013, the leasing cost for 108 frames would be over $8.1 m pa.

3.1.1.2.4 Power and cooling requirements of E25K

The E25K can be considered a high-density rack that draws a lot of power in comparison to a standard rack. Based on the Sun Fire E25K system site planning guide, the basic cooling requirements are shown in Table 3.4.

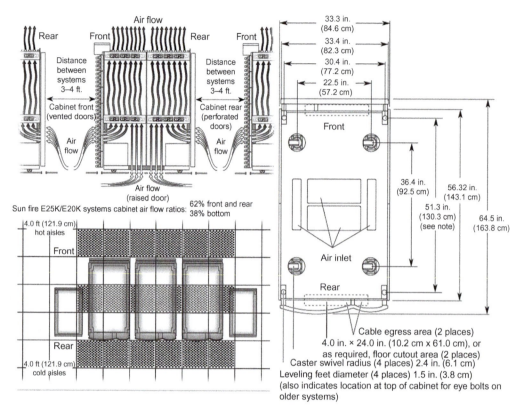

FIGURE 3.4

Physical dimensions of E25K frame or rack.

It is known that the traditional telecommunication rack's power consumption would be below 5 kW per rack and even with a common standard computer rack, the power consumption would be between 5 kW to 10 kW per rack (assume the computer is not a blade server). Now, the E25K needs over 28 kW per frame. The conventional computer data center or traditional telco data center cannot accommodate E25K frames. In order to load a E25K in a conventional data center, there are basically three solutions:

1. Reduce the number of system boards or system boards in each frame.
2. Upgrade the data center's air-conditioning system. Normally, the frame may need a full duct supply (refer to Section 8.6.4).
3. Control the workload or the utilization rate of each frame.

Perhaps this explains why the system board frames were not fully populated. According to the E25K's specification, there should be $240 \times 18 = 4{,}320$ system boards or system boards for 240 frames or racks if each frame is fully populated with system boards, but based on the latest monthly report, the total number of system boards was only around 800. The average number of system

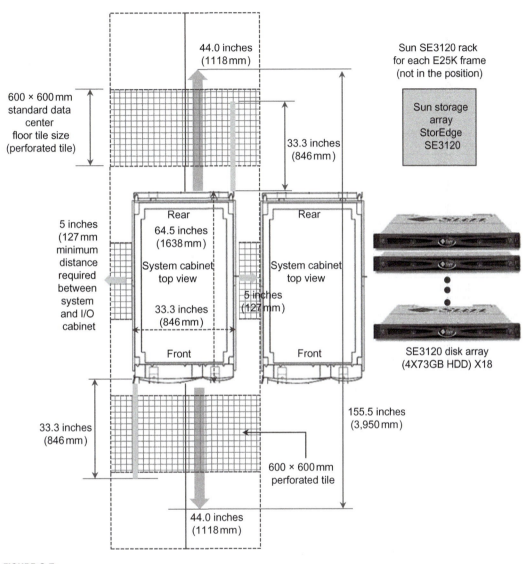

FIGURE 3.5

Required space for each E25K frame.

board per frame is between three and 8 (see Table 3.5). Because the service provider is charging the service and support price based on the number of frames rather than the number of system boards, it has opened the door to finding a cost reduction solution, that is consolidating each E25K frame if the leasing data center does meet the high density rack criteria. We will analyze this solution when we define the business problem in the later part of this chapter.

Table 3.2 Data Center Location for Each E25K System

	C Data Center	E Data Center	SL Data Center	U Data Center (Leased)	Total
Qty. & FL 1 frames	Level 1 = 22		Level 1 = 106	Level 1 = 60	188
No. of uniboards	158	0	714	350	1222
Qty. & Other FL frames	0	Level 8 = 2	Level 7 = 2	Level 3 = 48	52
No. of uniboards	0	6	12	328	346
Qty. Gold ($147.4 k pa)	8	0	30	80	118
Qty. Bronze ($62.4 k pa)	14	2	78	28	122
Total qty. of frames	22	2	108	108	240
Break/fix cost per annum	$2.053 m	$0.125 m	$9.289 m	$13.539 m	$25 m
System Board Details					
	Level 1		Level 1	Level 1	
No. production UB	50		146	308	504
No. nonproduction UB	108		568	42	718
		Level 8	Level 7	Level 3	
No. production other UB		6	12	284	302
No. nonproduction other UB				44	44
Total no. of UB	50	6	146	**592**	794
Total no. of non-UB	108	0	580	86	774
Total qty. of uniboards	158	6	726	678	**1568**
Average system boards per frame	7	3	7	7	

3.1.1.2.5 Application requirements of E25K

Since 2006, there have been about 80 applications and database workloads that have been moved onto the E25K platform. One of the major applications is Siebel (a CRM application for billing), which takes up 127 system boards (the total number of system boards is 785), or over 16% of the total number of system boards. We can classify all these applications into nine operational categories with four different types of state (active, inactive, physical and virtual) (see Table 3.5).

3.1.1.3 Service contract for all RISC servers

We will now look at how the rest of the $4 million has been spent to support other types of RISC servers. In addition to SPARC servers, IBM, HP, and Intel also produce RISC servers. The question is, "Do other types of RISC servers impact the service contract cost?" (See Table 3.6.)

Table 3.3 Data Center Room of E25K Systems

	C Data Center	E Data Center	SL Data Center	U Data Center (Leased)	Subtotal
Level 1/Room 0		2			2
Level 1/Room 2			20		20
Level 1/Room 3			12		12
Level 1/Room 7			24		24
Level 1/Room 8			30		30
Level 1/Room 9			16		16
Ground/Room 11			2		2
Ground/Room 12			4		4
Level 1/ Room 1				60	60
Level 3/Room 4				24	24
Level 3/Room 5				24	24
Level 8	22				22
Total	22	2	108	108	240

Note: "UB" stands for system board, "pa" = per annum, FL = floor level.

Table 3.4 Sun Fire E25K System Maximum Power and Cooling Requirements

Sun Fire System	Qty. of System Boards	Power (VA)	Air Conditioning (BTU/Hr)
E25K	Up to 18	28,701	97,538*

Note: 1 BTU/Hr = 0.29307107 W, 97,538 BTU/Hr = 28.6 kW.

Based on the above table, we can see that over 90% of the RISC servers are SPARC servers. HP, IBM, and others have very little impact on the cost of the service contract. So, let's investigate SPARC servers excluding the E25K server.

Based on the monthly report, there were 67 SPARC models bought between 1996 and 2012. Surprisingly, the ICT Company still has 40 antique SPARC servers (from before the year 2000) that are still supported by this contract (see Figure 3.6) and about 90% of the SPARC servers should be targeted hardware for cycling (or end of life by the vendor's roadmap).

The average maintenance and support cost for each RSIC server would be $1,300 pa or over $100 per server per month. If we spend $4 million on capex to purchase new servers supported by a virtualized infrastructure rather than opex for maintenance and support cost, it would be able to cover the workload for these 5,760 instances. (Of course, our conclusion assumes that the risks of both installation and migration costs are tightly controlled.) The main reason to support this proposition is that the virtualized infrastructure can significantly increase the server utilization rate

Table 3.5 Application Categories of E25K System Boards

Application Status	Product Development	Disaster Recovery	Production	Staging	Standby	Test	Training	Blank	Others	Total
Physical	128	16	792	24	2	570	6	24	6	1568
Virtual	112	0	0	10	0	136	2	18	0	278
Active	240	16	792	34	2	706	8	42	6	1846
Inactive	12	0	46	0	0	120	0	220	10	408
Subtotal	252	16	838	34	2	826	8	262	16	2254

Notes:

1. All physical and virtual instances are active.

2. "Virtualized" E25K means a "partition" of the system board into a number of domains. As we discussed above, each system board has four Ultra SPARC IV+ processors and each processor is a dual-core CPU. Theoretically speaking, if each core can handle one workload then each system board can be partitioned into eight instances or domains.

3. Two E25K frames have been allocated to install a LDoM or RISC virtualization program, which represents is a complete misunderstanding of the E25K system. This program had spent over $20 million over 18 months. The remarkable thing was none knew why the project had failed. We will have more details about this topic in the Chapter 11 of this book.

Table 3.6 SLA of All Other RISC Servers

RISC Vendors/ SLA	2 Hrs*	4 Hrs*	Platinum	Gold	Silver	Bronze	2 Work Days	Time and Material	EOSL	Not Supported	Subtotal
Oracle/Sun	52	2	0	1928	422	862	2	2056	0	4	5328
HP	0	0	4	190	94	54	0	166	2	0	510
IBM	0	0	0	0	0	0	0	0	8	0	8
Others	0	0	0	0	0	0	154	0	0	0	154
Total	52	2	4	2118	516	916	156	2222	10	4	6000

Note: 2 and 4 hours turn around time for Service Level Agreement (SLA) means that these physical servers are still within the warranty period.

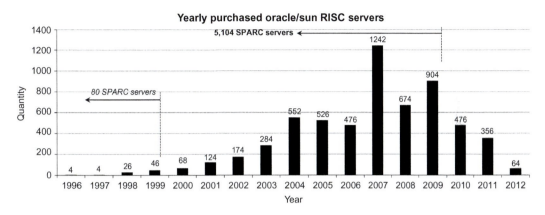

FIGURE 3.6

Oracle/Sun RISC servers: distribution of purchases by year.

(up to 75%). In comparison, the average utilization rate of a traditional standalone server would be approximately between 7% and 15%. For some applications it is even less than 1%.

Overall, the IT group of the ICT Company has not been managing server assets very well, especially with regard to the life cycle of the assets. The main reason is that the people who are managing the assets have no idea how to manage these IT assets. What they do is to just use their asset management power to set a lot of roadblocks for other line of business (LoB) units. We will have a further discussion on this topic when we define the business problem.

3.1.2 STORAGE

In addition to the server assets, one of other the important IT assets in a data center is the storage hardware. Referring to Figure 3.1, we can divide the storage assets and costs into four categories:

- NAS (major vendor: NetApp, qty. = 360, cost = $0.5 m)
- SAN (major vendor: EMC, qty. = 240, cost = $5.4 m)
- DAS (major vendor: Oracle/Sun, qty. = 4,500, cost = $2.6 m per annum)
- Others (major vendors: IBM/HP/Hitachi, qty. = 300, cost = $0.5 m per annum)

3.1.2.1 NAS

Traditionally, most NAS hardware equipment and systems for the IT group were provided by one of the major storage vendors.

Because of high capex spending on the NAS storage life cycle program ($84 m), many storage devices are still within the warranty period. Therefore, the cost for NAS hardware is only $0.5 m.

3.1.2.2 SAN

SAN storage equipment presents a much more complex picture because the cost of $5.40 m pa does not cover all storage assets in the IT group. This means that 240 devices or $5.40 million only

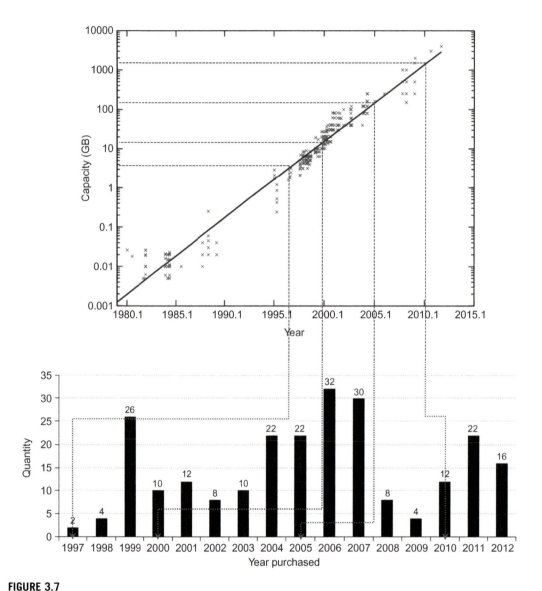

FIGURE 3.7

Distribution of EMC storage hardware purchased per year.

supports less than 30–40% of the total number of SAN assets. One part (over 40%) is managed by another person who is dedicated to SAN assets within the IT group. The rest of the SAN assets (or 20%) are managed by a person who belongs to another LoB unit outside of the IT group.

The IT group has 16 types of SAN models supported by this service contract. Over 70% of the assets were bought before 2007 or are more than 7 years old (see Figure 3.7).

Table 3.7 Maintenance and Support Costs for EMC Storage

SLA	4-Hour Response in Qty.	Gold in Qty.	Costs	Grand Total
Data Domain DD860	4		Another account	4
Data Domain DD880	4		Another account	4
Data Domain DD890	8		Another account	8
EMC Clarion CX600		4	92,000	8
EMC Clarion CX700		12	400,000	12
EMC Symmetrix 3430		6	188,000	6
EMC Symmetrix 3630		4	298,000	4
EMC Symmetrix 3830		28	1,592,000	28
EMC Symmetrix 3930		2	180,000	2
EMC Symmetrix 8430		4	108,000	4
EMC Symmetrix 8530		2	60,000	2
EMC Symmetrix 8830		8	516,000	8
EMC Symmetrix DMX		32	1,966,000	32
EMC Symmetrix DMX-3	94		Under Warranty	94
EMC Symmetrix DMX-4	10		Under Warranty	10
EMC Symmetrix VMAX	18		Under Warranty	18
Grand Total	138	102	$5,400,000	240

Table 3.7 shows that over 65% (or $3.6 million) of the break/fix cost supports two types of SAN storage equipment:

- EMC Symmetrix 3830 (qty. = 28, $1.6 m pa)
- EMC Symmetrix DMX-2000 (qty = 32, $2 m pa)

All 28 EMC Symmetrix 3830 storage arrays were bought between 1999 and 2002 and all 32 Symmetrix DMX-2000 storage arrays were bought between 2002 and 2005 (see Table 3.7).

Again, based on the above data, it is quite clear that the IT group is doing a very poor job in terms of life cycle. Even the storage equipment bought in 1997 is still in operation. In comparison with the relative new storage devices (less than 3−4 years old), the ICT company has more than 80% of old EMC or SAN storage equipment still in operation.

3.1.3 STORAGE SWITCHES

The last IT asset supported by this contract is the storage switch. Based on Figure 3.1, although there are 400 storage switches, most (or over 72.5% or 290 devices) of the assets are EMC storage switches. These EMC switches are actually rebranded Cisco switches. Moreover, these assets are

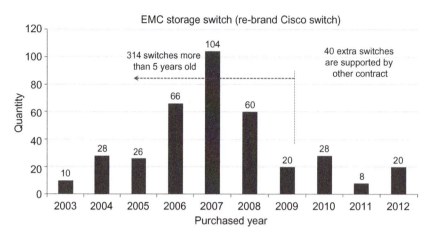

FIGURE 3.8

EMC storage switches (Rebranded Cisco Switches).

more than 5 years old (see Figure 3.8). The asset details show that the IT group has 26 different types of switches (see Table 3.8).

Most of these devices (75% or 316) are SAN port switches and 84 of them are director port switches, which are too expensive to support and maintain. Just 76 director port switches cost nearly 1 million dollars for a break/fix service contract.

The most interesting point is that because the company is in the ICT business, it has a separate contract with Cisco, which is worth over $50 million. Based on the contract terms, Cisco would support all Cisco network switches for $50 million pa, no matter how many devices the ICT has. It is a fixed price contract. The support contract price was significant, up from about just over $32 million (in 2007/2008 financial year) to $50 million in 2009. It was also called an umbrella support agreement. The contract was signed by another LoB unit of the ICT Company.

It was not clear whether the rebranded Cisco switches (or EMC storage switch) should be a part of the deal or not. Theoretically speaking, these switches should be included in the contract. After all, EMC cannot support these switches and only Cisco can do it. Even if EMC storage switches were not included in the deal, it would be a good idea for the IT group to buy the Cisco switches directly from Cisco rather than EMC.

Unfortunately, the people who maintained and managed these switch assets did not understand EMC storage switches were rebranded Cisco's switches. As a result, the IT group has to pay about $4 million pa extra for the break/fix costs.

So far, we have presented information about the business problem from three perspectives in terms of the break/fix service contract provided by one of the leading global service companies:

- Servers
- Storage
- Switches

All three types of IT assets are part of the problem; the IT group of the ICT has to spend over $48 m dollars to maintain a large amount of very old IT assets. Among these assets, the E25K is

Table 3.8 EMC and Other Storage Switches		
Type of Switches	**Qty.**	**Total Value**
EMC Cisco 9506-CDS	4	$38,000
EMC Cisco 9509-CDS	58	$1,292,000
EMC Connectrix DS-24M2 SAN Switch-CDS	6	$8,000
EMC Connectrix ED1032-CDS	8	$90,000
EMC Connectrix ED140-M-CDS	8	$84,000
EMC Connectrix ED64-M-CDS	56	$440,000
EMC Connectrix MDS-9140-CDS	40	$58,000
EMC MDS 9120 SWITCH-CDS	16	$10,000
EMC MDS-9513 Cisco Director-CDS	76	$1,960,000
EMC MDS-9513 Cisco Director	2	$0
CISCO NEXUS 5020	2	$0
EMC CISCO 9509	2	$0
EMC Connectrix EC-1100-CDS	4	$0
EMC Connectrix EC-1200-CDS	2	$0
EMC Connectrix ED1033-CDS	2	$0
EMC Connectrix MDS-9216A-CDS	2	$0
EMC Connectrix MDS-9506-CDS	2	$0
HP Switches	80	$8,000
Other Switches	30	$12,000
Total	400	$4,000,000

the major issue because it is worth more than 50% of the total break/fix support contract ($25 m pa for the E25K server and $2.6 m for direct attached storage (DAS). If we can solve the E25K server problem, we can save at least 50% of the break/fix cost or solve 50% of the business problem.

In this example, because of the absence of the problem owner, we cannot interactively communicate with the business owner to verify the business problem, so we have to slightly modify the standard BA process step. In other words, we have to analyze the problem from different angles.

3.2 DEFINE THE PROBLEMS

On understanding all the issues of IT asset management, life cycle, and the break/fix service contract, you may wonder how this could happen and why? Why does this IT group manage IT assets so poorly? To answer this question, we must understand how the ICT Company organizes its operation for IT management.

In the last chapter, we emphasized that for any IT project, if it achieves success, it is the people's success and if it fails, it is people's failure. Similarly, for any kind of IT asset management, any good IT asset management is because the right people are managing them; if there are poorly managed IT assets, it is because the wrong people occupy the wrong positions.

When we are trying to define the problem and find a right solution for it, it is very important to include the issue of people in the considerations. Sometime, if you exclude consideration of people, you can never find the right solution for the business problem. After all, it is IT people who manage the IT assets rather than an object or a robot. When you include people in the solution equation, politics or political issues will be inevitable.

Of course, you do not have to start with the people involved, which sometimes may become very tough or complex due to multiple issues intertwined together. What you can do is identify the number of problems first and then find their relationship.

If you are a BA consultant, you should be very careful in selecting your targeted problem, especially if the problem is closely associated with people or organization issues, because there may be many hidden and historic politics behind those fundamental problems.

Of course, the real business problem of this case is quite simple on the surface. Actually, we have already stated in the information briefing that it is the high cost for the break/fix support contract provided by the service vendor. However, many issues behind this problem are very complicated. Why is this so?

1. The support cost is much higher than the value of the assets. For example, no one would spend $1,000 in warranty to maintain a laptop computer that is worth only $500. Common sense says that if the laptop is broken down, you would throw it away and buy another new one. In this case, some assets are more than 10 years old and their values are zero or negative because they consume power and occupy valuable data center space.
2. The cost of the asset is not transparent. This means that the total cost of ownership (TCO) of the asset has no direct relationship on the assets and the supported business. From a business perspective, it does not matter how much the IT asset costs as long as it can generate business revenue and profit.
3. The service vendor increases the support contract's cost each year. The increase rate is based on the inflation rate rather than the asset value and the business value that the assets support.
4. About 57% of the support cost (or $25 million + $2.6 million) is for maintaining 240 E25K frames and DAS storage assets. Moreover, the majority of these frames (206) are more than seven years old and all these assets are end-of-life products and at the end of support based on the vendor's product roadmap.
5. Sufficient funds were allocated for the life-cycle program but it was unfortunate that a large amount of the budget ($84 million) had been spent on the wrong assets (NAS). The decision was not only incorrect but also so costly and it eliminated other assets (especially for the RISC server fleet) that badly needed to be refreshed. This indicates that the IT group has no good strategy to manage its IT assets although it has spent millions of dollars in consultants fee and taken more than six months for a IT infrastructure five-year strategic plan. (It was not quite clear why the IT group should waste millions of dollars to generate another substrategy at the IT infrastructure level, when the overall IT strategy had already been created. The substrategy

gave no concrete details but a very high level view that had been already presented at the CIO level. It was an absolutely useless exercise.) This leads to another issue.

6. IT people are talking too much in slogans but not enough about tangible results or deliverables. Even if something had been delivered, customers were often not satisfied with the results.

7. In order to decommission some antique assets, some applications running on these assets have to be migrated to new assets. The cost and risk of this migration is too high. None of the IT executives want to make this risky decision. "If it's not broken, why fix it?"

8. Due to frequent organization changes and the utilization of a large amount of IT contracts, some application owners cannot be found. In other words, the IT people do not know who should be responsible for running certain applications.

We can list more issues behind this simple surface problem. Overall, we can categorize all these issues into three root causes (see Figure 3.9)

- Decision motivation and decision process
- Cost transparency
- Application migration

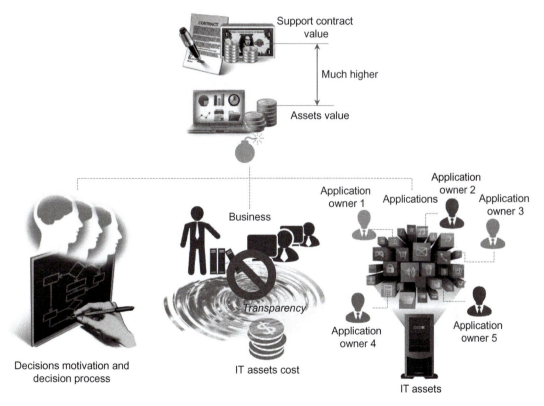

FIGURE 3.9

Root causes of the business problem.

3.2.1 ELICIT MULTIPLE ISSUES

The primary problem of higher cost for the supporting contract was not triggered by a single issue, but rather multiple issues. In order to solve this problem, we have to identify the many issues or root causes behind the problem. Let's walk through each category of the issue.

3.2.1.1 Decision making

First, we have the issue of decision motivation. The question is if some decision makers already know what the real problem is, why did they not make the right decision and fix it? This leads to the issue of decision motivation and the decision process. In order to make the right decision, we should have three decision components (see Figure 3.10):

- Decision motivation
- Decision information and knowledge
- Decision process

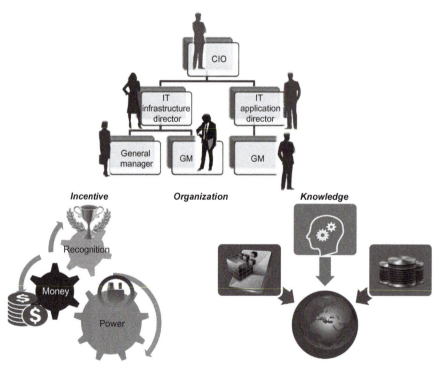

FIGURE 3.10

Decision motivation and process.

3.2.1.1.1 Decision motivation

For many investment projects or businesses, one of the most popular analysis tools for a decision maker to make a sound strategic decision is the Strength, Weakness, Opportunities, and Threat (SWOT) or Satisfaction, Opportunity, Fault, and Threat (SOFT) analysis method, which was developed by Albert Humphrey in the 1960s. In simple terms, the strength (S) means the company's capability or capacity to do the business. It is an internal element of analysis. The weakness (W) is the gap between the capability to do the business and the company's capacity. It can also be considered the company's resources gap. Opportunities (O) represent the external influences or market development or business opportunities to achieve the business profits. Threat (T) is also an external factor that may bring some disadvantages for the business or investment project, such as competition pressure, major vendors, and soft market demand or overall economic climate.

If the IT cost is not transparent, then an IT investment project can basically ignore two external factors, namely "Opportunities" and "Threat." Subsequently, the SWOT model may become a similar model such as Benefits, Opportunities, Cost, and Risk (BOCR) [61] (see Figure 3.11).

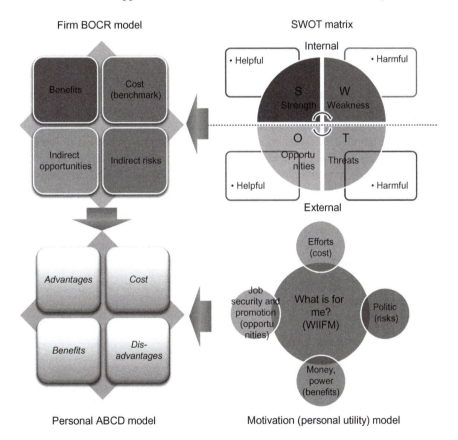

FIGURE 3.11

Evolution of decision models.

When the external competitive pressures are reduced, the opportunities and risks become indirect components for an investment project. Moreover, if the decision maker's motivation puts personal interests ahead of a company's or shareholders' interests, the BOCR decision model turns into a personal ABCD model, which is basically driven by personal motivation or a utility decision model. Ironically, if someone puts a company's interests ahead of personal ones, he/she cannot survive when the company's culture is highly politicized and some senior executives have hidden agendas. Of course, many of these personal motivations and hidden agendas will be sugarcoated to look like the only rational choice among different decision alternatives.

Final decisions are driven by many personal motivations or interests. Although nearly everyone knows that over 70–90% of existing IT assets, especially E25K frames (servers), should be refreshed immediately, no one wants to make this highly political and risky decision. Why is this such a highly risky and political decision? None can correctly estimate the overall costs of this life-cycle program

- No one can know how big a risk application migration is because some applications are so critical for the company's business, such as Seibel CRM.
- The company has many organization silos with shared IT infrastructure. It is unclear who is responsible for which application and how the IT infrastructure resources are allocated.
- Some critical information cannot be shared among internal IT people. Communication brick walls are pervasive. Many IT people see the information as protection for their job.
- Although the life-cycle program should be done very urgently, none of the decision makers would like to make this tough and almost suicidal decision (from a career perspective) because the decision to adopt expensive server hardware or the E25K frame was a big mistake in the first place. It was a political decision when it was made. Now, no one wants to touch this hot potato. This is why no one can give a correct cost and risk estimation for this life-cycle project.
- The life-cycle project or program also means some kind of change. It will certainly hurt or have an impact on some interest group, such as service support vendors. These vendors may have a lot of influence on the senior leadership team of the company.

The pervasive phenomenon of a communication brick wall has created intense politics within the IT group because it is a survival strategy in a frequently changing environment. The fundamental issues behind this phenomenon are:

- Improper corporate structure
- Wrong incentive system
- Incorrect decision process

We will discuss these issues in the subsequent sections.

3.2.1.1.2 Decision information and knowledge

Frequent reorganization and reporting line changes not only disrupt the normal processes of daily operation but also wipe out much valuable historic information and knowledge, which is terribly important for making critical decisions such as cycling products and application migration.

Lack of operation continuity, critical information loss, and insufficient or superseded knowledge had led to many senior IT executives or key decision makers not having enough confidence to make up their mind on many IT investment projects. A common approach for many decision makers or senior executives is to hire a bunch of consultants. There is nothing wrong with using consultants but the problem is that unless the decision maker knows what he/she wants, the consultant cannot provide valuable help. The result might not be what the decision maker wants but rather what the consultant thinks the decision maker wants.

The lesson that we can learn from previous experience is that when dealing with external consultants consider the following:

1. As a decision maker, you have to know what you really want.
2. Consultants alone will not provide enough decision information and knowledge.
3. The outside can only add value if you know what you really want.
4. Political motivation may drive you ahead of others for a short period but in the long run, you could end up losing.

We often say that a choice or direction is far more important than effort. An outside consultant can only assist you in the effort, not in the choice. A choice has to be made by the decision maker, not by the consultant. Now, the question is, how do we select the right direction?

The right approach is to listen to all opinions. We often say, "let a thousand flowers bloom." So before a choice is selected, decision makers should do the following:

• Listen to enemies to avoid deception
• Listen to outsiders (or consultants) to avoid prejudices
• Listen to ordinary people to avoid common mistakes
• Listen to competitors to avoid misdirection
• Listen to a sages to learn what is not understood
• Listen to predecessors to save lot of time

We should always remember that modesty is a type of strategic resource. If you can embrace all opinions, you will be enlightened; if you just listen to one side, you will be overtaken by darkness.

Any decision maker is dependent on three ingredients: determination (or correct judgment or choice), planning, and opportunities. If you think you can merely rely on an external consultant to make the right choice for you, you will fail miserably. How can we make the correct judgment? It will depend on the decision information and knowledge. When we are talking about decision information and knowledge, it is important to understand that decision information is achievable within a relative short time period but decision knowledge has to be accumulated over a long time period. Moreover, you can rely on the consultant to obtain the decision information but you can hardly rely on consultants for decision knowledge, because decision knowledge has to be taught and understood.

Because many decision makers for the IT groups did not have sufficient decision information or knowledge or the right motivation, many decisions made for IT investment projects were ridiculous, such as spending $84 million to save $50 million, where the net loss was $ 34 million.

3.2.1.1.3 Decision process

In addition to issues of decision motivation, information, and knowledge, the IT group also does not have the right decision process in place to prevent some common human decision biases, such as social proof, the sunk cost fallacy, the overconfidence effect, self-serving actions, chauffeur knowledge, the primacy and recency effects, and default effect biases.

Before we start our journey into the decision process, let's visit a true scientific story written by Dava Sobel, *Longitude* [73], as the kick-off point. The story took place more than 300 years ago. Here, we are not going to recap the story of John Harrison's genius sea clock that had beaten Isaac Newton's predication, but rather focus on the tragedy of Admiral Sir Clowdisley Shovell and his English Fleet, which was the real motivation behind the sea clock.

It was the foggy night of October 22, 1707. Sir Clowdisley and his fleet were on their way back home after a small victorious battle with French warships from Gibraltar. Sir Clowdisley and his decision-making executives believed that they were heading west of Île d'Ouessant, a small island outpost of the French (see Figure 3.12).

Unfortunately, they suddenly discovered that they had been trapped in the Scilly Isles which is full of hazardous reefs, just about 20 miles from the southwest tip of England because they were misguided by their longitude readings. They had no accurate longitude gauges at that time.

The flagship, the Association, sank first and before the rest of ships could realize the danger, two more ships, the Eagle and the Romney, were swallowed by the seawater. In the end, four of five warships disappeared that night.

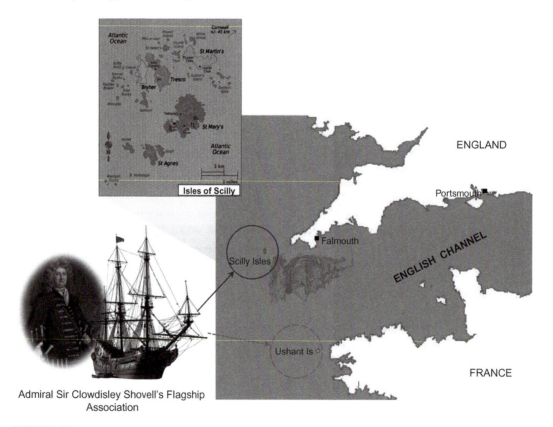

Admiral Sir Clowdisley Shovell's Flagship
Association

FIGURE 3.12

The story of Sir Clowdisley and his fleet.

Surprisingly, Sir Clowdisley himself washed ashore alive and was discovered by a local greedy woman. Unfortunately, the woman had more interest in his emerald ring on his finger than his life. She eventually killed him to retain his ring. Thirty years later and just before she died, she confessed that she murdered Capitan Clowdisley. What a tragedy this story was.

It seems that the tragedy was inevitable. Well, this is not true. Sir Clowdisley had an opportunity to avoid this tragedy. Just about 24 hours before, one of his crew members stuck his neck out and told him that the fleet had deviated from their original shipping route during cloudy days and was heading towards the wrong destination based on his experience and records. At that time, such behavior was not allowed. Royal Navy regulations would sentence anyone to death if he tried to influence the Capitan's navigation decisions. It was quite understandable back then because there was no accurate instrument to decide the longitude. Navigating a ship was purely based on the Capitan's sailing experiences and gut feelings. It is similar to today's investment decisions for a cloud-computing project. Imagine a ship sailing on a wide and wild open ocean; if every sailor was allowed to cast his opinion on how to navigate, the Capitan would be unable to decide how to navigate the ship. This was why Admiral Shovell ordered hanging the man for mutiny on the deck. The death sentence was due to the system—Royal Navy regulations. From the Captain's perspective, there was nothing wrong with this decision but before Sir Clowdisley made this automatic and direct decision about his crewman (so-called "system 1" thinking), he should ask himself some conscious, rational, and logical questions, such as:

- Why did the man want to stick his neck out and to risk his life? Surely, he would have had years of experience on the sea. He should understand the Royal Navy's regulations quite well.
- The ship had been sailing in foggy weather for many days. Would be it a good idea to review the navigation direction again?

If the Captain did ask these questions, he might have reached a different answer and the tragedy could have been avoided. This is so-called "system 2" thinking, if we can borrow Daniel Kahneman's vocabulary [74]. In the real world, system 1 thinking dominates our daily life. It is our gut feeling or pattern recognition. It saves time and energy. It is fine for us to use to solve certain type of issues, such as simple, linear, static, predicable, and less consequential problems. However, it is incapable of solving complex, nonlinear (exponential and percentage), dynamic, hard-to-predict problems. For many complex issues we need "system 2" thinking. This is why we have emphasized that a good leader should always focus on the abnormal rather than the normal and pay close attention to the exceptional rather than the regular.

Unfortunately, many decision makers in the IT group did not have this capability. Some decision makers cannot even differentiate between exceptional and regular issues. Even if they understand the difference, they always adopt the "system 1" way of thinking and solve the problem based on their personal perspective, interests, and intuition rather than taking the "system 2" approach of thinking, which is to focus on the long-term total cost of ownership and return on investment. They often shout the buzzwords and throw out technical jargon during the meeting, but some people hardly understand the real mechanisms between the business applications and the latest IT technologies. Many multimillion dollar investment decisions they made were short-sighted due to time pressures. One of the primary reasons was rushing to spend the capex at the end of each financial year. The decision to purchase the last patch of 16 E25K frames would be a typical example of system 1 thinking because the purchase cost might only be between $40 m–$48 m, but the cumulative ongoing support cost is well over $16 million even without regard for other cost items such as special installation, configuration, leased space, and power consumption costs.

In order to overcome system 1 thinking for system 2 problems, such as a decision about a multimillion-dollar IT investment project, the best approach to make a system 2 decision is to set up decision process and criteria, and to generate decision reference points or a list (strategic goals and objectives). In the remaining time, what you can do is to consult these reference points when time pressure exists.

The standard forward decision process is a part of the business problem solving process, which consists of seven steps (see Figure 3.13). The decision process has five steps embedded in the problem solving process [64].

This process is similar to five-phase process for E2E problem solving in Chapter 2. Of course, we can also adopt the other 19 types of problem solving strategies to solve system 2 problems (see Table 2.8).

In summary, the current situation for the IT group is that it is incapable of making a rational and correct decision for the business problem due to the different political motivations and lack of sufficient information and knowledge, as well as the incorrect decision process. The fundamental issue is the wrong people occupy the wrong positions.

The take away is that if a person's decision power is greater than his/her talent, foolish activities will follow and disaster will eventually be inevitable. If the person pretends to know more than he/she really does, tragedy will eventually arrive.

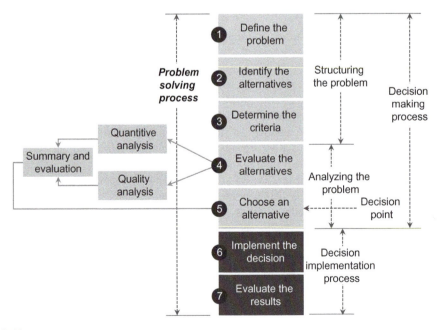

FIGURE 3.13

Seven steps of problem solving.

3.2.1.2 Cost transparency issue

From the evolution of decision models (see Figure 3.11) we can see that cost transparency has dramatically shifted the focus for many decision makers. If there is no cost transparency, the external threats and opportunities are taken away from the decision model. This leads to a release of external pressure and less urgency for many IT decision makers in many large corporations. As a result, when the IT decision makers make investment decisions, their focus will be shifted from the business needs to the indirect or internal financial measurements, which are often aligned with an industry benchmark. A benchmark is good for an indication, but is too general for a practical implementation.

As we know, the common business rule is that it does not matter how much the cost of the business is as long as the business can generate profits and maintain a high profit margin. Now, if the decision model has been shifted from a business-wide to an internal financial benchmark, some of the business has to be abandoned or scaled down. From the business perspective, IT does not make a contribution, but rather harms the business or drags it down.

From a user's perspective, the complicated approval process for allocating IT resources has triggered many IT resource consumers to overallocate the IT resources. They do not care whether the IT resources are idle or not as long as they do not pay for what they use. This not only causes a much lower IT resource utilization rate and aging IT assets, but also results in difficulties in identifying the owner of IT resources because many users totally forget how many IT resources they have allocated. After all, they consider the IT resources free or infinite.

In short, the lack of cost transparency in IT causes the following:

- The IT group may use incorrect measurements or a non-business-related benchmark for IT investment decisions.
- It adds to the complexity of IT administration. Often, the cost of administrating is more than the job itself.
- It is a root cause of internal political fights within the IT group.
- Users believe that IT resources are free. This leads to IT resource capacity overallocation, which triggers a lower IT resource utilization rate.

3.2.1.3 Application migration issue

In addition to IT resource overallocation, many applications are never decommissioned or switched off even they no longer serve a purpose for the business. Moreover, due to frequent senior leadership team changes, the IT contractors and FTEs (or the IT labor force) have a higher than normal churn rate. Many valuable IT records or pieces of information are either incorrect or incomplete.

This has created big risks for many application migrations. The higher risks of application migration have led to many IT decision makers being reluctant to make the risky decision of implementing a life-cycle program.

The cost to find the owners of many applications and make sure the existing applications can be implemented on the new IT assets may exceed the cost of the life-cycle project itself. In other words, the IT hardware life-cycle project is heavily dependent on the applications that are still running on these IT assets. Here, we have two issues:

1. Finding application owners. This is an auditing issue due to frequent re-organization and improper IT asset management and operation practice.
2. Making sure the existing applications are still compatible with new IT assets.

3.2.2 IT ASSET OPERATION PRACTICE

3.2.2.1 Horizontal brick wall effects

If all the above issues are concerned with the decision-making process that causes the problem of support costs, then the following issues that we will discuss are related to IT operational practice. Taking the E25K frame as an example, the ICT Company has at least seven either direct or indirect groups involved in E25K server (or frame) operation. Among these seven groups, there are five internal groups and two external groups of an external company that provide outsourcing services (see Figure 3.14). It makes the operational process and coordination quite complex.

However, only four groups of people are involved in daily E25K service operation. Two of them are internal groups. One has control of IT resource allocation but does not have control of

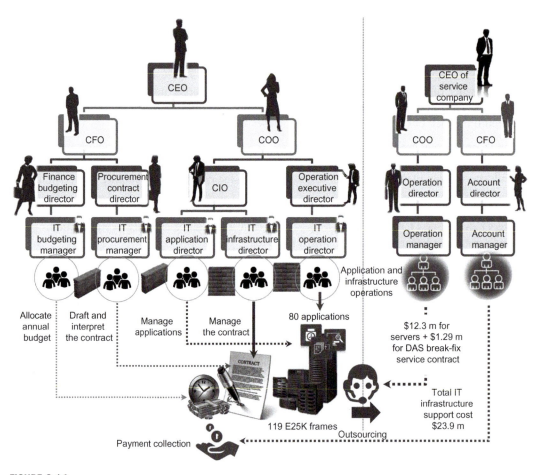

FIGURE 3.14

Organizational structure for managing 119 E25K frames.

budgeting. The other group, which is responsible for IT infrastructure, has control of IT budgeting but does not know how the resources are allocated. The other two groups belong to the external outsourcing company. One works in conjunction with the internal IT operation group and has full visibility of each E25K frame, including usage and resource allocation. The function of the other group is to collect monthly payments and manage the account. These people work closely with the IT infrastructure group.

The IT operations group was a part of the IT organization or structure under the CIO but the group has been split and integrated into the ICT operations group due to its operational nature. In other words, IT operations do not belong to IT and the CIO is not responsible for IT operations. In order to protect the group's interests, communication brick walls are very pervasive. This generates many barriers for information flow. It also creates a space for people to point fingers at each other when a problem occurs. This can be considered a horizontal operations issue.

3.2.2.2 Vertical filtering effect

From a vertical perspective, the structure of each IT group, such as infrastructure, applications, and operations, is not only complex but also changes very often; it is restructured nearly every 6 months due to IT leadership changes. Nearly every new CIO will bring his/her own people or close friends into the IT senior leadership team. There is nothing wrong with this if his/her close friends can make good decisions for the company. Unfortunately, many of them are unqualified IT professionals. They are chasing money, power, status, and promotion.

Because many unqualified managers are chasing power, status, and promotion, you will often find the reporting structure of IT operations is complicated. The common practice for many IT directors is to build own castle with more than 4 vertical reporting or management layers (see Figure 3.15).

Too many layers have led to the information filtering effect. Quite often people who are processing the most valuable information do not know the value of the information and people who want the valuable information to make the right investment decision never receive it. Most operational people have no idea what was is going on in terms of the ICT Company's strategy and where the company is heading. They do not know it and do not want to know it. They are the process robots (see Figure 3.16). The monthly COO IT asset report created by the bottom level of staff is a typical example. It is worthless because it reports everything, but has no value. The 30–40 page monthly report is full of raw data and tables, but has no valuable business analysis or problem highlights. Moreover, many potential issues have been covered up in order to protect different managers' interests. This is so-called vertical filtering effect.

Whether the information is deliberately or accidentally filtered out, the senior IT management cannot foresee when the disaster will occur. For example, the risks of 118 frames having Gold SLA and 122 having Bronze SLA would never reach the IT executives unless catastrophe occurs. The managers will only report that they have created $14 million in opex savings but they will never tell the CIO or COO that there are 166 critical applications on Bronze SLA support and 200 non-production applications on Gold SLA support. Of course, these managers themselves might not know how many critical or production applications are at risk. Just as former US Secretary of Defense Donald Rumsfeld said philosophically, there are things that we do not know that we do not know.

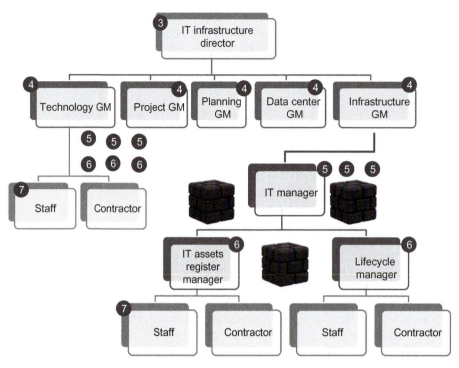

FIGURE 3.15

Organization of IT infrastructure group.

We can safely say that the most IT managers have no idea what they are really managing. They do not have to understand the mechanism of IT assets, such as the E25K, and they do not want to know because:

- First, it is not their business.
- Second, understanding the technology requires system 2 thinking. It requires a lot of brainpower.
- Third, the technology is not very useful in the corporation arena.
- Finally, the most important issue is that the corporation will not reward people who understand technology better and come up with better business solutions for tough business problems in an innovative way, but rather those who have sophisticated and savvy political skills.

Of course, we do not say that political skill is not important for problem solving, especially for some highly politicized organizations with frequent IT reorganization (constantly changing environment). However, if politics dominates all levels of the IT manager's agenda, then it will become a serious issue for the IT operation. Moreover, if it becomes a part of the company's culture, it will be very difficult to undo it. Ideally, a company should encourage and reward its staff for constantly upgrading their technical knowledge and skills and for having a more innovative way of thinking in solving business problems. This leads to two critical issues for any IT operation:

- IT operational structure
- Incentive system

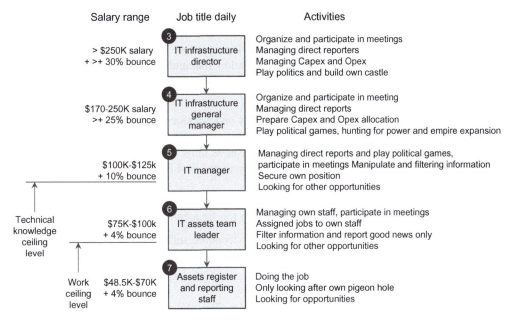

Salary range	Job title daily	Activities
> $250K salary + >+ 30% bounce	③ IT infrastructure director	Organize and participate in meetings Managing direct reporters Managing Capex and Opex Play politics and build own castle
$170-250K salary >+ 25% bounce	④ IT infrastructure general manager	Organize and participate in meeting Managing direct reports Prepare Capex and Opex allocation Play political games, hunting for power and empire expansion
$100K-$125k + 10% bounce	⑤ IT manager	Managing direct reports and play political games, participate in meetings Manipulate and filtering information Secure own position Looking for other opportunities
$75K-$100k + 4% bounce	⑥ IT assets team leader	Managing own staff, participate in meetings Assigned jobs to own staff Filter information and report good news only Looking for other opportunities
$48.5K-$70K + 4% bounce	⑦ Assets register and reporting staff	Doing the job Only looking after own pigeon hole Looking for opportunities

Technical knowledge ceiling level

Work ceiling level

FIGURE 3.16

Example organization chart for IT infrastructure service.

3.2.3 IT OPERATIONAL STRUCTURE

3.2.3.1 Too many management layers

Although we have entered the information age, surprisingly, many organizational structures for IT business units are still the same as 150 years ago, emphasizing the division of labor or the scale of production. The decision makers of the company believe that the division of labor or Taylor's processing model can bring productivity. In order to achieve operational efficiency, the company has been running an integration program for many years through a number of organizational restructurings. It is fine to eliminate organizational duplication and bureaucracy when the company is being transformed from a government corporation to a privatized enterprise. However, if it is overdone, the program quickly becomes political power wrestling and the "market for lemons" [5] effect occurs because the bigger the business unit is, the more power it has. Moreover, once many business units have been lumped together, the cost reduction becomes simply an across the board cut based on the average overhead rather than targeting some particular duplicated functions. This has led to people needing savvy political skills to survive. It is "cutting a business corner rather than cutting the cost." Finally, in order to maintain control of a bigger group, many executives or directors of large business units are running either dictatorships or military-style operations (think of the saying "my way or the highway"). As a result, the innovative thinking and different opinions of many employees has been suppressed. The culture of the company is to keep your opinion to yourself.

The main issue at the heart of the IT operational structure is the ICT Company uses an old organization structure to operate a new business. Scaling of production can only provide a marginal efficiency increase. The main driver for the company in increasing productivity has to be to rely on new ideas and smart ways of doing business.

Having seven or more management or reporting layers for an IT organizational structure only creates more room for political games and information manipulation and filtering. It does not matter how many restructures that the IT unit has had, if the seven reporting layers remains the same, the problems will stay because:

- The information is only partially flowing vertically and not shared horizontally.
- The information flow is too slow.
- There are many brick walls among different IT business units.
- The management team will divert too much energy to political fights and empire building rather than business problem solving.
- The IT staff's royalty is at an all time low.
- The management team will inevitably be changing too frequently.

Without enough accurate information provided by frontline staff, none of the senior directors is capable of making the right decision even if some of them were willing to get something done.

3.2.3.2 Too many IT organization changes

From 2005 to 2011, the IT group had seven new CIOs. The senior leadership team of the IT unit had been restructured again and again. Every new CIO would bring his friends and close allies into his/her management team. IT leadership team changes have become a half-year event. This led to many decision makers not being willing to or incapable of making long-term decisions, such as those that concern the life cycle of the RISC server. "Status quo" or "doing nothing" was the most safe, intuitive, and automatic choice for any incoming executive. As a result, 90% of 6,000 (or 5,400) RISC servers are waiting for replacement (7 or more years old).

Every time the reorganization occurs, many managers will be deeply involved in internal political fights to defend their empire or castle. Ordinary staff are fighting for their job or surviving. The situation is eat or be eaten. Overall, everyone will be in limbo for as long as 6 or 12 months. During the reorganization period, people are focusing on internal fights, political games, surviving, and job security rather than real work. The first priority of many managers is to grab a bigger piece of budget and more staff rather than making a good decision for the business because the bigger the operation unit is (or the more people you manage), the much safer you will be in the ever-changing environment. This has bought about another major problem, a misguided incentive system.

3.2.4 MISGUIDED INCENTIVE SYSTEM

The simple explanation for a misguided incentive system is that the company wants result "A" but rewards for "B." The desired goal and incentive system is completely mismatched. Based on basic economics theory, people will response to incentives. Different incentive systems will create different behaviors. The mismatch problem has three different perspectives:

- Wrong reason for promotion
- Short-term IT contractor labor managing permanent full-time employees
- Salary bottlenecks

3.2.4.1 Wrong reason for promotion

Promotion is the biggest incentive within the ICT Company. It not only means you gain the corner office but also a large salary increase, authority, status, and above all the power of decision making.

By standard HR performance theory, a promotion should be based on individual performance or contribution to the company rather than the number of staff that are under control. Unfortunately, this is often not a case for many companies. The common criterion for many promotions is to see how many employees someone manages. It leads to many managers maintaining a warlord mentality and acting as the king of an animal kingdom, with every manager trying to expand his empire or territory. You will rarely hear that a middle manager put his/her hand up and said that he/she had surplus employees due to the team's productivity increase due to innovative thinking and process improvement unless there is budget pressure. In other words, many managers do not have real motivation to actively improve his/her team's productivity in many large organizations. This absolutely contradicts the principle of cost efficiency.

3.2.4.2 IT contractors managing permanent employees

It is common practice for many large organizations to implement IT outsourcing strategies. By HR theory, the original goal of IT outsourcing was to rationalize the internal IT workforce. Unfortunately, many IT managers have abused IT outsourcing strategy or policy for their personal advantage or for managing internal politics. It has backfired for the IT group. Moreover, the IT outsourcing strategy has become the penicillin of any IT problem. To some degree, it has become an ideology or religion for many IT decision makers when they encounter any IT issue.

Due to this ideological mentality, the number of full-time employees was less than 45% of the total labor force. This means that over 55% of the IT workforce is either IT contractors or under a statement of work (SoW), which outlines a fixed amount of work within a fixed time period for a particular project. Normally, it is the capital type of work. IT contractors are normally paid over 100% more than full-time employees but there is no performance appraisal. Some IT contractors or SoW contractors have been working for the IT group for as long as 10 years and many of them are acting as managers and managing not only many IT contractors but also full-time employees. One of the main reasons for IT managers to use contractors to control internal full-time employees is to eliminate potential competitors. Generally, SoW and IT contract laborers will be much easier to manage and control than full-time employees because they are a money-oriented workforce.

Furthermore, some particular IT contractors have been promoted to a management position and hold the management and authority power to ask other contractors to divert their HR agent to the HR company owned by them. In other words, these contractors who have management power can leverage their management authority to generate extra cash for themselves.

The full-time employees' loyalty has hit an all-time low because full-time employees have to do more but be paid less while many IT contractors or SoW contractors do less but are paid more. Many full-time employees' performance appraisals were done by IT contractors. This was one of the typical examples that demonstrated the company's incentive and workforce management system was wrong. This is why nearly 99% of contractors would like to stay in the contract system. In 2011, the company tried to convert all IT contractors to full-time staff. Unfortunately, most contractors decided to leave the company rather than stay with the company and become full-time employees.

In contrast to the high payment for contractors, full-time employee fact the salary bottleneck effect. Let's have a look at the details of the bottleneck issue.

3.2.4.3 Salary bottleneck

Normally, the company's HR policy allows an average 3—4% salary increase every year in order to beat the inflation rate. This increase is often guaranteed for everyone if you are not a potential challenger to a management position or doing stupid things. This is a quite common practice for many large corporations or government agencies, especially when a union is involved. However, there is a catch. If a full-time employee stays in the same job for more than 10 years, the person's salary will hit a celling or a bottleneck. In other words, whether the person likes it not, he/she has to accept a salary deduction in comparison with the inflation rate once the salary hits the ceiling. The salary increase will have nothing to do with your performance (see Table 3.9 and Figure 3.16).

This means that everyone has to find alternatives for either moving up or out in 10 years' time. If you were quite successful during the early years of your career, say you were working hard and getting an 8% pay raise in year 4 or 5, you might fall victim to your own success because you will have less time to prepare to be a manager.

On the other hand, the organizational structure is like a pyramid. The higher up the corporate ladder, the fewer positions their are. The fact is that there are not many management positions. Furthermore, the incentive system primarily rewards management or political skill rather than productive workers or employees. Even if good employees have an opportunity to be promoted, this does not mean that good staff will automatically become good managers. As a result, the majority of people are chasing promotion and management positions rather than delivering the good results to the customers and the company.

In summary, everyone wants a good result but at someone else's expense. The older centralized management system and incentive system doesn't work well for many large corporations. It only generates more politics in the workplace and everyone will shift their focus from their work to the politics. To some degree, the symptoms are similar to the tragedy of commons (a game theory term).

The purpose in highlighting these issues is to identify the real problem behind these surface problems or symptoms. If the incentive system is not working quite well, it will distort people's decision motivations. Subsequently, it will lead to terrible consequences and cause business disasters.

3.3 REQUIREMENTS

Based on the above information brief and problem discussion, we can probably see there are five different types of business requirements for these IT assets, which include servers, storage, and storage switchs:

- Business application requirements
- Architecture requirements
- Operational requirements
- Vendor requirements (supplier requirements)
- Stakeholder requirements

The main purpose of gathering business requirements is to establish the solution assumptions and criteria for the business problem. Let's walk through each requirement.

Table 3.9 Salary Celling Level

Year	Level 7 Salary	Annual Growth Rate 4%	Level 6 Salary	Annual Growth Rate 4%	Level 5 Salary	Annual Growth Rate 4%	Level 4 Salary	Annual Growth Rate 4%	Level 3 Salary	Annual Growth Rate 4%
1	$48,500	$1,940	$70,469	$2,819	$125,000	$5,000	$175,000	$7,000	$250,000	$10,000
2	$50,440	$2,018	$73,288	$2,932	$130,000	$5,200	$182,000	$7,280	$260,000	$10,400
3	$52,458	$2,098	$76,219	$3,049	$135,200	$5,408	$189,280	$7,571	$270,400	$10,816
4	$54,556	$2,182	$79,268	$3,171	$140,608	$5,624	$196,851	$7,874	$281,216	$11,249
5	$56,738	$2,270	$82,439	$3,298	$146,232	$5,849	$204,725	$8,189	$292,465	$11,699
6	$59,008	$2,360	$85,736	$3,429	$152,082	$6,083	$212,914	$8,517	$304,163	$12,167
7	$61,368	$2,455	$89,166	$3,567	$158,165	$6,327	$221,431	$8,857	$316,330	$12,653
8	$63,823	$2,553	$92,732	$3,709	$164,491	$6,580	$230,288	$9,212	$328,983	$13,159
9	$66,376	$2,655	$96,442	$3,858	$171,071	$6,843	$239,500	$9,580	$342,142	$13,686
10	$69,031	$2,761	$100,299	$4,012	$177,914	$7,117	$249,080	$9,963	$355,828	$14,233

3.3.1 BUSINESS APPLICATION REQUIREMENTS

In order to target the main issue and achieve a quick win, we begin by solving the E25K server problem first, where the aim is to reduce the high cost of the $25 m + $2.6 m maintenance and support contract and $8 m leasing fee. By doing so, we not only slash more than 70% of the total contract cost but also obtain experience from the E25K life-cycle project to solve other RISC server life-cycle problems.

There are over 160 applications running on the E25K frames. The business application requirements actually identify all requirements for each application. It is impossible for us to list all requirements in this book for 160 applications, but we can list one of the primary application requirements as an example, in this case for the Siebel Customer Relationship Management (CRM) software.

To define the Siebel CRM requirements is not an easy task. It could be a very costly journey. If the business requirement is to deploy this for thousands of end users aross different regions, it would require many IT professionals and business analysts because Siebel CRM is a complex system (see Figure 3.17). Of course, the purpose of this exercise is not to deploy the new Siebel application but rather to find an alternative server platform that can replace E25K frames and move Seibel from E25K frames to a new hardware platform in a cost-effective manner.

We can probably visit the Siebel CRM URL and find the latest information regarding the system requirements and supported platform documents [75] and then obtain the existing components and parameters that have been installed on E25K frames. Based on the above figure, we can identify the minimum requirements for each server and database and file system (see Tables 3.10 and 3.11).

The minimum requirements are just a starting point. The real hardware requirements are dependent on many other factors:

- Hardware vendor (HP, IBM, Cisco, Oracle, or Dell)
- Operating system type (Windows, AIX, HP-UX, or Solaris)
- Database vendor (DB2, Oracle 10g, 11g, or MS SQL)
- Expected volume of data and indexes
- Network bandwidth
- Maximum number of concurrent user sessions
- High availability and failover requirements

Furthermore, we can identify more details of the database requirements (see Table 3.12).

Clearly, we can use the x86 platform to replace RISC servers according to Tables 3.10 and 3.12. Siebel's technical requirements (or parameters) would allow us to select a possible solution that replaced RSIC with x86 servers. Of course, there are other applications running on E25K frames, but Siebel is the critical application for the ICT Company. If we can safely switch it from E25K to x86 and move other applications to T series RSIC servers, we can probably achieve the business goal. We will discuss the details later chapters.

This is just a very small part of the application requirements involving the physical computer infrastructure. Other application requirements may include target cost, availability, scalability, security, reliability, performance and capacity for compute, storage, backup, and disaster recovery.

Siebel CRM is a very complex and enterprise-class application. It often involves various hardware (such as compute, storage, backup, and network components), different network protocols, and many third-party vendors. Moreover, hundreds and thousands of end users may require server cluster access at the same time (such as lunchtime) and the application developers may try to

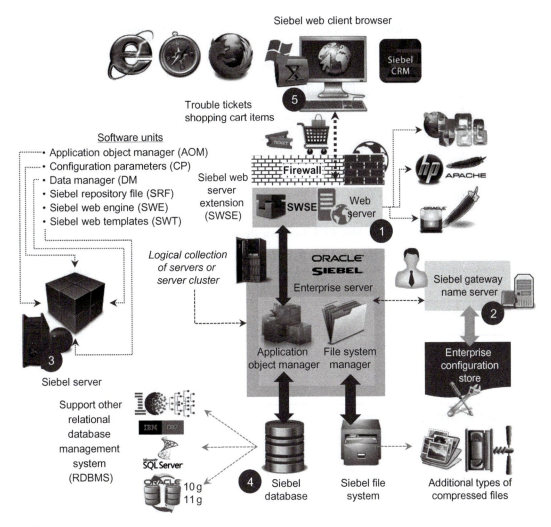

Siebel web client browser

Trouble tickets
shopping cart items

Software units
- Application object manager (AOM)
- Configuration parameters (CP)
- Data manager (DM
- Siebel repository file (SRF)
- Siebel web engine (SWE)
- Siebel web templates (SWT)

Siebel web
server
extension
(SWSE)

Firewall

SWSE   Web
server

Logical collection
of servers or
server cluster

ORACLE
SIEBEL
Enterprise server

Siebel gateway
name server

Application
object manager   File system
manager

Enterprise
configuration
store

Siebel server

Support other
relational
database
management
system
(RDBMS)

IBM DB2

Microsoft
SQL Server

ORACLE 10g
11g

Siebel
database

Siebel file
system

Additional types of
compressed files

FIGURE 3.17

Siebel CRM functional architecture.

modify the configuration and optimize the application at the same time in order to meet end user demands. Overall, the Siebel CRM migration from one hardware platform to another could be very complex. Therefore, it would be a good idea to analyze the following historic performance records in order to better understand the application volume, variety, and variation requirements:

- Server component event logging
- Siebel Application Response Measurement (SARM)
- Client-side logging
- Siebel usage collection

Table 3.10 Example of Siebel CRM x86 Processor Requirements and Supported Platforms for V8.1

Siebel Component	Min. x86 Processor Requirements	Min. Memory Requirements
Siebel Servers (3)	2 × P3 Xeon 500 MHz or Celeron 800 MHz	1 GB
Siebel Gateway Name Server (2)	P3 Xeon 500 MHz or Celeron 800 MHz	256 MB
Web Server (1)	P3 Xeon 500 MHz or Celeron 800 MHz	512 MB

Table 3.11 Example of Siebel CRM RISC Processor Requirements and Supported Platforms for V8.1

Siebel Component	Min. RISC Processor Requirements	Min. Memory Requirements
	Ultra SPARC-I, II, III, III HP-UX: PA-RISC 2.0, AIX Power, Power 2, 3, 4 , 4 + , Power PC	
Siebel Servers (3)	2 × 800 MHz	2 GB
Siebel Gateway Name Server (2)	800 MHz	2 GB
Web Server (1)	800 MHz	2 GB

Table 3.12 Database Requirements Details

Parameter	Name/Value	Description
Database vendor	Microsoft SQL	
Database version	SQL Server 2012	
Operating System	MS Windows Server	
Platform	IA-64	X86-64 processor
Database server account	SYSDBA	Directly connect to the DB to run the SQL script
Database host name	Dbsrvr0	
Database admin User	Admin	
Database server ID	MSSQLSRV12	
Database server port	1434	
Siebel DB index table space	SIEBELDB_IDX	This table space will hold the indexes of the Siebel CRM schema.
Siebel DB data table space	SIEBELDB_DATA	This table space will hold the data tables of the Siebel CRM Schema.

3.3.2 ARCHITECTURE REQUIREMENTS

In this context, architecture requirements means the ICT Company has set up its strategic goal to move all possible applications from RISC servers to the x86 platform. It called a "go x86" strategy. There are a few reasons that the ICT Company adopted the "go x86" strategy.

1. First, the price of an x86 server is significantly cheaper than a RISC server because the x86 server has been commoditized. Although the price of a RISC server, especially SPARC, has been declining dramatically since the 1990s, it is still quite expensive in comparison with x86 servers.
2. Intel has always encouraged the company to adopt x86 technology. Some trial initiatives for RISC migration were funded by Intel.
3. Since 2004, the ICT Company has spent over $50 million capex and tried to virtualize the x86 server platform. There have been at least five different internal LoB units that had implemented five different projects in order to virtualized x86 servers, but the results for most of projects could be considered failures, including one project named Virtual Server Farm (VSF), which was implemented by the IT group itself. In late 2011, the x86 project that was initiated by the IT unit has started to deliver only nonproduction applications on the virtualized x86 server clusters from five different data centers (see Table 3.13).
4. Of course, this very limited result ("very limited" means the server farm cannot run critical applications because it does not have disaster recovery) was built on the lesson of the Virtual

Table 3.13 Virtualized x86 Server Project Delivery Result

	CW-DC	C-DC[1]	E-DC	SL-DC	U-DC	Total x86 Capacity
No. of racks	4	20	8	20	8	60
No. of clusters	2	10	4	12	4	32
Physical server	20	94	36	96	32	278
HP server types[2] (Number of Physical Servers in different models)	DL585G5 (20)	DL585G5 (48)	DL585G5 (20)	DL585G5 (68)	DL585G5 (16)	172(4 socket Q-core)
		DL385G7 (34)	DL385G7 (16)	DL385G7 (28)	DL385G7 (16)	94(2 socket 12 core)
		DL585G7 (12)				12(4 socket 12 core)
AMD core no.	320	2160	704	1760	640	5,584
Specified vCPU no.	800	4,728	1568	3,584	960	11,640
No of VM[3]	618	1966	530	1520	368	5,002

[1]In C-Data Center, cluster 19 is dedicated to the Stress Volume Test (SVT).
[2]DL585G5 = AMD Opteron 8378, 2.4 GHz quad core. DL385G7 = AMD® Opteron®, 6174/2p, 2.66 GHz, DL585G7 = AMD® Opteron® 6100 Series processors 6174/se, 2.66 GHz.
[3]The monthly report at the end of June 2011 provided this information (there were only 2,470 VMs in April 11).

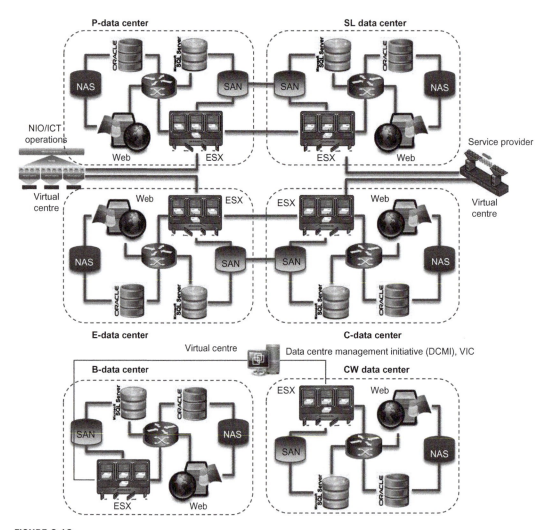

FIGURE 3.18

Virtual Server Farm (VSF) project.

Server Farm (VSF) project that started back in January 2005 (see Figure 3.18). Phase 1 of the project was to build the virtualizing x86 server farm in the C data center and phase 2 was to expand to the E, CW, B, P, and SL data centers between July 2005 and January 2006. Phase 3 was to establish disaster recovery in the C, CW, SL, and B data centers as well as migration from VMware ESX 2.X to ESX 3.

5. Based on the Requirement Definition Document (RDD), the project was trying to target 600 nonproduction hosts. According to the project plan, there were four nonproduction data centers (P, SL, E, and C). Furthermore, there were two test and development data centers (B and CW).

Each data center had five Dell Power Edge 6650 physical servers or nodes. Each node had four Xeon MP 2.7 MHz processors. Unfortunately, the project did not deliver anything and it was completely abandoned in 2007 and replaced by another virtualized x86 project. Surprisingly, the key people involved (virtualization project director and IT technology general manager) could get away with having responsibility for a multimillion dollar investment failure. It led to the RISC virtualization project failure later. In essence, the IT group had two trials to virtualize x86 servers and had limited success.

6. While the IT group implemented the virtualized project for x86 platforms, it also spent almost $20 million dollars and over 18 months to virtualize the RISC server platform. Unfortunately, the project was going nowhere. It was a disaster. We will spell out the main reason why the project failed.

For these reasons, the IT group has adopted the policy of "go x86," which is about trying to move as many RISC servers as possible onto a x86 virtualized hardware platform.

3.3.3 OPERATIONAL REQUIREMENTS

Operational requirements consist of two types of requirements: shared infrastructure and hardware support requirements for the infrastructure in the operational phase. If the application is an independent application running on a standalone IT infrastructure, there will be no sharing requirements. Today, it is hard to find any new application that would independently run on standalone IT infrastructure. Actually, one of the key ideas behind the cloud is infrastructure sharing so that IT can increase the IT infrastructure's utilization and efficiency.

3.3.3.1 Shared infrastructure requirements (constraints)

There are a number of shared infrastructure requirements that should be considered. The common shared IT infrastructure would be network, storage, platform, security, logging, billing, backup system, and data center facility for many large organizations. These shared infrastructure requirements will set up the baseline of constraints for future solution options.

3.3.3.2 System integration or transition requirements

When the solution is deployed, it may require the system to be integrated into the existing operation environment. The typical example of an existing operation system is the condition monitoring system. Ideally, you would not like to build another independent monitoring system for a particular solution or system. If so, it would increase the operational cost.

Today, many IT vendors provide a standard protocol to monitor their IT devices or system, such as Simple Network Management Protocol (SNMP) for hardware components. It would be possible for users or customers to integrate these IT systems into the existing monitoring environment.

3.3.3.3 Service monitoring requirements

In order to provide better service, service monitoring is essential. The Siebel server infrastructure provides a logging model to monitor each event. This model monitors different types of event. By controlling the log level of each event type, we can control the amount of information stored in

Table 3.14 Siebel Event Log Level [76]	
Log Level	**Description**
0	Fatal—Only severe errors are written to the log file. Recommended for productive operation.
1	Errors—The default setting: all error messages are written to the log file. Recommended for productive operation.
2	Warnings—Messages with warning characteristics are included in the log file. Recommended to trace configuration issues.
3	Informational—Messages with informational content are included in the log file. Recommended for troubleshooting and debugging.
4	Details—The log file will include detailed information about the process. Recommended for more detailed troubleshooting and debugging.
5	Diagnostic—All message output from the process will be written to the log file. Only recommended when lower levels do not yield the desired output or when requested by Oracle's technical support team.

log files. The Siebel logging model provides six different log levels for fault diagnosis (see Table 3.14).

Siebel suggests the customer set level 4 for fault diagnosis and "0" and "1" for normal operation. We have to be aware that the size of the log file can grow very quickly and devour valuable storage resources if the log level is set too high. It may also increase the difficulty for the admin staff in retrieving valuable information.

Of course, the business owner will make the final decision. The different log levels may be set up for different events in different periods (see Table 3.15).

For example, we can set up a higher log level at the first three or six months and once the application has been stabilized, we can wind back the log level.

3.3.3.4 Service maintenance and support requirements

Service maintenance and support requirements often include support time and fault or problem notification, response, and resolution or restoration time. It is more like a SLA specification for the service. The following three tables show examples of service support requirements (see Tables 3.16−3.18).

3.3.4 VENDOR REQUIREMENTS

Vendor requirements mean the interfaces of this business application with other third-party software. For example, Siebel CRM may create Siebel Application Response Measurement (SARM) output files that have comma-separated values (CSV) or XML format. You may want to load into some common third-party software, such as Microsoft Excel or other spreadsheet tools for further analysis.

Overall, the vendor requirements are the interface requirements of the third-party applications that enable the end users to complete their business process effectively (see Table 3.19).

Table 3.15 Siebel Event Type List [76]

Event Type	Description
Component Tracing	Various informational messages about parameter values and more.
General Events	Information about event points is written to the log file. Example: a background component enters its sleep interval.
Task Configuration	All parameters for the current task will be written to the log file header.
SQL Profiling	Extended summary of SQL prepare, execute, and fetch statements.
SQL Summary	Writes the timings for SQL statement preparation as well as fetch and execute operations to the log file.
SQL Error	Traces all erroneous SQL statements.
SQL Parse and Execute	Writes all insert, update, and delete SQL statements to the log file.
Event to track the flow of a message	For tracking messages exchanged between the Siebel Web Server Extension (SWSE) and the application object manager.
Object Manager Session Operation and SetErrorMsg Log	For capturing user session information.
Event Context	Traces screen, view, and applet names for the user session.
Security Adapter Log	Writes information about the Siebel security adapter to the log file.

Table 3.16 Service Support for Different Fault Levels

Fault Level	Notification Method	Response Time	Restoration Time
Fault Severity Level 1	Within 15 minutes Telephone or email	Less than 2 hours from the time of notification	Within 8 hours from the time of notification
Fault Severity Level 2	Within 30 minutes Telephone or email	Less than 2 hours from the time of notification	Within 16 hours from the time of notification
Fault Severity Level 3	Within 45 minutes Telephone or email	Less than 4 hours from the time of notification	Within 48 hours from the time of notification
Fault Severity Level 4	Within 60 minutes Telephone or email	Less than 4 hours from the time of notification	Within 72 hours from the time of notification

Table 3.17 Service Support Requirements

Support Hours	Additional Information
24 hours a day, 7 days a week	Includes public holidays and time is the local time at the place of the fault

Table 3.18 Fault Severity Level Definition for Operation Requirements

Fault Severity Level 1	Fault Severity Level 2	Fault Severity Level 3	Fault Severity Level 4
Severe Problem: Major functionality faulty.	Issue has or will affect customer productivity.	The fault can be worked around but problem must be fixed.	No customer impact fault.
All end users or 90% of end users cannot perform normal job functions.	System degradation and impact on the level of service, workaround solution required.	System starts to degrade but the application performance is within the acceptable level.	The system provides misleading information. Although it doesn't impact on the application, it may impact on productivity.
Faults have impacted on customers' business.	System cannot serve the end customer within the specified time.		
Examples: Major system failure, or unavailable to end user.	*Examples:* Failure of a redundant component that impacts customer performance.	*Examples:* Failure in a software component that is noncritical.	*Examples:* Monitoring system created false alarm.
System down.	Repeated failures.	Failure of a redundant component that does not impact customer performance.	Weekly storage backup system is not working quite well.
Data loss.	Problem will create intolerable delays if not addressed.		
Data unavailable.			
Workaround unavailable.			

Table 3.19 Third-Party Software or Vendor Requirements

Software from Third-Party Vendors	Scenario Description
Microsoft Office or other office applications, such as Google Apps or Open Office	For working with Word documents generated by the Siebel Document Server or attached to Siebel records.
Adobe Reader for PDF file	Either attach PDF file to Siebel CRM or read one that is created by Siebel BI publisher.
Microsoft Excel or other third-party spreadsheet tools	To work with Siebel's SARM CSV files.
Microsoft Outlook or other email applications	To synchronize calendar and contact data between Siebel CRM and MS outlook.
Adobe Flash Player (ActiveX)	If Oracle Business Intelligence Enterprise Edition (Oracle BI EE) is deployed. The default chart format of the integrated chart engine in Oracle BIEE is flash (swf).

3.3.5 OTHER STAKEHOLDER REQUIREMENTS

Referring to Table 2.3, we have addressed five key stakeholder requirements. Others stakeholder requirements are closely associated with solution deployment, such as implementing SME, testing, and project management. It should be a part of project management. They are beyond the scope of this book. In the rest of the book, we will focus on solution definition.

3.3.6 IDENTIFY HIDDEN REQUIREMENTS

When we identify requirements from each stakeholder, we should always be aware that each requirement has a motivation. Behind each motivation, there are always different incentives to support every motivation. In many circumstances, the stakeholder's requirement might not explicitly be spelled out. This may be either deliberate or unconscious. If you are confused with or can not understand the logic of a stakeholder's requirements, you should always ask yourself what incentive might lie behind it. Normally, you will find that 90% of people are driven by external incentives and 10% of people are driven by internal incentives.

For example, the unstated motivation and incentive for the IT asset support company is to maintain the service revenue and profit margin. The primary interest for the company is either to increase the support cost or to maintain the existing service charge. This is exactly opposed against the IT group's business objective.

Moreover, the internal IT asset manager who is controlling the opex budget is not willing to give up the opex budget. In other words, he does not want to reduce the IT operations costs because the bigger the budget is, the more resources the group will need, and his/her position will become much secure. This may sound ridiculous from a business perspective but it is the reality for many large corporations.

In conclusion, a BA should always be aware of these unstated or hidden requirements or interests and manage them properly. These hidden requirements will never be spelled out but a BA should understand that each stakeholder has his/her own motivations or interests. Understanding these hidden motivations or agendas can help us to solve the real business problem effectively.

3.4 SOLUTION

Assume we have confirmed all the business problems that we have identified above. The next step is generating a solution to resolve these problems. As we can see there are two aspects for the problem to deal with in the solution. One is from the organizational or human perspective and the other is from the technical perspective.

3.4.1 ORGANIZATIONAL PERSPECTIVE

We should understand that the root cause of many IT project failures for many large ICT companies or IT groups is often due to the dilemma of information transparency and power of authority at each management level. This means that each management level in many large

Table 3.20 Fundamental Differences between Industrial and Knowledge Ages

	Industrial Age	Knowledge Age
Human	Human as resource or object	Human as capital or subject
View of Job	Task-based work	Project-based and problem solving work
Performance	Average and benchmark	Real-world scenarios and case by case
Mentality	Competitive and zero-sum game	Collaboration and win-win solutions
Working practices	Rule- and procedure-based activities	Discovery- and innovation-based activities
Management function	Supervised and directed tasks	Unsupervised, service provider role
Management mentality	Rigidly controlled	Open, flexible and on-demand
Working environment	Static environment	Dynamic and interactive environment
Way of finding a solution	Pigeonhole focus and drill down	Critical thinking and creative inquiry
Use of capex	Buy	Lease
Employer's function	Employer as dictator	Employer as platform
Information transparency	Roadblocks	Fully transparent

organizations likes to set up information road blocks in order to achieve power of authority or control. If you have been working in any large organization, one of the common working protocols is that you should never try to send your information beyond your manager unless ether you are approved to do so by your manager or are not preparing to continuously stay in the same company or group. By the logic of a traditional organizational structure, this is reasonable. If you jump over your manager and directly report or send your information to a manager one level up, then your manager will eventually become redundant. It may lead to your manager losing his/her job or role. You can imagine the response of any person who feels his/her job is under threat.

However, the ultimate goal of the cost modeling exercise is trying to create cost transparency. The bottom line of cost transparency is actually information transparency. Now, you can see the dilemma, as any ICT company would like to make information as transparent as possible in order to rationalize its IT cost, but any management hierarchy would like set up information roadblocks in order to maintain power and control.

It is OK when we were living in the industrial age because the working environment was moving very slow. The management hierarchical structure is similar to early generation neural networks. It will eventually give the final desired output but it is a very slow learner and not very efficient.

However, we have been now moving from the industrial age to the information age and from the information age to the knowledge age. The fundamental differences between the industrial and knowledge ages are in Table 3.20.

Since our working environment has changed, the organizational hierarchy must be changed. The question is how to change and in what direction. Perhaps, Joshua Cooper Ramo's book [77] may give us a clue. He argued that the old and centralized organization structure will not work well because it is a slow, selfish, unethical, highly political, static, and broken environment. Ramo provided the solution, which he called "The management secrets of Hizb'allah." "It was in creating a system that allowed them to shift and learn and change—and that did all of those things even better when they were under attack." Hizb'allah proved their point when they leveraged fewer than 500 guerrillas fighters to frustrate a 30,000 man Israeli assault in 2006. Ramo argued that a better or winning organization must be a creative, innovative system that allows its staff to learn and change. Of course, there is one critical factor, which is dedication.

The critical successful factor for IT management is how to motivate others, not how to control or dictate others, because as a manager, if you would like to complete a small task, it is dependent on your command or order; if you would like to complete a big job, it is dependent on your brain; and if you would like to finish a large project or a program, it is dependent on other people's brains.

As we have indicated at the beginning of this chapter, if we boil it down to very basic issues, the primary reason for the IT group suffering multiple failures was the IT leadership. The ICT services must find the right IT leader. He/she must be the universal genius. He/she should have the following characteristics:

- Foresee others who cannot foresee
- Endure others who cannot endure
- Tolerate others who cannot tolerate
- Forgive others who cannot forgive
- Understand others who cannot understand
- Accept others who cannot accept

If the organization cannot adjust itself to meet new challenges, it doesn't matter how big and how powerful the organization is now, it will eventually be like Kodak, Nokia, Motorola, Enron, and Lehman Brothers.

Life-cycle issues or constantly rationalizing maintenance and support costs is an ongoing operational issue, not a once-off one. Therefore, unless the issue of IT organization can be solved properly, the high maintenance costs would come back again even if we solve the current problem for IT assets.

In this book, we will not give too many details about how to build the IT organization structure, how to select the right leadership team, and how to manage IT group. These issues are beyond the topic of this book. What we will concentrate on are the details of IT asset management or cloud infrastructure and associated technical issues. These are the essential material for IT decision makers to make the right decision.

3.4.2 TECHNICAL PERSPECTIVE

In order to reduce the maintenance cost for IT hardware assets, many IT people or consultants proposed different solutions, such as outsourcing, leasing, and insourcing but none of the solutions hits the nail and is quite compelling. Most of the solutions can be categorized as "No pain, no gain" or

Table 3.21 E25K Decommissioning Cost Savings Estimate

Cost Items/Year	Year 0	Year 1	Year 2	Year 3	Year 4	Total
Floor Space ($000)	0	14	907	2040	2040	5460
Power Usage ($000)	0	2043	4088	10800	10800	20288
Maintain ($) E25K vs. T4-4 ($000)tai	10000	470	17820	36140	36140	100570
Carbon Tax ($ 000)	0	164	1000	1960	1960	5480
Total Savings ($000)	10000	2988	24670	50940	50940	139,538

Table 3.22 Oracle/Sun T4-4 SPARC Server Procurement and Migration Cost Estimate

Capex Items/Year	Year 0	Year 1	Year 2	Year 3	Year 4	Total
Total Purchase Cost ($000)	14,750	15,750	22,450	0	0	$52,950
Build & Provisioning Cost ($000)	7,944	8,566	12,118	0	0	$28,628
Internal Resource Cost ($000)	7,406	7,406	7,406	0	0	$22,218
Total Investment Costs ($000)	30,100	31,722	41,974	0	0	$103,796
Net Cost Savings ($000)	–$20,100	–28734	–$17,304	$50,940	$50,940	$35,742

Note: Net Cost Saving = Total Saving – Total Investment Cost.

part of the "It will get worse before it gets better" fallacy. One of typical examples is the solution proposed a global leading consultant firm. It intended to solve the problem via few steps or phases. We will analyze the consultant firm's solution and see what was wrong with it as a starting point and then propose a comprehensive cloud solution that will be described in the rest of this book.

First the consultant firm claimed its proposal or solution could bring five benefits to the ICT Company:

1. Significant reduction in operational cost
2. Provision of a service-oriented platform to a large proportion of ICT's IT processing fleet, which means less time to market for deployment of business functions
3. Further development of ICT's virtualization capability in order to support IT's vision to be the best IT operation in the Asia Pacific (APAC) region
4. Support for ICT business principles by provision of an IT recovery capability to the disaster recovery program
5. Support for ICT's data center strategy with the end result of exiting from the U data center (Leased), further reducing the operational cost of IT to the business

Tables 3.21 and 3.22 support the consultant company's claims that its solution could save nearly $35.7 million (net savings) and the saving would begin from year 3 to 4.

3.4.2.1 Problem statement

Based on their understanding of the problem, the problem statement was described in the following five points from a maintenance and support perspective:

1. Cost to maintain: To maintain 240 E25K would cost $24−$36 m in the 2014 financial year. (Actually the maintenance and support cost was $25 million for 118 frames for Gold SLA support and 122 frames for Bronze SLA support in the 2012/2013 financial year.)
2. Limited capacity for growth: No current platform allows for growth.
3. High power usage: The T4 solution uses 71% less power than E25K frames.
4. Age of E25K fleet: The average E25K frame is 4−6 years old and 29% of IT servers fleet are more than 7 years old.
5. Floor space: The T4 solution uses 92% less space than E25K frames.

In summary, the ICT pays a significantly high maintenance and support cost for E25K servers. The data center floor space utilization rate is low and not efficient. The E25K frame cannot support business critical applications because the frames do not have disaster recovery (DR) capacity.

We have to point out the problem statement was not very accurate because the E25K server utilization rate is very low. So, the E25K server fleet still has enough capacity for market growth. Moreover, all these problem statements did not address the primary concern of the IT strategy, which is "go-x86."

3.4.2.2 ICT's IT strategy or business requirements

In order to be competitive in the market, the IT group has established the following IT strategic criteria for future IT hardware deployment:

- Target server platform is X86
- Desired operating system is an open source operating system such as Linux's Ubuntu, Red Hat, Debian, SUSE, or Fedora
- Purchased IT hardware should be competitive or commodity price

3.4.2.3 Assumptions

However, the consultant company estimated that the current virtualized x86 server farm fleet by itself did not have enough capacity. (Of course, the consultant firm was not sure. The assumption had not been confirmed.) Another assumption that should be confirmed is that the IT group would like to switch the x86 server vendor from HP to Cisco, to adopt Cisco UCS and a unified network and security architecture (expected to be available in 6−12 months).

Furthermore, they reviewed the existing RISC technology that is supported by Oracle/Sun, especially the SPARC T4-4 server. In comparison with the E25K frame, they concluded that the T4-4 would be one option or temporary solution to replace E25K frames to save on maintenance and support costs (see Table 3.23).

3.4.2.4 Proposed interim solution

According to the problem statement, IT strategy, business requirements, and IT infrastructure assumptions, the consultant firm suggested a transitional solution to resolve the problem of high maintenance and support costs for E25K frames.

Table 3.23 Technology Comparison between E25K and T4-4			
Feature	1 × E25K Frame	3 × T4-4	Performance
Processing Power (CPU)	144 core	96 cores	290% up
Memory (Max)	1152 Gb	3072 Gb	266% up
I/O M Value Report	TBC	TBC	
Power Consumption	22.5 kW	3.6 kW	84% down
Purchase Cost	$2.2 m	$0.3 m	
Maintenance Cost	$0.15 m	$0.027 m	
Space Requirements (Volume Includes Boot Disk)	8.4 m^2	0.5 m^2	83.3% down

In conclusion, the proposed solution is very simple, replacing one E25K frame with three SPARC T4-4 series servers over a five-year period. They called it a like-for-like refresh program (see Figure 3.19).

The pros of this solution are:

- Almost no risk for the migration of business applications
- Avoiding significant migration costs in isolation
- Saving maintenance and support cost after the third year of the program
- Increasing overall compute performance
- Reducing power consumption and leasing space

3.4.2.5 Issues with the proposed solution

However, they did not spell out the cons of the proposed solution:

- The solution does not meet the IT strategic requirements (target server platform x86).
- The OS is not open source software.
- The T4-4 server is not commodity hardware.
- It did not take into account NPV.
- The cost saving would start in the third year. In other words, the IT group may be trapped in the "it'll get worse before it gets better" fallacy because the ICT Company has to keep both hardware platforms for three years.
- The operational cost of the T4-4 has not been taken into account.
- Increasing processing power by 296% does not mean you can fully utilize the processor's capacity. It is dependent on the network I/O bandwidth. If the I/O bandwidth is limited, the powerful processor will be meaningless or wasted. In the assumption table, the I/O value is "To Be Confirmed" (TBC). It indicates that the choice of T4-4 does not make any sense. Actually, the utilization rate of many servers is below 15%.
- The real E25K replacement model is the M9 series server. Some risks may still exist, as some of 160 applications cannot run on the T4-4 SPARC server.
- If the proposed solution is a transitional one, the consultant failed to address how to reach the final solution. After five years, the T4-4 SPARC servers will become targeted hardware to be recycled.

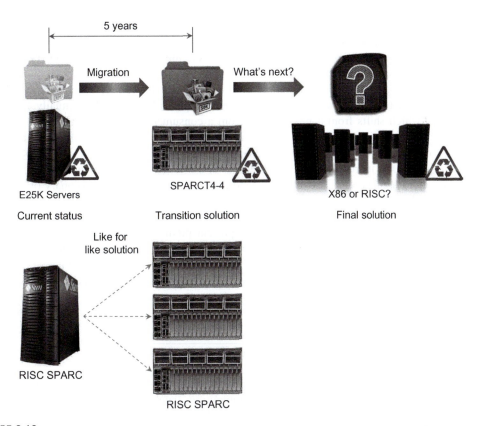

FIGURE 3.19

Proposed solution to replace E25K.

Overall, the proposal provided by this international consulting firm is an immature solution because it cannot meet any ICT's major business requirements. It only focused on the tactical issues, such as power consumption, carbon footprint, and leased space. It failed to address many strategic concerns that the ICT Company would like to solve, such as targeting the x86 platform, open source software, and commodity hardware.

Clearly, this proposed solution is not the right solution for the IT group. The risk is too high to spend almost $104 million capex in first three years and deliver the bulk (or 73%) of cost savings in the last two years. What if the solution cannot deliver the bulk of the savings? The solution did not spell out the risks. Moreover, the solution cannot achieve any of the IT strategic goals that the ICT Company has specified. It fails to solve the fundamental issue beyond the transitional solution. The IT group may have to continuously spend both capex and opex just to refresh its aging hardware compute platform. It would lead to a downward spiral of spending both capex and opex.

We believe the problem of the high cost of maintenance and support cannot be solved by a single solution, such as refreshing server hardware. It has to be resolved by multiple solutions from at least two different perspectives that we have described above. If we insist on using a single technical solution or tool to tackle the problem, then we may fall into the fallacy described by Mark Twain as follows: "If you only tool is hammer, you tend to see every problem as a nail."

So, what is the right solution? The simple answer is cloud computing, which will consist of multiple solutions across different disciplines. These multiple solutions will eventually lead to a paradigm shift, which shifts from capex to opex from a consumer's perspective and from opex to capex from an IT asset owner's perspective. This is the real meaning of the cloud business model.

In order to provide a correct and comprehensive solution for a high support cost problem like E25K, we have to build it from the ground up and establish a cloud cost framework from the data center facility up to applications. This is not a Band-Aid solution, but rather a visionary or strategic solution for the IT group.

What is the visionary or strategic solution? It is when a strategic decision maker can stand in the future looking at the present (not stand in the present predicting the future). A good decision maker can find the best path within numerous possible routes to reach the desired and strategic goal. How do you stand in the future? You need many assumptions, a mental framework, logical reasoning, risk analysis, and future probability estimation. This is the core content that this book will unveil in subsequent chapters.

3.5 SUMMARY

Cloud computing has now become a pervasive phenomenon that occurs in nearly every sizable organization. In contrast to other kinds of computing, such as grid, parallel, and high-performance computing, the cloud has been developed neither to chase the speed of computing nor to search for academic or theoretic results. It exists to solve real business problems. From the last chapter to this chapter, we try to use BA theory for a practical purpose, which is to address business needs.

In the beginning of this chapter, we first raised a $48 million question, which is how to save or reduce the $48 million dollar service contract that maintains and supports the aging IT infrastructure or assets for one of the leading ICT companies. Then we quickly provided the cost details associated with each IT asset category, namely servers (x86 and RISC), storage (NAS, SAN, DAS, and tape libraries), and storage switches.

When we analyzed the server cost of maintenance and support, we especially focused on a particular server asset, the E25K or RISC server platform. In order to understand the business problem, we described all the details and issues associated with the 240 E25K frames:

- Leasing space
- Power consumption
- Aging frames
- SLA and higher supporting costs
- Contract management
- Application issues
- People issues

The purpose of focusing on the E25K frame is that, if we can solve the E25K problem, we can solve at least half of the problem because the support cost for the E25K is more than $25 m per annum. If we include leasing space, power, and DAS storage equipment, the total cost can quickly be piled up to over $40 million per annum.

After we defined the major problems, we moved on to the definition of business requirements. According to BA process theory, we spelled out the business requirements from five different perspectives, namely applications, architecture (IT strategy), operation, vendors, and other stakeholders.

At last, we presented a Band-Aid solution presented by one leading international consulting firm to the ICT Company. Although they might understand the ICT's long-term IT strategy quite well, they still thought that a single technical solution would solve the real business problem.

We believe that their Band-Aid (platform refresh) solution may mitigate some surface problems but it would never solve the real problem. For the long term, this is a waste of money and time. In order to solve the problem for the long run, we believe that the company should adopt the approach of a systematic cycle for IT assets (see Figure 3.20).

If we follow the systematic cycle of IT asset approach, it would be quite easier to understand why we should reject the "platform refresh" or Band-Aid solution and embrace cloud computing.

In the rest of this book, we will address all issues regarding all IT assets from the bottom of the data center facility (or below the floor) up to all business applications. We will adopt the cloud business

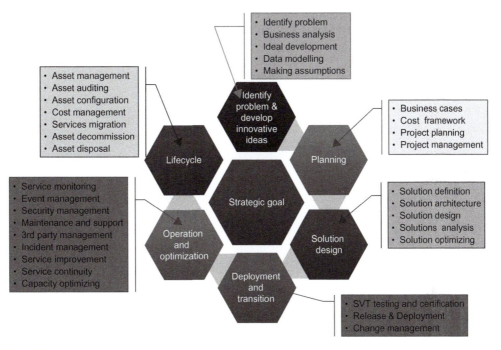

FIGURE 3.20

The cycle of IT infrastructure.

model to solve this problem. If you are an IT asset owner, the cloud business model can eliminate your opex. If you are IT asset consumers, the cloud business model will eliminate your up-front capex.

Theoretically speaking, a good cloud business model with fully virtualized infrastructure can remove the IT maintenance and support cost all together by leveraging high-availability (HA) and fault-tolerant (FT) tools and virtualized infrastructure. As noted in Chapter 1, this is the significant advantage of cloud computing for solving business problems, which we highlighted in this chapter to save nearly $24m in maintenance and support costs.

3.6 REVIEW QUESTIONS

1. Based on the above case briefing, what do you think the real problem behind the high maintenance and support cost for this ICT Company is?
2. If you were the business analyst, can you think of other methods or approaches to identify the real problem for this case?
3. If you were the decision maker, how do you resolve the people issues for this case?
4. What is your opinion of the above solution provided by the consulting firm?
5. If you were the decision maker, how do you work with the consulting firm to come up with a better solution?
6. Is cloud computing the right solution for the above case? If so, why is it? If not, why is it not?
7. If you were given the above business analysis task, what is the first step you would take?

DATA CENTER FACILITIES AND COST

There are many people who believe that cloud usage can be free. Louis Rosas-Guyon [83] argued that it is possible to use cloud resources (mainly, Infrastructure as a Service or IaaS) almost for free, especially for micro and small businesses. To some degree, the claim appears to be true. There are many cloud service providers that give away some initial cloud storage resources. This kind of free cloud resource may vary from 2 to 16 GB of cloud storage space depending on the marketing strategy [see Appendix E Nineteen Free Cloud Storage Options]. The website for "the top 10 best online backup" services provides good comparisons, tips, and a buying guide for small cloud users [84].

However, for medium and large enterprises or organizations, there's no such thing as a free lunch. The real cost of cloud services must land somewhere. In other words, someone somehow has to pay for cloud services. From an end-to-end cloud infrastructure perspective, the large proportion of cost (both capex and opex) lies within the data center facility. Therefore, it is absolutely critical for us to understand what a data center facility is. How is it associated with cloud computing infrastructure? Ultimately, how will the cost impact the cloud business solution?

To better illustrate the data center facility, it is a good idea to adopt the Open Data Center Alliance (ODCA) conceptual framework v1.0 [63] with some modifications. This framework presents the big picture of cloud cost components (see Figure 4.1).

The data center facility is the first layer of cloud computing. Sometime, it is also called Data Center as a Service. It can be considered the foundation of the cloud cost model. It consists of five basic components. We can formulate it as a "3 + 2" model. Here, "3" means three key functional components, space, power, and cooling, and "2" means two auxiliary components, fire suppression and physical security. In the following chapters, we will organize this into seven chapters for the purpose of cloud cost analysis:

- Data Center Facilities
- Data Center Power
- Power Distribution Unit and Cabling
- Data Center Cooling
- Effective Air Distribution in Data Centers
- Cooling Strategies
- Fire Suppression and Physical Security

There have been a plenty of books and articles that discuss cloud computing costs at the cloud infrastructure level (namely servers, storage, and networks) but they have barely touched on the costs of the data center facility. It seems to be free. Actually, it costs more than many people think. Therefore, we believe that these cost components should be brought to your attention.

It doesn't matter what the size of the data center is. The primary goal of the data center is to serve the business needs. Different businesses will need different size data center facilities. There are three different ways to measure the data center size or capacity:

1. The total number of racks installed in the data center
2. The total physical size of the building in square meters or square feet
3. The total power capacity in megawatts

All these measurements are complementary. From a cost modeling perspective, we group all these components together because the depreciation rates of these components (or assets) are the same, but they are different with IaaS assets (servers, storage, and networks). Normally, the lifetime of these assets is between 7 to 10 years. In contrast, the devices installed in a rack, such as servers, storage devices, switches, routers, and load balancers only have 3 to 5 years. Strategically speaking, the data center facility is an essential part of cloud computing. An elegant data center architecture and cost-effective solution can provide a solid foundation for any cloud company to get ahead of other competitors in the cloud market. Data center facility efficiency is a core competence for any cloud service provider.

In short, the data center facility is the first layer of cloud computing. It is the foundation of the cloud computing infrastructure. The relationship between cloud computing and the data center facility is similar to the dependence between an airplane and the airport infrastructure. Without it, no airplane can land on the ground. In the next seven chapters, we will unveil the key components of the data center facility.

DATA CENTER FACILITIES

This chapter (1) defines the data center, (2) provides brief information on how to plan data center capacity, (3) discusses the site selection process if the business decision is to build new data center facility, (4) provides performance metrics for a data center, and (5) describes the details of data center space and the cost estimation that underpins one of three pillars (space, power, and cooling) of the data center facility cost foundation (see Figure 4.1).

4.1 BASIC UNDERSTANDING OF A DATA CENTER

Before discussing the technical details of a data center facility, the first few questions that we may encounter are: What is a data center anyway? How does it matter to the cloud computing solution or cost modeling? What are differences between a conventional data center and a cloud data center?

To answer these questions, let us look at the data center from a historical perspective. Actually, there have been many names for a data center. We can summarize various names into four different perspectives (see Table 4.1).

4.1.1 DEFINITION OF DATA CENTER

Surely, some names describe certain data center functions. Others just mean different sizes of data center in terms of capacity. Still others are just spelled differently. All these names are right if one is just focusing on one aspect of data center function but they are not very comprehensive. Eric Bauer et al. [85] tried to define this term comprehensively:

> A data centre is a physical space that is environmentally controlled with clean electrical power and network connectivity that is optimized for hosting servers. The temperature and humidity of data centre environment are controlled to enable proper operation of the equipment and the facility is physically secured to prevent deliberate or accidental damage to the physical equipment. This facility will have one or more connections to the public Internet, often via redundant and physically separated cables into redundant routers. Behind the routers will be security applications, like firewalls or deep packet inspection elements, to enforce a security perimeter protecting servers in the data centre. Behind the security appliances are often load balancers which distribute traffic across front end servers like web servers. Often there is one or two tiers of server behind

the application front end like second tier servers implementing application or business logic and a third tier of database servers. Establishing and operating a traditional data centre facility – including IP routers and infrastructure, security applications, load balancers, servers' storage and supporting systems – requires a large capital outlay and substantial operation expenses, all to support application software that often has widely varying load so that much of the resource capacity is often underutilised.

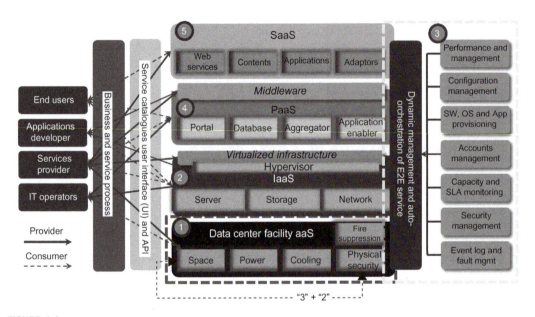

FIGURE 4.1

The big picture of the cloud cost framework.

Table 4.1 Different Data Center Names			
Engineering Perspective	**Communication Perspective**	**Storage Perspective**	**Computer Perspective**
Mechanical rooms	Wiring closet	Network storage room	Server room
Electrical rooms	LAN rooms	Storage space	Computer room
	Network closet or room	Backup room	Data center
	Telecommunication room	Disaster recovery site	Datacentre
	Console room or Network operation center		

Eric Bauer and colleagues' definition of data center is quite comprehensive. It includes data center space, power, cooling, physical and virtual security, IT infrastructure (server, network connection, storage, and load balance), IT applications, redundancy, data center operations, and management. The term does not only include hosting servers but also a mainframe. However, it seems to be too long.

Maurizio Portolani et al. [86] gave the definition of the data center from a network perspective as follows:

Data centers house critical computing resources in controlled environments and under centralized management, which enable enterprises to operate around the clock or according to their business needs. These computing resources include mainframes; web and application servers; file and print servers; messaging servers; application software and the operating systems that run them; storage subsystems; and the network infrastructure, whether IP or storage-area network (SAN). Applications range from internal financial and human resources to external e-commerce and business-to-business applications. Additionally, a number of servers support network operations and network-based applications. Network operation applications include Network Time Protocol (NTP); TN3270; FTP; Domain Name System (DNS); Dynamic Host Configuration Protocol (DHCP); Simple Network Management Protocol (SNMP); TFTP; Network File System (NFS); and network-based applications, including IP telephony, video streaming over IP, IP video conferencing, and so on.

Maurizio et al.'s term is a relatively narrow definition. It only emphasizes the functionality of hosting and networking. Perhaps this is because the majority of existing data centers are very small, what we often call a micro data center or computer room. Normally, they only accommodate a few racks. It may just utilize existing comfort cooling or the office air conditioning environment rather than a precision cooling facility. They are only to host a few applications and websites.

In order to serve the purposes of this book, we define a data center facility as follows:

The data center is a place where can accommodate many computing resources that collect, store, share, manage, and distribute a large volume of data. It consists of all necessary data center facility elements (space, power, and cooling) and IT infrastructure elements (server, storage, and network) based on business requirements.

A data center can be varied from a micro data center with a few servers to a warehouse scale that can accommodate thousands and even millions of racks that are configured with thousands or millions of servers. This is dependent on the particular business requirements or needs. Table 4.2 illustrates that different sizes or types of business may need different size data center facilities.

Table 4.2 Business Size and Data Center Scale Correlation

Business Size	No. of Employees	Data Center Size	No. of Racks
Micro Business	1–4	Office base	None
Small Business	5–19	Computer room	None or 1–5
Medium Business	20–200	Small or medium DC	5–20 or 20–100
Large Business	More than 200	Medium or large DC	20–100 or >1,000
Huge Enterprise Business	More than 10,000	Mega DC	>10,000

4.1.2 DATA CENTER ARCHITECTURE

Once the size of data center has been decided, the next step is to plot out the data center architecture. A typical contemporary data center should have nine basic function rooms or areas to support data center facility services (see Figure 4.2).

These nine basic function rooms are:

- Entrance Room
- Main Distribution Area (Computer Room)
- Telecom Room
- Mechanical Room
- Electrical Room
- Network Operation and Support Room (or NOC)
- Staging Area, Storage Room, Loading Dock
- Common Areas
- General Office

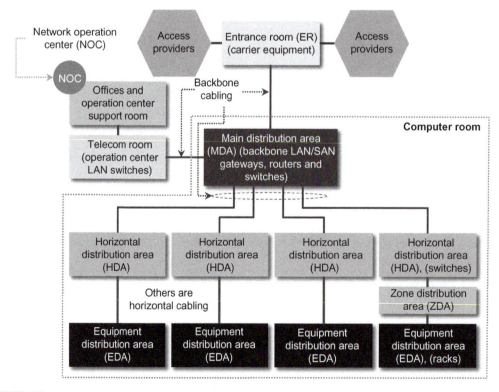

FIGURE 4.2

TIA-942 data Center topology (2005).

Each function room should provide unique features for the data center infrastructure. The architecture of these functional rooms is basically based on the TIA-942 standard data center topology. Before we further discuss these nine functional rooms in the section on data center space, we have to decide on data center capacity first. This exercise is a part of data center planning. In order to have the right data center architecture, it is important to have the right data center plan in terms of capacity. This plan will not only satisfy the existing business requirements but also fulfill future business needs.

4.2 DATA CENTER CAPACITY PLANNING

Business requirements will decide the data center workload, capacity, and tiering. It does not matter what size the business is. Whether it is a small, medium, large, or mega size business, the goal of data center capacity planning is to build or find the right data center facility for the business activity. It should not only meet the normal or existing business activities or operations but also accommodate the growth volume of future business demands. It is a long-term investment.

If we are talking about future growth, forecasting would be an inevitable step for our planning process. By human nature, we are not very good at predicting the future, particularly when we encounter the distant future, because there are so many uncertainties and variables. As a common idiom says, "I do not know what the future is, anything is possible." The longer the period of time the more inaccurate the prediction may be. It is quite obvious. We may be able to estimate the outlook of a business in 10 months but it would be very challenging to forecast the future business demands in 10 years.

However, as John Allspaw indicated, "You wouldn't begin mixing concrete before you know what you are building. Similarly, you shouldn't start to build a data center facility before you determine your data center's capacity. Capacity planning involves a lot of assumptions related to why you need the capacity. Some of those assumptions are quite obvious, others are not." [87] Actually, only very few assumptions may be quite obvious or direct and the majority of them are uncertain or fuzzy. Many assumptions involve subjective judgments or guesses. Others may have to be defended by certain probabilities, especially when we add the time domain for a longer period.

Why is this so? One of reasons is our subjectiveness in how we understand the world, as Mortimer J. Adler described: "Men are creatures of passion and prejudice. The language they must use to communicate is an imperfect medium clouded by emotion and coloured by interest, as well as inadequately transparent for thought" [89]. This means that the decision or judgment that we make is often highly subjective and based on personal perception or opinion. Very often, we see the world through an incomplete or even incorrect information medium.

Another reason may be that just as the German scholar, Reinhard Selten indicated, we only make the decision or judgment to the certain point of own satisfaction rather than to be rational [90]. In other words, when we make assumptions, we might not have enough time or patience to find a rational or perfect answer. An assumption could be the truth, but it is ultimately just what people think. Until it is proved by the time, the assumption may also be false or incorrect.

The last reason is probability. An assumption may be true at this moment but it might not be true at another moment. We are facing a dynamic world. Nothing holds still. When a prediction or assumption is made, we often defend it with the certain probability, which measures or estimates the likelihood of the assumption being true. Unless the probability is 0% or 100%, for a particular event, anything may occur. It actually makes the world much more interesting. If everything were predictable, the world would become very boring.

In essence, we should always be aware of the nature of assumptions when we make a series of assumptions for both the near term and future status of data center capacity. Assumptions are assumptions. They are not facts. Good future assumptions are those that you can probably defend with a definable certainty or probability. If the assumption cannot be defended by probability, it should be explicitly spelled out. Once we understand the nature of assumptions for capacity planning, we should be able to make the assumptions of capacity planning much more objective or scientific for our cost modeling exercise.

If we look from a major cost components' perspective at the data center facility, there are three key cost categories. These cost components should consist of more than 90% of the total data center facility costs:

- Space
- Power
- Cooling

Moreover, there are also four additional mandatory cost components that we should take into consideration for a TIA-942 standard tier data center facility:

- On-site security
- Fire suppression system
- Cable and cabling
- Racks or cabinets

How can we predict these key cost components when we are planning the capacity of the data center? We can probably adopt some common analytic methodologies, such as the cost benefits analysis (CBA), benchmark analysis, SWOT, agile, Delphi, and analytic hierarchy process (AHP) methods. (In addition to the common approaches, there are many other analytic approaches to define the cost. Readers can refer to Chapter 14 and see Appendix E for the details). We can also use these methodologies or processes in combination. It is really dependent on the phase of data center planning. In addition, we can also leverage different mathematic tools, especially statistical analysis or simulation techniques, to predicate future status. The ultimate goal is to eliminate subjective opinions and to have more scientific evidence so that we can use this evidence to support our assumptions and future forecasting results.

When we are talking about capacity planning for a data center facility, we may face one of the following seven scenarios due to different business circumstances:

- Building a brand new data center
- Purchasing or selecting colocation space
- Expanding the existing data center capacity
- Consolidating the existing data centers
- Moving or migrating current business applications into the cloud
- Building a business continuity facility
- Data center relocation

There may be other possible scenarios, but the above seven scenarios should be sufficient for us to discuss the cost models or framework. Once we understand these scenarios, we should be able to translate the business requirements into two series of key parameters for different scenarios:

- Performance of data center facility
    - Service Level Agreement (SLA)
    - Customer experiences
    - User or stakeholder expectations
- Resource capacity of data center facility
    - Resource ceilings
    - System capability
    - Reliability and availability

The purpose of data center planning is to make sure that all these parameters will be aligned with business requirements. One of the common approaches to specify these parameters is the so-called SMART approach recommended by Armando Fox and David Patterson [91]. SMART stands for:

- **S**pecific
- **M**easurable
- **A**chievable
- **R**elevant
- **T**ime boxed

"Specific" means each business requirement should be explicit, which implies that the expected result of the business requirement is measureable in dollar value. "Measureable" means the metric can be measured by a specified value, time, or dollar term. Here is an example of a specific and nonspecific metric:

- "The business requires that the hosting data center should be very reliable." This requirement is too simple, nonspecific, and unmeasurable.
- In contrast, the business requirement should state: "The hosting data center must exceed 99.95% availability, the number of unplanned outages in one month should be less than 0.01%, impacted customers should be less than 50; if an unplanned outage occurs, the impacted customers should be not more than 100, the response time should be less than 5 minutes, and the resolution time should be less than 2 hours." This requirement is specific and measurable.

"Achievable" means the result would be realistic based on the current technology level. For example, the business asks for a guarantee of no unplanned outages for a large-scale data center facility within the next 12 months. This may be an unachievable target for a tier 1 data center. The data center facility service (DCaaS) provider has to also review its database infrastructure and understand its data center capability in terms of meeting business demand.

"Relevant" means the business requirements must have business value to one or more stakeholders (data center facility's investor or sponsor). Suppose the business asks you to build a data center facility that requires a backup generator; one of the techniques to drill down to the real business value (also suggested by Armando Fox and David Peterson) is to keep asking five "why" questions. For example:

1. Why does the business require a generator? Because the business needs a very reliable hosting data center facility.
2. Why does high reliability matter to the business? If the data center is down, the business will lose significant sales revenue.
3. Why will the downtime impact the sales revenue? Because all CRM clients connected to the hosting server will be down as well.
4. Why will the hosting server be down? If we lose power in the data center.
5. Why will the data center lose power? If the power supply is disrupted and we do not have a generator.

Figure 4.3 is a simple flowchart to ask several "why" questions to determine whether the data center needs a generator or not. This process will drive the business value for both customers and stakeholders.

"Time boxing" means that you know where to stop if the business requirements have exceeded time and technology capabilities and/or budget limit. Of course, it is possible to divide a large amount of business requirements into a number of manageable and deliverable tasks or functions and then go back to stakeholders and fully communicate with them and get their approval for further resource (time, capex, and third-party support) commitment.

Once we understand how to effectively identify both performance parameters and resource metrics for data center facility, it is easier to follow the process of determining the data center capacity during the planning phase (see Figure 4.4).

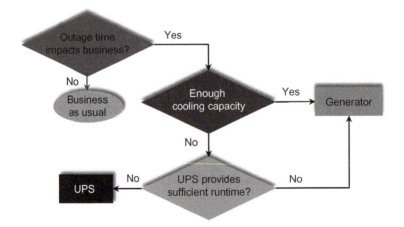

FIGURE 4.3

Determine if a generator is required.

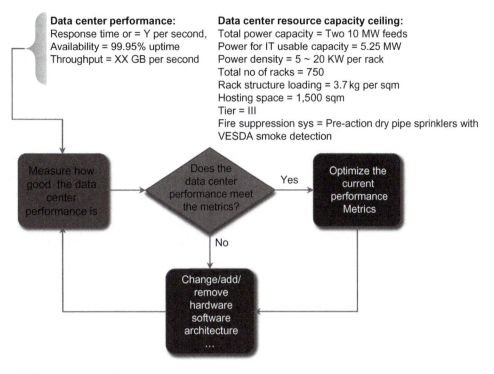

FIGURE 4.4

A simple process for data center planning.

When we implement the above process, there are a few important questions that should be asked. The art of capacity planning is dependent on asking the right questions in the right order. There are four main types of questions that should be asked:

1. What is strategic goal of the business? You must figure out the strategic goal of the business and how this strategic goal will be implemented in orderly way by subdividing it into a number of tactical objects.
2. What is being described by stakeholders in detail? As a data center facility planner you must discover the main facts and assumptions along with defendable probabilities to support the strategic goal and tactical objects within a specified time frame.
3. Is the defined strategic goal achievable in whole or in part? Surely, you cannot answer this question until you have answered the first two. You have to know what is being defined before you can decide whether the goal is achievable or not. If it is not achievable, you have to work it out in a different way.
4. How significant is the strategic goal? You have to understand why the goal is so important to the stakeholders. What is the business value in both explicit and implicit dollar terms?

Here is a typical example of asking the right questions in the right order for data center capacity planning:

1. What is your sales revenue target for the hosting service business in three years? How can you achieve it in each year or each quarter?
2. What are the main assumptions for your target? For each quarter's sale target, what is the probability, most likely, likely, or unlikely?
3. Is the defined sales revenue realistic? What are the risks in term of the current market conditions?
4. How significant is it for the company to achieve this strategic goal? What is the dollar value?

If the business is not new and just asking for business expansion, the second level of questions should be as follows: Does the existing data center facility meet the current business demand? If so, how well it is working? If not, why not? Do we need to expand the existing data center capacity? If the workload is growing at x% per annum for existing infrastructure, will it maintain the current performance? If not, what is the right strategy to expand the data center capacity?

- Build a brand new data center?
- Purchase colocation?
- Expand the existing capacity?
- Move a part of workload to a cloud?
- Consolidate the existing infrastructure?

By investigating like this, we will be able to make the cost of the data center facility align with the business goal and objects and the cost of data center will become much more transparent to both customers and stakeholders. Subsequently, it will also drive the unit cost of the data center facility to be more competitive.

Finally we have to point out the above assumptions we have made here are based on a so-called linear process model or single point of revenue prediction. It is the baseline estimation plus some standard deviation. We will have further discussion on this topic regarding a nonlinear model of revenue predication in Part V of this book.

Once we have fully understood how to effectively translate or interpret what the business wants, namely the strategic goals and the process of data center capacity planning, the next step is to examine the contents of data center facility planning in detail, which will include three critical elements:

- Data center site selection
- Data center performance
- Data center resource ceiling

4.2.1 DATA CENTER SITE SELECTION

A data center facility will be strategic assets or critical infrastructure for any enterprise that owns the infrastructure, especially for a business that provides Data Center as a Service (DCaaS) or Infrastructure as a Service (IaaS). The selection of a data center at the right site or location will be absolutely critical if the business is to be competitive in the marketplace. It will not only impact on return of the capex investment but also operational efficiency. It will ultimately impact on the unit cost of DCaaS and IaaS.

Table 4.3 Australian Data Center as a Service Catalog [92]

Service Categories	No. of Cloud Services	Percentage
IaaS	858	54%
PaaS	105	7%
SaaS	225	14%
Managed services	350	22%
Others and blank	51	3%
Total	1,589	100%

The cloud market is very competitive. Based on the latest Australian government's DCaaS service catalog (Department of Finance and Deregulation, version 5.1, releases date: June 26, 2014) there are 104 cloud service providers that supply more than 1,589 cloud services; nearly 54% of them are IaaS, 22% of them are managed services, and only about 21% of them are either PaaS or SaaS (see Table 4.3). Within this DCaaS catalog, some big global players, such as Amazon AWS and Rackspace, are not present. However, they have formed different alliances with different companies and provide IaaS for the Australian government. In short, they have already gained their foothold in Australia, where they have built a few data centers, especially in Sydney and Melbourne.

In comparison with the United States, United Kingdom, or even HongKong (see Appendix C) [93], the Australian cloud market is relatively small. For such a small market, over 104 providers and 1,589 cloud products is quite a crowd. In addition, the number of cloud service providers is not fixed. It is growing. This is good news for cloud consumers but for many cloud services providers, it means increased data center competitiveness and a need for efficiency in terms of building and operating DCaaS and IaaS. We believe the efficiency of data center infrastructure will be at the heart of the competition for many cloud service providers. However, when you make a decision either to build a new data center or to select one of the DCaaS providers, two primary issues must be considered. They are data security and data center efficiency. It doesn't matter what the size of the business is, whether it is small, medium, or large, even if the business is searching for colocation capacity. The bottom line of site security and efficiency will ultimately determine how to select the data center site. A decision maker has to implement a due diligence process for data center site selection.

When we implement a due diligence process for data center site selection, John Rath [94] suggests two primary factors to be examined:

- Natural disasters (mainly weather) and unnatural disasters
- Workforce resources and business climate

In addition to these two primary factors, John Rath also believes that a decision maker should also examine many different categories of issues. Some of them may be very special. However, the first thing would be the natural disaster and weather issue. When we talk about natural disasters, we can probably categorize these events into three types:

- Climatic
- Geological
- Hydrological

A climatic disaster event would include a blizzard, cyclone, hurricane, tornado, severe hail, excessive rain, heavy snow, ice and/or high wind, an electrical storm, or a severe weather pattern sustained over a period of time including very low or very high temperature. A geological disaster event will be events such as earthquakes and volcanoes. Hydrological disaster events will be tsunamis and floods. Despite these disaster events, other disaster events may be triggered by climatic, geological, and hydrological disaster event or events that are a combination of these natural disasters. The typical types of these disasters are:

- Fire/wildfire
- Avalanche
- Landslide/mudslide
- Drought

In contrast to natural disaster, some unnatural disasters events should also be taken into consideration for data center site selection, such as terrorist attacks and pandemics.

There is another way of making assessment of data center location, which was proposed by Karl F. Rauscher et al. [95] from Lucent Technologies. They suggested an eight-ingredient model. It is presented from a business continuity perspective (see Figure 4.5). The eight ingredients are environment, power, payload, policy, human, network, hardware, and software. Let's walk through these ingredients in detail.

4.2.1.1 The environment

Within the generic framework of the ingredients required for a data center facility to operate, the environment is the foundation. This means the geographic location of the data center. It should include climatic, geological, and hydrologic factors, which we have mentioned above. In addition, the site environment should also include the following five elements:

- Average temperature pattern
- Aa central location to all major customers, relatively
- Close to a power plant that provides the power

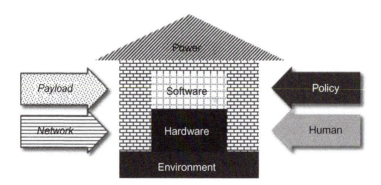

FIGURE 4.5

Eight-ingredient model.

- Many dark fibers
- Site has potential space for data center expansion

The main reason of including the average temperature pattern is to maximize the benefit of free cooling by leveraging economizers (for details, refer to Chapter 9) so that we can reduce the operating costs of the data center facility.

The meaning of having a central location to all major customers is that a data center should be close to the sources of major traffic or data streams so that the majority of customers can backup and retrieve data easily. For example, if all major customers are located in Sydney, it would be a good idea to allocate a data center in Sydney rather than Melbourne or Tasmania.

In order to reduce power transmission loss, a data center should be allocated as close as possible to the power plant. This will increase a data center's Power Usage Effectiveness (PUE) factor.

The dark fiber is another very important issue to consider. When you select the potential data center location, you would prefer the location already has many dark fibers that are ready via different carriers so that you can obtain a competitive price for the traffic of the data center network (see Figure 4.15 for the network ingredient).

During the last one year or so, unstructured data is growing dramatically at an exponential rate. According to IDC and EMC's forecasting in 2012, the digital universe will grow 50 fold (from 800 EB to 40ZB) between 2010 and 2020 (see Figure 4.6) and the latest IDC study in 2014 indicated that by 2020, digital data will reach 44 ZB (IDC updates this study every year http://idcdocserv.com/1678). This means that data growth is accelerating. To experience the real data growth, we can visit a live statistics site on the Internet [97]. Therefore, it is important to consider future growth for data center expansion.

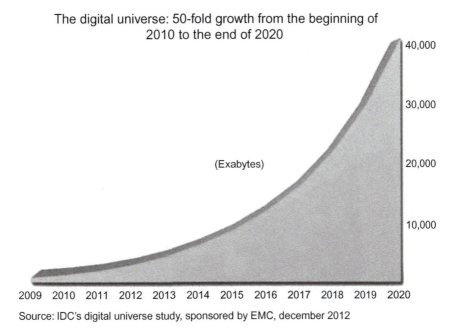

The digital universe: 50-fold growth from the beginning of 2010 to the end of 2020

Source: IDC's digital universe study, sponsored by EMC, december 2012

FIGURE 4.6

Data growth between 2010 and 2020 [96].

4.2.1.2 The power

Power means the external power supply from a power plant. For internal data center power distribution, we will give more details in the next chapter. When considering the data center location, the price of the power should be one of the key factors. It should be very competitive, reliable, and sufficient for future growth capacity. For example, when Priest Rapids Dam started supplying abundant cheap and renewable energy in Quincy, Washington (WA), it bought many high profile data centers to Quincy (see Figures 4.7 and 4.8).

Based on Colo & Cloud's information [100], the dam provides hydroelectric power at a price even lower than Rock Mountain Power, which was claimed to be the lowest price in the United States. The commercial power price for a data center is around US$0.025 per kWh. Microsoft reports its price is only about US$0.019 per kWh.

In contrast, the average price of electricity in Australia was around A$0.25/kWh in 2011−2012, which is one of the highest prices in the world according to the report by the Energy User Association of Australia (EUAA) (see Figure 4.9).

FIGURE 4.7

Priest Rapids Dam and hydroelectric project [98].

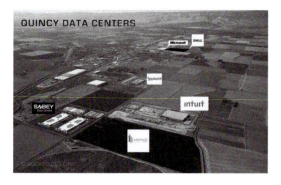

FIGURE 4.8

High-profile data centers in Quincy, WA, USA [100].

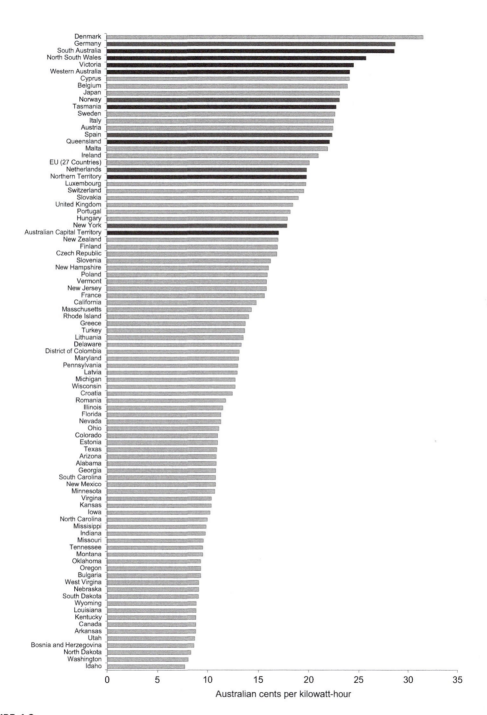

FIGURE 4.9

Electricity price by country, state, and province [103].

This is about ten times higher than Quincy, WA, USA. Of course, this comparison is not very accurate because the retail price is different from the commercial or the wholesale price. However, the power price is Washington is still the second cheapest in the EAAC price list. Normally, the commercial price would be lower than the retail one.

Based on the above EAAC's figure, if you would like to select a new data center location in Australia and just consider the power price factor alone, the favorable state would be ACT (around A$0.17/kWh) and the worst state is South Australia (around A$0.28/kWh). However, we have to be aware of the population density of the data center location. If the location of the data center is far away from a higher population density area, for example Sydney and Melbourne in Australia, the power consumption cost for network distribution may exceed the cost savings for power.

4.2.1.3 The payload and IT workload

If the price of the external power supply is uncontrollable, then the alternative to reducing the power supply cost is increasing the data center efficiency, which is the workload. The power usage efficiency is dependent on accurate prediction of data center workload because the higher the utilization of the data center the higher the efficiency is. Normally, the average operation cost for a data center will be five times more than its capex because the average life cycle of a data center facility is over 20 years. In other words, the opex is more than 25% of capex per annum. (This opex should include a 12.5% maintenance and support cost for many hardware components.) The optimal power supply load level is between 40% and 60% capacity (see Figure 4.10). It is dependent on what type of PDU is used.

Ideally, the data center should be operated at 100% (see Figure 4.11) for IT workloads. The higher the IT load, the better the data center efficiency is.

4.2.1.4 The policy

This refers to a local government policy that hopefully encourages data center facility investment. It is any kind of understanding and agreement between governments and data center facility companies. It can also be the government agreements, standard, policies, and regulations (ASPR). It may consist of a tax break for a high-tech data center facility that is built locally or incentives from by federal and local governments. The government policy could be considered a part of the business climate.

4.2.1.5 The human factor

This is the human capital. For example, when Google built one of its mega data centers in Council Bluffs, Iowa (see Figures 4.12–4.14) in 2007, Google was not only looking for clean energy, namely hydroelectric power, very close to the power source, but also looking to establish a partnership with nearby education institutions. Since 2009, Google has awarded more than $665 k to local schools in Council Bluffs, Iowa. Additionally, Google also partnered with City of Council Bluffs to launch a free WiFi network.

4.2.1.6 The network

This means the availability of dark fiber for a potential data center location. When the workload of a data center is growing, the demand for dark fiber capacity will be absolutely critical for data center scalability. This is because the demand for security enhancement and more bandwidth or traffic between the data center and head office or operations center will be increased. Moreover, if the data

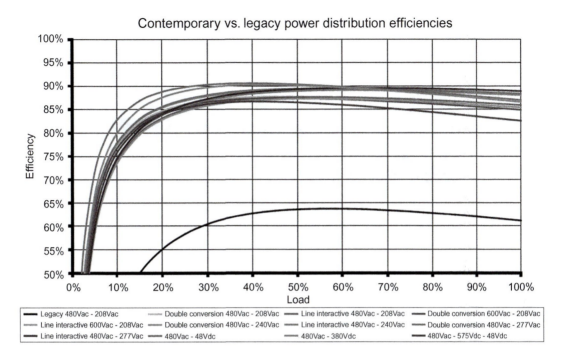

FIGURE 4.10

Power distribution or power supply efficiencies vs. workload [104].

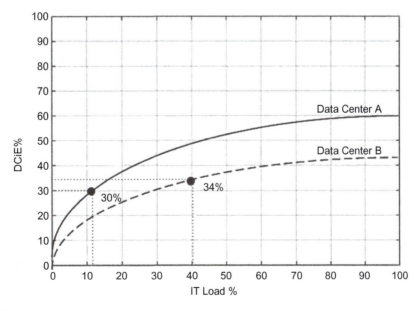

FIGURE 4.11

Data Center Efficiency (DCiE) metrics as a function of IT load [105].

FIGURE 4.12

Cooling towers of Google data center in Council Bluffs, Iowa [106].

FIGURE 4.13

Google's data center hovering above the floor in Council Bluffs, Iowa [107].

center workloads are designed for mission critical applications, the data center should not only be connected to disaster recovery sites with geographic diversity but also link to multiple backup data centers.

Taking the example of the Quincy, WA, area, the connectivity is provided by many wholesale dark fiber providers such as NoaNet and Grant County PUD built the fiber network. Some carriers, such as Zayo, Level3, Verizon, and Frontier have purchased capacity from them in order to offer their services to the data center facilities (see Figure 4.15).

In the US, state or local governments will point you in the right direction for dark fiber wholesale carriers. Of course, some companies such as Fibrelocator.com (http://www.fiberlocator.com/)

FIGURE 4.14

Google's data centers use color-coded pipes to indicate what they're used for. Referring to Google's URL, you can see all the details of color-coded pipes (Council Bluffs, Iowa) [108].

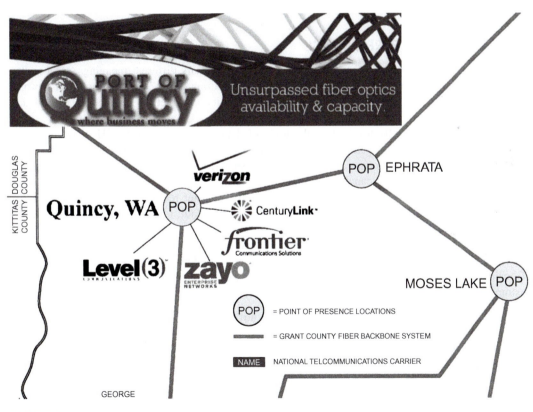

FIGURE 4.15

Dark fiber connectivity in Quincy, WA [100].

and CFN Services (http://www.cfnservices.com/) will provide research services concerning alloca-tion of dark fibers.

In Australia, a new company established in 2008, Vocus Communications, may be able to pro-vide information about dark fiber and connectivity for data centers both in Australia and New Zealand. The traditional carriers, such as Telstra, Optus, and AAPT, will provide their wholesale services for optical fiber network connectivity across Asia or the world.

In terms of data center hardware and software ingredients, we will give details in the following chapters.

The selection of a data center site is not only one of the essential processes for building a new data center but also a critical step in the selection of colocation and disaster recovery sites, migra-tion of an existing data center to a cloud, consolidation of a number of data centers, and even mov-ing legacy data centers to a new data center. It holds the future for many companies.

As a rule of thumb, the life cycle of a data center is about 20 years. The ongoing opex cost will be five times more than the initial capex investment. Data center site selection cannot only be based on the traditional criteria that are either just being close to head office or based on decision makers' intuitions. It should be vigorously analyzed via a proper process, such as the eight ingredients meth-odology. Once the site is selected, then we can work out the data center performance, which we are going to have a close look at in the following.

4.2.2 DATA CENTER PERFORMANCE

What does performance mean? Actually, "performance" has many different meanings, such as "an act of presentation" or to "play" a role in a movie, or "executing a task" or "fulfillment of a prom-ise," etc. Here, the meaning of performance means "quality of function" against an agreed and measurable standard or metrics.

In Section 4.2, we briefly touched on the topic of data center performance. Here we will give more details about data center performance based on the business requirements or needs.

Data center performance means a set of metrics. It should measure all aspects of the data center facility, which may include capability, high availability, reliability, scalability, manageability, latency, response or resolution time, throughput, security, disaster recovery or business continuity, resource utilization rate, energy efficiency or carbon footprint, fault tolerance, return on investment (ROI), and total cost of ownership (TCO).

At a glance, there are too many performance parameters to be measured. Which one is the most important? Which one is the least important? It is really dependent on who you are and what kind of business you are running or what kind of business applications you are hosting. From a cloud customer's perspective, data center performance may mean:

- Data center availability or reliability (cost of downtime)
- Security or data protection
- Throughput
- Latency
- Scalability
- Problem response and resolution time
- Business continuity or disaster recovery

For a cloud service (IaaS) provider, data center performance should include all aspects of measurements from the data center facility to the hosted applications and from cloud computing resource utilization to ROI/TCO. Let's have a look at the following critical performance metrics that will impact significantly on both data center service consumers and providers in terms of cost:

- Site availability
- Problem response and resolution time
- Scalability
- Utilization rate
- Latency and throughput

4.2.2.1 Site availability

From an end-to-end perspective, the most important performance measurement that every business will pay attention to is the system or data center availability. According to the NSI/TIA-942 standard (see Appendix H), one of the key metrics is site availability. It differentiates four tiers of data centers. This can be translated into a resource allocation, in terms of construction cost per square meter.

For traditional dedicated hosting services, we know that the application and hardware infrastructure is not shared. It is a one-to-one relationship. Subsequently, if one hardware component fails, it will not impact on other applications or customers. In contrast, the cloud environment is built on a virtual infrastructure or shared hardware. An issue with one piece of hardware may impact on many applications. In other words, one problem with a hardware device could lead to not only one but many applications that have performance degradation issues.

Therefore, if you are a cloud service provider and host many applications for your end users, availability does not only mean to one end user but also to all of your end users, so the availability measurement should include the number of end users. For example, a cloud service provider may claim that it can guarantee 99.95% availability (see Table 4.4). Does this mean to all end users or just 99% of end users per month or per annum. When a cloud service business customer signs a Service Level Agreement (SLA) with a cloud service provider, the service contract should be specified very clearly because it may impact on response and resolution time.

Table 4.4 Summary of Availability Information of ANSI/TIA-942 for Data Center Tiering				
Attributes	**Tier I**	**Tier II**	**Tier III**	**Tier IV**
Power & Cooling Delivery Paths	1 active	1 active	1 active + 1 passive	2 active
Redundant Components	N	N + 1	N + 1	2(N + 1)
Support Space to Raised Floor Ratio	20%	30%	80 ~ 90%	100%
Annual IT Downtime due to Site	28.8 hours	22.0 hours	1.6 hours	0.4 hours
Site Availability	99.671%	99.749%	99.982%	99.995%

4.2.2.2 Problem response and resolution time

From a cloud service operator's perspective, a cloud problem or a fault that impacts on the quantity of end users will decide the severity level of the fault. Consequently, it will trigger different levels of response and resolution time. For example if a cloud fault impacts more than 100 end users, the response time should be less than $5 \sim 10$ minutes and the resolution time should be within 2 hours. However, if the fault just impacts one end user, the response and resolution time will be much longer, such as a 2 hour response time with an 8 hour resolution time.

Very often, the service operator may use an operational metric to measure the availability with different levels of support. These metrics are mean time to repair or recover (MTTR) and mean time to failure (MTTF). There is a relationship between availability, MTTF, and MTTR:

$$Availability = \frac{MTTF}{MTTF + MTTR}$$

Here the MTTR is equal to the resolution time. Based on the reliability engineering theory, we often use another metric to measure system reliability, which is mean time between failure (MTBF). The relationship between MTBF, MTTF, and MTTR is equal to:

$$MTBF = MTTF + MTTR$$

To support the above availability, a cloud service may use different service levels, such as Platinum, Gold, Silver, Bronze, on call, normal business hours, etc. The price for different SLAs will vary from very expensive to very economic. Many managed service providers adopt this metric to differentiate their products and services in the cloud market. Table 4.5 shows an example of different cloud service support levels.

4.2.2.3 Scalability

From a cloud customer's perspective, cloud scalability means a cloud's elastic characteristics or flexibility. In other words, the end user only pays for what he/she has consumed of the cloud resources. The cloud resources cannot only be quickly scaled up but also be rapidly shrunken down.

Table 4.5 An Example of Cloud Operation Support Levels

Support Type	Support Time	Response Time	Resolution Time	No. of Impacted End Users
Platinum	24×7	<5 min	<2 hours	>100
Gold	24×7	<10 min	<4 hours	>50
Silver	$7 \times 21 \times 7$	<30 min	<8 hours	>5
Bronze	$7 \times 21 \times 5$	<45 min	<24 hours	>2
On Call	Call based charge	<60 min	To be decided	To be decide
Normal	Normal business hours excluding public holidays	<4 hours	Next business day	<1

From a cloud service provider's perspective, scalability means to accommodate various users' demands. This means that the cloud service provider does not only have the capability to scale its resource pool but also to scale it up.

In order to increase the cloud infrastructure utilization rate during resource idle times, the cloud service provider has to have a different price structure. For example, Amazon's EC2 and S3 services include a so-called "Spot Instance" price model. Others, such as Salesforce.com adopt the subscription price model, from which the cloud service provider can forecast or predicate the potential resource demand.

The question may be raised, "Despite having different price models to regulate cloud consumer's behavior during idle times, how is it possible for a cloud service provider to accommodate peak demand?" The simple answer is hardware virtualization and software multitenancy. Based on Artur Andrzejak et al.'s [101] research across six different corporate data centers, the typical utilization rate for a traditional hosting server is around 10% ~ 35%. Will Forrest et al.'s [52] discussion paper from Mckinsey also indicated that a typical data center's utilization rate is around 10%. Gartner's report [39] suggested that over 50% or 60% of the storage capacity would be idle in a typical company's data center. Our data also shows that the average utilization rate for some of hosting servers (mobile contents) was below 1% and the peak utilization rate was only around 7%.

Consequently, there will be enough infrastructure headroom for a cloud service provider to work with and still make enough profit while accommodating cloud customers' demands or workloads. The only question is how to optimize the resource pool and to synchronize each infrastructure component, including power, cooling, space, server, storage, and network. This is the topic that we are going to discuss in the next few chapters.

4.2.2.4 Utilization

The utilization rate is the key financial performance index when measuring the cloud. Theoretically speaking, the higher the utilization rate is, the lower the cloud infrastructure cost is. The fundamental reason that many enterprises move their IT workloads to a cloud environment is not to share IT resources or utilize advanced cloud technologies. It is because the existing standalone or traditional IT infrastructure is heavily underutilized. A cloud service provider can bring cloud services to its customers and increase the IT utilization rate significantly. Therefore, the cloud service provider can return cost benefits to its customers while still maintaining healthy profits.

As we will see in the later chapters, the cloud infrastructure utilization rate will be a critical factor in cloud cost modeling. It doesn't only require that the cloud service provider utilize proper capacity planning based on the business and IT workload profile but also requires a cloud service provider to build a data center in a modular fashion.

Before we move on the next topic of data center capacity, let's have a look two more key concepts of data center metrics, which are latency and throughput.

4.2.2.5 Latency and throughput

Latency and throughput are two very important performance metrics for any end user. These two performance indicators will measure all other data center performance metrics when a cloud service is online. Based on Adrian Cockcroft et al.'s [102] definition for Internet services, latency stands for "the time that it takes to complete a well-defined action" and throughput means "the number of defined actions performed in a given period of time." In very simple terms, the latency is the execution time and the throughput is the required bandwidth to execute a task.

To illustrate these two concepts of performance clearly, we will use both airplane and bullet train transportation as examples. Suppose an airplane that can carries 100 passengers per flight has to transfer 20,000 people from one airport to another and each flight would take 60 minutes per one way flight[1] (just ignore the time for loading and unloading passages). The question is, "How long would it take to complete this mission?" (See Figure 4.16.)

- Airplane capacity = 100 per flight
- Latency = 20,000/100 × 60 × 2 = 24,000 minutes or 400 hours to complete the mission
- Throughput = 20,000/400 = 50 people per hour (PPH)

If I use a bullet train to transfer the same amount of people (or 20,000) and each bullet train's capacity = 10,000 per trip and the time from one place to another destination would take 240 minutes or 4 hours,[2] what is the latency for the bullet train? (See Figure 4.17.)

- Bullet train capacity = 10,000 per trip
- Latency = (20,000/10,000) × 240 × 2 = 960 minutes = 16 hours to execute this mission
- Throughput = 20,000/16 = 1,250 people per hour (PPH)

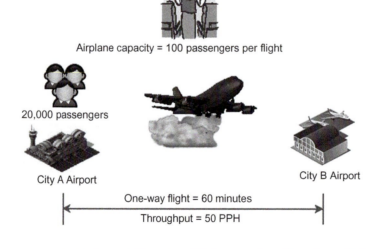

Airplane capacity = 100 passengers per flight

20,000 passengers

City A Airport

City B Airport

One-way flight = 60 minutes

Throughput = 50 PPH

FIGURE 4.16

An example of airplane latency, throughput, and capacity.

[1] Assume that the average passenger airplane's speed = 800 km per hour.
[2] Assume that the average bullet train's speed = 200 km per hour.

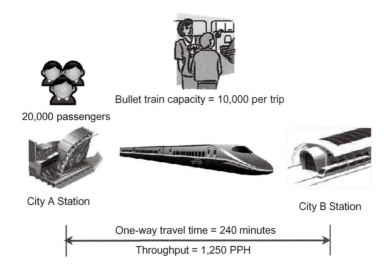

FIGURE 4.17

An example of bullet train latency, throughput, and capacity.

In comparison, the airplane is 240/60 = 4 times faster than the bullet train. Although the bullet train is slower in terms of latency, its throughput is 1250/50 = 25 times larger than the airplane.

Once we understand these two concepts, it would be easier for us to apply these concepts to the application of a high-speed link between two data centers.

Suppose we have a file of TCP window size = 1 MB (megabyte) to be transferred from data center A (in city S) to data center B (in city M). The core network connection between the two data centers is a 10GbE link with an average round-trip latency (RTT) of 20 milliseconds. Now, the question is, "What is the maximum throughput I can get? (See Figure 4.18.)

- 1 megabyte window size = $1024 \times 1{,}024 \times 8 = 8{,}388{,}608$ bits
- 8,388,608 bits/0.020 second = 419,430,400 bits per second throughput, which means the maximum possible throughput = 419 Mbps

Here, the example shows that although the pipe size is a 10GbE link, the maximum possible throughput is only 419 Mbps. So, how can we increase the throughput for the given 10GbE? The answer would be to either increase the TCP window size or reduce the RTT latency. This is similar to the story of the airplane or bullet train, where you can either increase the number of passenger per flight (from 100 passengers to 200 passengers per flight) or reduce round-trip time, by increasing the airplane speed (from 120 min to 100 min).

If the pipe size and latency are fixed, what is my maximum throughput?

- The pipe size is a 10 GbE link and round-trip time (RTT) = 20 ms.
- 10,000,000,000*0.02 seconds = 200 MBits/8 = 25 megabytes per second.

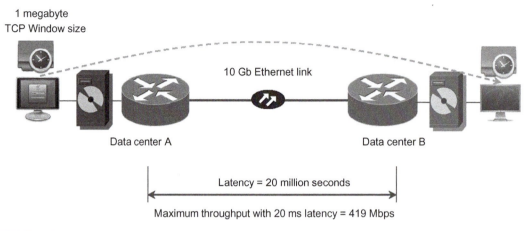

1 megabyte
TCP Window size

10 Gb Ethernet link

Data center A

Data center B

Latency = 20 million seconds

Maximum throughput with 20 ms latency = 419 Mbps

FIGURE 4.18

An example of the relationship between throughput, latency, and capacity between two data center links.

If the TCP window size is fixed, and is 1 megabyte, what is the maximum latency for transferring the file in the GbE link?

• Maximum latency = 8,388,608 bits (file size)/10 Gbits per second (desired throughput) = 838.8 microseconds = 0.838 millionths of a second.

4.2.3 DATA CENTER RESOURCE CELLING

We have touched on the topics of performance and capacity in the above sections. However, data center performance and capacity are very often misunderstood. Although they have a dependent relationship, these two measurements have different purposes.

As we have spelled out above, the purpose of performance is to meet business requirements within the specified quality or to exceed the customer's expectations. Capacity determines what the customers want and when they want it based on the current performance baseline.

From a financial perspective, most capacity planning work will be part of capex activities. In contrast, performance or performance management should be a part of opex activities. The International Standard Organisation (ISO) defines a framework for support and operation activities. We have five subactivities to underpin IT infrastructure operations including performance management (see Figure 4.19).

Similarly, we can establish a framework for data center capacity planning from a cost modeling perspective (see Figure 4.20).

There is a dependent relationship between data center capacity planning and performance management, which is the data center resource capacity (see Figure 4.21).

Why do we need data center capacity planning? It is because the resources are neither unlimited nor free and there is a resource celling in any data center. In order to meet unlimited customer demands with a limited resource pool, performance management is essential.

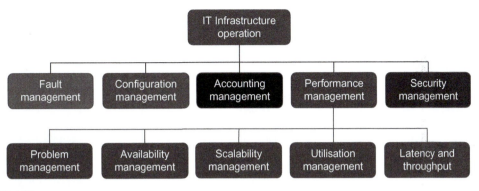

FIGURE 4.19

ISO for high-level IT infrastructure operation framework (FCAPS).

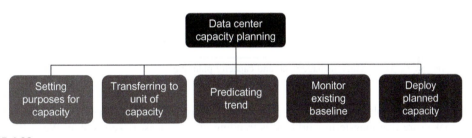

FIGURE 4.20

A framework of data center capacity planning.

Just in the above example, the 10GbE link between two data centers is the limited fixed resource capacity. In order to maximize the throughput, we have to either increase the TCP window size or reduce the RTT. If the RTT is fixed, then the only choice to increase the throughput is to increase the size of the TCP window. The formal description of this relationship is as follows:

$$Throughput\ (B) = \frac{TCP\ Window\ Size\ (W)}{RTT\ (D)}$$

For a cloud service provider, the data center resource celling will always be an issue. The right strategy to resolve this issue is to combine both data center capacity planning and performance management or performance tuning. Any cloud service provider should be aware of the risks of long-term workload trending down within a certain life cycle. The famous Amazon on-demand computing diagram (refer to Figure 1.15) only shows one scenario (growth). However, in reality, the IT workload may also trend down.

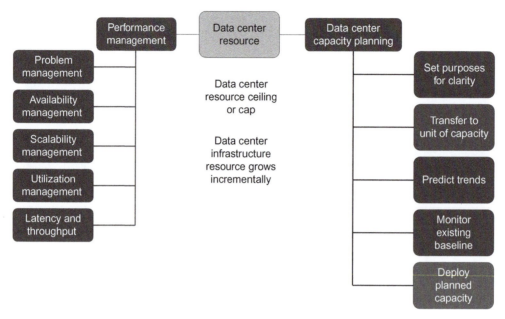

FIGURE 4.21

Data center resources, performance management, and capacity planning.

Therefore, it is absolutely critical for a cloud service provider to have the right marketing strategy and make sure that long-term workload is trending up or at least is kept stable. We will discuss more details in the last chapter concerning investment strategies.

4.3 DATA CENTER SPACE

We mentioned in the section on data center architecture the layout of a data center or its topology, which can be based on the TIA-942 (April 2004) standard (see Appendix H, TIA-942 Telecommunication Infrastructure Standard for Data Center Tier). However, this standard is basically using a telecommunication exchange perspective and is driven by the purposes of telecommunication.

Although it has covered some of the important functions of data center space that are also essential for a cloud data center, such as the entrance room, telecommunication room, office support room, and computer room, it hasn't touched on the topics that are very important from a computing perspective. Therefore, in addition to the data center functions disussed above, we should also pay close attention to the following five types of space:

- Total space (building shell)
- Total adjacent lot size (raw lot size)
- Whitespace (raised floor)
- Effective usable space (rack space)
- General Space

4.3.1 **FIVE TYPES OF SPACE**

4.3.1.1 Total space (building shell)

The total space is easy to understand; it is the building shell of the data center. It represents the building roof that covers all data center equipment. If you are building a new massive data center, then site selection would be the first step (refer to Section 4.2.1) and then you will build a data center in a new shell. However, many data centers are built in an old building shell, utilizing the existing building infrastructure, such as the Barcelona Supercomputing Center [109] that built a data center inside of Barcelona's Torre Girona chapel in 2005. It is a building from the 1920s (see Figures 4.22−4.24).

The main reasons to build a new data center in an old building shell were:

- Limited time (only four months) for installation
- Close to the research group at the Technical University of Catalonia

The pro is that it is very quick, which you can save a lot of time in laying the infrastructure foundation for the building shell. However, the con of utilizing an existing building is that it is not scalable or there is not enough space for expansion. In addition, the site may only have limited power and bandwidth capacity. The time to renovate an old building is quite difficult to estimate.

Selecting an old building shell may be only applied for small and medium data centers that have limited IT workload growth. It is more like a data center in a box (container) type of solution, where you would like to build a point of presence (POP) close to where your customers are, for example, a multimedia data center application.

FIGURE 4.22

Inside of Barcelona's Torre Girona Chapel [109].

FIGURE 4.23

Inside of Barcelona's Torre Girona Chapel, above the floor (in 2007).

FIGURE 4.24

Inside of Barcelona's Torre Girona Chapel, below the floor (in 2007).

4.3.1.2 Total adjacent lot size (raw lot size)

"Lot" is a real estate term. It refers to a "land lot." The term "total adjacent lot size" means that the data center will have enough potential land nearby for expansion purposes. There is another real estate term that known as "plottage" [110]. It is the process of combining adjacent parcels of land (or lots) to form one large parcel. It refers to merging or consolidating a number of adjacent lots into one large lot (see Figure 4.25).

Figure 4.25 shows an example of total adjacent lot size, which is three times larger than the original land dize of the data center space. It is a part of an investment strategy of building the data center in a modular fashion. However, when you are in the planning stage, it is important to understand the expandable land capacity, the total adjacent lot size. In other words, during the first phase of investment, the cloud workload may be difficult to predict so that you only build what you need, but when your business takes off, you should have enough land capacity to expand your business. Of course, the price of future land and specifically electrically active land is different. Based on the Uptime Institute Inc.'s research data in 2006 and 2007 [113], electrically active land was US$1,120 per square meter per month. If the inflation rate assumption is 3–4%, then today's price would be just over US$1,500 per square meter per month. We will discuss the cost model in later chapters. Empty future space may cost approximately 2/3 that of electrically active land.

4.3.1.3 Whitespace (raised floor)

The term "whitespace" means the usable raised floor data center environment that is measured in square meters or feet (it could be up to few thousand square meters). Many data centers, such as Facebook's data centers, do not use a raised floor, but the term "whitespace" may still be used to refer to the usable square footage [111] (see Figure 4.26).

Regarding the different methsod of air distribution, each air distribution approach has its pros and cons. We will discuss the strategy of cooling air distribution in Chapter 8.

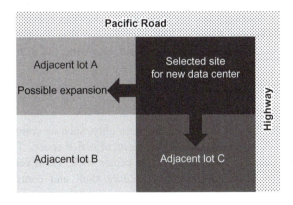

FIGURE 4.25

Total adjacent lot size.

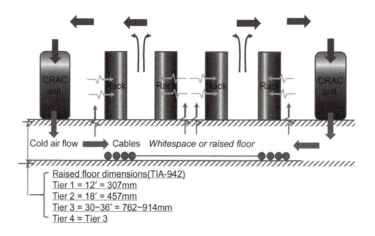

Cold air flow ▶ Cables *Whitespace or raised floor*

Raised floor dimensions(TIA-942)
Tier 1 = 12′ = 307mm
Tier 2 = 18′ = 457mm
Tier 3 = 30~36′ = 762~914mm
Tier 4 = Tier 3

FIGURE 4.26

Whitespace (raised floor).

4.3.1.4 *Effective usable space (rack space)*

Effective usable space is the rack space for installing IT equipment, such as servers, storage, network equipment (routers, switches, and load balancers), and firewall equipment. A typical size of a rack is 42RU high, which is about 6 feet or 1,866.9 mm. Each rack unit (RU) is 1.75 inches or 44.45 mm high. The width of the standard 42RU (EIA-310D or E) rack will be either 19 inches (482.6 mm) or 23 inches (584.2 mm). The depth of 42RU varies from 600 mm (24 inches) to 1,000 mm (42 inches). Normally, the rack depth size is roughly that of a standard floor tile size, which is 2 feet (600 mm) $\times$ 2 feet (600 mm), if there is cold airflow via a raised floor (see Figures 4.27 and 4.28).

Based on research from Kailash Jayaswal [164], only about 50% of data center space is occupied by racks or standalone hardware and the other 50% is for data center facilities, such as power, cooling, aisles, and ramp. Douglas Alger's [109] data showed that useable rack space varies from about 14% to 80% for 14 data centers around the world. However, the average percentage is below 50%, or 43.64%.

4.3.1.5 *General space*

Furthermore, there are many areas for general purposes only, such as common areas (for example, parking spaces), the network operation center, and general office space. These spaces should also be considered during the phase of building the data center shell. However, the network operation center can be built outside of the data center building shell and controlled by a head office remotely.

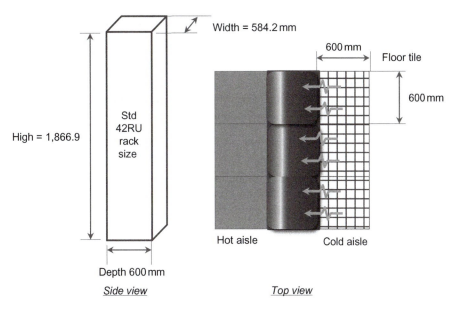

FIGURE 4.27

EIA-310 standard 42RU rack size.

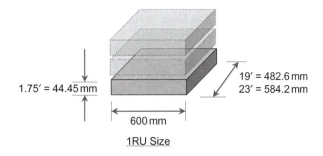

FIGURE 4.28

Standard 1RU size.

4.3.2 DATA CENTER FUNCTIONAL ROOMS

Referring to Figure 4.2 and the TIA-942 standard, a typical data center should have nine functional rooms. If we group them together, we can probably divide them into three types of special function categories:

- Utility support functions
- Computing functions
- Operational functions

Descriptions of these functions are shown in Figure 4.29. Let's explore the details of these functional rooms.

4.3.2.1 *Utility support functions*

The utility support function consists of three functional rooms: mechanical rooms, electrical rooms, and the staging Area including the storage and loading dock.

4.3.2.1.1 Mechanical rooms

A mechanical room is for installing cooling, compressors, water pumps, condenser units, and ventilation equipment or heating, ventilating, and air conditioning (HVAC) equipment. The room supports all HVAC or cooling functions for the data center facility.

4.3.2.1.2 Electrical rooms

An electrical room accommodates all uninterruptible power supply (UPS) units, batteries, generators, transient voltage surge suppression (TVSS), primary power panels, and service entrance transformers. The room supports a data center's power functions.

4.3.2.1.3 Staging area

This room is designed to store spare parts, faulty equipment to be sent off for repair, and all test equipment, tools, and other work gear (such as occupational and safety gear). This area also includes the loading dock for equipment transportation.

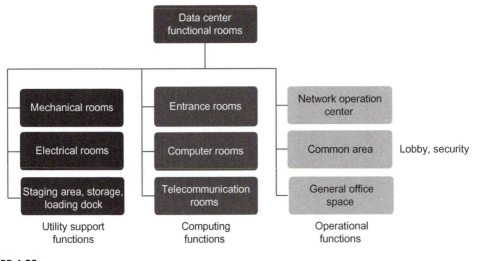

FIGURE 4.29

Data center functional rooms.

4.3.2.2 Computing functions

There are also three functional rooms in this group: entrance rooms, computer rooms, and telecommunication rooms. These functional rooms are mainly to serve the purposes of the servers, storage, and networks.

4.3.2.2.1 Entrance rooms

This is where the outside carriers' equipment meets the internal network. It is the demarcation. Normally, the equipment connects to the backbone network. Sometimes, there are many outside carriers connecting to one data center. In some instances, a carrier broker may optimize different carriers' capacity and become a reseller for a data center's customers, such as colocation customers.

The entrance room is normally located outside of the computer room so that other carriers' technicians can have access without compromising the data center security policy. In order to improve entry point redundancy and reduce excessive cable length, a large data center may have more than one entrance room to provide additional redundancy or to avoid exceeding maximum cable lengths for access provider-provisioned circuits. The entrance room interfaces with the computer room through the main distribution area. The entrance room may be adjacent to or combined with the main distribution area.

4.3.2.2.2 Computer rooms

Computer rooms are the main functional rooms for any data center. Without them, it cannot be called a data center. As we have described in the above section, normally the computer rooms will take up more than 50% of the total data center space. The key difference between a computer room and usable rack space is that the computer room has both hot and cold aisle functions but the rack space may not have both a hot and cold aisle. A rack space is within the computer room. Moreover, the computer room is divided into four different areas:

- Main distribution area (MDA)
- Horizontal distribution area (HDA)
- Equipment distribution area (EDA)
- Zone distribution area (ZDA)

Main distribution area (MDA): The MDA is the central point of distribution for all data center cabling systems. As we can see in Figure 4.2, this area is within the computer room. It may be locked into a dedicated room or area for security reasons. Normally, Private Branch Exchange (PBX), core network switches, and core routers are located in the MDA room. Some provisioning equipment for access providers, such as carrier class high-density M13 multiplexers may also be installed in the MDA room rather than the entrance room. One MDA may support multiple HDAs and multiple EDAs plus operational function rooms.

Horizontal distribution area (HDA): The purpose of the HDA is to support a dedicated area that is within a large computer room or hall for special functions or additional security. It is a centralized distribution point or horizontal cross connection (HC) for cabling to EDAs. A typical HDA may include SAN and LAN switches for the equipment within an EDA.

If a data center has multiple computer rooms that cross different floors, each floor will have its own HC to serve equipment on this floor. For a micro or small data center, an HDA would be unnecessary because one MDA should have enough capacity to handle all IT equipment within the entire computer room. However, for a large or mega size data center, there will be many HDAs.

Equipment distribution area (EDA): The name here explains itself, as this area is for connecting the end equipment or racks consisting of servers, storage disk arrays, access network switches, and other telco equipment. It should not be used for other cabling purposes, such as for an entrance room, MDA, or, HDA.

Zone distribution area (ZDA): This is another subcentralized distribution point between HDAs and EDAs. It provides the flexibility to accommodate frequent reconfigurations, such as "moves," "adds," and "changes." It is particularly useful for DCaaS providers to support colocation services.

4.3.2.2.3 Telecommunication rooms

These are dedicated to equipment related to telecommunication services. They are the common access point for backbone and horizontal pathways. The LAN network switch is also located in these rooms for the purpose of network operations. From Figure 4.2, the TIA-942 typical data center architecture or topology, we can see the telecommunication room is connected to the offices and operation support room, which is the operation center.

4.3.2.3 Operational functions

The next functional group is the operational function rooms. These are the network operation room, common area, and general office space. These three functional rooms support data center operational processes.

4.3.2.3.1 Network operation rooms

The network operation room is also called the network operation center. If it is operating a number of data centers around the world, it may be called a global operation center (see Figure 4.30). It can be located in the data center building shell. It can also be located outside the data center building and communicate via a remote control LAN or WAN. The main purpose of the operation center is FCAPS (see Figure 4.19).

4.3.2.3.2 Common area

The common area would include the lobby, site security, car parking, and cafeteria space. These areas are regularly accessed by data center staff and customers, and are designed for human comfort.

4.3.2.3.3 General office space

General office space is similar to other office areas except it is part of data center security monitoring based on the data center tiering. Again, the purpose of this space is for human comfort so the air conditioning system will be differentiated from the computer or server room.

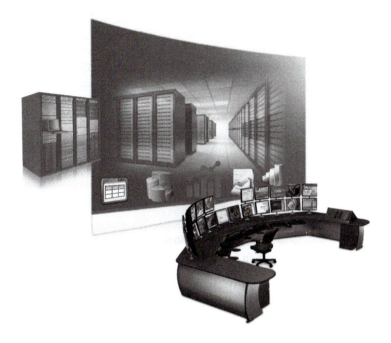

FIGURE 4.30

An example of a network operation center.

4.4 **HOW TO ESTIMATE COST OF SPACE**

Many vendors have published the average cost of space. In March 2008, the Uptime Institute [112] published research that indicated the average price for usable space is about US$1,249/square feet/ year or US$13,440/square meter/year for electrically active floor area. This can also be translated as US$4,840 per rack per year (with the assumption of the standard 42RU rack dimension 0.6 m × 0.6 m).

However, the author didn't give further details on how to calculate the result and how to make the assumptions for the calculation. Surely, land value will fluctuate from one location to another. Even the construction cost will also fluctuate from time to time, and place to place. It is quite challenging to pinpoint a particular number.

The best approach is to work out how to calculate or estimate the land or space value. Eric Shapiro [113] provided five different approaches to estimating the land value:

- The market approach or comparative method
- The income approach or investment method
- The residual approach or development method
- The profits approach
- The cost approach or contractor's method

Overall, the space will be counted as 15% of the total cost for a typical rack located in a data center that has 2N high availability. It doesn't matter if it is a traditional or cloud data center, they all need rack space or data center space. It is an illusion if people think that cloud computing means the data can be processed in a cloud (up in the air) without any physical infrastructure. From an IT resource usage perspective, there is no difference between cloud computing and traditional computing, such as utility, dedicated, distributed, and grid computing. They all have to consume data center facility resources. The only difference is that cloud computing uses data center resources much more efficiently by leveraging virtualization technologies, such as server virtualization and multitenancy.

4.5 SUMMARY

A data center facility is a physical place to accommodate computing resources that collect, store, share, manage, and distribute large volumes of data. The primary focus of a data center facility is the IT equipment or hardware rather than human resources. In this chapter, we have discussed two main topics:

- Site selection
- Data center space

One topic mainly focuses on the external space and the other predominantly regards the internal rooms or the area under the shell.

When we are planning to build a new data center facility or even extend one of the existing data centers, the first question that we encounter is how to select the data center location. We listed six fundamental issues or factors to be considered and weighted. Among these issues, workload and power are the most important factors because they will impact data center performance.

Because the decision on site selection will have long-term consequences (20 years), all data center ingredients should be carefully balanced out. Ultimately, the decision will impact the data center's performance from a long-term perspective. Data center performance consists of five metrics: site availability, scalability, utilization, latency plus throughput, and reliability. The reliability can also be represented with the common term mean time between failure (MTBF), which includes both mean time to failure (MTTF) and mean time to repair (MTTR). Moreover, MTTR includes both response and resolution time. Any mission critical application requires a specified response and resolution time, which we often call an SLA.

From a data center space perspective, a traditional data center facility has five different types of space: total space, total adjacent lot size (or potential expendable space), whitespace, effective usable space, and general space. As a general rule of thumb, the ratio of usable data center space is around about 50%. In other words, if the rack space needs one square meter then the supporting space of the data center facility will also need one square meter. This is not including the space for disaster recovery (DR). If we consider the DR space, the ratio of usable space for IT workload will be even lower or just above 40%.

If we look from a functional perspective, the data center can be divided into three basic functional group areas: utility functions, computing functions, and operational functions. Each function has three functional rooms. The utility function has mechanical and electrical rooms plus the

Table 4.6 Unit Cost of Data Center Space

Data Center Types	Tier 1	Tier 2	Tier 3	Tier 4
Electrically Active Floor Space	$1,120 per sqm per month or $13,440 per sqm per annum			
Future Empty Space Cost	$700 per sqm per month or $8,400 per sqm per annum			
UPS Redundant Cost per Annum	$12,000 per kW	$13,000 per KW	$24,000 per KW	$25,000 per KW
Redundant Configuration	1 active	1 active	1 active + 1 passive	2 active

staging area. The computing function has entrance, computer, and telecommunication rooms. The operational function has a network operation room, common area, and general office space.

Based on the Uptime Institute's research white paper [115], we can summarize the average cost of usable space would be US $13,440 per square meter per annum or $1,120 per square meter per month in 2007. This would include both capex and opex costs (see Table 4.6).

4.6 REVIEW QUESTIONS

1. What are the different names you know for a data center?
2. How can we define the meaning of data center facility in very simple terms?
3. Why do we need the data center if the data can be retrieved and stored in the cloud?
4. Is the cloud really free?
5. Why do we need data center capacity planning?
6. How can we ask the right questions for data center capacity planning?
7. How can we select a data center site if the plan is to build new data center?
8. How many factors should we consider when selecting the data center site?
9. What does we mean by data center space?
10. Why is the space so important?
11. How many types of spaces are there?
12. How many different functions and function rooms does a common data center have?
13. What is the average ratio of usable data center space in comparison with the total space?
14. What is the average cost per square meter or per square feet per annum for usable space?

DATA CENTER POWER

5

Power consumption is one of biggest cost components for data center operators. Power costs have been estimated to represent between 10%−25% of data center cost. For some companies, data center power has become the biggest hurdle to growing the cloud business.

In this chapter, we will first review some fundamental concepts of power, such as basic power metrics and the power factor of AC power. Then we will focus on five topics including power panels or circuit breakers; transfer switches, including static transfer switches (STSs) and automatic transfer switch (ATSs), generators, uninterruptible power supplies (UPS), and UPS batteries.

Finally, we will discuss the issues such as how to estimate the cost of power consumption, UPS, UPS batteries, and generators. We will cover the following seven topics:

- Basic concepts of power
- Power panels or circuit breaker
- Transfer switches (both STSs and ATSs)
- Generators
- UPS
- UPS types and UPS topology selection
- UPS batteries

5.1 INTRODUCTION

In Chapter 4, we discussed data center space. Although space is a very important issue, we often find the data center runs out of power before running out of space. From an energy perspective, data center power is the only driving force behind every IT device. Without power, specifically electricity, no IT equipment will work in the data center. Therefore, power is one of three critical elements (space, power, and cooling) for any data center. Based on Jonathan Koomey's [112] and Albert Greenberg et al.'s [116] research data, data center power represents 10% to 15% of the total cost. Gartner claimed that energy-related costs account for approximately 12% of the total data center expenditure in 2010 [114]. If we would like to save on data center costs, the energy bill is one of the major items for us to pay close attention since it is an ongoing opex component. Moreover, if a government regulation imposes a CO_2 emission tax, the data center has to pay extra for energy consumption if it is not green energy.

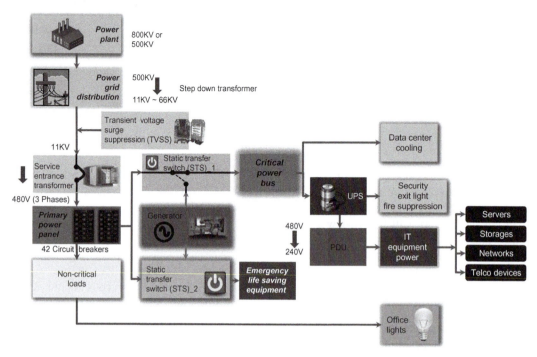

FIGURE 5.1

Data center power distribution system.

Let's examine the power distribution system (see Figure 5.1) and see why it costs so much. Let's also look at the mechanisms of the power distribution system that could lead to power loss.

From outside the data center, we can view a power distribution system as consisting of three parts:

- Power plant
- Power grid distribution (normally a step-down transformer)
- Transient voltage surge suppression (TVSS)

These factors trigger power or energy loss. That is why some warehouse or mega size data centers (such as some of Google's data centers) are built next to power plants in order to minimize the power transmission or distribution loss.

If we draw the boundary of a data center power system from the service entrance transformer, this will be the starting point of the data center power distribution system for our discussion. First, we will provide a brief discussion on the basic concepts of electricity and highlight specifically alternating current (AC) power. Second, we will change the topic to power panels or circuit breakers. If we cannot select the right circuit break and configure it correctly, it will cause many unnecessary and unplanned power outages. Third, we will shift our focus to STSs and ATSs as well as generators. The primary purpose of STSs, ATSs, and generators is to protect against external power supply disruption. Fourth, this chapter will raise the issue of UPS. As we know, there is a time gap between disruptions in an external power supply reaching the data center generator to establish stable power. That is why we need UPS. Of course, different business requirements will have different UPS configurations. Finally, we will move on to the topic of UPS batteries and monitoring them.

5.2 FUNDAMENTALS OF POWER

In order to understand data center power and power distribution systems, it is important to clarify some very basic electrical power concepts first. Many of them are concepts that we have already learned in high school, such as Ohm's law. Here, we just refresh your memory.

5.2.1 THREE BASIC POWER METRICS

Power is measured by three basic metrics: voltage, amps, and resistance (for DC power) or impedance (for AC power). Because of alternating curren (AC) and direct current (DC), we have apparent power that is represented by volt-amperes (VA) and real or active power that is represented in watts (W).

The relationship between voltage (V), amps (I), resistance (R), and power (P) is decided by Ohm's law, which is expressed as follows for DC:

$$P = VI$$
$$V = IR \ \textit{(Triangle formula)}$$
$$P = I^2 R$$

If the power is transmitted via AC with a single-phase sine wave, the equation will be a sine equation (see Figure 5.2) and the value is a complex number or a vector:

$$v = iR \ \text{ and } \ i = I_m \sin \omega t$$
$$p = p_R = V_m I_m \sin^2 \omega t = \frac{V_m I_m}{2}(1 - \cos 2\omega t)$$

If we use a complex number or equation to rewrite the above three equations, we will have the following three alternative equations that are presented in phasor form:

$$\dot{i}_A = I e^{j0°} = I_m$$
$$\dot{i}_B = I e^{-j120°} = I_m \left(-\frac{1}{2} - j\frac{\sqrt{3}}{2} \right)$$
$$\dot{i}_C = I e^{-j240°} = I_m \left(-\frac{1}{2} + j\frac{\sqrt{3}}{2} \right)$$

The single-phase voltage or current is often for residential customers, but for commercial and data center purposes, three-phase power will normally be adopted (see Figure 5.3). If each phase's voltage V_m is given, we can calculate the real output voltage V_r (see the following example):

If $V_m = 240$ V, then $V_r = 1.73 \times 240 = 415.2$ V.

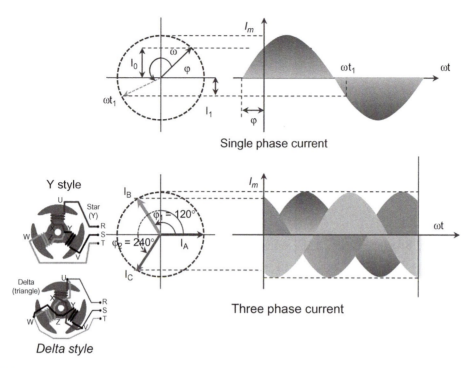

FIGURE 5.2

Single- and three-phase alternating current.

$$I_A = I_m \sin \omega t,$$
$$I_B = I_m \sin(\omega t - 120°)$$
$$I_C = I_m \sin(\omega t - 240°)$$

For power transmission, it is better to use high voltage with lower current rather than lower voltage with a higher current because a smaller diameter wire is much more economical. Table 5.1 illustrates an example to demonstrate the relationship among voltage, current, and wire diameter.

5.2.2 POWER FACTOR FOR AC POWER

In addition to understanding alternating current, it is very important to remember that the power a data center gets is not the real power but rather is the apparent power. The energy bill is based on the apparent power, not the real power. However, when we are talking about the power for the data center we are referencing the real power. As we have indicated above, the apparent power is for transmission purposes.

Therefore, in order to calculate the real power for data center energy consumption, we have to introduce a power factor (see Table 5.2). It is similar to the conversion between AC power and DC power.

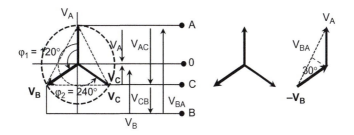

FIGURE 5.3

Three-phass voltage calculation.

$$\text{Assume } V_A = V_B = V_C = V_m$$

$$\dot{V}_{BA} = \dot{V}_B - 1\dot{V}_A = V_r$$

$$\frac{1}{2}V_r = V_m\cos 30° = \frac{\sqrt{3}}{2}V_m$$

$$V_r = \sqrt{3}V_m$$

Table 5.1 Voltage and Current Relationship in Transmission

Configuration Types	Type 1	Type 2	Type 2
Distribution Voltage	700	500	350
Current (Amps)	50	70	100
Transmission Power (KVA)		35	
Transmission Cable Size Ratio	1	40% of Type 1	100% of Type 1

Table 5.2 Power Factor Table

Voltage (V)	500					
Amps (A)	100					
Apparent Power (VA)	50,000					
Power Factor	1.0	0.9	0.8	0.7	0.6	0.5
Real Power (KW)	50	45	40	35	30	25

Here is an example. Suppose we need a pump for a chilled water system (a recirculating pump) to circulate the condenser water to a cooling tower (see Figure 5.4). The specified power consumption is 45 horsepower (HP) = 45 × 746 = 33,570 W. The question is, "How many amps are required for this pump to draw 240 AV/three phases with an efficiency rate = 0.9 and a power factor = 0.7?"

The answer is 128 A.

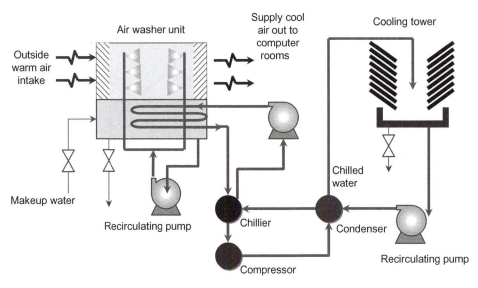

FIGURE 5.4

Chilled water system.

$$Amps = \frac{Power\ consumption}{volts \times efficency \times PF \times 1.73} = \frac{33,570}{240 \times 0.9 \times 0.7 \times 1.73} = 128\ A$$

5.3 POWER PANEL (CIRCUIT BREAKER)

A power panel (or circuit breaker) is one of the critical components in the data center's power distribution system. Based on many researchers' papers and vendors' whitepapers [117], almost 70% of power system failures are associated with circuit breakers (see Table 5.3).

We will now explore the root causes of circuit breaker failures.

5.3.1 TYPE OF CIRCUIT BREAKER AND SELECTION

The purpose of circuit breakers is to stop either current overload or short circuits to protect the other equipment in the data center. Normally, there are two types of circuit breakers:

- Thermal circuit breaker (for overload protection)
- Magnetic circuit breaker (short circuit protection)

A typical power panel consists of both thermal circuit breakers and magnetic circuit breakers (see Figure 5.5). A normal magnetic circuit often can handle as high as 2,000 times its current rating for short current.

Theoretically speaking, a standard circuit breaker is supposed to trip at 100% of its rated threshold level, but the industry code requires the rating to be 80% of the continuous current load.

Table 5.3 Power System Failure

Types of Failure	Percentage of Failures
Uninterruptible power supply (UPS)	18%
Power distributed unit (PDU) and associated circuit breakers	32%
All other power system circuit breakers	38%
Other power failures	12%
Total	100%

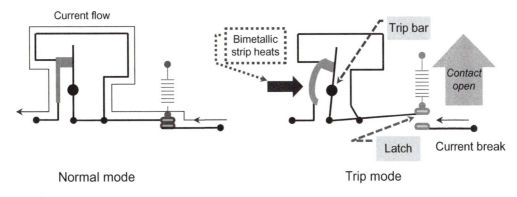

FIGURE 5.5

Thermal circuit breakers: normal and trip mode.

Table 5.4 Selecting the Right Circuit Breaker Value

Value	Description	Meaning
33 A	Allows 110% short-term current overloads	Maximum overload value
30 A	Specified value for circuit break	Marked value
24 A	80% of continuous current load	Selected value by code

In other words, when we see a device specified as a 30 A circuit breaker protection, the 24 A circuit breaker should be selected. This is because the typical circuit breakers are designed to trip at 110% of short-term overload (see Table 5.4 and Figure 5.6).

Because many IT devices have different power loads, the size of circuit breakers should be decided upon using a systematic approach. Otherwise, there may be many power system failure problems.

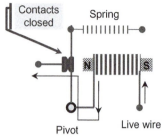
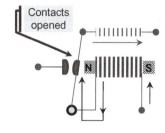

Spring force keeps contacts closed   Electromagnetic force opens contacts

FIGURE 5.6

Magnetic circuit breakers: closed and open modes.

5.3.2 CIRCUIT BREAKER COORDINATION

This part could also be placed in the section on PDUs or rack panels since they are closely associated with the circuit breaker. If we configure the circuit breaker incorrectly, it will cause many headaches during data center operation. To illustrate this issue, let's have a look the following example.

As we can see it on the left of Figure 5.7, when server A is connected to a rack, server A can draw a maximum of 20 A current or power. If the rack panel circuit breaker is configured with 16 A, this will cause trouble because if the rack panel circuit breaker is blown out, all other servers (servers B, C, and D) connected to this rack panel will lose their power.

The purpose of a circuit breaker is to protect IT equipment when the power is overloaded or a short circuit occurs. The circuit breaker is supposed to be open if the current is higher than the specified level. However, circuit breaker coordination may become very complicated. When the setup isn't designed carefully, it could bring other IT equipment down and trigger many unnecessary, unplanned outages. An example is illustrated on the left side of Figure 5.7.

In contrast, if we can configure the circuit breaker value correctly, unnecessary server outages can be avoided. On the right side of Figure 5.7, if we increase the value of the rack panel circuit breaker from 16 A to 25 A and reduce the outlet circuit breaker from 25 A to 16 A, basically swap the two circuit breakers, the rack panel circuit breaker will not trip if server A is overloaded.

5.4 TRANSFER SWITCHES AND GENERATORS

The transfer switch is another critical component for data center emergency power (see Figure 5.8). It switches between normal utility power and a standby generator. When the normal utility power source is lost, a transfer switch can immediately detect this fault and send a "kick off" signal to the standby generator to break the utility power source and divert the generator power to the data center load. Of course, the generator has the proper frequency and voltage.

We can see there is a gap between utility power loss and generator power kick-in, where no power sources are available for data center loads. This period is called "runtime." The typical time for this

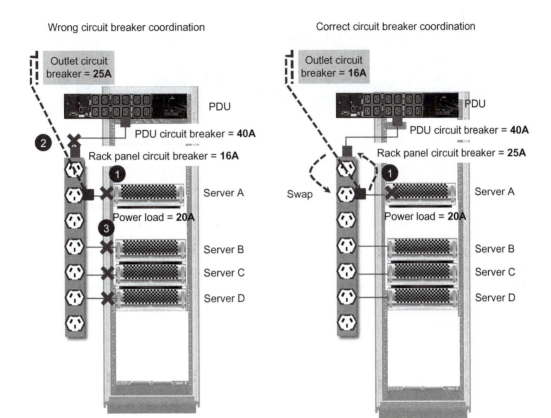

FIGURE 5.7

Wrong and correct circuit breaker configuration.

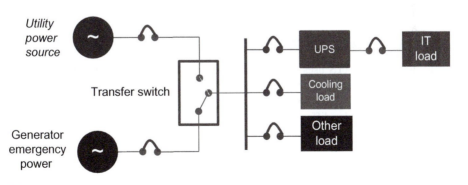

FIGURE 5.8

Function of transfer switch.

FIGURE 5.9

AETES 19-inch 2RU rack mount static transfer switch.

"runtime" gap is about 10 seconds. A well-designed data center allows for 20 to 45 seconds of buffer time. This is dependent on the generator's preparation time to reach the right parameters for the data center load. To bridge this runtime gap, we use a so-called uninterruptible power supply (UPS), which normally uses battery power. We are going to discuss this topic in later sections of this chapter.

When the utility power comes back, the transfer switch should be able to switch back to normal mode. The function of the transfer switch is to exchange between two live sources and minimize or eliminate power disturbances for some critical applications. There are two types of transfer switches:

- Static transfer switch (STS)
- Automatic transfer switch (ATS)

5.4.1 STATIC TRANSFER SWITCH (STS)

An STS is a switch that uses a semiconductor to divert the data center load between the utility source and emergency power. It is controlled by a sensor circuit. When the sensor circuit detects the utility power is out of the specified tolerance, it diverts the data center loads from the normal power path to the emergency one. This takes only about a few milliseconds depending on the type of STS (see Figure 5.9).

However, STS may sometime stand for something else. We should be very careful about what the exact meaning of the acronym is as some vendors may use the same acronym to mean "source transfer switch," which could be a relay switch or ATS.

5.4.2 AUTOMATIC TRANSFER SWITCH (ATS)

In contrast to the STS, an ATS uses a mechanical relay to make the switch. The response time of this kind of switch is normally longer than an STS, about 8 to 16 milliseconds (see Figure 5.10).

We can use either an STS or ATS for different purposes. Table 5.5 shows the selection criteria for both STSs and ATSs under different circumstances.

5.4.3 GENERATOR

The generator is the backup power source so a large data center can run for a certain period of time when utility power is down. The length of the runtime will decide the need for a generator. The bottom line is, "Do I really need a generator for my data center load or critical applications?" or "Would

FIGURE 5.10

1RU rack mount KWX-ATS.

Table 5.5 Comparison of STS and ATS					
Type of Transfer Switches	**Total Cost of Ownership (TCO)**	**Transfer Time**	**Power Range**	**Installation Requirements**	**Scalability**
Rack mount ATS	$100–200/kW	8–16 ms	5–10 KVA	Rack mounted, no wire	Scalable
Rack mount STS	$500–700/kW	4 ms	5–10 KVA	Rack mounted, no wire	Scalable
Large STS	$200–300/kW	4 ms	20–35 MVA	Electric hardwiring	Not scalable

my business tolerate any period of downtime?" If not, what is the consequence of downtime and how can we bridge this runtime gap? If yes, what is the maximum time that can be tolerated?

In Figure 5.1, we outlined the process to determine whether the data center needs a generator or not. Let's consider the first question: what is the cost of downtime to my business? The *Data Center Journal* (in 2010) [118] published research papers indicating the average cost of downtime per hour for all industries is about $1 million per hour. This is similar to the Meta Group's data published in October 2000 (see Table 5.6).

However, Emerson [119] estimated that the average cost of downtime per minute would be $5,600 per minute = $336,000 per hour in 2011, which was based on an "activity-based cost model" (see Figures 5.11 and 5.12).

Based on the above methodology or other ways of cost estimation for business, we can probably get an estimated cost for the business downtime. If the downtime cost is too high to be ignored in terms of business impact, then we should consider a generator. In order to decide on the right generator, we should have the right process for generator selection (see Figure 5.13).

The threshold level of the decision is the total cost of ownership (TCO) of the backup system equipment versus the desired runtime. It is quite clear that if a longer runtime is required, more

Table 5.6 Downtime Cost per Hour [120]

Industry Sector	Revenue Lost per Hour	Industry Sector	Revenue Lost per Hour
Brokerage Operation	$6,450,000	Utilities	$643,250
Energy	$2,817,846	Healthcare	$636,030
Credit Card Sales Authorizations	$2,600,000	Metal/Natural Resources	$580,588
Telecommunications	$2,006,245	Professional Services	$532,510
Manufacturing	$1,610,654	Electronics	$477,366
Financial Institution	$1,495,134	Construction and Engineering	$389,601
Information Technology	$1,344,461	Media	$340,432
Insurance	$1,202,444	Hospitality and travel	$330,654
Retail	$1,107,274	Pay-per-View TV	$150,000
Pharmaceuticals	$1,082,252	Home Shopping TV	$113,000
Banking	$996,802	Catalog Sales	$90,000
Food/Beverage Processing	$804,192	Airline Reservation	$90,000
Consumer Products	$785,719	Tele-Ticket Sales	$69,000
Chemicals	$704,101	Package Shipping	$28,000
Transportation	$668,586	ATM Fees	$14,500
Average Cost			$944,395

costly battery backup equipment is needed. The relationship between runtime and TCO of the backup system is grows linearly. In contrast, the generator capex is a once-off cost. Once the generator is bought, the rest of the cost would be fuel and maintenance and the runtime is unlimited.

Putting all these three cost factors (runtime, battery backup, and generator) together, we can draw a diagram and find an optimizing cross point for TCO vs. runtime (see Figure 5.14). The costs of the generator solution and backup solution have different characteristics against the runtime.

The optimizing point is where the cost of a battery backup solution has exceeded the cost of the generator solution. (Here, the cost means TCO). Of course, this optimizing point is not fixed and it is dependent on the workload.

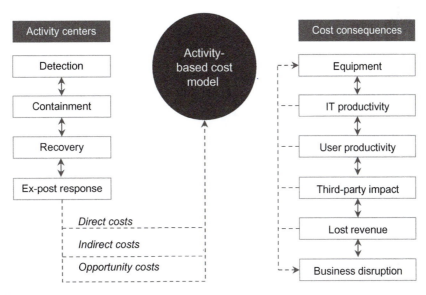

FIGURE 5.11

Activity-based cost frameworks.

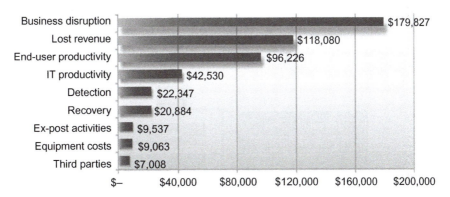

FIGURE 5.12

Average cost of unplanned data center outages for nine categories.

The higher the workload is, the shorter the runtime. Now, the question is where do these two lines cross? The answer is dependent on the size of the workload (see Figure 5.15). If the workload is 12 kW, the threshold level of the runtime will be less than 20 minutes. In contrast, if the workload is 2 kW, the threshold level of runtime will be greater than 70 minutes, which is three times more than the 12 kW workload.

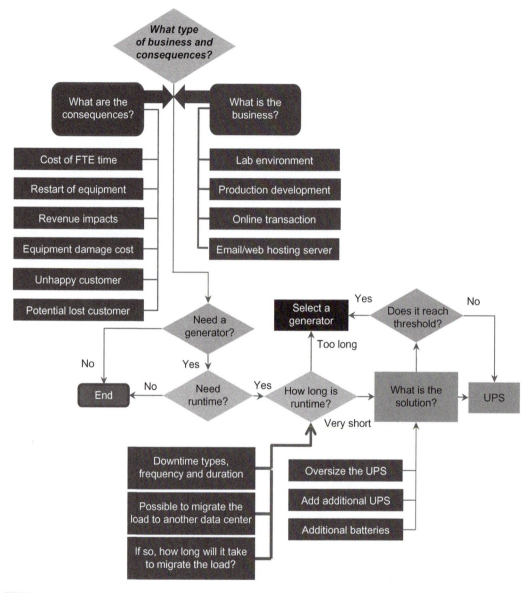

FIGURE 5.13

Details of process to decide runtime and generator.

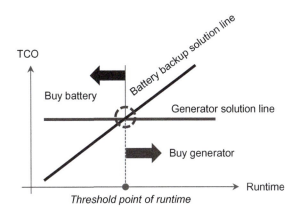

FIGURE 5.14

Choose between generator and batteries.

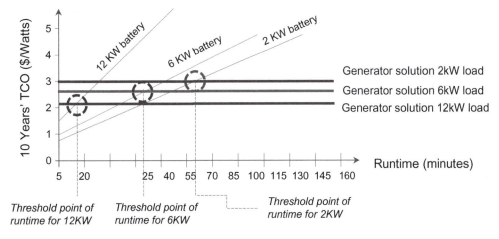

FIGURE 5.15

Workload decides the crossing point of TCO$/watts vs. runtime (minutes).

5.5 UNINTERRUPTIBLE POWER SUPPLY (UPS)

The purpose of UPS is to provide a reliable and quality power source to a data center. It has three alternative paths for three different functions or modes (see Figure 5.16).

The normal mode is "1," in which the utility power is converted from AC power to DC power and from DC to AC again. It is called "double conversion." Path number 2 is for the preventive maintenance bypass operation. Path number 3 is for charging the batteries. Normally, as much as 20% of AC power will go to battery charging until the battery is full.

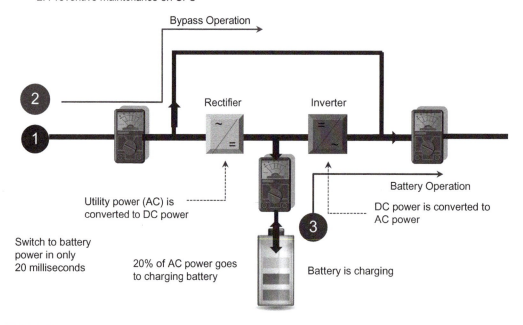

1. Power comes from utility power (normal operation)
2. Preventive maintenance on UPS

FIGURE 5.16

Uninterruptible power supply (UPS) double conversion.

Now, the first questions that we encounter are: "Why do we need UPS or double conversion?" "Is it waste of money and energy?" The answer is, "Of course not." As we know, the power provided by the power plant has many quality issues. There are at least eight types of typical common power problems from a power plant:

- Interruptions
- Impulsive transients
- Sags and undervoltages
- Swells and overvoltages
- DC offset
- Harmonic distortion
- Voltage fluctuation
- Frequency variations

The function of the UPS is to prevent these power problems and protect IT equipment (see Figures 5.17 – 5.21). This is the primary reason to have the UPS installed in the data center. Another reason for the UPS is to charge the battery. However, it is very costly because of energy loss.

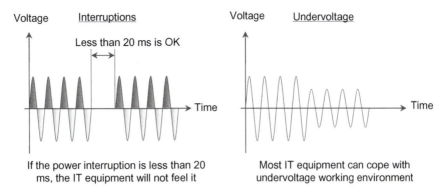

Voltage   Interruptions

Less than 20 ms is OK

→ Time

Voltage   Undervoltage

→ Time

If the power interruption is less than 20 ms, the IT equipment will not feel it

Most IT equipment can cope with undervoltage working environment

FIGURE 5.17

Common power interruptions and undervoltage.

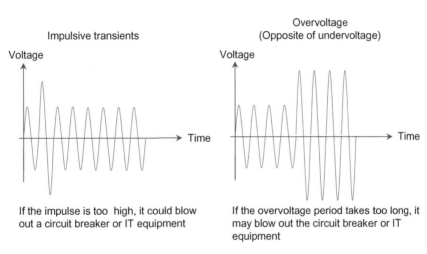

Impulsive transients

Voltage

→ Time

Overvoltage
(Opposite of undervoltage)

Voltage

→ Time

If the impulse is too high, it could blow out a circuit breaker or IT equipment

If the overvoltage period takes too long, it may blow out the circuit breaker or IT equipment

FIGURE 5.18

Impulsive transients and overvoltage.

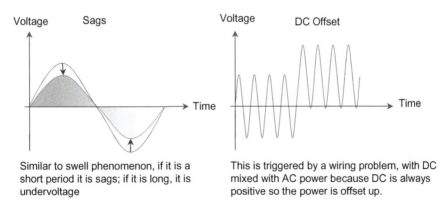

Voltage   Sags

→ Time

Voltage   DC Offset

→ Time

Similar to swell phenomenon, if it is a short period it is sags; if it is long, it is undervoltage

This is triggered by a wiring problem, with DC mixed with AC power because DC is always positive so the power is offset up.

FIGURE 5.19

Sags DC offset.

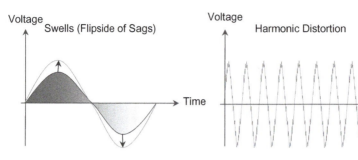

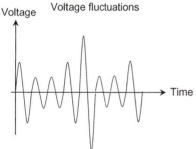

Swells are also associated with overvoltage; if it is a short period it is swells, if it is a long period it is overvoltage

There are a lot of problems that may cause harmonic distortion. For example, nonlinear loads, circuit impedance mismatches. These issues will create second- and third-order harmonics of the original frequency (50Hz or 60Hz)

FIGURE 5.20

Swells and harmonic distortion.

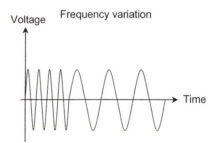

This is a combination of under- and overvoltage or sags and swells problems.

This is because the generator or small co-generator sites are being loaded and unloaded. This unstable frequency may cause erratic operation, data loss, system crashes, and equipment damage

FIGURE 5.21

Voltage functions and frequency variation.

5.5.1 DIFFERENT TYPES OF UPS TOPOLOGIES

In order to improve power source quality and protect IT loads, we have to use different types of UPS solutions to solve different types of power source problems as stated above. There are five basic UPS topologies:

- Standby or offline single UPS topology
- Line interactive UPS topology
- Online double conversion topology

- Delta conversion UPS topology
- Rotary UPS topology

This is not only way of categorizing UPS topologies. There is another way of categorizing UPS, which is the so-called International Electrotechnical Commission (IEC) standard 62040-3. It classifies all UPS into three major types based on the way the UPS delivers power to the critical loads:

- Passive standby (IEC 62040-3.2.20)
- Line interactive (IEC 62040-3.2.18)
- Double conversion (IEC 62040-3.2.16)

For the second type of line interactive UPS (IEC 62040-3.2.18), there are two common styles of UPS:

- Static
- Rotary

The static line interactive UPS is also named as the delta conversion topology and the rotary line interactive is also called a rotary topology. In other words, delta conversion and rotary should be a part of the line interactive UPS, which means there are only four different topologies. It doesn't matter how we categorize these UPS topologies, each UPS topology is designed for a particular power solution. Let's investigate each UPS topology in detail.

5.5.1.1 Standby or offline single UPS topology

The Standby UPS topology is a lower cost solution for power problems, such as sags and power surges, or impulsive transients. During normal operation, utility power supports the data center load, and utility voltage and frequency variations are not controlled by the UPS but pass through to the IT equipment (see Figure 5.22).

Only when utility voltage and frequency variations exceed the specified limit does the UPS convert DC battery power to AC power to support the data center load. The issue with standby UPS is that it doesn't react very quickly to prevent IT equipment shutdown.

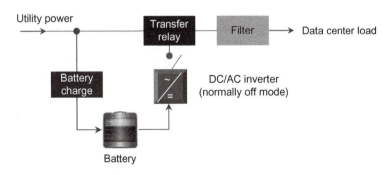

FIGURE 5.22

Standby or offline UPS topology.

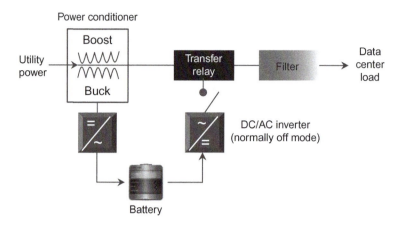

FIGURE 5.23

Line interactive UPS topology.

5.5.1.2 Line interactive UPS topology

The line interactive UPS is similar to the standby one, in which the utility power directly flows to the data center load. However, it has an inductor (auto-transformer) in the input path, which provides a certain kind of filtering capability to correct some power variations, such as sags and surges (see Figure 5.23).

The main advantage of line interactive is that you pay very little cost for a better quality of utility power. The major drawback is that it doesn't have the full capability to cope with all power problems. Some power problems with short duration will slip through the inductor and impact on the critical workload.

5.5.1.3 Online double conversion

This is one of the two comprehensive static UPS topologies. In contrast to the previous two topologies, it provides full power protection. It isolates the data center equipment from all types of utility power problems by continuously regulating the AC power (see Figure 5.16). For example, some critical IT applications require a maximum harmonic distortion tolerance of not more than 5%.

The main drawback of this topology is that it is very expensive and less efficient than standby and line interactive topologies. However, it is the most popular topology for the majority of data centers.

5.5.1.4 Delta conversion topology

The delta conversion topology combines both online and offline advantages, minimizes their disadvantages, and presents a hybrid solution to the data center load. The way delta conversion works is that it uses a special transformer configuration between the load and utility power. It controls the utility power magnitude, wave, shape, frequency, and other power metrics very accurately (see Figure 5.24).

When the utility power is normal, it does not use double conversion and lets the utility power pas through to the data center load. Only when utility power has problems does it isolate all power problems. It is utility power conversion "on-demand."

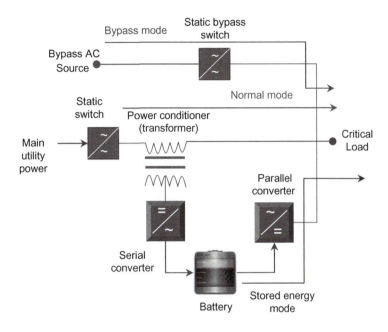

FIGURE 5.24

Delta conversion.

5.5.1.5 Rotary UPS topology

All of the above four UPS topologies are in a sense "static" because they do not adopt rotating machinery to re-create the AC sine wave. Instead, these static UPS topologies only take AC sine wave current and rectify it, or "chop" it up. This is one method of AC to DC conversion.

In contrast, the rotary UPS topology utilizes the same rectifier technology as static topologies in the opposite direction, from DC current to AC. It uses spinning motor-generators (MG) or a spinning wheel with mechanical energy to re-create the sine wave on the output. The advantage of this is AC power is a pure sine wave with very high quality (see Figure 5.25). The disadvantage is that it doesn't last very long. Fortunately, over 95% of power outages are less than 10 seconds and the flywheel or rotary UPS can normally provide 25–30 seconds of runtime.

5.6 HOW TO SELECT UPS TOPOLOGIES

The selection of UPS topologies is basically dependent on the business requirements, namely the requirements for the quality and reliability of power source. Edward R. Furlong [121] presented the relationship between reliability and cost for different types of UPS topologies (see Figure 5.26).

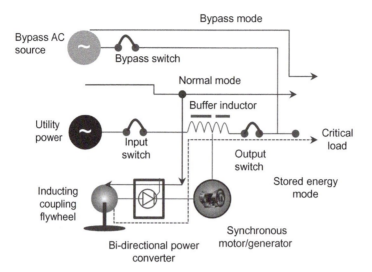

FIGURE 5.25

Rotary UPS topology.

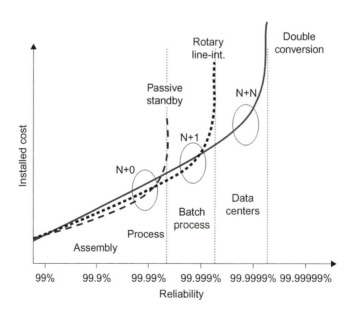

FIGURE 5.26

Reliability vs. cost for different types of UPS topologies [121].

5.6.1 UPS REDUNDANCY AND COST EFFICIENCY

When we come to select the UPS system for a particular business application, there are five key requirements that must be met:

1. Functionality
2. Maintainability
3. Fault tolerance
4. Reliability
5. Cost efficiency

Functionality means that the UPS must have all functions to protect the data center workload from all types of power problems. It may mean that online double conversion is a necessary solution.

Maintainability means having the capability to keep the UPS alive when a planned outage occurs, allowing for the performance of maintenance tasks.

Fault tolerance means the UPS system has the ability to continuously work without impact on the data center workload when some components fail. In other words, it is dependent on the reliability of the UPS, and we have to come up with a redundancy solution for the UPS system.

Based on reliability engineering theory, we know the relationship between reliability and downtime per year or per month. These are important performance metrics during operation. It is similar to Table 4.4 (see Table 5.7).

The reason to have monthly "downtime" in the above table is because a performance report is normally generated every month and very often the SLA will be reviewed on a monthly basis.

5.6.1.1 Configuration of UPS redundancy

If the business has different reliability requirements, we can configure the UPS system in four different ways as shown in the following:

- Single module system (SMS)
- 1 + 1 or Two UPS systems sharing the full load
- N + 1 or "N" for full load
- 2(N + 1) configuration

Table 5.7 No of 9s, Availability, Downtime per Year and per Month				
Number of 9s	**System Availability**	**Downtime per Year (mins)**	**Downtime per Month (mins)**	**UPS Configuration**
2	99%	5,256	438	SMS
3	99.9%	525.6	43.8	SMS
4	99.99%	52.56	4.38	1 + 1 or N + 1
5	99.999%	5.256	0.438	2(N + 1)
6	99.9999%	0.5256	0.0438	2(N + 1)

Single UPS supports the full load

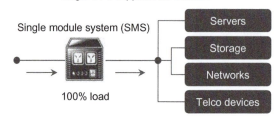

Single module system (SMS)

100% load

Servers

Storage

Networks

Telco devices

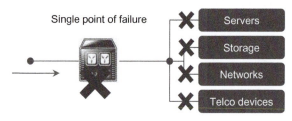

Single point of failure

Servers

Storage

Networks

Telco devices

If it fails, workload cannot be supported

FIGURE 5.27

Single module system (SMS) for UPS.

These different UPS configurations also represent different tiers of a data center facility. Let's investigate this topic in further detail.

5.6.1.2 Single module system (SMS)

This simply means only one UPS supports the full load (see Figure 5.27). The issue with SMS is that it causes a single point of failure if the UPS fails. The availability of an SMS system is below 99.92%. In other words, this UPS system can only achieve 2−3 9s system availability.

5.6.1.3 1 + 1 redundancy or two module system

One way to improve the availability of the UPS system is to add another UPS module into the system to create a 1 + 1 redundancy or two-module sharing system. Each UPS module can take 100% of the workload but it only shares 50% of the workload (see Figure 5.28).

As we can see in Figure 5.8, the UPS system has become very reliable, but it is not very efficient because most of the time, this system only works at 50% of its capacity and the other 50% is in idle mode.

5.6.1.4 N + 1 redundancy

In order to improve the efficiency of the 1 + 1 redundancy system, we can configure the UPS system as N + 1 redundancy, where N UPS modules carry the full workload (see Figure 5.29).

In the above case, N is equal to four, and each UPS module carries 25% of the total workload. Here, the capacity of each UPS is smaller than the "1 + 1" configuration in term of kW. Normally,

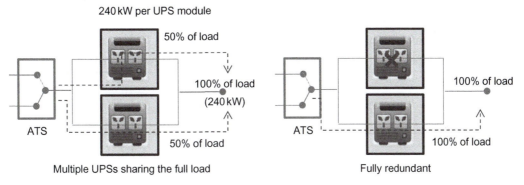

FIGURE 5.28

"1 + 1" redundancy UPS system.

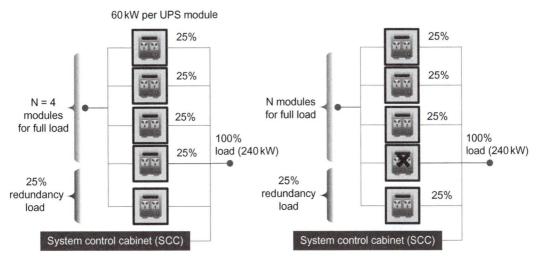

FIGURE 5.29

N + 1 redundancy UPS system.

the smaller the capacity is, the lower the cost is. In comparison with "1 + 1" redundancy, the N + 1 configuration has increased the UPS module's efficiency because all "N" UPS modules are operating at full capacity and only "1" is on standby mode. The system control cabinet (SCC) is a kind of monitoring system that manages and controls all UPS modules to make sure all modules are working properly. Table 5.8 shows an example of UPS loading and redundancy configurations. The larger "N" is, the higher the efficiency of UPS loading per module, but the lower the reliability or availability becomes.

Table 5.8 UPS N + 1 Redundancy Configuration					
UPS Redundancy Configuration	**1 + 1**	**2 + 1**	**3 + 1**	**4 + 1**	**5 + 1**
No. of UPS modules and type	2 × 240 kW	3 × 120 kW	4 × 480 kW	5 × 60 kW	6 × 48 kW
Critical load	240 kW				
Total UPS capacity	480 kW	360 kW	320 kW	300 kW	288 kW
UPS load per module	50%	67%	75%	80%	83%
Availability/capex/opex	Very High	High	Medium	Low	Very Low

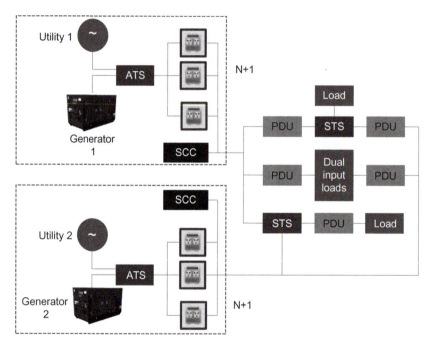

FIGURE 5.30

2(N + 1) UPS redundancy configuration.

With the N + 1 redundancy configuration, the UPS system cannot break down two modules at the same time. In order to increase the reliability of the N + 1 redundancy system, we can configure the UPS system as 2(N + 1).

5.6.1.5 2(N + 1) redundancy

Based on the TIA-942 standard, a Tier 4 data center must have a 2(N + 1) configuration. It consists of two "N + 1" systems, where the data center has two independent substations. This solution basically doubles the data center's infrastructure capacity (see Figure 5.30).

This 2(N + 1) UPS redundancy should have two utilities that feed to two subsystems. There are two ways to feed the data center load:

- Single feed
- Dual feed

With dual input loads, the data center power is fed from two different utility sources. Using STS, we can also feed the power from two different utility sources.

5.6.1.6 How to balance UPS availability and cost

Normally, a high availability UPS system is very costly. The aim of adopting it is because we want to support some mission-critical applications and increase the availability of the data center facility. Now, the question is, "Do we have other alternatives to balance the UPS system cost against the availability of data center?" The simple answer is "yes." There are some common solutions to balance the availability and overall UPS system cost:

- Divide the data center into different power zones
- Differentiate each power zone with different availability
- Scalable architecture (built-in modular UPS)
- Build small footprint for high power density per rack
- Ease of installation/hot-swappable components
- Parallel system for N + 1 redundancy

Among these solutions, the modular architecture would be key to balancing the UPS cost with UPS system availability. Suppose the data center facility requires 60 kW workload for UPS capacity; we could have three 20 kW UPS units or UPS modules in the system rather than one single 60 kW UPS module (see Figure 5.31).

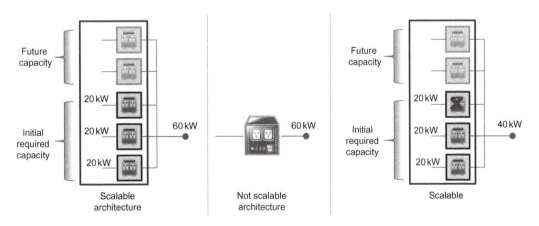

FIGURE 5.31

Build scalable UPS architecture with a modular style.

The advantages to have smaller UPS modules are:

- If one module fails, the data center still has a certain % of power rather than losing all the data center power. In this case, it has 40 kW capacity or nearly 70% of the total power.
- When more capacity is needed in the future, it can be easily expanded using a small footprint.
- It is very cost effective. It can reduce both capex and opex for data center investment.
- It can reduce UPS provisioning time, which helps the business increase speed to market.

Smaller UPS systems are normally applied for backing up workstations and telecommunication equipment. The power range varies from 700 VA to 2,000 VA. Most UPS modules within this range are rack-mountable UPSs. They are the best fit for backup at a rack level.

Now that we fully understand the UPS redundancy configurations, let's have a look at the unit of the UPS that forms the UPS redundancy topology, which is the UPS battery.

5.7 UPS BATTERIES

In Figure 5.16, we showed the double conversion UPS system. As we can see, one of the major components for the UPS system is the battery. There are three common types of batteries:

- Vented (flooded or wet cell)
- Valve regulated (VRLA)
- Modular battery cartridges (MBC)

5.7.1 VENTED (FLOODED OR WET CELL) UPS BATTERIES

The mechanism of a vented or flooded battery is releasing hydrogen through vents during normal operation; the electrolyte is sulphuric acid diluted with water (see Figure 5.32). It is the oldest battery technology. The common applications are cars and boats. The power requirement for this type of battery is above 500 kW.

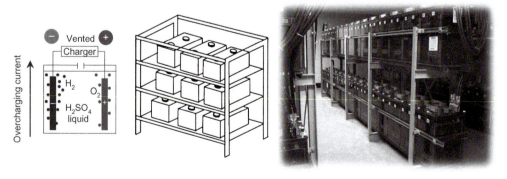

FIGURE 5.32

Vented (flooded or wet cell) battery.

Stephen McCluer [122] indicates that vented UPS batteries have following 12 characteristics:

- Nonsealed system for serviceability
- Continuously vents hydrogen and oxygen
- Requires periodic water replenishment
- Electrolyte stored in liquid form
- Usually too heavy to be lifted manually
- Transparent container allows inspection of plates and electrolyte level
- Operates at high currents
- Connected by large bolted terminals
- Stored in open frames or large cabinets
- Requires spill containment and hydrogen detection
- Typically 15−20 year life
- Usually considered part of the facility

Very often, this kind of battery system is installed in open racks located in a separated battery room, which has a dedicated ventilation system.

5.7.2 VALVE REGULATED (VRLA) UPS BATTERIES

This is most widely adopted UPS system. In contrast to a vented battery, it is a properly sealed battery, which does not allow any evaporation or adding of liquid. Therefore, it doesn't require a dedicated ventilation system. It is often installed in cabinets (see Figure 5.33). The life cycle of a VRLA battery is on average only 5 years (or 3−10 years). Typically, VRLA batteries are designed for below 500 kVA UPS systems.

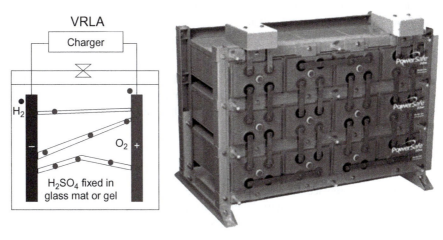

FIGURE 5.33

VRLA battery.

Stephen McCluer in his whitepaper listed the following 13 characteristics for this type of battery:

- Sealed system for electrolytes ("nonspillable")
- Hydrogen and oxygen recombine internally
- Opaque container
- Electrolyte is immobilized (absorbed glass mat or gel)
- "Starved electrolyte" makes it weigh much less than vented cells
- Operates at high currents
- 6- and 12-volt "Monobloc" for small and medium UPS
- 2-volt steel-clad modules for large DC systems
- Connected by bolted terminals or quick-connects
- Stored in open frames or large cabinets
- Pressure relief valves open under fault conditions
- Typically 3–10 year life
- Usually considered part of the electronic equipment

5.7.3 MODULAR BATTERY CARTRIDGE (MBC) UPS BATTERIES

MBC technology has just been introduced recently in comparison with the other two technologies. It is strings of VRLA batteries packaged into cartridges. The parallel-series architecture allows for easier installation and replacement. Similar to a VRLA battery, the life cycle is only about 5 years. It doesn't require a special ventilation system. The typical application for an MBC is a data center, network room, or office environment.

5.7.4 COMPARISON OF THREE COMMON UPS BATTERY TECHNOLOGIES

When we decide how to select one of these three UBS battery technologies, we have to consider the following issues (see Tables 5.9 and 5.10).

5.7.5 BATTERY MONITORING

When we discussed the issue of balancing availability and cost in Section 5.6.1.6, we suggested adopting a modular approach. This means there will be many UPS batteries. This has triggered another issue; we need a monitoring system to monitor the battery system. Battery life will be decreased by two major issues:

- The number of charges or discharges
- Operating temperature

What is the right time to replace the UPS battery? IEEE recommends that if the battery's capacity has dropped below 80% of its full capacity level or dropped 20% of its capacity, the UPS battery should be replaced. The 80% capacity line is sometimes also called the failure line (see Figure 5.34).

If you continuously use it after the "cutoff point" the battery will run in a deep discharge mode. Of course the opposite of deep discharge is called "shallow discharge." When the battery is running in deep discharge mode, it becomes very unreliable.

Table 5.9 Comparison of Three Common UPS Battery Technologies

Issues to Be Considered for Cifferent Battery Technologies	MBS	VRLA	Vented
Average Life Cycle	5 years	5 years	15 years
Maintenance cycle	Not required	12 months	3 months
Hazard zone	No	Varies	Yes
Acid filling	No	No	Yes
Separate room & ventilation	No	Varies	Yes
Spill containment	No	Varies	Yes
Site special requirements	Minimum	Medium	High
Scalability (runtime)	Easier	Moderate	Difficult
Portability	Easier	Moderate	Difficult
Weight	Moderate	Moderate	Heaviest

Table 5.10 Design Life vs. Expected Lifetime [122]

	Flooded	VRLA Large	VRLA Medium	VRLA Small	MBC
Designed life (years)	20	20	7–10	5	7–10
Expected life (years)	15	7–13	5	3	3–5

Instead of measuring voltage capacity for a UPS battery's life cycle, some battery vendors recommend monitoring the internal impedance of the battery. In other words, if the internal impedance rises 30% above the reference level or line, the UPS battery should be replaced.

The most reliable way to monitor the UPS battery's life cycle is to measure both voltage capacity and internal impedance.

For every 7.8 °C above the normal operation temperature (or 25 °C), the battery's life will be decreased by 25%. For example, suppose we increase the data center battery room's operating temperature from 25 °C to 32.8 °C; the battery's lifetime will be reduced from 5 years to 4 years.

Here are some important facts regarding batteries, which we should always be aware of:

• More than 80%–90% of all UPS faults are due to battery problems.
• Because of the series architecture, one battery fault can bring the whole string of batteries down.
• Within the first year, as many as 2–5% of UPS batteries can blow out.
• Within the first 4 years, the percentage of replacement batteries can reach as high as 65–70%.

Therefore, a battery monitoring system is mandatory for a data center although the monitoring system may cost as much as the battery purchase price.

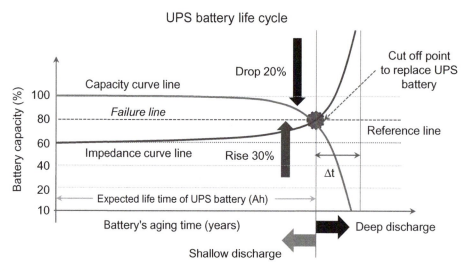

FIGURE 5.34

UPS battery's life cycle.

5.8 SUMMARY

Power is one of the major cost components for a data center facility. The data center power system consists of seven elements, namely the power panel (circuit breaker), transfer switch, generator, UPS, UPS battery, and power distribution unit (PDU), which we will discuss in the next chapter.

We started with recapping basic power concepts (current or amps, voltage, and resistance or impedance), including Ohm's law. Then, we focused on power panels and transfer switches along with generators. For the circuit breaker, we demonstrated how to configure and coordinate the circuit breaker properly in order to avoid unexpected power failure.

In term of capex, the generator is one of the big cost items. This chapter presented a flowchart to decide whether a data center needs a generator or not. Then, we shifted the focus to the UPS system; we discussed eight common power problems that are the major reason why we need a double conversion UPS for an enterprise class data center.

Furthermore, we have discussed five different types of UPS topologies or technologies and three different types of UPS battery technologies. Finally, this chapter discussed how to monitor UPS batteries.

UPS and UPS batteries are one of the major cost items for a power system. Having UPS redundancy increases data center availability. When we design or configure a UPS system, we should balance cost and UPS availability.

5.9 REVIEW QUESTIONS

1. Why should we use AC power to distribute the power in a data center?
2. What does circuit breaker coordination mean?

3. How do we select circuit breakers?
4. What is the power factor?
5. What are the differences between STSs and ATSs?
6. How do we decide the average cost of an unplanned outage?
7. How do we decide whether a data center needs a generator or not?
8. What is the process to decide runtime?
9. How many different types of UPS technologies are there?
10. How do we select the right topology for a data center?
11. How do we balance cost and UPS availability?
12. What are the most common power problems?
13. Why do we need double conversion UPS?
14. How many different types of UPS battery technologies are there?
15. What does a modular style of UPS architecture mean?
16. If our only requirement is to minimize the maintenance cycle, what is the best battery technology?
17. How can we maximize a UPS battery's life cycle?

POWER DISTRIBUTION UNIT AND CABLING

This chapter covers three major topics, namely the power distribution unit (PDU), data center power calculations, and strategies for reducing data center power, or increase power efficiency. In the first section, we discuss three types of PDUs: basic, metered, and switched. Next, we will discuss how to install power cables or power cable architecture and then we will illustrate the nine-step process for calculating data center power. Finally, we discuss how to avoid wasting power in a data center.

6.1 INTRODUCTION

When people talk about a PDU, they often use different names, such as cabinet distribution unit (CDU), Enclosure Power Distribution Unit (EPDU, Eaton), Intelligent Power Distribution Unit (iPDU, HP), power strip, or smart power strip. It does not matter what name is used, the primary function of the PDU is to distribute power, especially at the rack level via cabling within a data center.

In this book, we use the term PDU to mean power distribution unit because of its primary functionality. Based on the functionality of a PDU, we can classify it into three different types:

- Basic
- Metered
- Switched

All these PDUs have their pros and cons. Each type of PDU is applied to a particular circumstance or application with different costs. Let's walk through the details of each type of PDU.

6.1.1 BASIC PDU

With the basic type of PDU, the power distribution is very simple in terms of rack utilization. It is the same as a power strip attached to a rack. There are no additional functions for the basic PDU. It is quite economic in terms of the cost. The popular applications for a basic PDU are test, research and development, or a production development environment. Usually it is not a good option to select a basic type of PDU for a production environment.

6.1.2 METERED PDU

In contrast to the basic type, a metered PDU has a remote monitoring function. It monitors power usage. Some monitoring systems have additional probes or sensors to monitor temperature and the humidity of rack environment. The typical monitoring protocol for monitoring is the Simple Network Management Protocol (SNMP), which has been widely adopted in other network monitoring systems, such as for server clusters, data center networks, etc. Therefore, it can be integrated into the entire Data Center Infrastructure Management (DCIM) System. In comparison with the basic PDU, a metered PDU is much more expensive, but it provides extra value in information that can be used to reduce power consumption because the monitoring function can control the usage of the entire rack or the whole power strip or one individual power outlet.

6.1.3 SWITCHED PDU

A switched PDU has all the metered functions plus a remote switching function to control the power for individual power outlets. It has a precise control function for each power output. It can reboot any IT equipment remotely. The data center operation staff can use this function to isolate some intermittent faults. Therefore, costs more than a metered PDU. Actually, the switched PDU is the most expensive type of PDU.

6.2 RACK POWER DISTRIBUTION UNIT AND REDUNDANCY

Power redundancy at the rack level is very important. We have to design it properly. If the power redundancy is not right, it can cause many troubles during operation. We have already touched on the topic of PDU redundancy issues in Section 5.3.2. Here, we will unveil further details to illustrate some issues in terms of redundancy at the rack level (see Figure 6.1).

On the left side of Figure 6.1, there are three power points that are connected serially; the UPS connects to the PDU and the PDU connects to a rack PDU (or power strip). If one rack PDU fails, the rest of the servers will be out of power. In order to improve the availability, we have to add another rack PDU on the right side of the rack so that the rack servers can be connected to both rack PDU strips. This creates a slight improvement by removing the single point of failure at the rack PDU level. However, it is not good enough. There are still two single points of failure in this system at both the PDU and UPS level.

The way to improve all three power point connections is to add another UPS/PDU pair to the rack for power distribution. We can eliminate all three single points of failure and we can achieve high availability of power distribution (see Figure 6.2).

It may appear that the power distribution system has very high availability. However, we have to be very careful with just connecting dual system modules. Actually, connecting to dual power system modules doesn't mean that a power distribution system is fully redundant. It might seem to be redundant but actually, it is not. Let's walk through the following scenario (see Figure 6.3).

Assume we have two servers A and B. Each server's workload is the same, which is equal to 15 A. Consider connecting two servers to a pair of rack PDU strips that are connected with 25 A each. It shouldn't have any issues when all components of the power distribution system are

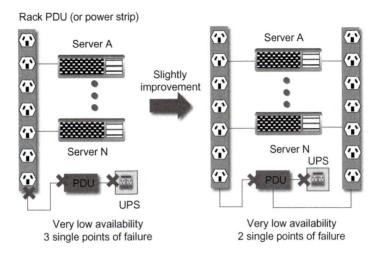

FIGURE 6.1

How to improve power distribution redundancy at the rack level.

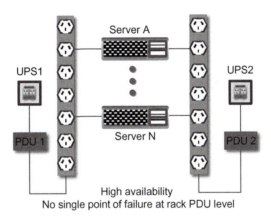

FIGURE 6.2

High availability of power distribution.

working fine because each server load will not exceed more than 80% of rack PDU (or 20 A) (see left side of Figure 6.3).

However, if UPS1 fails (see the right side of Figure 6.3, step 1), two servers on the rack of PDU1 will be out of power (see step 2 of Figure 6.3). As a result, all servers are trying to switch to rack PDU2. Now, the problem occurs. As we know, rack PDU2 only has 25 A maximum power load and the sum of the two servers' load is 30 A (or 15 A + 15 A). This will lead to a blowout for rack PDU2.

Clearly, this is not the right configuration for rack PDU and we will not achieve high availability for PDUs for this configuration. How can we improve this configuration?

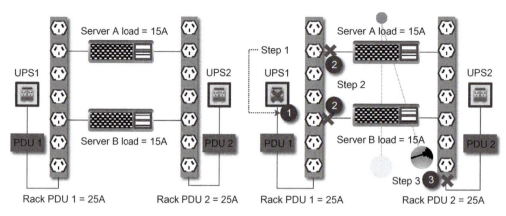

Can we achieve high reliability for this configuration?

If UPS1 fails, then server A and B will switch to PDU 2

FIGURE 6.3

False high availability configuration.

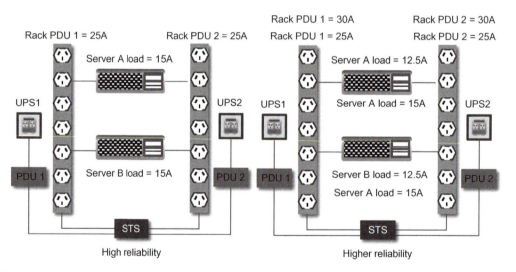

High reliability

Higher reliability

FIGURE 6.4

Improvement of false high availability configuration.

In order to improve the above false high availability, we have to introduce an STS between the two rack PDUs (see Figure 6.4). Consequently, when one of the UPS or PDU components fails, the STS can balance the power load between two rack PDUs.

Of course, if one UPS fails, the power distribution system will be at risk of a single point of failure at the rack PDU level again. Overall, the availability of the power distribution system has been increased dramatically.

If we would like to improve the power distribution system further and eliminate all single points of failures in the above case, the sum of the server load cannot exceed 25 A. In other words, each server's load cannot exceed 12.5 A. Alternatively, we can increase each rack PDU's workload to 30 A.

6.3 POWER FEED TO 42RU RACK

When we are powering IT equipment, it is important to coordinate between people who manage and operate the data center facility and IT professionals who allocate the IT equipment and design IT loads. It is important to map out which power cable to feed to which rack or how many power cables to feed one rack. Normally, the data center operation people do not know what IT professionals exactly want. Table 6.1 shows simple calculation for the power feed.

Note: In Table 6.1, we make the following assumptions:

- Assumed power factor $= 0.8$
- 1RU server draw $= 350$ W
- 2RU server draw $= 550$ W
- Blade Chassis draw $= 4,000-4,500$ W

Based on the above assumptions, if we would like to fully populate one 42RU rack with dual-corded 1RU servers, how many power feeds should we have?

Table 6.1 Simple Calculation for the Power Feed[1]					
Power Feed	**Details of Power Calculation**	**Available Power**	**No. of Blade Chassis (4–4.5 kW)**	**No. of 2RU Server (550 W)**	**No. of 1RU Server (350 W)**
240 V 5 A	$240 \times 5 \times 0.8 = 0.96$ kW	0.96 kW	0	1	2
240 V 10 A	$240 \times 10 \times 0.8 = 1.92$ kW	1.92 kW	0	3	5
240 V 20 A	$240 \times 20 \times 0.8 = 3.84$ kW	3.84 kW	0	7	10
240 V 30 A	$240 \times 30 \times 0.8 = 5.76$ kW	5.76 kW	1	10	16
240 V 30 A 3 phase	$240 \times 30 \times 1.73 \times 0.8 = 9.97$ kW	9.97 kW	2	18	28
240 V 50 A 3 phase	$240 \times 50 \times 1.73 \times 0.8 = 16.61$ kW	16.61 kW	4	30	47
[1]*Nameplate value = assume highest power draw CPU running 100% with full memory load running very low line condition.*					

Table 6.2 Power Cable Feed for One 42 RU Rack with Different Server Configurations

Type of 42RU Rack Configuration	No. of Power Feeds (240 V 10 A)	No. of Power Feeds (240 V 20 A)	No. of Power Feeds (240 V 30 A)	No. of Power Feeds (240 V 30 A 3 Phase)	No. of Power Feeds (240 V 50 A 3 Phase)
42 × 1RU servers (350 W)	10	4	3	2	1
21 × 2RU servers (550 W)	6	4	3	2	1
3 × 10RU blade chassis (4−4.5 kW)	7	4	3	2	1
10 × 1RU + 5 × 2RU + 2 × 10RU blades	8	4	3	2	1

Just WITH a simple calculation, we know that each 1RU server would draw 350 W. For 42 servers, the fully populated rack will need a 14.7 kW power feed. Here are five options that we can use to feed the rack. Moreover, if we replace 42 1RU servers with 21 2RU servers or three blade chassis, how many power feed cables do we need? (See Table 6.2.)

How can we check the power value for each IT component? One way to check it is to look at the nameplate value, but this is not very accurate. It is the highest power draw or maximum power. Another way to check the power draw at the rack level is to search the vendor's URL. Many major vendors, such as Cisco, Dell, HP, Oracle/Sun, and IBM provide calculation tools to estimate the power draw for different scenarios.

If you have mixed brands of IT equipment, you might have to run multiple tools to estimate the power draw. In comparison with the nameplate value, the vendor calculation tools provide more accurate power draw values.

6.4 DATA CENTER POWER CABLING INSTALLATION

6.4.1 TRANSFORMATION OF THE DATA CENTER

The traditional data center is constructed with a centralized approach. The main reason to build in a centralizing manner is because this approach is quite cost effective in serving the purposes of a telecommunication network. Today, many traditional data centers are converted to modern IT data centers. The issue with traditional telco data centers is that the power density of each rack is very low, less than 5 kW per rack. Quite often the data center runns out of power before running out of space because traditional IT equipment takes up more space than modern IT equipment.

In contrast, the modern data center mainly accommodates servers, storage disks, and network equipment. The architecture is based on the so-called federal model. The power density of each rack is much higher than the traditional one. For some blade server racks, the power density is as high as 35−45 kW per rack or over six times higher than a typical traditional rack. Subsequently, the approach to data center installation is different. Figure 6.5 shows different installation approaches between traditional and modern data centers.

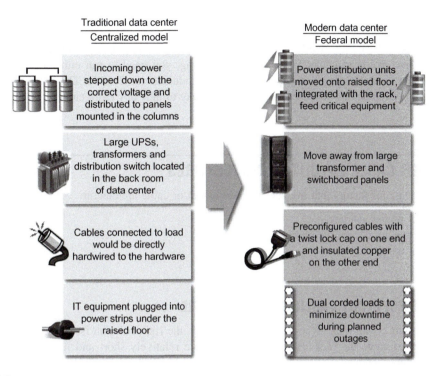

FIGURE 6.5

Traditional data center vs. modern data center.

Due to this move or transformation, power cabling installation will be also done differently. For the traditional data center, nearly all power cabling installation is a single cord under the raised floor. Today we can have either overhead cabling or raised floor cabling. Each rack has dual cords. Cabling design is dependent on:

- Size of data center
- Type of IT equipment to be installed
- Data center capex budget, especially cabling budget
- Forecasting for growth

6.4.2 UNDER THE FLOOR CABLING

With raised floor cabling, the data center looks very clean. No cable will be visible. Making a small change or connection between a major PDU and rack PDU is relatively easy. However, if the raised floor is opened up, it is going to impact other data center critical systems, such as cooling airflow. Furthermore, if the data center needs major changes or significant expansion, the data center may require additional construction for the raised floor to accommodate more cables. Otherwise, a bunch of cables could block cooling airflow. We will discuss the cooling issue in the next few chapters.

6.4.3 OVERHEAD CABLING

In contrast to raised cabling, overhead cabling is visible. Of course, it is personal preference, but some do not like overhead cable. With overhead cabling, you need to run either cabling trays or conduit to guide the cables to the equipment but the conduit is not flexible. The best practice is to use the preconfigured cables because there will be no way to hide any extra cable.

6.5 POWER CABLE LAYOUT ARCHITECTURES

There are three major factors that impact on cable layout or cable architecture:

- Location of power sources
- Size of power draw from the racks
- Distance of workload

6.5.1 STAR TOPOLOGY CABLING ARCHITECTURE

If the power sources and rack locations are not far apart, the right solution is to use a star topology or architecture to cable the racks because the cables are relatively short and it is relative easy to handle and connect them.

For example, assume there are six racks and each rack has a dual-corded load. Each rack is connected to two different PDUs or power sources. As a result, we will need 12 cables to run the power feed. The star topology cabling works well for a small computer room with a limited number of cables and conduits (see Figure 6.6).

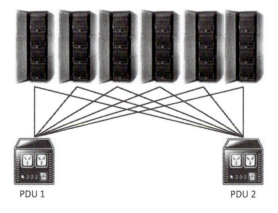

FIGURE 6.6

Star topology cabling.

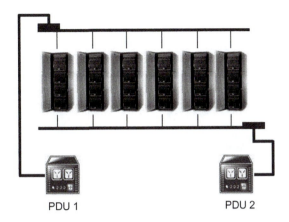

FIGURE 6.7

Bus topology cabling.

6.5.2 BUS TOPOLOGY CABLING

However, when the power sources are far away from the workload or racks, it is not a good idea to adopt star topology cabling. An alternative is to adopt bus topology cabling (see Figure 6.7).

In the above case, the cabling distribution system is only running two long cables and the rest of the 12 cables are quite short. Therefore, it is easier to manage, less expensive with regard to cable cost, and much more resilient to physical incidents. Here are a few points to keep in mind when you manage the data center cabling system:

- Cable maintenance should always pay attention to power cable connectors.
- Due to Moore's law, racks or IT equipment will be rearranged or reorganized very often. Normally, the change will occur every 18 months to 36 months in computer rooms.
- When we reorganize the current data center floor space, power cable failures will often occur.
- If you have the and infrared thermal scanner, you should inspect hot termination points.
- Thermal heat is a good indicator of either power overload or loose connections. More than 80% of electrical faults are not visible.

6.6 DATA CENTER POWER CALCULATION

Since the dot-com boom and bubble, many research reports have been published regarding data center power usage distribution. The pattern of power distribution varies from one data center to another. One of the widely cited research reports was published by Rumsey Engineers Inc. [123] and sponsored by Lawrence Berkeley National Laboratory (LBNL) in 2003. The report compared two case studies for two different data centers and concluded that computer or IT loads could vary from 38% to 63% (see Figure 6.8)[1] because of different configurations and workloads (see Table 6.3).

---

[1]We adjusted the term "HVAC" to "Cooling," "UPS loss" to "UPS loss/charging," and "Computer loads" to "IT workload or load." HVAC = heat, ventilation, and air conditioning.

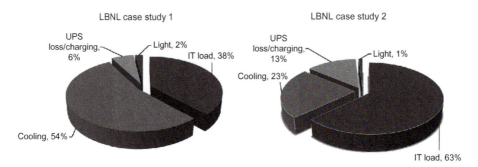

FIGURE 6.8

Data center power consumption breakdown.

Table 6.3 LBNL Data Center Case Studies for Power Consumption						
Case No.	Data Center Area (sqft)	Computer or IT Load (kW)	Computer or IT Load Energy Density (W/sqft)	Occupancy (%)	Total Power (kW)	Projected Computer Load Energy Density (W/sqft)
LBNL Case1	26,200	222	8	30%	580	27
LBNL Case 2	73,000	1,059	15	30%	1,700	50

Based on the Table 6.3, we can see that the major influence on power usage efficiency was the IT workload or utilization rate. The IT workload in the second case was nearly five times more than the first case.

In 2008, both APC and Emerson published whitepapers [125, 126] and provided a typical breakdown of how data center power was distributed in a data center. In the APC case, the assumption for the floor space was about 456 square meters or 5,000 square feet, the IT workload was 50 kW, and future forecasted load was 50 kW. Their result indicated that IT loads were only 36%. In contrast, Emerson's results show that IT loads were over 52% with similar assumptions (see Figure 6.9).

How can we calculate the real power usage? First, we should make these key assumptions accurate:

- Required workload
- Future workload (forecasting growth)
- Type of power redundancy

It is very important to make these assumptions right. If we overestimate the power load, we will have higher capex and opex. The unit cost for the data center facility or cloud infrastructure will be higher, TCO will become higher, and ROI will be lower. However, if we underestimate the workload, we will end up having power disruptions.

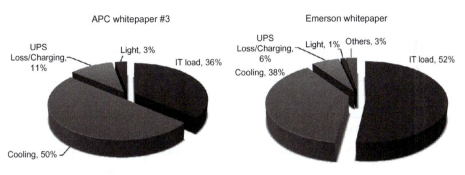

FIGURE 6.9

Recent data center power breakdown results published by major vendors.

6.6.1 PROCESS OF CALCULATING DATA CENTER POWER REQUIREMENTS

Now, our question is how to calculate the data center power requirements. This is a process issue. As we indicated in the above, the first step is to understand the business needs. Based on the business requirements or assumptions, we should be able to determine data center space and number of racks.

The second step is to make an assessment of requirements for both IT and non-IT equipment workloads; we have to decide on the size or power consumption of the following equipment:

IT equipment load:

- Servers
- Storage devices (SAN, NAS, iSCSI, and FC)
- Routers and switches (core, distribution, and edge)
- Load balancing
- Firewall

  Non-IT equipment load:

- Network nonitoring system
- On-site security
- Fire suppression system

  The third step is to verify and list all the above devices' power parameters:

- Type of power supply source (single or three phase)
- Power rating
- Voltage

We use the following example to demonstrate this process. Based on our understanding of the business requirements, we assume that a data center needs 1000 square meters of space, 120 racks, and the capability for 25% future growth (see Table 6.4).

We also assume that the average IT workload for each 42RU rack has the configuration in Table 6.5.

Table 6.4 Major Assumptions of Example

Data Center Space	No. of Racks	Future Growth
1,000 sqm	120	25%

Table 6.5 Required IT Workload per Rack

Devices	Unit Power Rating (W)	Qty. of Devices	No. of RU	Power Draw (kW)
Server 1 (1RU)	350	3	$3 \times 1RU$	1.05
Server 2 (2RU)	450	2	$2 \times 2RU$	0.9
Server 3 Blade Chassis	2500	2	$2 \times 10RU$	5
Storage Array 1	300	2	$2 \times 2RU$	.6
Storage Array 2	520	3	$3 \times 2RU$	1.56
Network Devices	100	2	$2 \times 1RU$	0.2
Total Rack Power	4,220	14	39RU	9.31

Table 6.6 Peak Power Overhead Adjustment

Workload for 120 Racks	25% Future Growth	Peak Power Multiplier Factor	Peak Power Draw	Peak Power Adjustments
1,117.2 kW	279.3 kW	1.10^1	1,536.15 kW	139.65 kW

[1]Note: This peak power draw multiplier factor has a variation. It could be 1.05, 1.08, or 1.15. It is dependent on the business application. For example, the business is a retail shop. During the Christmas season, the IT equipment usage could be well above the average usage. We can make this peak power multiplier factor even larger than 1.15. This is a business assumption.

Because the data center has 120 racks, the total power draw for the data center would be:

$$120 \text{ racks} \times 9.31 \text{ kW} = 1,117.2 \text{ kW}$$

The fourth step is making further workload adjustments with peak power capacity (see Table 6.6).

$$1,117.2 \text{ kW} \times 0.25 = 279.3 \text{ kW (Future Workload Estimation)}$$
$$1,117.2 \text{ kW} + 279.3 \text{ kW} = 1,396.5 \text{ kW (Total IT Load Including Future Growth)}$$
$$1,396.5 \text{ kW} \times 1.1 = 1,536.15 \text{ kW (Total Peak Power)}$$
$$1,536.15 \text{ kW} - 1,396.5 \text{ kW} = 139.65 \text{ kW (Net Peak Power)}$$

The fifth step is to calculate the UPS load. We assume that UPS efficiency = 90% and under the normal operation mode, the power needed for battery charging is very little and can be neglected. However, when the battery is partially and completely discharged, it will draw 20% of the UPS power load (see Table 6.7).

Table 6.7 Calculating UPS load

Total Workload	Inefficiency of UPS & Battery	Subtotal
1536.15 kW	10% (UPS)	153.62 kW
	20% (Battery Charging)	307.23 kW
Total	30% (Subtotal)	460.85 kW

Table 6.8 Summary of all Power Load Estimates in the Data Center

Power Draw Estimates	Power Load
Total Required IT load	1,117.2 kW
Future Load	279.3 kW
Peak Power Draw	139.65 kW
UPS and Battery	460.85 kW
Lighting & Others	25 kW
Total Power Draw	2,022 kW

Table 6.9 Summary of All Cooling Loads in the Data Center

Cooling Calculation Items	Cooling Efficiency Factor Calculation	Cooling Load
Chilled Water Power[1]	$2,022 \times 0.49\% = 990.78$ kW and $990.78 \times 0.7 = 693.55$ kW	693.55 kW
Direct Expansion Power[2]	$990.78 \times 1.0 = 990.78$ kW	990.78 kW
Total Cooling Power		1,684.33 kW

[1]Note: Regarding the cooling efficiency factor, we will give more details in the next chapter. Here, we evenly split the power load into two different cooling methods: chilled water cooling and direct expansion. Direct expansion is not as efficient as a chilled water system.
[2]A direct expansion air conditioning (DX) system is another way of cooling. It is different than chilled water cooling. It adopts a refrigerant vapor expansion/compression (RVEC) cycle to directly cool the air in an occupied space.

The sixth step is to estimate lighting and other power load. We assume 2.5 W per square meter so that we have the following result:

$$1000 \text{ sqm} \times 2.5 \text{ W} = 25 \text{ kW}$$

The seventh step is to summarize all power loads that we have just figured out and listed in the following table and then to estimate the cooling power (see Tables 6.8 and 6.9).

Table 6.10 Standby Generator Capacity Calculation

Load Components	Power Load	Generator Factor[1]	Subtotal
Total Power Draw	2022 kW	1.25	2.53 MW
Cooling Load	1684.33 kW	1.55	2.61 MW
Total Required Generator Capacity			5.14 MW

[1]*Note: The generator factor should be decided differently for different power draws. For the cooling system, many mechanical components, such as pumps (see Figure 6.9), are involved, so the factor would be greater. In this case, we use 1.55.*

Now we have the total power draw for this data center example:

$$\text{Total Power} = 2,022 \text{ kW} + 1,684.3 \text{ kW} = 3,706.3 \text{ kW} \approx 3.71 \text{ MW}$$

The eighth step is to tell power utility company how much utility power the data center needs.

This is the demanded power load for the data center, but when the data center operation people are asking for utility power voltage, the total power draw should be no more than a certain percentage of a threshold, such as 80% or 85%. This is dependent on national utility regulations. Therefore, the total power should be multiplied by this utility threshold factor. In this example, we use 80%. Therefore, the data center operator should ask125% more than the actual required power from the utility company. Here is the estimate data:

$$\text{Total Utility Power} = 3.71 \text{ MW} \times 125\% \approx 4.63 \text{ MW}$$

As we can see, the total utility power requirement is more than four times the critical IT load.

The ninth step is to calculate the standby generator capacity. When we calculate the generator capacity, we divide the workload into two components (see Table 6.10).

Based on the Table 6.10 calculation, the required generator capacity to support standby mode is 5.14 MW.

Overall, if we follow the nine-step process, we should be able to calculate the data center power (see Figure 6.10). The critical issue for power calculation is to make the right or correct assumptions. This impacts on the data center TCO/ROI.

We notice that the power of usage is not very efficient based on the total utility power (see Figure 6.11).

Ideally, all power draw should be consumed by IT equipment but due to power transmission and conversion, power loss is inevitable. For a green data center, we use Power Usage Effectiveness (PUE) to measure the energy efficiency of a data center:

$$\text{PUE} = \frac{\text{Power to Data Center}}{\text{Power to IT Load}}$$

Some people believe that PUE should not include HVAC [125] but others [128] argue that HVAC must be included in the PUE measurement. For many traditional data centers, the typical PUE is higher than 2, which is not very efficient. The ideal PUE should be equal to 1. If the PUE figure is very high, it indicates that there is a lot of room for data center operators to consolidate and improve data center energy efficiency. Based on Figure 6.9, we can break the power consumption items of a data center facility down into further detail (see Figure 6.12).

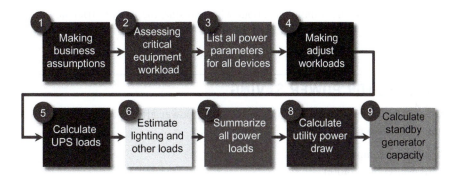

FIGURE 6.10

Nine-step power calculation process.

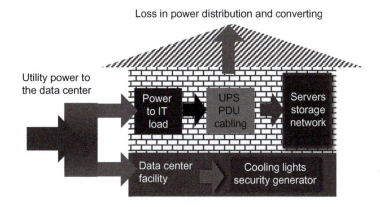

FIGURE 6.11

Data center power usage and efficiency.

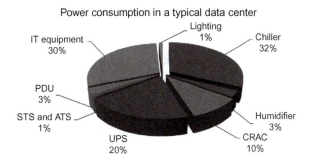

FIGURE 6.12

Power consumption of a typical data center.

The above diagram gives us some clues about where to start the power efficiency plan. We will discuss the issue of improving data center efficiency in Chapter 9.

6.7 STRATEGIES FOR POWER SAVING

What we are going to discuss here is mainly operational power efficiency. We will address power saving strategy from five perspectives:

- Redundant power equipment
- Improper power configuration
- Reducing capacity
- Data center server
- Inefficient cooling

6.7.1 IMPROVE EFFICIENCY OF UPS OR REMOVE REDUNDANT POWER EQUIPMENT

Based on the data center statistical analysis, the majority of existing enterprise data centers are running at less than 30% of their total power capacity. If we can improve the workload usage, we can improve data center power efficiency. The reason is that all power distribution has to go through a UPS for any enterprise size data center. If the UPS has double conversion, power loss is inevitable. The only way to improve the power efficiency is to increase the power usage or IT workload (see Figure 6.13).

Here is an example that can illustrate how much power can be saved. Suppose we have an average power density of each rack = 3 kW. For a detailed example of a power bill savings calculation, see Table 6.11.

When we select the UPS model for a data center power system, we should always check the TCO rather than just the purchase cost. The following example shows how to compare two UPS modules (see Table 6.12).

In summary, UPS B is $37,449 (or $51,246 − $13,797) better than UPS A per annum. If the UPS life cycle is 7 years, UPS B can save $262,143 ($37,449 × 7) over seven years without taking into consideration NPV. Today, real cost savings should rely on both capex and opex, which is TCO, rather than just capex or purchase cost.

6.7.2 IMPROVE POWER CONFIGURATION

When the utility power goes to the data center, we feed the power into the UPS. The traditional UPS has a transformer inside (see Figure 6.14). It is a step-down transformer with a lower voltage of 120 V instead of 240 V, which means power loss (see Section 8.5.3 for details on UPS loss).

In order to improve power efficiency, we can adopt two methods:

- Auto-transformer
- Higher voltage power output

These eliminate the power loss for the voltage step down (see Figure 6.15).

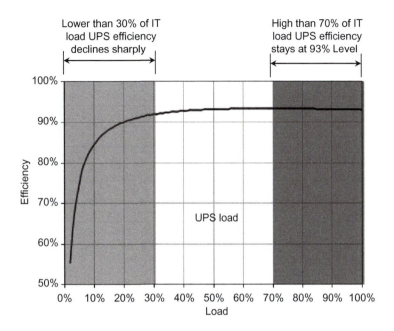

FIGURE 6.13

Improving power efficiency by increasing the workload.

Table 6.11 Example of Power Bill Savings Calculation

Assumptions	Calculation
	3 kW × 24 hours × 365 days = 26,280 kWh per year
$0.15 kW/per hour	26,280 × $0.15 = $3,942 per rack per year
200 racks in 700 sqm data center	200 × $3,942 = $788,400 per annum for the power bill
If we increase workload from 30% to 50%	UPS efficiency increase from 79% to 89% = 10%
Power bill saving	$788,400 × 10% = $78,840 per annum

   The solution of using an auto-transformer and running high voltage to increase the power efficiency by a certain percentage in terms of cost (2% cost savings for this particular case) is dependent on the particular UPS. Table 6.13 shows details of the calculations for two different scenarios for comparison. The cost savings is about $15,768 per annum if we use the same assumptions of power cost from Tables 6.12 and 6.13.

Table 6.12 Selection of UPS for Power Efficiency

UPS Dimensions	UPS A	UPS B
UPS efficiency	85%	95%
UPS power	150 kW	150 kW
Required power inputs	176 kW	157 kW
Power loss after UPS	26 kW	7 kW
Cooling cost to support extra heat ($0.15 kW/hour)	$17,082 per annum	$4599 per annum
Cost of inefficiency	$34,164 per annum	$9,198 per annum
Total cost of inefficiency	$51,246 per annum	$13,797 per annum

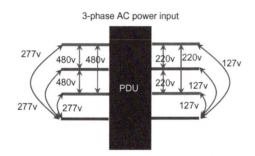

FIGURE 6.14

Example of PDU power input and output.

6.7.3 REDUCING DATA CENTER CAPACITY

For many enterprise data centers, being over capacity is always an issue because the IT budget is a yearly exercise. When a capacity planner is predicting capacity growth, overshooting is a preferred option rather underestimation because once an annual budget is locked in, it would be always easier to be underspend the budget rather than apply for extra funding.

In addition, if the IT capacity provisioning time is often longer than what should be, a data center manager would prefer to have an overcapacity data center to meet the extra demands of growth. Subsequently, most enterprise data centers are over capacity. Figure 6.16 is an example of forecasting overcapacity.

However, this doesn't mean there is no possibility that the actual data center power capacity could exceed the aggressive forecasting. What we discuss here is the normal case.

When we decide on the data center capacity, we design based on the capacity forecast. In addition, we may also have a design capacity ceiling. For example, the data center power capacity cannot be more than 85% of the total power capacity.

Consequently, this leads to a lot of wasted power capacity. What does this mean? It means inefficient up-front capex investment with power devices running in an idle mode. It wastes power or simply wastes data center opex. How can we resolve this issue?

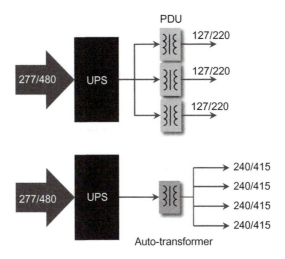

FIGURE 6.15

Comparison of traditional UPS and UPS with auto-transformer.

Table 6.13 Cost Savings Comparison		
Power Delivery Characteristics	**127/220 V**	**240/415 V**
UPS delivery voltage	480 V	480 V
UPS output transformer	No	Yes
PDU transformer	Yes	No
Power loss	9,000 W	1,000 W
240 V support	No	Yes
Cost of power loss[1]	$17,739 per annum	$1,971 per annum
[1]Using the same power cost assumptions as in Tables 6.11 and 6.12.		

Again, we grow the data center capacity in a modular style. When we are planning for data center capacity, we should forecast for a short time span, such as 1 year or 3 years rather than more than 5 or 10 years. It is always easier to predict next year's data center capacity rather than 5 years later.

If there is a long-term forecast capacity, we should constantly review and upgrade this long-term forecast prediction with Real Option Theory and Monte Carlo simulation, which we will discuss later chapters of this book. By doing so, we can increase data center power efficiency.

Data center server and cooling power saving strategies will be discussed in later chapters.

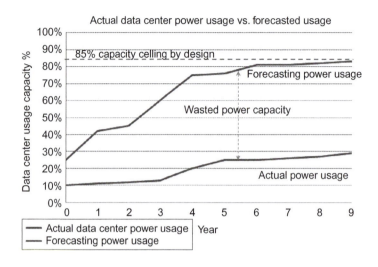

FIGURE 6.16

Actual vs. forecasted power usage.

6.8 SUMMARY

This chapter covered three main topics, namely the PDU, data center power calculations, and power saving strategies. We introduced three different types of PDU. The selection of a PDU type is really dependent on the business requirements, such as monitoring, security, and control. In addition, the architecture of a PDU and cabling is very important. Regarding power cabling, we discussed the pros and cons of both raised floor and overhead cabling. An efficient architecture for a PDU can increase power distribution availability. Of course this adds to the cost. The best solution is to balance the cost and availability based on the data center business requirements.

For the data center power calculation, we showed step by step how to calculate the power. It is a nine-step process. The critical part of this process is making the right assumptions, such as rack power density, future growth, and the inefficiency factor of UPS and UPS batteries.

Finally, we walked through a number of options to improve data center power efficiency. Basically, there are five different strategies to improve power efficiency. In this chapter, we only focused on redundant power equipment, power configuration, and overcapacity. We leave the other two topics to later chapters.

6.9 REVIEW QUESTIONS

1. How many types of PDU are there?
2. What is the main function of a switched PDU?

3. How can we improve PDU availability and reliability?
4. Is under the floor cabling better than overhead?
5. What are the pros and cons of under- and overhead cabling?
6. When should we adopt overhead cabling?
7. What is the right cabling topology?
8. How many steps are in the data center power calculation process?
9. Assume a data center has 150 racks and the average power density of each rack is about 5 kW. The size of the data center is 2,000 square meters and the forecasted future growth is 10–20% per annum in the next 3 years. How much power does this data center need?
10. How many ways are there to improve data center power efficiency?
11. Can we improve data center power efficiency by increasing data center workload?
12. What is the average data center workload?

DATA CENTER COOLING

Cooling is one of the three major concerns for a data center. As this is a major topic, we cover it over three chapters. This chapter offers a brief introduction to concepts of cooling or heat transfer, which are generally considered part of the fluid dynamics or mechanical engineering discipline. As many IT professionals are not familiar with these topics, we will illustrate them pictorially to enable grasping of concepts with ease.

First, we introduce basic terms and concepts and then we discuss cooling load; after that we present three cooling ingredients: pressure, temperature, and volume. We describe humidity and air distribution in Chapter 8 and different cooling strategies in Chapter 9.

7.1 INTRODUCTION

Cooling is one of the three keys or critical elements for any enterprise class data center. Without a cooling system, the data center would not work properly. It could quickly go bust. It is very important, but also costly. For some high-density data centers, the cooling capex could be as high as 50% of the total project cost. Therefore, if we can save costs in cooling, we can save large proportion of data center cost (both capex and opex).

7.2 UNDERSTANDING COOLING, COMFORT, AND PRECISION COOLING

From a cooling perspective, we have two different types of cooling. One is called comfort cooling. It is designed for humans. The other is called precision cooling; it mainly focuses on IT or other equipment. Principally, they appear to be the same, but they are different in many aspects. Let's walk through these two different cooling systems in the following sections.

7.2.1 UNDERSTANDING COOLING

What is cooling? Cooling is the process of removing heat (here, we have to emphasize that no one can destroy heat) and maintaining the right temperature conditions either for humans or objects.

Heat is one type of energy. It can be transferred from one body to another in varying quantities and intensities. The right cooling conditions consist of three critical metrics:

- Temperature
- Humidity
- Airflow

If the operational temperature and humidity cannot be kept at an adequate level in the data center, it causes downtime for the IT equipment and reduces system availability and reliability. Ultimately, it impacts on business applications running on the hardware platforms.

As we have already indicated in the previous section, cooling is the largest operation expenditure item (especially cooling opex) for a data center. One of the obvious reasons is that most enterprise data centers are operating around the clock ("always on") or $24 \times 7 \times 365$. In comparison with typical data center capex, the data center opex would be four to five times more than its capex. Moreover, many critical business applications require a redundant cooling system to be built into the data center facility. Therefore, if we would like to reduce the overall data center opex, we should not only design and build the cooling system properly, but also operate and optimize it just for the business needs.

7.2.2 COMFORT COOLING

Comfort cooling systems are designed for humans. They are operated in an intermittent mode, not $24 \times 7 \times 365$ all year round. The system may fluctuate with steep temperatures but people can tolerate rapid temperature swings. The primary focus is to maintain a comfortable environment for people and space, not for IT equipment. The amount of airflow (in and out) is moderated or limited. It is not engineered to be capable of regulating humidity and temperature within precise margins.

If we look for a sensible heat ratio for comfort cooling systems, it varies between 0.6 and 0.7. In other words, the system diverts 60%−70% of energy to temperature and 30%−40% to humidity.

If we use comfort cooling for a data center facility, the TCO of a comfort cooling system will be very high compared to precision cooling. Based on Emerson Network Power's whitepaper [129], "the TCO for comfort cooling is significantly higher − up to 60% more than a precision cooling system over the life of the equipment." You might think no one will use comfort cooling system for IT equipment or a data center but in reality, there are many micro and small data centers that are built within an office environment, which is within a comfort cooling zone. The reason for using a comfort cooling for IT equipment is the initial capex to build a new precision cooling system is too costly.

7.2.3 PRECISION COOLING

In contrast, the purpose of precision cooling is to cool IT equipment in a data center that requires precise and stable environment control. A precision cooling system has to work around the clock 24×7 and every day. It has to maintain a constant temperature and precise humidity and airflow because the IT equipment constantly produces a concentrated heat load and is very sensitive to both temperature and humidity changes. A precision cooling system is designed to achieve a 0.8 to 1.0 heat ratio.

7.2.4 ISSUES WITH NOT USING PRECISION COOLING

If the data center doesn't have a precision cooling system, it may trigger two issues: temperature and humidity. Temperature issues mean big temperature swings. Electronic devices do not like big temperature swings (very high at one moment and switching back to a very low temperature at another time). It could corrupt data processing and shut down the entire system. It may also cause latent defects for electronic chips and printed circuit boards. Sometimes, it may generate an intermittent problem, which is very difficult to detect or even simulate. Humidity issues may mean both high and low humidity problems. Higher humidity may lead to surface deterioration, condensation, and corrosion. Lower humidity may lead to increasing static electric discharge, corrupt data, and damage to electronic components.

7.2.5 HEAT SOURCES IN A DATA CENTER

Heat sources are the cooling loads. In a typical data center, the heat comes mainly from six different sources (see Figure 7.1). Here, other heat sources may come from external sources through walls, windows, and the roof.

The IT equipment may generate as much as 80% of the total data center heat. We can categorize these heat sources into four different origins or levels:

- CPU socket or core
- Rack unit level or individual equipment
- Rack
- Room

Traditionally, the cooling method is focused on room level but for modern high-density racks, this is not sufficient, so we change the cooling strategy from room cooling to CPU socket, individual server, or rack cooling.

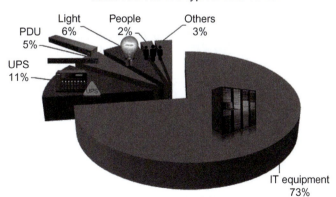

Heat sources in a typical data center

FIGURE 7.1

Heat source distribution in a typical data center.

7.3 TEMPERATURE, PRESSURE, AND VOLUME

Before we continue with further discussion of data center cooling in detail, we introduce some basic concepts and thermodynamic laws to refresh our knowledge. The triangle in Figure 7.2 summarizes information about these cooling concepts and basic laws.

7.3.1 HEAT

What is the concept of heat? From a comparative perspective, heat is the opposite of cooling. It is a relative term. Generally, what we mean by heat may include three types of heat:

- Sensible heat
- Latent heat
- Specific heat

Sensible heat is dry heat, which is generated by IT equipment. On the other hand, latent heat is associated with moisture. Physically, the heat is absorbed or released by changing physical state with changing temperature, such as water changing from vapor to water and from water to ice. Therefore, sometimes, it is also called heat transformation. When the heat is transferred between two substances, the transfer rate of each substance is different. Specific heat means the amount of heat to raise 1°F with 1 lb. of substance (or 4.1868 joules/gram °C).

If we make a comparison between a general office heat and a data center heat, we can find the ratio of sensible and latent heats is very different. The heat density is also different (see Figure 7.3).

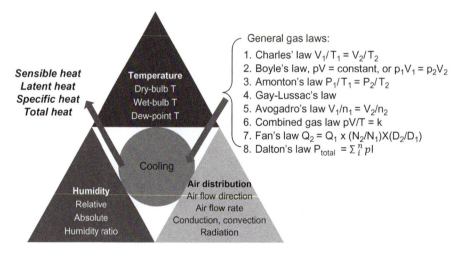

FIGURE 7.2

Basic cooling concepts and general gas laws.

Note: In Figure 7.2, T = temperature, V = volume, p = pressure, K = constant, Q = volume flow rate, N = rotational speed, and D = fan size.

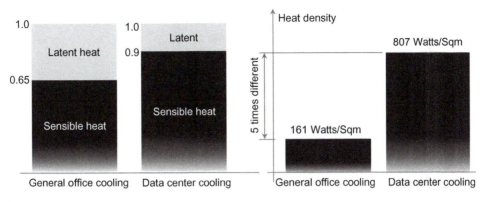

FIGURE 7.3

Comparison of sensible and latent heat and heat density between general office and data center.

7.3.2 TEMPERATURE

What is temperature? Based on Bill Whitman et al.'s [130] explanation, "temperature can be thought of as a description of the level of heat and also may be referred to as heat intensity. Both heat level and heat intensity should not be confused with the amount of heat, or heat content. Heat can also be thought of as energy in the form of molecules in motion." We can summarize Bill Whitman and colleagues's definition of temperature in the following two points:

- Temperature measures both level and intensity of heat.
- Temperature doesn't mean the amount of heat or quantity of heat, which is measured by British Thermal Unit (BTU) or watt (1 W = 3.41 BTU per hour). It means how much heat is contained in a substance.

Wilbert F. Stoecker et al. [131] express the term "heat" in a different way. They defined temperature as follows: "a substance indicates its thermal state and its ability to exchange energy with a substance in contact with it."

When we consider the temperature and humidity, we should consider three types of temperature:

- Dry-bulb temperature
- Wet-bulb temperature
- Dew-point temperature

7.3.2.1 Dry-Bulb Temperature (DBT)

The definition of "dry bulb" means the temperature is measured with a dry sensing element. It records the temperature of a substance in moist air (see Figure 7.4). In very simple terms, it is measuring air temperature with a normal thermometer. The method of measurement is just placing the normal thermometer in free air, but it has to be isolated from radiation heat and moisture. In essence, DBT is nothing but the atmospheric temperature.

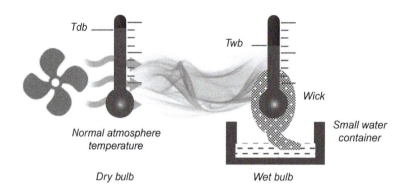

FIGURE 7.4

Dry bulb and wet bulb.

7.3.2.2 Wet-Bulb Temperature (WBT)

In contrast, wet-bulb temperature (WBT) shows the temperature of the air measured by a thermometer with a sensing element permanently wetted by a wick immersed in a container (see Figure 7.4). If the normal atmosphere comes through the WBT and into contact with the wick, the wet material will always absorb some moisture and release some heat. Subsequently, the WBT is always lower than DBT if they are placed in the same conditions.

In essence, the wet-bulb temperature always is cooler than the dry-bulb temperature because of the cooling effect of the wet wick around the wetbulb.

7.3.2.3 Dew-Point Temperature (DPT)

The DPT is the temperature point where the air cannot keep all of the moisture in the air and some water vapor in the air must condense or transform into a liquid water state. In other words, if the temperature is below the DPT level, the water vapor starts to condense. There are two ways to reach the DPT:

1. Decrease the temperature while the moisture or relative humidity is kept the same.
2. Increase the moisture in the air while the temperature is kept the same.

For a pure substance, dew point and boiling point are the same at a given pressure. If the DPT is equal to the air temperature, we will achieve 100% relative humidity. The DPT is the cutoff point before water starts to condense. Further details will be discussed in the following sections.

7.3.3 HUMIDITY

You may have a rough idea of the meaning of humidity based on the above concept of DPT. The term "humidity" means the amount of water vapor in the air. An amount of evaporated water is held in the air and this is dependent on the temperature of the air. This is also a relative measurement, which is often represented in absolute or relative humidity or humidity ratio. Therefore, we have three metrics to measure the humidity:

- Relative humidity
- Absolute humidity
- Humidity ratio

7.3.3.1 Relative humidity

The term "relative humidity" means the amount of moisture with a given amount of air, compared with the amount of saturation moisture with the same amount of the air under the same conditions of temperature and pressure. It is a ratio presented in percentage:

$$Relative\ Humidity(\emptyset) = \frac{Actual\ mositure\ content}{Saturation\ mositure\ content} \times 100\%$$

When the relative humidity reaches the saturation point, which is equal to 100%, the dry-bulb, wet-bulb, and dew-point temperatures are all equal.

7.3.3.2 Absolute humidity

This is the quantity of water vapor in a given volume of air. It is also called simply the humidity. It is a measure of the actual amount of water vapor in a particular sample of air. The unit of measurement is a mix ratio (gm water vapor/kg of dry air).

7.3.3.3 Humidity ratio

This is the mass of water that is interspersed in each kilogram of dry air:

$$w = \frac{kg\ of\ water\ vapor}{kg\ of\ dry\ air}$$

As we have already indicated in Section 7.2.4, both high and low humidity states will cause problems for data center equipment so we should have precise control of humidity. It is the essential part to increasing data center availability and reliability. We should understand how the humidity will impact data center cooling. There is a strong relationship among humidity, airflow, and temperature. Subsequently, when we are managing and operating a data center cooling system, we should pay close attention to the humidity measurement because it is one of the essential elements for a data center cooling system.

7.3.4 RELATIONSHIP BETWEEN TEMPERATURE AND HUMIDITY

When the data center air gets warmer or hotter, the amount of moisture that is held in the air is more than with cold air. The relative humidity will drop. We use the example in Figure 7.5 to illustrate this phenomena and the relationship between temperature and relative humidity.

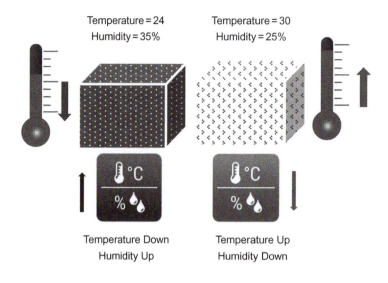

Temperature = 24
Humidity = 35%

Temperature = 30
Humidity = 25%

Temperature Down
Humidity Up

Temperature Up
Humidity Down

FIGURE 7.5

Relationship between temperature and humidity.

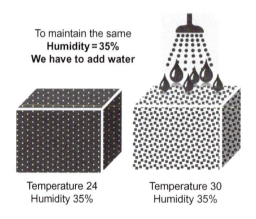

To maintain the same
Humidity = 35%
We have to add water

Temperature 24
Humidity 35%

Temperature 30
Humidity 35%

FIGURE 7.6

If the temperature goes up, the quantity of water goes up when humidity is kept the same.

If you want to maintain the same amount of humidity, we have to add water into the air. If we keep the humidity at 35% with different levels of temperature (in this example the temperature has been raised from 24°C to 30°C), the left data center will hold more water (see Figure 7.6).

Vice versa, if we decrease the temperature, water vapor cannot be held in the air; the environment has to condense or expel water vapor out from the cooler air. One of the typical examples of this phenomenon is when we bring an iced drink outside from an air conditioned pub during the summer; the condensation phenomena will occur on the surface of the glass (see Figure 7.7) because the hotter

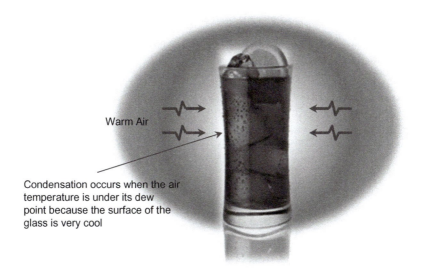

Warm Air

Condensation occurs when the air temperature is under its dew point because the surface of the glass is very cool

FIGURE 7.7

Condensation occurs when warm air meets the glass with the cold drink.

air encounters the cold glass surface. However, if we bring a glass of hot water out, the condensation phenomena will not occur. This is one of the intuitive ways to describe the relationship between temperature and humidity.

7.3.5 THE PSYCHOMETRIC CHART (HUMIDITY CHART)

If we place all the above metrics into one chart, we will have a so-called psychometric chart [132, 133]. This chart represents different properties of all three temperatures and relative humidity. If we know any two of the values, we can find out the rest of the values or the other two properties (see Figure 7.8).

From Figure 7.8, we can see that vertical line 1 is the dry-bulb temperature line, the horizontal line is the dew-point temperature line or marked as number 2, the angled line marked as number 3 is the wet-bulb line, and the curved line marked as number 4 is the relative humidity line.

For example, if we know dry-bulb temperature = 30°C and dew-point temperature = 14°C, we can find the wet-bulb temperature is around 19°C and the relative humidity will be 40%. The cross point of these four lines is their relationship point.

The American Society of Heating, Refrigerating, and Air Conditioning Engineers (ASHRAE) in 2004, 2008, and 2011 published guidelines for a data center to be operated within a recommended and allowable envelope of temperatures and relative humidity (see Figures 7.9 and 7.10).

For many major vendors, their equipment warranty range may be well beyond the ASHRAE recommended envelopes. The following example demonstrates HP Blade System c-Class Chassis' psychometric chart; the allowable operating environment for the c-7000 chassis is well beyond the recommended operation zone (see Figure 7.11). When the equipment is bought, it is important to

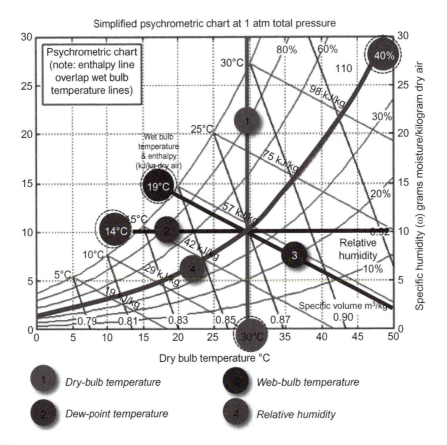

FIGURE 7.8

Psychometric Chart.

ask about its operation range or envelope. For x86 servers, HP, IBM Cisco, Dell, and Oracle should be able to provide this information. For RISC servers, Oracle, IBM, and HP will also supply this kind of information for their customers.

The purpose of having a psychometric chart is to achieve better control of data center temperature for IT equipment. How can we have a better control of data center conditions? The answer is refrigeration.

7.3.6 REFRIGERATION

Refrigeration is the process of removing heat, transferring the heat from one substance to another. From a data center perspective, it is transferring the heat from inside of the data center to the outside atmosphere. The heat cannot be eliminated or destroyed but is rather transferred, which means a substance's temperature can only be transferred from hot to cold. The process cannot be reversed. For example, you can transfer the data center's heat from inside to outside, but you cannot transfer cold from inside the data center to outside.

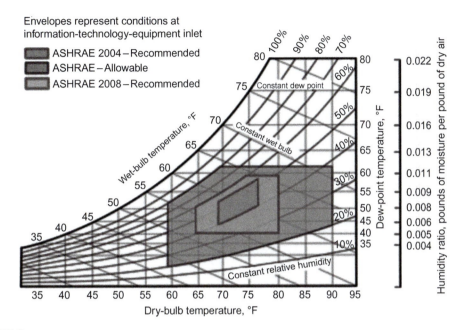

FIGURE 7.9

American Society of Heating, Refrigerating, and Air-Conditioning Engineers (ASHRAE) recommended temperature and relative humidity envelopes for data center, 2004 and 2008 [134] (US standard).

7.3.7 REFRIGERATION UNIT

In order to make it easy for us to calculate the cooling load of the refrigeration process, we have to first understand some basic calculation units and their relationship:

- Ton of refrigeration = the power to melt down 1 ton of ice within 24 hours
- 1 ton of refrigeration = 12,000 BTU/hour = 3.517 kW
- 1 bar = 100,000 pa (Pascal = pa) = atmospheric pressure on Earth at sea level

7.3.8 REFRIGERATION CYCLE

As we have mentioned above, refrigeration is the process of removing heat. Now, let's have a look at this process in detail. Based on the principles of heat transfer, the refrigeration process or cycle has four phases: three within the data center and one outside of the data center (see Figure 7.12):

1. Evaporation
2. Compression
3. Condensation
4. Expansion

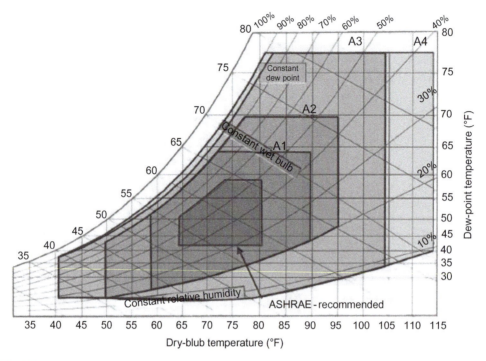

FIGURE 7.10

ASHRAE envelope guidelines for data center in 2011 (ISO standard).

7.3.8.1 Evaporation (state 1)

Evaporation is one of the two thermodynamic states. The common materials to absorb and remove heat are called refrigerants; examples include primary refrigerants like R-11, 22, 502, R123, and R134a, and secondary refrigerants including water, various brines, and antifreezes. Normally, the primary refrigerants have a lower boiling point, high heat of vaporization and high density in gaseous form. During the evaporation stage, the liquid state of a refrigerant is at a very low temperature and lower pressure (between −5°C and 7°C, 3.21 bar), which means it can absorb the heat from the data center, which makes the refrigerant boil and change to a vapor, which is shown in step 1 in Figure 7.12.

7.3.8.2 Compression (state 2)

During the compression cycle, the refrigerant is pumped into a compressor. The compressor loads with very high pressure that is greater than 13 bars or 13 times higher than normal atmospheric pressure; the temperature of the refrigerant is increased to a very high level, as high as 50°C, and it is sent to the condensation state or step 3.

Psychrometric chart

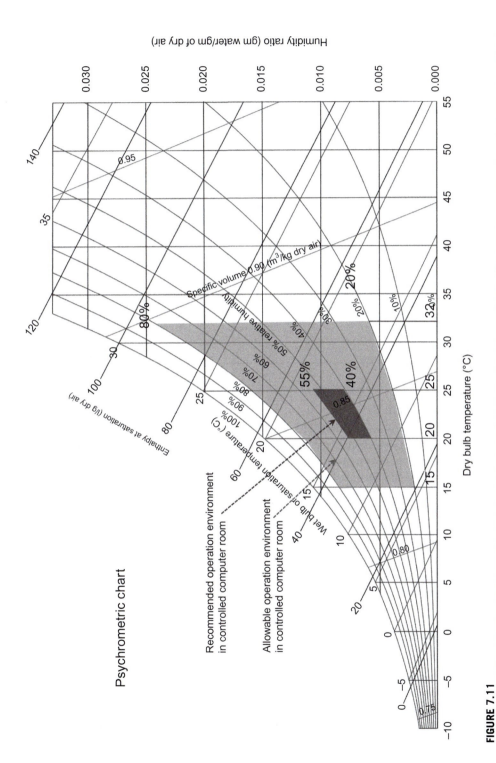

FIGURE 7.11

HP Blade System c-Class site planning guide.

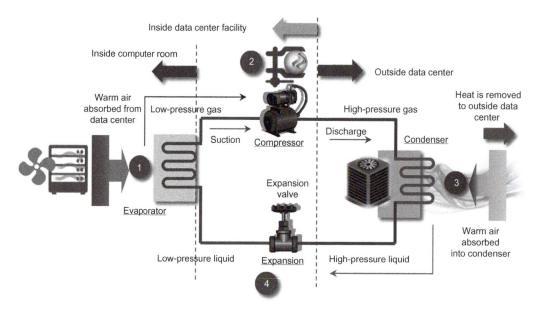

FIGURE 7.12

Completed refrigeration cycle process.

7.3.8.3 Condensation (state 3)

This is the opposite process to evaporation. The outside air is coming through over the condenser or high temperature coil. As we know, the outside air is much cooler than the condenser coil temperature so that the heat is now transferred to outside the data center. Therefore, cooled refrigerant with high pressure now has become liquid and is sent to the state of expansion or step 4.

7.3.8.4 Expansion (state 4)

This is the reverse of the process of compression. The function of an expansion valve is to increase the volume of refrigerant. By doing so, it decreases both the temperature and pressure, which comes back to the evaporation state.

These four states complete the full cycle of the refrigeration process so that it serves the purpose of removing heat from the inside of data center to the outside atmosphere.

7.3.9 AIRFLOW AND AIRFOW RATE

In Figure 7.2, we briefly touched on the topic of the fan law (or fan laws), which are associated with airflow and measure air movement (the unit of measurement = cubic meter per second or per minute). Without airflow, the refrigeration process would not occur. There would be no heat transfer. Let us investigate these fan laws in detail. However, before this investigation, we should first clarify the relationship among temperature, pressure, and volume by looking at the three famous gas laws in the thermodynamic process.

7.3.9.1 Gas laws

The gas law is also called the "general gas law." It defines the relationship among temperature, pressure, and volume. It is very important to understand these laws when we want to calculate a data center cooling temperature. Without understanding this law and its derivatives, there will be no precise control of data center temperature. We can present the gas law in the following equation:

$$V \propto \frac{nT}{P}$$

Here n is equal to Avogadro's constant. Three basic laws can be derived from this law:

- Boyle's law [temperature (T) = constant]
- Charles' law [pressure (P) = constant]
- Gay-Lussac's law [volume (V) = constant]

7.3.9.2 Boyle's law

When temperature is equal to a constant, the volume and pressure relationship obeys Boyle's law (see Figure 7.13), which means if we maintain the temperature at a constant level, the relationship between air pressure and the air volume is inverse. In other words, if the pressure is high, the air volume will be small. Vice versa, if the pressure is low, the air volume will become large:

$$V \propto \frac{1}{P}$$

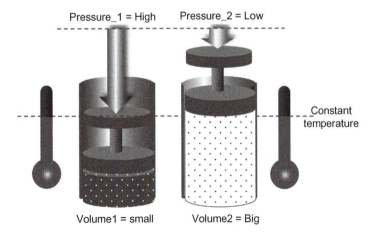

FIGURE 7.13

Boyle's law.

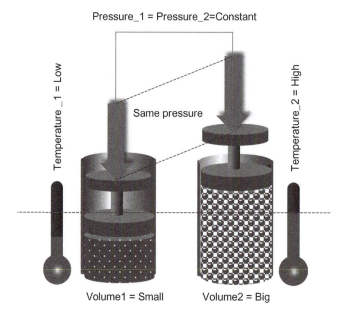

FIGURE 7.14

Charles' law.

7.3.9.3 Charles' law

Boyle's law explains the phenomena when the temperature is kept constant. Of course, we can also hold the pressure constant. If we maintain the pressure as a constant, it will lead to Charles' law, which shows that the relationship between temperature and volume is direct or proportional (see Figure 7.14). This means that if we increase the temperature value, the air volume will also be increased and if we reduce the temperature value, the air volume will become smaller:

$$V \propto T$$

7.3.9.4 Gay-Lussac's law

You may wonder what happens if we hold the volume constant. This actually becomes the third gas law, which is called Gay-Lussac's law. What Gay-Lussac's law says is that if you keep the volume unchanged, the relationship between temperature and pressure is direct or proportional, which means if you raise the temperature, the pressure will become high and if you lower the temperature, the pressure will also follow (see Figure 7.15):

$$P \propto T$$

7.3.10 FAN TYPES AND FAN LAWS

There is no doubt that without air movement, we cannot transfer heat. In order to transfer heat, we must have a fan. Fans are adopted by data center air condition systems extensively from circulating

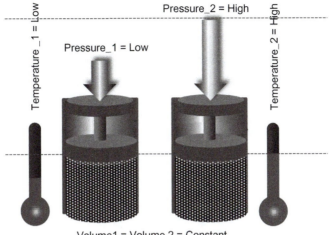

FIGURE 7.15

Gay-Lussac's law.

FIGURE 7.16

Typical axial fan and its blades.

air through to evaporators, condensers, computer room air condition (CRAC) units and computer room air handling (CRAH) units. We can classify fans into two types:

- Axial and propeller
- Centrifugal and radial

7.3.10.1 Axial and propeller fans

The principle of an axial fan is that it generates aerodynamic power by its blades and pushes the air forward (see Figure 7.16). This type of low pressure and high volume propeller fan is widely applied for heat exchangers, such as evaporators and condensers.

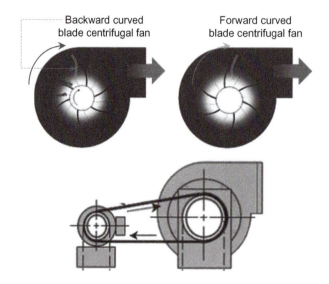

FIGURE 7.17

Centrifugal fan.

7.3.10.2 Centrifugal and radial fans

In contrast to the propeller fan, centrifugal fans can generate not only higher speed air low but also higher air pressure. Actually, it can create much more air pressure than a typical axial fan. It is most widely used in a data center's air conditioning system because it can effectively move large quantities of air with higher pressure. The centrifugal fan with forward-curved blades is commonly applied to low-pressure circumstances and the fan with a backward-curved blade and aerofoil type is often designed for higher pressure systems (see Figure 7.17).

7.3.10.3 Fan laws

Based on G.F. Hundy's description [135], fan laws mean that when a fan's diameter and inlet air density are certain, the air volume, pressure, power, and fan speed have the following relationship:

- Quantity of airflow volume (Q) varies as speed or velocity (V)
- Pressure (P) varies as square of speed (V^2)
- Power (W) varies as cube of speed (V^3)

On the other hand, if the speed is fixed, then air volume, pressure, and power will have the following relationship with the size of a fan's diameter:

- Quantity of airflow volume (Q) varies as cube of diameter (D^3)
- Power (W) varies as fifth power of diameter (D^5)
- Pressure (P) varies as square of diameter (D^2)

7.4 DATA CENTER COOLING COMPONENTS

Inside of a data center, we must have four controllable devices to implement the refrigeration cycle. Without these critical components, it would be impossible to maintain the right temperature and humidity in a data center. These four components are:

- Computer room air conditioning (CRAC) units
- Computer room air handling (CRAH) units
- Chiller
- Humidifier

7.4.1 CRAC

Normally, the CRAC unit is the floor-mounted equipment inside of the data center. It provides the refrigeration cycle function with cooling and humidity control systems. It can be installed in a centralized location or between the racks (see Figure 7.18).

7.4.2 CRAH

This unit is also located within a data center. The purpose of a CRAH unit is to circulate chilled water to remove data center heat. It must be used in conjunction with a chillier. The difference between a CRAH and CRAC unit is that the CRAC unit adopts chemical material that we have mentioned above, such as primary refrigerants R-11, 22, 502, and R123 to reduce data center temperature, but the CRAH unit uses a chilled water-based system to transfer the data center's heat. A CRAH unit must be used in conjunction with a chiller unit.

7.4.3 CHILLER

The chiller unit is located outside of the data center. It produces large volumes of chilled water that is distributed to the CRAH unit. It has the same function as a refrigeration cycle system (see Figure 7.19).

7.4.4 HUMIDIFIER AND DEHUMIDIFIER

The function of a humidifier is to increase moisture in the air of a data center to raise the relative humidity level. It can be a separate component or a part of a CRAC unit (see Figure 7.20).

There are basically three types of humidifiers for data center applications:

- Steam canister humidifiers
- Infrared humidifiers
- Ultrasonic humidifiers

Some other humidifiers, such as evaporator wicks, are designed for domestic applications. In contrast, the function of a dehumidification system is to remove moisture in the air (see Figure 7.21). Normally it is applied for residential purposes for air conditioning. Data center

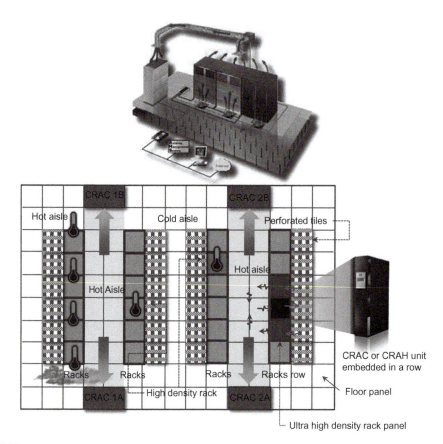

FIGURE 7.18

CRAC units.

hardware will normally produce enough dry heat because of the IT equipment. Therefore, it is unnecessary to have a dehumidification system. If you really need it, it may mean you have allowed outside wet air to invade the data center.

7.5 DATA CENTER COOLING CONTROL

CRAC units often have four different functions: heating, cooling, humidifying, and dehumidifying. Actually, one pair of functions is complementary to the other, as we have heating and cooling and humidifying and dehumidifying. Each unit can perform more than one function at the same time. For example, it can provide both cooling and humidifying. However, if we let these complementary functions occur in the same computer room (also known as "demand fighting"), it will significantly reduce data center efficiency. Some estimates show that "demand fighting" may lead to 20–30% less data center cooling efficiency.

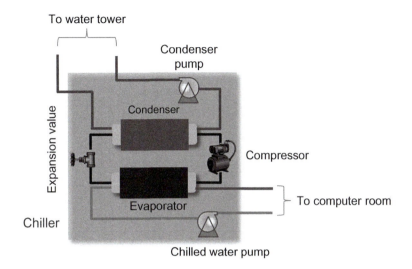

FIGURE 7.19

Chiller and CRAH.

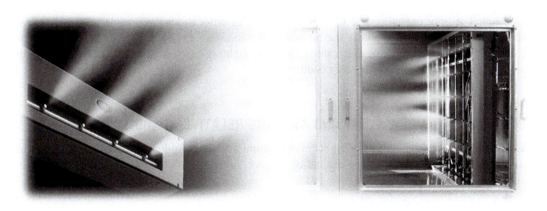

FIGURE 7.20

Humidifier.

7.5.1 DEMAND FIGHTING AMONG DIFFERENT CRAC UNITS

Ideally, all CRAC units within the same computer room should perform the same function. If somehow two CRAC units are against each other or complementary to each other, such as having one performing cooling functions and the other heating, it will be extremely wasteful. As noted above, the term for this phenomenon is "demand fighting." It is the largest contributing factor to energy inefficiency.

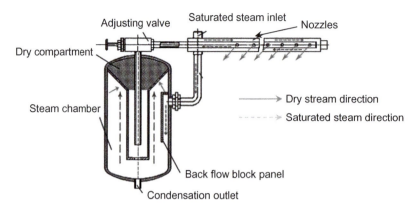

FIGURE 7.21

Mechanisms of a dehumidifier.

The following example demonstrates the issue of demand fighting. Suppose we have two CRAC units in the same computer room; one is operating at 23°C and the other at 21°C. If we keep the relative humidity around 40%, then we have to add more water into CRAC unit 2 because as the temperature is higher, more water can be held. However, at the same time, the temperature of CRAC unit 1 is only operating at 2°C less than unit 2. In order to keep the same level of relative humidity, the unit has to dehumidify the air or take the moisture out of air. This is a typical example of relative humidity control that causes "demand fighting" (see Figure 7.22). This is not an efficient way of controlling data center conditions.

7.5.2 ADOPTING A DEW POINT AND AVOIDING RELATIVE HUMIDITY CONTROL

The correct way of maintaining the right level of humidity and avoiding "demand fighting" is to focus on the dew-point temperature instead of relative humidity. With dew-point control, we can achieve the following:

- Use less energy to maintain the humidity level.
- Reduced demand fighting among CRAC units.
- A more cost-effective way to control data center humidity.
- Overhumidification won't be triggered by a large difference of return air temperatures.
- By keeping the same dew point, temperature fluctuation will have no impact on the amount of moisture in the air.

The bottom line is that by keeping the same dew point, the amount of water in the air will also be the same. So even if two CRAC units have different return air temperatures, unit 2 will not add more water or moisture into the air. It will allow two units to work together with more energy efficiency.

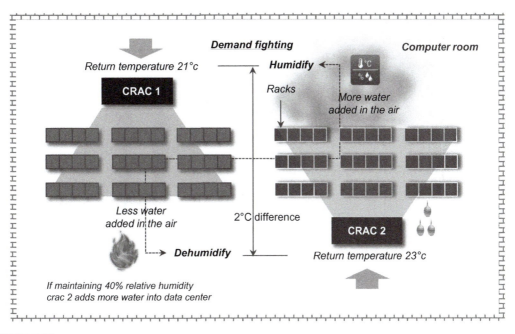

FIGURE 7.22

Relative humidity control resulting in demand fighting.

7.5.3 HOW TO CONTROL HUMIDITY AND TEMPERATURE

Outside the data center, the weather temperature and humidity fluctuates with different seasons, time of day, and weather patterns. An effective way of controlling both external and internal humidity and temperature will maximize the data center system performance or cooling efficiency.

The best way to control both internal and external humidity and temperature is to isolate the external impact on the internal data center conditions (see Figure 7.23). Some common practices are:

- No windows for computer room
- Seal door and opening cracks
- Minimize external infiltration
- Adopt vapor barriers to control moisture gain and loss

7.5.4 CONSEQUENCES OF UNDER- OR OVERHUMIDIFICATION

Within the data center or computer rooms, the relative humidity should be restricted within the so-called "dead band," which is in the 35−45% range (see Figure 7.24). The benefit of having operating humidity in this dead band is that the humidifier does not have to work. This means there is no energy consumption. If it is either over 45% or under 35% , there will a waste of both energy and water.

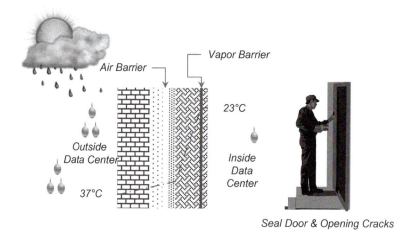

FIGURE 7.23

Control the data center's external and internal humidity and temperatures.

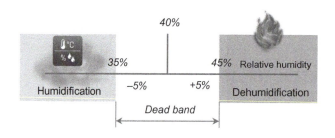

FIGURE 7.24

Setting the relative humidity within the dead band range.

Of course, all CRAC units should have the same configuration so that the data center operation can avoid a "demand fighting" situation.

7.5.5 MANAGING THE DATA CENTER TEMPERATURE

Again, as we have mentioned above, data center management is all about managing space, power, and cooling because these three components take more than 90% of data center operating costs and cooling is the largest cost component among these three. If we want to manage data center cost effectively, we have to manage cooling properly. This means that we should know how the temperature is distributed, how the data center environment is changing and where is the hot spots are. Actually, these questions are really questions of how to measure a data center's temperatures.

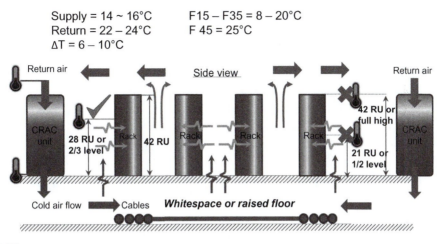

FIGURE 7.25

Rack level temperature measurements.

7.5.5.1 Rack temperature measurement

Some monitoring systems ask for the placement 10 or 15 temperature measurement points inside a rack. This appears to be excessive. The most important spot to measure the temperature of the rack is 2/3 up the rack, particularly if the data center is adopting parameter cooling, with a raised floor and perforated tile. The 2/3 up the rack position is an adequate level to measure the temperature. If it is too low, for example, one and half ways up the rack, it might not be the right rack temperature to measure, but rather the temperature coming from the perforated tiles. In contrast, if you place the temperature measurement spot too high, you might measure the mixing of the hot aisle and cold aisle, which is tunneling through over the top of the racks.

Therefore, the 2/3 up of rack position is a quite good spot to measure the rack temperature. Is it a good idea to measure every rack? It is really dependent on your resources but is not recommended.

Some places are so important for data center cooling temperature control that we have to allocate temperature measurements, such as the location of the mixing of the hot aisle and cold aisle. Now the question is where this most likely occurs. Normally, the hot and cold air will be mixed at the end of a row of racks. In order to get a full picture, we should also place a few measurement spots in the middle of the row (see Figure 7.25).

In addition, if a data center has one or a few high-density racks in the row, we should take measurements for these high-density racks (see Figure 7.26).

7.5.5.2 CRAC temperature measurement

To this point, we understand how to place temperature measurements at the rack level. However, it will not be sufficient to just place temperature measurements at the rack level for data center temperature control. We also need to measure temperatures at the CRAC level because the CRAC units are the source of cooling. The primary reason to measure the temperature at the CRAC level is that we can only control CRAC cooling air supply temperature in order to control data center temperature.

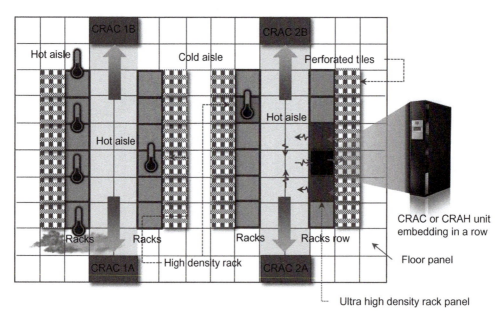

FIGURE 7.26

Place temperature measurements for high-density racks.

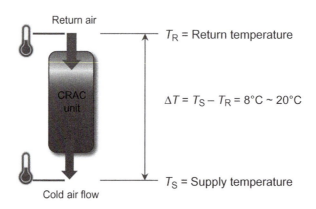

FIGURE 7.27

Measuring CRAC temperatures.

In order to control the CRAC temperature, we have to measure two positions at the CRAC unit. One is at the outlet, where we measure the supply temperature (or T_S) and the other is at the inlet to measure the return air temperature (or T_R) (see Figure 7.27).

The desired temperature gap between supply temperature T_S and return temperature T_R is around 8°C to 20°C. Some vendors [140] suggest that by eliminating hot and cold air

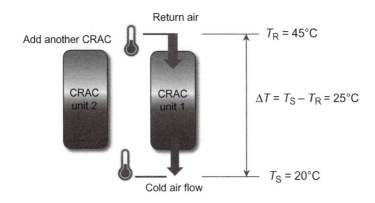

FIGURE 7.28

Not enough cooling air when $\Delta T > 25°C$.

Class	IT Equipment	Environment Control
Table 7.1 ASHRAE Thermal Guidelines		
A1	Enterprise Server, storage products	Tightly Control
A2	Volume servers, storage products, personal computers, workstations	Some Control
A3	Volume servers, storage products, personal computers, workstations	Some Control
A4	Volume servers, storage products, personal computers, workstations	Some Control

contamination (mixing, leaking, and bypassing) both supply and return air temperature can be increased by 5 or 6°C and the ΔT can be controlled at around 10°C.

If the ΔT is equal to only around 1 or 2°C, the CRAC unit should be turned off because the CRAC unit is not making too much of a difference and not working effectively in terms of cooling the computer room of a data center.

In contrast, if the ΔT is greater than 25°C, for example the supply temperature $T_S = 20°C$ and return temperature $T_R = 45°C$, it might indicate that there is not enough cooling in the data center. Perhaps the data center needs to add another CRAC unit (see Figure 7.28).

7.5.5.3 ASHRAE thermal guidelines for controlling temperature

If we refer to the Figure 7.9, the ASHRAE envelope guidelines for data centers in 2011, we can find ASHRAE classified four classes of IT equipment and corresponding control (see Table 7.1).

Based on the above table, the classification from A2 to A4 looks identical, but there are some details that spell out how to break down between these three classes. For a data center application, we will only focus on the A1 class.

ASHRAE's recommendation is quite conservative. As we can see from Table 7.2, the recommended dew point should be around about the 10 degree range. This does not mean that the data

Class	Humidity Range	Dry-Bulb Temperature	Maximum Dew-Point Temperature
		Allowable	
A1	20%–80% RH	15–32°C	17°C
A2	20%–80% RH	10–35°C	21°C
A3	8%–85% RH	5–40°C	24°C
A4	8%–90% RH	5–45°C	24°C
		Recommended	
A1–A4	5.5–15°C Dew Point	18–27°C	

Table 7.2 Details of ASHRAE Recommended and Allowable Thermal Control

center temperature can have a sudden swing between 5.5 and 15°C (see Table 7.2). As noted in Section 7.2.4, IT equipment does not like rapid temperature and humidity swings. Therefore, we have to have vigorous control of both temperature and humidity so that the data center can avoid big temperature and humidity fluctuations.

7.5.6 MAKING TEMPERATURE CHANGES BASED ON THE HEAT TRANSFER EQUATION

When heat is transferred from one substance to another, it has three different ways of moving heat:

- Conduction
- Convection
- Radiation

"Conduction" heat transfer is when one body directly touches another. "Convection" heat transfer is moving heat by a fluid medium to carry heat from one body to another and "radiation" is transferring heat by infrared wave.

If an air-conditioning system is designed to reduce the temperature of a data center, it will use the convection mechanism to transfer heat. The fluid medium is the air. Based on the gas laws, we will have the following equation:

$$Q = \rho \times V \times C_p \times \Delta T$$

- Q = the amount of heat transferred (kW, joule/hr or BTU/hr)
- 1 kJ/hr = 0.9478171 BTU per hr, 1 kW = 3600 kJ/hr
- V = velocity of air movement (cubic meter of air per minute or M^3 per min)
- ρ = density of sir (kg/m^3)
- ΔT = Temperature difference within the rack
- C_P = Specific heat of air (kJ/kg °C)

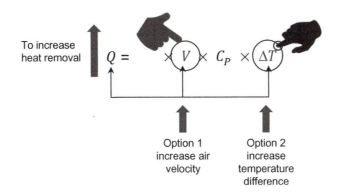

To increase
heat removal

$$Q = \quad \times \left(V\right) \times C_P \times \left(\Delta T\right)$$

Option 1
increase air
velocity

Option 2
increase
temperature
difference

FIGURE 7.29

Increasing heat removal by increasing air movement and temperature difference.

From Figure 7.29, we see that the $C_P = 1.0$ kJ/kg °C if the air is under the normal atmospheric pressure $p = 1.013$ bar and the value of the air density ρ is also moving within a very small range even when the atmosphere temperature has a large variation.

Subsequently, we will have two options to increase the efficiency of heat transfer, which are:

1. Increasing the temperature difference
2. Increasing the velocity of air movement

Both options require energy consumption, which will increase opex. Therefore excessive airflow speed and temperature differentiation is not economically sound.

For example, based on the fan laws, we know that power consumption and fan speed is a cubic relationship. If we reduce fan speed by 10%, we can save 27.1% in power. If we reduce fan speed by 20%, we can save 49% in power. Furthermore, if we use only 50% of the original fan speed, the power usage is only 12.5% of the original consumption.

7.5.7 FIVE DIFFERENT TECHNOLOGIES FOR REMOVAL OF DATA CENTER HEAT

Tony Evans from APC published whitepapers in 2004 and 2012 [139] regarding different air conditioning technologies. In the whitepaper published in 2004, Evans summarized the five basic IT environment heat removal methods or techniques.

7.5.7.1 Air cooled DX system (two piece)

The air-cooled DX system has been widely adopted for the IT environment. It is also referred to as a split air-conditioning system. It is very popular for many small and medium computer rooms. The letters of DX stand for Direct Expansion. The system consists of two components. One is located inside of a data center or a computer room, and is also named a CRAC unit. The other piece, the condensing coil is located outside of the data center (see Figure 7.30).

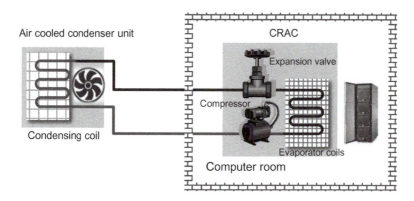

FIGURE 7.30

Air-cooled DX system.

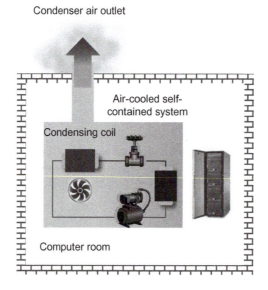

FIGURE 7.31

Air-cooled self-contained system.

7.5.7.2 Air-cooled self-contained system (one piece)

An air-cooled self-contained system is where all components of the refrigeration cycle are compacted within one unit, but the exhaust air is routed away from the data center to the outside or into an unconditioned space so that the system can provide effective cooling. The air that is cooling the condensing coil should be supplied from outside the data center. Otherwise, it will create a vacuum condition and suck the warm air into the data center. Normally it has very limited cooling capacity (up to 15 kW) (see Figure 7.31).

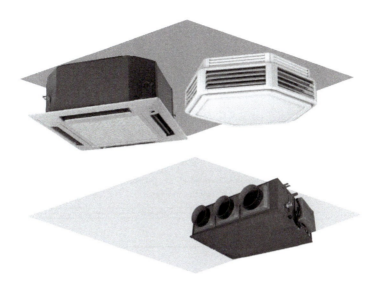

FIGURE 7.32

Different types of ceiling mounted cooling systems.

7.5.7.3 Ceiling mounted system

The technology of a ceiling mounted cooling system can be either DX, self-contained, or glycol cooling. It is basically a different installation rather than a different way of cooling. The cooling device is very small and is mounted on the ceiling (see Figure 7.32).

7.5.7.4 Glycol-cooled system

The glycol-cooled system is similar to the air-cooled self-contained one, where all refrigeration cycle components are enclosed in one unit, including the heat exchanger component. The heat exchange medium is the glycol, which is similar to automobile anti-freeze, which mixes water and ethylene glycol. Glycol can absorb much more heat than air. A system pump circulates glycol liquid and makes sure the warmer glycol is transported from the CRAC unit to an outdoor fluid cooler. Heat is removed by outside atmosphere air, which is fan-forced through the fluid cooler coil unit (see Figure 7.33). The glycol-cooled system is quite popular for many small- and medium-size data centers.

7.5.7.5 Water-cooled system

A water-cooled system is similar to a glycol-cooled one, where all refrigeration cycle components are packed into one unit and located inside a data center (see Figure 7.34).

However, in contrast to the glycol system, it has two different features:

- The heat exchange medium is water instead of glycol.
- Heat is transferred to outside atmosphere by a cooling tower rather than a fluid cooler.

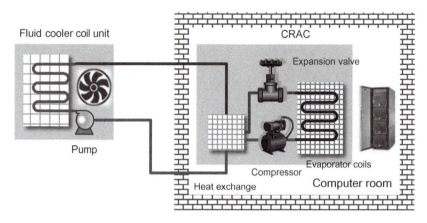

FIGURE 7.33

Glycol-cooled system.

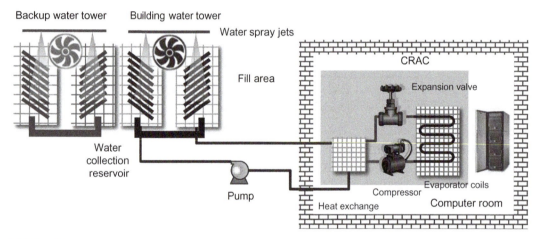

FIGURE 7.34

Water-cooled system.

This is widely adopted by all sizes of data centers. Normally, it is attached to a building cooling tower and another cooling tower is added for backup purposes or to increase cooling system reliability.

7.5.7.6 Chilled water system

For a chilled water system, all components to perform the refrigeration cycle are built in to a unit called a water chiller. In comparison with other cooling technologies, it moves all refrigeration cycle components out of the data center (see Figure 7.35).

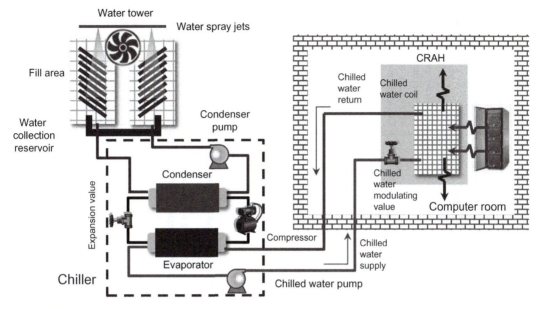

FIGURE 7.35

Chilled water system.

The aim of a chiller is to produce chilled water. Normally, the temperature of chilled water is around 8°C or even lower. Once the chilled water is created, the chilled water is pumped into computer room air handler (CRAH) units that are located inside a computer room. In comparison with a water-cooled system, the chilled water system produces lower temperature water. The way of removing heat is not to supply cooling air but rather to suck the warm air into chilled water coils filled with circulating chilled water. When the air flows out of the chilled water coils, which are inside of the CRAH unit, the air is cooler. At the inside of a chiller, the method of heat rejection is similar to a water-cooled system. The system is normally used for medium and large data centers.

In summary, we list all cooling systems' advantages and disadvantages in Table 7.3.

Based on the above selection criteria, we should be able to make the right decision to select the right cooling technology for different sizes of data centers that have a specified workload (see Table 7.4).

The classification of data center size and workload is just based on rules of thumb.

7.6 SUMMARY

At the beginning of this chapter, we made a comparison between two different types of cooling, comfort and precision, and then we discussed the heat sources of a data center. After discussing data center heat issues, we introduced three key concepts of thermal dynamics, heat, temperature, and humidity, as well as their relationship. One of the key concepts for data center cooling is that heat

Table 7.3 Cooling Technologies Comparison

Cooling Technologies	Advantages	Disadvantages	Applications
Air-Cooled DX	1. Lowest TCO 2. Easiest to maintain	1. Refrigerant piping must be installed 2. The pipe cannot be run very long, less than 60 m 3. Multiple CRAC units impossible for one system 4. It is a one-to-one relationship	For wiring closets, small & medium data centers with moderate availability requirements
Air-Cooled Self-Contained	1. Lowest installation cost 2. Very reliable 3. Portable 4. Easy and quick to be adopt	1. Smaller heat removal capacity 2. Requires ductwork 3. Less energy efficient 4. Not for precision cooling application	For wiring closets, laboratory environment with moderate availability requirements Use to fix hot spots in data center
Celling Mounted	Do not need IT floor space	Complex installation and maintenance	Cooling 3-17 kW IT equipment
Glycol Cooled	1. High reliability 2. Not much space required 3. Glycol pipes can be longer than DX 4. It is capable of supporting several CRAC units with one outdoor unit 5. When temperature drops, it can directly flow to specially installed economizer coil, which provides "free cooling." 6. Reducing opex	1. Requires additional components (pump package, valves) 2. Increased capex in comparison with DX 3. Additional glycol maintenance required	For small to medium data center with moderate availability requirements
Water Cooled	1. The system has the highest reliability 2. Condenser water can easily be run long distance 3. One outdoor cooling tower can support multiple CRAC units 4. Less expensive than chilled water system	1. High initial capex for cooling tower, pump, and pumping installation 2. Very high maintenance cost due to frequently cleaning and water treatment requirements 3. If no dedicated cooling tower, it may reduce system reliability	In conjunction with building cooling system for small, medium, and large data centers with moderate to high availability requirements
Chilled Water	1. CRAH is often less expensive and capable of removing a large amount of heat with the same footprint of air conditioners 2. Chilled water pipe loops can run very long distances 3. One cooling tower and one chiller unit can support several CRAH units 4. It can be extremely reliable 5. For large installations, the unit cost (per kW) is the lowest	1. It has the highest capex cost for installation below 100 kW of workload 2. CRAH unit removes more moisture than CRAC unit so it needs extra humidifier	In conjunction with other systems in medium and large data center with moderate to high availability requirements or high availability dedicated solution in large enterprise data centers

Data Center Size and Workload/ Cooling System	Air-Cooled DX		Air-Cooled Self-Contained		Glycol Cooled		Water Cooled		Chilled Water	
	Floor	Ceiling	Floor	Ceiling	Floor	Ceiling	Floor	Ceiling	Floor	Ceiling
Wiring closet or micro data center 1−5 rack, 1−15 kW	√	√	√	√	X	X	NA	NA	X	√*
Computer room 1−10 racks 1−30 kW	√	√	√	√	√	√	NA	NA	√	√*
Small data center 5−20 racks 10−100 kW	√	√	√	√	√	√	NA	NA	√	√*
Medium data center 10−100 racks 50−500 kW	√	X	X	X	√	X	√	X	√	X
Large data center >100 racks, >500 kW	X	X	X	X	√	X	√	X	√	X

Table 7.4 Making the Right Decision to Select the Right Cooling System

Note: If the building chilled water system is very close to the wiring closet or computer rooms.

can never be destroyed but only transferred from one place to another. Moreover, we discussed the psychometric chart (or humidity chart), the ASHRAE standard, and the four stages of the refrigeration cycle.

Further, we spelled out the three gas laws as well as the fan laws. We laid out the relationship between the three gas laws, which is the relationship between volume, temperature, and pressure. These laws and relationships are the foundation of the refrigeration cycle.

In addition, we also described key cooling components that make up of a data center cooling system: CRAC units, CRAH units, chillers, and humidifiers. Among these cooling elements, the chiller is the critical element for many enterprise data center cooling systems.

Finally, we discussed two essential cooling topics, data center cooling control and temperature management, along with five different technical options to select from when choosing the right cooling system. These two issues will ultimately impact the bottom line of both capex and opex of a data center.

7.7 REVIEW QUESTIONS

1. What is the difference between comfort and precision cooling?
2. Why does a data center need precision cooling?
3. Can we use comfort cooling for a data center?
4. What are the key elements for controlling data center heat?
5. What is the best way to control data center temperature, dry bulb, wet bulb, or dew point?
6. What is the relative and absolute humidity?
7. What are the gas laws?
8. If we reduce fan speed by 10%, how much power can we save?
9. Do the majority of server vendors provide a psychometric chart for their equipment?
10. What are the four stages of the refrigeration cycle?
11. What is the most costly and important component in a data center cooling system?
12. How many technologies are there to remove data center heat?
13. What is the most popular technology for a data center cooling system?
14. For a large data center (more than 100 racks and power consumption of more than 500 kW), which cooling technology would be the best fit?
15. How can we avoid demand fighting among different CRAC units?

EFFECTIVE AIR DISTRIBUTION IN DATA CENTERS

This chapter covers five topics that are closely related to data center air distribution. First, we cover 10 different methods of air distribution based on two different floor architectures: hard floor and raised floor. Second, we will briefly touch on the guidelines of air distribution methods. Third, we introduce computational fluid dynamics (CFD) analysis for data center temperature distribution. Fourth, we cover aspects of data center cooling calculations. Finally, we discuss how to manage and optimize a cooling system.

8.1 INTRODUCTION

Many scholars and research institutes have done much research regarding data center air distribution. Many results indicate that enough data center cooling capacity does not mean effective control of all IT equipment temperature in a data center. An Uptime Institute study showed that one data center had one-quarter of its IT equipment running too hot while the cooling capacity was ten times greater than the workload. Why is this so?

In order to answer this question, let us walk through the thermal equation again that we have already presented in Section 7.5.6 and find out how to control heat or workload via air distribution.

We already know that there are two major influencing factors that impact on heat load in the following equation. One is temperature difference and the other is velocity of airflow:

$$Q = \rho \times V \times c_p \times \Delta T$$

We can rewrite the equation in the following format, which is driven by airflow:

$$V = \frac{Q}{\rho \times c_p \times \Delta T}$$

Let's have a look what the airflow really means to the heat load by plugging some real data into the equation:

- $Q = 1\ kW = 3600\ kJ/hour = 60\ kJ/minute$
- $\rho = 1.2\ kg/m^3$
- $CP = 1.005\ kJ/kg\ °C$
- $\Delta T = 10°C$

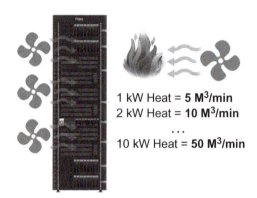

1 kW Heat = **5 M³/min**
2 kW Heat = **10 M³/min**
. . .
10 kW Heat = **50 M³/min**

FIGURE 8.1

Cold air velocity vs. amount of heat to be removed.

$$V = \frac{3600}{1.2 \times 1.005 \times 10} = 298 \ m^3/hour = 49.75 \ m^3/hour \approx 5 \ m^3/min$$

In other words, for 1 kW of rack heat load, we need five cubic meters per minute of air to cool it down for a 10-degree Celsius temperature difference. If the rack heat load is increased to 2 kW, we need 10 cubic meters per minute of airflow. This is a good example that gives us the simple relationship between the airflow rate and temperature (see Figure 8.1).

Although you might have enough cooling capacity in the cooling system, if the airflow rate is not adequate, the heat still cannot be removed.

8.2 METHODS OF AIR DISTRIBUTION

Based on Neil Rasmussen's whitepaper [136], there are three different types of air distribution approaches for a data center:

- Flooded
- Targeted or locally ducted
- Fully ducted or contained

8.2.1 FLOODED APPROACH FOR HARD FLOOR

With the flooded approach, both supply and return air is not properly guided and there is no duct work to the targeted load but rather the load or heat is flooded. The only constraints to the airflow are the data center wall, ceiling, and floor. For most comfort cooling systems, such as an office air conditioning system, we adopt this approach. Basically, there is not much air control. The consequence of this approach for data center is the heavy mixing of hot and cold air flows (see Figure 8.2).

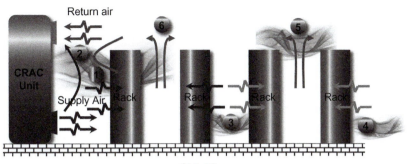

Side View

FIGURE 8.2

Flooded approach.

With this flooded approach, there will be two major problems with cold and hot air mixing:

1. Hot return air mixing with cold supply air at the rack intake
2. Cold supply air mixing with the hot return air at the CRAC unit

In addition to mixtures at position 1 and 2 in Figure 8.2, there will be an inevitable mixture of cold and hot air in the supply air delivered to positions 3 and 4. Likewise, there will be a hot and cold air mixture for the return air moving back to the CRAC unit at positions 5 and 6.

As a result, the air mixture will reduce the ΔT value, which will make the CRAC unit working hard and reduce the efficiency of heat removal.

8.2.2 TARGETED OR LOCALLY DUCTED APPROACH FOR HARD FLOOR

In order to improve the flooded approach, we can adopt a so-called targeted or locally ducted air distribution method. For this approach, either the supply or return air distribution is locally ducted to partially control where the air is going. "Locally" means three meters from the IT load or a back of the rack exhaust (see Figure 8.3).

However, the issue with locally ducted return air is how to avoid supply or cold air mixing with hot air in the last row from CRAC unit, which is position 1 in Figure 8.3. It appears to be inevitable. Therefore, this air distribution approach has improved the air mixture situation, but it still hasn't fully resolved it yet.

8.2.3 FULLY DUCTED OR CONTAINED APPROACH FOR HARD FLOOR

When we want full control of air distribution, we use a fully ducted or contained air approach, where the air is directly ducted into or out of the load.

With the fully ducted or contained approach, we have installed a so-called chimney system at the back of the rack to collect hot or return air. By doing so, there will be no hot and cold air contamination (see Figure 8.4).

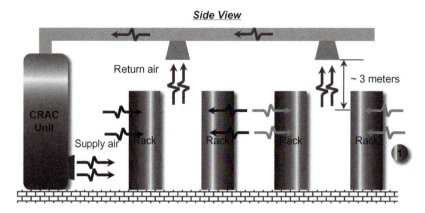

FIGURE 8.3

Targeted or locally ducted approach.

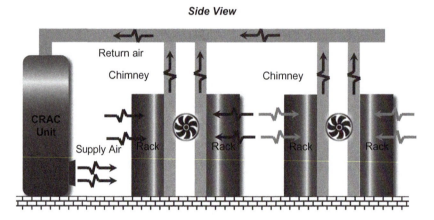

FIGURE 8.4

Fully ducted or contained air distribution approach.

There are some mechanical fans in the chimney system, which suck the hot air away and avoid hot and cold air mixtures. It is a part of the backdoor system.

8.2.4 LOCALLY DUCTED FOR SUPPLY AIR WITH HARD FLOOR

In contrast to containing the return air, we can use local ducts for supply air. In this scenario, the system is ducted for cold air rather than hot air (see Figure 8.5).

As we can see in Figure 8.5, there will be an issue in terms of hot and cold air mixture if we allow the return or hot air to flood everywhere, because some cold air will be right near the CRAC unit.

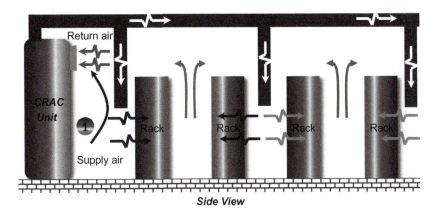

Side View

FIGURE 8.5

Targeted or locally ducted for supply air with hard floor.

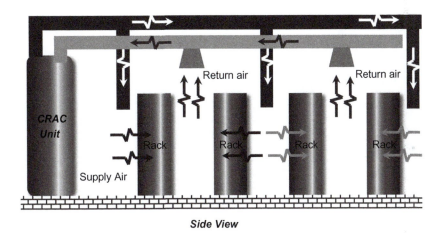

Side View

FIGURE 8.6

Locally ducted or targeted supply and return air.

8.2.5 FULLY DUCTED FOR BOTH SUPPLY AND RETURN AIR WITH HARD FLOOR

In addition to locally ducted supply air, we can add locally ducted return air. This ducted system may become quite complex but it will be relatively energy efficient (see Figure 8.6).

Furthermore, we can improve the ducted return air with a fully ducted return air system (see Figure 8.7). In other words, there will be no hot and cold air mixture in the computer room. This is good for energy efficiency but it is inflexible for relocation of racks. Any ducted system will face this issue. In order to improve the flexibility of data center rearrangement, the alternative is to adopt a raised floor approach.

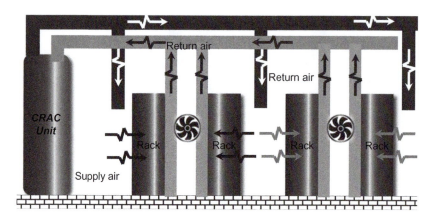

FIGURE 8.7

Locally ducted supply and fully ducted return air system.

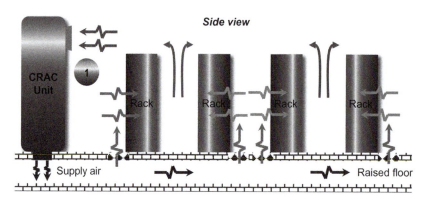

FIGURE 8.8

Locally ducted or targeted approach with raised floor.

8.2.6 LOCALLY DUCTED OR TARGETED APPROACH WITH RAISED FLOOR

Most of the above diagrams (except Figure 8.2) show a locally ducted or targeted approach for air distribution with a solid floor scenario. For the raised floor scenario, we can control the supply (or cold air) by rearranging perforated tiles on the raised floor rather than changing the supply air duct system (see Figure 8.8).

With the raised floor approach, the supply air has been fully ducted, but the issue with this approach is that the cold air may come back straight away to the return air intake of the CRAC unit in the first row. It will cause a cold and hot air mixture due to the flooded air return approach (see Figure 8.8, position 1).

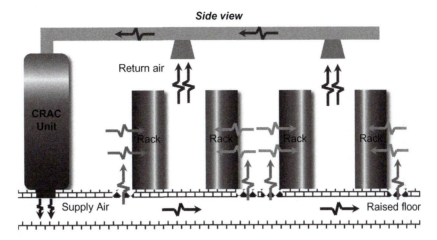

FIGURE 8.9

Locally ducted or targeted return air with raised floor.

8.2.7 FULLY DUCTED RETURN AIR WITH RAISED FLOOR

In order to improve this air distribution approach, we can add locally ducted return air to eliminate the cold and hot air mixture in the first row with the CRAC unit.

Actually, this is the most popular or typical air distribution approach for many data centers. There will be some cold and hot air mixture but it has been minimized. This is quite an efficient air distribution approach (see Figure 8.9).

Of course, we can make this scenario more energy efficient by installing fully ducted or contained return air, which will take all return air away without any cold and hot air contamination (see Figure 8.10). It is more energy efficient but it costs more.

8.2.8 FULLY DUCTED SUPPLY AIR WITH RAISED FLOOR

Likewise, we can also have a fully ducted system for supplying air with a raised floor. Because the supply air is fully ducted, although there is flooded return air, it will not mix with cold air. It is quite efficient (see Figure 8.11).

8.2.9 FULLY DUCTED SUPPLY AIR AND LOCALLY DUCTED RETURN AIR WITH RAISED FLOOR

With the above air distribution configuration, we can make a further improvement with locally ducted return air (see Figure 8.12).

Side View

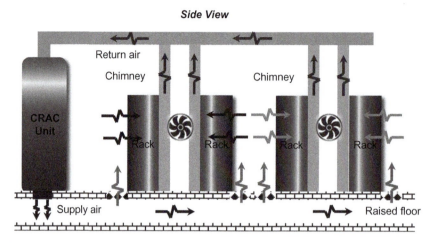

FIGURE 8.10

Fully ducted return air with raised floor scenario.

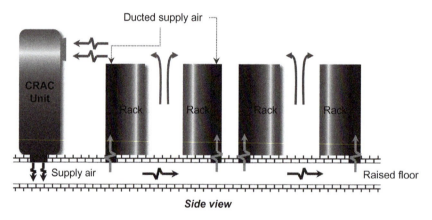

Side view

FIGURE 8.11

Fully ducted supply air with raised floor.

8.2.10 FULLY DUCTED SUPPLY AND RETURN AIR WITH RAISED FLOOR

Similar to the hard floor scenario, we can fully duct both the supply and return air with a raised floor (see Figure 8.13). This approach is at the top of the range in terms of cost and energy efficiency. It is the most energy efficient system that we can get but it is obviously very expensive because there is not only the additional cost of duct installation but also the additional space (about 200 mm + 200 mm) for both the front and the back of each rack. Furthermore, it is the most inflexible air distribution system because you cannot rearrange the data center floor layout. Once the ducted system is done, the rack position is fixed. Therefore, the fully ducted system needs proper capacity planning.

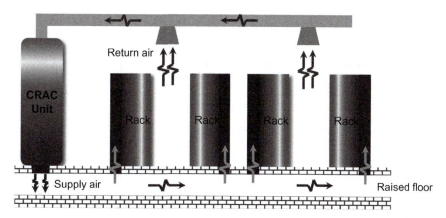

FIGURE 8.12

Fully ducted supply and locally ducted return air with raised floor.

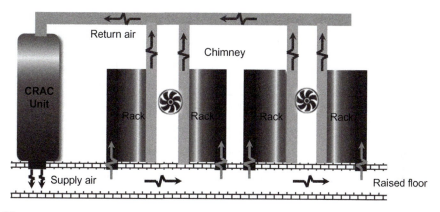

FIGURE 8.13

Fully ducted supply and return air with raised floor.

8.3 GUIDELINES FOR AIR DISTRIBUTION METHODS

In summary, we have discussed three different methods of air distribution for both supply and return air. Regardless of using a hard or raised floor, we have a 3×3 matrix, which is a combination of nine different air distribution approaches. These nine approaches are listed and summarized in Table 8.1.

In addition of these nine different air distribution approaches, we also have two different floors namely hard floor and raised floor. A raised floor is actually a type of targeted ducted supply air, but it has a flexibility of allowing floor layout rearrangement.

Table 8.1 Air Distribution Guidelines for Nine Approaches

Supply/ Return Air	Flooded Return	Targeted Ducted Return	Fully Ducted Return
	1. Small LAN rooms	2. General use	3. Large data center/colo.
Flooded supply	Not recommended for most data centers Up to 100% cold and hot air contamination Up to 3 kW per rack Simple installation Low cost It is very flexible for moving racks	Not recommended for most data centers Up to 6 kW per rack Low cost Easy to install No raised floor	Upgradeable Suitable for hot racks 70–100% hot exhaust air captured Up to 30 kW per rack No raised floor CRAC quite efficient
	4. Data center with static power densities	5. Small to medium data centers	6. Hot spot problem
Targeted ducted supply	Not recommended for new design Up to 6 kW per rack	80% of hot exhaust air captured High performance High efficiency Cost effective Up to 8 kW per rack Typical data center use	Upgradeable 70–100% of hot exhaust air captured Good for high-density racks Increasing CRAC's temperature leads to economizer hours Up to 30 kW per rack
	7. Mainframes/rack with vertical airflow	8. Mainframes/rack with vertical airflow	9. Harsh non–data center environments
Fully ducted supply	Limited economizer hours Supply air more predicable with very little hot air to be mixed Up to 30 kW per rack	More energy efficient than targeted supply but less efficient than fully ducted return Very minimum or no hot air contamination Up to 30 kW per rack	Very good for high-density racks Specialized installation More space required Up to 30 kW per rack

8.4 COMPUTATIONAL FLUID DYNAMICS (CFD) ANALYSIS

We have had an extensive discussion about different methods of air distribution in a data center. All of these methods are targeting the rack level because every rack is one of the major sources of heat load. However, we cannot differentiate every rack unit (RU) or CPU socket or core. This only discusses the static situation in the data center. It cannot deal with rack relocation or data center layout rearrangement due to the IT equipment life cycle. Moreover, the temperature sensors only measure the temperature at an isolated point rather than dynamic airflow.

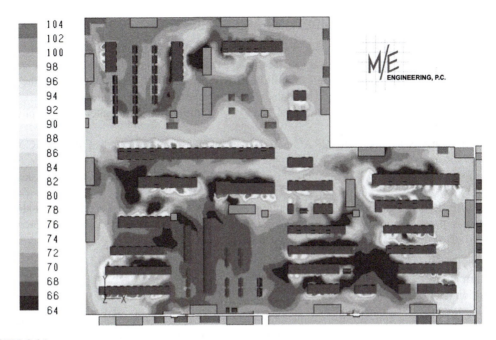

FIGURE 8.14

An example of a CFD modelling process [124].[1]

The above nine air distribution options can only provide a preliminary solution for a data center cooling system. If we would like to know precise airflow, dynamic temperature patterns, or a 3D model of temperature distribution down to the RU or CPU socket level, we have to adopt CFD simulation analysis. It can predict airflow in the data center.

8.4.1 WHAT IS DATA CENTER CFD ANALYSIS AND SIMULATION?

CFD analysis and simulation is not new. It has been applied in many industries, such as automobile, airplane, ship, and building design. HVAC is just one of the applications (see Figure 8.14).

CFD analysis and simulation is basically established on four mechanical engineering disciplines:

- Numerical computation
- Numerical modeling
- Fluid mechanics
- Heat transfer or thermodynamics

---

[1]Computational fluid dynamics (CFD) is used to model the air temperatures in a data center. The figure shows a temperature contour map at 5 feet (or about 1.5 meters) above the floor.

8.4.2 THE PROCESS OF CFD MODELING AND SIMULATION

This is an iterative process to make the simulation closer to the real-world scenario. The first step is to take all the inputs from the data center's computer room, such as its dimensions, racks, and all other objects inside the room and then find all heat sources of non-IT load. This will be the most time-consuming part of the exercise if the data center has never done CFD modeling before.

The second step is to set up all the initial boundary conditions of a computer room or physical environment for the CFD model.

The third step is to model the CRAC unit, which includes measuring all of the CRAC unit's parameters, such as fan speed, supply, return air temperatures, etc.

The fourth step is to find IT heat sources or IT load. This goes all the way to individual devices, even to a CPU socket.

The fifth step is to execute the CFD simulation based on all the inputs. Because it is a simulation process, it may require a large amount of computing power to execute the calculation process.

The sixth step is to validate or calibrate the simulation results, such as:

- Supply airflow
- Return airflow
- Position temperatures

This is basically to compare the simulation result against the real temperature measurements. If there is a big difference, it may mean the simulation model may be incorrect or not very accurate. The simulation model may need further improvement or fine-tuning. If there is a small difference, we can put the real measurements into the simulation model and execute the simulation model again; it is an iterative process. If the iterative results converge, it means we are on the right track.

The seventh step is to optimize the data center conditions such as increasing or decreasing the temperature and fan speed or moving the rack unit around to achieve an optimal solution for minimum data center energy consumption. Once the hard work has been done, we can repeat this iterative process again and again based on different "What if?" scenarios (see Figure 8.15).

In summary, CFD analysis is used to simulate dynamic airflow in a data center. The simulation for the air movement is not only at a single level of a rack but at all levels. With the assistance of a CFD simulation tool, we can complete the following tasks:

- Completely avoid supply and return air mixing
- Block any supply air short circuiting
- Eliminate low raised floor static pressure
- Optimize airflow rate from each perforated tile
- Control airflow to improve energy efficiency without jeopardizing data center availability

We can move the CRAC unit around in the data center and find the best or at least optimized location for airflow. Sometimes, even switching off some of the CRAC units can improve the data center cooling conditions.

There are a number of CFD software solutions on the market. The prices vary from US$7K to US$55K per CPU socket per annum. Table 8.2 presents a list of CFD software for data center purposes.

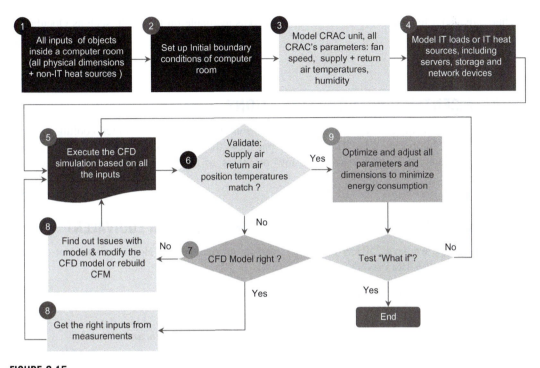

FIGURE 8.15

A flowchart of the CFD modeling process.

Table 8.2 CFD Software List			
CFD Software Name	**List Price per License (US$)**	**License Environment**	**Applications**
6 Sigma DC	55,000	Per CPU socket	Very accurate and for data center application
CoolSim	10,000	Standalone	Data center application
Tile Flow	13,000	Per CPU socket	Data center application
Autodesk Simulation CFD (Blue Ridge)	25,000	Per CPU socket	Various applications
Autodesk Simulation CFD 360	7,000	Cloud base	Suitable for data center application
Flovent	55,000	Standalone	Good
ANASYS Airpak	Less than 500	Standalone	Various applications

There are also a few open source CFD software tools available on the Web, such as OpenFoam and Open Flower.

8.5 DATA CENTER COOLING CALCULATIONS

Up to this point, we have discussed key concepts and theories of data center cooling and air distribution. Now, the question is, "How can we put these theories into practice?" or "How do we calculate data center cooling? We will use few problems to demonstrate how to calculate data center cooling.

8.5.1 CONVERTING ENERGY IN KW TO TONS OF ICE COOLING EQUIVALENT

Problem 1: Assume we have 250 kW critical IT load in our data center. How many tons of cooling do we need to cool the data center?

$$\frac{1 \ ton \ cooling}{3.517 \ kW} = \frac{x}{250 \ kW}$$

$$x = \frac{1 \times 250}{3.517} = 71 \ tons = 12,000 \times 71 = 852,000 \ BTU/hour$$

It is very easy and very straightforward to be calculate.

8.5.2 IT LOAD CALCULATIONS

8.5.2.1 Assumptions

Problem 2: Suppose I have 30 racks and install 480 2RU servers (each 2RU server power draws 4.9 amps at 240 AV), 120 1RU 24-port network switches (each has a power draw of 1 amp at 240 V, one for network traffic, and the other for the network management system), and 240 1RU storage disk drives (each has eight HDDs, 3 amps at 240 V) (see Table 8.3). How much cooling do I need for 30 racks with this kind of configuration?

Table 8.3 Computer Equipment for Small Data Center					
IT Equipment	**Quantity**	**Qty. per Rack**	**Installation Size**	**Amps per Unit**	**Voltage AV**
Server	480	16	2RU	4.9	240
Storage devices	120	4	1RU	3.0	240
Network switches	60	2	1RU	1.0	240
Rack	30	22	42RU		

8.5.2.2 Cooling load calculations

If we calculate the IT load per rack base, we will have following current draw:

- Server load: 16×4.9 amps $= 78.4$ amps
- Storage load: 4×3.0 amps $= 12$ amps
- Switch load: 2×1.0 amps $= 2$ amps
- Total current draw $= 92.4$ amps per rack

Total amps for this small data center $= 92.4 \times 30 = 2,772$ amps
Total watts (volts $\times$ amps) $= 240 \times 2,772 = 665,280 = 665.3$ kW
Total cooling required for IT load $= 665,280/3,517 = 189$ tons of equivalent ice required

8.5.3 TOTAL COOLING REQUIREMENT CALCULATION

The total data center heat should be the sum of all outputs of components within the data center. In Figure 6.12 and Section 6.6.1, we indicated there are six types of heat output:

- IT devices
- UPS
- PDU
- Light
- People
- Other, such as the air conditioning unit itself and security devices

Let's have a look at one of the examples for a medium size data center. Assume a data center has:

- Space $= 2,500$ square meters
- UPS $= 300$ kW with only 20% load, UPS (20%) $= 60$ kW
- Full-time equivalent (FTE) $= 25$ people working in data center

8.5.3.1 UPS heat output calculation

Table 8.4 UPS Heat Output			
Energy Loss Type	**Loss Factor**	**Calculation**	**Heat Output**
No-load loss	0.03	300×0.03	9 kW
Proportional loss	0.05	60×0.05	3 kW
Square-law loss	0	0	0
Total			12 kW

Notes:
1. No-load losses are also called tare, constant, fixed, shunt, and parallel losses. They independent of the power load. They are contributed by UPS transformers, capacitors, logic boards, and communication boards.
2. Proportional losses means the power losses are proportional to increasing power. This is because the power is processed by various power paths in the UPS system, such as switches, transistor, conductors, semiconductors, and rectifiers.
3. Square-law loss is due to power load increasing to a very high level, with the electrical current running through the components also being very high. Based on Ohm's law, the current squared multiplied by resistance becomes the power. When power load is between 50% to full load, the square-law loss will be around 1−4% (see Figure 8.16).

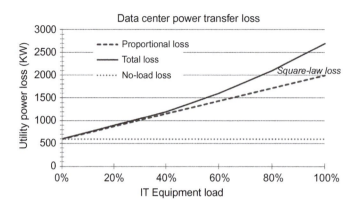

FIGURE 8.16

Example of power transfer loss graph [141] and [137].

Now, we should be able to calculate power distribution unit (PDU) heat loss.

8.5.3.2 PDU heat output calculation

Table 8.5 PDU Heat Output

Energy Loss Type	Loss Factor	Calculation	Heat Output
No-load loss	0.02	300×0.02	6 kW
Proportional loss	0.015	60×0.015	0.9 kW
Square-law loss	0	0	0
Total			6.9 kW

8.5.3.3 Light heat output calculation

Table 8.6 Light Heat Output

Energy Loss Type	Loss Factor	Calculation	Heat Output
Light	3 W/per sqm	2500×3	7.5 kW

8.5.3.4 People heat output

Table 8.7 Light Heat Output

Energy Loss Type	Loss Factor	Calculation	Heat Output
People	100 W per person	25×100	2.5 kW

8.5.3.5 Summary of all heat outputs

Table 8.8 Total Heat Load for Cooling Requirements

Type of Heat Generated	Factor	Calculation	Heat Output
IT Equipment	20%	300×0.2	60 kW
UPS	0.03, 0.05	$300 \times 0.3 + 60 \times 0.05$	12 kW
PDU	0.02, 0.015	$300 \times 0.02 + 60 \times 0.015$	6.9 kW
Light	3 W per sqm	2500×3	7.5 kW
People	100 W per person	25×100	2.5 kW
Total			88.9 kW

8.5.3.6 Other consideration for cooling requirements

In addition to typical IT load, other considerations should be taken into account because every data center has different circumstances. We list some common factors that might have to be considered during the process of calculating cooling requirements:

- Additional heat loads due to windows, exposed walls, and the roof.
- Additional heat load due to humidification compensation on the CRAC unit.
- Additional cooling capacity for redundancy if required.
- Additional cooling capacity for a large data center, 1.2 to 1.3 times the IT load rating as a safety margin.
- If the cooling system has a high level of cold and hot air contamination, add 30% extra capacity.

8.5.3.7 High density blade server cooling considerations

As ASHRAE predicted in 2005, IT equipment power density has been increasing dramatically since 1992. In comparison with 1994, server power density has been increased by more than 20 times (see Figure 8.17).

Traditionally, the power density of most data centers was only about 3−5 kW per rack. When cloud computing took off in 2008, the average power density per rack was around 5−8 kW per rack. By 2010, a full load of server blade enclosures, which only has 10RU, consumed about 10−15 kW.

However, most data center facilities for telecommunication purposes were built to accommodate 3−5 kW per rack and data center cooling systems were also made for lower power density racks.

Table 8.9 lists the latest blade servers provided by major blade vendors.

Bomara Associates' [142] research indicated that most cloud infrastructure has now adopted ultra-high density blade technology. A typical rack with a full load of blade chassis can suck as much as 30−40 kW. Subsequently, this puts more pressure on the conventional cooling system (see Table 8.10).

In contrast to traditional racks, these high and ultra-high density racks are not just operating at 5−15% of CPU utilization rate as a traditional standalone server does. They are running at over 75−80% utilization rates. This would be a big challenge for many conventional data center cooling systems. This is why many data centers have experienced running out of power before running out of space.

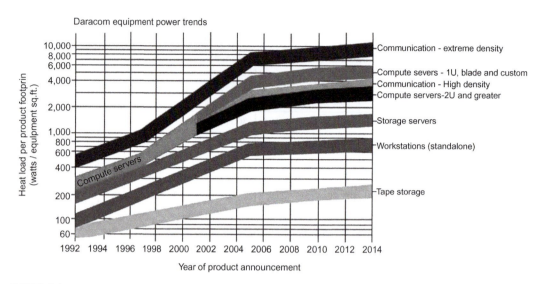

FIGURE 8.17

© 2005 ASHRAE TC 9.9 datacom equipment power trends and cooling applications.

Table 8.9 Power Draw of Blade Server Products from Major Vendors (Full Load)

Server Vendors	Products	Max Dimension	Power Draw (Full Load)
Oracle Sun	Sun B6000, Sunx6270 (10)	10 RU	12−13 kW per enclosure
IBM	IBM Blade Center H (14)	9 RU	11−12 kW per enclosure
HP	HP c7000 BL460c (16)	10 RU	14−15 kW per enclosure
Cisco	Cisco UCS 5180, 6120 (8)	6 RU	12−13 kW per enclosure
Dell	Power Edge M1000e (16)	10 RU	16−17 kW per enclosure

Table 8.10 Most Cloud Infrastructure Moving towards High-Density Racks

Power Density Level	Infrastructure Application	No. of Servers per Rack	Power Draw per Rack
Standard density	Client-server	5−15 1RU	1−3 kW
Medium density	Virtualized server	15−30 1RU	3−8 kW
High density	Virtualized server/cloud	42 1RU or 2−3 blade chassis	8−15 kW
Ultra-high density	Cloud	4−6 blade chassis	15−30 kW

8.6 MANAGING AND OPTIMIZING COOLING SYSTEMS

Earlier in Section 4.2.1.3, we indicated that the operating cost could be as high as five times the initial investment data center capex. Power consumption is one of the major operating cost items; it is around 20% of opex and half of this 20% (or 10%) is due to cooling.

Therefore, it is absolutely critical to implement the best practices for data center operation and make sure that the data center cooling system has been optimized according to the current workloads.

Normally, we can look from three perspectives to improve data center cooling efficiency:

Regularly review the configuration of the cooling system and make sure it has been optimized:

- Do we have enough cooling capacity for the total workload demand?
- Is the cooling system operating according to design specifications?
- Is the delta T (ΔT) greater than 8°C?

Plan and implement regular cooling preventative maintenance:

- Are the coils cleaned regularly?
- Is the airflow rate right?
- Are the testing points calibrated regularly?

Decommission unused equipment and consolidate very low utilization devices:

- If the equipment is not for hot standby, it should be switched off.
- If the equipment has a very low utilization rate, less than 1%, the workload should be consolidated with other hardware and the device should be switched off.
- Decommission any alien[2] (or ghost) equipment if no one uses it. It could create over 15% energy savings.

8.6.1 RESOLVE EASY ISSUES IMMEDIATELY TO IMPROVE COOLING EFFICIENCY

In order to improve data center cooling efficiency, there are a few easy things that could be done, which often get ignored.

8.6.1.1 Install blank panel

If there are empty RUs between the lower and higher positions of a rack, a blank panel should be installed. It can prevent hot and cold air contamination (see Figure 8.18).

8.6.1.2 Manage racks and cables properly

If the rack cables are not installed properly, they could block the hot airflow from the back and cold air may not get through. Consequently, the cold air cannot remove the IT equipment heat. This would create a cooling problem even the cooling system has enough capacity for the IT load (see Figure 8.19).

---

[2]If IT equipment has no owner or no one to be responsible for it, we often call it alien or ghost equipment. It is quite common in many large organizations due to structure changes.

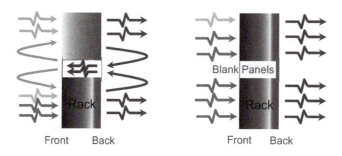

FIGURE 8.18

Installation of blank panel to prevent hot and cold air contamination.

Cable mess, block cooling air flow   Proper cabling on two sides

FIGURE 8.19

Install and manage rack cabling properly.

The rack should not be too shallow. It may cost extra to purchase a deeper rack, but it is worthwhile to have enough space for cable installation.

The rack door should have enough open perforation. It must be greater than 50%. The average open perforation is around 65%. Some data centers may remove rack doors altogether or even server covers in order to increase the velocity of airflow.

8.6.1.3 Optimizing raised floor height for cooling

If a data center uses raised floors for racks' air supply, then the right floor height is absolutely essential. The TIA-942 recommends different heights (from 12 inches to 36 inches) for different tiers of data centers. The general rule of thumb is the floor height should be higher than 500 mm and less than 900 mm. If it is too high, there will be not enough air pressure. If it is too low, the underground cabling may block the airflow.

FIGURE 8.20

Data center airflow dampers.

8.6.2 GUIDELINES TO MANAGE PERFORATED TILES AND RACKS

A perforated tile should be always placed in a cold aisle; never leave it in a hot aisle. If you place perforated tile or tiles in a hot aisle, it would be the same thing as mixing cold and hot air. It wastes energy. A hot aisle should be hot. Never try to reduce the temperature in a hot aisle.

When airflow dampers (see Figure 8.20) are placed in the data center, we should be always aware that the dampers might decrease airflow by a maximum of 33%.

Place a perforated tile where a rack has IT load or where it is necessary. If the rack doesn't have IT load or heat, the perforated tile shouldn't be allocated, even within a cold aisle. If one perforated tile can handle the IT load, you should never allocate two perforated tiles to the floor so you can save the cooling energy for another place or purpose. For example, if a standard density rack has 3 kW of IT load and one specified perforated tile can cover this rack with 15 m^3/min airflow (5 m^3/min airflow per kW, see Figure 8.1), then it is not necessary to leave two tiles with 30 m^3/min airflow. In other words, perforated tile is a cooling tuner. We only place it where the heat load needs it.

For a standard perforated tile, the open surface (or space) should cover approximately 25% of the total tile surface. As we mentioned before, one 1 kW rack needs 5 m^3/min airflow. One perforated tile has 15 m^3/min airflow, so one perforated tile can cool a 3 kW rack. If the rack becomes medium density or 6 kW density, it will require double perforated space for 25% to 50% of the total tile surface (see Figure 8.21).

Moreover, if the rack becomes a high-density rack, we do not only need more perforated space on the tile but also have to increase airflow velocity. For example, if the high-density rack has a 15 kW load, we should have 75 m^3/min airflow of perforated tile.

In order to make a CRAC unit work more efficiently, it is not good practice to place racks on a longer row. There should be less than 20 racks in one row.

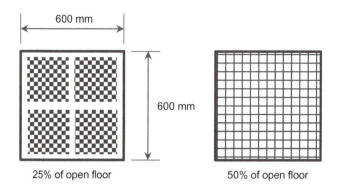

FIGURE 8.21

Perforated tile open floor.

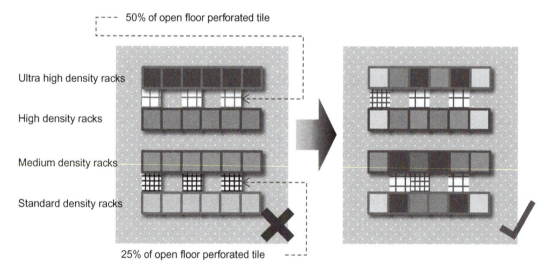

FIGURE 8.22

Mixing with different density racks in a data center.

When we have mixed numbers of high-, medium-, and standard-density racks, it would be a good idea to place high-density racks with standard ones so that we can leverage underutilized cooling capacity around the standard rack rather than concentrating high-, medium-, and low-density racks together (see Figure 8.22). A few additional things we should always remember when we place high-density racks in a data center are:

1. Never place a high-density rack at the end of a row because of air mixing.
2. Never place a high-density rack in the corner.

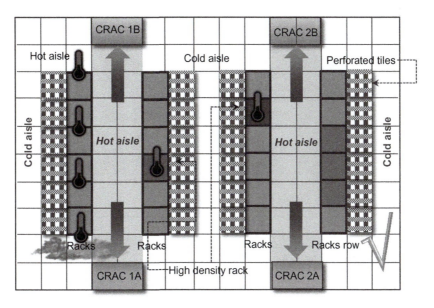

FIGURE 8.23

Align CRAC units with hot aisles.

How do we place CRAC units? Should we align them with cold aisles or hot aisles? The answer is hot. The simple reason is that hot air is much lighter because of lower air density and easier to move around so we have to make sure that the hot air has the shortest distance or path and can be quickly removed out of the data center rather than kept within the data center. By doing so, we can reduce the chances of hot and cold air contamination. For this reason, we should place CRAC units as close as possible to hot sources so when the hot air comes out of the back of the racks, it can be immediately taken away (see Figure 8.23).

8.6.2.1 Avoid the Venturi effect

When we place a perforated tile, we should avoid the so-called Venturi effect, which occurs if a perforated tile is too close to a CRAC unit; the supply air won't come out of the perforated tile. Instead, the hot air will be sucked into the raised floor (see Figure 8.24).

This is because negative pressure is generated when the velocity of cold air is too close to the CRAC unit. Good practice is to place a perforated tile at least two floor panels (closed tiles) away from a CRAC unit. Some vendors suggest that it should be at least 5 floor panels away, which is 3 meters (see Figure 8.25). It is really dependent on the size of the computer room and supply air pressure and velocity. The best way to decide this distance is to use CFD simulation.

In case there is not enough distance between the CRAC unit and first perforated tile to avoid the Venturi effect, we can put some air velocity damping to slow the velocity of supply air. Ideally, we should place perforated tile away from the CRAC unit to avoid the Venturi effect rather than placing damping under the raised floor.

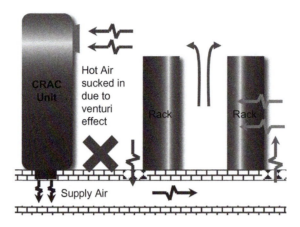

FIGURE 8.24

Avoid the Venturi effect when placing perforated tiles.

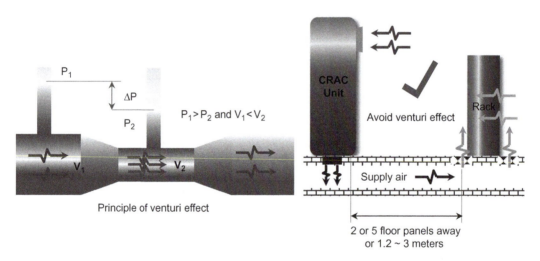

FIGURE 8.25

Avoid the Venturi effect.

8.6.2.2 Avoid the supply short circuit

Avoiding the Venturi effect is not only an issue for the perforated tile arrangement. We have to also avoid the supply air short circuit and bypass effect, which means if the short circuit effect does occur, the supply air goes directly back to the return air inlet of the CRAC unit without cooling any IT load. When the bypass effect occurs, the supply air doesn't make any contribution to cooling the IT equipment but rather mixes with hot air (see Figure 8.26). This is the result of either misplacing the perforated tile at the wrong spot or running cable cutouts. Some data center statistics indicate that between 50% and 80% of cooling energy can be lost to these effects.

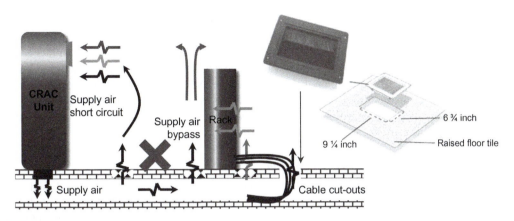

FIGURE 8.26

Avoid cold air short circuit and bypass.

Both effects would decrease the ΔT value, which will lead to reducing the CRAC unit's efficiency. In order to avoid these pitfalls, we should pay close attention to avoid short circuit and bypass effects. With cable cutouts, we can use grommets to seal cables, which we show in Figure 8.26.

8.6.3 CONDITIONAL MONITORING FOR COOLING SYSTEM

We should not consider a data center is a static system. Actually, it is a dynamic system, especially if some corrective and preventive maintenance or IT device retrofit or decommissioning activities occur from time to time.

A monitoring system can provide an alarm due to temperature or supply air changes or any cooling issues. These changes include not only air volume changes but also the velocity or rate of change. It can help us to make an immediate response and get a rapid resolution if it is a critical alarm. It also can provide valuable information for us to target the right component to take the right activities for preventative maintenance. For example, if the data center temperature is changing very slowly, it may mean that the air-conditioning system doesn't have enough capacity. So, the operations staff should bring the issue to the capacity planning manager. On the other hand, if the temperature change is very sudden, it could be that a CRAC unit has broken. The data center operations staff should find the root cause of the issue and ask for an air-conditioning tradesman to fix it if necessary.

The other important advantage of a monitoring system is that it can provide correlation information. For example, if the cooling water temperature and electricity consumption doesn't match very well or doesn't work efficiently, it may mean the system has some issues due to clean water or airflow.

8.6.4 HANDLING HIGH-DENSITY RACK COOLING

In Section 8.5.3.7, we expressed that the utilization rate of a high-density rack is much higher than a standard density rack, as much as 80% higher. If this utilization rate of a server is not evenly distributed, which is highly likely, then there will be potential issues in cooling the high-density rack. A lot of research indicates that for some virtualized cloud infrastructures, the variation of server utilization rate could be as high as 70%. In other words, when it is quiet, the server utilization rate is only around 10%, but when it is very busy, the utilization rate could reach 80%. It is really dependent on what kind of applications are running on the virtual machine (VM) and when they are running.

When we design the cooling capacity, we will always want to cover the peak load or full IT load. If the servers or a high-density racks are on either light or idle mode while the cooling system is switched on at full capacity, it will waste energy.

8.6.4.1 Row-based and rack-based cooling

The solution to resolving the high-density rack issues is to adopt either a row- or rack-based cooling strategy. Row-based cooling is where the supply air from a CRAC or CRAH unit is dedicated or embedded into a high-density rack row and the return air can be captured immediately and travel the shortest distance back to the CRAC unit. Likewise, the cold air doesn't have to travel a long distance and directly reaches the IT load so that energy is not wasted forcing cold air across a long distance under a congested raised floor. The solution trys to minimize the chances of cold and hot air contamination (see Figure 8.27).

In addition, the cooling system will place a number of thermal sensors at the rack level to measure the temperature changes due to utilization rate change or IT load variation. If the temperature is lower, then the speed of the fan will be lower as well. This means that when the rack temperature gets higher, the fan will blow harder or faster and when the rack temperature is lower, the fan speed will slow down.

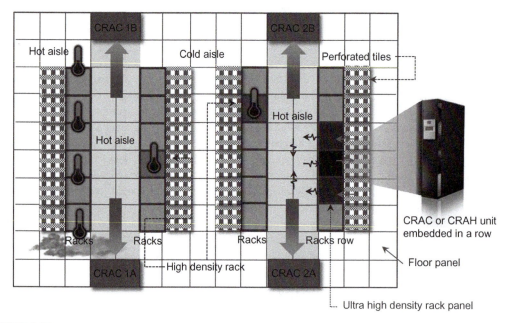

FIGURE 8.27

Row-based cooling system for high-density racks.

In Section 7.5.6, we indicated that if we can reduce fan speed by 20%, we can reduce power consumption by about 50%. Therefore, if the row-based cooling system has an automatic fan speed control, it would save energy consumption significantly. Ultimately, it will save on operating costs for the data center.

8.6.4.2 Cold and hot aisle containment

In Section 8.2, we discussed a number of solutions to distribute air. Some options involve either fully ducted supply or return. With the fully ducted option, the advantage is avoiding the mixing of hot and cold air but the disadvantages are that it is very costly and it is difficult to rearrange the floor layout.

Instead of adopting a fully ducted solution, we can use so-called hot aisle or cold aisle containment. The basic idea is to seal either the hot aisle or cold aisle to avoid mixing of cold and hot air (see Figures 8.28–8.30).

Similar to the fully ducted air distribution, the cold air containment cannot only unify the temperature for the cold aisle but also lift the CRAC's return temperature by an average of 5–6°C so that the CRAC unit can work more efficiently. For a traditional data center, the supply air temperature of a CRAC unit may be around 12–13°C. This lower temperature setting is to compensate for

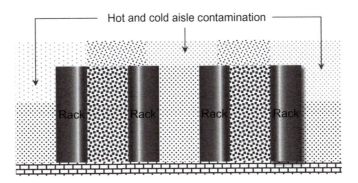

FIGURE 8.28

Contaminated hot and cold aisles.

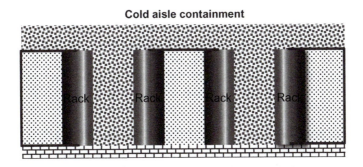

FIGURE 8.29

Cold aisle containment.

Hot aisle containment

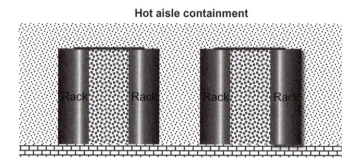

FIGURE 8.30

Hot aisle containment.

cold and hot air mixing or a cold air short circuit. With cold aisle or hot aisle containment, the supply air temperature can be lifted to 18−19°C. For the same size of IT load, we can save a few CRAC units. Ultimately it can save both capex and opex for a data center.

Both Pacific Gas and Energy (PG&E) in 2007 [143] and Gartner [144] in 2008 research indicated that the cold aisle containment can save 20−30% in cooling costs. Rittal [145] claimed that cold aisle containment can increase efficiency up to 40% in comparison to a data center without any containment. The CRAC unit is capable of supporting ΔT ranging from 23−38°C depending on the IT load conditions. In other words, if the supply air temperature is 20°C, the return air temperature can reach as high as 50°C. Therefore, existing data center cooling infrastructure, which was only designed to support 3−5 kW per rack, can be improved to handle a 20 kW high-density rack if cold aisle containment is implemented.

However, there are some costs for cold or hot aisle containment. First it is quite obvious that this will add to the initial investment capex. Second, it will block the data center luminaire and interfere with the fire suppression system. Third, the hot aisle temperature may be too high to be acceptable, as high as 40°C, which is above the Occupational Safety and Health Administration (OSHA) guideline temperature of 38°C. Fourth, in case the power fails, the hot aisle temperature will increase much faster than a noncontainment aisle.

In some cases, the hot aisle temperature can reach an unacceptable level in a few minutes. In contrast, a noncontainment aisle will take around 30 minutes or more. Subsequently, the data center will be shut down very quickly. One of the possible solutions to combat this emergence failure is to automatically open up the self-closing door and roof panels if hot and cold aisle containment has been built with this kind of infrastructure (see Figure 8.31).

In comparison with a door and panel system, the curtain infrastructure is very economical and cost effective. It does work but it doesn't look very attractive (see Figure 8.32).

8.6.4.3 Summary of pros and cons of different containment approaches

Both hot aisle and cold aisle containment can improve data center energy efficiency significantly, but some vendors, such as Liebert or Emerson Network Power [146], Rittal, and Eaton [147] emphasize that cold aisle containment is the better solution because these vendors believe cold aisle

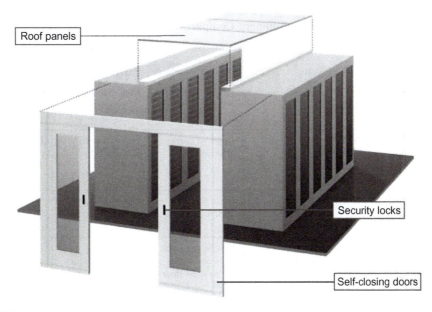

FIGURE 8.31

Hot and cold aisle containment with door and roof panel infrastructure.

FIGURE 8.32

Curtain containment infrastructure.

Table 8.11 Hot and Cold Aisle Containment Comparison

Features	Hot Aisle Containment		Cold Aisle Containment	
	External Cooling	Internal Cooling	External Cooling	Internal Cooling
Focus on cooling availability & efficiency	Cold air distribution open and exposed to surrounding disturbance		Minimize exposure of cold air distribution to surrounding disturbance	
Energy efficiency to lower opex	Improve efficiency but add cooling load due to large fan or fast fan speed to combat additional pressure drop	Improve energy efficiency	Improvs energy efficiency by 30%	Improve energy efficiency by 30–40%
Capability to cool high-density rack	10–15 kW per rack	More than 30 kW per rack	10–15 kW per rack possible	More than 30 kW per rack possible
Ability to retrofit for traditional data center in raised floor condition	Aisle celling panels doors and hot air return ducting/plenum required	Can be done but does not work with raised floor	Aisle celling panels and doors required	Aisle celling panels, doors, and cooling units required

containment can be implemented with both hard and raised floors and it is easier to retrofit into existing raised floor data centers. Other, such as APC [148] argue that hot aisle containment is superior to the cold aisle containment solution because hot aisle containment can channel the hottest air directly into the coolers or CRAC units. Since it prevents hot air from impacting on the data center environment, it will be deployed anyway.

In addition to hot or cold aisle containment solutions, some data center solutions, such as the PTS data center solution [149] remind data center operations staff that "end of row" containment is also a good option because most air mixing will occur at the end of a row. With end of row containment, the cooling efficiency could reach up to 80–95% while eliminating some of the disadvantages of full-size containment, such as interfering with fire suppression and blocking room lighting. Furthermore, it will leave some breathing room for hot air so that the data center can have some spare time to switch on the redundant system in case the power fails.

In terms cold and hot aisle containment solutions, PTS recommends both. It is really dependent on which cooling object is focused on. If the focus is on perimeter cooling, PTS suggests cold aisle containment; if it is on in-row cooling, PTS recommends hot aisle containment.

Emerson Network Power [146] has created a very good and comprehensive summary of cold aisle and hot aisle containment with different configurations of CRAC units located either in the internal or external containment zone (Table 8.11).

8.6.4.4 Which one is better?

There has been an ongoing debate in terms of which type of containment is most efficient. Whether it is hot aisle or cold aisle, it appears there is not a foregone conclusion yet. An experiment conducted by both Intel and T-system [150] in 2011 has indicated there are no significant differences between cold and hot aisle containment. Subsequently, the decision on whether a data center should adopt hot aisle or cold aisle solution rest on other business and finance variables and personal preference. We will give more detail in later chapters.

8.7 SUMMARY

In this chapter, we covered five main topics: data center air distribution, its efficiency, CFD analysis, data center cooling calculations, and optimization of the cooling system. The most important topic covered is how to calculate data center cooling and this involves many assumptions. If we can get the assumptions right, the result of the cooling calculation should be very accurate.

The method of data center air distribution is based on two different scenarios: hard floor and raised floor. Each scenario has five different air distribution methods. Altogether, we have 10 different air distribution methods. The selection of a particular air distribution method can refer to a 3×3 matrix table.

CFD analysis is one of the simulation tools to analyze cold and hot air flow and distribution within a data center or in a server room. The biggest advantage of CFD is that it can help the data center manager to optimize the cooling temperatures and airflow rates to achieve the best energy efficiency.

The final part of this chapter introduces guidelines on how to manage and optimize the cooling system, such as cold and hot aisle containment.

8.8 REVIEW QUESTIONS

1. If one rack's power density is 5 kW and the temperature difference from front to back or $\Delta T = 10°C$, what is the right airflow rate (air velocity) for the rack? (Assume air density $\rho = 1.03$ kg/m^3 and $C_P = 1.0$.)
2. When a few rack servers are idle, I can switch off these servers. If I can reduce fan speed by 20% on average, how much power can I save? If I reduce fan speed by 50%, can I significantly reduce power consumption? If so, please explain why?
3. How many methods of air distribution are there?
4. What is the best method of air distribution to avoid cold and hot air mixing?
5. What is the common air distribution approach for the majority of data centers?
6. Please explain the pros and cons of the common air distribution approach for the majority of data centers.
7. Please describe the guidelines for selecting air distribution methods.
8. What is CFD analysis?
9. How do we process a CFD analysis for a data center air distribution?
10. What are those most popular software tools for CFD analysis?
11. Assume I have 300 kW critical IT load in a data center. How many tons of cooling do I need to cool the data center?

Table 8.12 Total Cooling Requirement Calculation

IT Equipment	Quantity	Installation Size	Amps	Voltage AV
Server	800	2RU	5.2	240
Storage devices	200	1RU	3.5	240
Network switches	100	1RU	1.5	240
Rack	50	42RU		

12. If I have 50 racks (42RU) installed with the number of server, storage, and network devices listed in Table 8.12 in a data center, what is the total cooling required?
13. Assume I have a 3,500 square meter data center, and UPS = 350 kW with only 25% load. There are 35 people working in this data center. What is total cooling requirement?
14. How many different ways are there to optimize a data center cooling system?
15. How do we handling a high-density rack for an existing data center?

COOLING STRATEGY

In this chapter, we will take a close look at different cooling solutions or different cooling strategies for different cooling objects under different circumstances. Basically, we cover three different cooling strategies: room-based, raw, and rack-based cooling. Moreover, we can combine these cooling strategies for a particular requirement. Finally, we discuss how to leverage free cooling using economizers.

9.1 COOLING CONTROL FOR WIRING CLOSETS

There are many names for data centers and one of them is "wiring closet," which is a mini or micro data center that is allocated a small room or shares general office space. All data center components are packed in a few racks and with limited IT capability. If we quantify it in details, we have the general dimensions for a wiring closet shown in Table 9.1.

You may wonder, "Why should we discuss wiring closet cooling strategies first?" A wiring closet is very popular for many small, medium, and even startup businesses. The right cooling strategy will save a lot of opex.

Basically, we have five different strategies or options to handle the cooling for a wiring closet (sometimes called a network room):

- Just share cooling capacity with comfort cooling or office-based cooling, where IT heat load is transferred by building air conditioning
- Conduction cooling, where heat flows through walls
- Passive ventilation cooling, where heat is removed via a ventilation system
- Fan-assisted cooling, where heat flows out through a vent with assistance from a fan
- Dedicated cooling, where heat is removed by a dedicated cooling unit

9.1.1 SHARING COMFORT COOLING SYSTEM

When a wiring closet shares a comfort cooling system, the closet doesn't have full control of cooling temperature. The cooling system may be switched on or off during the night and on the weekend. The sensible heat ratio for comfort cooling is lot lower than precision cooling, where it could be as low as only 0.6 rather than 0.8 to 1.0 for precision cooling. The comfort temperature may have big swings, which will lead to harm for the IT equipment in the wiring closet.

Table 9.1 Wiring Closet Measurements

Measurement	Quantity
Floor space	Less than 10 square meters
Contents	1−3 racks of equipment (server, network, storage, UPS, and PDU...)
Heat load per rack	Average 1.0−3.0 kW per rack
Typical cooling strategy	None or share with building cooling during day
Location	Separate office room or remote location of building
Security	Medium (locked door or locked cabinet)
Average Cost	$150 k to $300 k

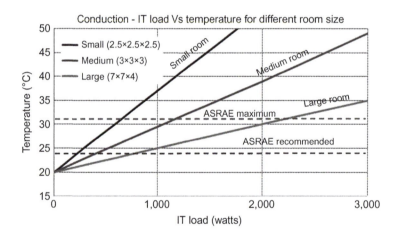

FIGURE 9.1

Conduction: temperatures versus room sizes [151].

9.1.2 CONDUCTION COOLING

Conduction cooling means natural cooling. It is really dependent on a room's size and ambient temperature. IT load can increase along with room size (see Figure 9.1).

Based on Figure 9.1, we have one small, one medium, and one large room for the conduction cooling. Even for the large room shown as a green line, the maximum IT load can only be just a little more than 2 kW if we would like to keep the IT load within the ASRAE maximum and recommended limit band. Therefore, room-based or natural passive cooling is not suited for a rack IT load that is more than 2.5 kW. Are there any other solutions for an IT load that exceeds 2.5 kW per rack? Let's take a look at other alternatives, namely passive and fan-assisted ventilation solutions.

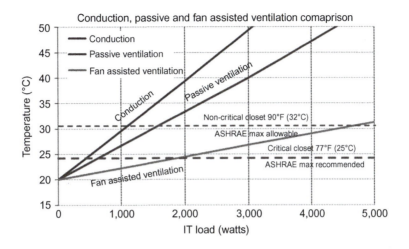

FIGURE 9.2

Comparison of conduction, passive, and fan-assisted ventilation [151].

Table 9.2 Recommended Cooling Solutions for Wired Closet		
Total Critical Load	**Noncritical Load**	**Recommended Cooling Solution**
400 W	1000 W	Conduction
700 W	1,750 W	Passive ventilation
2,000 W	4,500 W	Fan-assisted ventilation

9.1.3 CONDUCTION, PASSIVE, AND FAN-ASSISTED VENTILATION

Passive ventilation is based on using natural airflow to cool a wiring closet or IT load. It does not get any assistance from air movement. In contrast, fan-assisted ventilation uses fan assistance to accelerate air movement. Based on the heat transmission principle, the faster the air movement, the more heat load can be transferred out (see Figure 9.2).

Table 9.2 shows the recommended cooling solutions for different sizes and types of IT loads within a micro data center or wired closet.

9.2 ROOM-BASED COOLING

Many traditional data centers are using room-based cooling. The CRAC units focus on the entire heat load in the data center room rather than an individual rack or IT equipment. It is less granular in terms of airflow and temperature due to the physical constraints of the room including the ceiling

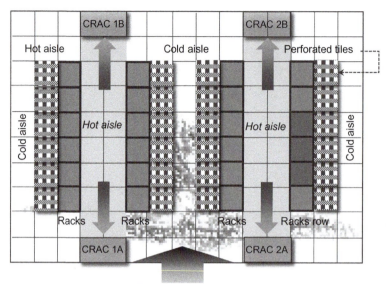

Room based cooling

FIGURE 9.3

Room-based cooling.

and CRAC unit location (see Figure 9.3). Furthermore, any IT equipment change or relocation will impact room-based cooling.

Because there is a higher probability of air mixture for room-based cooling, a large amount of energy has been wasted if the airflow is not contained. The cooling performance is quite difficult to predict. Therefore, CFD simulation may be required to help both designer and operator minimize a cold air short circuits and bypass issues. This will certainly decrease the the CRAC units' cooling capacity.

Typically, we use room-based cooling for lower density racks. The IT load of each rack varies between 1 to 3 kW per rack.

9.3 ROW-BASED COOLING

With row-based cooling, the CRAC or CRAH unit is dedicated to a particular row. Normally, the CRAC unit will be embedded into the row. The airflow path becomes short and is much more predicable than with room-based cooling. This increases the air distribution efficiency and reduces power consumption (see Figure 9.4).

Very often, a rack-based cooling scenario is applied to hard floors, in which no raised floor is required. It is quite simple to define. No room geometry emission issues will impact row-based cooling. As a result, the efficiency of the entire CRAC unit can be increased up to 95%. This supports both N + 1 and 2N redundancy.

The row-based scenario can handle up to 30 kW per rack, which means that it has the capacity to deal with medium- and high-density racks.

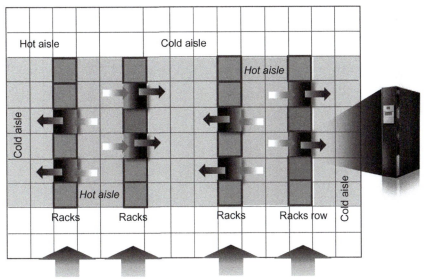

Row based cooling

FIGURE 9.4

Row-based cooling.

9.4 RACK-BASED COOLING

A rack-based cooling scenario is a very simple predefined layout. Each CRAC unit will be dedicated to a particular rack. A raised floor is not an essential requirement for rack-based cooling, but piping is necessary for each CRAC unit. It can support up to 50 kW heat load per rack (see Figure 9.5).

Because each CRAC unit is dedicated to a single rack, there is no support for redundancy. Furthermore, it requires a large number of AC devices. Rack-based cooling is particularly designed for ultra-high-density racks.

9.5 COMPARISON OF ROOM-, ROW-, AND RACK-BASED COOLING

Every cooling strategy has its pros and cons. The question is, how can we select the right cooling strategy for our data center orbusiness needs? The Kevin Dunlap et al. whitepaper [152] from APC summarizes the issues quite well (see Table 9.3).

The paper compares three different cooling strategies from the perspective of five categories:

1. Agility
2. System availability
3. Life cycle cost (TCO)
4. Serviceability
5. Manageability

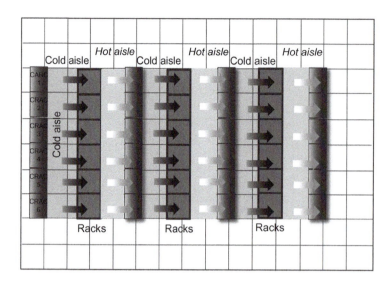

FIGURE 9.5

Rack-based cooling.

These five categories are performance measurements for a well-designed and managed data center. Moreover, Dunlap et al. listed additional six various criteria in terms of data center performance measurements in the comparison of the three cooling methods (room, raw, and rack):

1. Initial cost (capex)
2. Electrical efficiency (PUE)
3. Water piping or other piping near IT equipment
4. Cooling unit location
5. Redundancy
6. Heat removal method

9.5.1 MIXING WITH ROOM AND ROW BASED COOLING

A conventional data center is designed to work with standard density racks and not high-or ultra-high-density racks. When a business requests that high- or ultra-high-density racks be fitted into the traditional data center, it might not be the right solution to retrofit the entire conventional data center for a few high-density racks because:

- There are still many standard density racks in operation if the data center has not been built from scratch.
- Capex investment is normally on a yearly or granular base rather than in one big bang.
- It is not cost effective to retrofit the entire data center for high-density racks.
- In addition, not all racks will be fitted with high-density IT load equipment. Some racks will install network and storage equipment.
- For a conventional data center, there will always be a mix with standard-, medium-, and high-density racks.

Table 9.3 Comparison of Room-, Row-, and Rack-Based Cooling

Selection Criteria	Pros/ Cons	Room-Based	Row-Based	Rack-Based
Agility	Pros	Easier to redistribute cooling air pattern for rack below 3 kW	Flexible for deployment with any rack density; cooling capacity can be shared with different density racks	Capable to handle any density rack
	Cons	Inefficiency if cold or hot air cannot be contained	Must have hot and cold aisle layout. Less flexible than room-based cooling system	Cooling capacity cannot be shared with other racks
Service Availability	Pros	CRAC units and redundancy can be shared with all racks in the data center	Redundancy can be shared with all racks within a row. Close coupling between racks and CRAC eliminate vertical temperature increases	Close coupling eliminates hot spots, standardized solution minimizes human error
	Cons	Containment required to separate air streams	Redundancy needed for each row of racks	Redundancy required for each rack so it is very costly
Life Cycle Cost	Pros	Much easier to reconfigure floor layout, less piping installation cost	High flexibility with wide range of power and density types. Less provisioning time	Easier to deploy due to standardization, ongoing installation cost is lower
	Cons	Overcapacity cooling, initial capex is higher due to higher air mixing, long-term opex is higher	Initial capex investment may be quite high in comparison with room-based cooling	Initial capex is higher and It could be overcapacity due to different applications, wasting opex
Serviceability	Pros	CRAC unit is located on the perimeter or outside the room; may avoid some human error	Modular approach, reduce downtime, standardized unit, reduce MTTR	Due to standardized CRAC unit, it is easier to perform routine services
	Cons	Requires special technician or expert to complete regular services.	CRAC units mix with IT racks; may increase human error	If redundancy is required 2N components should be installed
Manageability	Pros	System is quite simple and also easier to manage	Both hot and cold air predictable; cooling system faults can be isolated	Cooling issues easier to be isolate
	Cons	Requires advanced service training, impossible to do real-time analysis?	In comparison with room-based cooling, it needs more connection points, increased operational costs	More components are required; less reliable and manageable

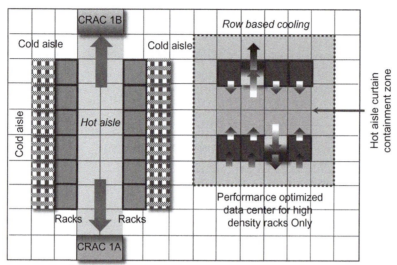

FIGURE 9.6

Mixed cooling strategy.

Therefore, it is a good idea to have two different cooling approaches in one data center, with both room-based and row-based cooling or isolated zone-based cooling (see Figure 9.6).

The zone-based cooling strategy means that any heat generated within the high-density zone will be immediately transferred out without any impact on the other racks within the data center. There are three different approaches to establish a high-density zone:

- Hot aisle containment
- Rack containment
- Uncontained (least desirable scenario)

9.5.2 HOT AISLE AND RACK CONTAINMENT FOR HIGH-DENSITY ZONE

When the high-density zone is established in a conventional data center, we will always build hot air containment so it can prevent the return air from impacting other standard density racks. The containment can be either row-based hot air containment or rack-based containment with a chimney structure to remove the return air. It is also possible to have both supply and return air containment (see Figure 9.7).

Rear containment is similar to hot aisle containment except panels are used to form a rear air channel in the back of a row of racks. It adds 200 to 300 mm depth to a rack. If we have both supply and return air containment, the size of a rack would be doubled.

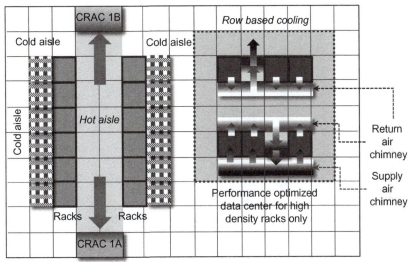

FIGURE 9.7

Rack-based cooling with rear door chimney containment.

9.5.3 UNCONTAINED

An uncontained high-density zone is the most undesirable approach. However, sometimes the physical conditions do not allow for the containment of both hot air and cold air, such as when we different rack sizes or racks come from different vendors. This would require more cooling capacity to ensure that the high-density heat load will not impact on other zones.

If a mixed cooling strategy is adopted, when data center capacity planning you should think ahead because you would like to know where the CRAC unit will be located and how the pipe will be run. Obviously, the shorter the distance, the lower the installation cost. The bottom line is to minimize the initial investment capex.

9.6 RACK REAR DOOR–BASED COOLING STRATEGY

The latest technology for data center cooling is to adopt a so-called "laminar airflow" strategy. It is actually a rear rack door cooling strategy for the IT load. This approach doesn't require the conventional hot and cold aisle configuration. All the racks face one direction. The air is only delivered to the first row. Heat containment doesn't require extra installation material, such as curtains and doors. The heat load is removed immediately within a rack.

Except for the first row of the racks, the cooling system is passive, which means it doesn't require assistance from external fans. This configuration can deliver cool air from one side of data center to the other. It is quite efficient (see Figure 9.8).

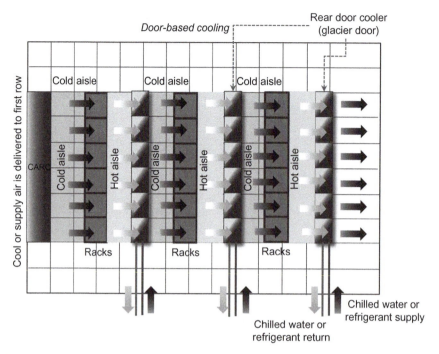

FIGURE 9.8

Rear door-based cooling.

Although it is quite efficient, this configuration also adds installation costs or initial investment capex. It is similar to rack-based cooling. Although this cooling strategy has many benefits, it is quite challenging to build door-based redundancy. If one of the rear cooling doors fails, the impact on the IT load is much less than with other containment system. There are many vendors that provide rear door cooling products, such as:

- Vette (RDHX)
- IBM (Rear Door iData Plex)
- Sun (Sun Glacier)
- Liebert (XDR Passive Rear Door)

9.7 RAISING THE DATA CENTER TEMPERATURE

Raising floor temperature is also considered another cooling strategy to save on opex, and optimize or minimize operating costs. Many IT heavyweights such as Google, eBay, Amazon, HP, IBM, Microsoft, Oracle/Sun, Dell, Yahoo, etc. have been trying to raise data center temperature to save millions of dollars in power consumption opex. Some data center experts and facility managers [153] believe that many temperature settings or floor temperatures are too lower or too conservative.

These settings are very often recommended by IT equipment vendors. For example, some temperature settings are as lower as only 12−13°C. The average temperature is around 20−22°C. Google believes the temperature can be increased to around 26−27°C.

During a 2007 data center conference, Oracle/Sun indicated that if a data center temperature can be raised by one degree, the energy bill can be reduced by 4%. Based on Google's recommended settings, the average cost of energy consumption can be reduced between 20−28%. Microsoft said that it saved $250 k per annum by raising the temperature 2 to 4 degrees in its Silicon Valley data center.

However, this doesn't mean that there is no cost to raising temperature. Some data center managers warn that if the operational temperature is set to higher than a vendor's recommended level, the warranty will be voided. Furthermore, in the case of a power failure, a data center with a higher temperature setting wouldn't have enough buffer time for the system to switch to a backup mode. It may lead to a system being shut down. Still further, Nosayba El-Sayed et al.'s [154] study showed that when temperature approaches 40°C, some IT devices will become unreliable. Overall, the authors were trying to find three relationships with temperature:

- Temperature and reliability
- Temperature and performance
- Temperature and energy consumption

Based on their data from a dozen data centers within thre different organizations, their conclusions were:

1. The impact of high temperature on system reliability is less than what we have often assumed.
2. There is no clear evidence between high temperature and some IT component (server nodes and DRAM) failures or outages.
3. Temperature variation is more important than average temperature level in terms of system reliability.
4. CPU power consumption will increase sharply after 30°C because of increasing server fan speed, but when the temperature reaches 40°C, power consumption will again stabilize. This may be due to the limits of fan speed. In the increase from 30 to 40°C, power consumption goes up by 50%. This conclusion appears to be aligned with the fan law.
5. If the temperature increases linearly while it is below 50°C, the number of errors for an IT device will also grow linearly, not exponentially.
6. The performance will deteriorate if the temperature is above 50°C, but it is dependent on the device. Some disk drive performance starts declining at 60°C.
7. Power leakage for both processors and internal server cooling fan speeds seems to be negligible due to poorly designed algorithms of controlling data center fan speed.

In summary, the authors made a general conclusion that most organizations could run their data center at a higher temperature than the current temperature configuration without making significant sacrifices in system reliability.

This research paper indicated one of the cooling strategy options is to increase the current data center temperature if it has been configured too low. However, we should be very careful in configuring the temperature settings because a data center doesn't only accommodate servers and storage disk drivers but also network gear, such as routers, switches, load balancers, security devices, and network management systems. Each hardware device will have different response in terms of different temperatures settings. As a general rule of thumb, the recommended upper temperature limits for a data center would be:

- Server $= 32-35°C$
- Storage devices $= 35-40°C$
- Telco or network equipment $= 40-45°C$

Ultimately, when the temperature setting is decided upon, the data center manager should consult each vendor and ask for the psychometric chart for the equipment. It would be unwise to set the temperature point too high and beyond the warranty boundary of the psychometric chart.

Most major vendors, such as Cisco, HP, Dell, Oracle/Sun,[1] and IBM provide the operating temperatures for their hardware devices. For example, HP states the operating temperature of its HP ProLiant DL 380G8 (one of HP's x86 servers) is between 10 and 35°C and relative humidity (RH) is from 10% to 90% (see Figure 9.9). However, it indicates that if the dry-bulb temperature is over 30°C, the system performance may deteriorate. Moreover, the maximum wet-bulb temperature should be kept below 28°C and the maximum rate of change should not be more than 10°C per hour (or 18°F per hour).

Of course, the nonoperating boundary limit (when keeping device in storage for example) is larger than the operating one, with the dry-bulb temperature ranging from $-30°C$ to 60°C and RH from 5% to 95%.

However, for every 300 meters a data center location is above sea level, the upper limit of dry-bulb temperature should be dropped by 1°C due to the lower atmospheric pressure (see Figure 9.10).

The recommended approach is to increase data center temperature incrementally rather sudden increasing it a large amount more than 10°C. After the setting has been increased, we should monitor the response of all IT devices very closely and carefully. Of course, before doing so, it is essential to fully understand the data center environment conditions, such as RH and dry- and wet-bulb temperatures because we need to make an assessment after the temperature is raised.

9.8 FREE COOLING USING ECONOMIZERS

One of most effective cooling strategies to reduce cooling cost and increase cooling efficiency is using free cooling by leveraging economizers. Economizers introduce outside cool air when the outside temperature is lower than the inside temperature of a data center. Currently, we can adopt two types of economizers:

- Air-side economizer
- Water-side economizer

---

[1]The lower boundary dry temperature of the X3-2B server blade, Oracle/Sun's x86 series product, is 5°C.

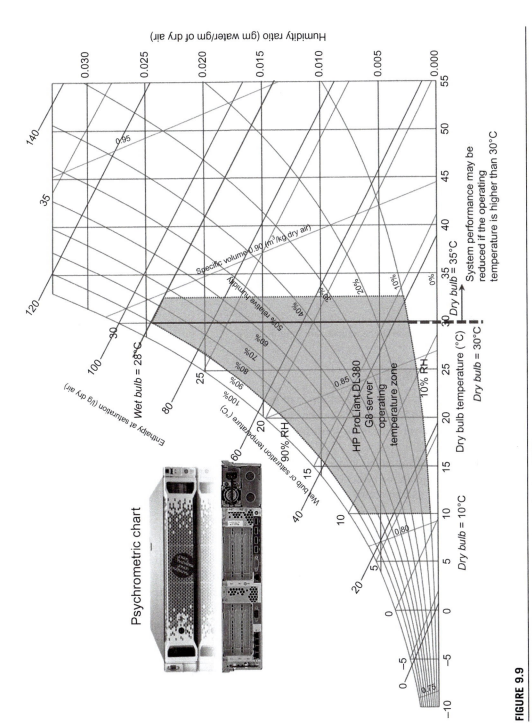

FIGURE 9.9

HP ProLiant DL 380 G8 warranty psychometric chart [155].

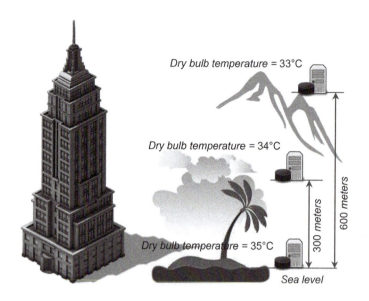

Dry bulb temperature = 33°C

Dry bulb temperature = 34°C

Dry bulb temperature = 35°C

Sea level

300 meters

600 meters

FIGURE 9.10

For every 300 meters above sea level, the temperature limit drops by 1°C.

9.8.1 AIRSIDE ECONOMIZER

An airside economizer directly draws cool air from outside of a data center, while the hot or return air is directly rejected to outside the data center building. However, this doesn't mean just "opening the window.". The supply or outside air must be monitored and conditioned for the correct relative humidity level (see Figure 9.11).

Theoretically speaking, when the temperature of outside air is below the data center's return air, the airside economizer should be switched on for the IT load. The ideal situation is that the climate has a stable temperature and humidity profile.

9.8.2 WATERSIDE ECONOMIZER

In comparison with an airside economizer (or directly drawing on the outside air), a waterside economizer indirectly cools the data center, using outside air to reduce the temperature of chilled water within an external water tower rather than using electricity to cool the chilled water. The chilled water is then distributed to CRAH or CRAC units (see Figure 9.12).

Many researchers have conducted different studies [157, 158] to compare airside and waterside economizers. Which one is better or more energy efficient? It is really dependent on the location of the data center. At some geographic locations, an airside economizer is more efficient than a waterside one. At other locations, the waterside type may be better than an airside economizer.

The Green Grid organization [159] provides cooling map web tool to estimate energy efficiency in the US, Europe, and Japan. Figures 9.13 and 9.14 show both waterside and airside cooling maps for Europe.

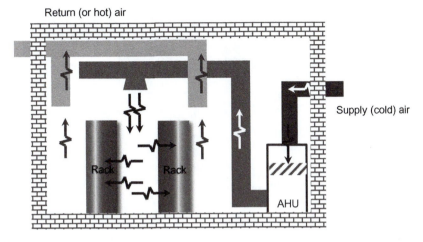

FIGURE 9.11

Airside economizer.

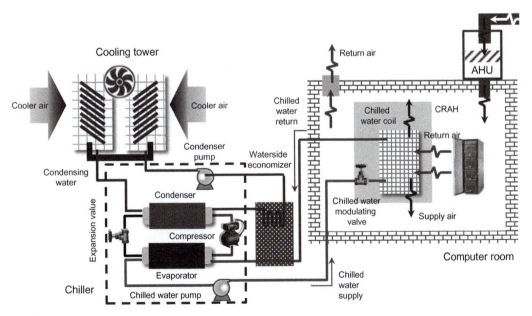

FIGURE 9.12

Waterside Economizer.

FIGURE 9.13

Airside cooling map for Europe [156].

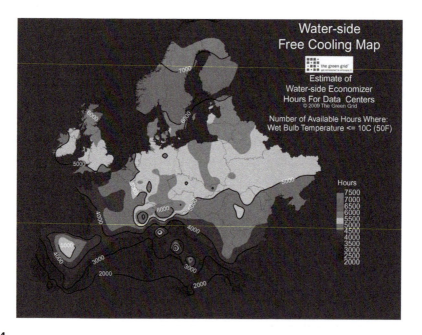

FIGURE 9.14

Waterside cooling map for Europe.

Based on the above airside cooling map, we can see that the Scandinavian countries, the United Kingdom, and Ireland have more than 8,000 hours of free cooling per year. In other words, if we build a data center in these countries, we can have at least 11 months of free cooling. In comparison, looking at Figure 9.14, waterside cooling only offers between 5,000 and 7,000 hours free cooling. This is more than one month less free cooling. Therefore, it would be better to adopt the airside economizer approach in these countries.

However, there are some advantages for waterside (fluid-side) economizers. The heat is directly transferred from the chilled water or glycol loop to the outside and the inside cooling temperature is provided by cooler air from outside without using the refrigeration cycle.

It is less risky because the heat exchange process is isolated between outside and inside systems rather than using direct introduction of outside air. There will be very little impact on data center space. It is best suited for colder climates or weather when the outside temperature is colder than the chilled water loop, which runs from 4°C to 10°C.

The same website [160] also provides a calculation tool to estimate free cooling savings (see Figure 9.15). We can use this tool to estimate operation costs in term of cooling. Ultimately, this

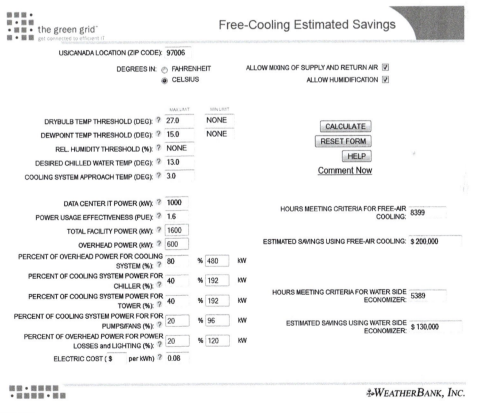

FIGURE 9.15

Free-cooling estimated savings.

can help us to calculate total cost of ownership (TCO) and return on investment (ROI). These estimated results can help decision makers and stakeholders make the right investment decisions for a data center investment project, which we will discuss in detail in later chapters.

The Green Grid free-cooling map and estimated assumptions are based on the ASHRAE recommended ranges for both temperature and humidity. Since 1999, ASHRAE has published four different versions of its specification, in 1999, 2004, 2008, and 2011. ASHRAE already released the 2013 version. Therefore, when you are trying to estimate free-cooling savings, you have to be aware of what ASHRAE version you are using. Different versions of the ASHRAE specification may give you different free-cooling results. One of the significant changes made for ASHRAE 2011 was with the class zones (see Tables 9.4 and 9.5).

Table 9.6 makes a clear comparison among three versions of ASHRAE, 2004, 2008 and 2011, for both dry-bulb temperature and relative humidity (RH).

Based on the 2008 and 2011 version of ASHRAE, Green Grid released its corresponding airside free-cooling map in both 2009 and 2012 (see Figures 9.16 and 9.17).

As we can see in the above figures, Green Grid has relaxed the airside free-cooling map. With the 2011 version of ASHRAE, the new class A2 zone has 8,500 hours free cooling per year and covers 75% of North America. In comparison with the earlier map of Europe, the new free-cooling map now covers 99% of Europe. The only location where one cannot use free cooling is Spain (see Table 9.7 and Figure 9.18).

If we compare Figure 9.18 with Figure 9.13, we can see that there is a significant improvement in using airside free cooling on this map.

9.9 SUMMARY

In comparison to Chapter 8, this chapter covered much wider topics in cooling. This is why we call it "Cooling Strategy" in contrast to the optimization topics in the last chapter. We started with a wiring closet cooling strategy, which is just to adopt a comfort cooling system or the existing office cooling system. Then, we offered details of three different methods of cooling in terms of focusing on an object, such as room-, row-, and rack-based cooling. In order to select the right strategy for cooling, we provided pros and cons for these different cooling approaches.

After these basic cooling approaches, we introduced mixed cooling strategies in order to deal with the many lower power density data centers. Further, we discussed a new method of cooling, which is the rack rear door-based cooling strategy.

Finally, we touched on the topic of raising the floor temperature and using free-cooling economizers in order to reduce data center power consumption, which can ultimately reduce data center operating costs.

Table 9.4 ASHRAE 2008 Temperature and Humidity Ranges for Data Centers

	Equipment Environment Specification										
	Product Operation[a,b]							Product Power Off[b,c]			
	Dry Bulb Temperature (°C)		Humidity Range Non Condensing		Max Dew Point (°C)	Max Elevation (m)	Max Rate of Change (°C/hr)	Dry Bulb Temperature (°C)	RH (%)	Max Dew Point (°C)	
Class	Allowable	Recommended	Allowable (% RH)	Recommended							
1	15 to 32[d]	18 to 27[e]	20 to 80	5.5°C DP to 60% RH and 15°C DP	17	3050	5/20[f]	5 to 45	8 to 80	27	
2	10 to 35[d]	18 to 27[e]	20 to 80	5.5°C DP to 60% RH and 15°C DP	21	3050	5/20[f]	5 to 45	8 to 80	27	
3	5 to 35[d,g]	NA	8 to 80	NA	28	3050	NA	5 to 45	8 to 80	29	
4	5 to 40[d,g]	NA	8 to 80	NA	28	3050	NA	5 to 45	8 to 80	29	

[a]Product equipment is powered on.
[b]Tape products require a stable and more restrictive environment (similar to Class 1). Typical requirements: minimum temperature is 15°C, maximum temperature is 32°C, minimum relative humidity is 20%, maximum relative humidity is 80%, maximum dew point is 22°C, rate of change of temperature is less than 5°C/h, rate of change of humidity is less than 5% RH per hour, and no condensation.
[c]Product equipment is removed from original shipping container and installed but not in use, e.g., during repair maintenance, or upgrade.
[d]Derate maximum allowable dry-bulb temperature 1°C/300 m above 900 m.
[e]Derate maximum recommended dry-bulb temperature 1°C/300 m above 1800 m.
[f]5°C/hr for data centers employing tape drives and 20°C/h for data centers employing disk drives.
[g]With diskette in the drive, the minimum temperature is 10°C.

Table 9.5 ASHRAE 2011 Temperature and Humidity Ranges for Data Centers

Class[a]	Product Operation[b,c]					Product Power Off[c,d]		
	Dry-Bulb Temperature (°C)[e,g]	Humidity Range Non Condensing[h,i,j]	Max. Dew Point (°C)	Max Elevation (m)	Max Rate of Change (°C/hr)[f]	Dry Bulb Temperature (°C)	RH (%)	Max Dew Point (°C)

Recommended (applies to all A classes; individual data centers can choose to expand this range based upon the analysis described in the ASHRAE paper)

Class[a]	Dry-Bulb Temp	Humidity Range	Max Dew Pt	Max Elev	Max Rate	Dry Bulb	RH	Max Dew Pt
A1 to A4	18 to 27	5.5°C DP to 60% RH and 15°C DP						

Allowable

A1	15 to 32	20% to 80% RH	17	3050	5/20	5 to 45	8 to 80	27
A2	10 to 35	20% to 80% RH	21	3050	5/20	5 to 45	8 to 80	27
A3	5 to 40	−12(°C) DP & 8% RH to 85% RH	24	3050	5/20	5 to 45	8 to 80	27
A4	5 to 45	−12(°C) DP & 8% RH to 90% RH	24	3050	5/20	5 to 45	8 to 80	27
B	5 to 35	8% RH to 80% RH	28	3050	NA	5 to 45	8 to 80	29
C	5 to 40	8% RH to 80% RH	28	3050	NA	5 to 45	8 to 80	29

[a]Classes A1, A2, B and C are identical to 2008 classes 1, 2, 3 and 4. These classes have simply been renamed to avoid confusion with classes A1 through A4. The recommended envelope is identical to that published in the 2008 version.

[b]Product equipment is powered on.

[c]Tape products require a stable and more restrictive environment (similar to Class A1). Typical requirements: minimum temperature is 15°C, maximum temperature is 32°C, minimum relative humidity is 20%, maximum relative humidity is 80%, maximum dew point is 22°C, rate of change of temperature is less than 5°C/hr, rate of change of humidity is less than 5% RH per hour, and no condensation.

[d]Product equipment is removed from original shipping container and installed but not in use, e.g., during repair maintenance, or upgrade.

[e]A1 and A2 - Derate maximum allowable dry-bulb temperature 1°C/300 m above 950 m.
A3 - Derate maximum allowable dry-bulb temperature 1°C/175 m above 950 m.
A4 - Derate maximum allowable dry-bulb temperature 1°C/125 m above 950 m.

[f]5°C/hr for data centers employing tape drives and 20°C/hr for data centers employing disk drives.

[g]With diskette in the drive, the minimum temperature is 10°C.

[h]The minimum humidity level for class A3 and A4 is the higher (more moisture) of the −12°C dew point and the 8% relative humidity. These intersect at approximately 25°C. Below this intersection (~25°C) the dew point (−12°C) represents the minimum moisture level, while above it relative humidity (8%) is the minimum.

[i]Moisture levels lower than 0.5°C DP, but not lower −10°C DP or 8% RH, can be accepted if appropriate control measures are implemented to limit the generation of static electricity on personnel and equipment in the data center. All personnel and mobile furnishings/equipment must be connected to ground via an appropriate static control system. The following items are considered the minimum requirements (see Appendix A for additional details):
1. Conductive Materials
   a. conductive flooring
   b. conductive footwear on all personnel that go into the datacenter, including visitors just passing through;
   c. all mobile furnishing/equipment will be made of conductive or static dissipative materials.
2. During maintenance on any hardware, a properly functioning wrist strap must be used by any personnel who contacts IT equipment.

Table 9.6 ASHRAE 2004, 2008, and 2011 Temperature and Humidity Range Comparison for Data Centers

Year	Recommended			Allowable		
	2004	2008	2011	2004	2008	2011
Temperature Range	20–25 (°C)	18–27 (°C)	18–27 (°C)	15–32 (°C)	10–35 (°C)	5–45 (°C)
Relative Humidity Range	40%–55% RH	5.5°C DP to 60% RH and 15°C DP	5.5°C DP to 60% RH and 15°C DP	20%–80% RH	20%–80% RH	−12(°C) DP & 8% RH to 90% RH

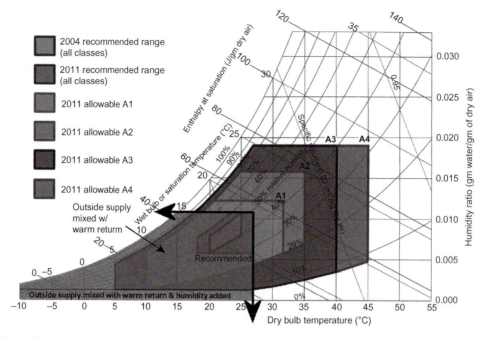

FIGURE 9.16

Airside free-cooling map based on ASHRAE 2008 [99].

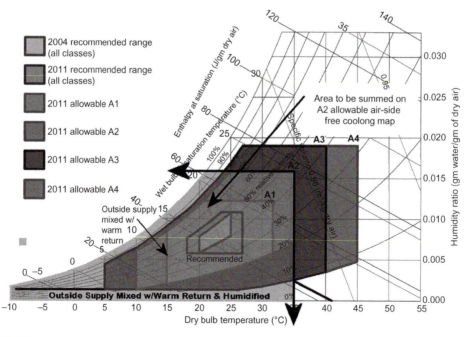

FIGURE 9.17

Airside free-cooling map based on ASHRAE 2011 [99].

Table 9.7 Green Grid Airside Free-Cooling Comparison between 2009 and 2012		
Version	**2009**	**2012**
Recommended Max Dry Bulb	27 (°C)	35 (°C)
Dew Point	15 (°C)	21 (°C)

FIGURE 9.18

Airside free-cooling map for Europe (Green Grid 2012).

9.10 REVIEW QUESTIONS

1. What is the best strategy to cool a wiring closet? The closet only has five racks and each rack's power density is 3.5 kW.
2. What is conduction cooling?
3. What are the pros and cons of room-based, row-based, and rack-based cooling?
4. What is the best fit for mixing room- and row-based cooling strategies?
5. How many types of free economizers are there?
6. Where is the best place to utilize free economizers?
7. What are the disadvantages to raising the data center temperature in order to save power?
8. How can we install a high-density rack in the existing data center that can only handle low-density racks?
9. What does "rack containment" mean?
10. What is the new technology for data center cooling?

FIRE SUPPRESSION AND ON-SITE SECURITY

10

This chapter covers two major topics: fire suppression (sometimes called a fire sprinkler system) and physical security. The first topic can be considered a part of chemical engineering, but we will just focus on how to select the best solution for a data center. We divide this topic into two parts. One is fire detection or the fire alarm system and the other is fire suppression.

The second topic of this chapter is on-site or physical security systems. Based on the TIA 942 standard, different tiers of data center should have different physical security systems. We can discuss physical security with reference to three layers:

- Physical layer
- Organzational layer
- Infrastructure layer

We will focus on the physical and organizational layers. Actually, the weakest security link is at the organizational layer because of frequent organizational changes.

Finally, we discuss the cost of physical security systems. The more the sophisticated security system is the more it will cost. We have to find the balance between security risks and the cost of the system.

10.1 INTRODUCTION

Right from the start of Part II, we have mainly focused on the three major cost components of a data center, which are space, power, and cooling. There are also two additional and essential issues that we should not ignore, which are fire suppression and on-site or physical security systems. These components are absolutely critical for any enterprise-class data center and even for a wiring closet because any IT equipment damage will have devastating consequences. This is not only very costly due to unplanned outages that trigger interruptions in normal business operations but also could lead to unrecoverable damage to the business and sometime even at a personal level. Therefore, a fire suppression system is mandatory. Many developed countries have legislation, codes, and standards to prevent fire hazards.

Table 10.1 Temperature Comparison

	Temperature °C
Upper limit for server	35
Hard disk damage	65
IT equipment damage	80
Car ignition	150
IT device smoking	200–275
Sprinkler activation (fire)	300–320

Fire suppression systems are not new. They have been widely applied in the building industry. The mechanisms of fire protection systems are well understood. Many vendors or manufacturers provide a wide range of products and services for fire protection systems. We will not reproduce this information or material. For many data center decision makers and managers, the most important questions are the following: How do I select a fire suppression system for the data center? How do I manage it? How can I make a comparison among different fire suppression technologies and what is the TCO/ROI for the selected fire suppression system? What is the benchmark cost for a fire suppression system?

Before we answer these questions, let's examine what are we going to protect in a data center and what kind of fire could occur. Table 10.1 outlines various typical temperatures for comparison and provides a rough idea of when a fire suppression system might activate.

10.2 ISSUES WITH TRADITIONAL FIRE SUPPRESSION SYSTEMS

Our previous experience demonstrates that smoke causes more than 95% of IT device damage, lost data, and early component failures. When the fire suppression system has been switched on, the IT devices might already be melted or damaged. However the fire suppression system can protect other data center equipment, such as PDUs; UPS, CRAC, and CRAH units; cables; and generators. Therefore, it is absolutely critical to select the right fire detection and suppression system.

During the last few decades or so, many vendors and manufacturers have developed different innovative fire suppression systems in order to find a better way to protect IT equipment in a data center because the traditional fire suppression system not only creates many side effects for IT equipment but also does not suit the latest IT equipment. Some obvious issues are:

- Water sprinkler systems can lead to irreversible damage in a data center.
- Traditional fire suppression systems will damage the Earth's ozone layer, which triggers global warming.
- Traditional systems are too expensive to be install and maintain.
- Because of Moore's law, today's IT equipment is much smaller, compact, and powerful. The heat density is much higher than traditional IT equipment.

10.3 FIRE CLASSIFICATION AND STANDARDS

In order to prevent fire, we have to understand what type of fire we will encounter in a data center. The United States, Europe, and Australia have different classifications for fire, but they are closely correlated (see Table 10.2).

Referring to Table 10.2, the combination of A, B, C, and E will be encountered in a typical data center. When we make a selection for a fire solution, all these fire types should be taken into consideration.

It doesn't matter what size the data center is. The fire system must meet the minimum requirements based on National Fire Protection Associated Code 75 in the US or AS-1850 in Australia; the system must have:

- Fire detection
- Alarm components
- A sprinkler system
- Portable fire extinguisher
- Emergency power off (EPO) ability

A clean-agent suppression system can be considered an "add-on" for medium and large enterprise data centers.

10.3.1 FIRE DETECTION

Obviously, before the fire is extinguished, it must be detected. Now, the question is, where should the detector be placed? We can set fire detectors everywhere, but it would cost too much. Based on the best practices of fire protection in a data center, the recommended places for smoke alarms would be two areas: around the computer room and in the power room as described in the following.

Table 10.2 Different Standards of Fire Classification

United States	Europe	Australia AS-1850	Fuel or Heat Source	Explanation
Class A	Class A	Class A	Ordinary combustibles	Everyday flammable substances like wood, cloth, paper, rubber, and many plastics
Class B	Class B	Class B	Flammable liquids	Liquids, greases, and oils and similar substances that are flammable and combustible
Class B	Class C	Class C	Flammable gases	Gas substances are the source of combustion
Class C	–	Class E	Electrical equipment	Energized electrical devices such as computer equipment or fuse boxes are the sources of these fires
Class D	Class D	Class D	Combustible metals	Combustible metals provide the basis for combustion
Class E	–	–	Radioactive materials	
Class K	Class F	Class F	Cooking oil or fat	Restaurant, kitchen, or other fires beginning in overheated cooking oils and fats

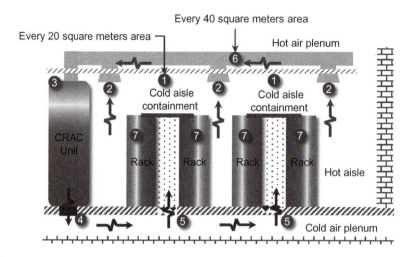

FIGURE 10.1

Typical locations for fire detection in a data center.

10.3.1.1 Computer room detection

- Sensitive electronic equipment
- Raised floor (because invisible)
- High velocity airflow
- Aisle containment system

When we place fire detection sensors in a computer room, there are at least seven basic locations that should be considered (see Figure 10.1).

1. For a cold aisle with containment, one air sampling detection point should be placed every 20 square meters.
2. For a hot aisle, one air sampling detection point should be placed at each colleting point of return air.
3. For a CRAC unit, one air sampling detection point should be set at the entry of the CRAC unit.
4. At the supply air outlet of a CRAC unit, one air sampling detection point should be placed.
5. At the each perforated tile or just before the supply air exit point, one air sampling detection point should be placed.
6. For early warning fire detection (EWFD), one air sampling detection point should be set every 40 square meters.
7. For each rack, one air sampling detection point should be set.

10.3.1.2 Power room detection

- Emergency generator room
- Automatic emergency power off (EPO) & power distribution
- Fire retardant material (smoke)

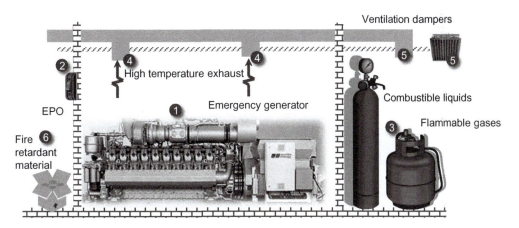

FIGURE 10.2

Typical fire detection for power room and other flammable objects.

For a data center power room, the recommended detection points should be near:

- Combustible liquids
- Flammable gases
- High temperature engine surface and exhaust
- Interlocks: dampers, ventilation, and fuel

Refer to Figure 10.2 for typical fire detection for a power room and other flammable objects.

10.3.1.3 Fire detection system

The fire detection system consists of three major components: air sampling smoke detection sensors, sampling pipe, and a centralized detector (see Figure 10.3).

Ideally, the air sampling smoke sensors will give a very early warning and detect the fire at the incipient stage rather than beyond stage 2 or visible smoke (see Figure 10.4).

In order to increase fire detection performance, NFPA[1] 72 (National Fire Alarm Code) suggests the following parameters for airflow rate, air change per hour (ACH), and spacing per detector (see Table 10.3).

10.4 FIRE SUPPRESSION SOLUTION SELECTION

Once we fully understand what types of fire to detect and where to place air sampling detectors, the next issue is how to select the right fire suppression system for the business. If a data center is just leased space, such as an office complex, it would be too expansive to purchase and install fire system because it will become a permanent fixture which will not be portable when a lease contract

---

[1]National Fire Protection Association.

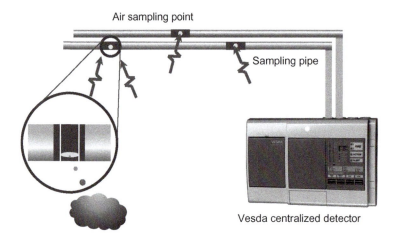

FIGURE 10.3

Air sampling smoke detection system.

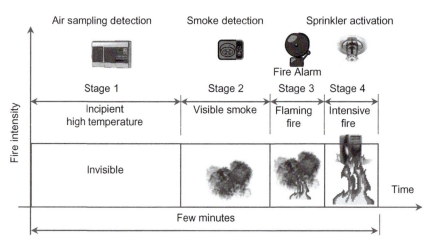

FIGURE 10.4

Four stages of fire development.

expires. In addition, if a company would like to expand or downsize its operation, such a system becomes very inflexible.

The ideal system should be a standardized module that can be uninstalled and reinstalled and and is not a permanent fixtures. Thus the investment for fire suppression becomes a portable asset. This would be similar to a computer room or containerized data center.

Some fire suppression systems require very little cleanup; they use what is called "clean agent gases." Others require a cleaning crew to spend a few days to clean up the mess after a fire. Even

Table 10.3 Airflow Rate and Spacing per Detector

Minutes per Air Change	Air Change per Hour (ACH)	Spacing per Detector (m²)
1	60	12
2	30	23
3	20	35
4	15	46
5	12	58
6	10	70
7	8.6	81
8	7.5	84
9	6.7	84
10	6	84

if it is a tiny fire, it might lead to a few days of business downtime. Furthermore, when the cleaning job is completed, the fire suppression system has to be recharged. This is a time-consuming and a very expensive process. In addition to these costs, there is an extra issue to be considered: the environment. The old popular fire suppressant "halon" has been banned since 1995 because of ozone depletion potential (ODP) and global warming potential (GWP). Based on environmental considerations, the Table 10.4 [161] presents a comparison among different agents using seven different characteristics.

10.4.1 TRADITIONAL FIRE SUPPRESSION SOLUTIONS

Traditional fire suppression solutions commonly refer to three types of fire extinguisher: carbon dioxide or CO_2, water, and halon. These solutions have been widely adopted throughout the 20th century.

10.4.1.1 Carbon dioxide (CO₂) fire suppression

Carbon Dioxide (CO_2) is quite effective generally but it is an especially effective solution for Class B and Class E fire according to AS-1850. However, CO_2 is harmful when inhaled at high concentrations (>5% by volume or 50,000 parts per million (ppm)). The threshold limit value (TLV) for healthy adults for eight hours per day is 0.5% (or 5,000 ppm). Therefore, people must be vacated before the CO_2 system discharges.

10.4.1.2 Water-based (or water mist) fire suppression

In comparison with CO_2, a water solution has no toxicity and asphyxiation problems. It is environmentally friendly and has a lower cost. It is highly efficienct in suppressing certain fires, specifically class A and B, and controlling liquid and solid fuel fires. However, a water-based

Table 10.4 Characteristics of Each Fire Suppression Solution

Fire Suppression Solution	Carbon Dioxide CO₂	Water	Inergen	FE-227 ENCARO-25	Aerosol (Aero-K)
Agent Type	Invisible pressurised CO_2	Water sprinkler or water mist	Inert gas (52% nitrogen, 40% argon, and 8% carbon dioxide)	Liquefied compressed gas	Potassium-based aerosol using pyrotechnic-based chemistry
Toxicity (GWP, ODP)[1]	GWP = 1.0 ODP = 0	GWP = 0 ODP = 0	GWP = 0 ODP = 0	GWP = 2900 ODP = 0	GWP = 1.0 ODP = 0 Environmentally friendly and nontoxic
Cost of Installation	Higher (more than $10 k)	Medium (less than $1 k)	Medium (less than $1 k)	Higher (more than $10 k)	Lower (less than one hundred)
Space Required for installation	Piping & floor space required	Piping & sprinkler head installation	Large space & weight requirements for storage	Piping & floor space required	Wall space required. No piping minimal space and weight requirements
Cleanup	None	Potentially extensive	None	None	Vent with fan, minor residue on surface requires dusting
Unique Features	1. Displaces oxygen in the environment 2. Toxic. Not safe to breathe upon 3. Discharge 4. Must pass an air integrity test/room must be pressurized 5. Not intended for Class A fires	1. Flooding effective for class A fires only 2. Can damage electrical equipment beyond repair	1. Breaks down in the presence of heat 2. Extinguishes fires by reducing the oxygen level 3. After discharge pressure must be relieved to avoid damage to the enclosure 4. Does not create a fog 5. Breathable during discharge	1. Must pass an air integrity test/room must be pressurized 2. Free of residue 3. Noncorrosive 4. Low toxicity 5. Nonflammable	1. Room integrity test not required 2. Uses a fire suppressing aerosol of extremely small particles of potassium compounds suspended in carrier gasses 3. Noncorrosive, nontoxic
Effectiveness	Very	Dependent upon fire type	Very	Very	Very

Note:
[1]*The ozone depletion potential (ODP) and global warming potential (GWP) values are from Table 1.5 and 1.6 of The Scientific Assessment of Ozone Depletion, 2002, a report of the World Meteorological Association's Global Ozone Research and Monitoring Project. All GWP values represent global warming potential over a 100-year time horizon.*

solution is not suitable for a computer room or class E fire (based on the AS-1850 standard) or class C (based on NFPA). Cleanup and safety issues are the biggest concerns when electronic components get wet.

The downtime after water discharge may be as long as a few weeks for a water sprinkler system. Moreover, a water sprinkler system is not portable. It cannot be uninstalled and reinstalled in a new location. It would become a fixture of the building. If the business plan involves a short period of time, a water sprinkler is not an ideal solution for fire suppression.

10.4.1.3 Halon

Halon can be considered a "clean agent" because it is a nonconducting, volatile, or gaseous fire extinguishing substance that does not leave a residue on the equipment but evaporates quickly. There are two very common types of Halon, which is a chlorofluorocarbon (CFC) based substance. They are:

- Halon 1211 (a liquid streaming agent, 85% liquid + 15% gas)
- Halon 1301 (a gaseous flooding agent)

They are remarkably safe for human exposure, have low toxicity, and are chemically stable. Based on the research [162], Halon is quite effective for class A (common combustible), class B (flammable liquids) and class E (electrical) fires.

Halon is an extraordinarily fire suppression agent, even at lower density. The way that Halon works is not only to suppress three fire ingredients but also to break the fire chain reaction in these three ways:

- Suppresses burning material, which is the source of fire or anything can be burnt
- Reduces oxygen, which is an essential element for fire to continue
- Eliminates ignition sources (high heat can trigger fire even without any spark or open flame)

Halon is similar to CO_2 in terms of leaving no residue on the devices. However, in contrast to CO_2, Halon does not displace the air out of the area where it is dispensed. Even for the toughest fires, less than an 8% ppm concentration of Halon should be enough to suppress the fire and leave plenty of air to use in the evacuation process. Also, unlike CO_2, there is no danger of "cold shocking" avionics or other sensitive electrical equipment.

Because of these benefits, Halon became very popular starting in the 1960s. It was in widespread use as one of the fire suppression agents in the protection of data center and telecommunication rooms around the world.

However, since the Montreal Protocol in 1987 [163], Halon has been identified as an ozone depleting potential (ODP) chemical because it is a CFC-based compound production ceased on January 1st, 1994.

ODP is a relative scale that measures a compound's ability to destroy ozone. Common refrigerants used in domestic refrigerators and automobile air conditioners have been assigned an ODP value 1 as the baseline.

Halon 1301 has a value between 10 and 16, which mean it can have 10 to 16 times the potential to destroy ozone layer. It is estimated that overall Halon accounts for about 11%–20% of ozone depletion.

Following in the footsteps of the Montreal Protocol, the Kyoto Protocol created in December 1997 was committed to reducing gases with global warming potential (GWP) in by cutting industry CO_2 and hydrofluorocarbon (HFC) emission.

GWP is also a relative measurement. It is to quantify how much heat is trapped in the atmosphere. It is the globally averaged relative radioactive force impact of a particular greenhouse gas. This radioactive force (both direct and indirect effects) is a cumulative quantity, which is integrated over a period of time from the emission of a unit mass of gas relative to some reference gas. The International Panel on Climate Change (IPCC) selected CO_2 as this reference gas in 1996. GWP = mass (metric tons) of carbon dioxide equivalents/mass of gas.

If Halon is not a solution, what is an alternative? This is the topic we are going to discuss in the next section.

10.5 INERT GASES, HALOCARBONS, AND AEROSOL

10.5.1 INERT GASES

Inert gases are a compound of nitrogen (52%), argon (40%), and CO_2 (8%). There are some health concerns in relation to the use of inert gases because they are similar to CO2 in that the fire suppression is based upon the effectiveness of reducing oxygen content within the protected space.

Inert gases are not toxic but a discharge of inert gases results in approximately a 3% concentration of carbon dioxide. Although it is still breathable, evacuation is recommended for humans. Since it is not stored in a liquid state, it requires a considerable amount of space.

10.5.2 HALOCARBONS

A halocarbon is any chemical compound that consists of carbon combined with one or more halogens. Two of characteristics of halocarbons are that they are nonflammable and nonreactive. However some halocarbons will be stimulated by ultraviolet radiation in the upper atmosphere and can damage the ozone layer.

Table 10.5 lists five common halocarbon materials for fire suppression. The method of halocarbon fire suppression is 80% chemical reaction plus 20% cooling.

10.5.3 AEROSOL

Aerosol is the newest technology for fire suppression. It was approved by the NFPA in 2005. It has no postcombustion byproducts. One of the typical products is Aero-K. It consists of ultra-fine particles that are expelled via generators. When it is discharged, it generates a fog-like environment and remains in the air for up to one hour to eliminate any chance of reignition. Cleanup activities are just venting the room and a light dusting of the surfaces. It is not toxic or corrosive.

In contrast to gaseous systems, it doesn't need operational pressure or pump installation. It is very cost effective in terms of installation and maintenance and requires minimal space.

Table 10.5 Inert Gas Agent versus Halocarbon Agent

Inert Gases	How Does It Work?	Halocarbons	How Does It Work?
Inergen		FM-200 (HFC227, FE227)	
Argonite		FE-13	
Nitrogen	Reduction of oxygen to less than 15% concentration	Ecaro-25 (FE-25)	80% chemical reaction + 20% cooling
Carbon Dioxide		CEA-410	
ProInert		NAFS-III	

10.5.4 FLUORINATED KETONE (LIQUID) (NOVEC 1230)

This is a nonhazardous clean agent. The method of fire suppression is through 80% cooling and 20% chemical reaction, as it works based on a cooling effect rather than reducing oxygen. It is a safe solution for both people and the environment. It has the lowest GWP ($=1$) and ODP ($=0$) in comparison with other clean agents.

The energy discharge is through a pipe and nozzle that causes vaporization. The common water pressure at home is between 40−80 psi (pounds per square inch or 2−6 bars). Novec 1230 has 360 psi or 25 bar pressure with nitrogen. Its boiling temperature is only 49.2°C. The heat of vaporization is 25 times less than water.

At room temperature, Novec 1230 is liquid. It can be regarded as the third generation of clean agent. It is one of the potential gaseous fire suppression agents that can replace traditional Halon. Actually, it has already been widely adopted in Europe.

10.5.5 MOST COMMONLY USED AGENTS IN TODAY'S DATA CENTER

We summarize the characteristics of the above clean agents and the environmental profiles for the Halon alternatives as well as associated costs in Tables 10.6 and 10.7. These are the most commonly used agents in today's data center for fire suppression.

10.6 FIRE SUPPRESSION SYSTEM COST FOR DATA CENTERS

The common practice to estimate fire suppression system cost is based on the size of data center or cost per square meter. We will determine the amount of fire agent required to suppress the fire and the amount of equipment needed to deliver the fire agent. This will also be the basis for an air smoking sampling detection system.

The fire agent density level will be different for different classes of fire. In addition, the cost is not just a once-off purchase cost. The total cost of ownership (TCO) includes operation and maintenance costs from a life cycle perspective.

Table 10.6 Most Commonly Used Agents in Today's Data Center for Fire Suppression

Clean Agent	Chemical Name	Manufacturer	Category	Fill Weight	Installation Cost	Agent Refill Cost
FM-200	HFC-227ea	Dupont	Halocarbon	12–13 kg	$34 k	$8.5 k
FE-25	HFC125	Dupont	Halocarbon	12–13 kg	$34 k	$8.5 k
Novec 1230 Sapphire	FK-5-1-12mmy2	3M	Floroketone	15–16 kg	$35 k	$9.1 k
Inergen	IG-541 (52%, N2, 40% Ar, 8% CO2)	Tyco Ansul	Inert Gas	122–123 liter	$41 k	$2.2 k (labor)
Argonite/ ProInert	IG-55 (50% N2, 50% Ar)	Fike Corp.	Inert Gas	122–123 liter	$41 k	$2.2 k (labor)

Table 10.7 Environmental Profiles of Different Fire Suppression Solutions

	Halon 1301	FM-200	FE-25	Novec 1230
ODP	12	0	0	0
GWP	6900	3500	3400	1
Atmospheric lifetime (years)	65	33	29	0.014 (5 days)

According to Info-Tech, the average mandatory fire suppression cost for a data center would be around $90–$92 per square meter. The average additional cost, such as for a fire detection system would be around $400 per square meter. Overall, the total cost will be $487–$492 per square meter.

10.7 SUMMARY OF FIRE SUPPRESSION SELECTION

On top of all of the above issues, such as fire types or class, efficiency of fire suppression, space to be covered, detection systems, TCO/ROI and environmental issues, we should also consider the following two additional issues:

- Will the space be occupied by people? If so, CO_2 and some inert gases solutions will be less favorable.
- The storage space requirement for a clean agent various amongst agents. Some occupy very little space, others more space.

Overall, the selection of a fire suppression system including fire detection should involve weighing the pros and cons of different options. It cannot just be focused on the purchase cost alone. The bottom line is to serve the business requirements. Different business requirements for various sizes of data center will have different fire suppression solutions. In Table 10.8, Douglas Alger [109] listed different fire suppression systems in 18 different data centers across the globe.

Table 10.8 Data Center Fire Suppression System Comparison

Organization	Countries	Launched	No. of Racks	Total Space (sqm)	Fire Suppression
ACT Inc.	US	Mar-08	150	623	Double pre-action wet sprinklers, FM-200 gaseous
AISO	US	Apr-05	15	186	Aerosol
Behnhof (Sweden)	Sweden	Sep-08	140	1,000	Novec 1230
Barcelona Supercomputing Center	Spain	Apr-05	48	160 (hosting)	Water mist system
Calcul Québec (Compute Québec)	Canada	Aug-09	56	217 (hosting?[1])	Double-action dry pipe sprinkler system
Cisco	US	Apr-11	754	15,050	Pre-action dry pipe sprinklers, with VESDA smoke detection
Citi	Germany	May-08	2,722?	21,182	Pre-action sprinklers
Digital Realty Trust	US	2005	15,385?	105,295	Dual interlock pre-action system with heat and smoke detection above and below
eBay	US	Oct-11	256	3,902	Double action, pre-action interlocked system; VESDA detection system
Facebook	US	May-11	N/A, 4,949?	13,657	Pre-action dry pipe system with VESDA monitoring
Green House Data	US	Jan-08	200	883	Novec 1230
IBM	US	Nov-09	960	14,865	Wet pipe system, with VESDA detection
Intel	US	Jul-06	268	1,672	Wet pipe sprinkler system with VESDA detection system
IO	US	Jun-09	3,000	49,982	High sensitivity smoke detection, pre-action dry pipe
NetApp	US	Mar-09	2,136	11,613	Double-interlock dry-pipe
Syracuse University	US	Dec-09	70	1,115	Novec 1230
Terremark	US	Jun-01	Various	66,677	Pre-action dry pipe
Yahoo	US	Sep-10	2,800	17,652	Dual interlock, pre-action dry pipe

Note:
[1]This is an estimated figure for hosting space not the total space.

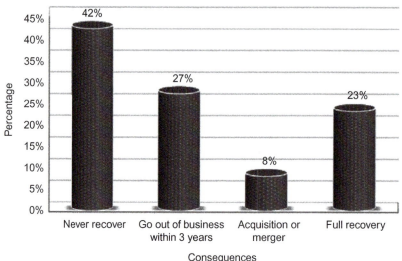

FIGURE 10.5

Consequences for businesses that suffered a major system failure.

10.8 ON-SITE OR PHYSICAL SECURITY

When we start to discuss the topic of data center physical security, the first questions that we encounter are, what does data center physical security mean and what is the context of physical security? These two questions can be simplified with four "W"s:

1. Why do we need protection (purposes)?
2. What is the focus (objects)?
3. Who are we protecting against (threats)?
4. What is most likely to occur (possibilities)?

In contrast to logical security, physical security protects the data center facility. The main purpose of physical security is to protect the business. *Wirtschaftswoche* magazine published the consequences of a major system failure, in Issue 18, April 24, 1997 (see Figure 10.5).

In order to protect business, US lawmakers established a legal framework in order to protect data and information security. This framework is supported by the following legislations:

- Statement on Standard for Attestation Engagement (SSAE) No 16 (2010), which has replaced Statement on Auditing Standard (SAS) No 70 Audit
- Payment Card Industry Data Security Standard (PCI DSS)
- Gramm-Leach-Billey Act (GLBA) (1999)
- Health Insurance Portability and Accountability Act (HIPAA) (1996)
- Sarbanes-Oxley Act (SOX) (2002)
- Federal Information Security Management Act (FISMA) (2002)

Table 10.9 Physical Site Security and Access Control (TIA-942)

Tiering/Objects	Tier 1	Tier 2	Tier 3	Tier 4
Generators	Industry grade lock	Intrusion detection	Intrusion detection	Intrusion detection
UPS telephone & MEP rooms	Industry grade lock	Intrusion detection	Card access	Card access
Fiber vaults	Industry grade lock	Intrusion detection	Intrusion detection	Card access
Emergency exit doors	Industry grade lock	Monitor	Delay egress	Delay egress
Accessible exterior windows	Off-site monitoring	Intrusion detection	Intrusion detection	Intrusion detection
Security operations center	N/A	N/A	Card access	Card access
Doors into computer rooms	Industry grade lock	Intrusion detection	Card or biometric access	Card or biometric access
Perimeter building doors	Off-site monitoring	Intrusion detection	Card access	Card access
Doors from lobby to Floors	Industry grade lock	Card access	Single person interlock	Single person interlock

However, the physical part of data center security is based on TIA-942 (see Tables 10.9 and 10.10).

The International Standard Organisation (ISO) has a similar standard, ISO/IEC 24764. The European Union (EU) has the EN 50173-5 standard. The Australian government released the "Physical Security Management Protocol" (PSMP) in 2011.

The ultimate object to be protected in a data center is the data. In order to protect the data, the underlying infrastructure also must be protected. Physical security means the protection activities should focus on three issues:

- Prevent any catastrophic damage, such as natural disasters, where the data becomes irrecoverable.
- Keep any irrelevant or unauthorized people out of the data center premises.
- Maintain data center integrity. This means only authorized people can have authorized access; not every data center staff member will have all levels of security clearance.

In terms of security implementation, we will have following three layers:

- Physical layer (perimeter, building, data center, computer room, rack)
- Organizational layer (people, organizational structure, and processes)
- Infrastructure layer (servers, storage, and network)

Table 10.10 CCTV Requirements (TIA-942)

CCTV Monitoring	Tier 1	Tier 2	Tier 3	Tier 4
Building perimeter & parking	No requirement	No requirement	Yes	Yes
Generators	N/A	N/A	Yes	Yes
Access controlled doors	No requirement	Yes	Yes	Yes
Computer room floors	No requirement	No requirement	Yes	Yes
UPS, telephone, and MEP rooms	No requirement	No requirement	Yes	Yes
CCTV				
CCTV recording on all cameras	No requirement	No requirement	Yes, digital	Yes, digital

We will leave the infrastructure layer of security to the next part of this book. It mainly involves access to the infrastructure layer and the network management system. This chapter will focus on both physical and organizational layers.

10.9 PHYSICAL LAYERS

Physical security can be divided into five different layers or zones. The closer you get to the core, the higher the security level is. The highest security will be at the physical server or the node in the rack.

The physical security layers or zones are:

- Site perimeter (or public zone)
- Perimeter security (or reception zone)
- Facility control (or operation zone)
- Computer room control (or security zone)
- Cabinet or rack control (or high-security aone)

There two terminologies represent the same concept (see Figure 10.6).

As we can see in the diagram in Figure 10.6, each layer corresponds to a physical security zone. Physical protection means to protect every possible entry point for a data center. In other words, we should think about each entry gate and access door to a rack or high-security zone.

10.9.1 PROTECTING DATA CENTER PERIMETERS

Perimeter protection is the first layer of physical security. The following components make up the baseline protection for the first layer of physical security (see Figure 10.7):

Security envelope

- Fencing
- Moat
- Walls

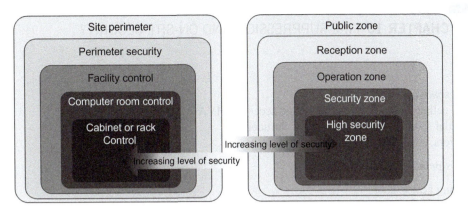

FIGURE 10.6

Five physical security layers of data center.

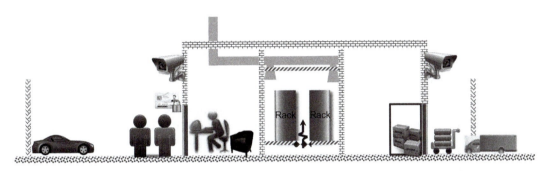

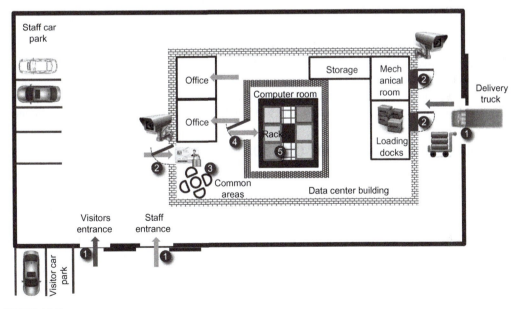

FIGURE 10.7

A typical data center security map.

- Open space clearance
- Roof, celling, windows, internal walls, access to HVAC and wiring
- Potential sources of concealment for intruders
- Exteriors, sight lines, and signage

  Access points: doors and control

- Building access doors
- Rack door locks

  Cameras or CCTV control and monitoring

- Cameras and recording or closed circuit television (CCTV) system
- Monitoring and alarm system

  Human security control

- Security guards

10.9.2 SECURITY ENVELOPE

The fencing, walls, and moat are all part of the physical security envelope to separate public space and the restricted data center. The security envelope may coincide with the data center building footprint or a proportion of it, where a part of the interior security wall is merged with the security envelope. The security envelope doesn't only encompass the fencing and walls but also the roof and ceilings. Various data center facility elements within the physical security envelope must be considered.

"Open space clearance" means there should be at least 3 to 5 meters of clear space from the fence or from the data center building. There should not be any trees, plants, or shrubs that provide points of concealment or allow unauthorized entry to the data center facility. This should be a part of data center landscaping.

There are many potential sources of concealment for intruders, such as foliage, ceilings, ducts, and cages. The security envelope should eliminate these potential sources of concealment.

Exterior sight lines and signage should be kept to a minimum. The data center is not a showground.

10.9.3 ACCESS POINTS AND DOOR CONTROL

From a physical security perspective, the weakest link of a data center is the number of building access points. The more access points the data center has, the more risky the data center is. There are many different approaches to protecting the access points, namely doors. A very basic way of having secure doors is to use key locks or electronic locks. At the next level, for more sophisticated or programmable door locks, we can have card readers or security codes. This is much better when the data center has a colocated business, from which the customer may come and go from time to time. It would not be convenient to change the door lock for every customer that comes and goes. Furthermore, we can use biometrics readers, such as fingerprint, hand, iris, face, retina, and handwriting scans and voice recognition at more secure access points, such as the computer room or server room.

Door control has both physical and logical or policy control elements. The physical control elements involve revolving doors and mantraps to prevent tailgating or piggybacking at the doors.

The logical or policy control is to have a policy under which people sign in and out in logs with regular review of the door access log book and security logs. Door control means not only entry the data center but also exit from it.

10.9.4 CAMERA OR CCTV CONTROL

A camera or CCTV system is part of the real-time monitoring system. If we look from an end-to-end perspective, it is one of 14 critical components of security information and event management (SIEM). Based on the TIA-942 standard, tier 3 and 4 centers must have a CCTV system. When the CCTV system is installed, it must be protected by a UPS system. The recording media should be kept in a very secure place. The recording media has to be regularly reviewed because the quality of the recording media has to be guaranteed. Therefore, during the review process, the following questions should be raised:

* Is the CCTV system functioning properly as per the design specification?
* Can every person accessing the area be identified clearly?
* Can you see all assets that are being removed or relocated?
* Will the recording media be stored securely off-site and be retrievable?
* What is the procedure for access to the recording media?
* How long will the media will be maintained before being destroyed?
* Who can access the media and who can approve the access request?
* Does any camera need to be relocated or justified for a particular object?

    Normally, there are seven critical locations where cameras or CCTV systems need to be placed:

* Entry gates and building entry doors
* Visitor area/lobby or common area
* Electrical and cooling equipment
* Utility and wiring closet rooms
* Loading docks
* Office space
* Media storage

10.9.5 SECURITY GUARDS

If the business requires on-site security guards, the data center must have 24 × 7 security guards. It may cost more in comparison with other physical security solutions but with humans on the premise 24 × 7, the security guards cannot only filter out any possible false alarms, but also can detect security threats in concealed locations that are difficult to detect, such as in bathrooms.

    Ultimately, the function of physical security is to screen every person who wants to get into the data center. It can be boiled down to three fundamental issues:

* Who are you?
* Why are you here?
* When should you be here?

    These issues covered in the next section.

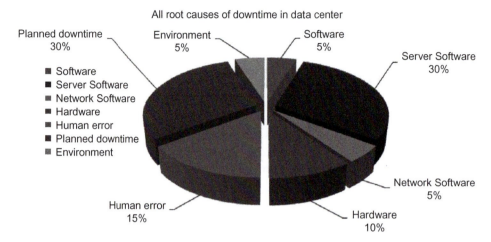

FIGURE 10.8

All root causes of downtime in data center [164].

10.10 ORGANIZATIONAL LAYER

For many data centers, the most vulnerable point in the data center security chain is the humans because only humans make many mistakes and errors. Actually, human error is a major issue for service breakdown in the data center due to change requests (both accidental changes and scheduled changes). Security can prevent some human errors with 24×7 monitoring.

10.10.1 PEOPLE

There is much statistical research showing that people or human errors cause about 15% of unplanned outages or downtime (see Figure 10.8). Within the planned downtime category (30%), there is also a certain percentage of human errors that trigger the data center downtime.

If we exclude all planned downtime or outages, human error increases to 18% (see Figure 10.9).

If we just focus on the critical applications, human errors rise to another level; they could account for 40% of operation errors and system outages, which make up 55% and 22% of the critical applications downtime, respectively (see Figure 10.10).

As shown in Figure 10.11, 7% of the 22% section that represents system outages involves security-related incidents.

If we can reduce human errors in data center operations, we can decrease a significant amount of data center downtime and system outages. Now, the question is, why do human errors occur in a data center? The main reason is because of changes, such as software upgrades, patches, system reconfigurations, scheduled maintenance activities, etc. Is it possible to ban all changes? The answer is definitely "No" because the world is always evolving. Change is inevitable, especially for the IT industry. Of course, it is possible to have a system embargo during special periods, such

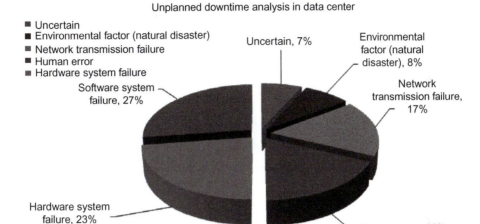

FIGURE 10.9

Unplanned downtime analysis [289]

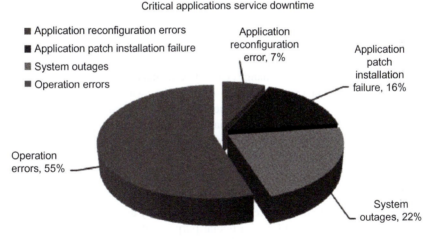

FIGURE 10.10

Critical applications service downtime.

as before a new product launch, during special events, and at Christmas. However, eventually, the changes have to be implemented for business reasons to improve the system.

Change on its own will not cause outages. The outages are triggered by the mistakes or accidents of inexperienced staff or by intentional and malicious activities of certain employees. With the first root cause, staff training and well-documented operating procedures will help decrease the possibility of outages. With the second cause, physical security and well-implemented security policies can reduce the possibility of any security incidents.

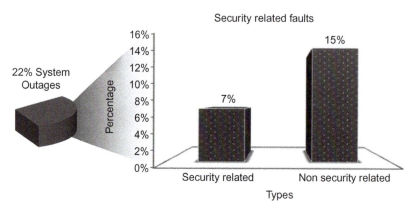

FIGURE 10.11

Breakdown of system outage category from Figure 10.10.

10.10.2 ORGANIZATIONAL STRUCTURE AND POLICY

Due to market competition, the organizational structure is always changing. "The information technology revolution has driven the pace of competition and rapid globalization. Consequently, enterprises increasingly need to consider and pursue fundamental change transformation — to maintain or gain competitive advantage" [289].

When an organization is changing the business, the organizational structure also has to be changed along with the policies. If all these changes cannot be managed properly, it will lead to security incidents or system outages. For example, if the organization switches the maintenance vendor or service provider due to the cost rationalization, the new service provider may make some mistakes and cause system downtime because it isn't familiar with existing operational procedures.

The security policy defines who can access which security zones. It ensures that security systems protect the data center facility properly. In other words, there are four security access criteria for a data center:

- Identify the person who is trying to gain access (Who are you?).
- Ask for the reasons access to the data center is required (Why are you here?).
- Grant access to a particular person for a particular purpose (What is the reason for access?).
- Allow the identified person to access the particular security zone within the specified time period.

There are many security technologies that can provide different security identification protocols, but the most widely popular technologies for data center facilities are:

- Key or identification card
- Keypad with security code or personal identification number (PIN)
- Biometrics (fingerprint/hand, iris, face, retina, handwriting, and voice recognition)

We can combine these different technologies or methods to increase security levels for different access zones of data center facilities (see Figure 10.12).

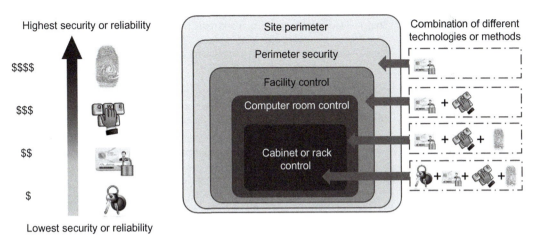

FIGURE 10.12

Combination of different technologies to increase the level of security.

The policy should also require all employees to follow up on the security process. For example, the security policy should make sure that a system password is changed regularly. If the security policy cannot enforce this password policy, malicious hackers will likely easily be able to crack passwords. Similarly, if any employee leaves the data center permanently, the access code should be reprogrammed.

10.10.3 SECURITY PROCESS

The security process is a set of rules and a flowchart for data center employees to follow. For example, the logging process tracks each person in and out of the data center and also tracks the purpose of entry. In case any outage occurs, data center management can find the root cause of the outage and then fix it. This can prevent the same incident from happening again.

10.11 ESTABLISHING PHYSICAL SECURITY

When we are trying to build up the physical security for a data center facility, we have to consider three essential elements with six critical steps:

The first element is to define the physical security problems for the data center facility. This consists of two steps:

1. Determine the security areas and the level of each security area or zone: What needs to be secured?
2. Define the access policy for each security zone: Who can access where?

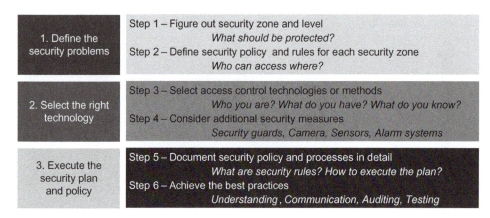

FIGURE 10.13

Construction of physical security.

The second element is to select the right security technology for different security zones. It also has two steps:

3. Select access control technologies with different combinations. The questions to be answered for granting access are: Who are you? What do you know and what do you have?
4. Consider additional security measurements and monitoring tools: cameras, sensors, alarm systems, and security guards.

The third element is to execute the physical security plan or policy and manage any upcoming changes due to business strategy changes or variations:

5. Document security policies and processes.
6. Achieve the best practices of physical security: create access control in layers, communicate with security staff, empower employees on security, conduct internal audits and test breaches, and understand what needs to be protected and what threats are coming from.

All the above steps are summarized in Figure 10.13.

10.11.1 COST CALCULATIONS FOR PHYSICAL SECURITY SYSTEMS

We have to understand that the more reliable a security system is, the higher the cost will be (see Figure 10.12). There is no free lunch. Therefore, when we establish a physical security system for a data center facility, it is essential to balance the business risks (or potential cost) and physical security system cost (see Figure 10.14).

We can find a balance point between the potential costs of security measures and the cost of implementing a physical security system. In terms of physical security cost calculations, we have three or four basic approaches for data center facilities:

1. Proportion of data center infrastructure cost
2. Cost per watt per month + capex
3. Cost per TB data storage + capex
4. Baseline cost + incremental cost per square meter of computer room

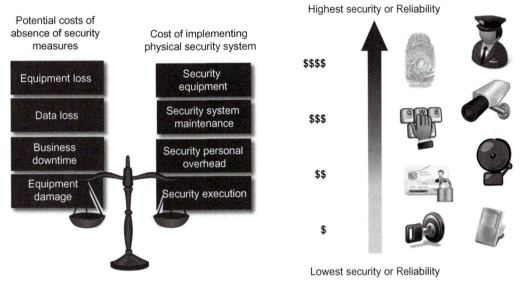

FIGURE 10.14

Balance between business risks and security system costs.

10.11.1.1 Proportion of data center infrastructure cost

This is basically focused on the capex or investment costs for a data center facility. When it is calculated, we only include the data center building costs or anything below the floor. In other words, all server, storage, and network component costs are not included. Furthermore, any software and data center monitoring system costs will be excluded too. This is often applied to the situation where the operating costs for physical security are negligible, which means the data center facility will have no security guard on-site during the operating phase. The percentage of the total data center facility costs that are needed for physical security is between 3.25% and 7.08%.

For example, if the data center facility construction costs are $10 million, the investment for physical security would be between $325 K and $708 K.

10.11.1.2 Cost per watt per month (opex) + capex

If the data center facility is not a brand new structure, the capex investment cost calculation will become much more complex. We will discuss this in later chapters. However, if we would like to calculate the opex cost, Luiz André Barroso et al. [291] from Google suggested that the cost ratio is from $0.02 to $0.08/W per month.

For example in Section 6.6, the total power draw of a data center facility is 2.0 9MW; the opex of physical security would be 41.8 k to 167.2 k per month or between $0.5 million and $2 million per annum.

10.11.1.3 Cost per terabytes data storage (opex) + capex

Similarly, instead of power consumption, we can use storage capacity to calculate the physical security cost based on terabytes of storage. If we do not take account of all other factors, such as storage tiering and type of connection (DAS, NAS, or SAN) the average cost per TB for physical security opex would be from $1,000 per terabyte per month to $4,000 per terabyte per month.

10.11.1.4 Baseline cost plus incremental opex per square meter of computer room

This is normally applied to the situation where the business grows very slowly at the beginning but accelerates after the initial period. This cost model is the combination of the above three cost structures.

For the baseline cost, the cost calculation is based on the proportional cost of the data center facility infrastructure. For the incremental cost, the cost is based on utilization per square meter of computer room or cost per watt per month or cost per terabyte per month.

Physical security features can be added during data center capacity growth. For example, initially, the data center may have no security guard. When the data center business expands to health-care, finance, or banking, we can add 24×7 on-site security guards or optical sensors and adopt more sophisticated security technologies, such as biometric scans.

10.11.2 SUMMARY OF PHYSICAL SECURITY

The purpose of data center physical security is to separate the data center facility from public sightlines. It is also to keep any unauthorized and/or bad guys out of the important physical boundaries.

The goal of the implementation of physical security is to screen every person who is trying to access the data center facility and make sure that the particular person is only granted access for a specified security zone within a certain time period.

A physical security system is focused on humans. It is not only focusing on external people, but also monitoring internal personnel because only humans make errors and about 15–20% of data center downtime is due to human errors.

When we try to build up a physical security system, we should follow the six steps outline above and create a map for the data center physical facility.

When we prepare a business case or physical security budget, we can adopt four different methods to calculate both capex and opex. The choice is really dependent on the particular business case as we have illustrated above.

10.12 SUMMARY

We have discussed both fire suppression and physical security systems for data centers. If we do not have these two systems, the data center will still be operational but will be taking on a lot of risk. These system are necessary to protect the data center.

For medium and large data centers, we should not only have a fire suppression system but also a fire alarm detection system. In order to suppress a fire during the first stage, we suggested placing fire alarm detectors in seven different locations. The number of alarm detectors is dependent on both airflow rate and the size of the data center space.

When we discussed fire suppression solutions, we highlighted three typical traditional solutions. Halon, which was one of the popular solutions, has been banned since 1987 due to the Montreal Protocol but it still may exist in many traditional data centers.

In order to eliminate traditional fire suppression solutions, we described the most commonly used fire suppression solutions in today's data center and then we unveiled the costs and characteristics of these fire suppression solutions.

On the topic of physical security, we answered four fundamental questions (purpose of security, objects, threats, and possibilities) in this chapter. The TIA-942 guidelines suggest different levels of security for different tiers of data center. Practically, data center physical security can be divided into five different security zones. The security system is built around these five security zones. The main function of a physical security system is to scan people. Ironically, the weakest link point is also the people, or the organizational layer. Therefore, the physical security system is important, but the logical (or organizational layer) security system cannot be ignored.

We concluded the chapter with details on how to calculate the physical security cost for both capex and opex.

10.13 **REVIEW QUESTIONS**

1. How many types of fire would typically occur in a data center based on the Australian classification?
2. What kind of fire equipment must a data center have based on the fire protection code?
3. What are the essential locations where placement of alarm detectors should be considered?
4. If fire development has four stages, what is the right stage for detection?
5. Please list two or three different fire suppression solutions and their characteristics, including costs.
6. What are the common fire suppression solutions in traditional data centers?
7. What fire suppression solution has been banned since 1987?
8. What is the most popular fire suppression solution for today's data center?
9. If a data center has 2,000 square meters, please estimate the cost for a fire suppression solution that has $ODP = 0$ and $GWP = 1$.
10. Why do we need a physical security system for a data center?
11. If we have a tier 3 data center, what kind of physical security system do we need?
12. Normally, how many physical security layers are there?
13. What is the weakest link in a data center physical security system?
14. How do we calculate the cost for a physical security system?

CLOUD INFRASTRUCTURE AND MANAGEMENT

Part III focuses on the IaaS layer of cloud computing. We will unveil the details of all physical elements of the cloud infrastructure. In comparison with Part II, all components that we are going to introduce are "above the floor," namely, servers, storage, networking equipment, and hypervisors (see Figure 11.1). We have to note that a hypervisor is not a physical hardware component. It is a software layer that is built on top of hardware components (server, storage, and network). From an operations perspective, a hypervisor is a kind of file or operating system that is stored in a database. We will briefly touch on the topic of the hypervisor in Part III because it is closely associated with server, storage and network components.

We are going to describe each item in detail in order from left to right in Figure 11.1. The order also implies the weight of the amortized cost for each cost item.

CLOUD INFRASTRUCTURE SERVERS: CISC, RISC, RACK-MOUNTED, AND BLADE SERVERS

11

In this chapter, we first present the history of server or client/server architecture and then focus on the internal physical architecture of a server. Once we understand the internal architecture of a server, we will discuss its relationship with the external environment, such as storage, the network, load balancers, PDUs and UPS units. Finally, we will focus on the hypervisor for RISC servers (see Figure 11.1).

11.1 CLOUD SERVERS

From Figure 11.1, we note that the first physical infrastructure item is the server is within the second layer. It is not only one of the critical components of a cloud, but also the most expensive item in the cloud cost framework. A Microsoft research report [116] indicated that the amortized cost of servers is as high as 45% of the total capex of a cloud data center.

When people are talking about server virtualization or cloud computing, we often hear a lot of technical jargon, such as x86, RISC, bare metal, guest OS, host, instance, workload, cluster, server farm, node, vMotion, vSwtich, hypervisor, etc. Many people, especially people who come from a non-IT background, such as finance, are confused by this technical jargon in comparison with traditional computing terms in a nonvirtualized environment. You might wonder why we have to bother to know this jargon. The simple answer is because a lot of the jargon represents the units to measure the virtualized or cloud infrastructure. As we have indicated before, the cloud is not a simple one-to-one relationship. In order to better understand the cost of the cloud, we have to understand this jargon and its meaning first.

Most cloud computing books only mean x86 servers when they are discussing servers. There are only a few books or papers that have focused on the topic of RISC servers (basically UNIX). One of the main reasons is that x86 servers have almost caught up with RISC server performance but the cost is often significantly lower. Based on IT Candor research [182], the revenue of the RISC server market has dropped nearly 50% from 2003 to 2014 (see Figure 11.2).

However, in this chapter, we will not only cover x86 servers but also discuss RISC servers, particularly Oracle/Sun SPARC servers. The reason to cover the topic of RISC servers is because

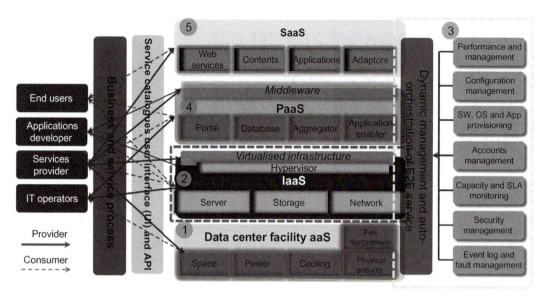

FIGURE 11.1

IaaS layer.

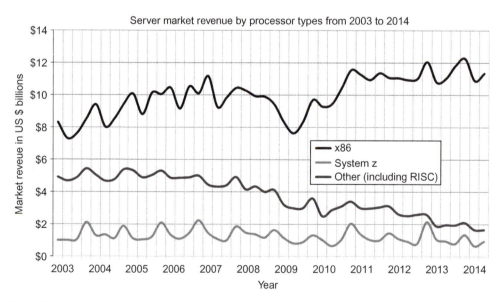

FIGURE 11.2

IT Candor 10-year server market revenue [182].

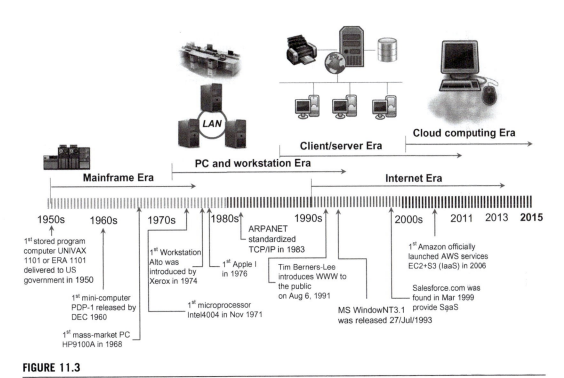

FIGURE 11.3

Last 60 years of server evolution.

many large enterprises and government organizations have a certain amount of Sun SPARC servers in their server fleets. For some telco companies, the number of SPARC servers may be more than the number of x86 servers in their data centers. It is absolutely critical for these companies to have the right cloud strategy and cost model to deal with those SPARC servers.

Now, the first questions we face are: What is a server and what is a client? Why do we have a server, not a mainframe or PC? How many server types are there? To answer these questions, we should take a close look of the history of computer or server evolution in the last 60 years (see Figure 11.3).

As we can see in Figure 11.3 (this Figure appears to be similar to Figures 1.2 and 1.3 but each figure has a different emphasis), the history of computing has gone through four or five eras. Beginning in the early 1950s through to the 1970s was the mainframe era. The computer was a heavy and huge colossus that occupied a large amount of space. People had to personally go to a data center to get access to a computer or mainframe. The usage time had to be precisely scheduled. It was not only very costly but also very inconvenient. For some large calculations, such as finite element analysis or numerical computation, people had to work around the clock 24x7 to get a satisfactory result. During this period, the IBM mainframe took over 70% of the world's computer business. This period was an era of centralized computing.

Beginning the late 1960s, and through the 1980s, in order to make computers much more accessible for many ordinary businesses, IT professionals were trying to make computers lighter, smaller, and portable. It was the era of PCs and workstations. The most famous PC was the Apple I in 1976 and IBM compatible PC (or IBM 5100) in September 1975. The most popular workstation vendors were Digital Equipment Corporation (DEC), Sun and Apollo, HP, Silicon Graphics International (SGI), and IBM. In comparison with mainframes, the workstation computer was much cheaper and more affordable for many ordinary companies. It successfully ran many applications, especially office applications, project management, 3D graphic displays, desktop publisher (DTP), and computer-aided design/computer-aid manufacturing/computer-aided engineering (CAD/CAM/CAE, such as AutoCAD and CATIA).

For most of large CAD/CAM projects, team collaboration is essential. Subsequently, workstation computers were required networking. Actually, Apollo initially ran the Aegis operation system but that was later replaced with the Distributed On-line Multi-access Interactive Network/Operating System (Domain/OS).

It has a proprietary token-ring network feature that can support relatively small networks up to dozens of workstation computers in a typical office environment. It was an elegant network design that gave a certain degree of network transparency but it could not inter-operate with any other existing network hardware and software. The IT industry went on to adopt Ethernet and TCP/IP. In the early 1990s, when the Internet started become widespread, the client/server architecture became a better solution for many organiaations and companies to utilize computer resources because it is accessible, affordable, open source, and cost effective (see Figure 11.4). Due to improvements in network connectivity, it also became increasingly reliable.

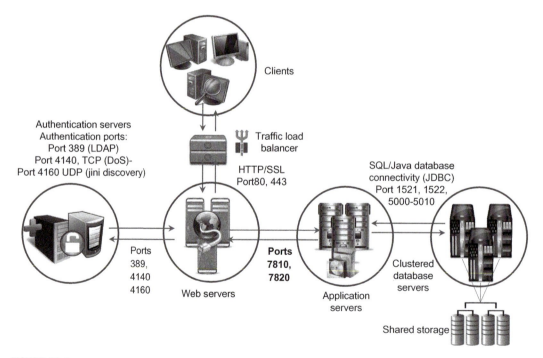

FIGURE 11.4

Typical client/server architecture.

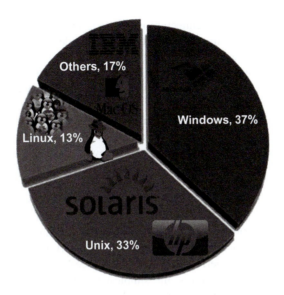

FIGURE 11.5

Server OS marketshare in 2009: data sources are Forrest Research and IDC.

One of the reasons client/server became so popular is because of its open platform or system. An open system defines a series of formal standards that allow different vendors to support it. In contrast to the mainframe computer, a customer has very limited choices or bargaining power in terms of price. Now, customers could purchase any hardware and software from different vendors. Open system allows for "mix and match" (MnM) or "plug and play" (PnP).

Because of the open system, software has been slowly separated from hardware. And many software companies have come to dominate the computer industry. Software defines everything.

One of the most successful software companies throughout the client/server era has been Microsoft. Since July 27, 1993, Microsoft has been continuously releasing new versions of its server operating system every two to three years from Windows NT 3.1 to Windows 2012R2. Through October 18, 2013, it has released 10 versions of the Windows server OS. It dominates in server OS marketshare (see Figure 11.5).

11.1.1 A CLIENT/SERVER ARCHITECTURE

From Figure 11.4, the mechanisms of the client/Server architecture is quite easy to understand. The software or application installed in a client machine (a PC or desktop or laptop computer) is the front end of the application. It manages local client resources, such as the monitor, keyboard, mouse, RAM, CPU, and other peripherals. If we replace it with a virtualized infrastructure, the remote virtual desk infrastructure (VDI), it will become a cloud VDI.

In comparison with mainframe terminals, the client is no longer a dumb machine. It has become a more powerful PC because it has its own computational environment. The client can be considered a customer who requests services. A server is similar to a service provider who serves many clients.

At the other side of client/server architecture is a server. The function of the server machine is to fulfill. all client requests. This means that the server-provided services can be shared among different clients. The server (or servers) is normally in a centralized location, namely a data center, but we also call it a server room or network room or LAN room or wiring closet or network storage room. It is really dependent on the size of the server fleet. The connection between clients and servers is via either a dedicated network or the Internet. Theoretically speaking, all servers are totally transparent to clients. The communication between client and server is based on standard protocols, such as Ethernet or TCP/IP. Once the clients initiate the service requests, the server will respond and execute these requests, such as data retrieval, updating, dispatching, storing, and deleting. Different servers can offer different services. A file server provides file system services, such as document, photo, music, and video files. A web server provides web content services. A storage server hosts storage services with different service levels, such as platinum, gold, silver, bronze, backup, and archive storage services. An application server supports application services, such as office applications or email. In addition, a server can also act as a software engine that manages shared resources such as databases, printers, network connectivity, or even the CPU. The main function of a server is to perform back-end tasks (see Figure 11.6).

Among these different types of servers, the simplest server is the storage server. With a file server, such as an FTP (File Transfer Protocol) or SMB/CIFS (Server Message Block/Common Internet File System) or NFS (Network File System, Sun) server, a client may request a file or files over the Internet or LAN. It is dependent on the file size. If the size is very large, the client's request needs a large amount of network bandwidth. This will drag the network speed down. Database, transaction, and applications servers are more sophisticated.

Since the 1980s, the number of hosting servers has been growing exponentially (see Figure 11.7). When ISC begun to survey host count in January 1993, the number of hosts was only 1,313,000; however in July 2013, the host count reached 996,230,757. It has increased almost 760 times, but the

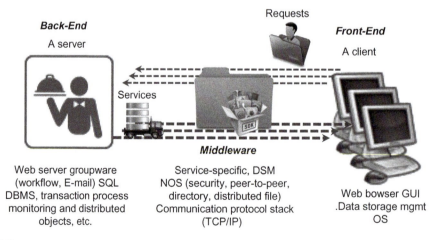

FIGURE 11.6

Client/server relationship.

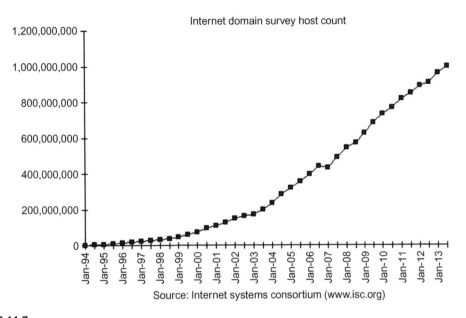

FIGURE 11.7

Internet domain hosts [184].

average hosting server's utilization rate is much lower. Based on Gartner's report in November 2008, the average utilization rate of x86 servers for most organizations was only between 7% and 15% [185]. Our experiences indicate that for some mobile content servers, the utilization rate is even below 1%. This has led to server consolidation by leveraging dramatic improvement from virtualization technology. In essence, Internet technology and service sparked the acceleration of host server growth and growing server volume has triggered server virtualization, which lays the basic infrastructure foundation for a cloud.

Now that we have clarified the concepts of client, server, and client/server architecture, in the following sections, we will take a close look at both x86 and RISC servers.

11.2 X86 SERVER

When IT professionals are talking about the server virtualization, they often mean x86 servers. So, what is an x86 server? How is it different from other types of servers?

An X86 server is a server is running an x86 CPU. An z86 CPU is one type of processor or instruction set architecture (ISA) that is built into a CPU chip. Currently, there are two types of processors on the market:

- Complex instruction set computers (CISC)
- reduced instruction set computers (RISC)

All x86 CPUs are CISC processors. Just as the name indicates, CISC processors adopt quite complex instructions. For example, to implement a very simple instruction of adding two integers (2 + 2), a CISC processor has to copy an element from one array (data structure) to another and then upgrade both array subscripts. In contrast, a RISC processor only uses very simple instructions, such as load and store. Furthermore, a RISC processor cuts operations to main memory. It assumes all required operands are within the processor's registers.

You may wonder what ISA is anyway and why we need it. The simple answer is that ISA is a well-defined interface between hardware and software. It is a kind of "contract" between hardware and software. It is similar to a protocol in the network domain. It gives a set of functional definitions of computing, which a computer can understand. It precisely describes how to invoke and access the hardware resources. Another way to define the x86 ISA is that it is one type of machine language (see Figure 11.8).

From a high-level language (HLL) perspective, the x86 ISA is the medium to make HLL that can be independent of hardware binary code or an individual vendor's hardware code (see Figures 11.9 and 11.10). Without ISA, the software programming task would become a tedious job, where one program that runs on one type hardware is not compatible with others. If you wanted to run the same program on different processors, you would have to rewrite the program for different hardware instructions or codes. This really wastes resources. This is the reason why we need ISA as a common medium that can talk to different hardware code. x86 is one the types of ISA.

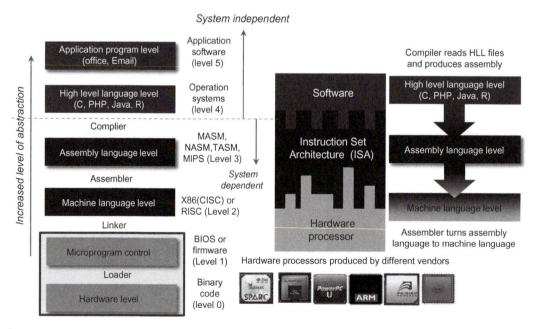

FIGURE 11.8

A computer system.

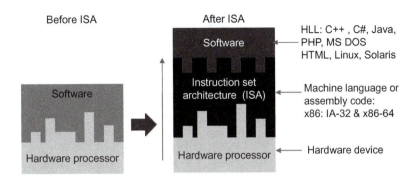

FIGURE 11.9

ISA function.

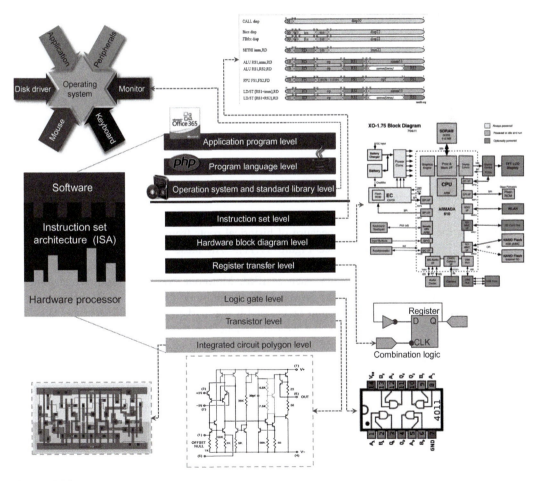

FIGURE 11.10

More details of computer system layers.

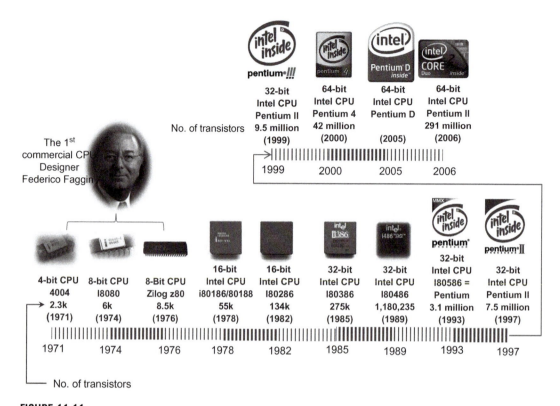

FIGURE 11.11

A brief history of the Intel x86 CPU.

The reason for the name "x86" is because of historical roots from the 8-bit Intel 8080 or Zilog z80 and Intel 16-bit 80186/i80188 (see Figure 11.11).[1] All these processors follow a common assembly language and computer architecture standard, namely 80x86 or simply x86.

There have been many x86 vendors, such as IBM, Motorola, NEC, National Semiconductor, Intel, AMD, VIA, Cyrix, Transmeta, and NexGen but currently there are only three major vendors, which are Intel, AMD, and VIA (see Table 11.1). Intel is the market leader for x86 processors.

We have explained what the x86 is, but we only touched on the topic of the CPU. x86 servers not only have a CPU but also other server components, including caches, RAM, motherboards, local storage, networking components, PCI cards, and NUMA. Why is this so important? The reason is that these components not only impact on the performance of the virtualization infrastructure or virtual machines but also decide the unit cost of the virtual machine. Ultimately, it decides the TCO/RO. This is the most difficult part of cost modeling for a virtual infrastructure because the unit cost is closely related to virtual machine (VM) density or physical node (or server)

---

[1]Pentium means "5" because US law bans number-based trademark. (It originally comes from the Greek word "Pente" meaning "5.")

Table 11.1 Total x86 CPU Market Share

Overall x86 CPU Market	2013 Q1		2012 Q4		2012 Q1	
	Units (K)	**Market Share**	**Units (K)**	**Market Share**	**Units (K)**	**Market Share**
Intel	70,618	85.2%	76,208	84.8%	79,230	80.2%
AMD	11,816	14.3%	13,177	14.7%	11,816	19.1%
VA	441	0.5%	490	0.5%	682	0.7%
Total	82,875	100%	89,875	100%	98,780	100%

to virtual machine (P2V) ratio. Theoretically speaking, the higher the density, the lower the unit cost is. However, there is a physical ceiling that restricts the number of VMs that can fit on one physical node.

This physical ceiling is decided by not only by a server's physical components such as CPU, cores, caches, RAM, motherboard, PCI cards, storage, network components, and NUMA but also by the type of hypervisors, types of workload, and workload diversity. Moreover, if the physical server fleet is purchased at different times or years, the configuration of servers would not be the same. This leads to enormous challenges to establish a cloud cost model. That is why we should understand every detail of the physical node or server hardware here.

11.2.1 CPU

When we discuss x86 CPUs, we have to realize that there has been so much different jargon and so many different names for CPUs due to different technologies. We often hear different terms referring to CPU functionality, such as socket, chip, core, n-way, processor, multithreading, and hyperthreading.

What do these terms exactly mean? Are they important to know for the cost modeling? The simple answer is "Yes" because most software vendors will charge license fee costs per socket unit, but some license fees are per core and not per physical server or node. We will now clarify these technical terms.

11.2.1.1 Socket

The socket means a physical connection between a CPU and a computer motherboard. The part that is installed on the motherboard is called a "carrier socket"; it carries the central processing unit (CPU). Traditionally, one computer motherboard only has one socket so it can be fit with one CPU. However, many recent motherboards have more than one carrier socket (see Figure 11.12) to increase the processing power of a server.

We have to be very careful not to confuse a physical CPU socket (or carrier socket) with a network socket between a client and a server. Although the name is the same, a network socket refers to one endpoint of a link between a client and a server running on the computer network.

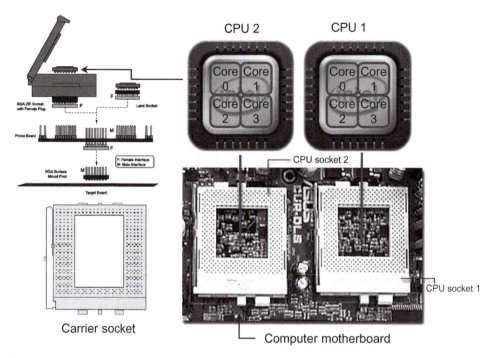

FIGURE 11.12

CPU sockets.

The network socket is a virtual interface between a client and a server port over a network so that the TCP layer can identify the application data that will be sent.

From the TCP/IP layer's perspective, a network connection socket is the combination of the IP address and port number (see Figure 11.13 and Table 11.2).

11.2.1.2 Chip

A chip is a physical printed circuit or integrated circuit (IC) board. The term actually has much wider implications. It refers to the many tiny components made by semiconducting materials that are embedded on an integrated circuit, such as memory chips, floating-point chips, CPU chips, BIOS chips, and graphic processing Unit (GPUs).

11.2.1.3 Core, multicore, processor, and CPU

The terms "core," "processor," and "CPU" are very confusing due to rapidly changing technology. In many circumstances, these terms become interchangeable. Traditionally, the terms "processor" or "CPU" were very straightforward and simple. They represented a microprocessor chip that implemented a series of processing tasks based on input. They executed the tasks one by one in series. There was not a clear definition of processing tasks that should be included in one CPU.

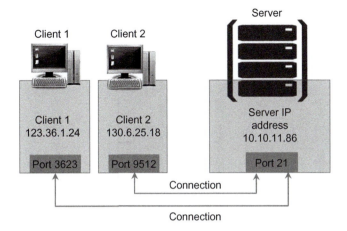

FIGURE 11.13

TCP/IP socket.

Table 11.2 TCP/IP Port and Sockets			
Value	Server	Client 1	Client 2
IP Address	10.10.11.86	123.36.1.24	130.6.25.18
Port	21	3623	9512
Socket	10.10.11.86:21	123.36.1.24:3623	130.6.25.18:9512

However, when the clock speed of a microprocessor or CPU starts to hit the heat barrier (see Figure 1.9), microprocessor designers and engineers looked for other alternatives to increase CPU speed, and they came up with the multicore architecture or parallel computing. With a multi-core architecture, hardware engineers can jump out of the "heat/performance" dilemma. In other words, the term "multicore" means multiple smaller CPUs within a large CPU.

However, how can we define the core boundary? Referring to the first commercial CPU 4004 architecture, we know that it just consisted of only a few very basic execution blocks or functions, such as an arithmetic logic unit (ALU), instruction fetcher, decoder, register, pipeline interruption handler, and I/O controller unit (see Figure 11.14).

Later, cache memory was added into big CPUs and the very basic or smaller execution parts of processors could be duplicated. These physical self-contained execution blocks that are built along with shared cache memory are now called "cores."

Each core is capable of independently implementing all computational tasks without interacting with outside components (they belong to a big CPU), such as the I/O control unit, interrupt handler, etc. which are shared among all the cores.

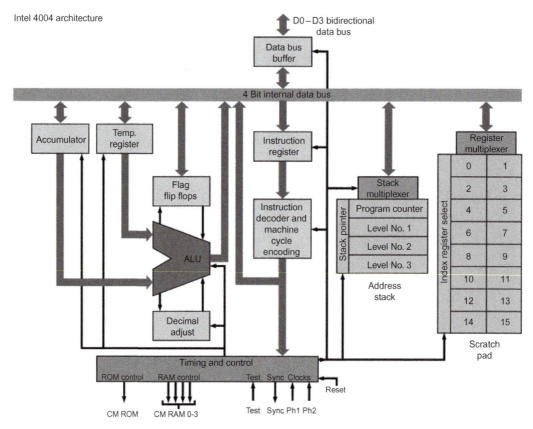

FIGURE 11.14

The first commercial CPU: Intel 4004 [186].

In summary, a core is a small CPU or processor built into a big CPU or CPU socket. It can independently perform or process all computational tasks. From this perspective, we can consider a core to be a smaller CPU or a smaller processor (see Figure 11.15) within a big processor.

Some software vendors, such as Oracle, charge license fee on a per core base rather than per socket.

11.2.1.4 N-way servers

If a server has a number of multicore processors, it has a number of independent execution units. A server with two sockets where each socket has four cores can be described as an 8-way server (see Figure 11.12). This means that this server can have eight independent processors that are running simultaneously. If a server has 32 cores, we can call it a 32-way node or 32-way server. From an executing task' perspective, we can say that each core is equal to a way. In essence, N-way is the total number of cores or processing units within a physical server or node.

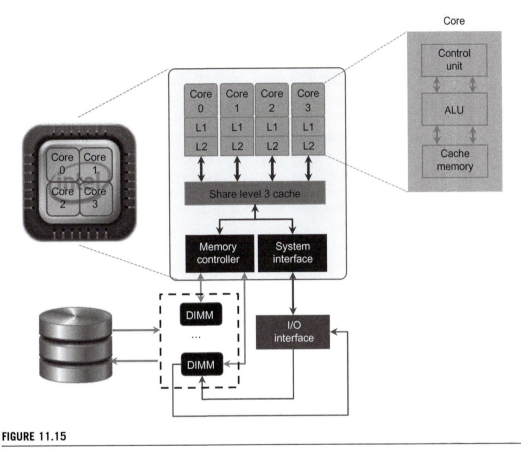

FIGURE 11.15

Multicore processors.

11.2.1.5 Multithreading and processes

Once we have resolved all the physical terms of the CPU, we can focus on the terms that deal more with the virtual, such as multithreading, processes, and hyperthreading. A thread is a scheduled process without a full stack of memory associated with it. We can consider a thread a data stream that is passed through a physical processor or CPU. Normally, we use the concept of a thread in comparison with a process. A process is a special case of a thread; it is a single thread with dedicated and full memory allocation, privileges, etc. Both a process and a thread are an abstraction of a unit for execution. Sometime, we call these units tasks. A process can only implement tasks one at a time on one physical CPU or a CPU socket. In other words, process performance is serial. If the CPU socket has more than one core, other cores will be in idle mode. Furthermore, if a parent process creates child or subprocesses, the parent process cannot terminate until the child process completes its tasks. If the parent process is much faster than the child processes, the parent process will have nothing to do but wait.

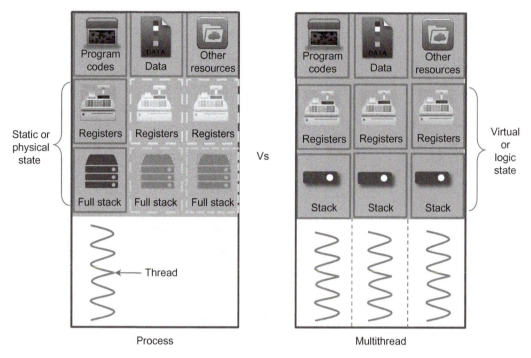

FIGURE 11.16

Process vs. multithreading.

In contrast, multithreading can perform many tasks concurrently. A kernel schedule can allocate shared resources for multithreading to implement tasks asynchronously in the same CPU socket but on different cores. It can interrupt each thread from time to time to give the other a chance to execute tasks in parallel (see Figure 11.16).

If a server is running more than one process at the same time, tis is called multiprocessing. Normally, the server has to have multiple CPUs to do multiprocessing, such as multiple cores or multiple sockets.

The benefit of multiprocessing is that it can isolate an error in one process. If one process has a problem, it will not bring down other processes. In contrast, multiple threads can impact each other. If one thread has an error, it will bring down other threads. However the benefit of multithreading is sharing resources, such as register address space and the memory stack. Very often, multi-threading occurs within a process spontaneously. That is why we sometime call it a "lightweight" process. In other words, the mechanism of multithreading is to divide a process into a number of scheduled processes and run them in parallel.

11.2.1.6 Hyperthreading

Hyperthreading is an Intel technology from before its multicore architecture became available. Hyperthreading makes a single CPU chip have many logical multiple cores. Intel introduced it in

2000 for the Pentium 4 but it was quickly abandoned due to issues of high power consumption, heat intensity, inability to increase clock speed, and inefficient pipelines.

However, the technology was reintroduced again in 2008. Hyperthreading has demonstrated that it can improve CPU performance by sharing the computational workload among multiple cores. It can schedule more than one core. It has been widely adopted by all current Intel CPUs, such as the Core i3, i5, and i7.

Imagine you have many applications, such as Microsoft Office, a web browser, iTunes, Skype, and AutoCAD all opened at the same time. If there is only one CPU, then each application has to run one after the other. What hyperthreading technology does is that it divides one physical CPU into two logical processors by sharing, partitioning, and duplicating various CPU resources. Hyperthreading enables users to leverage idle CPU resources and use more than one application at the same time without slowing down processing speed.

11.2.2 SERVER CPU CACHE

The word "cache" means a collection of items of the same type stored in a hidden place. The term in the context of a server means special high speed storage. When cache memory is embedded into a microprocessor, we call it a CPU cache. The first CPU cache was introduced by the Intel 80486 microprocessor in 1989. It only had 8 K memory and one level, located right next to a micro-processor. Therefore, it was named a level 1 cache or L1. The size of the L1 cache is the smallest. Typically, the size varies from 8 KB to 1 MB. In 1995, the Intel Pentium Pro launched with a so-called on-package level 2 cache or L2 cache, which is slightly further away from the processor. The size of the L2 cache is from 516 KB to 2 MB or greater. The next level of cache is level 3 or L3 cache. Referring to Figure 11.15, the L3 cache is shared among multiple cores.

There are two different types of cache in term of manufacturing. One is "on-die," which is physically embedded into the microprocessor. It is part of the same silicon chip. The other is "off-die," which is separated from the microprocessor chip. Most L1 and L2 caches are "on-die" caches. The L3 cache is an "off-die" cache. The cost of an L3 cache would be around 5% of the total cost.

Cache is very important for virtual infrastructure, especially for hypervisors. Taking as an example VMware's ESXi host, the larger the cache size, the better ESXi will run, especially for fault tolerance (FT) and vMotion.

11.2.3 RAM

For any computer, memory is the next most important physical component after the CPU. Actually, the first product made by Intel was not a CPU but rather a memory device: the Intel 3101 released in 1969. This occurred just one year after Intel was founded. It was the world's first solid-state memory chip or 16X 4-bit Static Random Access Memory (SRAM) (64-bit memory). In 1970, Intel produced the Intel 1103, the world's first Dynamic Random Access Memory (DRAM) with a capacity of 1 K that was adopted by HP 9800 series computers. It was the best-selling memory chip in 1972.

From a virtual infrastructure perspective, the physical memory or RAM size is vital to VM performance and the scalability of the virtual environment. You may have enough processing speed

Table 11.3 RAM Considerations

Physical and Virtual Assumptions	Quantity	Summary	Total
Sockets per physical server or node	2		
Cores per socket	4	Total no. of core per node	8
Virtual machines per core	8	Total no. of VMs per node	64
Max. virtual CPUs per core	12	Maximum no. of vCPU per node	96
Average vCPUs per VM	1.5		
RAM per VM	4 GB	Total size of RAM for VM	256 GB
Hypervisor required RAM*			2 GB
Average overhead to manage per VM*	53 MB	Total overhead	14 GB
Total required RAM per node			272 GB

Table 11.4 Memory Overhead for Common VM Configurations [187]

Memory Allocation	1vCPU(MB)	2vCPUs (MB)	4vCPUs (MB)	8vCPUs (MB)
1 GB	26	30	38	54
4 GB	49	53	61	77
18 GB	140	144	152	169

capacity with CPU power but if you have limited RAM capacity, the number of VMs will be restricted. Ultimately, this would impact on the physical server's utilization rate, which will translate into increasing the unit cost of the cloud infrastructure.

Therefore, the size of RAM should be aligned with physical CPU capacity and the number of VMs and vCPUs to be installed on this physical node. For example, if the physical server has two sockets with 4 cores per socket and we also assume the number of VMs is 8 per core and the maximum number of vCPUs is 12 per core, then the total number of VMs would be 64 per physical node and the total number of vCPUs[2] is 96 per physical node. If the average RAM size per VM is 4 GB, then the total RAM required for the physical many be as much as 272GB (see Tables 11.3 and 11.4). We can round up the total size of RAM to 288GB.

11.2.4 NUMA

NUMA stands for nonuniform memory access. Sometime, it is called nonuniform memory architecture. The recent x86 CPUs provided by both AMD and Intel along with many current motherboards will support this architecture. The reason to have NUMA is to resolve the bottleneck issue due to multiple cores or processors trying to access the same memory via the limited size of the memory bus.

---

[2]One VM can have more than one vCPU. One physical core can have many vCPUs.

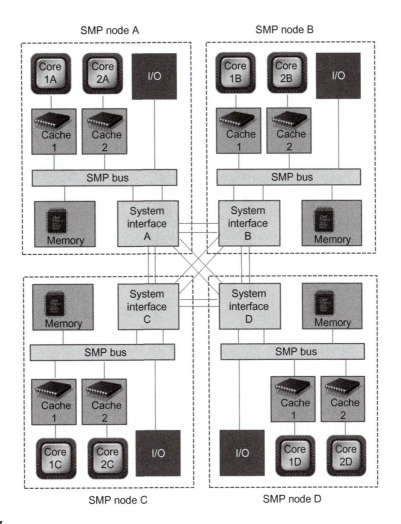

FIGURE 11.17

NUMA architecture.

The way NUMA works is that it allows one core process to access memory that belongs to other cores. Under the NUMA architecture, a physical server's CPUs are reorganized into symmetric multiprocessing (SMP) style nodes. Each node has its own localized RAM modules that have much lower latency (see Figure 11.17).

Many hypervisors, such as VMware vSphere, can leverage NUMA architecture to manage VM placement by tuning the NUMA CPU scheduler. By default, NUMA is disabled in the BIOS setting or "node interleaving" is disabled. Subsequently, the physical server will ignore the NUMA

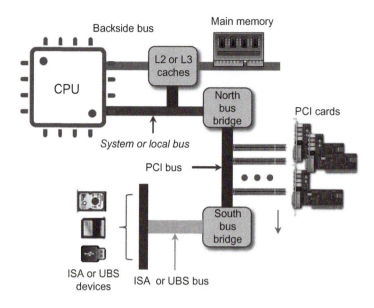

FIGURE 11.18

Server bus architecture.

mechanism, and NUMA will not try to optimize localized memory. This is fine for a physical node that only has one core or a single CPU. Normally, some experts suggest that if the NUMA is enabled, hosts should have at least four cores across at least two NUMA nodes.

If you have the NUMA feature, you have various options for your virtual architectures. The bottom line is to minimize VM latency and maximize VM performance. It is nice to have, but it will indirectly impact on the cost of the virtual infrastructure.

11.2.5 SERVER PCI CARDS

With a modern server, there are a few bus channels in the system. The first one is the backside bus (BSB), which is directly connected to the CPU cache, normally the level 2 cache if the L2 cache is off-die. The next one is the main bus, also called the front-side bus (FSB), or system or local bus. It is also directly connected to the CPU. It is mainly connected to main memory via the memory controller. The slower bus called the Peripheral Component Interconnection (PCI) bus. It is connected to the system bus through the north bus bridge. The PCI bus was derived from the ISA bus. It mainly connects to PCI cards, which are used to connect all types of PCI devices, such as printers, monitors, mice, and network components. The last bus we highlight is the Industry Standard Architecture (ISA) bus developed by IBM, which is mainly for connection of hard drives. The ISA bus is connected to the PCI bus via the south bus bridge (see Figure 11.18). A bridge is a part of a computer chipset, and acts as a traffic controller to manage data traffic flow.

Table 11.5 PCI Bus Speeds

Bus	Year	Max Bandwidth (Bytes)
PCI	1992	33 MB/s
PCI-X v1.0	1999	133 MB/s
PCI Express 1.0a	2003	250 MB/s per lane (8x is 2 GB/s, 16x is 4 GB/s, 32x is 8 GB/s)
PCI Express 2.0	2006	500 MB/s per lane (8x is 4 GB/s, 16x is 8 GB/s, 32x is 16 GB/s)
PCI Express 3.0	2010	1 GB/s per lane (8x is 8 GB/s, 16x is 16 GB/s, 32x is 32 GB/s)
PCI Express 4.0 or PCIe	2011	16 GB/s per lane

Table 11.6 PCI Slot Bandwidth

PCIe Slot Type	Single Direction Bandwidth (Bits)	Dual Direction Bandwidth (Bits)	Slots
X1	2.5 Gbps/200 Mbps	5 Gbps/400 Mbps	
X4	10 GBps/800 Mbps	20 Gbps/1.6 Gbps	
X8	20 Gpbs/1.6 Gbps	40 Gbps/3.2 Gbps	
X16	40 Gbps/3.2 Gbps	80 Gbps/6.4 Gbps	

The cost of a PCI card varies from less than a hundred dollars to a few hundred dollars. It is dependent on the speed of the PCI bus. Higher bandwidth means higher cost (see Tables 11.5 and 11.6.)

When we allocate high-speed slots for I/O network cards, we should make sure there is enough bandwidth for both network and storage traffics. In other words, the allocated bandwidth for high-speed slots on the motherboard should match the bandwidth of both network and storage cards, such as FCoE, FCHBA, 10GbE, CNA, or Infiniband. For example, if I have a single port 10GbE card for network traffic connection, we have to use at least PCIe 2.0 × 4 slot and for a dual port card (see Table 11.6).

11.2.6 SERVER STORAGE

When we purchase a server, it is quite common to purchase local storage as well. The size of local storage or a hard disk drive (HDD) is often smaller, for example less than 200GB. It is normally applied to booting local systems, such as the ESXi boot image, or to auto-deploy images. Of course, the server is also connected to any shared external storage. We will have further discussion about this topic when we discuss storage in a later chapter.

11.2.7 SERVER NETWORK

We have mentioned the topic of the server network interface (or PCI interface). It is one of the three critical elements of the cloud infrastructure that is located above the floor. We will have further discussion about network mechanisms in a later chapter of this book.

11.2.8 SERVER MOTHERBOARD

We have already touched on issue of the motherboard above. It also has many other names, such as mainboard or system board. However, the main function of a server motherboard is to aggregate all the server components into one system.

In contrast to a PC, a server motherboard does not need a GUI interface, expensive video adaptors, an audio interface, or other peripherals. What a server motherboard needs is a reliable power supply or UPS and fan, a high-speed bus, and I/O interfaces. One of the critical components in a server motherboard is the chipset, because it controls all bus workloads.

A server has to support multiple users. As we know, a server could be a web server, database, content, or application server. One of the common characteristics is that a lot of processes will be running in the background. If a server has multiple cores with enabled multithreading, then the workload of the CPU, RAM and I/O interface will increase dramatically. It means both the backside bus (BSB) and the frontside bus (FSB) have to be very fast. If the BSB and FSB are not fast enough, they will create a bottleneck for a server's processing speed. Therefore, if a server has multiple cores and multiple sockets, the server's motherboard should have adequate bus speed.

Because a physical server node will generate many VMs, it must have the right reliability, availability, and serviceability (RAS) features, such as built-in circuit redundancy, remote monitoring functions (especially fan speed and CPU temperature), etc. The bottom line is to make sure that the number of CPU cores is matched by adequate bus speed or bandwidth. This is not only from a physical perspective but also from a virtual infrastructure point of view. This ensures that we can have a higher density of VM for each physical node without impact on VM performance. As a result, we can minimize TCO and maximize ROI.

To this point, we have discussed all physical components inside a server. In the following section, we will look at how to group many servers together and install them into data center racks.

11.3 RACK-MOUNTED SERVERS AND VENDORS

A rack-mounted server or standard racked server or simply a rack server is the standard server box that can be fit into a standardized 19-inch-wide rack. The height of a rack server can vary from 1 rack unit (RU), to 2 RU, 4 RU, or even 8 RU (one RU = 1.75 inches = 44.45mm). In general, high-end servers are powerful and costly.

Currently, many server vendors provide a wide range of rack-mounted servers beginning with entry level servers all the way up to very high-end servers in term of performance and capacity. Taking HP as an example, it provides the entry level HP ProLiant DL320e G8 or DL360e G8 (see Figure 11.19 and Table 11.7) and the high-end DL385p G8 and HP DL 585 G7.

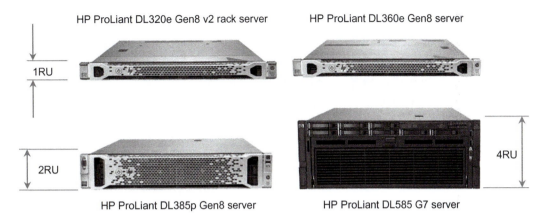

HP ProLiant DL320e Gen8 v2 rack server   HP ProLiant DL360e Gen8 server

1RU

2RU

4RU

HP ProLiant DL385p Gen8 server   HP ProLiant DL585 G7 server

FIGURE 11.19

HP ProLiant DL series rack servers.

Table 11.7 HP ProLiant Series Rack Servers				
Configurations/ Models	HP DL 320e G8 v2	HP DL360e G8	HP DL 385p G8	HP DL 585 G7
No. of CPU sockets	1 (Intel Core i3)	1 or 2 (Intel Xeon E5)	1 or 2 (AMD 6200)	2 or 4 (AMD)
No. of cores	2 or 4	4 or 6 or 8	4 or 8 or 12 or 16	8 or 12 or 16
Cache size	8 MB L3	10 MB L3	16 MB L3	16 MB L3
Max RAM size	32 GB	384 GB	768 GB	1.5 TB
Memory slots	4 DIMM or 4X8	12 DIMM 12X32	24 DIMM 24X32	24 DIMM or 24X64
PCIe 3.0	One X 16	One X16	3 PCIe2, X16	11 PCI-X, PCIe 2.0 x16
Warranty (parts/ labor/on-site)	1/1/1	3/1/1	3/3/3	3/3/3
Physical size	1RU	1RU	2RU	4RU
Max. internal storage	4.8 TB	9.6 TB	30 TB	8 TB
Starting price	$949	$949	$2,185	$13,000

Of course, many other server vendors, such as IBM, Dell, Lenovo, Huawei, Oracle/Sun, Fujitsu, and Cisco provide many competitive products similar to HP offerings (see Figures 11.20 and 11.21).

HP, Dell, and IBM are traditional vendors for the x86 server market. Huawei, Cisco, and Lenovo have just gotten into the server market recently. Oracle/Sun and Fujitsu traditionally provide RISC servers, such as the SPARC T and M series servers. Now, they also offer x86 servers.

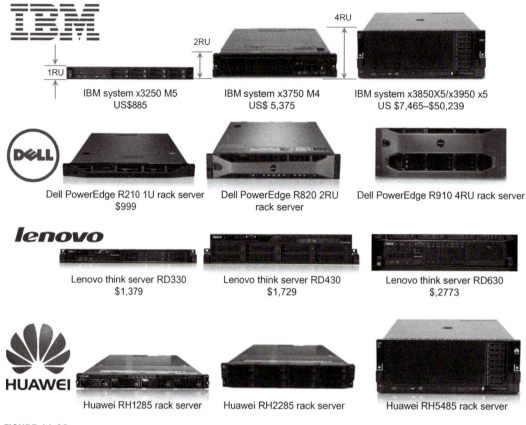

FIGURE 11.20

IBM, Dell, Lenovo, and Huawei rack servers.

In terms of server price, Huawei and Lenovo may be very competitive, but overall, the prices have become very similar because most of vendors adopt "just-in-time" models due to Moore's law. They will not stockpile a large quantity of different models of rack servers in their warehouse. The common practice is to take an order from a customer and then build with an Original Design Manufacturer (ODM) in China. The final step is to stamp the company's logo on the product. The profit margin for servers has been squeezed down quite lo, especially for entry level servers. In other words, the rack server has become a commodity product. The only difference is hardware support, management software, and other additional services (see Appendix G for a comparison among the different server vendors).

All rack server prices listed in the above table and figures are current online prices provided by the vendors at the time of writing. This is a retail price for a small quantity or volume. However, if the quantity is very large enough or a customer has a long-term procurement relationship with a particular vendor, the discount price could more than 30%.

| Sun server X3-2 (former sun X4170 M3) US$ 5,296–US$23,378 | Sun server X3-2L (former sun X4270 M3) US$6,418–$47,563 | Sun server X2-8 (former sun X4800 M2) US$ 40,277–US $102,156 |

Fujitsu primergy RX100   Fujitsu primergy RX300   Fujitsu primergy RX350

Cisco UCS 22M3 (US1,349)   Cisco UCS 420M3 (US7,837)   Cisco UCS 460M3 (US8,519)

FIGURE 11.21

Oracle/Sun, Fujitsu, and Cisco rack servers.

Generally speaking, the price for an entry-level server would be less than $1k. The next level or middle range 2RU rack server would be between $3k and $7Kk depending on the brand and server configuration. The 4RU rack server is normally designed for enterprise customers. The starting price for such a high-end server would be around $10k.

There is no doubt that the price of rack servers is trending down and a 1RU rack server will continue to become more powerful. The rack server and blade server may be converging. After the following section discussing blade servers, we will compare the pros and cons of rack and blade servers, but first let's have a look at blade servers.

11.4 BLADE SERVERS

11.4.1 WHAT IS A BLADE SERVER?

A blade server is just a physical node with a different appearance. In comparison with a rack or tower server, it is much more compact and has a high density within a rack. Therefore, it often

| Huawei E6000 | HP c7000 Enclosure $24,000 –$31,000 | Dell M1000e |

FIGURE 11.22

Common vertical arrangement for blade servers.

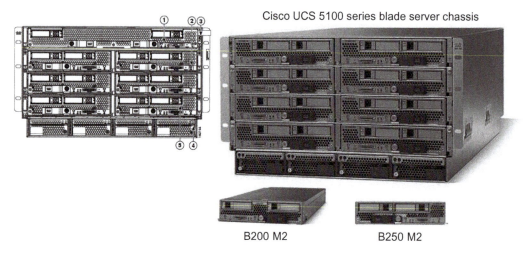

Cisco UCS 5100 series blade server chassis

B200 M2   B250 M2

FIGURE 11.23

Cisco UCS 5100 Series Blade Server Chassis and B200, B250 blade modules.

consumes more power than traditional tower and rack-mounted servers. In comparison with the rack server, the majority of vendors provide blade servers in a vertical format or arrangement (see Figure 11.22).

Cisco is the only major vendor to build a horizontal arrangement, with 8 B22M3 or B200 M3 or B230 M2 or B420 M3 blade modules in the UCS 5100 Series Blade Server Chassis (see Figure 11.23). HP has both vertical and horizontal blade server arrangements.

All the above major vendors that provide rack-mounted servers also supply blade servers. However, the price of a blade server is higher than a rack server. According to Forbes Guthrie [187], the rack server still holds a dominant position in the world server market. The proportion of the rack server market share is as high as 85%. Of course, this does not mean that blade servers are not good. Blade servers are very efficient for large scale or warehouse type data centers and quick deployment.

11.4.2 **HISTORY OF BLADE SERVERS**

Based on Christopher G. Hipp's biography [188], the original idea for the blade server was due to the dot-com boom. Many IT professionals were frustrated with the heavy workload (especially for cabling) to deploy a massive amount of 1RU rack-mounted server (the so-called "pizza box") in many data centers for web hosting and colocation business during the late 1990s.

Chris Hipp with the help of his colleagues came up with the idea of a blade server. In December 1999, Chris Hipp and his friends established a company named Rocket Logix or RLX technologies to focus on the blade server business. One year later, RLX released its first blade server: the RLX System 324 in May 2001 (see Figure 11.24).

Although RLX logged six US patents with a total of 187 claims regarding blade computing throughout 2000s, the RLX System 324 was very similar to a PC-on-a-Card or single-board-computer (SBC) server; Citrix had achieved a dominant position for theses blade-like servers in the late 1990s. One of the early players in the blade server market was Egenera. It was established by the CTO of Goldman Sachs, Vern Brownell [189] in March 2000. Its pBlade series of blade servers especially targeted enterprise customers. In comparison with the RLX System 324, the pBlade was arranged in a horizontal manner (see Figure 11.25).

FIGURE 11.24

RLX System 324.

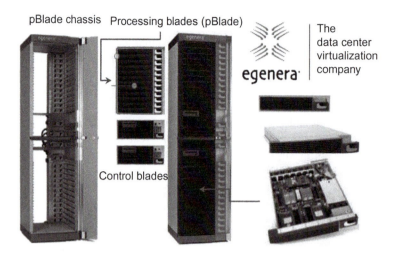

FIGURE 11.25

Egenera's pBlade and Blade Frame EX chassis.

As the blade server market was booming, many traditional server vendors, such as HP, IBM, Sun, and Dell, jumped into the blade server market in late 2002.

However, after the dot-com bubble burst between 2003 and 2004, the blade server market became very sluggish. Many blade startup companies faded away. RLX Technologies had shifted focus to the High-Performance Computer Cluster (HPCC) while Egenera concentrated on financial processing. In 2004, RLX Technologies only had 36 employees and about 200 customers. It got out of the blade hardware business and concentrated on Linux-based management software. In October 2005, it was sold to HP for $102 million.

When the server market became very quiet, some major players, such as Dell, suspended their blade business due to it cannibalizing their rack and tower server business. However, Dell came back again when the blade technology had crossed the "chasm" [12] after the initial peak inflation period (see Figure 1.5).

According to IDC, in 2005 the blade server market has already exceeded 500,000 units and generated $2.1 billion dollars. In comparison with 2004, blade volume had grown 63% and revenue had grown 84%. IBM was the market leader and took about 39% market share or $819 million. HP had 35% market share or $735 million. Dell was in the third spot and only had 9% market share (see Figure 11.26).

By 2013, although server blade market size had tripled in terms in terms of volume, its market size was still relatively small in comparison with rack servers (see Figure 11.27). However, most server market growth has been contributed by blade servers.

After almost 10 years, HP has climbed into the number one spot for server market share with Dell in second and IBM in third position in terms of server volume (see Figure 11.28). Noticeably, many Chinese companies, such as Huawei, Inspur, and Lenovo have gained momentum in the server market.

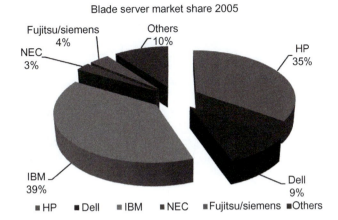

FIGURE 11.26

Blade server market share in 2005.

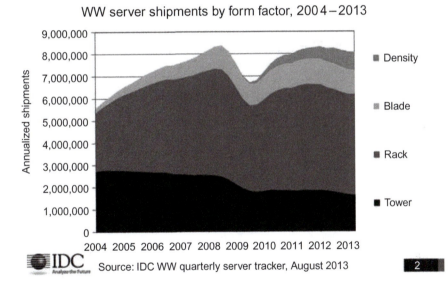

FIGURE 11.27

IDC Statistic Data of Server Shipments between 2004 and 2013.

However, if we look from a server revenue perspective, IBM has climbed back to the number one position from one year ago. This was mainly due to IBM System z sales. However, IBM suffered about a 10% decline in comparison to 2012.

For the x86 server market, the rack server market gained 3.9% in volume and 2.4% in revenue for the second quarter of 2013 (see Figure 11.29). In contrast, the x86 blade server market declined

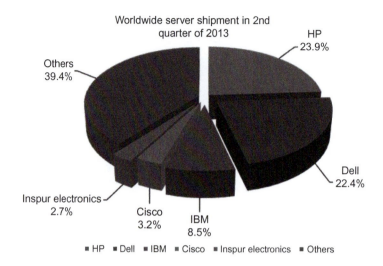

FIGURE 11.28

IDC WW server shipment in second quarter of 2013 (volume or quantity).

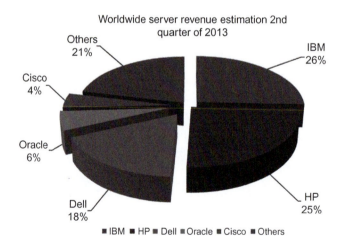

FIGURE 11.29

Gartner's WW server revenue estimation in second quarter of 2013 (revenue estimation).

by 3% in volume and 4.5% in revenue. In contrast to other major vendors, Cisco is a new player (it just got into the server market in early 2009) made significant progress with 16.6% growth and jumped into the second position of the blade server market in terms of revenue while all other major blade server vendors, such as HP and IBM, have been losing market share since 2009 (see Figure 11.30).

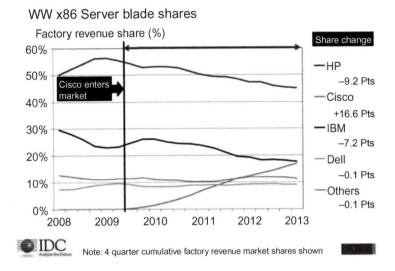

WW x86 Server blade shares

FIGURE 11.30

Worldwide x86 Server blade market between 2004 and 2013.

11.4.3 RACK VS. BLADE SERVER

Is a rack server better than a blade server or vice versa? It is really dependent on what your business requirements are. If you would like utilize existing data center infrastructure, the blade server is subject to the power conditions because normally blade servers require more power than rack servers. On average, blade server power density is between 10 to 15kW per rack. Some ultra-high-density blade server racks are as high as 50kW per rack. In comparison, the average power density for a rack server is only between 3 kW and 5 kW per rack. In other words, the average power density of a blade server is about three to five times higher than a rack server. In some extreme cases, it could be 10 times as high.

The biggest issue with a blade server is lack of granularity in terms of capacity expansion. As we know the blade chassis can carry from 8 to 16 blades; it would be quite challenging to make such a purchase decision for hardware unless you require a very large size server fleet. This means that you either have 16 blades or nothing if you want to have a blade server. Of course, you can purchase a few blades along with a blade chassis first and add more blades later on. If you make this decision, you have to control the time between two purchases. Normally, it should be less than three years. If the time gap is too long, you will not only find the model is out of date but also that your vendor will not support your existing blade servers that you have already purchased. You may be able to find a third-party vendor but the cost would be very high because it would be quite difficult to find any spare parts. In these circumstances, you may find the best solution is to buy the latest blade server and decommission the existing blade server fleet. This leads to a very low utilization rate for the blade server chassis. Normally, a blade chassis is quite expensive.

In order to make clear comparisons between rack and blade servers, we can review blade and rack servers from 10 different perspectives (see Table 11.8).

Table 11.8 Pros and Cons of Blade and Rack Servers

Server Types	Blade Server		Rack Server	
	Pros	Cons	Pros	Cons
Space	Less space			More space
Power density		High power density	Lower power density	
Cabling	Less cabling			More cabling
Scale up		Difficult to scale up	Easier to scale up	
Scale out	Easier to scale out			Difficult to scale out
Capex		High initial capex	Less initial capex	
Speed to market	Quick deployment			Slow deployment
Power savings	Power efficiency per unit			No power savings
Redundancy		No redundancy at chassis level	Easier to make redundant	
Remote management	Easier to manage			Difficult to manage

In summary, if you have a limited budget and relatively small server fleet, the rack server solution is better than blade servers. Even if you have a server fleet between 50 and 150 servers but the market outlook is very uncertain or sluggish, the rack server is still a relatively good solution because today, a pizza box has become much more powerful than ever before. With a virtualized infrastructure, you can quickly scale out even with rack servers.

However, if your business goal is to get a foothold in a massive market, the blade server would be a better solution. Of course, it is subject to power supply in your data center. Overall, whether it is a rack or blade server, most x86 servers are ODM or OEM in China. It has become a commodity product. It is not worth paying a high price for a fancy blade product. When we make a purchasing decision, we should always consider it from a life cycle and TCO/ROI perspective rather than just purchasing price alone.

11.5 RISC SERVER

So far, what we have focused on is x86 or CISC servers. We should also be aware there are a lot of RISC servers in many medium and large corporations and government agencies. Therefore, it is absolutely critical for us not only to understand the mechanisms of RISC servers but also to know the cost of cloud migration for these RISC servers if both the capex and opex for the RISC servers are too high.

If server virtualization is a precondition of cloud computing, then we have to virtualize RISC server fleet. Obviously, VMware vSphere or Hyper-V or Xen are not a hypervisor solution for RISC servers because these hypervisors are designed for x86 processors, not for RISC chips. So, the question is, how do we virtualize a RISC server? And what is the cost to move a RISC server to the cloud? How many RISC servers are there? What is the most popular one? If an application is currently running on a RISC server, should we stay with the RISC server or move to x86?

11.5.1 HISTORY OF RISC SERVERS

Before we answer these questions, we should understand why we need RISC servers in the first place. We should begin with a review of the history of the RISC server, a look at how we got here. It will help us to understand why some companies have so many RISC servers in their data centers.

We already presented the term "CISC" in Section 11.2, which stands for complex instruction set computer (CISC). Here, "complex" means the design of the instruction set is not simple. It was the result of the intent of chip designers to avoid using expensive memory. During the 1960s, the unit cost of memory was around $32 per KB. In the early days, memory, such as DRAM, was a big business. Many companies were selling memory chips to replace magnetic tape memory. Because memory chips were quite expensive at that time, software programmers came up with a solution of using a few complex instructions to do heavy lifting rather than many simple instructions that are loaded into a large memory chip to complete equivalent tasks. The philosophy behind the CISC architecture was to move the complex instructions down to the hardware level. Generally, complex instructions lead to more complex hardware, which means it would be more expensive. However, Maurice Vincent Wilkes resolved this elegantly with a microprogrammed control solution in the 1950s. Therefore, it was unnecessary to have very complex hardware design (see Figure 11.31).

Although the implementation of the CISC ISA is much more complex than RISC, it did help programmers close the sematic gap between the machine language and high-level language. For example, in a CISC environment, the programmer can directly use the mircoprogram's "while" or "for" instruction, which is the same as a C program.

As computer hardware continued improving, in the early 1980s John Cocke realized that a a complex instruction set could be replaced with a very simple one when he was involved in the IBM 801 project. John Cocke is considered the father of the RISC ISA. Later, a group of IBM hardware and complier experts recognized that many complex instruction codes generated in CISC were not very useful. In contrast, a simpler instruction set could be implemented in an efficient pipeline structure, which would take far less hardware resources. Unfortunately, like the DOS system, IBM didn't take this advantage of this idea until 1991. IBM developed its Power and Power PC ISA.

In 1982 and 1983, David Patterson from UCLA led the RISC I project in collaboration with John Hennessy from Stanford University. Later, Sun built its SPARC platform based on the RISC I project. What David Patterson and others did was to use the quantitative approach for computer design; they found many special instructions were hardly used by any programmer and only small percentage of ISA instructions were making up the bulk of the workload. Therefore, those hardly utilized instructions could be taken out without any major impact functionality. This finding led to a reduced instruction set by eliminating most unnecessary and complex instructions, which now we call a reduced instruction set computer (RISC). Of course, RISC has made a lot of improvemens in term of ISA performance in comparison with CISC.

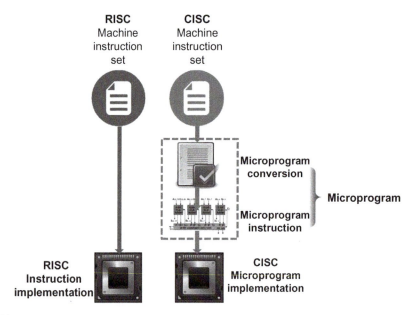

FIGURE 11.31

Different RISC and CISC implementations.

11.5.2 CISC VS. RISC

According to Randal E. Bryant et al.'s [190] findings, we can summarize at least eight different general characteristics between early RISC and CISC ISAs (see Table 11.9).

There have been many RISC processor vendors during the last 30 years or so (see Figure 11.32). Some of them, such as DEC and Compaq, were acquired by larger vendors, such as HP. Others have switched to different business applications, such as mobile handset and digital embedded devices.

The debate on whether CISC is better than RISC or visa versa is still going on among many computer experts and researchers. Theoretically speaking, the RISC processor seems to be the winner because a RISC chip takes less time to implement per instruction. However, this doesn't mean there isn't any cost. With a simpler instruction set, RISC has to use more instructions to accomplish a task. In contrast, CISC chips have less a instructions in their instruction sets. The bottom line of the RISC vs. CISC argument is whether we should have a simpler instruction set with a large quantity of instructions or a complex instruction set with less instructions.

For more than 10 years, RISC could not kick CISC out of the processor market. Instead, x86 or CISC processors have been gaining the momentum and taking over RISC market share. In 2012, x86 processors have about 74% of the server market pie (see Figure 11.33) in terms of revenue and RISC processors only have less than 18% of the server market.

It is quite obvious that x86 or CISC has already won the race. Well, does this mean that RISC will disappear or CISC will replace all RISC chips? Not quite, because it is not that simple. So far,

Table 11.9 x86 (CISC) and RISC ISA Comparison

Characteristics	CISC	Early RISC
Volume of instructions	A large number of instructions. The Intel document describing the complete set of instructions is over 1200 pages long.	Many fewer instructions. Typically less than 100.
Instruction execution time	Some instructions with long execution times. These include instructions that copy an entire block from one part of memory to another and others that copy multiple registers to and from memory.	No instruction with a long execution time. Some early RISC machines did not even have an integer multiply instruction, requiring compilers to implement multiplication as a sequence of additions.
Length of encodings	Variable-length encodings. IA32 instructions can range from 1 to 15 bytes.	Fixed-length encodings. Typically all instructions are encoded as 4 bytes.
Address mode	Multiple formats for specifying operands. In IA32, a memory operand specifier can have many different combinations of displacement, base, and index registers, and scale factors.	Simple addressing formats. Typically just base and displacement addressing.
Using of arithmetic and logical operations	Arithmetic and logical operations can be applied to both memory and register operands.	Arithmetic and logical operations only use register operands. Memory referencing is only allowed by load instructions, reading from memory into a register, and store instructions, writing from a register to memory. This convention is referred to as a load/store architecture.
Approach of executing a program on the hardware	Implementation artifacts hidden from machine level programs. The ISA provides a clean abstraction between programs and how they get executed.	Implementation artefacts exposed to machine level programs. Some RISC machines prohibit particular instruction sequences and have jumps that do not take effect until the following instruction is executed. The compiler is given the task of optimizing performance within these constraints.
Method of condition codes	Condition codes. Special flags are set as a side effect of instructions and then used for conditional branch testing.	No condition codes. Instead, explicit test instructions store the test results in normal registers for use in conditional evaluation
Method of using register	Stack-intensive procedure linkage. The stack is used for procedure arguments and return addresses.	Register-intensive procedure linkage. Registers are used for procedure arguments and return addresses. Some procedures can thereby avoid any memory references. Typically, the processor has many more (up to 32) registers.

Processors for RISC operating systems

Oracle/sun SPARC enterprise server workstation

MIPS

Apple IBM Motorola (AIM) IBM PowerPC

Smartphones, tablets, netbooks, eBook readers, digital TV, home gateways

HP-UX

Explicitly parallel instruction computing (EPIC)

Google's mobile handsets, tablets, digital TV, game consoles, cameras, and other digital embedded applications

DEC Alpha AXP

FIGURE 11.32

Major RISC processor vendors.

RISC still has a hold on the mobile digital device market. The typical example is that Apple products adopt RISC chips (Cortex). CISC will not kick RISC out of the CPU market completely in the foreseeable future.

There is reason to say that RISC and CISC have evolved towards each other (see Figure 11.34). In other words, the CISC (or x86) chip looks more like a RISC chip. For example, CISC chips have adopted RISC operations, while most acceleration mechanisms in RISC processors are now also available to CISC chips.

Likewise, RISC processors have gradually introduced more instructions and many of them take multiple cycles to execute. Today, a RISC chip has hundreds of instructions in its ISA library. It hardly fits the title of "reduced instruction set computer."

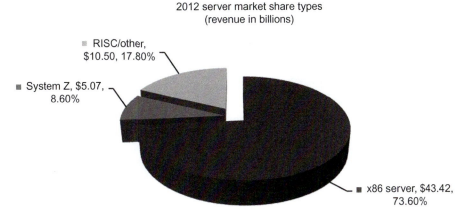

2012 server market share types
(revenue in billions)

RISC/other,
$10.50, 17.80%

System Z, $5.07,
8.60%

x86 server, $43.42,
73.60%

FIGURE 11.33

RISC, x86, and System z server market share in 2012.

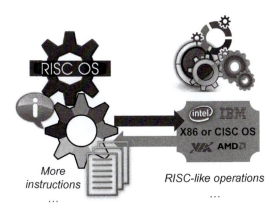

FIGURE 11.34

RISC and CISC processors are evolving towards each other.

After over 10 years' evolution, it is hard to find a clear distinction between the RISC and CISC ISAs in term of improving processor performance and efficiency. Although the instruction set of RISC and CISC looks very similar from a technical perspective, it is a totally different zero-sum game in the marketplace. Up to now, it appears that the x86 or CISC chip is winning the race in the server market.

Extremetech [191] illustrated that Intel x86 processors first took the PC desktop and laptop market in the 1980s and then grabbed the data center client/server market. During the last 10 years or so, Intel has started to crush the high-performance computer (HPC) market (see Figure 11.35) in terms of volume. Extremetech predicts that x86 processors will eventually conquer the mobile and network appliance market, which is now held by RISC processor vendors such as MIPS and ARM.

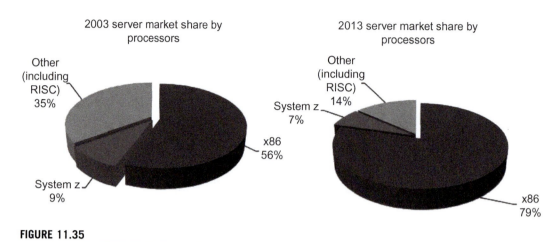

FIGURE 11.35

Markets conquered by Intel x86 chips in the last 10 years.

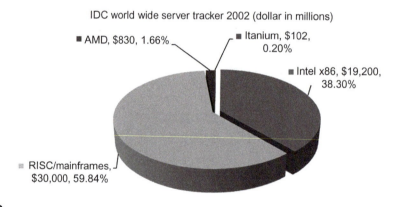

FIGURE 11.36

IDC WW server market share by processor types in 2002.

11.5.3 RISC SERVER MARKET SHARE

Speaking about server market share, IDC demonstrated that, overall, the RISC server market is shrinking down from nearly 60% market share in 2002 to only less than 30% (see Figures 11.36 and 11.37) in 2010.

   If RISC servers are losing market share, why should we bother to pay attention to them? The answer is that although the RSIC chips seem to be losing share in the server market, there have been many RISC servers purchased and installed by many data centers during the last 10 to 15 years or so, especially Oracle/Sun SPARC RISC servers. Therefore, it is absolutely essential for us to not only understand RISC servers but also have a clear strategy either to exit the RISC platform or stick with it.

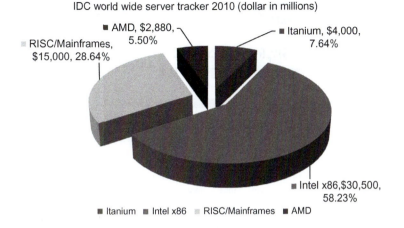

IDC world wide server tracker 2010 (dollar in millions)

■ AMD, $2,880, 5.50%

■ Itanium, $4,000, 7.64%

■ RISC/Mainframes, $15,000, 28.64%

■ Intel x86,$30,500, 58.23%

■ Itanium ■ Intel x86 ■ RISC/Mainframes ■ AMD

FIGURE 11.37

IDC WW server market share by processor type in 2010.

If we dive into further detail on the RISC server, we can find that there are three major vendors in RISC server market: Oracle/Sun SPARC, IBM PowerPC, and Intel's Itanium competing in the RISC market (strictly speaking, Itanium is an EPIC processor). However, the Sun/SPARC system mainly dominated the RISC server market during the 1990s and early 2000s. Subsequently, our discussion will concentrate on the SPARC server.

11.6 ORACLE/SUN SPARC SERVERS

The SPARC processor was originally developed by Sun Microsystems, which was established in 1982 by Vinod Khosla et al. SPARC means **S**calable **P**rocessor **Ar**chitecture. The chip architecture is based on the RISC I and II projects. However, when Sun Microsystems started its workstation business in 1982, it used Motorola's 68K chip, a CISC microprocessor, until 1987.

In contrast to other processor producers, Sun adopted the open standard approach and licensed different chip manufacturers to make their own version of processors that can fit with different product prices and budgets.

In 1987, Sun Microsystems and Fujitsu developed the first SPARC 32-bit processor. It was SPARC version 7. In 1990, they released SPARC version 8 and it was still a 32-bit architecture. Three years later, they introduced SPARC version 9. This was a 64-bit processor (see Figure 11.38). In comparison with Intel, which achieved its first 64-bit processor (Pentium 4) in 2000, Sun Microsystems was 7 years ahead of its competitors.

Because of the nature of open systems, SPARC customers can run many operating systems on SPARC processors. Sun Microsystems provides three operating systems for SPARC chips. One of the OSes is open source, Open Solaris. On top of the OS, there have been at least four different types of applications (see Figure 11.39) developed by various application vendors. Most of them are mission-critical applications for many medium and large enterprises.

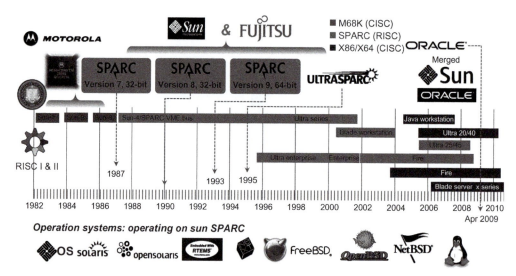

FIGURE 11.38

History of Sun Microsystems SPARC server.

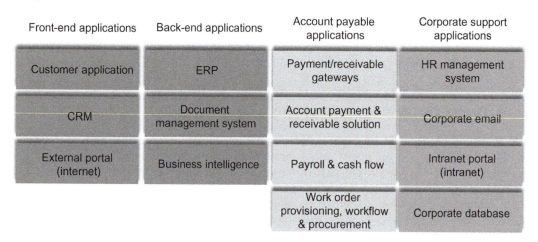

FIGURE 11.39

Four different types of common enterprise applications.

After almost 30 years of operation, Sun Microsystems were acquired by Oracle in April 2009. Following the merging of the two companies, Oracle/Sun quickly released its SPARC strategy for 2010 to 2015 (see Figures 11.40 and 11.41).

According to the Oracle/Sun technology roadmap, we can see that Oracle/Sun is trying to integrate M series and T series SPARC servers after 2014. One of the reasons to merge these two platforms is to simplify the SPARC virtualization infrastructure or environment because the M series server can only be partitioned and not virtualized.

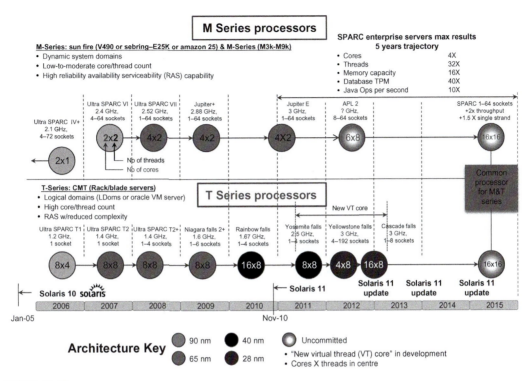

FIGURE 11.40

SPARC Processor five-year history and five-year outlook.

As we have indicated above, in comparison with x86 chips, Oracle/Sun uses a slightly different method to virtualize its SPARC environment. It adopts the so-called Chip Multithreading (CMT) technology. Oracle/Sun's virtualization concept classifies the virtual environment (VE) into three virtualization models.

The first model provides multiple isolated operating environments within one operating system instance. In essence, the aim of this model is to virtualize the operating system, which is known as operating system virtualization (OSV). This is actually an executable environment that has become a private copy or file within a container or bigger operating system. This means that OSV cannot directly utilize any ISA repertory or the computing resources below the operating system level.

The second model is often called the bare-metal model, in which the bigger operating system is replaced with a virtualized environment that is directly installed on the computer hardware. The name for such a virtual environment is the hypervisor. The key difference with the first model is that the hypervisor can cross multiple hardware resources rather than one big OS being tied up with individual hardware. A hypervisor will be responsible for virtual machine monitoring (VMM). Each VM can run a different OS. In this sense, a hypervisor can run a number of host VMs to manage computing resources. If a VM is running for a particular instance or software application rather than managing computing resources, it is called a guest VM. If an OS is running on the guest VM, we name it the "guest OS."

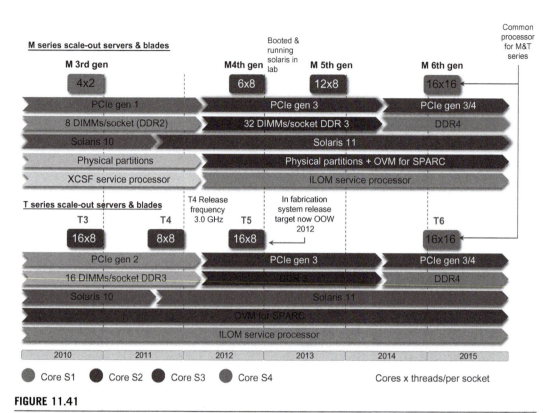

FIGURE 11.41

SPARC Processor and RAM roadmap.

The third model is not really a virtualized environment. It creates hardware partitions so that the computer hardware resources, such as CPU, RAM, and I/O, can be segregated into smaller, isolated, and multiple compartments. Oracle/Sun calls these isolated compartments partitions or domains.

Sun Microsystems used to have many different names for its server product series. It is often quite confusing when people are trying to distinguish which one is RISC and which one is a CISC server. In order to simplify Oracle/Sun product series as well as to align these products with classification of virtualization models, we use Figure 11.42 to clarify any confusion.

As we can see, Oracle/Sun currently has three major production series in conjunction with three different virtualized environments (VE). Of course, all production series can run the first virtualization model. The second model can run on both T-series and X-series servers. The key difference is the different type of CPU. The T-series server uses a RISC processor and the X-series server uses x86 chips. The M-series server can only be fit into the third virtualized model. Let's have a look the M-series server in detail.

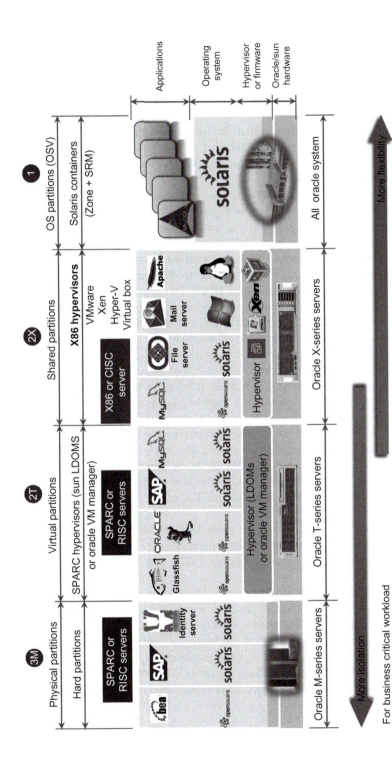

FIGURE 11.42

Three virtualized models.

11.6.1 ORACLE/SUN M-SERIES RISC SERVERS

Oracle/Sun M-series product is one of two types of RISC servers under the SPARC Enterprise series, Unix-based computers that support Sun OS, Solaris, Open Solaris, Free BSD, Open BSD, and other operating systems (see Figure 11.38). It was developed by both Sun Microsystems and Fujitsu.

This computer product range mainly targeted the middle and high end of the server market. According to Sun, the letter "M" means the features of an M-series server should be similar to a mainframe. Within the M-series server product line, Oracle/Sun currently has five different product models (see Tables 11.10 and 11.11).

The Oracle/Sun M-series server is the server model that replaced the SPARC-based Sun Fire system, such as the Sun Fire E25K or E20K. As Figure 11.41 showed, the M-series servers can only be divided (or virtualized) with a domain or a hard partition. Here, we see new usage of the term "partition." According to the hardware definition, the meaning of hard partitioning is to segment a single resource so that it looks like many resources. For example, we can segment a hard disk drive (HDD) into many HDDs. We can also group different segmented hardware components together, such as CPU, RAM, I/O, and local HDD. This segmented computer resource has another name, "domain." The domain is a totally independent computer system resource that can run the Oracle Operating System (OS). It is vertically isolated from other domains.

When we are trying to virtualize M-series servers, we have to be aware that M-series servers do not work with any hypervisors because the M-series processors (or SPARC64 chips) do not have the Hyper Privileged Mode (HPM) instructions.

The reason we emphasize this point here is because it brings to mind a very simple and stupid architecture mistake made by a famous consulting company for a large telco company. Basically, both the consulting and telco companies were trying to virtualize E-series SPARC servers. The virtualization project had wasted over about $20 millions in capex and more than 18 months valuable time. The real issue of this virtualization project was that one of IT professionals from the consulting company suggested installation of LDoM or Oracle/Sun's hypervisor on both SF E25K and T-series (or T5220) servers (see Figure 11.43). The aim of this installation was to create a virtualized environment (VE) across both E-serial and T-serial SPARC chips in order to utilize some idle E25K servers.

Clearly, the processors of SF E25K servers are either Ultra-SPARC III Cu or IV or IV+. These chips do not have the Hyper Privileged Mode instructions. Of course, they would not work with T-Series servers. It was a very stupid mistake to group T5220 with E25K servers to create virtual machines (VM).

The technology used in the Sun SPARC Enterprise M-series server is an embedded computer, the eXtended System Control Facility (XSCF). In other words, the hard partition or domain of the M-series server is created, configured, and altered from the XSCF.

The key difference between a hypervisor and hardware (or hard) partition is that a hypervisor can fully virtualize hardware resources. That is why people call it "bare metal." In contrast, the hard partition solution can only segment hardware resources. The bottom line is a fully virtualized environment controlled by a hypervisor has much more flexibility than a hard partition.

Table 11.10 Oracle/Sun M-Series Servers

Model	RU	Max No. of Sockets	Max. Cores	Threads	Processor Types	Processor Frequency (GHz)	Max. Memory (GB)	PCI Slots	On Board HDD (TB)	Hardware Partitioning	Listed Retail Prices	GA Date
M3000	2	1	4	8	SPARC64 VII, VII+	2.52, 2.75, 2.86	64	4	2.4	Not Support	$39,821	Oct-08 VII Apr-02 VII+
M4000	6	4	16	32	SPARC64 VII, VII+	2.15 GHz (VI) or 2.53, 2.66 GHz (VII)	256	25	0.6	2	$89,940	Apr-07 VI Jul-08 VII Dec-10 VII+
M5000	10	8	32	64	SPARC64 VI, VII, VII+	2.15 GHz (VI) or 2.53, 2.66 GHz (VII)	512	50	1.2	4	$167,037	Apr-07 VI Jul-08 VII Dec-10 VII+
M8000	N/A	16	64	128	SPARC64 VI, VII, VII+	2.28, 2.4 GHz (VI) 2.52, 2.88, 3.0 GHz (VII)	1,024	122	9.6	16	N/A	Apr-07 VI Jul-08 VII Dec-10 VII+
M9000	N/A	64	256	512	SPARC64 VI, VII, VII+	2.28, 2.4 GHz (VI) or 2.52, 2.88, 3.0 GHz (VII)	4,096	288	38.4	24	N/A	Apr-07 VI Jul-08 VII Dec-10 VII+

Table 11.11 Oracle/ Sun M-Series Server SPARC64 Processor Types

	SPARC64 VI	SPARC64 VII	SPARC64 VII+
Code name	Olympus-C	Jupiter	Jupiter-E or M3
Frequency (MHz)	2,150–2,400	2,400–2,880	2,667–3,000
Architecture version	V9/JPS1	V9/JPS1	V9/JPS1
Year	2007	2008	2010
Total threads	$2 \times 2 = 4$	$2 \times 4 = 8$	$2 \times 4 = 8$
Process (μm)	0.09	0.065	0.065
No. of transistors (M)	540	600	–
Die size	422	445	–
Power (W)	120	150	160
L1 D cache(k)	128×2	64×4	64×4
L1 I cache (k)	128×2	64×4	64×4
L2 cache (k)	6144	6144	12288
L3 cache (k)	None	None	none

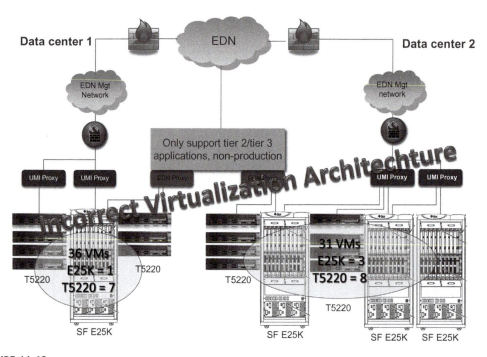

FIGURE 11.43

Example of incorrect virtualization architecture for SF E-series and T-series servers.

Table 11.12 Relationship of Physical Hardware and Virtual Machines (VMs) under a Hypervisor

Server Type	Virtual Machine	Description of Physical to Virtual (P2V) Relationship
Physical CPU socket	1-to-1	One physical server is assigned to one virtual machine
Physical CPU socket	1-to-many	One physical server is assigned to many virtual machines
Physical CPU socket	Many-to-1	Many physical servers are assigned to one virtual machine
Physical CPU socket	Many-to-many	Many physical servers are assigned to a few virtual machines

Table 11.13 Relationship of Physical Hardware and Hard Partitions

Server Type	Hard Partitions	Description of Physical to Virtual (P2H) relationship
Physical CPU socket	1-to-1	One physical server is assigned to one domain
Physical CPU socket	1-to-many	One physical server is assigned to many domains

Furthermore a hypervisor can create the relationship of many to one, many to many, and one to many between VMs and hardware but a hard partition can only have a relationship of one to one and one to many (see Tables 11.12 and 11.13).

The hard partition is also called a "dynamic domain." The meaning of "dynamic" is that you can reconfigure or regroup CPU, RAM, and I/O resources without shutting down the entire server. It is also called dynamic reconfiguration (DR).

Although the hard partition (or dynamic domain) does not provide enough flexibility for hardware resources, it can provide vertical isolation to share the powerful high-end physical server resources. It is normally designed for mission-critical applications that need very high SLA business applications.

Because M-series servers are targeting the high-end server market, the price is very high,, even for entry level M-series servers, in comparison with normal x86 servers. For example, the HP DL 585 G7 has a similar capacity as the M4000, but the price of the M4000 is nearly seven times more than the HP DL 585 G7. Perhaps this explains why RISC servers have been losing market share during the last 10 years or so.

The key issue is that servers have become commodity products. In order to address this challenge, Oracle/Sun provides T-series servers, which is our topic for the following section.

11.6.2 ORACLE/SUN T-SERIES RISC SERVERS

In comparison with M-series servers, "T" marks the entry and midrange level of Ultra-SPARC (or UNIX) servers. All SPARC T-series machines are rack-mounted servers. Oracle/Sun provides T-series servers to create SPARC versions of VMs. The SPARC hypervisor adopting this virtualized technology is different than x86 hypervisors such as VMware vSphere, Citrix Xen, and Microsoft Hyper-V. Oracle /Sun called the technology Logical Domains or LDoMs for short (now it has been replaced with VM Server for SPARC).

The LDoM hypervisor can only run those physical servers where SPARC Chip Multithreading (CMT) processors have been installed or enabled. These SPARC server models are basically T-series servers, which include the rack-mounted T5X20/T5X40 models ("X" roughly stands for the physical size of server. For example, if "X" is equal to "2," it represents a 2RU rack-mounted T-serial server.) Subsequently, we have the T5220 model and T6320/T6340 blade models as well as the earlier Sun Fire T1000/T2000 series (see Tables 11.14 and 11.15).

All T-series SPARC servers in Tables 11.14 and 11.15 have been superseded by SPARC servers showed in the both Tables 11.16 and 11.17. The reason we present the data here is to make it easier for readers to make comparisons with current SPARC servers and x86 servers. Table 11.16 is for rack-mounted SPARC server and Table 11.17 is for the SPARC blade servers.

In the above four tables, the server configuration is close to the high end but the price is close to the low end. In other words, the prices shown in the tables are just an indication. Table 11.16 shows the gap between the starting price and high-end price would be roughly double (or approximately 2.7 times) on average.

11.6.3 SPARC LOGICAL DOMAIN AND VIRTUAL MACHINE (VM)

All T-series servers enable the functionality of the logical domain, which can manage a virtual machine (VM). Each logical domain (LDoM) or VM can have its own virtual resources (see Figure 11.44). In comparison with the M-series, T-series chips have the Hyper Privileged Mode instructions built in to the processors. Subsequently, we can run a very small or thin hypervisor that resides in firmware (if the hypervisor is installed using a bare metal approach). The function of the SPARC hypervisor is similar to x86 hypervisors, which is to monitor, track, and manage logical CPUs, RAM, and I/O devices.

In addition, the SPARC hypervisor also provides logical communication channels between logical domains and the hypervisor or among the logical domains (see Figure 11.45).

The number of LDoMs or VMs is subject to the type of physical T-series SPARC server. Theoretically speaking, it should be that one thread or one strand is equivalent to one vCPU. If one LDoM or VM must have at least one vCPU, then the maximum number of LDoMs should be equal to the maximum number of threads (or CMT). Because the Oracle/Sun recommendation is to leave four threads for the control domain, the maximum number of VMs should be less than the maximum number of threads. We can use the following equation to determine the theoretical maximum number of VMs per physical T-series SPARC server:

$$VM_{Max} = Thread_{Max} - 4$$

For example, if a T5-2 SPARC server has 256 threads, the maximum number of VMs should be 252 based on the above equation.

However, if we adopt best practices to configure a physical T-series SPARC server, one physical core is assigned to one guest domain [193]. Therefore, the T5-2 server has only 32 cores. The maximum number of LDoMs or VMs should be 31. One is dedicated to the control domain.

Table 11.14 Oracle/Sun SPARC Obsolete T-Series Rack-Mounted Servers

Model	RU	No. of Sockets	Cores	SPARC Processor Type	Thread	RAM (GB)	HDD (GB)	PCI Slots	OS Solaris	L1 (KB) on Core	L2 (MB)	List Starting Price
T1000	1	1	8	U-SPARC T1, 1.0 GHz	32	32	292	1	10	24	3	$10,560
T2000	2	1	8	U-SPARC T1, 1.0/1.2/1.4 GHz	32	64	584	e3 + ×2	10	24	3	$11,284
T5120	1	1	8	U-SPARC T2, 1.2/1.4/1.6 GHz	64	128	2,400	e8	10, 11	24	4	$13,183
T5220	2	1	8	U-SPARC T2, 1.2/1.4/1.6 GHz	64	128	4,800	e16	10	24	4	$26,989
T5140	2	2	16	U-SPARC T2+, 1.2/1.4 GHz	128	128	2,400	e13	10	24	4	$22,613
T5240	2	2	16	U-SPARC T2+, 1.2/1.4/1.6 GHz	128	256	4,800	e16	10, 11	24	4	$36,413
T5440	4	4	32	U-SPARC T2+, 1.4/1.6 GHz	256	512	1,200	e28	10, 11	24	4	$42,658
T3-1	2	1	16	SPARC T3 1.65 GHz	128	128	9,600	e6	10, 11	N/A	6	$18,369
T3-2	2	2	32	SPARC T3 1.65 GHz	256	256	3,600	e10	10,11	N/A	6	$40,822
T3-4	5	4	64	SPARC T3 1.65 GHz	512	512	4,800	e16	10,11	N/A	6	$85,942

Table 11.15 Oracle/Sun SPARC Obsoleted T-Series Blade Model Server

Model	No. of Sockets	Cores	SPARC Processor Type	Thread	RAM (GB)	HDD (GB)	PCI Slots	OS Solaris	L1 (KB) on Core	L2 (MB)	List Starting Price
T6300	1	8	U-SPARC T1 1.0,1.2, 1.4 GHz	32	32	500	4	10, Linux	24	3	$3,695
T6320	1	8	U-SPARC T2, 1.2/1.4/1.6 GHz	64	128	2,000	2	10	24	4	$30,151
T6340	2	16	U-SPARC T2+, 1.2/1.4 GHz	128	256	4,000	4	10	24	4	$52,902
T3-1B	1	16	SPARC T3 1.65 GHz	128	128	TBA	4	10, 9/10	N/A	6	N/A

Table 11.16 Oracle/Sun SPARC Current T-Series Rack-Mounted Servers

Model	RU	No. of Sockets	Cores	SPARC Processor Type	Thread	RAM (GB)	HDD (GB)	PCI Slots	OS Solaris	L2 (KB)	L3 (MB)	List Starting Price to High End
T4-1	2	1	8	SPARC T4, 2.85 GHz	64	256	4,800	e6	10,11	128	4	$20,984–$52,404
T4-2	3	2	16	SPARC T4, 2.85 GHz	128	512	3,600	e10	10,11	128	4	$35,132–$95,192
T4-4	5	4	32	SPARC T4, 3.0 GHz	256	1,000	4,800	e16	10,11	128	4	$54,437–$$204,736
T5-2	3	2	32	SPARC T5, 3.6 GHz	256	1,000	3,600	e6	8,9,10,11	128	8	$53,948–$111,988
T5-4	5	4	64	SPARC T5, 3.6 GHz	512	2,000	1,800	e16	10, 11.1	128	8	$96,756–$236,062
T5-8	8	8	128	SPARC T5, 3.6 GHz	1,024	4,000	1,800	e16	10, 11.1	128	8	$165,842–$440,224

Table 11.17 Oracle/Sun SPARC Current T-Series Blade Servers

Model	RU	No. of Sockets	Cores	SPARC Processor Type	Thread	RAM (GB)	HDD (GB)	PCI Slots	OS Solaris	L1 (KB) on Core	L2 (KB)	L3 (MB)	List Starting Price to High End
B6000	10												$8,645
T4-1B		1	8	SPARC T4, 2.85 GHz	64	256	TBD	e4	10, 8/11	16	128	4	$17,291–$47051
T5-1B		1	16	SPARC T5, 3.6 GHz	128	512	1,200	e4	10, 11.1	n/a	128	8	$25,862–$53,922

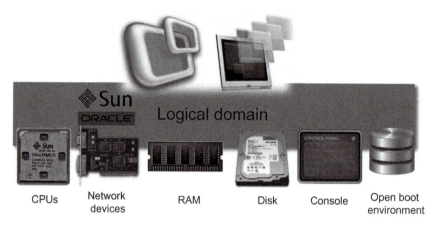

FIGURE 11.44

SPARC logical domain or virtual machine resources.

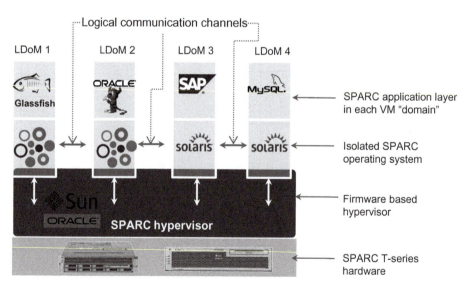

FIGURE 11.45

Logical communication channels.

11.7 **SUMMARY**

In this chapter, we concentrated on the server. We not only discussed x86 (or CISC) servers, but also explored the details of RISC servers, with a special focus on the Oracle/Sun SPARC server. From a computer evolution perspective, we can see why the client/server architecture has become the mainstream computer architecture in the data center:

1. The Internet has become widespread and has been integrated with our daily life. The number of hosts has increased exponentially or 900% during the last 20 years or so.
2. In contrast to a mainframe, the client/server architecture is very flexible and much easier to deploy.
3. The cost of server deployment is only a fraction of that for a mainframe.

We also presented brief information about the major vendors that provide these servers:

- X86 (CISC) processor: These are often produced by two major vendors, Intel and AMD.
- RISC (SPARC) processors: These are mainly provided by Oracle/Sun and Fujitsu.

We clarified all terms, units, and jargon with regard to servers and processors. We aimed at establishing the foundation for our cost modeling because these units and terms, such as sockets, cores, methods, domains, and multithreading, will be the physical baseline to measure the cost of a cloud infrastructure.

As Extremetech illustrated, the Intel x86 chip has not only taken over the PC/workstation market, but also server market in data centers during the last 30 years. In comparison with RISC servers, the x86 or CISC server has gradually become the dominant computer in the server market and RISC servers have been losing ground.

The landscape of the server market has changed a lot since 2005. Cisco has been gaining momentum in x86 server (blade server) market share since 2009. Based on IDC data from the second quarter 2013, traditional server vendors are losing x86 server market share and "others" (including some Chinese vendors, such as Huawei and Lenovo) have gained a significant amount of the server market (40% in volume and 21% in revenue). This has indicated that x86 servers have become a commodity type of product because many servers are OEM products made in China. This could be one of influential factors for many decision makers in making capex investment decisions. We will continue this discussion in later chapters. Despite major traditional server vendors (such as HP, IBM, and Dell) losing market share, they still hold over 50% market share in terms of volume and 70% in revenue (for all types of servers including mainframe, x86, RISC, and EPIC).

After we discussed the details of x86 servers or processors, we moved on to physical installation of servers. Traditionally, there were only two types of servers styles: tower and rack-mounted servers (or pizza boxes). During the dot-com boom era between the late 1990s and early 2000s, people started to develop blade servers in order to deploy servers on a large scale while saving physical space and cabling. From an incremental perspective, the rack-mounted server would be a better solution for TCO/ROI. We will give more detail in later chapters.

In the final part of this chapter, we unveiled the details of RISC servers. We explained what a RISC server is. And what the differences between x86 (CISC) and RISC servers are. We also looked at why the RISC server is losing market share to x86?

In particular, we focused on Oracle/Sun SPARC servers. We explained the difference between M-series and T-series SPARC servers. We also listed both M-series and T-series SPARC server configurations and listed prices for both obsolete and current models.

At the end of this chapter, we briefly touched on SPARC logical domains (LDoMs) or the VM manager for SPARC in order to explain how to make an assumption of the number of VMs per physical SPARC server.

11.8 REVIEW QUESTIONS

1. Why has the server dominated the computer market during the last 30 years?
2. What is the fundamental theoretical difference between RISC and x86 or CISC servers?
3. Why are x86 servers taking server market share in the data center?
4. Which one is better, blade or rack-mounted servers?
5. What is a SPARC server?
6. Can we create a virtual server farm (or a number of virtual machines) based on a mixture of SPARC M-series and T-series servers?
7. What is the maximum number of VMs per SPARC server based on theory?
8. What is the maximum number of VMs per SPARC server based on best practices?

CLOUD STORAGE BASICS

This chapter covers three main topics. It begins with an overview of data center storage. This includes storage hardware, power, building blocks, protocols, and different storage topologies. It introduces storage tiering and SLA. This is the availability and reliability of a storage system. Finally, it presents different storage options and their relationship with the hosting and cloud infrastructure. The main purpose of this chapter is to lay out the foundation foer cloud storage costs. In short, we divide this chapter into four sections:

- Storage types and storage hardware
- Storage application and performance
- Storage cost calculations, benchmarks, and vendors
- Traditional storage vs. cloud storage

12.1 STORAGE HIERARCHY

Storage is one of the key components for any cloud infrastructure. It supports server operations. Without it, the server will not be able to perform. Based on the topics of storage performance, capacity, and cost, we can basically classify computer storage hardware into five categories:

- Cache (static random access memory or SRAM)
- RAM (dynamic RAM or DRAM)
- Solid state disk (SSD) (NOR and NAND flash)
- Hard disk drive (HDD)
- Tape drive/optical storage

These five categories are different types of storage components with different technologies, installed in different locations on a server (see Figure 12.1). Cache storage is located within the CPU. A RAM chip is resident within a server motherboard. We have briefly touched on these hardware topics in previous chapters. In this chapter, we will concentrate on external (located outside a physical server) storage hardware components, such as SSDs, HDDs, and tape drives, or tape libraries. Because the HDD is currently the most popular external storage hardware and most cost-effective storage solution, we will begin with HDDs and then explore SSDs. Price G2 [194] predicted in 2014

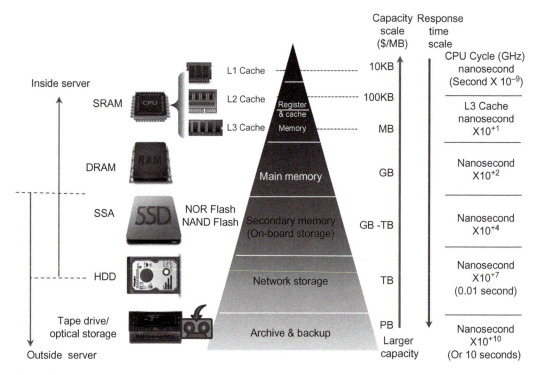

FIGURE 12.1

Memory and storage hierarchy.

that eventually, the price of SSDs will be the same as HDDs. Subsequently, they will replace HDD storage solutions. Finally, we will discuss tape drives and optical storage. These are mainly archive and backup solutions.

12.1.1 HARD DISK DRIVE (HDD) FUNDAMENTALS

HDDs have been the mainstream external storage medium for almost 60 years. Although they have been under strong challenge from SSD products and have physical limitations, they will still be accompanying us for next five years or so. So, we should not only understand the mechanisms of HDDs but also their value for your business. Based on the business type or market segment, HDDs can be divided into six different categories or types:

- Mobile
- Branded
- Consumer electronics
- Desktop or PC
- Enterprise high-performance disk
- Enterprise

12.1.1.1 *HDD physical metrics*

What we are going to focus on here is enterprise high-performance storage disks or enterprise HDDs. Despite different HDD market segments, the fundamental principles of all HDDs are the same. From an HDD capacity perspective, the size of capacity can vary from 50 GB per HDD up to a few TBs per HDD. However, there are only 5 different HDD speeds, which are 4,200 (70 Hz), 5,400 (90 Hz), 7,200, 10,000 and 15,000 RPM (revolutions per minute) but the most popular enterprise HDD types in the majority of data centers are:

- 7,200 (120 Hz)
- 10,000 (160 Hz)
- 15,000 (250 Hz)

Please note that the unit of RPM is not part of the International System of Units (SI units). The word "revolution" is just used to represent the physical action of the HDD rather than the standard unit of measurement. The real physical measurement unit should be the rotation or frequency (Hz). We have the following relationship equations between RPM and Hz (radians per second = rad/s):

$$1\ Rad/s = \frac{60}{2\pi}\ (rpm) = 9.55\ rpm\ (radian/per\ second),$$

$$1\ Rad/s = \frac{1}{2\pi} = 1\ Hz$$

$$\omega\ (Rad/s) = 2\pi f$$

$$f = \frac{\omega}{2\pi}$$

If we look at HDD physical dimensions, we find that the size of HDD can vary from an initial size of 24 inches in 1956 to the latest one that is 0.85 inches in 2004 (see Figure 12.2).

However, the most common physical sizes of HDD are 3.5 and 2.5 inches. For enterprise storage, these two sizes of HDD dominate nearly all applications because they are convenient to fit into either a 2 or 3RU rack-mounted storage disk array (see Figure 12.3).

Figure 12.3 shows two examples of an EMC 3RU rack-mounted hard disk array. As we can see, the individual HDD is not only similar to many consumer types of HDD in term of physical dimensions but also in terms of capacity and speed (RPM).

Normally, the cost of each individual HDD is dependent on a combination of data storage capacity, interface, speed (RPM), and even warranty (see Table 12.1 and Figure 12.4).

With regard to the storage interfaces, we have at least 12 common storage interfaces that connect to servers (see Table 12.2).

For enterprise applications, the common storage interface types are SATA, SAS, SCSI, and Fibre Channel (FC). These interfaces will be combined with three major types of storage protocol or network connectivity:

- Storage area network (SAN)
- Network-attached storage (NAS)
- IP network

IBM RAMAC 350 (5MB)
1956
Cost = $10,000 or $2,000/MB
Physical size = 24 inches

Seagate ST506 (5MB)
1979
Cost = $1,500 or $300/MB
Physical size = 5.25 inch

Rodime RO352 (10MB)
1983
Physical size = 3.5 inches

Prairietek 220 (20MB)
1988
Physical size = 2.5 inches

Integral peripherals
(21.4MB) 1991
Physical size = 1.8 inch

HP (21.4MB) 1992
Cost = $250 or $12/MB
Physical size = 1.3 inch

IBM (340MB) 1999
Physical size = 1.0 inch

Toshiba (4TB) 2004
Physical size = 0.85 inch

FIGURE 12.2

Physical dimensions of HDDs.

EMC CLARiiON CX-4G15-600
fibre channel drive

3RU 15 3.5-Inch Disk Drives

EMC VNX V3-2S10-300
300GB 10K SAS

3RU 25 2.5-Inch Disk Drives

FIGURE 12.3

Two types of EMC disk drive carrier or disk processor enclosure (DPE).

Table 12.1 Different Types of HP HDD

Capacity (GB)	Spin Speed (RPM)	Interface	Physical Size	Warranty (Year)	Avg. Rotational Latency and Seek	Watts (Sleep/ Idle/ Active)	Online Price (US$)
2,000	5,400	3G SATA	3.5" LFF	1	5.5 ms rotational + 10 ms seek	1.5/6/7	$120
1,000	7,200	3G SATA	3.5" LFF	1	4.1 ms rotational + 9 ms seek	1.5/7/10	$269
500	7,200	3G SATA	2.5" SFF	1	4.1 ms rotational + 9 ms seek	1.5/7/8	$229
500	7,200	6G SATA Dual port	2.5" SFF	1	4.1 ms rotational + 9 ms seek	1.5/7/8	$369
300	10,000	6G SATA Dual port	2.5" SFF	3	3.0 ms rotational + 4.0 ms Seek	2/7/12	$309
146	15,000	6G SATA Dual port	2.5 SFF	3	2.0 ms rotational + 3.3 ms Seek	1.5/7/10	$369

Table 12.2 Different Storage Interfaces

Enterprise Storage Interfaces	Consumer Storage Interfaces
SATA	IDE
SCSI	PATA
SAS	UATA
Fibre Channel (FC)	Wi-Fi
Thunderbolt	USB
	Fire Wire 400
	Fire Wire 800

FIGURE 12.4

HP P2000 G3 MSA FC Dual Controller SFF Modular Smart Array system.

These storage protocols can be mixed with different storage interfaces such as iSCSI or IP Fibre Channel or IP SAN to achieve different performance, measured by inputs and outputs per second (or IOPS). When we examine storage performance and return on investment (ROI), we often hear that many storage vendors claim that their storage products would be the best value for the money on the market. As Table 12.1 shows, each HDD has a different price due to different configurations. The question for us as customers is how can we find out which one is a better value for the money? In other words, how can we independently measure or estimate the HDD value?

12.1.1.2 HDD evolution

Hubbert Smith [128] suggested a decision-making process with four key storage metrics (or CP^3) to evaluate a particular storage component or HDD:

- Capacity (GB) (capex component)
- Purchase cost ($) (capex component)
- Performance (IOPS) (opex component)
- Power (watts) (opex component)

Clearly, the first two metrics measure the Capex component and the last two metrics are involved in opex components. As Hubbert Smith suggested, when we calculate these metrics, we should always put the benefit in the top of the fraction (numerator) and leave the expenses, such as power and purchase cost, in the bottom of the fraction (denominator). Then, we will have following four relative metrics or ratios to evaluate or compare different HDDs:

$$P_C = \frac{Performance\ (IOPS)}{Cost(\$)} \quad (1) \quad P_P = \frac{Performance(IOPS)}{Power(watt)} \quad (2)$$

$$C_C = \frac{Capacity\ (GB)}{Power\ (Watt)} \quad (3) \quad C_P = \frac{Capacity\ (GB)}{Power(Watt)} \quad (4)$$

Now, you may wonder how do we calculate IOPS? This is a critical question because IOPS is not only associated with an HDD's RPM but also associated with storage applications and network connectivity. There will be further discussion of these topics later.

We assume that HDD has latency when it reads and writes data from HDD medium, the platter. This latency is determined by the rotational latency (RPM) of the disk and the seek time of the actuator arm (see Figure 12.5). This latency is measured in milliseconds (ms).

Based on the above definition, we can establish the IOPS equation as follows:

$$IOPS = \frac{1}{Rational\ Latency + Average\ (Read + Write)\ Latency}$$

For example, assume the HDD rational latency is equal to 2 ms, read latency is equal to 3 ms and write latency is equal to 6 ms. Let's assume that a particular online transaction processing (OLTP) application spends 70% of its time "reading" and 30% of its time "writing." In this case, we will have the data listed in Table 12.3.

It will be quite straightforward for us to decide all the latency categories because HDD manufacturers will provide these physical metrics. The real issue is how to work out the proportional

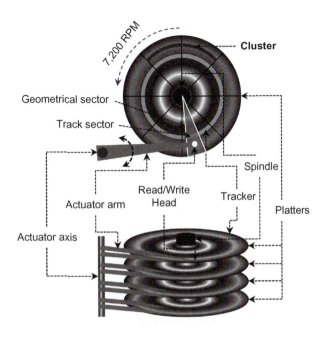

FIGURE 12.5

Inside of hard disk drive.

Table 12.3 Example of IOPS Calculation

Latency Category	ms	ms to s Conversion	Application Proportional %	Avg. R + W Latency	Subtotal	IOPS
Rational latency	2	0.002			0.002	
Read latency	3	0.003	70%	0.0021		
Write latency	6	0.006	30%	0.0018	0.0039	
					0.0059	169

% of reading and writing time for different business applications. Dell's whitepaper [195] provided 11 applications with different I/O workload profiles (see Table 12.4).

Once we know all four parameters of each HDD (capacity, IOPS, cost, and power consumption), we will be able to evaluate HDDs with different configurations and make a good comparison in terms of value for the money (see Table 12.5).

Based on these evaluation formulas, we can compare apple to apple among different configurations and different prices of HDD. We can use the HDD configuration in Table 12.6 and make a comparison for five different HDDs provided by different vendors.

Table 12.4 Application I/O Workload Profiles

Applications	Block Size in Bytes (KB)	Read %	Write %	Random %	Sequential %	I/O Performance Metric
Web file server	4, 8, 64	95%	5%	75%	25%	IOPS
Database online transaction processing (OLTP)	8	70%	30%	100%	0%	IOPS
Exchange email	4	67%	33%	100%	0%	IOPS
OS drive	8	70%	30%	100%	0%	IOPS
Decision support system (DSS)	1,000	100%	0%	100%	0%	IOPS
File server	8	90%	10%	75%	25%	IOPS
Video on demand (VoD)	512	100%	0%	100%	0%	IOPS
Web server logging	8	0%	100%	0%	100%	MBPS
SQL server logging	64	0%	100%	0%	100%	MBPS
OS paging	64	90%	10%	0%	100%	MBPS
Media streaming	64	98%	2%	0%	100%	MBPS

Table 12.5 Example of HDD Evaluation Formulas

HDD Parameters	HDD Value Assumption	Ratio Formula	Key Ratio	Results
Capacity	500 GB	IOPS/$	250/229	1.09
Performance (IOPS)	250	IOPS/watt	250/10	25
Unit cost	$229	GB/$	500/229	2.18
Power	10 watts	GB/watt	500/10	50

Table 12.6 Comparison of Five Different HDDs with Key Metrics

HDD Types (RPM)	7.2 K (1 TB)	7.2 K (500 GB)	7.2 K (500 GB)	10 K (300 GB)	15 K (146 GB)
Performance (IOPS/$)	0.45	0.52	0.33	0.97	1.08
Performance (IOPS/watt)	12.00	15.00	15.00	25.00	40.00
Capacity ratio (GB/$)	3.72	2.18	1.36	0.97	0.40
Capacity per watt (GB/watt)	100.00	62.50	62.50	25.00	14.60

From this exercise, we can see that this approach to evaluation can boil all HDD metrics down to a unit level. We can avoid any confusion due to different configurations of HDD when we make any comparison among different HDDs.

During the last few decades, we have experienced a very dynamic computer industry. The price of hardware may fluctuate at any time. One metric of HDDs alone, such as high capacity, cannot decide the best value for the money. We have to consider all aspects of an HDD because different applications will have different requirements in terms of performance metrics. This leads to another question, which is "How can we select different types of HDD (in term of size of capacity and rational speed) for different business applications?"

12.1.2 STORAGE SLA AND RAID ARCHITECTURE

To answer the above question, we have to introduce the concept of a Service Level Agreement (SLA). The service orientation is the foundation of IT business. It underpins an IT business's organization and IT architecture. The cloud business model actually drives the IT service orientation further from the physical world to the virtual realm.

However, any virtual realm must be supported by the physical world. "Nothing acts unless it's actual." So the question now is how to define the SLA and how to establish the relationship between SLA and different types of HDD. The common practice for hosting storage businesses is "tiering" (see Table 12.7). It is similar to data center tiering structures (see Table 4.2) but with different parameters.

In Table 12.7, you might notice that the lower the tier number, the higher the cost. The storage tiering should be closely aligned with the business SLA. For example, if the storage application is for OLTP business, you would need the highest SLA for OLTP applications because if the OLTP database falls over, it will certainly impact on your business revenue or cash flow. Table 12.7 is mainly focused on the capex of storage, but we should also find out the opex cost of tiering, which is the cost of the SLA.

Table 12.7 Example of Storage Tiering for Different Business Applications

Tier Cost	T0	T1	T2	T3	T4	T5	Total/Avg.
GB (Usable)	2,221	9,355	12,830	17,176	16,908	51,360	109,830
No of HDD	80	140	120	80	48	64	532
Drive cost/tier	$147,000	$77,560	$66,480	$66,000	$42,483	$47,775	$447,298
% allocation of fixed cost	1.7%	30.4%	26.1%	17.4%	10.4%	13.9%	100%
Fixed cost/tier	$3,727	$65,221	$55,903	$37,269	$22,361	$29,815	$214,296
Total tier cost	$150,727	$142,781	$122,383	$103,269	$64,844	$77,590	$661,594
Tier cost/GB	$68.48	$15.26	$9.54	$6.01	$3.84	$1.51	$17.44
Tier cost/GB/ month (48)	$1.43	$0.32	$0.20	$0.13	$0.08	$0.03	$2.19

Table 12.8 Example of SLA Metrics

Service Level	Inherent Availability = (MTTF)/(MTTF + MTTR)	Support Hours	Downtime (seconds per month)	No. of Failures per Month	Max. No. of Customer Impacts	Remedy Price
Business Critical	99.999%	24 × 7	26.28	≤ 1	5	$500,000
Platinum	99.995%	24 × 7	131.4	≤ 3	10	$300,000
Gold	99.990%	24 × 7	262.8	≤ 5	50	$250,000
Silver	99.950%	13 × 7	1314	≤ 7	100	$100,000
Bronze	99.900%	13 × 5	2628	≤ 10	500	$50,000
Basic	99.00%	8 × 5	26280	≤ 15	1000	$25,000

12.1.2.1 The common definition of an SLA

In Chapter 4, we briefly discussed the topic of SLAs in terms of data center sites. Here, we will give more details of storage SLAs in terms of cost. An SLA is the performance metric that both service providers and consumers have agreed upon for service availability within the specified period of time, normally one year or one month. It will help both parties to visualize the service cost and consequences if the service provider fails to meet the agreed SLA. The standard formula is actually to measure the service availability or inherent availability (IA):

$$Availability = \frac{Uptime}{Uptime + Downtime} \times 100 \ or \ A = \frac{MTBF}{MTBF + MTTR} \times 100$$

Here, MTBF stands for mean time between failure and MTTR is mean time to repair (see Table 12.8).

From Table 12.8, you might notice that this SLA does not only regulate inherent availability but also the number of faults that may occur within a one-month period. In addition, it also specified the number of impacted customers or service in operation (SIO) because this SLA is designed for business to business (B2B). For example, this could be the SLA for a cloud service provider that provides IaaS to a web content provider.

We have to indicate that in practice, a SLA may also include response and resolution time, which is reflected in the MTTR and the support hours. For example, if the SLA is designed for the Exchange email application, the required response time may be less than 15 minutes and resolution time should be less than 2 hours.

This is just common SLA operation, as we are looking at the SLA issue from an operational perspective. However, from an enterprise storage application perspective, the SLA not only means the availability or uptime, but also the service quality and business risks. In other words, we also have to consider access bandwidth and business continuity for storage SLAs (see Table 12.9).

In this table, we introduce the term Fibre Channel (FC) RAID-1, RAID-5, SAN, and Director Port in order to differentiate different tier levels. This addresses the SLA issue from the RAID architecture perspective to prevent HDD failure.

Table 12.9 Example of Hosting Storage Cost

	Tier 1	Tier 2	Tier 3	Tier 4	Tier 5		
Type of SLA	Platinum (GB)	Gold (GB)	Silver (GB)	Bronze (GB)	Archive (GB)	SAN Ports	Director Port
Infrastructure	FC RAID-1	FC RAID-1	FC RAID-5	FC RAID-5			
Capacity (H/W usage)	$0.84	$0.48	$0.35	$0.17	$0.18	$10	$20
Operation (mgmt. cost)	$0.80	$0.76	$0.48	$0.30	$0.21	$15	$20
Total hosting storage	$1.64	$1.24	$0.83	$0.47	$0.39	$25	$40

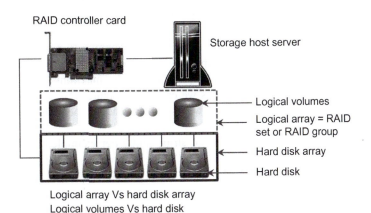

Logical array Vs hard disk array
Logical volumes Vs hard disk

FIGURE 12.6

Architecture of hardware RAID.

12.1.2.2 RAID techniques

What is RAID? RAID stands for redundant array of independent/inexpensive disks. It is a method or architecture involving combining a group of HDDs to prevent HDD failure. However, we have to remember RAID is just to prevent data loss due to hardware failure, not to protect the information or data from deleting accidently or software failure. Software failure protection is handled via backup activities.

When we implement RAID, we have two choices: one is software RAID and the other is hardware RAID. What software RAID does is to provide RAID options at the host-based software level from a storage host server. In contrast, hardware RAID has a dedicated hardware controller to manage RAID configurations. We will mainly focus on hardware RAID because it can provide very good performance for cloud storage. Hardware RAID consists of four basic components: storage host server, RAID controller card, logical array (logical volumes) and hard disk array (HDDs) (see Figure 12.6).

At the logical level, RAID options are defined by three basic techniques:

- Striping
- Mirroring
- Parity

12.1.2.2.1 Striping

The technique of striping is to spread storage data across multiple drives or HDDs so that all read/write heads can work in parallel. From a storage user perspective, striping makes multiple HDDs into a single disk in the logical system. In comparison with read/write from a single disk in series, the striping technique increases data processing performance.

As we can see, a logical array organizes a bunch of HDD arrays. Within each physical HDD, the number of addressable blocks for data has been fully mapped or predefined. These predefined blocks are named "stripes." One strip can cross all HDDs within a logical array (see Figure 12.7).

An HDD partition is a logical domain that is separated by HDD firmware. It can be checked in a partition table. In contrast, a volume is defined by the operating system. We can assign drive letters to volumes. One HDD can have many partitions and one partition can have many volumes. A column is a vertical section of an HDD's platters. A stripe size is a unit within a stripe. That is why it is also called a stripe unit or stripe depth. This is the maximum data block that can be assigned into one HDD for a logical array. As we can see in Figure 12.7, all stripes have the same stripe unit number across all HDDs. In other words, stream data is split into smaller units when it is written onto an HDD.

One stripe should have a certain number of stripe units. For example, stripe 1 has two stripe units. This is also called "stripe width."

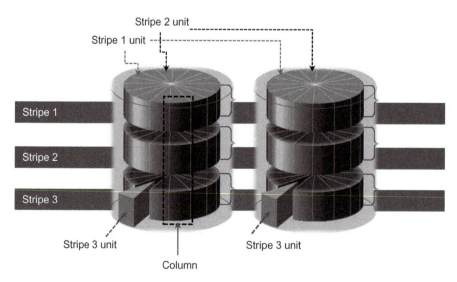

FIGURE 12.7

Diagram of a stripe and stripe unit or size or depth.

12.1.2.2.2 Mirroring

This term is quite easy to understand. It is one-to-one relationship in terms of HDD redundancy. In essence, the data will be written into two HDDs. This technique is normally for business critical applications, such as logging data or online transaction processing data.

12.1.2.2.3 Parity

The parity technique is a solution that is a combination of mirroring and striping. With a one-to-one redundancy solution (mirror), the utilization rate of an HDD is very low, only 50%. It would cost too much for non-business-critical applications. If it is not business critical, we still need some degree of data protection in case one HDD fails.

Parity adds an extra HDD into the physical array or RAID group so that we can increase stripe width to accommodate parity information or data. If any HDD fails, the parity technique can implement the lossless bitwise exclusive-OR (or XOR) algorithm, subtract the missing data value from other HDDs, and replace the failed HDD (see Figure 12.8).

You may notice there is a term referencing usable GB or storage capacity in Table 12.7. This is referring to different type of RAID or RAID options. In contrast to the usable storage capacity of a RAID setup, it is the storage capacity for the redundant capacity. Normally, five or six different RAID options or architectures are very common because they have better storage performance:

- Data redundancy
- Capacity utilization
- Read/write performance
- Minimum/maximum number of drives

Let's have a look pros and cons of each RAID option in detail.

12.1.2.3 RAID configurations

12.1.2.3.1 RAID-0

RAID-0 is the special case. Strictly speaking, it is not RAID because it doesn't have any redundancy. Any HDD failure will lead to data loss or destroy the entire disk array. For RAID-0, the advantage is quite obvious, as the capacity utilization rate is 100% because it doesn't have any disk for redundancy. The disadvantage is also very clear, which is there is a single point of failure. Actually, it increases failure rate because the data is spread across many HDDs. The more disks we have in the array system the higher the risk is. However, RAID-0 splits the data stream into many stripe units or stripe depths. The common sizes of stripe units are 16 KB, 32 KB, 64 KB, and

FIGURE 12.8

Parity technique.

128 KB. This lays out the foundation for other RAID options or nested RAID; we will discuss these options shortly (see Figure 12.9).

12.1.2.3.2 RAID-1

RAID-1 has 100% redundancy. This is why another name of RAID-1 is "mirroring." This adopts the mirroring technique to create HDD redundancy. In other words, any data will be recorded twice. If one HDD is faulty, we can retrieve data from a mirrored HDD. Because RAID-1 takes a mirroring approach, the usable capacity of the disk array is only 50% (see Figure 12.10).

12.1.2.3.3 RAID-5 (distributed parity with N + 1)

RAID-5 uses the parity technique to build HDD redundancy. However, there are two different types of parity models: one is having a dedicated HDD for parity and the other is distributed parity. RAID-4 adopts the dedicated parity model. RAID-4 sounds OK at the hardware level but it has many performance penalties at the software level. We will not spend too much space and time discussing RAID-4 because no cloud storage will use RAID-4.

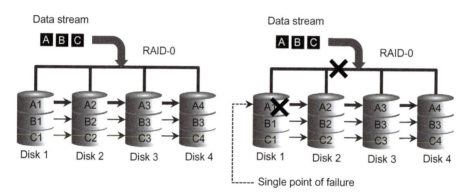

FIGURE 12.9

RAID-0 configuration.

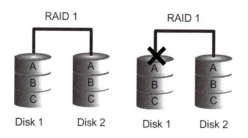

FIGURE 12.10

RAID-1 (mirroring).

In contrast to RAID-4, RAID-5 adopts a distributed parity model. It overcomes many performance issues and bottlenecks of RAID-4. It uses the mathematical parity calculation to reproduce a volume if one HDD is faulty (see Figure 12.11).

12.1.2.3.4 RAID-6 (distributed parity with double parity redundancy)

From a parity technique perspective, RAID-6 is the same as RAID-5. It also uses "distributed parity," but it adds one more HDD for redundancy. If we have "N" number of HDDs in the disk array, the usable capacity of the HDDs will be $N - 2$. In other words, if "N" is equal to 10, the usable space is 80% of raw capacity (see Figure 12.12).

12.1.2.3.5 RAID-10 or RAID-01 (nested RAID-1 and RAID-0 or RAID1 + 0)

RAID-10 is a combination of RAID-1 and RAID-0. Or simply, it is a mix of one mirroring with a few striping HDD groups or one striping with a few mirroring HDD groups. If we combine the striping HDDs first, it is nested as RAID-10. If we combine the mirroring HDDs first, it will become RAID-01 (see Figure 12.13).

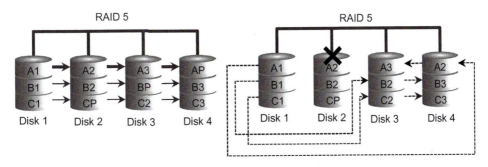

FIGURE 12.11

RAID-5 (distributed parity).

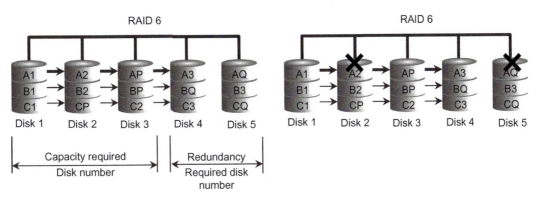

FIGURE 12.12

RAID-6 configuration.

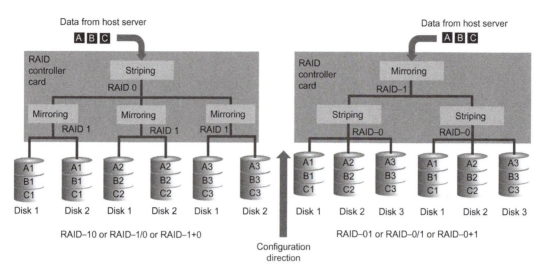

FIGURE 12.13

Nested RAID, RAID-10, and RAID-01.

In the RAID-10 option, the RAID configuration performs mirroring first and then striping. In contrast, RAID-01 is striping first and then mirroring. Subsequently, this RAID setup can afford to have three faulty disks without any operational impact. However if one the RAID-01 disks is faulty, it will bring down all the striping disks. In our case, this would be three HDDs. Therefore, RAID-01 is not a practical RAID option.

12.1.2.4 Comparison of RAID options

Each RAID option has its advantages and disadvantages. When we select RAID options, we have to balance among types of HDD or IOPS, data center conditions (such as power and cooling), RAID cost, and RAID performance based on different application requirements. For example, if a business requires a small SQL database application with very frequent and random access, RAID-10 will be a good solution to handle the workload because although RAID-10 capacity (50% of utilization rate) is small, it is very reliable.

IBM summarized the performance of 12 common RAID options using seven different metrics (see Table 12.10) [196].

What this table shows is that RAID level does impact on an HDD's IOPS. For example, both the read and write performance of RAID-0 are "superior" without any additional latency from the RAID setup. On the other hand for RAID-1, although both the read and write performance are still "very high," every write operation has to be executed on two disks (or HDDs). This means more I/O overhead.

Furthermore when the RAID-5 option is implemented, the "write" execution will have more latency because the RAID controller has to read, calculate, recalculate, and write a parity data block on the number of HDDs. From the RAID-5 controller perspective, it has to execute both two disk reads and two disk writes. One "read" and "write" operation is for the real data block and the other is

Table 12.10 Different Type of RAID Comparisons

RAID Level	Data Redundancy	Physical Drive Capacity Utilization	Read Performance	Write Performance	Built-in Spare Drive	Min. Number of Drives	Max. Number of Drives
RAID level-0	No	100%	Superior	Superior	No	1	16
RAID level-1	Yes	50%	Very high	Very high	No	2	2
RAID level-1E	Yes	50%	Very high	Very high	No	3	16
RAID level-5	Yes	67% to 94%	Superior	High	No	3	16
RAID level-5E	Yes	50% to 88%	Superior	High	Yes	4	16
RAID level-5EE	Yes	50% to 88%	Superior	High	Yes	4	16
RAID level-6	Yes	50% to 88%	Very high	High	No	4	16
RAID level-00	No	100%	Superior	Superior	No	2	60
RAID level-10	Yes	50%	Very high	Very high	No	4	16
RAID level-1E0	Yes	50%	Very high	Very high	No	6	60
RAID level-50	Yes	67% to 94%	Superior	High	No	6	60 (SCSI)
							128 (SAS, SATA)
RAID level-60	Yes	50% to 88%	Very high	High	No	8	128

for parity. As a result, the total operations for RAID-5 will be four. This number is called the write penalty (see Figure 12.14). This is why the "write" performance is only "high" (see Table 12.10).

For RAID-6, the write penalty will be six because RAID-6 has double parity redundancy.

The letter "E" stands for "Enhancement". It is normally placed after the RAID option. For example RAID-1E. We will not discuss this topic here.

12.1.2.4.1 Summary of common RAID characteristics, cost and write penalties

We summarize different RAID options in Table 12.11. As RAID-3 and RAID-4 are hardly used for most business solutions, we should pay close attention to RAID-1, RAID-5, RAID-6, and RAID-10 and associated costs.

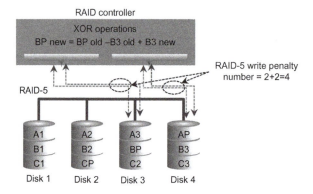

FIGURE 12.14

Write penalty for RAID-5.

Table 12.11 RAID Options			
RAID Options	**Main Characteristics**	**Cost**	**Write Penalty**
RAID-0	Striped array with no fault tolerance	Low	0
RAID-1	Disk mirroring	High	2
RAID-3	Parallel access array with dedicated parity disk	Moderate	4
RAID-4	Striped array with independent disks and a dedicated parity disk	Moderate	4
RAID-5	Striped array with independent disks and distributed parity	Moderate	4
RAID-6	Striped array with independent disks and dual distributed parity	High than RAID-5	6
RAID-10 & RAID-01	Combinations of RAID levels. Example: RAID-1 + RAID-0	High	2

You may wonder why we have to understand these details. The question will be answered through the following example.

12.1.2.4.2 RAID options and application IOPS

Suppose a content server requires that its storage performance have an average IOPS = 6,400 and 80% of IOPS is "read" and 20% is "write." If the performance metric is just cost, RAID-6 has more storage capacity than RAID-1. From an economic perspective, RAID-6 would be the first choice but if we select the RAID-6 option, does it meet the IOPS performance requirement? The question is how many HDDs can be saved if the RAID option is RAID-6?

Calculation Details:
Step 1: Find the total IOPS for RAID-6

- RAID-6 = 80% × 6,400 (read) + [20% × 6,400 (write)] × 6 (RAID-6 write penalty number)]
- RAID-6 = 5,120 + 1,280 × 6 = 12,800 IOPS

Step 2: Find the total IOPS for RAID-1

- RAID-1 = 80% × 6,400 + [20% × 6,400] × 2 = 7,680 IOPS

Referring to Table 12.1, we will have following results for different RAID options if we select the HP 300 GB option.
Step 3: Find the number of HDDs and their row capacity

- RAID-6 = 12,800/300 = 43, and 43 × 300 GB = 12.9 TB (row capacity)
- RAID-1 = 7680/300 = 26 and 26 × 300 GB = 7.8 TB (row capacity)

For the same IOPS performance, RAID-6 has to have 17 or 66% more HDDs than RAID-1.
Step 4: Find the usable capacity

- RAID-6 (usable capacity) = (43 − 2) × 300 GB = 12.3 TB
- RAID-1 (usable capacity) = (26/2) × 300 GB = 3.9 TB

If RAID-1 needs the same amount of usable storage capacity as RAID-6, RAID-1 should have:

- 12.3 TB/0.5 = 24.6 TB

The number of HDDs should be 24,600 GB/300 GB = 82. Of course, 82 HDDs can provide 24,600 IOPS for the RAID-1 option.

From a usable storage capacity perspective, RAID-6 can save 82 − 43 = 29 HDDs. If each HDD costs $309, we can save $8,961.

From this example, we understand that both the RAID-5 and RAID-6 options can give us higher or better IOPS performance. In contrast, RAID-1 will give us lower IOPS performance because RAID-5 and RAID-6 have higher storage utilization rates and higher "write penalties," but RAID-1 has lower storage utilization rate and a lower "write penalty." Overall, we have to balance between utilization rate and IOPS performance when we decide on a RAID option.

12.1.3 STORAGE LUN

By now, we should understand that the RAID architecture not only provides redundancy for any HDD failure but also aggregates a group of inexpensive hard disk drives (HDDs) into one chunk of storage volume for a hosting server. However, not all applications will require a very large volume of storage. For example, if one application only needs 500 GB storage, a RAID group (or logical array) provides 2 TB capacity. This may lead to 75% of the RAID group capacity being wasted.

In order to resolve this issue, people split a large RAID group into a number of logical volumes and each volume is assigned a unique number, which we call a logical unit number (LUN).

What a LUN does is partition a group of HDDs that form a RAID set. LUNs will represent the entire RAID set capacity. It divides the large volume of a RAID set into a number of smaller slices. Each LUN can be mapped to an individual host server (see Figure 12.15).

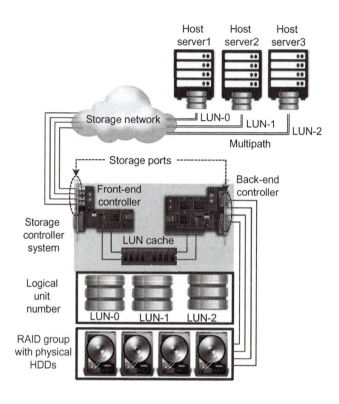

FIGURE 12.15

Logical unit number (LUN).

The above figure illustrates the mechanisms of LUNs and a storage network. We will give more details of storage networks in the following sections but here, we will focus on two more LUN terms: LUN expansion and LUN masking.

12.1.3.1 LUN capacity expansion

12.1.3.1.1 Meta LUN concatenation

When the existing LUN storage capacity is not enough for a particular business application, how can we increase the storage capacity? One of the solutions is meta LUN. The way to expand LUN storage capacity is to join other LUNs. This is also called "concatenation." Any mirror and parity types of RAID can be concatenated. For example, a LUN on RAID-1 can be joined with a LUN on RAID-5. However, a LUN on RAID-0 can be only joined with another LUN on RAID-0.

Concatenation LUN expansion is a quick solution to increase LUN storage capacity, but it will not provide any benefits for LUN performance. In order to improve not only the capacity but also performance, we have to adopt meta LUN striping.

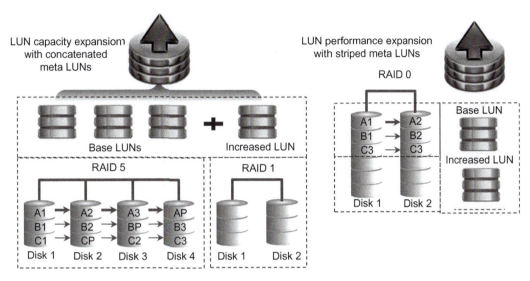

FIGURE 12.16

LUN expansion by concatenated and striped meta LUNs.

12.1.3.1.2 Meta LUN striping

In contrast to concatenation expansion, striping LUN expansion requires the same capacity and RAID type (see Figure 12.16). As we understand the principle, the more HDDs we have, the higher performance will be (see the above example in Section 12.1.2.4.2).

12.1.3.2 LUN masking

The function of LUN masking is to protect other unauthorized hosts that are accidently trying to access the LUN that has already been mapped into one host. It defines which host can access which LUN under a shared storage environment. For example, there are three LUNs mapped to different lines of business (LoBs), namely, finance, product, and procurement groups. Without LUN masking, each LoB can access all LUNs. This will raise data security issues and other problems. With LUN masking, each LoB can only access its own LUN.

12.2 **SOLID STATE DISK OR FLASH SSD**

So far, we have discussed the basic storage component based on hard disk drive (HDD) technology. Since IBM invented the first longitudinal HDD in 1956, it has been in use for almost 60 years, but now we are at the verge of replacing HDDs with SSDs for three main reasons:

1. The performance gap between the CPU and HDD has become greater during the last 17 years or so because CPU performance has improved by 30 times but HDD has only been lifted 30% during the same period (see Figure 12.17). HDD I/O performance has become the bottleneck over time.

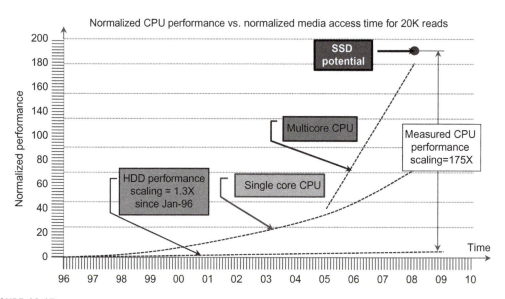

FIGURE 12.17

Huge scaling discrepancy between CPU and HDD [197].

2. HDD has reached its physical limitation based on existing technologies (see Figures 12.18 and 12.19) because the mechanical part of HDDs has reached the nanometer level.
3. The price of SSDs is almost equivalent to HDDs (see Figure 12.20).

If we make a quantified comparison between SSDs and HDDs in terms of 10 performance metrics, we can see that SSD is far better than HDD for 8 out of 10 performance measurements (read, write, low weight, low noise, low power consumption, better MTBF, and no operation shock (see Figure 12.21 and Table 12.12).

Although the SSD's cost per GB was quite high in comparison with HDDs in 2007, SSD market price is declining faster than for HDDs. Once the unit price of SSDs is equal or less than HDDs, data migration from HDD to SSD will be inevitable.

According to Deal news [200], consumer SSD products had a sharp drop in 2012. For smaller size (64 GB) SSDs, the unit price was only $0.47 per GB in August 2012 but it was still relatively expensive in comparison with HDD prices, for which the unit price was only $0.08 per GB in 2012 and $0.04 per GB in 2013. However, looking back at the history of SSD prices, we have reasonable confidence that SSD prices will match HDD prices (see Figure 12.22).

If the unit price of SDDs is equal or slightly higher than HDDs, it would open the door for the possibility of migration from HDD to SSD. When we evaluate SSD cost, what should we know from a TCO/ROI perspective? Basically, there are three fundamental issues that should be clarified:

- What is an SSD?
- What are the key differences between SSDs and HDDs?
- How does the TCO compare between SSDs and HDDs?

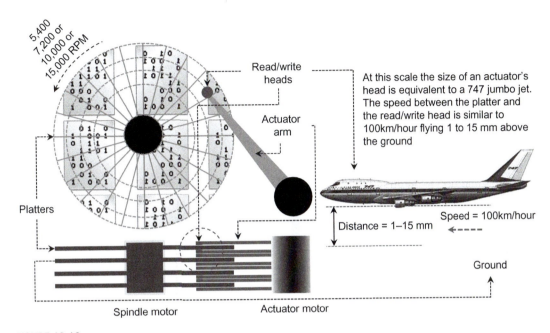

FIGURE 12.18

HDD read/write heads have reached their physical limits.

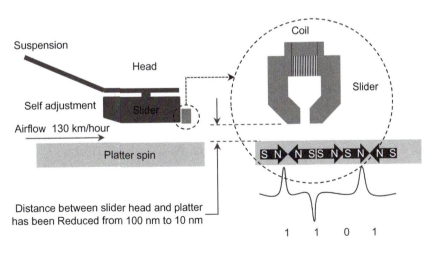

FIGURE 12.19

The distance between the HDD read/write head and platter.

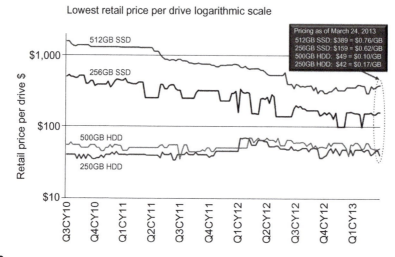

FIGURE 12.20

256 GB HDD and 256 GB SSD price history and forecast [198].

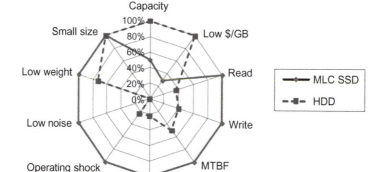

FIGURE 12.21

2.5-inch SSDs vs. HDDs in PC performance characteristics (by Forward Insights) [199].

12.2.1 WHAT IS AN SSD?

SSD stands for solid state drive. The solid state contrasts with a hard disk drive (HDD), which consists of components with hollow and moving states. It also means that when an SSD reads or writes information or data, it does not require moving parts.

SSD is flash technology-based storage as it does not require power. Hence, it is also called as nonvolatile flash memory. If it uses "Not AND" or "Negated AND" logic gates, the full name of

Table 12.12 Enterprise Storage Technologies and Key Metrics (Source: Violin Memory) [200]

Technologies	Capacity (GB)	Latency (μS)	IOPs	Cost/ IOPS ($)	Cost/GB($) in 2007
Capacity HDDs	2,500	12,000	600	13.3	3
Performance HDDs	700	7000	1,200	16.6	28
Flash SSDs	700	200	500	140	100
Flash SSDs (read-only)	700	45	50,000	1.4	100
DRAM SSDs	250	3	200,000	0.5	400

Notes:
1. The price is for the enterprise storage.
2. Metrics are all normalized for typical rack-mounted system statistics per U of height (1.75″).
3. Latency and IOPS estimates assume same numbers of random reads and writes.
4. Latency and IOPS estimates assume 4 K block sizes.

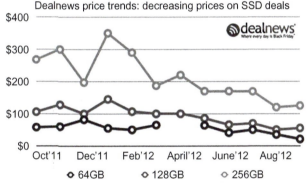

FIGURE 12.22

SSD price trends in 2011 and 2012.

the memory chip becomes nonvolatile NAND flash memory. NAND logic gates are generally applied for RAM, USB memory, and SSDs. Flash storage is in the realm of semiconductor memory. It captures information or data in an array of columns and rows that consist of a semiconductor cell across every intersection (see Figure 12.23).

There are two issues with flash technology. One of them is that memory cells do not like to be flashed too frequently because after many flash cycles (erasing), the transistor gate becomes worn out and eventually has to be broken down. This is also called the wear level. Another issue is that when the SSD does sequential writing for new data it has to follow the process of erasing and then writing. This leads to slower performance. Sometime, it may be slower than a high end HDD.

To resolve these issues, single level cell (SLC) has been adopted for many enterprise storage applications. SLC only stores a single bit, which is either a "1" or "0" bit. In contrast, multilevel

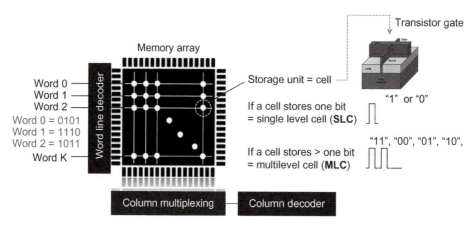

FIGURE 12.23

Flash technology-based storage.

FIGURE 12.24

SSD vs. HDD.

cell (MLC) will accommodate two bits, which are "00," "01," "10," and "11." In comparison with MLC, SLC has ten times the endurance (flash) of MLC but it comes with a high cost. There is another type of flash that Samsung adopted called is triple level cell (TLC). It has three bits.

Strictly speaking, SLC, MLC, or TLC doesn't last fever but they are protected by a flash controller that is always built into an SSD. It manages error correction, wear leveling, and data distribution so that all data written is spread evenly across all physical blocks of the SSD.

12.2.2 SSD VERSUS HDD

One of the obvious differences between an SSD and HDD is that an SSD doesn't have any mechanical parts. It consists of flash memory, an SSD controller, a connector, a DRAM buffer (or cache), and a printed circuit board (PCB) (see Figure 12.24). In comparison, an HDD has far more components than an SSD. It not only has electronic components but also mechanical components.

Based on Intel's test results for their products in July 2011 [201], an SSD's annual failure rate (AFR) was 87% better than an HDD (SSD = 0.61% versus HDD = 4.85%). Table 12.13 compares several key performance attributes of SSDs and HDDs.

Table 12.13 Key Metrics Enterprise SSDs and HDDs [199]		
Attributes	**Solid State Drive (SSD)**	**Hard Disk Drive (HDD)**
Physical size	2.5 inches	2.5 inches
Capacity	100/200/400 GB	146/300 GB
Media	SLC NAND	1−2 disks/2−4 heads
Interface	SAS 6 Gbps	SAS 6 Gbps
Avg. access/seek time	0.1 ms	3.0 ms(read)/2.7 ms (write)
Random read (IOPS)	90,000	385
Random write (IOPS)	16,000	325
Sequential read (64 K)	500 MB/s	200 MB/s
Sequential write (64 K)	250 MB/s	200 MB/s
Reliability MTBF	2.0 million hours	1.6 million hours
Nonrecoverable read errors	1 per 10^{17}	1 per 10^{16}
Voltage	5/12 V	5/12 V
Sleep/idle mode	<1 W	4.5 W
Operational mode	6.5 W	8.7 W
Noise	0 dB	3.3 dB
Weight	152 g	220 g
Warranty	5 years	5 years
Cost/GB	$0.47−$1/GB	$0.04−$0.075/GB

Note: In the last row of this table, we give a rough price range for both SSD and HDD during the last 2−3 years (2012−2014).
Figure 12.20 also shows the price trend between 2010 and 2013.

12.2.3 TOTAL COST OF OWNERSHIP OF SSD

As the above table has already indicated, the cost of SSDs is still six to eight times higher than HDDs but we should compare the TCO. SNIA provided a simple way to calculate the TCO [202] in October 2009. It is basically a consideration of four aspects:

- Acquisition
- Maintenance and repair
- Power and cooling
- Performance

Acquisition cost means high random I/O (input/output) per GB of data transactions for different applications, such as Exchange email, banking transactions, etc. It is basically the purchase cost or initial capex investment. Bearing this in mind, when we make assumptions, the unit price of SSD (per GB) is declining at an average of 30%−40% yearly over the last decade or so.

Maintenance and repair cost is looking at the annual failure rate. Based on Intel's whitepaper, SSD is 87% better than HDD.

Table 12.14 5-Years TCO Calculation for SSD and HDD

Parameters	SAS 15 K RPM 146 GB HDD	SATA 256 GB SSD
Power		
Power cost ($0.158/kWh)	$1,794	$34
Cooling cost	$2,153	$41
Disk array		
Cost of enclosures	$6,500	$3,250
Enclosure energy draw	$1,365	$683
Drive and maintenance		
No. of drives	18	2
Drive cost	$4,489	$2,000
Maintenance/warranty cost	$763	$340
Total cost of ownership		
Up-front cost	$13,177	$6,273
Per year cost	$987	$19
5-year TCO	$17,063	$6,348

Power and cooling cost is to examines data center power consumption. For some Tier 0 and Tier 1 storage systems, SSDs can save over 80% in total storage system energy requirements in comparison with HDDs. Performance cost compares the IOPS cost between SSDs and HDDs.

SNIA showed an example TCO calculation based on a Microsoft Exchange Email Server scenario. The email server is configured to serve 2,000 heavy Blackberry users with 100 MB storage per mail box and 3 IOPS per user. The further assumptions were:

- Workload read/write ratio: read = 65% and write = 35%
- Data block size = 4 kB random small block I/O
- HDD: 3.5-inch 146 GB drive, 15 K RPM, SAS interface, keep 479.7 IOPS (4 kB block size)
- SSD: 2.5-inch 256 GB drive, SATA interface, keep 30,000 IOPS (4 kB block size)
- RAID configuration = RAID-1 [write penalty (WP) = 2]

From Section 12.1.2.4.2, we know how to calculate the number of HDDs to meet the an application's IOPS requirements.

Because per user IOPS is equal to 3, the total IOPS requirement for the email server should be $2,000 \times 3 = 6,000$ for 2,000 users:

$$No \ of \ HDD = \frac{(IOPS \times R\%) + WP \times (IOPS \times W\%)}{HDD \ IOPS}$$

Therefore, we will have $[(6,000 \times 0.65) + 2 \times (6,000 \times 0.35)]/479.7 = 17$. (Because it is the mirroring configuration, the number of HDDs should be 18.)

With regard to SSD, only two SSD drives should be able to meet both IOPS and capacity performance requirements. In summary, the example listed the detailed data in Table 12.14.

Table 12.15 Intel TCO Calculation Based on SNIA model		
Costs	**7 Intel SSDs**	**48 15 K RPM HDDs**
Energy cost	$211	$10,523
Disk array cost	$3,933	$15,730
Drive cost	$10,483 ($1497.57/per SSD)	$9,815 ($204.48/per HDD)
Total cost of ownership	$14,416	$36,068

Similarly, Intel did a very simple calculation based on the SNIA model and three parameters. With an SSD, Intel can save about 60% off the HDD TCO (see Table 12.15).

12.3 STORAGE TOPOLOGIES AND CONNECTIONS

When we have enough storage resources, how can we utilize them effectively? Along with computer evolution, storage systems are also trending from decentralized to centralized. In this section, we will discuss four different storage connectivity scenarios for hosting servers.

12.3.1 DIRECT ATTACHED STORAGE (DAS)

Direct attached storage (DAS) is the connection between storage and a server/servers without a storage network or any network device, such as a router, switch, hub, or director. However, no network does not mean there is no interface connection. DAS can have many different types of interfaces that are connected to a server, such as a Host Bus Adapter (HBA), IDE/ATA, SATA, SAS, SCSI, eSATA and Fibre Channel (FC). These interfaces are also applied to other types of network storage. We will have further discussion on this in the next section.

If we use the storage disks' location as a distinguishing point, we can have two types of DAS: internal and external DAS.

12.3.1.1 Internal DAS

With internal DAS, the storage disk/disks are directly located inside of a hosting server. The common interface connection is through HBA. The main function of HBA is to provide high-speed bus connectivity or communication channels between a host server and storage devices or a storage network. In addition, HBA can also handle many heavy-lifting jobs in order to alleviate the hosting CPU's processing workloads (see Figure 12.25). Normally, the internal DAS allocates one or two disk drives for system boot. With an internal DAS, the physical space is limited. If a business application needs further expansion for larger storage capacity and the physical space within the host server is not available, then we have to locate a disk array externally.

12.3.1.2 External DAS

For an external DAS arrangement, the storage disk array is still directly attached to a server without any network device. However, it interfaces with the host server with different protocols. The

FIGURE 12.25

Internal DAS.

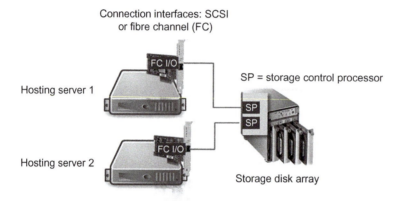

FIGURE 12.26

External DAS.

popular interface protocols are SCSI and Fibre Channel (FC). In comparison with internal DAS, external DAS overcomes the issues of physical space and distance between the host server and storage disk array. In addition, the storage array can be shared by more than one host server (see Figure 12.26).

Similar to dedicated computers, the major issues with DAS are inflexibility, high risk, difficult maintenance, and inefficiency or overprovisioning, which means more storage capacity is normally allocated than what a host needs. In order to resolve these issues, the next logical solution is networking storage arrays.

12.3.2 STORAGE AREA NETWORK (SAN)

If we understand the issues with DAS, the ideal SAN would not be too difficult to understand. In a very simple terms, SAN is just a bunch of computers and storage devices (or arrays) that are connected to each other with a high speed and dedicated network (or a number of network devices, such as a hub, switches, and routers). In the example in Figure 12.27, we see a Fibre Channel Arbitrated Loop (FC-AL) hub that connects to all hosting servers and storage arrays.

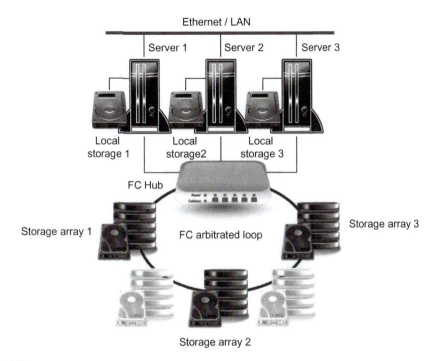

FIGURE 12.27

Basic storage area network (SAN) With FC-AL hub.

Actually, the FC-AL implementation is an early stage of SAN. The way the FC-AL works is that when a node (all hosting servers and storage arrays are considered a node within a SAN) fires or initiates an arbitrated (ARB) request for a communication channel with one of the other nodes, it will take a control of the loop if the request is received (see Figure 12.28).

This kind of configuration is fine but it has a number of limitations or issues:

- When the number of storage devices grows, the FC-AL configuration will not be sufficient because with 8-bit addressing, FC-AL can only support up to 126 devices or nodes within one loop.
- If we add more storage devices into this arbitrated loop, each device has to share bandwidth with other devices. Subsequently, it will reduce the high-speed FC efficiency.
- When we make any changes to the loop, such as increasing or decreasing the number of nodes, the loop has to be refreshed. It will freeze the entire SAN for a moment.

In order to resolve this issue, a solution called a Fibre Channel Switch (or FC-SW), a switch fabric network, has been developed. It allows tany number of computer server nodes to communicate with any number of storage nodes without scarifying bandwidth performance. This means that we can add more storage devices onto this FC-SW fabric network than with an FC-AL hub. The FC-SW configuration is now replacing the FC-AL hub (see Figure 12.29). It enables an "any-to-any" type of connection.

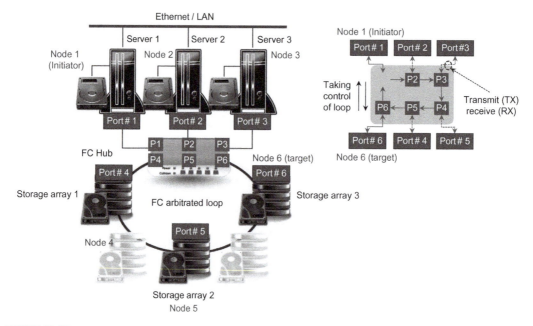

FIGURE 12.28

Mechanism of SAN FC-AL.

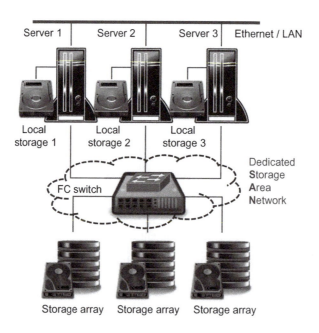

FIGURE 12.29

SAN connection with switch.

Because FC-SW adopts a 24-bit addressing mechanism, it can support over 15 million nodes and multiple pairs of ports with full bandwidth communication channels within a fabric.

The term "switch fabric" means that many switch elements can be assembled as a scalable fabric topology based on the number of nodes. For an enterprise application, an FC-SW topology can have multiple tiers (see Figure 12.30).

From Table 12.9, we can see the price of a SAN (FC switch) and director port is different. A director is a large switch for enterprise applications. It has fault tolerance capabilities. The number of director class switch ports (typically 128−516 ports) is double or triple times more than edge or midrange switches (typically 32−64 ports). Normally, the unit cost (per port) of a director tends to be much more expensive than a standard switch. The additional cost is due to the extra reliability and performance built into a director (see Figure 12.31).

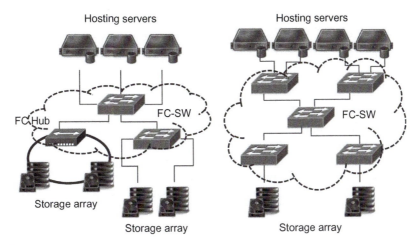

FIGURE 12.30

Different types of SAN FC-SW topologies.

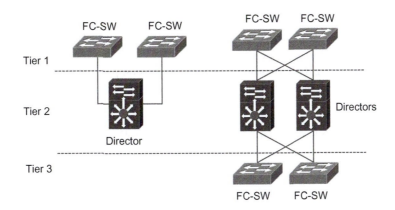

FIGURE 12.31

Tiered SAN FC-SW topology.

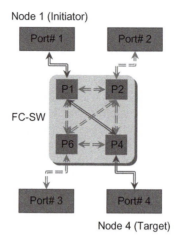

FIGURE 12.32

FC-SW SAN duplex (TX + RX) communication channel.

In comparison with the right side of Figure 12.30, the tiered SAN FC-SW topology architecture is just replacing a FC-SW with a director in Figure 12.31. With a mash-up connection, it builds fault tolerance capability into a Fibre Channel fabric switch SAN.

For any FC-SW SAN, there are two key components: the SAN switch and the port interface. FC-SW has an intelligence capability that can logically establish a duplex communication channel [transmission (TX) and receive (RX)] from an initiator node to a target node via switch ports (see Figure 12.32).

From Figure 12.32 we see that node 1 as an initiator can transmit data to target node 4 via FC-SW. Once the link is established, this link can be considered a dedicated line between the initiator and target nodes.

With the SAN architecture, we can have six different types of interface ports but with the FC-SW SAN, we can only have four types of interface ports (see Figure 12.33):

- N-port, where "N" stands for node. This is a node port. Normally, it means an HBA port on either a server site or storage array site.
- E-port, where "E" stands for expansion. This is an expansion port that connects two Fibre Channel (FC) switches. The link between the two FC switches is named a "inter-switch link" (ISL).
- F-port, where "F" stands for fabric. This is a switch port facing a node port (N-port).
- G-port, where "G" stands for generic. This can be either an E-port or an F-port. This is dependent on its function.

The reason to clarify the above issues is that different ports will have different prices. It will impact on the construction of the cost model. In the following section, we will first discuss NAS and then unveil the topic of storage protocols. This will lead to discussion of different bandwidths for SANs.

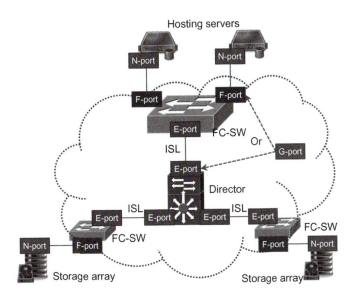

FIGURE 12.33

FC port types.

12.3.3 NETWORK ATTACHED STORAGE (NAS) AND FILE STORAGE PROTOCOLS

What is NAS and what are file storage protocols? Moreover, if we have DAS and SAN, why do we need a NAS architecture for data center storage? These questions will be answered in the following.

12.3.3.1 The idea of NAS

The initial idea of network attached storage (NAS) came from file sharing by many users via an interconnected network. During the early evolution of computers, file sharing was not an easy thing, especially when some users turned their computers off. It would be impossible for other people to access the files stored in their computers (see Figure 12.34).

This issue led to the idea of having a dedicated computer to host shared files so that every user can access the shared files throughout a file storage network. This was an early form of NAS architecture (see Figure 12.35).

As we can see in Figure 12.35, NAS is actually an IP-based file sharing environment that is attached to a LAN. Therefore, it needs protocols for users to communicate with file servers. If we use the UNIX operating system (OS), Sun Microsystem developed the Network File System (NFS) as a protocol to share files. However, if we adopt Windows, the protocol is the Common Internet File System (CIFS). Today, there are many software solutions that allow people operating across both the UNIX and Windows OSes to share files.

When more and more users need to access the file server to share files, the requirements to improve I/O performance and run different applications for diversified configurations become the priority. As a result, a NAS device that differentiates with a general-purpose server has

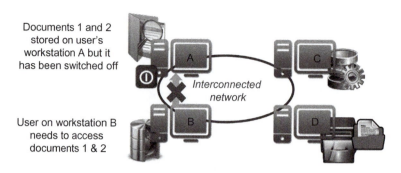

FIGURE 12.34

Early sharing issues via a network.

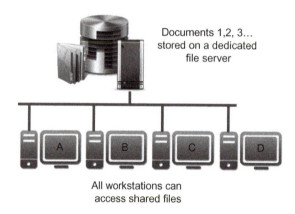

FIGURE 12.35

Early form of NAS.

been developed that is dedicated to NAS applications and clients. In contrast to a general-purpose server, it has own OS, namely the Real-Time Operating System (RTOS) for file serving (see Figure 12.36).

This OS adopts an open standard protocol so that many vendors can support it. A NAS device is capable of optimize the execution of file access and the connection of storage arrays. It has a "many-to-one" configuration that allows the NAS device to serve many clients simultaneously. It can also be configured as "one-to-many," which enables one client to access multiple NAS devices or shared file servers at the same time. With a UNIX environment, the NAS device can leverage the NFS system as a shared catalog for network users.

12.3.3.2 Elements of a NAS device

Figure 12.35 shows some components of a NAS device. Actually, there are more components that should be included, which are discussed below:

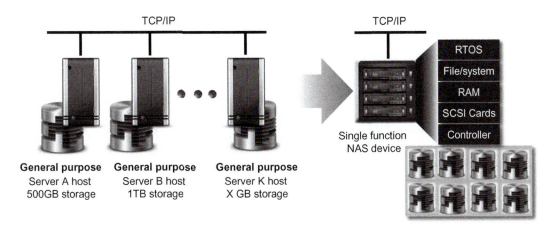

FIGURE 12.36

General-purpose servers moved to NAS box or device.

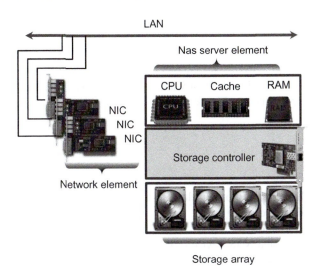

FIGURE 12.37

NAS device hardware elements.

12.3.3.2.1 Special server and network elements

- NAS head: This is a special server, which consists of a CPU, cache RAM, and bus channels.
- Network interface cards (NIC): This can be any type of network card, such as Gigabit Ethernet, Fast Ethernet and Fibre Distributed Data Interface (FDDI).

12.3.3.2.2 Storage elements

A disk controller provides RAID options and LUN (see Figure 12.37).

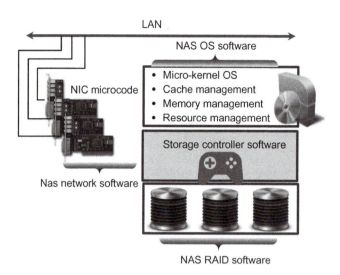

FIGURE 12.38

NAS device software elements.

12.3.3.2.3 Software elements and file system

Software elements include the NAS OS software, NIC microcode, and RAID software. The NAS OS consists of four components (see Figure 12.38):

- Micro-kernel OS
- Memory management
- Resource management
- Cache management

The file system is the most important element for NAS. It is an open standard or protocol to support file sharing (see Figure 12.39).

To implement a NAS solution, we have two options: one is an integrated solution and the other is a gateway one. With an integrated NAS device or solution, all NAS hardware and software components are integrated into one physical frame or enclosure. It becomes a self-contained environment.

12.3.3.2.4 Integrated NAS

An integrated NAS solution means that the NAS device serves storage clients via the IP network. It can be either a lower cost solution via an ATA type of interface connected to a single storage enclosure or a high-end solution with an FC interface connected to storage arrays.

A low cost integrated NAS solution is very common for departmental NAS applications because its primary focus is to consolidate many storage devices. In order to reduce opex, the flexibility and management for a NAS device's configuration is kept to a minimum. In other words, the solution is fixed. The device cannot be upgraded beyond its initial configuration. When any extra capacity is required, the solution just connects additional new boxes to the IP network (see Figure 12.40).

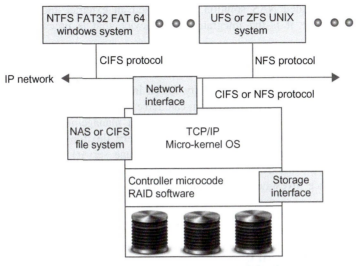

FIGURE 12.39

NAS file system.

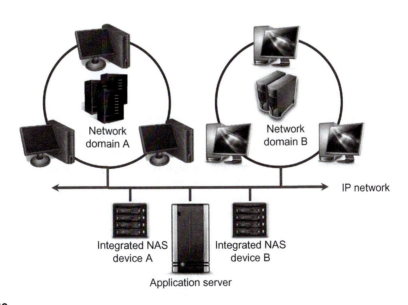

FIGURE 12.40

A low-end application-type of integrated NAS solution.

For a high-end integrated NAS solution, we can add an external and dedicated NAS device or storage array. Because it is the integrated NAS device that is preconfigured, it has limited scalability.

12.3.3.2.5 Gateway NAS

In order to have more scalability and flexibility for an integrated NAS, a gateway NAS device is a good solution. The gateway NAS solution can have an independent NAS head and one or more storage arrays. Subsequently, the configuration and management of this solution is much more complex than an integrated one. This solution is very flexible and has a higher scalability because you can scale up the NAS head (dedicated storage server) and storage arrays independently. This can increase the NAS capacity utilization rate by sharing the SAN environment. In essence, it can reduce investment capex but increase opex. We will have a detailed discussion about this topic later.

12.4 STORAGE PROTOCOLS

Throughout this chapter, we have mentioned the storage interface many times, such as when discussing storage ports and storage network connections. Wherever there is an interface, we must have a handshake protocol so that the communication can occur. We will walk through from a basic HDD interface to the Fibre Channel switch fabric.

A storage protocol is the communication channel between the storage devices (or storage array) and storage controllers. It defines the parameters of how they communicate. Normally, storage protocols can be classified into two categories:

- File-oriented protocol
- Block-oriented protocol

12.4.1 FILE-ORIENTED PROTOCOLS

File-oriented or file-based protocols are the communication specification for a client to access a file server or network attached storage (NAS). As we have described the mechanisms of storage disks in the above sections, they are just dummy hardware devices, whether they are HDDs or SSDs. It is quite obvious that these devices rely on high-level software to control their formatting, block addressing, security permissions, file names, and file directories. All these operations are processed by a file system according to file-oriented protocols. Typically, file-oriented protocols represent layer 6 and 7 of the OSI model. They are built on top of the bottom 5 layers.

When a client is trying to access a file, the file system in a file server or filer reads and writes data in blocks from a specified location on the disk. Blocks are a group of bytes controlled by the file system when it formats the disk.

In essence, the way that a file-oriented protocol works is that it reads and writes variable-length files and segments into blocks before they are stored on a disk or a tape. To implement this protocol, we need a file system. This is the key difference between a standard storage disk and a block storage disk. We should note that a block storage disk is supported by a file system to process data resources in a different way. This is a critical point what we would like to emphasize. As discussed above, the NAS approach is to use file systems to manage physical storage resources. If a file system is just an operating system, it is quite easy for us to understand that different operating systems will have different file-oriented protocols.

Based on Figure 12.38, we see two common file-oriented protocols are implemented by two different operating systems; Windows OS has the Common Internet File System (CIFS) protocol and UNIX OS has the Network File System (NFS). Although both names consist of the words of "file system," they are not really file systems but rather network protocols for file system access in terms of the operations of "open," "read," and "write." If we just focus on these operations for file retrieval, we might have to include two more file-oriented protocols: File Transfer Protocol (FTP) and Hyper Text Transfer Protocol (HTTP). These two protocols can be implemented under both the UNIX and Windows environments. However, FTP and HTTP do not have the full functionality that CIFS and NFS can support. They can only be applied for transferring files with simple read and write operations. Therefore, FTP and HTTP cannot be considered file-oriented storage protocols for NAS.

12.4.1.1 Server Message Blocks (SMB)/Common Internet File System (CIFS)

CIFS is a one of two standard protocols to provide an application protocol interface (API) for manipulating files and implementing remote administration functionality under the Microsoft Windows operation system. The root of CIFS can be traced back to the Server Message Block (SMB) technology designed by IBM in 1984. The SMB defined a network protocol for a client to submit file-oriented requests (open, read, write, and close file) to a file server. That is why it is quite often referred to as SMB/CIFS. SMB is based on the service of the Network Basic Input Output System (NetBIOS), not Windows sockets (Winsock) (see Figure 12.41).[1] SMB is supported by many UNIX and Linux operating systems via open source software, namely Samba, originated by Andrew Tridgell in 1991.

CIFS was first published by Microsoft in 1996. With the release of Windows 2K, CIFS finally replaced SMB under Windows operating systems. CIFS can normally be implemented in a NetBIOS environment, but CIFS also can be directly run on TCP or Winsock. Because Windows is a proprietary OS, CIFS is also a proprietary protocol and Microsoft has a copyright on the CIFS specification. However, Microsoft has published the specification to the open source community, and allowed other companies to implement the CIFS protocol without any royalty fees. Now, CIFS has become a competitor to both the Web NFS and NFS protocols.

12.4.1.2 Network File System (NFS)

The NFS protocol was developed by Sun Microsystems (now Oracle/Sun) in 1980. Again, NFS is another file-oriented protocol that Sun Microsystems allow people to use in the UNIX environment without any royalty fees. By 1986, Sun had extended the protocol capability to the PC market and allowed people to share files based on PC-NFS.

---

[1]IPX/SPX = Internet Packet Exchange/Sequenced Packet Exchange
NetBIOS = Network Basic Input Output System
NetBEUI = NetBIOS Extended User Interface
MS-BRWS = CIFS Browser Protocol = Microsoft Browser

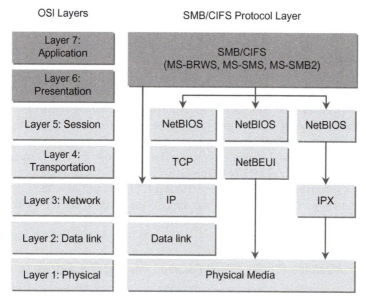

OSI Layers   SMB/CIFS Protocol Layer

IPX/SPX= Internet Packet Exchange/Sequenced Packet Exchange
NetBIOS= Network
NetBEUI = NetBIOS Extended User Interface
MS-BRWS = CIFS Browser Protocol = Microsoft Browser

FIGURE 12.41

SMB/CIFS protocol layer stack.

The first two NFS versions of protocol were classified as NFS version1, then after 1989 the IETF released the NFS v2 or RFC-1094 (1989), and NFS v3 or RFC-1813 (1995). Both NFS v2 and NFS v3 were widespread in the IT industry and become the standard protocol for file sharing under the UNIX environment. NFS v4 was introduced via RFC 3010 in 2000. The latest NFS version is also named NFS v4 but was introduced via RFC 3530. It was released in 2003. Since then, NFS v4 has been improved a lot in terms of optional features, such as security, caching, locking, and message communication efficiency in comparison with early NFS v4. Although NFS has PC capabilities, it has always been considered a file-oriented protocol for UNIX and Linux operating systems rather than the PC environment.

The method of NFS operation is quite simple. All versions of NFS employ Remote Procedure Call (RPC) and a data abstraction mechanism or external data representation (XDR) for file sharing (see Figure 12.42).

In the early versions of NFS such as v1 and v2, it used UDP to provide a stateless network connection between a client and a server. With UDP, there is no guarantee of packet delivery nor is there any data packet sorting feature. UDP is just streaming packets from one network device to the other. With v3, the protocol is capable of operating both with UDP and TCP for packet delivery.

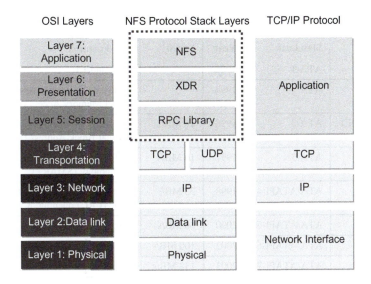

OSI Layers   NFS Protocol Stack Layers   TCP/IP Protocol

FIGURE 12.42

NFS protocol stack.

As we know the TCP/IP protocol suite also supports UDP. However, TCP is a guaranteed delivery protocol. In other words, if the packets are corrupted or missing, TCP can check it and resubmit the packet again. NFS v4 adopts a TCP stateful protocol and adds security enhancement features.

12.4.2 BLOCK-ORIENTED PROTOCOLS

Block-oriented protocols read and write individual fixed-length blocks of data. These protocols correspond to SAN. There are mainly three types of popular block-level storage protocols today:

- Advanced Technology Attachment (ATA); this includes PATA and SATA
- Small Computer System Interface (SCSI); this includes iSCSI and Fibre Channel over Ethernet (FCoE)
- Single-Byte Command Code Set (SBCCS)

12.4.2.1 IDE/ATA/parallel ATA or PATA

IDE/ATA stands for Integrated Device Electronics/Advanced Technology Attachment. Actually, IDE is the first ANSI ATA standard or ATA-1. ATA is an open-systems standard. It was initiated by the Common Access Method (CAM) committee and later regulated by the ANSI X3 committee in 1994. Since then, several ATA versions have been released (See Table 12.16). Each version of ATA specified a protocol at a data block level, a parallel electrical interface, and a physical interface.

The ATA specification allows no more than two storage devices per bus channel (one is the master and the other is the slave). For high-performance storage, sharing a bus channel is not preferred. Many servers have more than two ATA buses. Early ATA versions only supported HDD

Table 12.16 ATA Versions [203]

ATA Version	Standard	Year	Speed	Key Features
IDE	ATA-1	1986		Pre-standard
	ATA	1994		PIO (programmed IO) modes 0−2 multiword Direct Memory Access (DMA) 0
EIDE (Enhanced IDE)	ATA-2	1996	16 MB/s	PIO mode 3−4 multiword DMA mode 1−2, Logical Block Address (LBA)
	ATA-3	1997	16 MB/s	Self-Monitoring Analysis and Reporting Technology (SMART)
	ATA/ATAPI-4	1998	33 MB/s	Ultra DMA modes 0−2, Cyclic Redundancy Code (CRC) queuing, 8-wire
Ultra DMA 66	ATA/ATAPI-5	2000	66 MB/s	Ultra DMA mode 3−4
Ultra DMA 100	ATA/ATAPI-6	2002	100 MB/s	Ultra DMA mode 5, 48-bit LBA
Ultra DMA 133	ATA/ATAPI-7	2003	133 MB/s	Ultra DMA mode 6

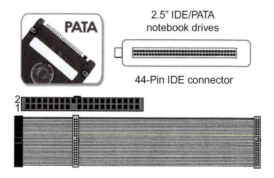

FIGURE 12.43

44-pin IDE/PATA interface connector.

commands but ATA Packet Interface (ATAPI) has the similar commands as SCSI (we will discuss this in the next section), which allows CD-ROM and tape drives to use the same ATA interface. All these ATA standards are parallel ATA or PATA. PATA drives can only support a single user or personal computer environment. It focuses on low cost and low capacity rather than speed and reliability. Moreover, PATA has another issue, which is that it has too many pins for its interface connector (see Figure 12.43).

12.4.2.2 Serial ATA or SATA

In order to improve performance and reliability, simplify drive configuration, enable server implementation, and lower the number of pins, Serial ATA or SATA was developed by the SATA working group, an industry consortium (see Figure 12.44). SATA version 1.0 was first published

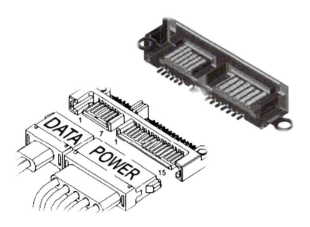

FIGURE 12.44

SATA interface connector (7 pins for data, 15 pins for power).

Table 12.17 SATA Versions				
SATA Versions	**Year**	**Raw Bandwidth**	**Transfer Speed**	**Key Features**
Serial ATA 1.0	2002	1.5 Gbit/s	150 MB/s	
Serial ATA 2.0	2005	3.0 Gbit/s	300 MB/s	
Serial ATA 2.6	2007	3.0 Gbit/s	300 MB/s	NCQ unload
Serial ATA 3.0	2008	6.0 Gbit/s	600 MB/s	NCQ with isochronous data transfers
Serial ATA 3.1	2011	6.0 Gbit/s	600 MB/s	Universal Storage Module
Serial SATA 3.2	2013	16 Gbit/s	2 GB/s	Combines both SATA and PCI Express buses

in 2001, and only has 150 MB/s transfer speed or 1.5 Gbit/s raw data rate. In Jan 2013, SATA version 3.2 was released; it can support 16 Gbit/s raw data rate and 2 GB/s transfer speed (see Table 12.17).

Clearly, SATA has many advantages over PATA for consumer types of applications. Both the IDE/PATA and SATA interfaces have been widely applied for desktops and laptops. They have higher bandwidth and lower cost. These characteristics have attracted the attention of enterprise server applications. The recent progress of SATA has often led to the following question: if SATA is capable of solving the problems that many enterprise storage applications have, why can't we replace SCSI with SATA or converge two, instead of using Serial Attached SCSI (SAS)?

One of the reasons is that the ATA-based protocols are typically designed for the consumer market. So, the design was kept relative simple. For example, SATA only provides 8 bits for failure report, while a similar SCSI protocol has up to 18 bytes for a similar function.

Although the ATA protocols are not applied to trunk storage networks, they can often be utilized in a subsystem of a storage network. Let's explore the details of SCSI.

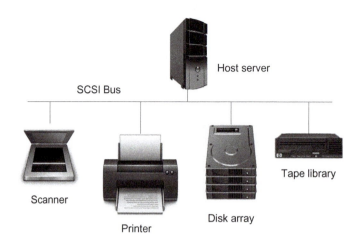

Host server

SCSI Bus

Scanner

Printer

Disk array

Tape library

FIGURE 12.45

Small Computer System Interface (SCSI).

12.4.2.3 SCSI

SCSI stands for Small Computer System Interface. It is an open standard. It was created by Shugart Associates in 1979. Therefore, the initial acronym was SASI, which means Shugart Associates System Interface, and the ANSI X3 committee standardized it in 1986. It is an interface protocol that transfers block-oriented data between a server and storage devices or any computer device (see Figure 12.45).

After many years' evolution, SCSI has become a set of standards that define three layers of a SCSI architecture model:

- Commands
- Protocol
- Interface connection

The first version of SCSI (or SCSI-1) could only support 8 devices with a bus topology and SCSI-2 was extended to 16 devices. With the SCSI-3 protocol, it cannot only support a variety of device interfaces but also different transmission technologies; the iSCSI protocol is one of the transmission protocols that is specified by the Internet Engineering Task Force (IETF). The early versions of SCSI are parallel based, and adopt a parallel bus architecture (see Table 12.18). Since 2008, the evolution of the SCSI protocol is similar to ATA; there has been a move to serial-attached interfaces, such as serial-attached SCSI or SAS. SAS 3.0 can support up to 16,256 devices and throughput is up to 9.6 GBits/s (see Table 12.19).

When storage devices attach to a server via a SCSI interface, they can be deployed with two types of connections: internal and external.

With internal deployment, storage devices such as HDDs or SSDs are directly connected to the SCSI bus. Previously, this SCSI bus was a SCSI Parallel Interface (SPI); this now has been replaced by SAS. If a storage device needs to access a traditional parallel SCSI bus, we will need a

Table 12.18 SCSI Parallel Interfaces (SPI) Standards

SCSI Versions	Interface Name	Year	Bus Width	No. of Devices	Raw Bandwidth	Max Throughput	Length
SCSI-1	Narrow SCSI	1986	8	8	40 Mbits/s	5 MB/s	6 m
SCSI-2	Fast SCSI	1994	8	8	80 Mbits/s	8 MB/s	3 m
SCSI-2; SCSI3 SPI	Fast-Wide SCSI	1993	16	16	160 Mbits/s	20 MB/s	3 m
SCSI-3 SPI	Ultra SCSI	2003	8	4 or 8	160 Mbits/s	20 MB/s	1.5 m−3 m
SCSI-3 SPI	Ultra Wide SCSI	2003	16	4,8,16	320 Mbits/s	40 MB/s	1.5 m−3 m
SCSI-3 SPI-2	Ultra 2 SCSI	2003	8	8	320 Mbits/s	40 MB/s	N/A
SCSI-3 SPI-2	Ultra2 Wide SCSI	2003	16	16	640 Mbits/s	80 MB/s	N/A
SCSI-3 SPI-3	Ultra 3 SCSI	2003	16	16	1280 Mbits/s	160 MB/s	N/A
SCSI-3 SPI-4	Ultra 4 SCSI	2003	16	16	2560 Mbits/s	320 MB/s	N/A
SCSI-3 SPI-5	Ultra 5 SCSI	2003	16	16	5120 Mbits/s	640 MB/s	N/A

Table 12.19 Some Serial Attached SCSI Interface Standards

SCSI Version	Name	Year	No. of Devices	Raw Bandwidth	Max Throughput	Length
iSCSI	IP SCSI	2001	2^{128} (IPv6)			Network dependent
SAS 1.1	Serial Attached SCSI	2006	16,256	2.4 Gbits/s	300 MB/s	6 m
SAS 2.1	Serial Attached SCSI	2011	16,256	4.8 Gbits/s	600 MB/s	6 m
SAS 3.0	Serial Attached SCSI	2013	16,256	9.6 Gbits/s	1.2 GB/s	6 m
SCSI Express	SCSI over PCIe (SoP)	2013		7.877 Gbits/s	985 MB/s	

storage controller or SCSI adaptor (or SCSI controller). A SCSI controller is special hardware that handles the SCSI protocol and access by SCSI devices.

If both the CPU and memory are embedded into a SCSI adopter or controller, it becomes a SCSI Host Bus Adaptor (HBA). If the SCSI protocol is transmitted over a Fibre Channel connection with a SCSI HBA, it is named FC HBA. If both SCSI HBA and FC HBA are supported by onboard CPU and memory, then they are capable of processing any type of workload, such as encoding and decoding, which is offloaded by the host CPU.

When the SCSI protocol is transmitted over IP network via the TCP/IP stack, the storage controller can be deployed by software drives via a standard network interface card (NIC). If a special NIC similar to an HBA card is embedded with both CPU and memory, we call it a TCP Offload

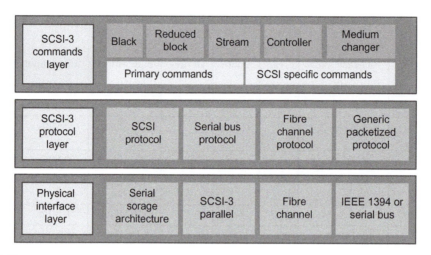

FIGURE 12.46

SCSI-3 Architecture Model (SAM).

Engine (TOE). Again, it can also process the workloads that are offloaded by the host CPU. Some TOEs can also handle iSCSI logic, which can assist the host CPU by diverting storage I/O processing.

12.4.2.4 ISCSI

The iSCSI protocol was created to address the issue of reducing TCO because of higher investment capex for the SCSI interface, network, training, and management software. It is not only designed to work with the existing TCP/IP network but also can integrate with the existing SCSI architecture.

From iSCSI protocol stack or architecture perspective, the iSCSI implementation is really the SCSI-3 standard (see Figure 12.46) over Internet Protocol (IP) with TCP transformation.

The SCSI-3 architecture is based on the client/server relationship model. If a client requests services, a server will prepare and then fulfill the client's needs. The second-generation SCSI-3 Architecture Model (SAM-2) is aligned with the OSI model. The three SCSI-3 layers shown in Figure 12.46 are actually the OSI model's Layer 7 (Application), Layer 6 (Presentation) and Layer 5 (Session) (see Figure 12.47). This is also equivalent to the Fibre Channel (FC) 4 or Upper Layer Protocol, which we will discuss just after the iSCSI protocol.

ISCSI is the transport protocol that is carrying the SCSI Command Description Block (CDB) from an initiator application client to the target SCSI device (see Figure 12.48).

As we can see in Figure 12.47, the basic transfer unit of the iSCSI protocol is the protocol data unit (PDU). It can encapsulate SCSI CDB and send it from an initiator to the target SCSI device. The iSCSI device driver or protocol within HBA will build a PDU with adequate CDB and LUN and then pass the packets over to the network layer (TCP/IP socket). The rest is the standard process of TCP/IP from the TCP segment to the IP datagram and from the IP datagram to the Ethernet frame (see Figure 12.49).

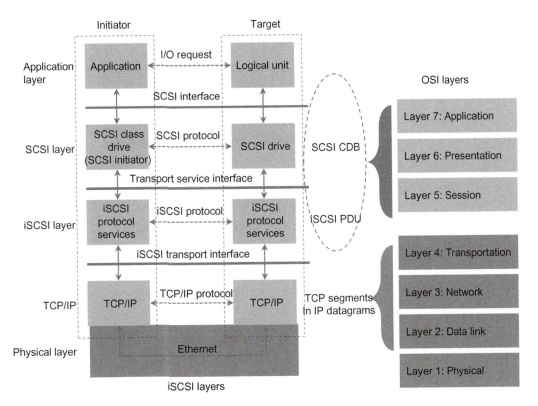

FIGURE 12.47

iSCSI layers.

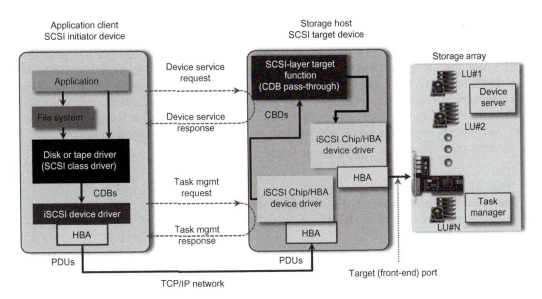

FIGURE 12.48

An iSCSI client/server model command flow.

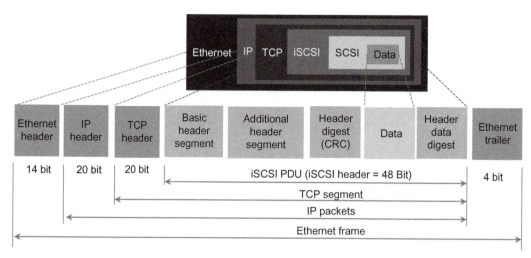

FIGURE 12.49

E2E description of the main processing path of the iSCSI protocol.

The iSCSI protocol has dramatically improved the SCSI protocol, especially with regard to the problem of limited distance between client and storage array and the limited number of devices that can be supported, which has improved from 16 (SCSI-3) to 2^{128}. However, there is one issue that iSCSI cannot resolve, which is the limited bandwidth or speed between the SAN switch and storage array. The alternative solution is the Fibre Channel Protocol.

12.4.2.5 Fibre Channel Protocol (FCP)

The Fibre Channel Protocol (FCP) is one of the communication protocols designed to carry serial SCSI-3 data over an optical fiber network. The throughput of a Fibre Channel network can provide from 100 MB/s to 1.6 GB/s and the distance can be extended from 500 meters to 10 kilometers. The max number of devices for FC-SW is 16,777,216 or 2^{24} (see Table 12.20).

Because Fibre Channel (FC) is a common data transmission protocol, it is capable of working with many current network protocols and interface or I/O interface protocols, such as:

Network protocols:

- IP
- IEEE 802.2 (MAC)
- Enterprise Systems Connection (ESCON) for Mainframe
- Asynchronous Transfer Mode (ATM)

I/O interface protocols:

- Intelligent Peripheral Interface (IPI)
- High Performance Parallel Interface (HIPPI)
- Single Byte Command Code Set (SBCCS)
- Small Computer System Interface (SCSI)

Table 12.20 Fibre Channel Standard

Name	Specification (ANSI XT11)	Year (Availability)	Raw Bandwidth (Mbits/s)	Max Throughput (MByte/s)	Full Duplex (MByte/s)	Length
1GFC	X3T11/94-175v0	1997	800	100	200	500 m/10 km
2GFC	X3T11/96-402v0 FC-PH-2	2001	1,600	200	400	500 m/10 km
4GFC	X3T11/96-402v0 FC-PH-2	2005	3,200	400	800	500 m/10 km
8GFC	X3T11/07-299v0	2008	6,400	800	1,600	500 m/10 km
16GFC	X3T11/09-276v0	2011	12,800	1,600	3,200	500 m/10 km
32GFC		2015		3,200	6400	500 m/10 km
128GFCp		2015		12,800	25,600	500 m/10 km

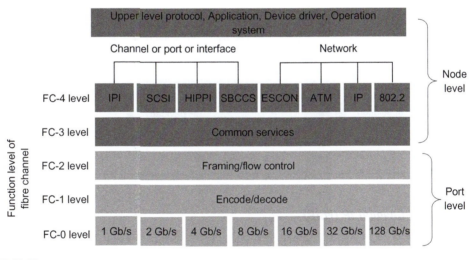

FIGURE 12.50

Fibre Channel protocol stack.

Figure 12.50 illustrates the functional levels of the Fibre Channel Protocol that can interface with many other network and I/O interface protocols.

FC does bring the benefits of storage network performance and scalability, but it also come with additional cost because of the extra components of FC HBA and FC switches. In addition, data over FCP can be transmitted no more than 10 km (see Table 12.20). If we want to extend the transmission distance longer than 10 km, the next solution is to adopt FCIP.

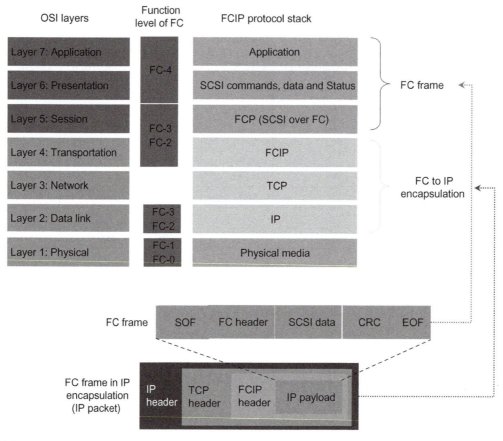

FIGURE 12.51

FCIP protocol stack.

12.4.2.6 Fibre Channel IP (FCIP)

FCIP is a tunneling or delivery protocol. The aim of the FCIP tunneling protocol is to deliver a Fibre Channel frame via an IP network because most networks used by enterprises are IP networks. In contrast to a payload protocol, this establishes a virtual pipe over the existing IP-based network (see Figure 12.51). Therefore, FCIP doesn't control and monitor data traffic flow. These functions are handled by FC-SW and devices within the FC-SW fabric.

The most popular application for FCIP is disaster recovery, where the data can be backed up and retrieved from a strategic data center site (see Figure 12.52).

From Figure 12.28, we can see that we now have two different physical IP networks. One is for the communication among hosting servers and clients. The other is for the storage network or SAN. It doesn't only increase the complexity for the IP network infrastructure but also add cost for both capex and opex. The solution to resolve this issue is to adopt Fibre Channel over Ethernet (FCoE), which we are going to discuss in Section 12.4.2.8.

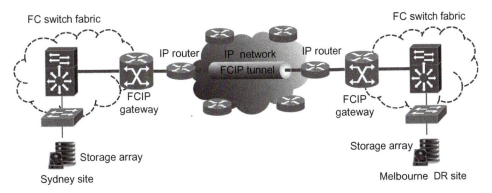

FIGURE 12.52

Example of FCIP topology.

12.4.2.7 Internet Fibre Channel Protocol (iFCP)

Along with FCIP development, the IETF also developed anther protocol called the Internet Fibre Channel Protocol (iFCP). The initial goal of iFCP was to replace both FC-SW and SAN with Fibre Channel (FC) over IP network, or simply an IP network. In essence, it is a specification that defines the communication protocol from one iFCP gateway to another iFCP gateway over the IP network for existing FC components. The protocol allows existing FC storage components to be directly attached to an IP network. From a protocol stack perspective, iFCP replaces the FC network's transport layer (FC-2) with an IP network (or Ethernet) transport layer, but still supports upper layer information (see Figure 12.50).

The key component of this solution is the iFCP gateway, which connects existing FC devices, such as FC HBA, and an IP network (see Figure 12.53). By leveraging the iFCP gateway, we can eliminate the FC switch fabric network. Ultimately, this is a consolidation solution. The idea behind this initiative is to reduce the total cost of ownership (TOC) by integrating two different networks into one IP network.

However, the solution will not be able to deliver cost savings because of the end node attachment with FC-SW. In addition, iFCP products do not have enough FC port density to accommodate the connectivity requirements of most modern FC-SANs. Therefore, iFCP gateways are usually deployed in conjunction with FC switches (see Figure 12.54). Due to these factors, iFCP solution has not been widely used in the IT industry. However, it could be another alternative solution for FCIP to support both FCP and SCSI commands, data, and status information between a SCSI initiator and SCSI target.

If iFCP is not an ideal solution for FC-SAN and IP network/Ethernet consolidation, what is the alternative solution? This is our next topic.

12.4.2.8 Fibre Channel over Ethernet (FCoE) Protocol

As we've stated above, the main purpose of FCoE is to consolidate the number of networks, so we can converge the NIC for host server to access the IP network and the HBA to connect the SAN

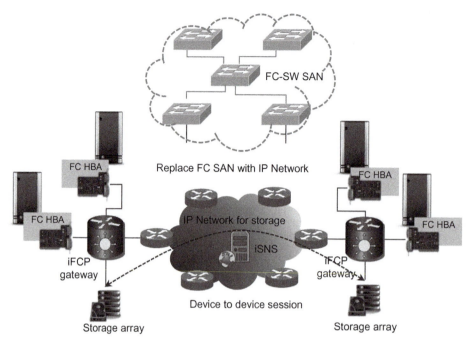

iSNS = Internet storage name services

FIGURE 12.53

Initial idea of iFCP: replace FC switch network with IP network.

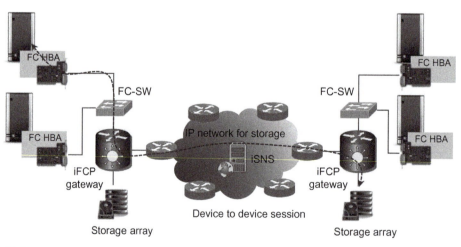

FIGURE 12.54

iFCP deployment model.

into one interface, which is called a Converged Network Adaptor (CAN) via the FCoE protocol. There are two key components for FCoE consolidation (see Figure 12.55):

- Converged Network Adapter
- FCoE switch

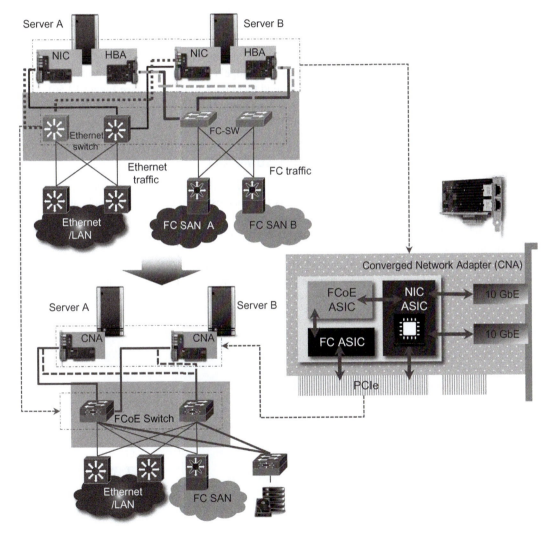

FIGURE 12.55

Adopt FCoE to consolidate storage networks.

12.4.2.8.1 Converged Network Adapter (CNA)

The function of a CNA is to embed both the NIC and FC HBA into one adapter and replace them with one or two high capacity I/O interfaces, namely 10 GBits/s Ethernet and a PCI express (PCIe) bus connected to a server slot so that both the NIC and FC HBA traffic is consolidated into one adapter. Within the CNA, the key engine to process FC and Ethernet convergence is the embedded chip called an Application Specific Integrated Circuit (ASIC) (refer to Figure 12.55).

12.4.2.8.2 Fibre Channel over Ethernet (FCoE) Switch

In order to consolidate both Ethernet/LAN and FC-SAN, an FCoE switch bundles FC and Ethernet functions; it uses an FC Forwarder (FCF) and Ethernet bridge to join the function of the FC switch and Ethernet switch.

What an FC Forwarder does is to encapsulate the FC packets from FC ports into FCoE frames and forward them to the Ethernet bridge. Thus the Ethernet bridge's function is to de-encapsulate the FCoE frame from the Ethernet ports into FC frames and send them back to FC ports (see Figure 12.56).

With FCoE consolidation, we reduce 50% of the adapters and cabling we use. In addition, it also reduces the complexity of the FC-SAN and system management.

12.4.3 STORAGE INTERFACE PROTOCOLS SUMMARY

The decision on storage interfaces or I/O protocols is really dependent on many factors or criteria but the key drivers behind any storage decision is the business requirements for applications (such as file data or block data), performance, operating system, throughput, flexibility, scalability, data mobility, and reliability. The bottom line of protocol selection is total cost of ownership (TCO) and return on investment (ROI) for the business.

From the original ideas of ATA and SCSI, we saw that the PATA set of protocols has been developed for the desktop and laptop storage domain and SCSI set of protocols has been designed for enterprise server environment. When we are looking from an evolutionary perspective at

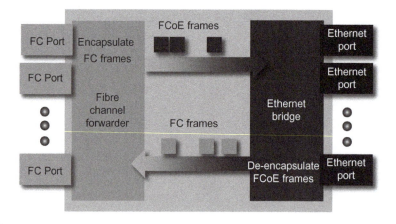

FIGURE 12.56

Function of FCoE switch.

internal storage disk connectivity, both ATA and SCSI have gone from parallel to serial, which have been developed as SATA and SAS, respectively.

For the external storage connection environment, the network storage protocol (or SCSI-3) was split into two branches based on SCSI-3 or the SCSI-3 Architecture Model (SAM):

- iSCSI
- FCP

ISCSI delivers SCSI CDB over TCP/IP. FCP transmits SCSI-3 data over an optical Fibre Channel network or Fibre Channel switch fabric. Recently (2009), the FCoE protocol was defined; it can consolidate (or converge) both TCP/IP and Fibre Channel networks into one IP network (see Figure 12.57).

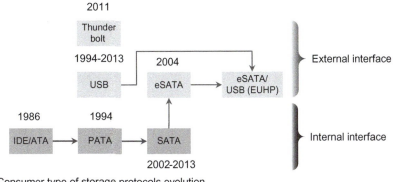

Consumer type of storage protocols evolution

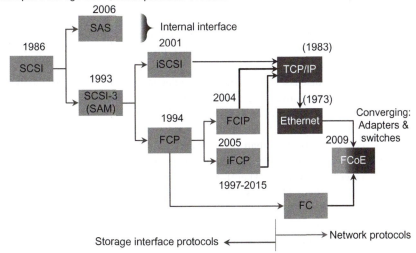

FIGURE 12.57

Block storage interface and network protocol evolution.

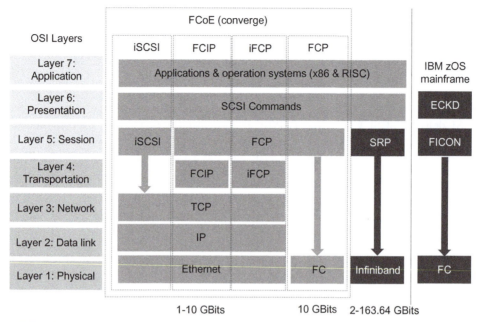

FIGURE 12.58

Storage interface block protocol stacks [125, 203, 204].

If we draw a correlation between the OSI layer model and storage interface protocol, we can find that although there have been many storage interface protocols, the trend is the convergence of many protocols (see Figure 12.58).

In this section, we have discussed most of the popular storage interface protocols. You might wonder, if these protocols are converging, why we have to know them? The reason is that any company will not purchase all its equipment in one batch. IT equipment within any data center is normally slowly built up over years. If an IT department is doing well at life-cycle management, the life span of IT assets will be less than 5 to 7 years. If not, the life span may be longer than 10 years. For some telco companies, the longest lifetime of IT assets is over 17 years, especially for some network management systems. Therefore, it is important for us to know all these technologies so that we can replace these IT assets with compatible interfaces and the right technology to meet business requirements if the business decision is moving to a cloud.

The other main purpose to describing all details of storage interface protocols is to lay the foundation and principles for consolidation of different types of storage so we can select the right protocol for the right storage application under a cloud storage environment.

From Table 12.21, we can see that each protocol has its pros and cons. Because many new technologies have rapidly been developed, each existing protocol should be examined very carefully.

Table 12.21 Block-Oriented Storage Protocols for SAN, MAN, and WAN

Network Types	MAN & WAN	Data Center SANs	All Networks	IP SAN
Interface Types	FC to IP to FC	FC to IP to FC	FC to IP to IP SAN	IP SAN to IP SAN
iSCSI (Native IP)			√	√
FCIP (Tunnelling)	√			
iFCP (Native IP)	√	√		
FCoE (Native IP)	√	√	√	√

Previous assumptions and concepts about the storage protocols should be scrutinized from time to time. Very often, we will find some assumptions might not be realistic or adequate. It will certainly impact on our cost model. Therefore, we should always go back to the business objectives and ask the question, "Why?

12.5 PROS AND CONS FOR DIFFERENT STORAGE TOPOLOGIES

Following the discussion of basic storage hardware, including hard disk drives (HDDs), the RAID architecture, and the HDD replacement, solid state disk (SSDs), we have unveiled the details of different storage topologies and network interfaces as well as storage protocols for these interconnections. For many people, these terminologies and descriptions of storage architectures are very confusing. As Ulf Troppens et al. [206] indicated, "The fact [is] that there is a lack of any unified terminology for the description of storage architectures.... There are thus numerous components in a storage network which, although they do the same thing, are called by different names. Conversely, there are many systems with the same name, but fundamentally different functions."

As a result, it is quite challenging for any customer to compare which topology and/or interface is better or which one is the best fit for his/her business or application needs. In addition, there are some vendors who often exaggerate one aspect of their product and ignore other parts of product functions. It could mislead customers into wrong conclusions. For this reason, the Technical Council of the Storage Networking Industry Association (SNIA) published the "Shared Storage Model" in 2001 (see Figure 12.59).

The model has five basic building blocks (see Figure 12.60).

These five building blocks are basically aligned with the seven layers of the OSI model (see Figure 12.61). From a vertical data flow perspective, this shared storage model or architecture has a total of eight possible paths from application to storage hardware, such as disk or LUN.

We can describe these eight possible paths as follows:

1. Application (App) to Block Aggregation (BA) to Storage Hardware (SH)
2. App to Database (DBMS) to SH
3. App to DBMS to BA to SH
4. App to DBMS to File System (FS) to BA to SH
5. App to DBMS to FS to SH

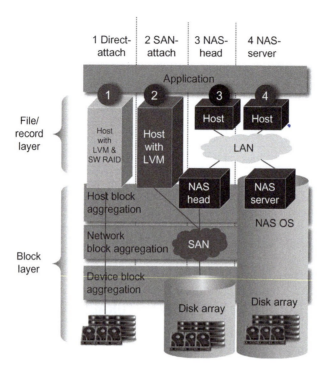

FIGURE 12.59

Storage topologies based on shared storage model.

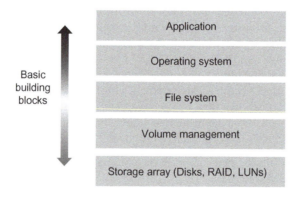

FIGURE 12.60

Five building block of shared storage model.

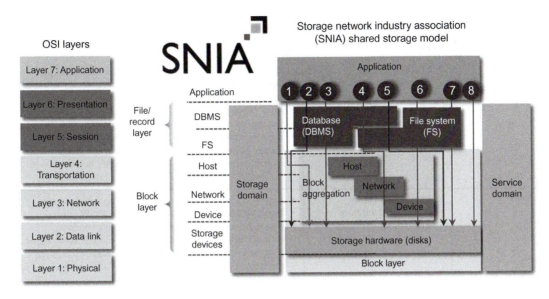

FIGURE 12.61

Eight possible paths of shared storage model.

6. App to FS to BA to SH
7. App to FS to SH
8. App to SH

Furthermore, SNIA drew the three common storage topologies based on the shared storage model. Based on SNIA terminology, we can now summarize the pros and cons of different storage architectures in term of performance, provisioning, manageability, configuration, security, scalability, reliability, configuration, and ultimately cost (TCO/ROI). A customer can use the following table to evaluate a storage product and make the right technology decision in term of TCO/ROI.

Table 12.22 Storage Types Pros and Cons

Storage Types	DAS	NAS	SAN
Topology	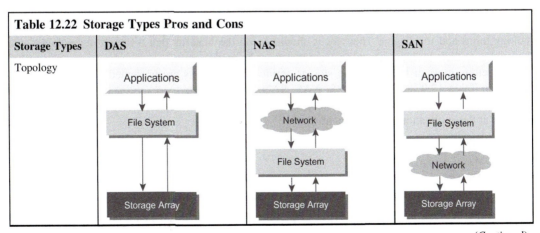		

(Continued)

Table 12.22 Storage Types Pros and Cons *Continued*

Storage Types	DAS	NAS	SAN
Pros	• Simplicity • Ease of configuration • Ease of manageability	• Standard TCP/IP network • Optimize performance • Improve scalability • Most efficient for file sharing tasks • Improve utilization rate • Simple network implementation	• Higher utilization rate • Enhance storage resource sharing • Significantly improve performance • Higher scalability • Higher reliability • Simplify business continuity process
Cons	• Limited scalability • Lower availability or single point of failure • Lower utilization rate and no resource sharing	• Add workload to LAN • Incompatible OS • Planned outages to maintain unique OS • High-level file abstraction not suited for some apps • Filer owns storage resources	• Interoperability issues with FC-SW from different vendors • Add more NMS systems • More training required for FC-SW network
Applications	Boot system (local drive)	Only file-oriented data (workgroups)	Both block- and file-oriented data, disaster recovery (data center)
Cost	Higher TCO	Lower cost	Reduce TCO Increase ROI

12.6 TRADITIONAL STORAGE VS. CLOUD STORAGE

So far, we have introduced many storage terms and technologies. These technologies support the business applications and services. They are the foundation of cloud storage. However, most business customers have no interest in these technologies. Very often, they are confused by these technology terms and the jargon. Their focus should be on the benefits that different technologies can contribute to their business versus the cost that must be paid.

Therefore, most of the enterprise storage services or products are presented in the data tiering shown in Table 12.9 rather than DAS, NAS, SAN, and associated storage interfaces or protocols. For traditional storage services, tiered storage services should be supported by three basic storage metrics at the application level (or metrics)

• Scalability
• Capacity
• Performance

Scalability and capacity are very straightforward. The term "performance" however, covers a board range. We can have differen types of performances, such as financial, operational, business,

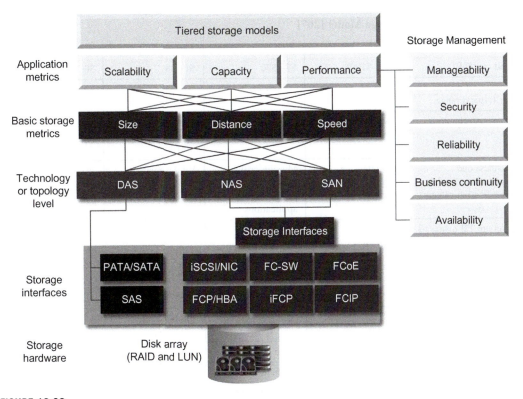

FIGURE 12.62

Translating storage technologies into application and business metrics.

application, management performance, etc. Subsequently, there is a managerial subcategory (or submetrics) to support performance (see Figure 12.62).

Under the application level, these metrics are supported further by three tangible components, which are:

- Size (no. of disk drives or GB or TB storage)
- Distance (between hosting servers to the storage location)
- Speed (read and write latency)

Underneath these tangible metrics, DAS, NAS, and SAN come to play their roles to underpin the basic storage measurements. So, instead of listing storage performance with a technology orientation, we can adopt Horizon Inc's approach, using service-orientated storage measurements with a tier-based model (see Table 12.23).

With this tiered storage model, we can easily define the relationship between storage cost and business performance. This model is very helpful for people to identify the unit cost of different storage topologies or technologies. Cloud computing or cloud storage adds extra features on top of traditional storage in terms of the business or service orientation. Based on the definition of cloud

Table 12.23 Tiered Storage Model [207]

Data Tier	Tier 0	Tier 1	Tier 2	Tier 3
Unit cost/GB[1]	$50–$100*	$7–$20	$1–$8	$0.20–$2.00
Amount of data in tier (typical range	1–3%	12–20%	20–25%	43–60%
Primary technology	SSD (Flash)	High performance disk arrays, FC	Midrange disk arrays, SAS, SATA	Tape libraries, offsite data vaults
Business and applications for data classification category	I/O intensive, response-time critical	Mission-critical, OLTP, revenue generating applications	Vital, sensitive, business important applications	Archives, fixed content, compliance, reference data
Average TB managed per administrator (open systems)	TBD	30 TB	30–100 TB	X TB–Y PB
Age of data (Day)	0–1	1–3	3–7	30–90 +
Availability	99.999%	99.999%	99.99%	99.0–99.9%
Probability of re-reference	>80%	70–80%	20–60%	1–5% or near 0%
Acceptable downtime	None	None	<5 hours/year	<1 day/year
Problem response	<2 hours	<2 hours	<5 hours	<24 hours
I/O performance capability	Highest >1 million IOPs	High 200–300 IOPs	Moderate 100–200 IOPs	Moderate, Low
Backup RPO	4 hours	<4 hours	<12 hours	1 day or more
Application RTO	<1–2 hours	<1–2 hours	<5 hours	<24 hours
Disaster protection	Required	Required	Select applications	Select archives
Data recovery	Mirrored, replication	Mirrored, replication	Scheduled backups	Local and remote backup
Interface connection (open systems)	FC multipath	FC, Multipath	FC and IP	FC and IP
Power consumption per GB	Low	Highest	High	Lowest

[1]The prices are from before December 2010. This unit price of SSDs is for enterprise applications. However, by 2013, the unit price should be below $10/GB because the price depreciation rate is around 30%–40% YoY.

computing noted in Chapter 1, we can easily figure out some of the additional measurements or metrics for cloud storage; in comparison with traditional storage, cloud storage should have the following four basic characteristics:

- Agility
- Flexibility

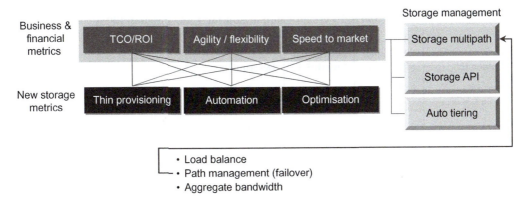

FIGURE 12.63

Additional storage metrics for cloud storage.

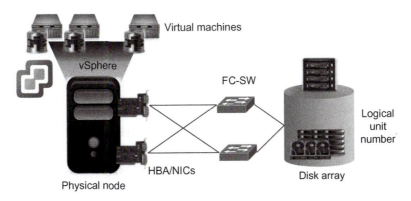

FIGURE 12.64

Storage multipath technique.

- TCO/ROI
- Speed to market

All these characteristic measurements of cloud storage are only reflected at the financial or business level. The underpinning of these financial and business metrics is new technologies and new storage management tools for cloud infrastructures, such as a hypervisor (see Figure 12.63).

However, not all hypervisors provide full cloud functionality because many cloud-enabling technologies are still evolving and improving. For example, VMware vSphere hosts can interact with physical nodes' HBAs/NICs and establish redundancy paths via storage process ports for virtual machine LUNs. This multipath technique is adopted by a host to decide on storage path access (see Figure 12.64).

Table 12.24 VSphere 5.1 and 5.5 Version Comparison for LAG function [208]

Functionality	vSphere Distributed Switch 5.1	vSphere Distributed Switch 5.5	Description
Support for multiple LAGs	No	Yes	• In Distributed Switch 5.1, the LACP support is enabled on an entire uplink port group and that port group acts as a single LAG for the switch. • vSphere Distributed Switch 5.5 supports multiple LAGs.
Configure distributed port groups to use LAGs as active uplinks	No	Yes	• On Distributed Switch 5.1, you can configure one LAG to handle the traffic for all distributed port groups on the distributed switch. • vSphere Distributed Switch 5.5 lets you use a LAG to handle the traffic for particular distributed port groups. You can set LAGs as the active uplinks in the teaming and failover order of port groups.
Multiple LACP load balancing algorithms	No	Yes	• The LACP support in Distributed Switch 5.1 supports only IP hash load balancing. In Distributed Switch 5.5, all load balancing algorithms of LACP are supported.

Theoretically speaking, the multipath function should support several features, such as:

• Load balancing
• Path management (failover)
• Bandwidth aggregation

Unfortunately, with previous versions of vSphere (before vSphere 5.1), vSphere only supports a single datastore with a single storage path for active I/O at any one time. In other words, the hypervisor cannot aggregate bandwidth across links. However, the latest version (5.5) supports this function, which is called Link Aggregation Groups (LAGs) (see Table 12.24).

Of course, different cloud infrastructures (such as Microsoft's Hyper-V or Citrix's Xen, even the same hypervisor but with different versions) may have different functions or configurations of cloud storage. When we build a cost model of cloud computing, we should take into consideration all of these aspects. Taking the above example, although vSphere 5.1 allows 32 datastores per datastore, the real number of datastores to be configured has to be reduced for some I/O intensive applications in practice because of the traffic bottleneck, asvSphere 5.1 doesn't not have the LAG function. We will have further discussion on this in later chapters.

12.7 MAJOR STORAGE VENDORS AND MARKET TRENDS

Based on IT Candor's statistics on external storage system market share in 2012 (up to the end of September 2012), there are eight major leading vendors, but HDS is excluded in the list of major vendors (see Figure 12.65). IT Candor might leave HDS in the "others" category. The total

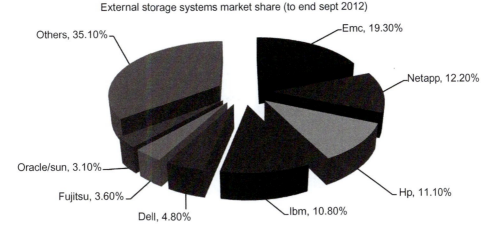

FIGURE 12.65

Global major storage vendors and market share in 2012 [209].

calendar year revenue was US$32.564 billion based on IDC data. In comparison with 2011 ($31.079 billion), the growth was about 4.8%.

As we can see from Figure 12.65, EMC is leading the way as the market leader, with 20% ∼ 25% of the total storage market share. It mainly provides high-end SAN storage products, such as CLARiiON and Symmetrix and the VMAX series of storage arrays. It is worth noticing that in January 2009, EMC completed its acquisition of VMware.

Following EMC, the next major storage vendor is NetApp. In contrast to EMC, NetApp mainly supplies NAS-oriented products, such as the FAS 6200 and FAS 3200 series. Just based on raw storage capacity, the price of NetApp is slightly cheaper than EMC. However, because it is file-oriented storage that needs a certain amount of storage space to load a storage OS, the utilization rate per gigabyte is relatively lower than EMC storage products.

In contrast to IT Candor's method of statistics analysis, IDC only lists vendors who have revenues above 5% of the total market share. If a vendor's revenue is below this threshold level, it will be sunk into the "other" category. As a result, there are six major vendors in the global enterprise storage market, EMC, NetApp, IBM, HP, HDS, and Dell (see Figure 12.66).

Figure 12.66 shows total storage system revenue, which includes external storage system. IDC published two sets of data, one for external and the other for total storage systems. EMC, NetApp, and HDS only provide external storage systems. The revenue gap between external and total was about $7 billion (see Table 12.25).

The main purpose of showing the market data is trying to find the correlation between the storage capacity growth and vendor revenue growth as this may help us to make reasonable cost modeling assumptions.

Based on the last eight years of storage growth data and IDC's analysis, IDC predicated that storage capacity would grow at the average rate of 35%−45% per year (45.6% for file-based data

Total storage systems market share (to end sept 2013)

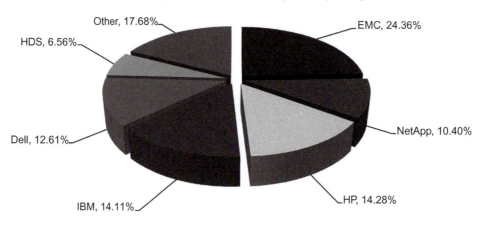

FIGURE 12.66

Global major storage vendor market share in 2013 [209].

Table 12.25 Global External Storage System Revenue 2008−2012 (millions)						
Year	2008	2009	2010	2011	2012	2013*
EMC	4,553	4,108	5,416	6,694	7,411	7,490
NetApp	1,601	1,560	2,352	2,911	3,054	3,196
IBM	2,665	2,560	2,922	3,183	3,155	2,087
HP	2,556	2,109	2,344	2,524	2,449	2,396
Hitachi (HDS)	1,858	1,647	1,741	2,068	2,209	2,017
Others	6,898	6,091	6,460	6,116	6,374	5,434
Total external	20,131	18,075	21,235	23,496	24,652	26,497
Dell	3,144	2,790	3,417	3,552		3,877
All storage disks total	27,761	24,465	28,718	31,079	32,564	31,497
*The data here is just an estimation for 12 months for 2013, using from the fourth quarter of 2012 to the third quarter of 2013.						

and 34% for block-based data) in next two to three years or so. Here, file-based data means unstructured data and block-based data is structured data (see Figure 12.67).[2]

If the above IDC prediction is right, global storage vendor revenue is flat or has just seen marginal growth over the last five years or so (see Table 12.25). One of the reasons may be that the unit cost of storage systems is declining at a similar rate.

[2]Source: IDC Worldwide File-Based Storage 2011−2015 Forecast: Foundation Solutions for Content Delivery, Archiving and Big Data, doc #231910, December 2011.

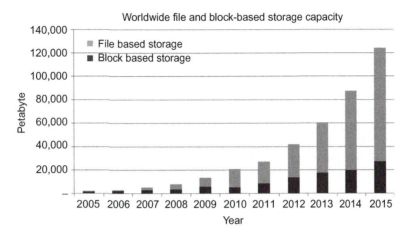

FIGURE 12.67

Forecasting of worldwide file and block disk storage capacity.

12.8 SUMMARY

In this chapter, we began with the overview of the storage hierarchy and then focused on the basic component of the storage system, which is the disk drive. From the storage disk drive, we built up to RAID setup and LUN and storage controllers. This is the bottom-up approach to unveiling the storage system.

Ultimately, the purpose of RAID, LUN, and storage controllers is to establish highly reliable enterprise-storage systems with a Service Level Agreement (SLA) in mind. Of course, an SLA supports storage tiering, where different storage tiers are designed for different business applications.

In terms of storage tiering, the chapter not only discusses the reliability of storage systems, but also describes the performance, which is the disk's IOPS for different RAID configurations or options. In the second part of this chapter, we mainly focused on SSD, because the price of SSDs is declining at an average rate of 30%−40% year on year over the last 10 years or so. According to the Price G2 prediction, the unit price of SSDs will be equivalent to HDDs in the middle of 2014. We believe this predication is quite reasonable because HDD has hit its physical limits (it has already reached nanometer scale). If this is right, there will be a major transformation for the enterprise storage industry in next three for five years or so. In other words, SSDs will gradually replace most HDDs.

From Table 12.11, we can see that RAID-5 and RAID-6 have higher write penalties than RAID-1 or RAID-10. Subsequently, we might increase the storage utilization rate but sacrifice storage access speed by using HDDs. If we select SSDs as the basic components for the storage array, the issue can be mitigated, especially for random access because the average random write speed (IOPS) of SSDs is six and eight times faster than HDDs. Actually, the majority of servers require random access (see Table 12.4).

Following the basic storage elements, this chapter discussed the three most important technical terms: DAS, NAS, and SAN. Due to server virtualization, many companies start to consolidate their DAS storage in order to avoid a single point of failure and increase storage utilization rate. Based on IDC's storage statistics, the DAS market (revenue) is quite flat or declining over the last five years. In contrast, the external storage system market grew 22.5% in the same period.

Speaking of external storage systems, this chapter discussed NAS, which is mainly file-based storage, and SAN, which is mainly for block-based storage. From the history of the technology, we can see that the initial purpose of NAS was to share files. In contrast, the original purpose of SAN was to share storage space or disk capacity.

Because both NAS and SAN are external storage systems, we need a storage network and interface to connect hosts and storage arrays. This leads to storage interface and network protocols. In 1986, IDE/PATA was initiated by CAM. In 1994, the ANSI-X3 committee took over the storage protocol standard and published a number of versions of PATA and replaced it with SATA and SAS. Now, most DAS solutions are using the SAS interface. Along with SATA and SAS development, the ANSI-X11 committee developed the SCSI protocol for external block-oriented storage systems. The advantage of the SCSI-3 or SAM-2 architecture is that it cannot only run on the TCP/IP network (via iSCSI), but also can go through a Fibre Channel network (via FCP). If the storage data goes through aTCP/IP network, the host and storage arrays have to use a few NIC adapters. If the data travels through an optical fiber network, the FC HBA cards have to be installed at both sides of the network. Commercially, it would be quite costly to run two storage networks. In order to consolidate both a Fibre Channel Switch (FC-SW) network and a TCP/IP network, FCIP was developed. However, FCIP is just a tunneling protocol. It does not control and monitor data traffic flow. Subsequently, iFCP was developed, but iFCP did not achieve its original goal, which was to eliminate FC-SW and FC-HBA altogether.

In order to resolve the issue of running multiple networks (both Fibre Channel and IP), FCoE was developed. It integrates both NIC and FC cards with one single adaptor: CNA. It also consolidates both network switches and Fibre Channel switches with a single FCoE switch. FCoE not only merges two networks but also reduce many network components. FCoE is a key direction for data center storage network.

When we touched on the topic of file-oriented storage, we discussed two types of protocols. One is NFS, designed for UNIX systems, and the other is CIFS, which is for Windows OS.

At the end of this chapter, we summarized pros and cons of different storage topologies and then we translated these storage topologies into a service-oriented model, specifically a storage tiering model. In addition, we also compared traditional and cloud storage. The main goal of this comparison is to highlight some issues that different versions of hypervisors might have with different storage functionalities. So, when we make any assumptions for our cloud cost model, we have to take all these factors into consideration.

Moreover, we briefly introduced major storage vendors and their market share and market trends during the last five years or so. We are trying to emphasize that the unit price of storage systems is declining YoY. This factor will have a significant impact for us in establishing a cloud cost model for computer storage.

12.9 **REVIEW QUESTIONS**

1. If an HDD's specification indicates that its speed = 10,000 RPM, what IOPS can we get if the rational latency assumption is 2.0 ms and we assume 80% read and 20% write?

2. There are two RAID options to be selected. One is RAID-10 and the other is RAID-01. Which one should be selected and why?

3. RAID configuration varies from RAID-0 to RAID-6. Why have RAID-3 and RAID-4 hardly been adopted?

4. If the purchase cost per GB of an SSD is slightly higher than for an HDD, for example 10% higher, would SDD still be a better option for the storage system if the application is Exchange email, the life cycle 5 years, and the required capacity is 2000 users and 100 GB per user? What is the threshold price for SSD to be better than HDD?

5. What is the main purpose of having LUN and LUN masking?

6. If we have a boot system to be installed in a cloud environment, which storage topology should be selected?

7. If a customer requires storage capacity for an SQL database and the I/O bandwidth requirement is the higher, the better, which topology should be selected and which network protocol would be the right choice if the capex budget is the secondary issue?

8. Assume a company has 250 TB storage capacity with average 25%−35% growth capacity per annum prediction and most storage components are lower speed HDDs, with 5,400 RPM (25%), 7,200 RPM (45%), 10,000 RPM (15%), and 15,000 RPM (5%). Based on application storage requirements, Tier-0 capacity requires 5%, Tier-1 10%, Tier-2 20%, and Tier-3 75%. The issue is that the storage hardware has become the bottleneck for many of the company's applications. Many online customers and partners are complaining about the slow response for web searching queries. What is the rational strategy to replace or upgrade the storage hardware with $250 k per year during the next three years? If the capex budget is not enough, what is the right amount of capex?

DATA CENTER NETWORKS

13

In the previous chapter, we briefly discussed storage networks, such as SAN and NAS. Now, we will focus on all data center networks. Data center networks are basically the switch fabric of inbound traffic network connections, if we just leave all outbound traffic and routing issues aside for a moment. The conventional data center network is a tree-based topology, which is a combination of star and bus topologies. We will begin to discuss the conventional data center network topology first and then move on to the topic of different network topologies, such as fat tree, Clos network, DCell, BCube, c-through, OSA, Butterfly, and Dragonfly. The main purpose in discussing these topologies is to make a comparison of these topologies against a list of network performance metrics, especially for three basic types of cloud network traffic, virtual machine (VM), hypervisor and management traffic.

Ultimately, we are trying to establish the basic cost components for a data center network based on different applications, various technologies, and investment strategies.

Before we start to touch on all the above topics, we will have to clarify some of the basic concepts for data center network components, such as NIC, switch, top of rack, end of row (EoR), middle of row (MOR), bridge, hub, load balance, router, and gateway. In addition, we will introduce some virtualized products and technologies that have been developed by various vendors, such as the Nexus series switch and HP Flex-10. Overall, we will cover the following:

- Network terms and key network components
- Data center network, topologies
- Network performance metrics
- Characteristics of data center network for cloud computing

13.1 KEY NETWORK TERMS AND COMPONENTS

In order to clarify some key network components, we have to understand some basic network terms first. The first question what we encounter is, what is a network anyway? A network is the multi-path that interconnects different end points. From a broad perspective, we may have many different types of networks, such as human networks, social networks, relationship networks, neural networks, radio networks, TV networks, telecommunication networks, computer networks, and data center networks. The various types of network actually reflect different business purposes and applications. In this chapter, what we are interested in is data center networks. They are supported by three functional subnetworks:

- Computer or server networks
- Storage networks
- Management networks

All these above networks can be divided into two categories: one is logical and the other is a physical network. To construct a data center network, we must have three network components:

- Network hardware (components, interface, and pipes or physical transmission media)
- Network topology and architectures (method of connection)
- Network software (protocols and programs to manage network and systems)

Let's explore the details of these network elements.

13.1.1 NETWORK HARDWARE

Physically, we need many different types of network hardware components to establish a data center network. Without these components, no one can build a data center network. Now, the question is, where is the starting point? Let's start with a typical data center network topology (see Figure 13.1) as an example, which is often recommended by one of the major network equipment vendors, Cisco.

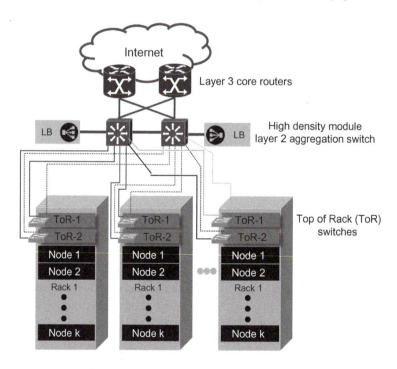

FIGURE 13.1

Typical data center network connection or topology.

Figure 13.1 is a basic three tier or layer data center network topology that has a core router, aggregation switch, and top of rack (ToR) switches. If we compare this topology with the standard OSI protocol stack model (see Figure 13.2), we find that the core router is handling layer 3 data traffic, which is also known as packets, and both the aggregation and ToR switches are processing layer 2 data traffic, which represents frames (see Figure 13.3).

If we follow this OSI or TCP/IP protocol stack model, it is quite easy for us to understand the function of each type of network hardware device. Based on these figures, we can see that the majority of data center network hardware can be classified into two types of devices: switches and routers. These elements (mainly switches) will become the major cost items in constructing a data center network. We can use these devices to connect many hosting servers. They can form a data center network fabric. That is why sometimes a data center network can be considered a switch fabric. Let's walk through each element of the switch fabric network.

13.1.1.1 Hub

The above figure demonstrated that we can probably use two types of network hardware to connect different network segments at layer 2: a hub and switch or perhaps a bridge. A bridge can be considered either a layer 2 or layer 3 device. We will depict further details of the bridge just before we start to discuss the topic of routers.

Both hubs and switches are the logical center of an Ethernet network for delivery of data streams that have been framed into logical packets of a certain length. To explain the mechanism of a switch, let's have a look at the function of a hub first.

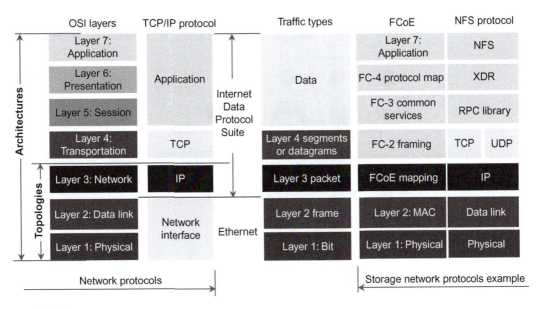

FIGURE 13.2

Protocol layer stack.

The function of a hub is to connect many different computer devices through a cable plugged into a port, which becomes an aggregation point of a network. It is a typical network star topology. We use the following example (see Figure 13.4) to illustrate the way a hub works.

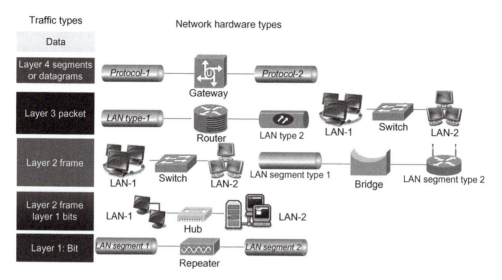

FIGURE 13.3

Network traffic and network hardware types.

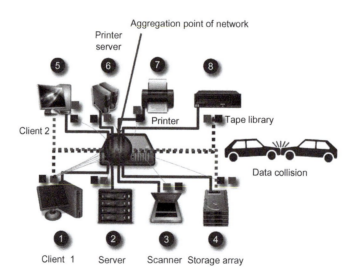

FIGURE 13.4

A typical hub connection (star topology).

When client 1 wants to write data onto the tape library or device number 8, it sends data packets to its hub port. The hub will broadcast these packets to all hub ports, and all devices that connect to the hub will receive these packets. Each device will check the address on the packets against their own address. If the address is matched, the device will accept these packets. If not, it will simply ignore them. You might wonder what happens when both client 1 and client 2 send data packets to the hub spontaneously. This is a good question. The simple answer is that it will cause a packet collision. For example, if client 1 [marked as no. 1] is trying to access the tape library [marked as no. 8] and at the same time, client 2 [marked as no. 5] is trying to write a file to the disk storage array [marked as No. 4], because the hub sends packets to every port, packet collision will be inevitable. In order to avoid this, LAN adopts a Carrier Sense Multiple Access with Collision Detection (CSMA/CD) method that has a collision detection feature, which can force both clients to stop sending packets and wait a fraction of a second (a random time interval or time slot[1]) before trying to resend their packets. If client 1 has established a communication channel with the tape library, client 2 has to wait until client 1 finishes its data transmission. Normally, the speed of a tape library is very slow. If the hub is capable of transmitting at 100 Mbps but the tape library can only work on 5 Mbps, then the whole network will only transmit at the speed of 5 Mbps or less. The more clients that try to access the hub concurrently, the slower the network will be.

We often classify a hub with three different categories: passive, active, and intelligent. It is dependent on the function of a hub. If a hub is simply transferring a digital signal (frames) through from one segment of network to another, it is a passive hub. Sometimes, it is also referred to as a concentrator. If a hub doesn't only deliver a signal but also amplifies it, we would name it an active hub or a multiport repeater at layer 2.

Normally, the hub is a very simple and slow network device. This is why a hub is considered a layer 1 device. Whether it is a layer 1 or 2 device, the function of a hub is to transport and monitor data frames. The media to join two separate network segments is either twisted-pair wire or fiber-optic cable. Fundamentally, a hub has a similar function as the layer 1 device but it has an additional feature that allows it to be connected to more than two segments of networks. A typical hub may have four, five, or eight ports. Some hubs may have 16 or more ports. A good five-port hub can build a small home network, which only costs between $15−$50 dollars. Traditionally, a simple hub is an unintelligent and unmanageable device. At the layer 2 level of the OSI stack model, a hub just reads any of the data frames passing through it and doesn't care about the source or destination of these packets. If all packets from different devices are flowing into the hub at the same time, the transmitting packets will easily collide. When the number of interconnected hubs increases, the collision rate of packets will grow exponentially. As a rule of thumb, a hub can only support a very small amount of networking. For a 100 Mbits bandwidth Ethernet network, the number of hubs should be less than two and the number of network segments should be no more than three.

If we build extra features into a hub, such as SNMP and virtual LAN (or VLAN) to support remote management capability, the hub can be considered an intelligent hub.

When a network is very slow or has limited bandwidth, a hub could act as a cheap and reasonablly reliable device to connect different network segments. However, when network bandwidth grows larger than 100 Mbps and beyond, the hub will not be an ideal device for any large network,

---

[1]Waiting slot times for all clients $= 2^c − 1$, where "c" is the number of collisions.

especially a data center network. Today, it is hard to find any hub product in the marketplace because there is no significant manufacturing cost difference between a hub and a switch. The switch has replaced the hub for any size of network.

13.1.1.2 Switch

Similar to a hub that we have mentioned above, a network switch is one of the key components to connecting many different network devices, such as clients, host servers, printers, storage arrays, and tape libraries. It forms a large area network and wide area network (LAN/WAN) to share information and computer resources.

If the network switch is the basic ingredient to establish LAN/WANs then a router is the essential component to join different LAN/WANs. It is capable of select the optimized route or the best path to deliver data packets. We will focus on the router shortly.

The function of a network switch is similar to a hub; it joins all computer devices so that they can communicate with each other. However, a switch does the job in a different way. Rather than flooding all packets to every port, a switch can read the address of a data frame from a source port and devote it directly to the destination port connected with the target device. The switch will establish a logical channel for data stream transmission between this source and the destination ports. In other words, other ports will not be interfered with by this transmission. If other computers are trying to transmit their packets, they can do it via unused ports. A switch allows many connected computers to transmit many data streams concurrently (see Figure 13.5).

If a switch can permit data to be sent and received concurrently, we call it full duplex mode. All these features will accelerate the speed of the data stream through a switch. Obviously, a switch is much faster than a hub.

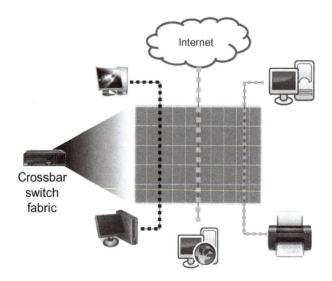

FIGURE 13.5

The mechanism of a typical switch.

A switch doesn't have a passive mode. It is always active. Very often, it can be shifted up and down among the different layers of the OSI stack model rather than just being stuck in layer 2. The term "switch" is not strictly defined by any standard, such as IEEE 802.1X. It is more like a commercial term rather than a technical term. This is why the term "switch" can be moved from layer 1 all the way to layer 4 of the OSI protocol model. Quite often, the term "switch" becomes interchangeable with the terms "hub," "repeater," "bridge," and "router." It is really dependent on a switch vendor's valuation for its customers or consumers. If the term "switch" is more valuable than "hub," "repeater," "bridge," or "router," it will be called a switch. If not, they will use different terms. Actually, the layer 2 switch is the same as a bridge by the definition of IEEE 802.1D.

In contrast to the hub, a basic switch has the capability to define a virtual circuit path for packets through it, but it doesn't have dynamic reconfiguration capability to provide optimizing routes based on different network traffic conditions. The intelligent ability to reconfigure other paths is often dependent on optimization algorithms built in to a memory controller (see Figure 13.6).

A switch can be either manageable or unmanageable; this depends on the category of switch. It is also reflected in its price. Switch prices range from below $50 to more than $500,000. A manageable switch has an SNMP agent, command-line interface (CLI), and web-based GUI interface built into it, which allows IT administrators to manipulate or reconfigure a set of switch parameters. Some vendors may provide additional advantageous features for their switch products, such as

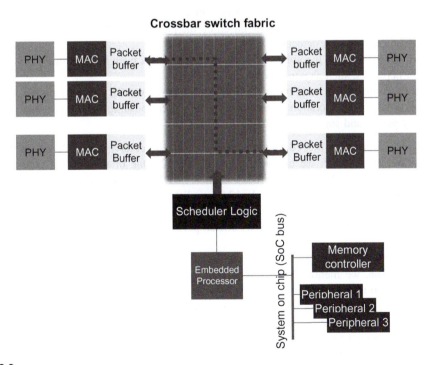

FIGURE 13.6

A typical switch functional block diagram.

backward compatibility that mixes traditional RJ45 ports and SFP+ (small form-factor pluggable plus) 10G ports, auto-negotiation between higher and lower speeds, advanced VLAN traffic segmentation, QoS prioritization, advanced security and Internet Group Management Protocol (IGMP) snooping, link aggregation, dynamic VLAN assignment, double VLAN tagging access control list (ACL) binding, static routing, and minimum load path (MLP) snooping. This kind of switch may be named a smart or intelligent switch. An IT administrator can create and store different configurations with a fully manageable switch. An enterprise class switch usually has a high-density port and fully manageable capabilities plus many smart features. It has its own CPU and memory on board. In contrast to a manageable switch, an unmanageable switch can't be remotely controlled or managed. All configurations are prefixed.

When you select or purchase a switch, you have to review the following 13 basic features for you application or business requirements:

1. Ports: the number of ports, yypes of port (such as RJ-45 and SFP+)
2. Size of packet buffer memory: provides capability to dynamically share memory resources across only used ports
3. Latency: with 64-byte frames, 10 Gbps copper 10GB-T, and fibre SFP+
4. Switch fabric: in Gbps
5. Port speeds: port speed and duplexing capabilities affect the throughput of the switch
6. Link aggregation: the ability to send data over multiple connections to the same endpoint
7. Management features: SNMP, smart control center, port mirroring, port prioritization, etc.
8. Filtering, the ability to segment traffic based on the physical identification of devices and QoS
9. Security: virus, intrusion detection
10. Network access control: the ability of a switch to provide a bridging function between two different networks, such as wireless and WiFi
11. VLAN: dynamic VLAN assignment, double VLAN tagging ACL binding, etc.
12. Physical dimensions, operation temperatures, and power consumption
13. Warranty period and supported SLA

In addition, if a switch is moved up to OSI layer 3, it will act as a router. People name this kind of switch a "director," which we mentioned in Chapter 12. One of the leading industry vendors, Cisco, provides the Cisco Multilayer Director Switch (MDS) or MDS 9000 series switch to serve this purpose. In Section 12.1.2.1 and Table 12.9, we listed the cost of a director port for storage. Actually, this port can switch between layer 2 and layer 3. That is why a director port normally costs 50% to 100% more than a normal SAN switch port.

13.1.1.3 Bridge

In the above section, we mentioned that a layer 2 switch is a bridge. The function of a network bridge is to join two network segments or divide one network into two separated network segments or LANs. Usually, two networks may adopt the same protocol, such as the Ethernet protocol, but this is not limited to the same protocol for two networks. Historically, a bridge may only have two Ethernet ports connected to each network segment. However, because a layer 2 switch is the same as a bridge, many switch vendors may provide a bridge that has more than two ports. One of most popular types of bridge is an Ethernet bridge. It can overcome some inherent obstacles of the Ethernet protocol by controlling data flow among different network segments. When a bridge is connected to an Ethernet network, its function is to make the network device transparent. Transparent bridging is the bridging method to route and manage data traffic efficiently. A transparent bridge has four operation modes:

- Frame or packet filtering
- Forwarding packets
- Broadcasting and learning addresses
- Loop resolution

The concept of a transparent bridge is to examine the incoming data stream of the Media Access Control (MAC) address for the packet destination first and then compare it to the destination MAC with the MAC address-forwarding table. If the destination address exists in the forwarding table, it will send these packets to the destination device. If not, it will broadcast the data packet to all devices and listen to the destination device's response. In other words, the bridge has

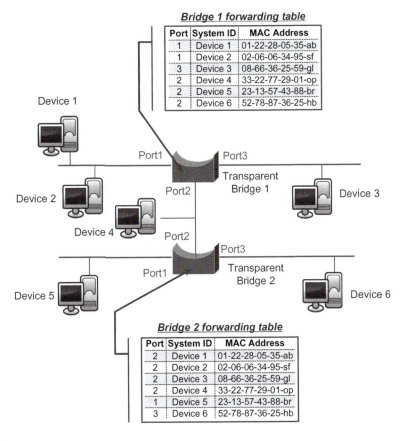

Bridge 1 forwarding table

Port	System ID	MAC Address
1	Device 1	01-22-28-05-35-ab
1	Device 2	02-06-06-34-95-sf
3	Device 3	08-66-36-25-59-gl
2	Device 4	33-22-77-29-01-op
2	Device 5	23-13-57-43-88-br
2	Device 6	52-78-87-36-25-hb

Bridge 2 forwarding table

Port	System ID	MAC Address
2	Device 1	01-22-28-05-35-ab
2	Device 2	02-06-06-34-95-sf
2	Device 3	08-66-36-25-59-gl
2	Device 4	33-22-77-29-01-op
1	Device 5	23-13-57-43-88-br
3	Device 6	52-78-87-36-25-hb

FIGURE 13.7

Transparent bridging on Ethernet network.

begun to search for the destination device in the network. Once the destination device responds to the broadcasting signal, the bridge will add the destination device's MAC address into its forwarding table and transmit packets to the destination device. The broadcasting time will be set for a certain interval. If the broadcasting time has expired and no destination device has responded to the broadcast signal, the bridge entry of the filtering database will become invalid (see Figure 13.7).

The reason for broadcasting and listening for a MAC address is not only to learn about the new devices that are plugged into the network but also to upgrade the forwarding table due to existing devices being moved around from time to time (see Figure 13.8).

All devices that are plugged into the network have a unique MAC address. It is the fingerprint of any physical hardware or device. This is why sometimes it is also named the hardware or physical address. It doesn't matter whether it is a network interface card (NIC), hosting server, printer, switch, hub, storage disk, or even the bridge itself, they all have this address. It is this address that a bridge can trace among different LANs.

One thing that we should remember is that when sending and receiving devices within the same network segment, this forwarding activity will not happen. This reduces overall network congestion. In short, the bridge will only occur between two network segments. However, if the destination device doesn't receive a quality signal over a longer distance, the bridge will retransmit the packets again.

For a bridge to operate correctly and effectively, all networks shouldn't have any network loops. Therefore, a transparent bridge will include a loop resolution process. The principle of the loop resolution process is quite simple to understand; the process will learn the network topology of all the network devices that have been bridged and calculate a spanning tree of the network. A spanning tree is a subset of the topology that links all network devices without any loops. A Spanning Tree Protocol (STP) is defined by the IEEE 802.1D standard. Actually, this protocol is one of the routing technologies to solve the problem of network loops via adaptive and dynamic routing. We will discuss STP and routing in detail in the following section.

A bridge can also talk to different types of physical networks or media, such as wireline and wireless networks such as 100Base-T and WiFi (see Figure 13.9).

A bridge can not only join a number of network segments, but also split a large network into a few smaller networks, which can reduce the number of network devices competing for transmission privileges (see Figure 13.10).

We often utilize bridges to separate internal groups for a large enterprise or government agent to improve network performance. For example, if salespeople are using iOS for their wireless iPad and R&D people adopt Linux systems for web hosting, a bridge can provide a partition to separate the traffic between these two internal groups.

In summary, a network bridge can't handle any network protocol higher than the Link Layer Control (LLC) protocol. It is like an unmanageable switch that doesn't accept any IP address and network commands. You can't "ping" it. For the TCP/IP network model (refer to Section 13.2), a network bridge can only interact with the Address Resolution Protocol (ARP), Neighbor Discovery Protocol (NDP), and Open Shortest Path First (OSPF). Regardless of how many ports are available, a bridge can only provide one port for packet forwarding and another for packet distribution. From a network perceptive, a bridge only has one network interface.

A bridge doesn't support routing paths but can transmit packets based on its destination MAC address. You can add as many network bridges as you like in a network, but you can't stretch the

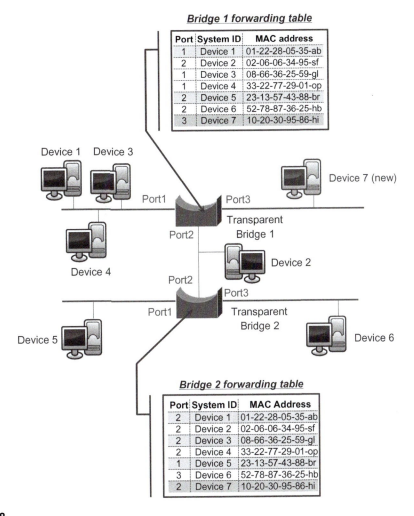

Bridge 1 forwarding table

Port	System ID	MAC address
1	Device 1	01-22-28-05-35-ab
2	Device 2	02-06-06-34-95-sf
1	Device 3	08-66-36-25-59-gl
1	Device 4	33-22-77-29-01-op
2	Device 5	23-13-57-43-88-br
2	Device 6	52-78-87-36-25-hb
3	Device 7	10-20-30-95-86-hi

Bridge 2 forwarding table

Port	System ID	MAC Address
2	Device 1	01-22-28-05-35-ab
2	Device 2	02-06-06-34-95-sf
2	Device 3	08-66-36-25-59-gl
2	Device 4	33-22-77-29-01-op
1	Device 5	23-13-57-43-88-br
3	Device 6	52-78-87-36-25-hb
2	Device 7	10-20-30-95-86-hi

FIGURE 13.8

Transparent bridge updating forwarding table.

network segment extension beyond a network bridge. For example, in Figure 13.8, if both bridge 1 and 2 have been connected with port 2, port 1 of bridge 1 can't be connected to port 1 of bridge 2. If so, the forwarding tables of both bridge 1 and 2 will not work properly. Because a port is kept by the MAC address-forwarding table, it can be considered a logical part of a bridge rather than a physical one. If extra ports have been detected by a bridge, they will be self-configured in the forwarding table. They are not managed by anyone. If the operating system is Windows, the network bridge will be software-based or a virtual network interface that extends two or more different networks. Normally, the bridge will store incoming frames into a buffer and take subsequent

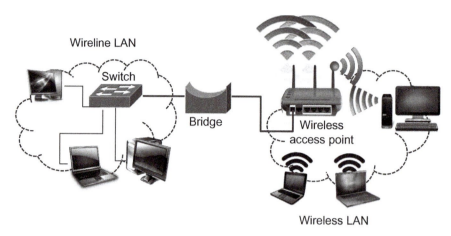

FIGURE 13.9

Bridge between different types of network segments.

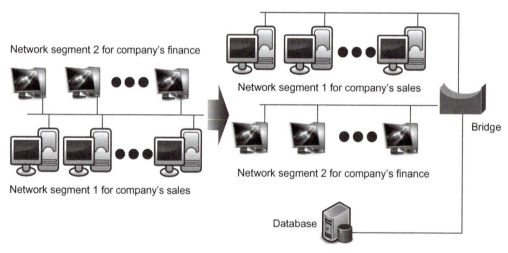

FIGURE 13.10

Split a large company network into two network segments.

actions based on the MAC address-forwarding table. Therefore, the throughput of a bridge will be less than a repeater.

In general, a bridge will be more expensive than a repeater or a hub, but will be cheaper than a switch or router. Normally, the price of a wireless enterprise grade bridge will vary from approximately $500 to a few thousand dollars.

13.1.1.4 Router

The solution to resolve layer 3 (or higher than layer 3) communication issues will be dependent on a network router. Similar to a bridge, a network router joins different types of networks. When it directs network traffic, it is based on packet IPs or logical addresses rather than MAC or physical addresses. As a result, a router can differentiate different types of network while a bridge can't.

Sometimes, people will refer to a layer 3 switch as a router, which is similar to a layer 2 hub being considered as a switch because the term of switch is just a commercial or marketing name rather than a strict and technical definition. When Bolt Beranek and Newman (BBN) Technologies[2] developed the router in 1978, it was actually a packet switch. In 1980, it was replaced by a DEC PDP-11 minicomputer that could configure IP traffic. During later 1980s and early 1990s, as the Internet started to boom, many ISPs bought Sun SPARC servers as a low-cost router. It was a Cisco system that created this special application of a computer system as a router. Cisco has become one of the major switch and router providers. It had 39% of the global market share in the second quarter of 2013 according to Infonetics Research (see Figure 13.11).

13.1.1.4.1 Principles of routing

The principle of a router is to read all incoming data packet logical addresses and then based on its own routing table forward these incoming data packets to their destinations. Because the router can not only read IP addresses but also has the intelligent power or computing capability to support incoming packet routing, it is capable of finding the shortest path in the network to the packet's destination. In this sense, a router can be an off-the-shelf or conventional computer that is

Top 5 service provider router and switch
vendors by 2Q13 global revenue share

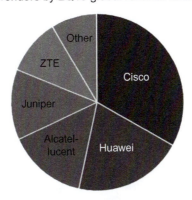

© Infonetics research, service provider routers and switches
quarterly market share, size and forecastes, August 2013

FIGURE 13.11

Top 5 service providers for routers and switches in second quarter of 2013 [210].

[2]In October 2009, BBN Technologies was acquired by Raytheon for $350 million.

specially configured for routing purposes. Normally, a router would be slower than a layer 2 switch (based on port ID) or a bridge (based on MAC) because it not only takes the time to read a packet's IP address, but also interprets it.

Actually, a typical router has a CPU, RAM, I/O interfaces, and an operating system (OS). For example, Cisco routers have an OS named the Internetwork Operating System (IOS). Juniper's routers have the Juniper Network Operation System (JUNOS) and Huawei's routers have the Versatile Routing Platform (VRP). All this hardware and software make up the two basic components of a router: the forwarding engine and routing engine (see Figure 13.12).

These two components will perform five primary tasks:

- Interface with different types of network, such as wireline and wireless, and accept incoming data packets from different network sources (forwarding engine).
- Examine the destination IP (routing engine).
- Find the best possible path to the packet's destination (routing engine).
- Forward the data stream or packet to the destination node (forwarding engine).
- If the primary path is blocked or down, find an alternative path if it is available and retransmit data packets to the destination node (both routing and forwarding engines).

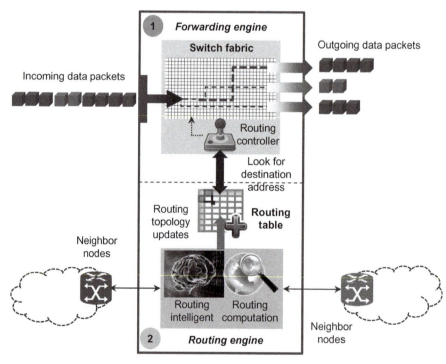

FIGURE 13.12

A typical network router architecture.

Cisco CRS3/16   NE5000E

Juniper T4K

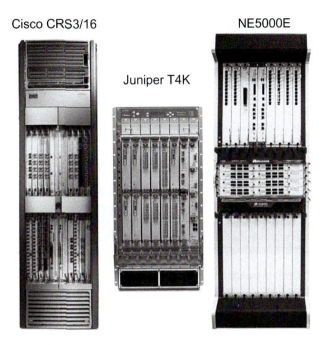

FIGURE 13.13

High-end enterprise router.

13.1.1.4.2 Router size

In addition to these basic routing tasks, many router vendors may add extra functions for their products, such as security, remote connectivity, traffic filtering and monitoring, and network management functions. The various network router types are similar to computers. They could vary from high end to low end based on the different capabilities of the router. A high-end router may cost over $100 k–$500 k, such as Cisco's CRS-3/16, Huawei's NE5000E, and Juniper's T4K (see Figure 13.13).

For middle-range routers, the price will be around $10 k. If the application is a home network or small office, the low end of router pricing will be below a few hundred dollars (see Figure 13.14). For many tiering data centers, high-end routers are the preferred choice.

13.1.1.4.3 Router types

If we look from a network size perspective, we can probably classify routers into three types: interior, exterior, and border (or gateway) router. An interior router connects many autonomous LANs within a large enterprise and can cross many different geographic locations. For example, an interior router may connect a sales group (located in Sydney) of a small and medium business with another sales group (located in Melbourne) of large enterprise customers. Normally, the interior router will not forward data packets within a LAN. This task will be controlled by a switch.

In contrast, the exterior router acts as an Internet backbone. The border or gateway router is the network device that connects interior and exterior routers. Routers in data centers are either interior or border (gateway) routers (see Figure 13.15).

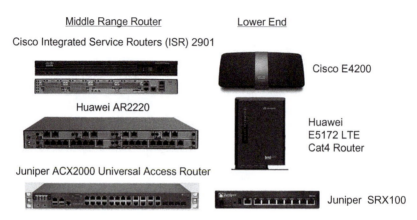

FIGURE 13.14

Middle-range and low-end routers.

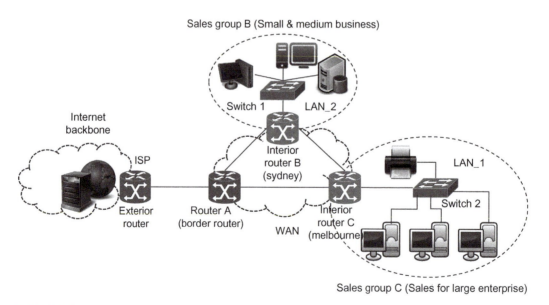

FIGURE 13.15

Router types based on network size.

13.1.1.4.4 Routing protocols

As we have mentioned above, the distinguishing feature for a router is whether a router has an intelligent engine or not. The basic components of this intelligent engine are routing protocols, routing algorithms, network topologies that can be automatically updated by the router itself, and calculation capabilities so that the router can handle all events due to network changes, network outages, network congestion, and the number of hops between the source and destination nodes. Among these components, the routing protocol is the key.

A generic router will depend on six basic routing protocols (RIP, RIPv2, BGP, OSPF, IS-IS, and EIGRP) and these protocols can be classified into three categories:

- Distance vector (or DV) (RIP, RIPv2, BGP)
- Link state (OSPF, IS-IS)
- Hybrid of distance vector and link state (EIGRP)

Distance vector (DV) routing protocols will provide the following distance-related information (see Figure 13.16):

- The best path between the source and destination
- The number of hops to the destination
- Latency and other network traffic characteristics

The Routing Information Protocol (RIP) is one of the earliest DV routing algorithms; it was originally defined by IEEE RFC 1058 in 1988. It is mainly applied for routing between interior and border routers. The latest version of RIP is version 2 or RIPv2, which was defined by RFC 2453. The maximum number of hops can't be more than 15 and the lifetime for any one path can't exceed more than 180 seconds. In contrast to RIPv1, RIPv2 doesn't update the routing table every 30 seconds, but rather slightly randomizes it, which overcomes the issue of overloading when too many routers update at once.

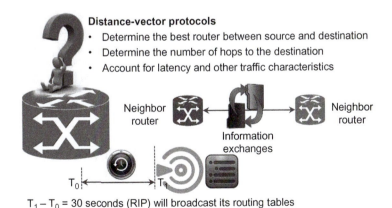

Distance-vector protocols
- Determine the best router between source and destination
- Determine the number of hops to the destination
- Account for latency and other traffic characteristics

Neighbor router   Information exchanges   Neighbor router

$T_1 - T_0 = 30$ seconds (RIP) will broadcast its routing tables

FIGURE 13.16

Distance vector protocols.

The other DV protocol is the Border Gateway Protocol (BGP). This is basically designed for WAN routing. RIP and RIPv2 use IP routing but BGP communicates routing messages to TCP sessions. It is a very complex routing protocol. A network administrator can configure a set of rules to differentiate one group of routers over another based on a certain routing policy. If RIP and RIPv2 are designed for routing between interior and border or gateway routers, then BGP is applied for routing between border and exterior or backbone routers (see Figure 13.17).

In comparison with DV protocols, link state protocols allow each router to independently figure out the best path to the destination nodes for its data packets rather than rely on neighbor routers for path information.

Open Shortest Path First (OSPF) is one of the link state routing protocols; it adopts a very complex routing algorithm to work out the best path. OSPF doesn't impose a ceiling on the number of hops. Normally, the shortest path is the most direct route between a source and a destination. If one path is slow due to traffic congestion or broken down, OSPF will find another alternative route that is the most efficient path to the destination.

OSPF is similar to creating virtual paths. Every running link will be installed in a router's database of possible links. Therefore, if OSPF finds any outages for the current link, the router can quickly recover an alternative path.

OSPF, IS-IS, RIP, and BPG are all open source protocols and can be applied on UNIX, Linux, and Solaris systems based on the Zebra project (www.quagga.net). Therefore, nearly all vendors support OSPF. OSPF is normally applied for links between interior and border routers or different LANs. You can adopt OSPF for routers provided by different vendors.

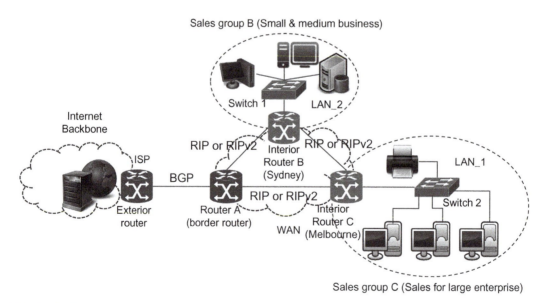

FIGURE 13.17

Different DV protocols for different types of router links.

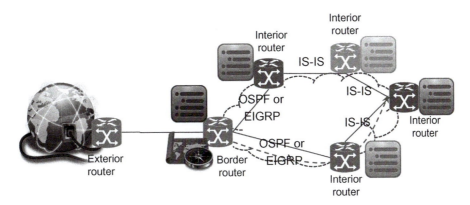

FIGURE 13.18

Link state and hybrid routing protocols.

The other link state routing protocol is Intermediate System to Intermediate System (IS-IS). It was originally developed by the ISO. Although the best path algorithm of IS-IS is similar to OSPF, it is designed for interior routers only. IS-IS is not as popular as OSPF.

Cisco Systems initiated a hybrid protocol, the Enhanced Interior Gateway Routing Protocol (EIGRP), in the mid-1980s. It has many good features in comparison with OSPF, such as fast convergence time, low network overhead, easier configuration, less CPU consumption, supporting for multiple routing protocols, and elimination of unnecessary routing traffic. However, it is a proprietary protocol that only Cisco supports (see Figure 13.18).

13.1.1.5 Gateway

In Chapter 12, we briefly discussed the topic of a gateway for NAS. Similarly, we have also mentioned a gateway router, which is a border router. The generic term "gateway" means a computer-like device supported by both hardware and software that can communicate with two or more different systems. A network gateway is a component that works with two different types of networks in terms of processing data comes from different physical media, formats, protocols, and architectures.

In order to communicate with different types of network, a network gateway must operate at multiple layers of the OSI model because it has to establish and manage sessions, decode encrypted data, and translate different logical and physical addresses. Because a gateway has to implement many tasks at different layers, it may potentially trigger network traffic congestion and significantly slow a network down. It is most certainly slower than a switch, hub, bridge, or router.

In comparison with a network router, a gateway is operating at the layer 4 or above, at the session, presentation, and application layers. A router may operate between layer 3 and 4 but will never move up beyond layer 4, such as to the application layer of the TCP/IP model. From this perspective, a gateway device can be a conventional computer that is running special software to serve the linkage function. If this is so, why is a border router also called a gateway router? This is because "gateway" has similar usage as "switch." It is a marketing or commercial term rather than a technical definition. A router may have different aspects of a gateway that have been built into it.

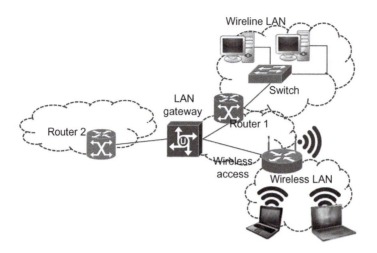

FIGURE 13.19

Example of LAN gateway.

The key difference between a router and a gateway is that a gateway is capable of operate in the upper layers of the OSI model (or the application layer of the TCP/IP model).

In spite of the above two types of gateway that we have already discussed, there are many other popular gateways that are provided by many computer and network vendors, such as firewall or proxy servers, credit card gateways, Internet gateways, email gateways, voicemail gateways, hosting gateways, data center LAN gateways, etc. (see Figure 13.19).

13.2 DATA CENTER NETWORK TERMS AND JARGON

Once we have clarified the concepts of basic network devices, the next logical question is how to effectively use these components to construct a scalable, reliable, high performance, and cost effective data center network (DCN). This is dependent on how to design and build a state-of-the-art large and flexible DCN topology.

In order to make it easier for readers to grasp the topic of DCN topologies, we will first explain some network topology jargon and concepts in the following section and then review some basic principles of a data center network. Following these basic concepts, the following section will focus on many different topologies as well as their pros and cons. At the end of this section, we will discuss several existing challenges and the limitations of some popular cost models for today's data center networks.

13.2.1 DCN TERMS, JARGON, AND DEFINITIONS

If we would like to understand data center network connections, topologies, metrics, and costs, the first thing is to understand the real meaning of many technical terms and jargon. In the following section, we will concentrate on these terms, jargon, and definitions.

13.2.1.1 Topology

A generic meaning of topology is as a mathematical term, used to define topological spaces and their continuous maps. It can be considered a part of geometry, set, graph, or even logic theory because we use these theories and routing algorithms to model different computer networks or data center networks. This is why there are many technical terms and definitions shared by both graph theory and network topology, such as nodes, vertices, paths, links, and edges.

13.2.1.2 Network topology

The term "network topology" is used to define the distribution or arrangement of many different network components, including the links and interfaces among network components. Normally, wireline networks will be linked by network devices, such as repeaters, hubs, switches, bridges, and routers, and joined by physical pipe, such as electronic and fiber cable. Wireless networks will be connected by many antennas or WiFi or WiMAX devices. Because almost all network devices have been digitized or packetized, network topology can also divided into physical and logical (or virtual) network topology. However, what we are focusing on here is the data center network (DCN) topology, which is only restricted to the boundary of the data center facility.

13.2.1.3 Data center network topology

The DCN is the part of the computer network that can be connected by either electronic or optical fiber or a mixture of connection types (see Figure 13.20). Looking from the OSI or TCP/IP model's perspective, the DCN is a layer 2 and layer 3 network because it operates between these two layers.

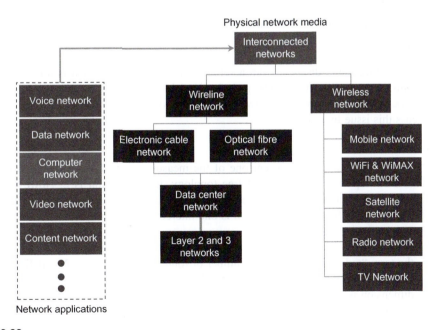

FIGURE 13.20

Data center network.

We can also consider DCN basically as a switch fabric because of the quantity of network switches in comparison with the volume of other network components. This also means that we can adopt commoditized network switches to reduce DCN cost.

The DCN topology will be designed to effectively connect all network components within a data center. These components should include NICs, HBAs, nodes (or hosting servers or computers), hubs, switches, routers, bridges, gateways, load balancers, firewalls, and storage components. In short, a DCN specifies how the switches will be wired together. It will impact on data traffic performance, which includes data packet routing, DCN reliability, scalability, throughput, latency, and flexibility. Above all, it will ultimately impact on the business applications and the long-term cost.

13.2.1.4 Node

In graph theory, a node means a point or a vertex without dimension. For a server farm or cluster, it means a physical hosting server. For a DCN topology, we mean the network endpoint, which can be either a switch or router.

13.2.1.5 Node degree

This is the number of links a node has with its neighbors. In short, it is the number of links per node. For a scalable network, the number of links should be a function of the number of nodes. It is linear. For example, for a bus topology, a node only has one degree or one link. However, for a ring topology, it has two degrees or two links.

13.2.1.6 Neighbor nodes

If two nodes are connected and next to each other, they are the neighbor nodes.

13.2.1.7 Diameter

This is the maximum routing distance from a source to a destination node. It is not only the maximum routing distance but also the shortest path for available nodes within a network topology. For a hierarchy type of DCN topology, the lower the number of degrees, the smaller the diameter is. We will discuss this issue in a bit.

13.2.1.8 Dimension

The term "dimension" is used to represent one of the measurements of space in the graph theory. For a popular DCN topology, such as a fat tree topology, the dimension is 2. However for other topologies, such as a hypercube, the dimension can be 2, 3, greater than 3, or even n dimensions. It can be the stage or tier. Simply, a dimension is one interconnection link.

13.2.1.9 Radix

For a DCN, the term "radix" just means the number of router or switch ports. Normally, we use the letter "N" to represent the number of nodes and the letter "k" is to indicate the number of ports per node. If the dimension is the same as the radix, it means the network topology is regular. The size of the radix can be low or high, which is equivalent to small or large. Based on Kachris et al.'s [211] conclusions, future data center networks will increase the radix of switches to reduce capex cost because a high radix will decrease the number of hop counts and latency. Villar et al. [212]

argued that for large switch-based interconnect networks, a high radix number will not only decrease the number of network components but also increase DCN performance.

13.2.1.10 Regular topology

In a regular topology, all nodes are linked with the same graph pattern. In other words, the graph of a DCN has the same structure. If the DCN has a regular topology, nodes can be connected with the same degree, and the routing of data packets can be predetermined by the coordinates of the nodes. Normally, the DCN topology is regular, for example fat tree, ring, crossbar, butterfly, and mesh, all of which we will discuss shortly.

13.2.1.11 Irregular topology

In contrast to a regular topology, an irregular topology means the nodes are constructed randomly without any pattern so that nodes don't have the same node degree. They are connected arbitrarily. A typical example of an irregular topology is the Internet or Web.

13.2.1.12 Nonblocking and blocking

If any permutation between sources and destinations can be connected, the topology can be considered nonblocking. Otherwise, the network topology is blocking. A connection between a free input and output pair is not always available because the pair may conflict with existing connections.

13.2.1.13 Direct network

For an interconnected network, a network topology can be categorized into two different types [213]. One is the so-called direct network, which means the endpoint of a node is directly connected to the backbone network. The endpoint of a node will be located inside the interconnected network. Any communication among non-neighboring nodes has to go through a few dimensions of devices. For example consider a DCN switch where node A is trying to communicate with another node E; it has to travel through a number of devices. One of the typical examples of a direct network topology is the mesh network topology.

13.2.1.14 Indirect network

In contrast to a direct network, an indirect network topology occurs where the endpoints of nodes only connect to the edge of network devices. In other words, the endpoints of nodes are located outside the interconnected network. For example, with a DCN indirect network topology, the physical server nodes don't connect to the core routers directly, but rather the top of rack (ToR) switches or end of row (EoR) switches. The typical example of an indirect network topology is the tree network topology (see Figure 13.21).

Based on work by Dennis Abts [234], the terms "radix" and "dimension" are interchangeable for both direct and indirect networks. "Radix" stands for the number of switch ports and "dimension" refers to the number of stages for an indirect network topology. However, for a direct network topology, both terms are reversed. So, just be careful when you encounter these terms. You should always check the context of these terms rather than just taking the surface meaning.

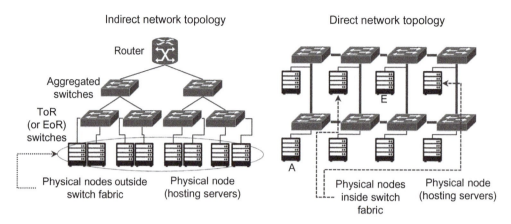

FIGURE 13.21

Direct and indirect network topologies.

Table 13.1 DCN Performance Measurements		
1. Scalability	2. Aggregation throughput	3. Reliability
4. Incremental scalability	5. Oversubscription	6. Security
7. Cabling or connectivity complexity	8. Fault tolerance	9. Latency
10. Bisection bandwidth	11. Energy consumption	12. TCO/ROI

13.3 METRICS OF DCN TOPOLOGY

Because of the high scalability of requirements, almost all DCN topologies lie within either the direct (or router-based) or indirect (or switch-based) network category. Now, the question is, how do we know which DCN topology is better for cloud applications with regard to cost or TCO/ROI? Perhaps Kaishun Wu et al.'s [220] paper will give some clues in terms of DCN performance measurements or metrics, which may include those listed in Table 13.1.

All above measurements are very basic or common principles in designing any data center network. In addition to these common criteria for a conventional data center, there are many extra measurements or costs that have to be properly considered for a cloud data center environment:

- Applications complexity: Many large enterprise applications are often dependent on shared services, such as directories and SQL databases, especially if the business needs a solution mixing both "on-premise" and "off-premise" applications. A DCN topology must support or work with these applications without migration or duplication of these shared services.

- IT silo: Due to complexity of the DCN, a data center should not duplicate tools, processes, and IT administration when operating and managing cloud data centers, especially for some cloud solutions that have to maintain an on-premise data center.
- Seamless network connectivity: Applications should be always on, no matter how the actual DCN topology changes (for example, some nodes may be online or offline from time to time).
- User transparency: When a user wants to move or create a VM, it can be quite confusing and might interrupt normal processes. "User transparency" can make sure the user is aware of the VM location.
- DCN compliance and auditing for data security
- Support agility and flexibility
- Multipath diversity
- Resiliency and maintenance
- Disaster recovery
- Backward compatibility

Once we have these performance measurements in our mind, we should be able to answer the earlier question: which DCN topology is better for cloud applications with regard to cost or TCO/ROI?

13.4 TYPES OF NETWORK TOPOLOGY

Today's DCN topology can be traced all the way back to the telecommunication network in 1950s. The aim of the telco circuit or packet switch network topology was to increase the efficiency of carrying capacity and performance. There have been many types of network topologies, but the most basic types of network topologies for computer network are outlined in Table 13.2 and Figure 13.22.

These topologies represent the shape of the physical network connection or linkage. In order to increase a network's reliability, throughput (or bandwidth), flexibility, and scalability and to reduce latency costs, many new network topologies have been developed on top of these six basic network topologies (Table 13.3).

The list of new network topologies could go on and on. We can't list all of them. Moreover, many new network topologies are still emerging.

In short, there are many different network topologies that have been developed for different purposes and different criteria. The issue is which one is the right one for a particular DCN with certain business applications. To answer this question, we have to classify all these topologies into the right category and then examine each topology to see whether it is fit for DCN purposes based on a

Table 13.2 Basic Types of Network Topologies	
Bus	Star
Token ring or linear and ring	Point to point
Mesh	Tree

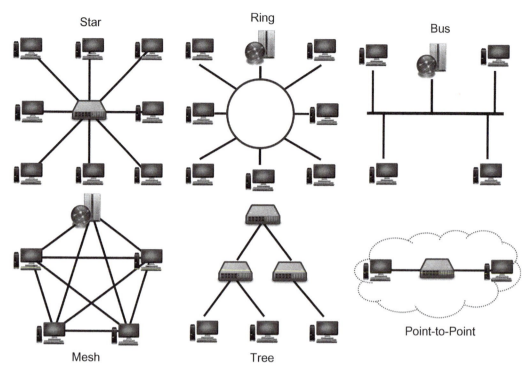

FIGURE 13.22

Basic network topologies.

Table 13.3 Other Types of Network Topologies			
Crossbar	**Omega**	**De Bruijn**	**c-Through**
Clos	Hypercube	Pyramid	Hellos
Bayan tree	Torus	FiConn	Portland
Fat tree	Flattened butterfly/2DFB	Optical Switch Architecture (OSA)	Al-Fares
VL2	Dragonfly	Benes	Hedera
B-cell, D-cell	Shuffle exchange	Batcher	HCN and BCN[1]
[1]*Hierarchical Irregular Compound Network (HCN) and Bi-dimensional Compound Network (BCN).*			

set of performance criteria, especially the total cost of ownership. Clearly, not all topologies are designed for DCN applications. Some are designed for telco applications (wireline or wireless phone) and others might be for the general purposes of computer networks, such as a client/server architecture.

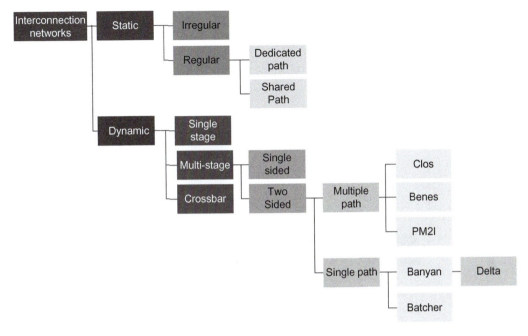

FIGURE 13.23

A simple classification of interconnection networks based on a multistage fast packet switching network.

In the late 1980s, Peter Newman [214] presented a network topology classification based on a multistage fast packet switching network (see Figure 13.23). The mechanism behind this classification was based on control mechanisms employed with the various classes of multistage network. More precisely, if we look from a network routing perspective, it is clear that this classification was designed according to static and dynamic routing, which is similar to a switch operating at layer 2 and 3 of the OSI stack layer model.

If the classification follows the routing mechanism, then static routing means the routing table can only be populated or entered through static routes (or manually preconfigured). To maintain a large network, static routing would be a tedious task. If a network becomes quite complex, static routing may become impossible. The term "static" means "fixed" or "predetermined." In contrast, dynamic routing is a kind of automated routing solution that uses routing algorithms. In a dynamic routing environment, routers can learn the network condition changes automatically and make adjustments accordingly. Dynamic routing doesn't need any human intervention. It is designed for any size and complexity of interconnected network. "Dynamic" stands for flexible. For example, if one router or switch is broken down, the routing table will automatically be upgraded for the existing routing environment.

Following in the fashion Peter Newman's classification, Yang Liu et al. [215] classified DCN topologies into two big categories: "fixed topology" and "flexible topology." Based on authors'

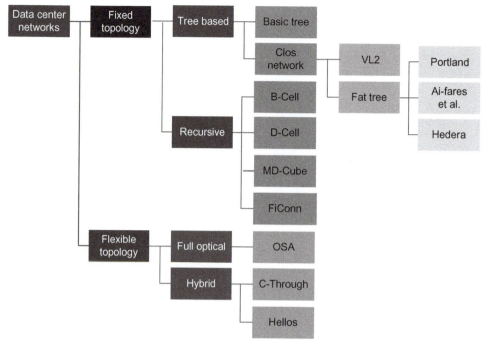

FIGURE 13.24

Classification of data center topology.

definition, "fixed" means the network topology is fixed when it has been deployed. It is not clear what exactly the term of "fixed" really means in this context. What properties of the network topology are fixed from the time when it is deployed?

Is it the physical DCN topology or logical topology or just the routing table configuration? The authors didn't give further explanation of the term or any examples. If the term "fixed" is the same as "static" and "flexible" corresponds to "dynamic," the different classifications of a Clos network do not make sense in the two classifications (see Figure 13.24).

Before Yang Lie et al.'s classification, Yueping Zhang et al. [216] proposed another method of DCN topology classification, which is to divide DCNs into two categories: hierarchical and flat architectures. Zhang et al.'s definition of hierarchical and flat architecture classification is similar to William J Dally et al.'s [213] direct and indirect network because in the DCN hierarchical architecture, server or end nodes are arranged in different levels and in the DCN flat architecture, all servers are placed in a single layer and are interconnected with switches (see Figure 13.25).

Further in the past, Lucian Popa et al. [217] addressed the classification issue from a DCN hardware (switch and server) cost perspective. What they did was classify the DCN topologies into

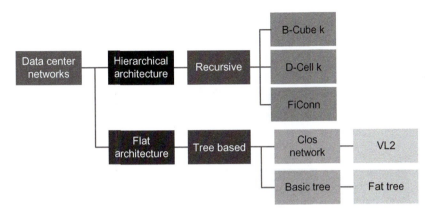

FIGURE 13.25

Classification of DCN into hierarchical and flat architectures (topologies).

three categories: switch only, server only, and Hybrid. Based on the definition of the switch-only topology, data packets forwarding is implemented by the switch fabric exclusively. In contrast, a server-only DCN topology has each server playing two roles:

- Running applications
- Routing or relaying data traffic between servers

Each server is connected to other servers to form a DCN fabric. The hybrid DCN topology adopts both switches and servers as the DCN fabric hardware. If switch-only and server-only are the two extreme solutions for a DCN topology, then the hybrid topology solution is g in the middle (see Figure 13.26).

Based on Section 13.1.1.4, we understand that the routing engine is actually a computer server. If we consider the routing function as being implemented by a server or part of the server as a router, then the DCN topology classification will revert to William J. Dally's interconnection network topology classification.

Jose Duato et al.'s [218] interconnection network classification is much comprehensive than William J Dally's (see Figures 13.27 and 13.28). The classification doesn't only include point-to-point networks, which are direct and indirect networks, but also covers shared medium and hybrid networks. Traditionally, the interconnection network classification focused on the operating mode (synchronous or asynchronous) and network control (centralized, decentralized, or distributed). Because of technology advantages from multicores chips and multiprocessors, the authors shifted the classification criteria from traditional measurements to more significant current benchmarks. The primary principle of Duato et al.'s classification is based on Lionel M. Ni's paper [219], which involved interconnection network (IN) scalability from an IN design perspective. In other words, a scalable IN can effectively accommodate a large range of processors and nodes and the basic building components of an IN are the commoditized network switches, especially cut-through switches or packet switches.

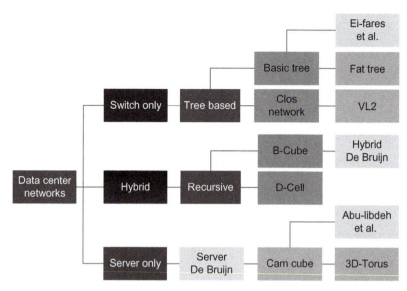

FIGURE 13.26

Switch-only, server-only, and hybrid DCN topologies.

Based on the scalability principle, INs have been classified into three major categories:

- Shared medium networks
- Point-to-point networks
- Hybrid networks

A shared medium networks is a small-scale and contentious network in comparison with other types of network. It allows only one endpoint or device to access the network medium at any given time. As Figure 13.27 shows, the most popular application for shared medium networks are LAN and backplane buses. The typical types of topology are "bus" and "ring." The main issue with the shared medium network is that it is not scalable due to the bandwidth limitations. Therefore, it is not recommended for DCN applications.

Hybrid networks are a combination of shared medium and point-to-point networks. Because the shares medium networks have become a bottleneck, the hybrid network's scalability is not as good as point-to-point networks. Therefore, we will just concentrate on point-to-point networks for DCN application.

From Figure 13.28, we can see that the point-to-point networks are divided into two big categories:

- Direct or router-based networks
- Indirect or switch-based networks

The reason to put both direct and indirect networks into the point-to-point basket is because both networks can be modeled by a graph function G (N, C), where G = graph, N = nodes, and C = communication channel.

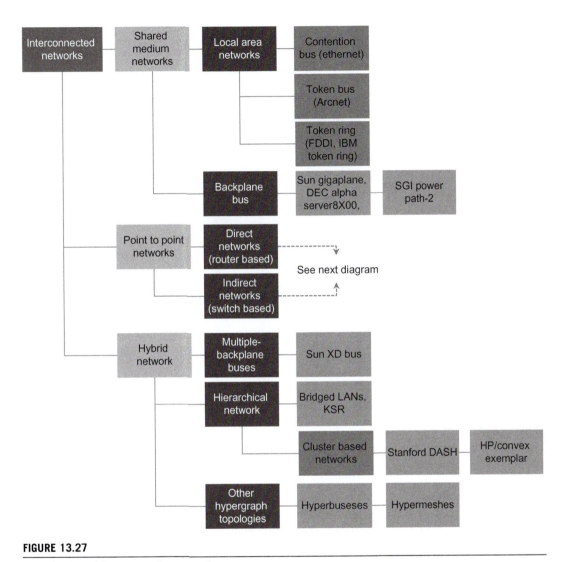

FIGURE 13.27

Classification of interconnection networks.

13.4.1 COMMON DCN TOPOLOGIES

To illustrate the DCN cost model, we will select few common DCN topologies and apply the above performance metrics. We will begin with the switch-based network or basic tree topology because it has been one of most popular topologies for both traditional and modern data centers.

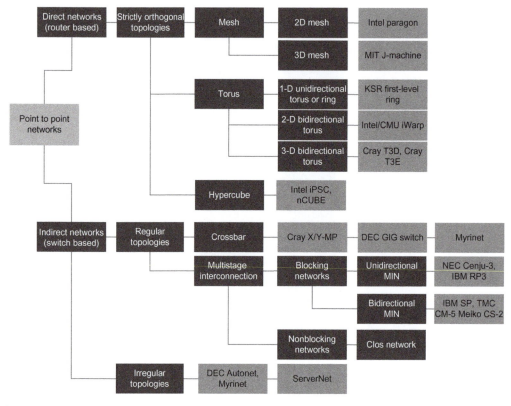

FIGURE 13.28

Point-to-point network topology.

13.4.1.1 Basic trees

The tree-based topology is one of most widely adopted solutions for DCN. It normally consists of three tiers: core, aggregation (sometimes called distribution) and edge (or access). Each tier corresponds to either layer 2 or 3 or both layers of the OSI model (see Figure 13.29).

The basic idea of a tree network topology is that there is only one possible simple path between any two nodes, namely the source and destination. The higher the tier of the tree is, the more severe the communication bottleneck becomes. It is a hierarchical topology where any connected part of the graph can represent the entire graph. It defines a routing algorithm for any irregular topology.

Pros:

- Easy to deploy
- Cheaper than torus and crossbar topologies
- Better for local traffic
- Latency only O(log N), which is relatively low
- Commodity price of network fabric nodes

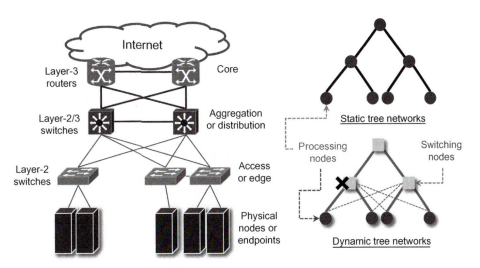

FIGURE 13.29

Typical DCN basic tree topology.

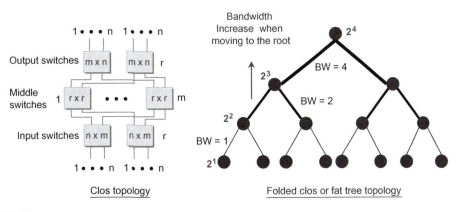

FIGURE 13.30

Clos and folded Clos or fat-tree network topologies.

Cons:

- Root can be bottleneck for data traffic
- Single point of failure

13.4.1.2 Fat tree

In order to improve the root bandwidth performance, one of the solutions is to adopt a fat-tree network topology. A fat tree is a folded Clos network topology. At each tier level, the bandwidth remains constant for any binary node (see Figure 13.30).

The total number of nodes (N) connected to a binary fat tree with k tiers or levels can be represented in the following formula:

$$N(k) = 2^0 + 2^1 + 2^2 + \cdots + 2^k = \frac{(2^k - 1)}{2 - 1} = 2^k - 1$$

Taking the example in Figure 13.30, the number of physical switches (or nodes) would be equal to 15 because k is equal to 4.

13.4.1.3 Commodity switch fabric-based fat tree (Al-Fares)

In 2008, Mohammad Al-Fares et al. [221] proposed a scalable DCN architecture or topology and adopted commodity switches as a network fabric. They argued that even when deploying the highest-end IP switches/routers (as we showed in the above sections, the typical highest-end switches/routers might cost over $100 k, and some types of core routers could be well above a half-million dollars), the nature of the network topology may only provide 50% of the available aggregation bandwidth for the nodes at the edge or access level. Unbalanced DCN bandwidth impacts on DCN performance and some application design and deployment. As a result, a substantial amount of capex and opex have been wasted due to the underutilized capacity of the highest-end switches/routers.

The solution that Al-Fares et al. provided was to leverage a large quantity of commodity Ethernet switches to deliver a DCN with high performance and lower cost. They claimed that this solution has the following advantages:

- Highly scalable interconnection bandwidth
- Backward compatibility
- Commercial off-the-Shelf (COTS) Ethernet switches
- All Ethernet switches identical (lower maintenance cost with one type of spare part)
- Fat tree topology by its nature is nonblocking

The COTS switch fabric organizes the DCN topology into a k-ary fat tree (see Figure 13.31). It consists of k pods and each has two layers (edge and aggregation) of k/2 switches. For every edge switch with k ports, only k/2 numbers are connected to hosting nodes and another k/2 will be connected to the aggregation switch (one level up) (see Figure 13.32).

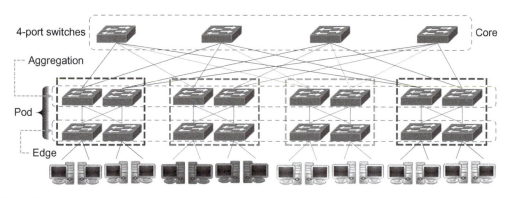

FIGURE 13.31

COTS switch fabric fat tree (k = 4).

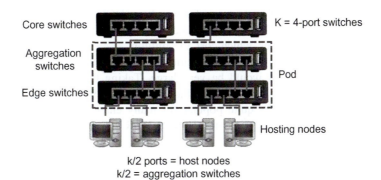

FIGURE 13.32

Connection details of fat tree by COTS Switch Fabric.

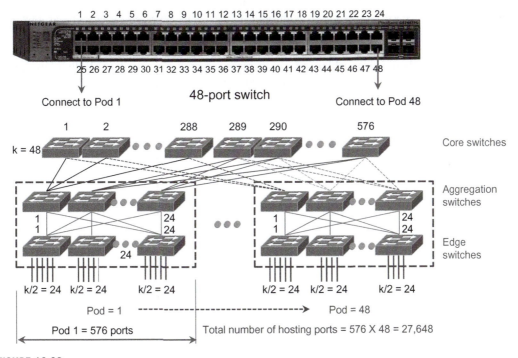

FIGURE 13.33

COTS switch fabric fat tree for cluster interconnects with k = 48.

The paper reviewed different numbers of port switches from 4 up to 48 ports. In general, if the switch has k ports, a fat tree of COTS switch fabric can support $k^3/4$ hosts. The total number of k-port switches is equal to $(k/2)^2$ and each core level switch will connect to each of k pods. The ith port of any core switch is connected to pod$_i$ at the aggregation layer (see Figure 13.33).

The paper claimed that the deployment cost for the above DCN would be $8.64 million dollars. In comparison with traditional DCN topologies and techniques, the COTS switch fabric fat tree solution was about 4.2 times cheaper, which cost $37 million.

However, one of the disadvantages for this solution is that the volume of copper cables or RJ45 to connect all the COTS switches would be very large. Taking the above 48-port switch as an example, the number of interconnection copper cables would be 82,944.

This is why the ToR solution is quite popular for many enterprise DCNs. Before moving to the next DCN topology, let's review ToR and EoR or MoR solutions with regard to the copper cable issue.

13.4.1.4 Top of Rack (ToR) solution

Referring to Figure 13.1, ToR is one of the popular tree-based DCN physical switch fabric designs or network device arrangements. The key advantages of ToR are the following. (1) All copper or RJ45 cables are relatively short and contained within the rack. (2) The Ethernet switches (at ToR) are connected to high density modular or aggregation or distribution Ethernet switches via only two optical fiber cables. Each rack is linked with optical fiber. This saves on expensive and long running copper cables. (3) As a result, we can reduce cold airflow obstacles if a data center facility adopts a raised floor solution. A a lot of Capex could be saved if we minimize floor height. (4) With relatively short copper cables, we can increase server access speed. (5) With a few optical fiber cables, rack management and relocation is made easier and cheaper. These are the key influential reasons why tmany DCN designers prefer ToR to end of rack (EoR) (see Figure 13.34).

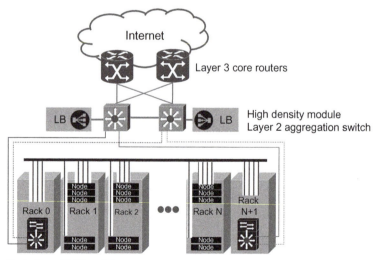

FIGURE 13.34

End of row switch connectivity solution.

However, there is one issue in selecting ToR solution, which is the added burden for management of each ToR switch. For a small size DCN, the ToR solution can get away with the issue of management workload for ToR switches. When the size of the DCN becomes quite large, for example 256 racks, the number of ToR switches would be double or 512. To manage 512 ToR switches would be a tedious task, especially when patching with new firmware or reconfiguring a large volume of ToR switches. It may require a longer planned outage, which is not acceptable for some mission-critical applications.

In addition to management issues, the aggregation switch could become the bottleneck for the ToR solution because the more ports an aggregation switch has, the more likely it is to have a scalability problem, such as a limited number of physical ports, issues with supporting high-bandwidth ToR switches (10 gigabit switches), and limited logical VLAN capacity per VLAN spanning tree (PVST). Taking the above case as an example, if each rack has to support 100 VLANs in single level 2 domain, there will be 25,600 VLANs to support at the aggregation switch site. However, some vendors' products only support a limit number of PVSTs. For example, the typical Cisco Cat 6500 aggregation switch only supports 10,000 PVSTs and the latest Nexus-7000 is only capable of accommodating 16,000 PVSTs.

In short, the ToR solution considers each rack as a single module to establish the DCN tree-based topology. It has the following advantages or pros:

- Flexible and modular setup using per rack solution
- Racks can be easily relocated or upgraded or changed
- Elimination of long running bulk copper cables
- Reduction of copper cable expense
- Ready for future optical fiber cable infrastructure
- Contain copper cables within a rack
- Less cold airflow resistance and lowering of raised floor height

Of course, there are some costs for the ToR solution:

- Logical VLAN capacity bottleneck
- More L2 switches to manage
- Potential physical port scalability issues at aggregation switch level

13.4.1.5 End of Row (EoR) and middle of ROW (MoR) solutions

If there are too many racks to manage, one of alternative is to adopt an end of row (EoR) solution for a tree-based DCN topology. Shown in Figure 13.34, the EoR switch rack can be located on either side or both sides of a row to connect all nodes within the row. Of course, it is not necessary that the location of the switch rack be at the end of row. It can be at any position of the row as long as it is within the row. One of the popular solutions is to place switch racks in the middle of the row (see Figure 13.35).

With the "MoR" solution, the use of extremely long copper cable can be avoided if the rack row is quite long. However, this may be not suitable for a room-based cooling strategy because the airflow is not stable at the end of row and the server racks will generate most of the heat.

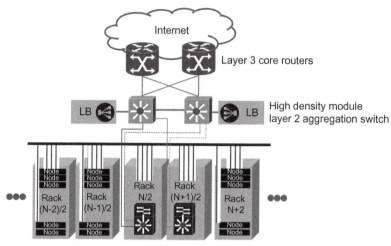

FIGURE 13.35

Middle of row switch connectivity solution.

The main idea of EoR is seeing the row as a module rather a rack. It can be aligned with row-based cooling (refer to Section 9.3). In comparison with a ToR based solution , an EoR-based solution works best with a stable data center environment, in which the infrastructure layout will last for more than three to five years or until the end of the life cycle.

One of the main advantages of the EoR solution is that it uses less switches than ToR. Taking the above example of 256 racks, the EoR solution only needs 64 switches compared with ToR needing 512 switches if each row has eight cabinets (32 rows). The EoR solution has 1/8 the number of switches. However, EoR may increase the switch port density. The higher the port density is, the higher the cost of the switch is. Overall, the switch cost savings may be slightly reduced. In other words, we have 512 commoditized switches vss 64 high-density port switches plus the bulk of longer copper cables.

The lower number of switches doesn't only lower the investment capex but also reduces the opex of a break/fix contract. In addition, the fewer network elements there are, the higher the reliability of the DCN is.

In summary, the EoR or MoR solution provides the following advantages that are almost opposite to the ToR solution; the ToR's cons become the EoR's pros and vice versa:

- Fewer switches to manage
- More reliable DCN
- Reduction in switch capex
- Lower maintenance cost
- Fewer aggregation ports
- Fewer SFP instances in layer 2 domain

The disadvantages of the EoR solution are quite obvious in comparison with the ToR solution:

- More and longer copper cables run
- Less flexible than ToR solution with an incremental investment approach
- Future challenges for optical fiber cable solution
- Higher raised floor to accommodate bulk of running copper cables

In summary, the value of tree-based network topology lies mainly in its good scalability and accessibility.

Up to now, we have reviewed tree network topology extensively from basic tree to fat tree to the latest new type of fat tree, a cluster interconnected fat tree with a COTS switch fabric. The reason to cover these topics is that the majority of past, current, and future data centers will adopt or have adopted a multitier tree topology solution. Actually, Cisco, one of dominant vendors for network hardware equipment, recommends [222] a multitier or hierarchy-based tree topology solution for a DCN.

In summary, a tree-based (common three levels or tiers) topology at least supports the following advantages for DCN infrastructure:

- Scalability
- Accessibility for troubleshooting
- Easier to deploy
- Cost effective
- Better for local traffic
- Lower latency

If we drill down further, we can find that a tree topology actually is a combination of multiple star and bus topologies. One of the major disadvantages is that if any fault happens at the root switch or primary node at the core layer, the entire tree will collapse.

In addition, for fat tree topologies such as the COTS switch fabric solution, one of the major drawbacks is the efficiency of switch use. This solution has only 20% switch port usage. In other words, 8 out of 10 switches will be used for interconnection. In order to overcome some pitfalls of tree-based DCN topologies, recursive DCN topologies have been developed.

13.4.2 RECURSIVE DCN TOPOLOGIES

As we can see in Figure 13.26, recursive DCN topologies basically consist of three major structures: DCell, B-Cube and FiConn. The basic idea is similar as "Fat-Tree" that is built by lower-end switch fabric. Let's investigate DCell DCN topology first.

13.4.2.1 DCell

13.4.2.1.1 Principles of DCell

The method of constructing a DCell structure is to build a standard DCN cell and then repeat it based on the principles of a defined topology. The main goals of DCell are:

- Scalable
- Fault tolerant: no single point of failure (link, server, and rack)
- High network capacity to support bandwidth hungry applications
- Efficient and distributed routing algorithm

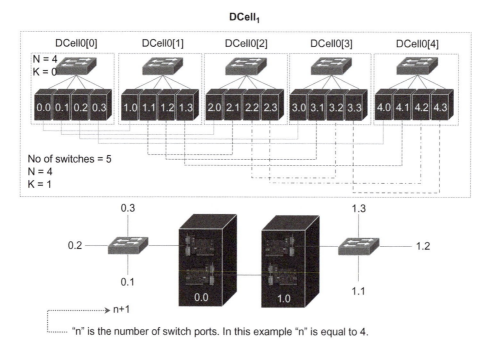

FIGURE 13.36

DCN topology: use $DCell_0$ to form $DCell_1$.

Chuanxiong Guo et al. [223] presented this topology in 2008. Basically, the idea of DCell is not only to rely on standard switches but also to leverage the network interface card (NIC) within the host servers (or physical nodes) to form a DCN topology. The number of NICs for each host is based on the level of DCell. A high-level DCell is built up on low level DCells. The lowest level of DCell is level 0. For example, if a DCell is at level 0, it is denoted as $DCell_0$; if the DCell is at level k, it is marked as $DCell_k$. The switches connected to all host servers are low end or commodity type switches, for example four-port switches (see Figure 13.36).

13.4.2.1.2 Structure of DCell

As we can see in the above figure, five $DCell_0$s form one $DCell_1$. The DCell one level up always has $n + 1$ (n represents the number of switch ports) DCells below, for example, $DCell_1$ has $4 + 1$ $DCell_0$s. If we want expand to $DCell_2$, each server has to have three NICs (see Figure 13.37).

It will be built starting with $DCell_0$ first and then $DCell_1$, and finally $DCell_2$. Because of the size of the page, we use two-port switches to illustrate the mechanism of how to build $DCell_2$. You might notice that each host server has a digital mark in both Figures 13.31 and 13.32. The technical term

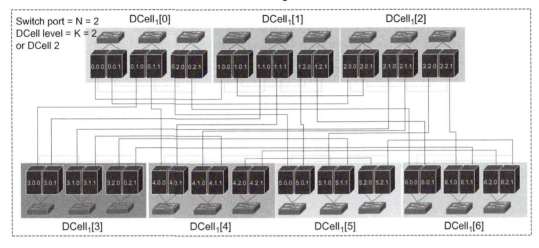

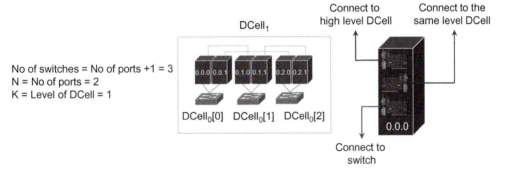

FIGURE 13.37

Use DCell$_1$ to form DCell$_2$ DCN topology with two-port switch.

is "tuple." The technical symbol is [a_1, a_0]. It is a server's unique identification (or ID) in a DCell. In Figure 13.31, the tuple has two digits, for example "0.0" or "1.0." This symbol has two real meanings:

1. The position of the particular server in a DCell (level of DCell).
2. The number of NICs or ports to form the DCell. If it has two digits, the server has two NICs or two ports.

If a server only has two NICs, it can only form DCell$_1$. In order to form DCell$_2$, the server must have at least three NICs (see Figure 13.37). One is to connect a commodity or mini-switch. The second NIC is to connect another server at the same level DCell. The third NIC is to connect to the one level up DCell.

13.4.2.1.3 DCell formula

Chuanxiong Guo's paper used "gk" (just "DC") to represent the number of $DCell_{k-1}s$ in $DCell_k$ (for example in Figure 13.32, k = 2, and the number of $DCell_{k-1=1}s$ is equal to 7) and t_{k-1} (or just "S") for the number of servers within each $DCell_{k-1}$. The total number of servers in $DCell_k$ one level up would be:

$$S_k = DC_{k-1} \times S_{k-1}$$

where k > 0. Taking the above example in Figure 13.32, we have:

$$S_2 = 7 \times 6 = 42$$

In general, we have:

$$S_k = DC_k DC_{k-1} \cdots DC_0 S_0 = S_0 \prod_{i=0}^{k} DC_i$$

and

$$\left(n+\frac{1}{2}\right)^{2^k} - \frac{1}{2} < S_k < (n+1)^{2^k} - 1$$

where k > 0 and "n" is the number of servers in a $DCell_0$. Table 13.4 shows the number of servers in a DCell topology can quickly grow exponentially.

13.4.2.1.4 DCell summary

In summary, the authors argued that the DCell topology is an alternative solution to providing a large-scale DCN with up to several million servers without connecting to expensive core switches or routers. Although many servers are connected to different DCell levels, all servers are on equal footing. The topology has overcome the issue of a single point of failure. Furthermore, it doesn't

Table 13.4 The Mean Value and Standard Deviation of Path Length in Shortest-Path Routing and DCell Routing [223]

N	k	S	Shortest Path		DCell Routing	
No. of Servers in $DCell_0$[1]	DCell Level	Total No. of Servers at $DCell_k$	Mean	Standard Deviation	Mean	Standard Deviation
4	2	420	4.87	1.27	5.16	1.42
5	2	930	5.22	1.23	5.50	1.33
6	2	1,806	5.48	1.18	5.73	1.25
4	3	176,820	9.96	1.64	11.29	2.05
5	3	865,830	10.74	1.59	11.98	1.91
6	3	3,263,442	11.31	1.55	12.46	1.79

[1]*The number of servers in a base unit cell.*

have the bottleneck problem the tree topology has. After all, the strategic direction of the DCell topology is to support all-to-all, many-to-one, and one-to-many traffic patterns.

However, Deke Guo et al. [224] indicated that both DCell and BCube are not truly expandable topologies for a DCN because of the additional NIC installation requirements and the expansion trend (exponential). A NIC may be relatively cheaper in comparison with other network devices but human labor and project management for hundreds of thousands of servers is not much cheap. DCell may be good for a mega data center or "big band" capacity growth but not good for an incremental approach. For example, $DCell_0$ with a four-port switch has four servers. $DCell_1$ with a four-port switch expands to 20 servers. $DCell_2$ with a four-port switch quickly reaches 420 (21 times). $DCell_3$ with a four-port switch explodes to 176,820 (or 421 times). Clearly, this approach to capacity growth is not practical for many enterprise data centers.

In addition to the above disadvantages, the traffic of DCell is imbalanced, which much more traffic carried by the level 0 DCell rather than evenly distributed to other links. In short, it still has not resolved the bottleneck issue for the tree topology.

13.4.2.2 *BCube*

In order to resolve some issues of the DCell solution, such as traffic bottlenecks and NIC installation, Chuanxiong Guo et al. [225] proposed another DCN topology in 2009, which was called BCube. Instead of adopting more NICs within hosting servers to construct a DCN, the BCube solution is to leverage more COTS switches to form a DCN so that the solution can save a lot of the trouble in upgrading a large quantity of physical nodes (or servers).

13.4.2.2.1 Principles of BCube

The core principle of the BCube topology is that it is a server-based network, where each server has multiple NICs or network ports (Guo et al. suggested that typically, the number of ports should be no more than four) to connect different BCube levels of switches. In essence, a hosting server doesn't only host many applications but also acts as network fabric to form a BCube topology (see Figure 13.38).

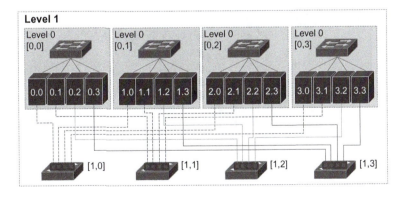

FIGURE 13.38

A typical level 1 BCube topology with four-port switch fabric.

The main goals of the BCube topology are to resolve the following issues:

- Support for bandwidth intensive applications
- Flexible to cope with all traffic patterns (one-to-one, one-to-many, one-to-all, and many-to-many)
- Fault tolerance with a gradual approach to performance degradation
- Container-based data center application (standard 20 or 40 feet or 12 m × 2.35 m × 238 m shipping container, see Figure 13.39), which is typically required to connect a few thousand servers

In comparison with the fat tree topology, the paper claimed that BCube's one-to-X (one-to-one, one-to-many, and one-to-all) traffic throughput is two times better than fat tree and a three times improvement over the MapReduce application. Similar to the fat tree topology, BCube still has to run a bulk of copper cables. However, because it is mainly focusing on the data center in a shipping container application, the length of copper cable is very limited, less than 12 meters.

In comparison with DCell, the authors argued that BCube provides bottleneck-free traffic throughput and supports much higher network capacity. For any network expansion, a server upgrade is not necessary.

13.4.2.2.2 Structure of BCube

Similar to DCell, the BCube network topology is also fabricated by two network components: a COTS switch and hosting servers (see Figure 13.33). The upper level BCube is built on lower level BCubes.

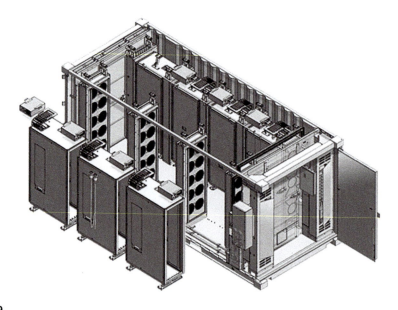

FIGURE 13.39

Shipping container-based modular data center (MDC)

13.4.2.2.3 BCube formula

The base level BCube is $BCube_0$, which consists of n number of servers with one physical n-port switch. For example, a particular $BCube_0$ may consists of four servers with one four-port switch. To build a $BCube_1$ in this instance, we will require four four-port switches with four $BCube_0$ modules. In general, a $BCube_k$ ($k \geq 1$) consists of n $BCube_{k-1}$ components with n^k n-port switches. Each server within a $BCube_k$ should have $k + 1$ NICs or ports. A $BCube_k$ topology can support N servers that are combined with S_k n-port switches at the $k + 1$ level:

$$N = n^{k+1} \text{ (no. of servers to be supported)}$$
$$S_k = n^k \text{ (no. of switches)}$$

Taking the above $BCube_0$ that consists of four servers with a four-port switch as an example, its $BCube_1$ can support 16 servers and combine with four four-port switches at level 1 ($N = 4^{1+1} = 16$ and $S_k = 4^1 = 4$). Further, the $BCube_2$ here can support 64 servers and combine with 16 four-port switches at level 2 ($N = 4^{2+1} = 64$ and $S_k = 4^2 = 16$) (see Figures 13.40 and 13.41).

In general, the way of forming $BCube_k$ is that it consists of "n" $BCube_{k-1}$s labeled from 0 to $n - 1$. Each server will be marked as $[a_k, a_{k-1}, \ldots a_0]$ ($a_i \in [0, n - 1]$, $i \in [0, k]$) in $BCube_k$. For example, a server of $BCube_1$ will be marked as [0,0], [0,1] ... [3,3] (see Figure 13.39) and a server of in $BCube_2$ with $n = 4$ will be marked as [0,0,0], [0,0,1] ... [3,3,3] (see Figures 13.41 and 13.42).

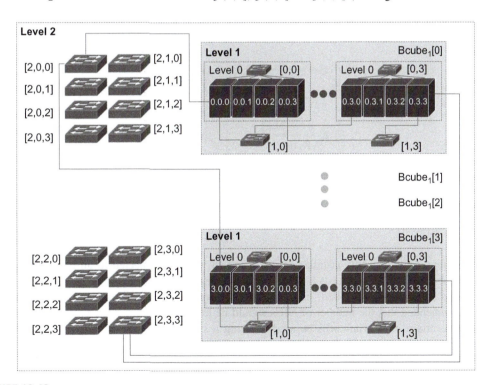

FIGURE 13.40

Level 2 BCube topology.

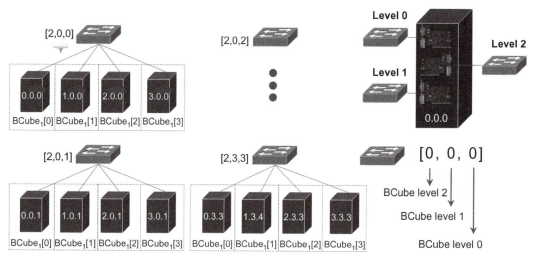

FIGURE 13.41

Level 2 BCube topology connection details.

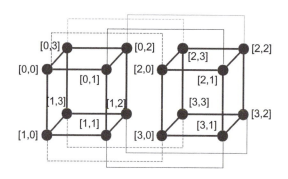

FIGURE 13.42

2-ary 4-cube (hypercube).

Each digit represents one NIC installed in a server that will be connected to an n-port switch. To form a BCube$_0$, a server only needs one NIC, For BCube$_1$, a server needs two NICs; for BCube$_k$, a server needs k NICs to be installed. Each NIC will be connected to its own level of switches. The paper recommended that the number of NICs should be less than four.

Likewise, the n-port switch will be marked using a similar approach as [L, s_{k-1}, s_{k-2} ... s_0], where the letter "L" stands for level ($0 < L < k$). For example in Figure 13.42, [2,0,0], [2,0,1] ... [2,3,3] means level 2 or BCube$_2$ switches.

In essence, the switches within the BCube topology can only be connected to servers. There will be no switch-to-switch direct connections in the BCube topology. The role of a switch is similar to dummy crossbars that connect many neighbor servers and let traffic flow.

Table 13.5 Performance Comparison of BCube and Other Network Topologies				
	Tree	**Fat Tree**	**DCell**	**BCube**
One-to-one	1	1	$k'+1$[1]	$k+1$
One-to-many	1	1	$k'+1$	$k+1$
One-to-all	1	1	$\leq k'+1$	$k+1$
All-to-all (ABT)[2]	n	n	$n/2^{k'}$	$n(n-1)/(n-1)$
Traffic nalance	No	Yes	No	Yes
Graceful degradation	Bad	Fair	Good	Good
Wire no.	$n(n-1)/(n-1)$	$n\log_{n/2}(n/2)$	$(k'/2+1)/n$	$n\log_n n$
Switch upgrade	No	Yes	No	No

[1] A level 2 ($k'=2$) DCell with $n=8$ is enough for a shipping container type of DCN. k' is smaller than k.
[2] Note: Aggregate Bottleneck Throughput (ABT).

If we replace the BCube's switches and their n links to servers with an $n \times (n-1)$ full mesh, the result will be a generalized hypercube (see Figure 13.42). The number of server ports for a generalized hypercube is $(n-1) \times (k+1)$ [n = number of switch ports and k is the level of the hypercube].

In comparison with hypercube topology, the number of server ports in the BCube topology is far less than in a generalized hypercube. For example, if the number of switch ports n = 16 and the cube level is k = 2, then for a hypercube, the total number of server ports will be 45. However, for a BCube, the total number of server ports will only be 3. This would save a lot on NIC costs. Of course, practically, 45 server ports would be too many for a computer network.

In addition to the physical structure of a BCube, it runs a Source Routing Protocol (SRP) logically. SRP will be installed in all BCube servers. What SRP does is take advantage of the multipath BCube topology and actively probe the network. It supports:

- BCube traffic balance
- Fault detection and handling without link state distribution
- Fine-tuning BCube capacity degradation as faulty servers or switches increase

13.4.2.2.4 BCube summary

The Virtual Layer 2 (VL2) topology (we will this in the following section) and BCube share many similar design principles, with both topologies providing high capacity to all servers. Guo et al. argued that the BCube topology is better for handling one-to-many traffic patterns because the BCube SRP adopts an active probing mechanism to process traffic load balancing while VL2 introduces IP address decoupling and a server location directory that is totally random (see Table 13.5).

In order to compare costs among common topologies, the paper provided Table 13.6 to highlight costs. As we can see from the table, the cost difference is not significant.

BCube is a server-based network topology. It does provide an alternative DCN topology other than nasic tree or fat Tree. However, one of issues with BCube is that like DCell, you can't build

Table 13.6 Cost and Power Comparison for Four Topologies

Topology	Cost ($k)			Power (kW)			Wire No.
Device[1]	Switch	NIC	Total	Switch	NIC	Total	
Basic tree[2]	55	10	4,161	4.4	10	424	2,091
Fat tree[3]	92	10	4,198	10	10	430	10,240
DCell	10	41	4,147	1.2	20	431	3,468
BCube	51	41	4,188	5.8	20	435	8,192

[1]The unit price of server = $2,000 and power consumption = 200 W.
[2]Switch of basic tree = 48-port D-Link DGS-3100-48 @ $1,250/103 W, quantity = 44 (the cheapest switch on the market).
[3]DCell, BCube and fat tree = 8-port D-Link DGS-1008D @ $40/4.5 W switch, quantity DCell = 256, BCube = 1280,
Fat Tree = 2304. A one-port NIC = $5 with 5 W power consumption and four-port = $20 with 10 W.

BCube partially. As the authors indicated in the paper, if it is partial, BCube routing will not work properly for some server pairs. It might still be able to establish network path, but it reduces the network capacity. In other words, server capacity increase is not very flexible in terms of rack by rack. This will lead to the issue of overcapacity investment.

13.4.3 OTHER DCN TOPOLOGIES

13.4.3.1 Virtual layer 2 (VL2)

When we discussed the topology of BCube, we mentioned VL2 in comparison with the BCube and DCell topologies. Here, we will explore the details of the VL2 mechanism. The physical appearance of the VL2 topology is actually a fat tree or folded Clos network. The focus of VL2 is not on the physical topology but rather the virtual layer of routing data packets. To borrow Cartesian's vocabulary, VL2 is for solving the "mind" problem rather than the body problem. Actually, all the previous DCN topologies are "body" problems.

If all previous DCN topologies that we have discussed could be considered as dealing with investment issues, then VL2's goal is to address an operations issue for the existing DC infrastructure. Just as Albert Greenberg et al. [226] indicated, today's DCN is facing four primary issues:

- Conventional DCN architectures, such as tree-based topologies, heavily rely on high-cost hardware (switch, router, and gateway). The capacity of physical resources among the different tree branches is not evenly distributed and very often oversubscribed by factors of 1:5 or 1:80. Some branches may oversubscribe as high as over 1:240. As a result, this really eliminates communication among hosting servers. For a virtualized environment, this will jeopardize the action of vMotion. It wil create congestion hot spots for one part of the DCN while other parts of the DCN have too many resources.
- Most data centers will host multiple different applications and many applications share the same physical resources. However, when one application experiences traffic congestion, others will not experience the issue and continue to flood the network that has already been congested, and all applications sharing this branch will suffer collateral damage.

- In order to achieve scalability, conventional networks divide IP addresses among VLANs and assign them to servers. This approach will VMs with the same IP address from being migrated out of the original VLAN (see Figure 13.43).
- The fragmented IP address pool will increase the workload for IT admins when hosting servers must be reassigned to different applications. Ultimately, this slows down the speed of server deployment and reduces IT agility.

13.4.3.1.1 Principles of VL2

The main issues that VL2 is trying to resolve are:

- Eliminate any traffic hot spots and balance the DCN resource pool.
- Perform isolation or traffic congestion alerts and stop traffic flooding within the DCN topology.y
- Use layer 2 semantics or flat addressing, where any IP address can be connected to any port of an Ethernet switch so that any VM can use vMotion to go to any physical node with a portable IP address.

The design principles of VL2 are:

- Randomizing to cope with traffic volatility by utilizing Valiant Load Balancing (VLB) (see Figure 13.44) and coping with traffic congestion by utilizing TCP's E2E control mechanism
- Leveraging existing proven networking technology, such as Equal-Cost Multipath (ECMP) forwarding IP anycasting and multicasting
- Separating server names from their locations, which is separating application-specific addresses (AAs) from their location-specific addresses (LAs)
- Relying on end systems by using data center hosts' programming capabilities (the VL2 directory system is located in servers rather than switches)

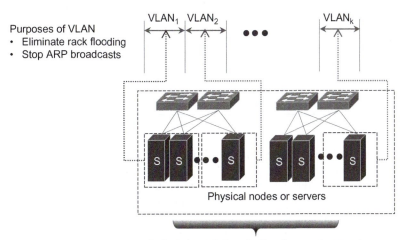

FIGURE 13.43

VLAN issues with virtualized environment.

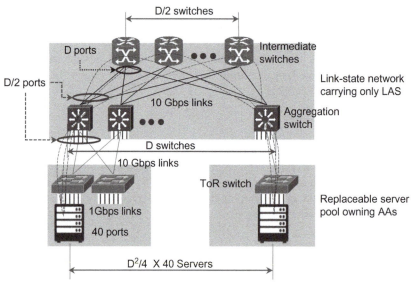

FIGURE 13.44

Valiant Load Balancing (VLB) to handle traffic volatility.

Table 13.7 Physical Node Degree (D) of Available Switches and No. of Servers in Resource Pool

No. of Ports per Aggregation Switch = D	Servers Connected to ToR Switch	Total No. of Servers in the Resource Pool
4	40	160
24	40	5,760
48	40	23,040
144	40	207,360

Based on Figure 13.44, we can see that the network topology is built with two separate address pools. One has LAs and the other uses AAs. The Clos topology can work quite well with VLB by indirectly forwarding traffic through an intermediate switch at the top tier or spin of the network. Any server will take a random path up to the randomly selected intermediate switch and reach down to its destination via a random path as well. If an aggregation switch radix becomes high, the total number of servers in the resource pool will become larger. Here is the formula to calculate the total number of servers in a resource pool (see Table 13.7):

$$Total\ no.\ of\ servers = \frac{D^2}{4} \times Servers\ connected\ to\ ToR\ switch$$

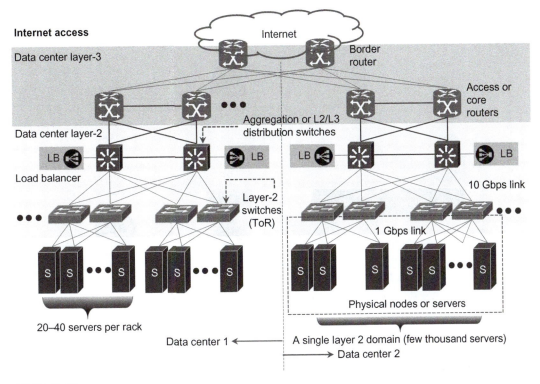

FIGURE 13.45

Conventional DCN with folded Clos or fat tree topology.

13.4.3.1.2 Structure of VL2

The physical part of VL2 consists of a folded Clos or fat tree network topology fabricated with low-end or low-cost switches. To illustrate the mechanisms of VL2, the authors connected the physical DCN as in Figure 13.45.

- 20–40 servers per rack are connected to two layer 2 switches.
- The links between servers and switches are 1 Gbps.
- The links between layer 2 switches (ToR and aggregation switches) are 10 Gbps.
- The links among different data centers are connected by border routers.
- The network is built with two separated address pools (LAs and AAs). The link state network is only carrying LAs but the replaceable server pool will have AAs.

In the virtual part, VL2 will deploy two software components:

- VL2 agents
- Directory system

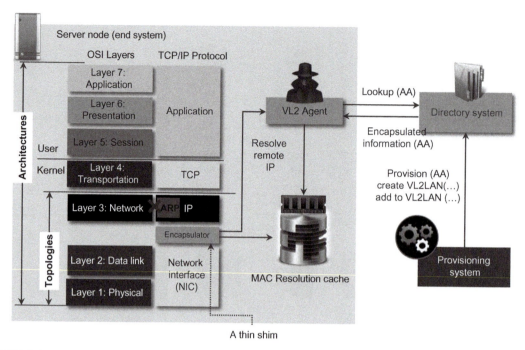

FIGURE 13.46

Logical part of VL2 topology.

This creates a so-called layer 2.5 or a thin shim of a protocol stack between layer 2 and layer 3 in the TCP/IP network protocol for servers to implement functions that are not available in "dummy switches" (see Figure 13.46).

This creates an illusion that hosting servers are connected to a big noninterfering data center that has a wide layer 2 switch pool (see Figure 13.47).

13.4.3.1.3 Summary of VL2

VL2 is a firmware-based DCN traffic balancer for network switches. Its aims are to resolve traffic balancing issues in the cloud environment of a data center network. It will increase the utilization rate of data center resources. Subsequently, it can reduce the unit cost of virtual machine (VMs) or reduce both capex and opex for an existing data center.

VL2 can potentially increase the oversubscription rate. For example, a typical 128-port switch may cost $10,000 and be physically able to connect to 64 servers (with half the switch ports used for switch interconnections). In a virtual environment, each physical node (server) may have a one to four VM ratio. VL2 will enable the switch to handle not only oversubscription traffic VMs (256 VMs) but also it will have the capacity of interconnection switch ports in terms of bandwidth.

The paper claims that building an oversubscription VL2 network can be approximately 14 times cheaper than any conventional data center network. The cost would be 14 to 20 times cheaper based on the oversubscription ratio ranging from 1:1 to 1:23.

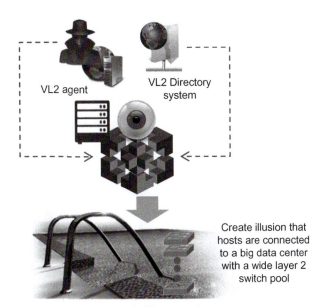

Create illusion that
hosts are connected
to a big data center
with a wide layer 2
switch pool

FIGURE 13.47

Logical components of VL2.

However, VL2 isn't without cost. One of the issues with VL2 is that VLB uses a randomization approach to handle data traffic. It can't differentiate the priority of data traffic. What VLB does is treat all data traffic equally and make them all average cases. In other words, VLB will reduce network performance for prioritized applications.

In short, if an application can tolerate the data traffic latency or performance degradation, VL2 is worthwhile to be implement to reduce both capex and opex. If the business application cannot tolerate data traffic latency, then VL2 shouldn't be considered.

Based on the VL2 topology analysis, we may be able to find another way to improve network utilization rate. The physical network topology doesn't mean everything. By leveraging TCP/IP protocol stack, we can dramatically improve the network utilization rate in a "good" data center, which may only have a 10% to 30% network utilization rate.

The VL2 approach is to liberate servers' additional capability into a large and uniform resource pool.

13.4.3.2 Conventional butterfly and flattened butterfly

In addition of VL2, people have also developed a dragonfly topology for DCN. It can save lot on cabling costs. In order to understand the dragonfly, we should clarify the concept of the conventional butterfly, flattened butterfly and Dilated Flattened Butterfly (2DFB) topologies.

The original butterfly network topology was developed when Bolt Beranek and Newman (BBN) Technologies (now merged into Raytheon) worked to resolve the issues with massively parallel computing in 1982.

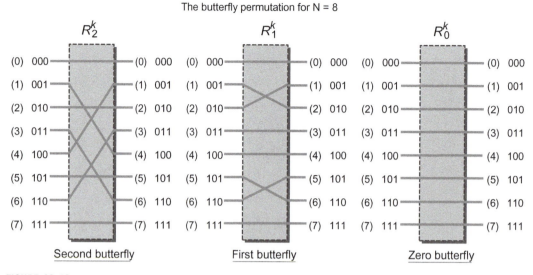

FIGURE 13.48

The butterfly permutation for N = 8 [218].

The term "butterfly" means a method of combining or permutating connections among multi-stage switches network in order to achieve switch or routing path diversity and increase network reliability or fault tolerance.

For any ith k-ary butterfly permutation R_i^k ($0 \leq i \leq n - 1$) we have:

$$R_i^k(a_{n-1} \ldots a_{i+1}a_{i-1} \ldots a_1a_0) = a_{n-1} \ldots a_{i+1}a_0a_{i-1} \ldots a_1a_i$$

where the a_i is an arbitrary port number. For example, the ith butterfly permutation interchanges the 0th and ith digits of the index. The following example (see Figures 13.48 and 13.49) illustrates the butterfly permutation for k = 2, i = [0,1, 2], and N = 8 (N is the number of nodes or inputs).

The flattened butterfly network topology was proposed by John Kim et al. [227] in 2007. The main idea of the flattened butterfly is to leverage a high radix switch network in order to improve the network cost efficiency.

13.4.3.2.1 Principle of flattened butterfly

The principle of the flattened butterfly is to combine or to flatten the data traffic routers in each row of the network into a single router (see Figure 13.50).

The conventional butterfly network topology consisting of higher radix switches with k-ary and n-fly is capable of reducing the network latency and cost, but the issue is that it does not have path diversity, which leads to lower throughput for adversarial data traffic pattern. In contrast, a folded Clos topology can support multipath and arbitrary traffic patterns without suffering any throughput degradation. However, the issue with folded Clos or fat tree is that they are too expensive. As we indicated before, the switch port utilization rate is only 20%. The cost of fat tree is nearly twice the

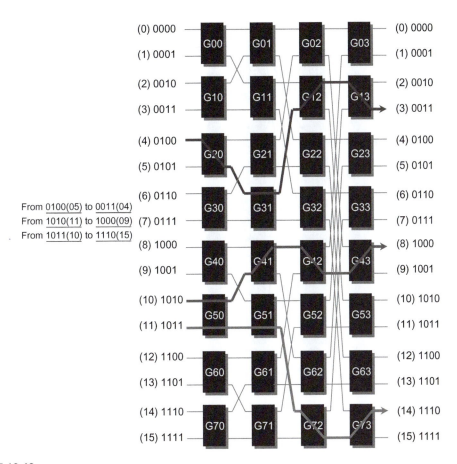

FIGURE 13.49

The conventional 2-ary and 4-fly butterfly.

conventional butterfly for the same amount of network capacity. The flattened butterfly solution can resolve this dilemma.

13.4.3.2.2 Structure of flattened butterfly

If we amplify the right side of Figure 13.50, the flattened butterfly data traffic routers, we find it is combining or flattening the routers in each row of the network into a single router (or path) (see Figure 13.51).

In the Figure 13.51, we extracted all the routers of the conventional butterfly from Figure 13.50 to illustrate how the butterfly routers (k-ary and n-fly) have been combined into single routes. The routers of R0 and R1 in Figure 13.50 have become R0′. Similarly, routers R2 and R3 has become R1′ and so on. After the combination, all butterfly channels have been flattened as a single bidirectional channel or two unidirectional channels (see the right side of Figure 13.51).

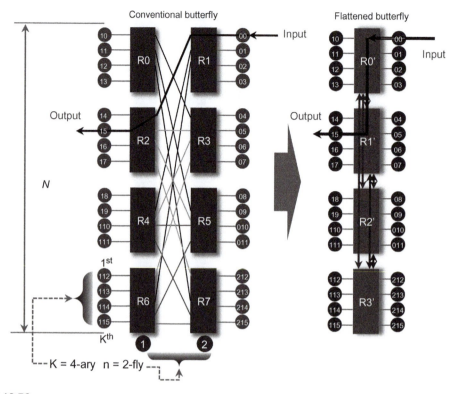

FIGURE 13.50

4-ary, 2-fly butterfly and 4-ary, 2-fly flattened butterfly.

13.4.3.2.3 Flattened butterfly formula

In general, for the conventional butterfly, we can calculate the size of a network with following formula:

$$N = (n + 1)2^n \text{ or } N = (n + 1)k^n$$

Where n = number of flies in the butterfly topology (n = 0, 1, ..., n) and k is the number of arrays of a node. If the interconnection is a fat-tree-based network topology, k is equal to 2.

For the flattened butterfly, we can defined the following formula:

$$j = i + \left[m - \left(\frac{i}{k^{d-1}} \bmod k \right) \right] k^{d-1}$$

$$k' = n(k - 1) + 1$$

$$N \leq \left\lfloor \frac{k}{n'+1} \right\rfloor^{(n'+1)} \quad and \quad n' = n - 1$$

$$k' = \left(\frac{k}{n'+1} - 1 \right)(n' + 1) + 1$$

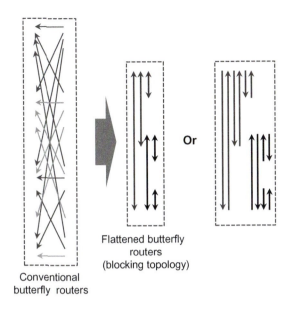

Flattened butterfly
routers
(blocking topology)

Conventional
butterfly routers

FIGURE 13.51

Conventional butterfly routers and flattened butterfly routers.

Where j is the any butterfly router connected to the i router, m is any number from 0 to k − 1, dimension d is any number from 1 to n′ = n − 1, and k′ is the radix. For example (see Figure 13.52), R4′ of the flattened butterfly is connected to R5′ in dimension "D" = 1, R6′ in dimension "D" = 2, and R0′ in dimension "D" = 3.

13.4.3.2.4 Flattened butterfly summary

Ultimately, the flattened butterfly topology can bring cost reduction benefits. John Kim et al. claimed that in comparison with the folded Clos or fat tree topology, flattened butterfly can save 35%−53% in cable link capex. The percentage cost reduction is dependent on network size. For example, a fat tree network with the size of N = 1k would require 2048 link cables. In contrast, the same size flattened butterfly network would only need 31 × 32 = 992 link cables. For a smaller size of network, such as N < 1k, the flattened butterfly would achieve 35%−38% cost savings over Folded clos. For large networks (N ≥ 4k), the flattened butterfly can achieve as high as a 53% cost reduction.

Obviously, the flattened butterfly is built upon the conventional butterfly network topology. If the radix size is quite high, such as 64, the conventional butterfly still can maintain a lower cost network as long as the size of network is within 1k < N < 4k and the number of flies are kept to no more than 2. However, for N > 4k and n > 2, the cost of the flattened butterfly will be much better than the conventional one.

If we fix the network size, for example N = 4k, we have different options for the flattened butterfly network in terms of different array, fly, and radix values (see Table 13.8).

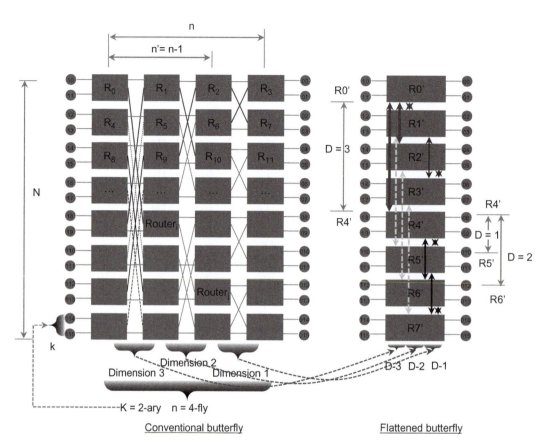

FIGURE 13.52

From a conventional butterfly to a flattened butterfly for k = 2-ary and n = 4-fly.

Table 13.8 Different k, n, and k′ Combinations or Options for Network Size N = 4k					
k-ary	n-fly	k′ Radix	Dimension n′ = n − 1	Cost Increase per Node	Network Size
2	12	12	11		
4	6	19	5	300% per n′ = 1	
8	4	29	3		N = 4k
16	3	46	2	45% per n′ = 1	
64	2	127	1		

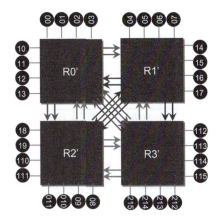

2-Dilated flattened
butterfly (2DFB) routers
(non-blocking topology)

FIGURE 13.53

2-Dilated Flattened Butterfly (2DFB) nonblocking topology.

The paper concluded that the higher the n-fly is, the lower the average cable cost should be. However, for a given N, the higher the radix or lower the dimension of the connection is, the higher the performance and the lower the costs. In other words, the average link cable cost decline will be offset by an increase in the number of links and n-flies. The cost per node can increase by 45% from $n' = 1$ to $n' = 2$ and by 300% from $n' = 1$ to $n' = 5$.

Overall, the flattened butterfly topology has the following advantages:

- Lower hop count than fat tree
- Better path diversity than a conventional butterfly
- About 50% cheaper than fat tree for the same network capacity with load-balanced traffic

The issue with the flattened butterfly topology is that network load imbalancing would occur for high radix routers. As Ajithkumar Thamarakuzhi et al. [228] indicated in their paper, the flattened butterfly is after all a blocking network, although it is a cost-effective topology. This blocking phenomenon will impact on the network performance when all network nodes are transmitting and receiving data at full network bandwidth.

13.4.3.2.5 2-Dilated Flattened Butterfly (2DFB)

In order to resolve this issue, Ajithkumar Thamarakuzhi et al. proposed a solution so called a 2-Dilated Flattened Butterfly (2DFB) switching network (see Figure 13.53).

The 2DRB topology adopts the Network Field Programmable Gate Array (or NetFPGA) [229] as a switch network fabric. In comparison with other network topologies (see Tables 13.9 and 13.10), the paper argues that 2DFB is a nonblocking high-speed network with reduced cost.

13.4.3.3 Dragonfly topology

The dragonfly topology is another interconnection network solution that was presented by John Kim et al. [230] in 2008 after the flattened butterfly network topology proposal. The term

Table 13.9 Network Topologies Comparison

Network Topology	Hypercube	Folded Clos	2DFB
No. of switches or routers	N	$\dfrac{N}{k}Log_kN$	$k^{[log_kN]-1}$
Internal bandwidth needed for each switch	$(Log_2N) + 1$	2k	$2([log_kN] - 1)(k - 1) + k$
No. of links	$\dfrac{N(log_2N)}{2}$	$N([log_kN] - 1)$	$\dfrac{(k^{([Log_kN]-1)})(k - 1)([log_kN] - 1)}{2}$

Table 13.10 Resource Comparison for Different Network Topologies

Total Number of Nodes	N = 256			N = 4,096			N = 65,536		
Network Topology	No. of Links	No. of Routers	Router Internal BW	No. of Links	No. of Routers	Router Internal BW	No. of Links	No. of Routers	Router Internal BW
Hypercube	1,024	256	9	24,576	4,096	13	524,288	65,536	17
16-ary folded Clos, k = 16	256	24	32	8,192	640	32	196,608	14,336	32
16-ary flattened butterfly, k = 16	120	16	31	3,840	256	46	92,160	4,096	61
16-ary 2DFB, k = 16	120	16	46	3,840	256	76	92,160	4,096	106
32-ary folded Clos, k = 32	256	12	64	8,192	320	64	196,608	7,168	64

"dragonfly" is used because the proposed topology has a wide body (local channel interconnections) but narrow wings (global channels).

A good network topology design is basically dependent on the performance and cost of the network. The network cost is determined by the cost of longer optical fiber cables, especially interrack cables. Therefore, reducing the amount or length of thes cables can lower the cost of a network.

Normally, a high-radix network requires longer optical cables than a low-radix one. The purpose of the dragonfly solution is to reduce both network diameter and optical cable costs to increase "pin-bandwidth" (or port) capability by leveraging high-radix routers. In other words, the aim of the dragonfly solution is to focus on increasing port quantity (or high radix) per router rather than bandwidth per port (or fat ports) with low radix.

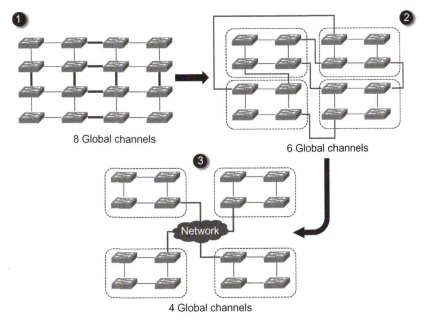

FIGURE 13.54

Evolution of reducing global channels.

13.4.3.3.1 Principle of dragonfly solution

The principle of the dragonfly solution is to increase the efficiency of a high-radix network. The dragonfly reorganizes a few high-radix routers into a virtual router with a few global channels. Only a minimal amount of routed packets will reach or pass through more than one global channel. In essence, it reduces the number of global channels of high-radix networks. Figure 13.54 shows the evolution of reducing the number of global channels for a 4×4 mesh interconnection network from eight global channels to four.

John Kim et al. indicated the dragonfly topology can save 20% in costs in comparison with a flattened butterfly topology and up to 52% versus a folded Clos for a network with 16 nodes.

13.4.3.3.2 Structure of dragonfly

A dragonfly topology is a typical hierarchical network that is composed of three levels of network components (see Figure 13.55):

- Routers or switches
- Groups
- System

At the bottom level, each router or switch can connect to "p" number of nodes with "a − 1" number of local channels (shown as yellow lines) that link with other routers in the same group, for instance group G_0 with "h" global channels to talk to other groups (shown as green lines).

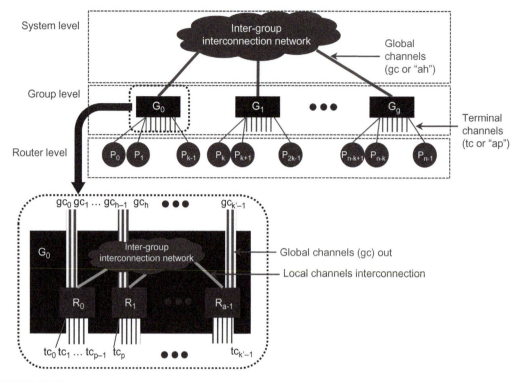

FIGURE 13.55

Structure of dragonfly topology.

Subsequently, we will have the k links or degrees for each router.

A group (blue color) of a dragonfly will have "a" routers (from R_0 to R_{a-1}) that are connected with both local and global channels. Each group has "ap" links to end nodes and "ah" connections to global channels. As a result, all routers will become a virtual router that has a total of $k' = a(p + h)$ channels. The size of k' will be far great than k (radix of the routers) or $k'7 \gg k$. This characteristic will enable the dragonfly to minimize the number of global channels.

13.4.3.3.3 Dragonfly formula

In a maximum-sized dragonfly, there will be only one global channel between each pair of groups. The formula for the maximum size of a dragonfly can be defined as follows:

$$N = ap(ah + 1)$$

The above equation illustrates that we can have up to "g" groups:

$$g = ah + 1$$

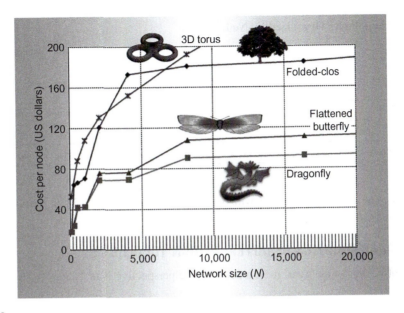

FIGURE 13.56

Cost comparison among different network topologies [231]

Each router has k radix:

$$k = p + a + h - 1$$

For each virtual router, we will have k' virtual radix:

$$k' = a(p + h)$$

The dragonfly parameters "a," "p," and "h" are arbitrary values. However, in order to balance the network traffic load, the network should have:

$$a = 2p = 2h$$

13.4.3.3.4 Dragonfly summary

Ultimately, the dragonfly topology sets up a virtual network boundary by dividing local and global traffic channels. It will be very helpful in reducing the data center's link costs by reducing the length of optical cable.

In term of cost comparisons, the authors provided other four alternative topologies: 3D torus, folded Clos (fat tree) and flattened butterfly to demonstrate that the cost reduction would be significant for a large size of network, >5,000 nodes (see Figure 13.56). It would be 20% better than flattened butterfly and 52% better than folded Clos for the same bandwidth.

However, Natasa Maksi et al. [232] argued that the assumption of the dragonfly topology is dependent on the commoditized price of a certain quantity of switches. In other words, the cost of a commoditized switch can be neglected in their cost model. This assumption should be reviewed or revisited if a high-end switch has many advantageous technologies and routing algorithms built in.

Table 13.11 Topologies Organized by Node Degree

Link Types	Type of Network Topology
Node degree 1	Shared bus
Node degree 2	Linear array, ring
Node degree 3	Binary tree, fat tree, shuffle exchange
Node degree 4	Two-dimensional mesh (illiac, torus)
Node degree greater than 4	n-cube, n-dimensional mesh, k-ary, n-cube

In essence, the dragonfly topology will only have cost saving benefits if the majority of data center traffic is localized in nature.

13.4.4 CHARACTERISTICS OF DIFFERENT DCN TOPOLOGIES

A summary of network topologies from a node degree perspective is in Tables 13.11 and 13.12.

13.5 CHARACTERISTICS OF CLOUD DATA CENTER NETWORK

Based on today's virtualization technology, a cloud data center network should have at least four types of networks either physically or virtually:

- Management network
- Kernel network (VMkernel or XenKernel or Windows Kernel)
- Virtual machine (VM) network
- Storage network

13.5.1 MANAGEMENT NETWORK

The management network manages the DCN virtual environment or hypervisor control system. For example, if the hypervisor is VMware vSphere, then VMware vCenter Server, ESXi Server Console and other management applications should be running on this network. It is the lifeline for a virtualized environment. The primary goal of a management network is to monitor, manage, create, deploy, configure, and upgrade VMs and hosts within the virtualized environment. If the management network is down, the network might still be running, but it would be like a car without a steering wheel.

For security reasons, some argue that remote access devices should be excluded from the management network, such as Dell Remote Access Controller (RAC) or HP Integrated-Light-Out (ILO) or Cisco UCS Cisco Integrated Management Controller (CIMC), but in theory, they should be included in the management network. There will be many pros and cons to including remote access from a management network.

If we separate the remote access network from the management network, then a cloud DCN will have an additional network. This could increase the network cost.

Table 13.12 Characteristics of Different Types of Network Topology

Type of Network Topology	No. of Nodes	Node Degrees	Diameter	Bisection BW	Edge Level
Bus/star	$K+1$	K	2	1	Variable
Crossbar	K^2+2K	4	$2(k+1)$	K	Variable
1D mesh	K	2	$k-1$	1	Constant
2D mesh	K^2	4	$2(k-1)$	K	Constant
3D mesh	K^3	6	$3(k-1)$	K^2	Constant
n-D mesh	K^n	2n	$n(k-1)$	K^{n-1}	Variable
1D torus	K	2	$k/2$	2	Constant
2D torus	K^2	4	K	$2k$	Constant
3D torus	K^3	6	$3k/2$	$2k^2$	Variable
n-D torus	K^n	2n	$nk/2$	$2k^{n-1}$	Variable
Hypercube	2^K	K	K	2^{k-1}	Variable
Basic tree	$(k-1)^3$	1	$2\log_{k-1} N$	$n/2$	Variable
Clos network	$n^2/4 \times n$ (ToR)	1	6	N/n(ToR)	Variable
Fat tree	$n^3/4$	1	6	$N/2$	Variable
DCell	$\leq (n+1)^{2k}-1$	$K+1$	$2^{k+1}-1$	$>N/4\log_n N$	Variable
BCube	n^k+1	$K+1$	$\mathrm{Log}_n N$	$N/2$	Variable
Butterfly	$(k+1)2^k$	$K+1$	$2k$	2^k	Variable
Flattened butterfly	$(n+1)k^n$	$K-1$	$N+1$	$n+1-(n-1)/k$	Variable
Dragonfly[1]	$ak(ah+1)$	$a(k+h)$	$ah+1$	$a=2p=2h$	Variable

[1] *"a" is an arbitrary number between 1 and n; similarly "h" also is an arbitrary number between 1 and k − 1.*

In addition to the hypervisor's management traffic, the management network should also carry other third-party management applications. For example, BMC's Remedy (or ITAM) is one of the mature network management systems for enterprise applications. It has built many management components (APIs) to interface with vCenter or the VMware vSphere hypervisor (see Figure 13.57).

Overall, when we calculate the cost of a management network, we should not only think about the hypervisor cost, such as vCenter or Microsoft's System Center or Oracle VM Manager, but also hardware vendors, third-party management applications, and system integration costs.

13.5.2 KERNEL NETWORK

A kernel network can be considered part of a management network because the traffic generated by a kernel network is for managing, moving, and conducting live migration of VMs; VM scheduling;

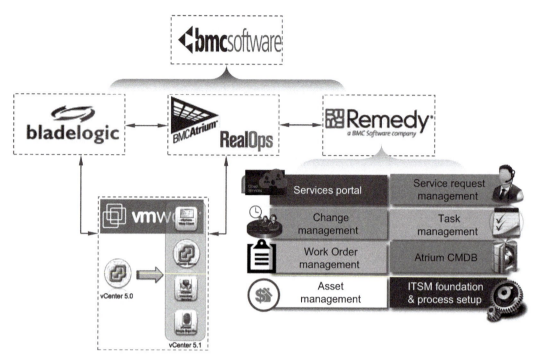

FIGURE 13.57

VMWare vCenter interface with BMC.

VM resource management; local support for consoles; and IP-based storage. If a hypervisor is installed with a bare metal approach, the kernel network traffic would be similar to a special network for operating system traffic plus other virtualized infrastructure traffic. Most kernel network traffic is local.

If we use VMware vSphere as an example, we find that the VMkernel is the engine of the VMware hypervisor. It has two kinds of logical interfaces. One is with the Virtual Machine Monitor (VMM) to carry VMs and the other is an API to connect with third-party applications. The physical interfaces are device drivers, for Peripheral Component Interconnection (PCI) and Host Bus Adaptor (HBA) devices and network interface cards (NICs) (see Figure 13.58).

Microsoft Hyper-V takes a slightly different approach for its hypervisor architecture. The kernel of the management OS (or parent partition), which is equivalent to VMware's host, is running at ring "0" on the host's processor (see Figure 13.59) and the Windows kernel is sitting on the VM bus. It is very similar to the Xen hypervisor's architecture (see Figures 13.60 and 13.61).

The Xen hypervisor has a special guest named Domain-0 or Dom0. When the hypervisor is booted, this special guest kernel is also loaded up. It can be loaded without any file system drivers. The major task of Dom0 is to process all input and output requests from other guests because it has special privileges to access real device drivers via the Xen bus or shared memory segment. In comparison with other domains that are named DomU, Dom0 has higher level of privilege than others. It provides the user interface to the hypervisor. For DomU, the letter "U" means unprivileged.

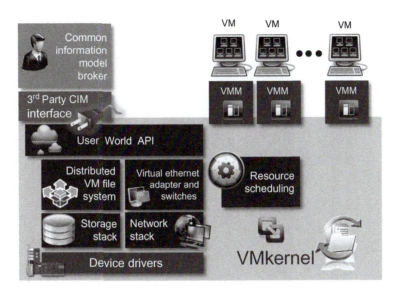

FIGURE 13.58

Inside of VMkernel (VMware architecture)

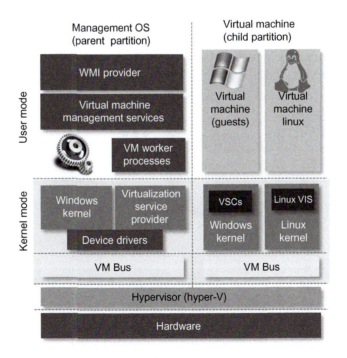

FIGURE 13.59

Details of Windows kernel (MS Hyper-V architecture).

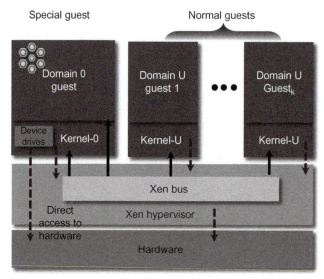

The xen hypervisor architecture

FIGURE 13.60

Xen hypervisor architecture.

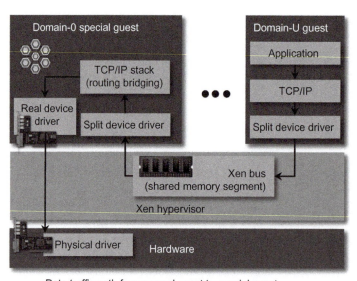

Data traffic path from normal guest to special guest

FIGURE 13.61

Data traffic among guests.

13.5.3 VIRTUAL MACHINE NETWORK

The hypervisor may generate a certain amount of data traffic, but the large amount of data traffic is generated by the many virtual machines (or VMs) hosted by a hypervisor. The virtual machine network may carry any type of data traffic from remote desktop protocols to file transfer protocols or application-specific protocols (see Figure 13.62).

13.5.4 VIRTUALIZED STORAGE NETWORK

The virtualized storage network can be either part of the kernel or management network. The reason to handle it separately is that the storage data created by VMs is mainly IP-based and the storage is originated by a hypervisor. It is mainly NFS-driven data traffic that should be handled differently. VMWare's vSphere architecture will differentiate between hypervisor-generated NFS/iSCSI traffic and VM-generated NFS/iSCSI data traffic. For hypervisor-generated storage, extra security and redundancy will be added. Overall, different storage data originating from different sources will be handled separately.

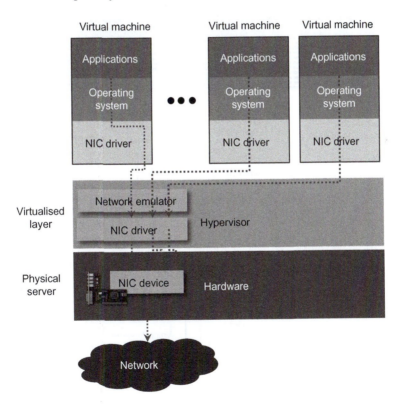

FIGURE 13.62

Data traffic generated by virtual machines.

13.5.5 EXAMPLE OF CONNECTION DETAILS

The following example illustrates the connections between one physical node and DCN switch networks for VMware vSphere 4.0 hypervisor installations (see Figures 13.63–13.65). The purpose of this example is to demonstrate that two connections between a hosting server and switches in a schematic may end up with more than 11 Category 6A (Cat-6A, unshielded twisted pair (UTP) cables to support 10 GBase-T) in the real world.

This is a typical x86 hosting server (HP 4RU machine) that was released in 2010. Based on Moore's law, it should be on the way to the end of its life cycle. This physical node has four processors and each processor has four cores. As we can see from Figure 13.63 through to 13.65, two physical ports (vmnic-0 and vmnic-7) or two 1-gigabit Ethernet trunked ports are dedicated to the

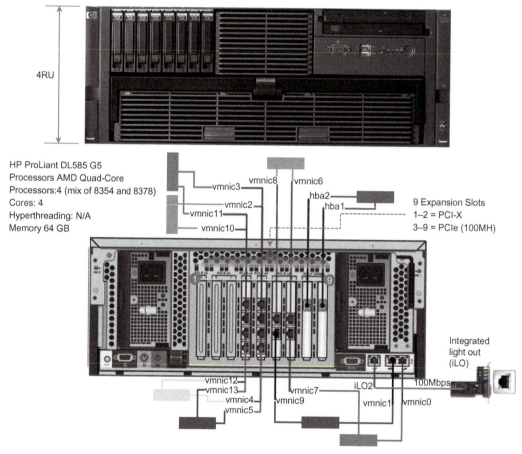

FIGURE 13.63

Example of network connection between Server and DCN switch networks.

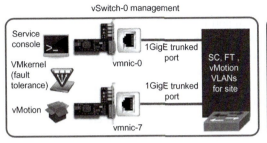

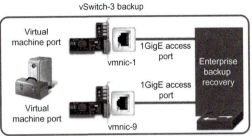

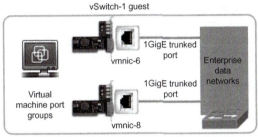

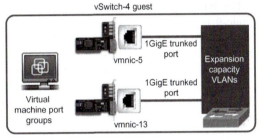

FIGURE 13.64

Switch network details.

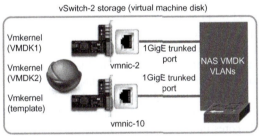

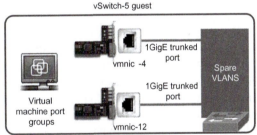

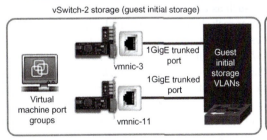

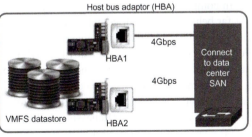

FIGURE 13.65

Switch network details (continued).

management network, which is for the console service, VMkernel (fault tolerance), SC, and vMotion functions. Both ports are assigned to vSwitch port 0.

vSwtich 2 is configured for VMkernel network traffic and guest initial storage. The physical ports are labeled vmnic-2 and vmnic-10 for VMkernel and vmnic-3 and vmnic-11 for guest initial storage. All network links are 1-gigabit Ethernet. This virtual switch is mainly dedicated to the VMkernel storage network.

vSwitch ports 1, 4, and 5 are allocated to guest virtual machine groups, for the virtual machine network. With an incremental approach, vSwitch-4 is on standby and vSwitch-5 is a spare for future expansion.

For backup storage, vSwitch-3 will be dedicated to the link. It consists of the vmnic-1 and vmnic-9 ports and each has a 1 GigE link. However, one of the backup ports, vmnic-1, is not located in the 9 expansion slots. It is the NIC connection port-1. For the technical specification of HP NIC, we can refer to HP's website (www.hp.com/go/ProLiantNICs). This also provides the unit cost of different types of HP server adapters.

As we can see in Figure 13.65, HBA ports (orange) do not have a virtual switch configuration. They are directly connected to a SAN for Virtual Machine File System (VMFS). Each link of the HBA port is 4 Gbps, which is four times bigger than each GigE trunked port. The common practical recommendation for any VMFS datastore is to adopt RAID-5 configuration (refer to Section 12.1.2.3.3). If the application running on a virtual machine requires better performance, we should consider a RAID-1 configuration. Overall, the link bandwidth and RAID configuration should be synchronized.

In comparison the with noncloud environment, we might have seven or nine connection ports or network links (two links for management network, two links for storage, two links for backup, two links for host traffic, and one for remote access) for each hosting server. With a cloud environment, we have to add two more links for kernel traffic. For a 42 or 44 RU rack, we fit it with nine to ten HP DL385 G7 boxes. The number of Cat-6 cables can quickly exceed 100. It wouldn't be easy to manage more than 100 Cat-6 cables. Sometime, ToR may be the only solution for a cloud DCN environment.

The HP DL385 G7 is one of the newer models, released by HP in March 2013 (see Figures 13.66–13.69). It has two CPU sockets and each socket is configured with 12 cores. It has more computer power (24 CPU cores) than the HP DL 585 G5 (16 CPU cores) and yet the physical size of the DL385 G7 is only 2 RU, which means it is much more compact than the DL585 G5. In other words, we can fit more physical nodes or CPU cores into one standard 42 RU rack.

In comparison with a server blade configuration, such as the HP BL460c G6, the HP DL385 G7 is not far behind in terms of computer power capacity per rack. If it is a 42 RU rack, the HP BL460c G7 can hold three c7000 enclosure chassis and 48 blades with a total of 576 CPU cores (see Figure 13.70). For the same size of rack, we can fit 19 DL385 G7 units with 456 CPU cores. The only issue is the number of Cat-6 cables. It may end up with more than 200 Cat-6 cables if the rack is fully populated.

In contrast, the blade has no cabling issues but it has heat dissipation problems. The data center has to consider a special cooling strategy for the blade configuration. The maximum power draw for a fully equipped c7000 chassis would be 14 to 15 kW (refer to Table 8.9). If we have three c7000 chassis, it would need 42 kW power draw per rack. As we indicated before, the power draw of a traditional rack is only between 3 to 5 kW per rack. If the server architecture selects the blade server option, it may lead to the need to upgrade the data center air conditioning system. This could cost millions of dollars in up-front capex. Unless a company needs large capacity for expansion, the standard rack-mounted server would be a preferable choice.

HP ProLiant DL385 G7

Processors AMD Magny-Cours Opteron 6147

Processors: 2

Cores: 12

Hyperthreading N/A

Memory 192 GB

PCI Slot-1 NC550SFP (10GbE Network)

PCI Slot-2 NC364T (1GbE Network)

PCI Slot-3 Free

PCI Slot-4 Free

PCI Slot-5 NC364T (1GbE Network)

PCI Slot-6 FC2242SR (4Gbs SAN)

FIGURE 13.66

HP ProLiant DL385 G7.

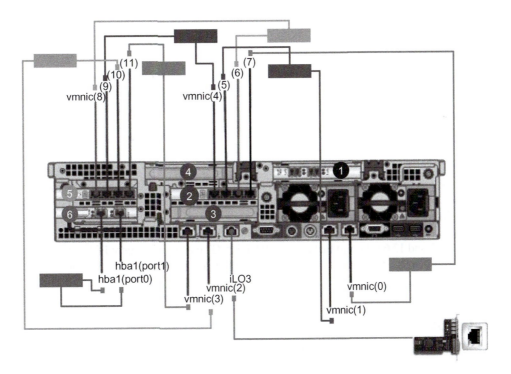

FIGURE 13.67

HP ProLiant DL385 G7 back panel configuration.

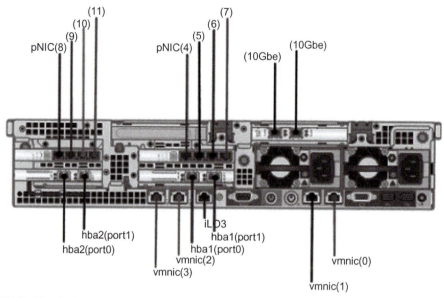

HP ProLiant DL385 G7
Processors AMD Magny-Cours Opteron 6147
Processors: 2
Cores: 12
Hyperthreading N/A
Memory 192 GB

PCI Slot-1 NC550SFP (10GbE Network)
PCI Slot-2 NC364T (1GbE Network)
PCI Slot-3 FC 2242SR (4Gbs SAN)
PCI Slot-4 Free
PCI Slot-5 NC364T (1GbE Network)
PCI Slot-6 FC22425R (4Gbs SAN)

FIGURE 13.68

Configuration 1 of HP DL385 G7.

Figure 13.66 shows one scenario for computer capacity expansion based on the original network configuration of the HP DL585 G5. It is fully backward compatible. The switch network doesn't need to be changed or upgraded unless there are other issues, such as bandwidth capacity, reliability, scalability, aggregation throughput, agility, and flexibility.

Figures 13.67 and 13.68 showed that a new HP DL385 G7 can have different PCI slot configurations to meet the requirements due to network upgrades from 1 gigabit per second to 10 gigabits per second.

13.6 CLOUD DCN SUMMARY

13.6.1 DCN COMPONENT SUMMARY

This is the longest chapter in this book. It has been divided into five big topics. First we clarified the key components of networks and their functions. We especially highlighted two network elements for both layer 2 and 3, namely the switch and router. Strictly speaking, the name "switch" is

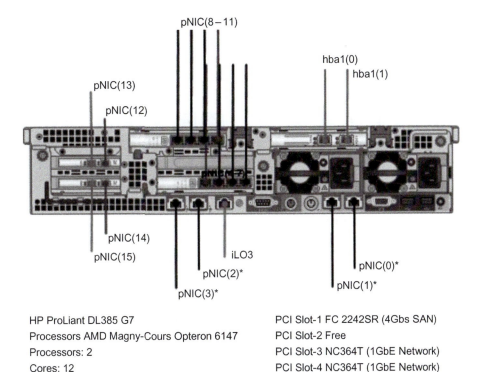

FIGURE 13.69

Configuration 2 of HP DL385 G7.

HP ProLiant DL385 G7	PCI Slot-1 FC 2242SR (4Gbs SAN)
Processors AMD Magny-Cours Opteron 6147	PCI Slot-2 Free
Processors: 2	PCI Slot-3 NC364T (1GbE Network)
Cores: 12	PCI Slot-4 NC364T (1GbE Network)
Hyperthreading N/A	PCI Slot-5 NC550SFP (10GbE Network)
Memory 192 GB	PCI Slot-6 NC550SFP (10GbE Network)

not a proper technical definition but rather a commercial term. That is why the term "switch" can be applied to many network elements from layer 1 all the way to layer 4 of the OSI or TCP/IP protocol stack; it is really dependent on vendors' descriptions of their products for customers. Practically, the common meaning of switch refers to layer 2 network element (frame). Sometimes, it may cover layer 3 (packet). It is really dependent on the real functionality and capability of a switch. The commoditized switch is much cheaper. The cheapest 48-port gigabit Ethernet switch would be less than $700 dollars. Even for a 10 Gigabit Ethernet switch + 4 SFP, such as the Cisco Catalyst 4948, the price is now below $3,000. A few years ago, it would cost over $10,000. This is due to vigorous market competition from Chinese vendors, such as Huawei. A similar product, Huawei's S5700S-52P-LI-AC, it sold for only $. It is only one-third of Cisco's cost. In essence, Huawei is selling a 10 gigabit switch at almost a 1 gigabit price. Perhaps this is why Huawei has become one of major players in the network equipment market during the last 10 years or so. If a customer doesn't believe the conspiracy theory that the network doesn't run EIGRP and doesn't hold any Cisco shares, Huawei's network equipment could be one of the options. After all, a 70%

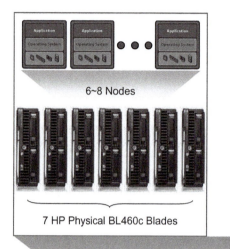
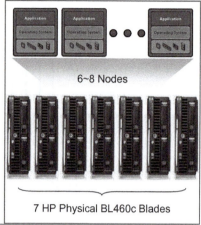

6~8 Nodes   6~8 Nodes

7 HP Physical BL460c Blades   7 HP Physical BL460c Blades

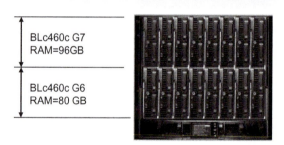

BLc460c G7
RAM=96GB

BLc460c G6
RAM=80 GB

C7000 enclosure

FIGURE 13.70

Example of HP BL460c G7 blades configuration.

discount price would be a very attractive choice for any business, especially if the network topology really needs a large volume of COTS switches, such as for DCell or BCube topologies.

Above the layer 2 switch is the router, which is a layer 3 network device. A router may cover both layer 3 and layer 4, but will never operate above layer 4. A router reads all logical addresses from incoming data packets and then forwards these data packets to its destination based on their logical IP addresses and an internal routing table. Because it reads incoming data packets, it is normally slower than a network switch.

In addition to reading IP addresses, a router can also have the capability of finding the shortest path in the network to a packet's destination. This is why a router should be considered a conventional computer that is configured for routing purposes. If we understand this basic concept of routing, it is quite easy for us to realize the logic behind server-centric topologies such as DCell, BCube and Dual-Port Server Interconnection [233].

When a network device is required to communicate at layer 4 or above, a gateway device is the preferred choice. A network gateway is ultimately a computer-like device that can support both hardware and software communication for two different types of network.

13.6.2 TERMS AND DEFINITIONS SUMMARY

In the second part of this chapter, we focused on many terms, jargon, and definitions related to the network. There are many terms that are borrowed from mathematical theory because many principles of network topologies are explained by mathematic topology theory. Among the 14 common terms that have been introduced, node, node degree, diameter, dimension, radix, and DCN topology are the most important definitions. They are the foundation of the fourth part of this chapter, namely the types of network topologies.

13.6.3 METRICS SUMMARY

Before moving to the DCN topology section, the third part of this chapter listed all the criteria that are used to decide which DCN topology should be considered the right one. There are 12 common criteria for any network topology. In addition, there are 10 metrics that have been developed for DCN topology. From a cost perspective, IT silo is one of the important issues for cost analysis because the more duplicated tools that are deployed or created, the higher the cost is.

Another important issue is backward compatibility. Practically all data center components should be backward compatible. If they are not, not only do the hardware components have to be upgraded but also the software components. The cost of a data center project will become unpredictable. Many IT decision makers have difficulty making up their mind for many replacement projects because of the backward compatibility issue, even if a vendor assures them that there shouldn't be any problem with backward compatibility.

After all the basic terms and concepts have been defined or clarified, we move on to the topic of DCN topologies. We have given the details of 9 or 10 different DCN topologies from the basic tree to the latest dragonfly model. The main focus of the fourth topic is how to reduce the DCN costs for both capex and opex while maintaining or even increasing network performance.

13.6.4 DCN TOPOLOGY SUMMARY

Each DCN topology has pros and cons. It is really dependent on the DCN traffic pattern or business applications. In earlier sections, we first explained 14 terms related to DCN topology and discussed types of network topology and different way of categorizing them. We divided DCN topologies into three groups:

- Common DCN topologies, such as star, tree, line, mesh, ring, bus
- Combinations of common DCN topologies, such as recursive, folded Clos or fat tree, and commodity switch fabric-based fat tree.
- Other DCN topologies such as VL2, which is a firmware based, and dragonfly, which is a virtual channel-based topology.

Each subsequent topology is trying to resolve some issues that the previous DCN topologies have.

We began with the basic tree topology. It can be considered a combination of star and bus topologies. It is recommended by one of the major network vendors, Cisco. The advantages with the basic tree are that it is easier to deploy, cheaper than the torus and crossbar topologies, better for local traffic, latency is relatively low, and there is commodity pricing for the access network fabric. However, the issues with the basic tree are root traffic bottlenecks and that there is a single point of failure.

In order to resolve the issue of root data traffic bottlenecks, researchers came up with the fat tree solution or folded Clos network topology. Fat tree has resolved the issue of root traffic bottlenecks but it creates scalability issues with the network topology, as some core switches are very expensive.

In 2008, Al-Fares et al. came up with a solution that we called a COTS switch-based fat tree. The solution proposed using low end or commercial-off-the-shelf (COTS) switches as the network fabric to make up a network topology. It is a highly scalable and backward compatible network. Above all, all Ethernet switches are identical. It can support $K^3/4$ hosts. However, the issue with this topology is that it needs a lot of copper cable and there is a poor switch port utilization rate (only 20%).

One of possible solutions to resolve Al-Fares et al.'s issue is the DCell topology, which leverages NICs in the hosting servers or end nodes. It is a server-centric solution rather than a pure switch-centric solution, such as the fat tree topology. DCell provides a scalable, fault tolerant, high capacity network for bandwidth hungry applications and an efficient distributed routing algorithm. However, it is not a truly expandable topology in terms of the small incremental footprint of the server host and NIC installation.

To improve the DCell topology, especially on the issue of NIC installation, the BCube topology utilizes more COTS switches in comparison with DCell. Instead of using server NIC ports for connections, the BCube topology lets one server connects to multiple switches. The advantages of a BCube are traffic balancing, fault detection and handling without link state distribution, and the ability to fine-tune network capacity degradation as faulty servers and switches increase. BCube is better fit with the solution of a data center in a shipping container.

Similar to the DCell topology, the BCube topology doesn't support partial network solutions so it can't be expanded in capacity using an incremental approach or a small footprint node.

How can we resolve the node capacity with a small footprint issue? Albert Greenberg et al. argued that physical network topology doesn't mean everything. They focus on the virtual layer of a switch or server by injecting a thin shim or layer 2.5 packets into the transmission TCP/IP protocol and redirecting the data traffic. VL2 is a firmware-based topology. It can make sure that the existing physical network capacity is being better utilized. It consists of two software components: the VL2 agent and a directory system. It creates an illusion that hosts are connected to a big pool of layer 2 switches in a data center.

VL2 sounds like a perfect solution but it isn't without cost. One of the issues with VL2 is that it can't differentiate traffic priority. The VLB adopts a randomization method to process or to balance data traffic. It treads all data traffic equally and converts them into the average case. VL2 is not for priority applications but it can liberate servers or switches' additional capacity for a large and uniform resource pool.

When we listed DCN metrics, we required multipath diversity and reliability. The conventional butterfly and flattened butterfly topologies support these features. The real purpose of the flattened butterfly is to save on cabling costs. In comparison with the fat tree topology, the flattened butterfly can save up to 53% in costs. However, the flatten butterfly is a blocking network topology. Ajithkumar Thamarakuzhi et al. proposed a better solution, the so-called 2-Dilated Flattened Butterfly (2DFB). It provides better performance.

In order to make further cost reductions, John Kim et al. proposed another topology, the so-called dragonfly topology. The approach of the dragonfly topology is to lift network performance by increasing the volume of switch ports (or leverage high radix) rather than reducing it and increasing each port's bandwidth.

The implementation of dragonfly involves reorganizing DCN switches or routers into a number of subgroups and dividing switches' links into local and global channels. By regrouping switches and routers, the dragonfly topology can reduce the total number of global channels that are often fabricated by optical cables. Longer or interrack optical fiber cables are expensive. By eliminating a number of global channel links, the dragonfly topology can deliver 20% cost savings in comparison with the flattened butterfly topology.

13.6.5 CLOUD DCN

In the last part of this chapter, the book focuses on the characteristics of a cloud data center network. It generally describes different types of networks in a cloud environment. Based on many practical experiences, we classified cloud data center networks into four different types:

- Management
- Kernel
- Virtual machine
- Virtualized storage

In comparison with a conventional data center network, a cloud environment will have an extra network dedicated to data traffic that is generated by a hypervisor. The reason to have a dedicated network for the hypervisor-generated traffic is because this traffic will handle different types of data in term of redundancy and security. That is why a cloud data center network may have more network links to switch networks than a conventional one. In the last part of the discussion on characteristics of cloud DCNs, we demonstrated an example of a cloud DCN that connects to x86 server with bare metal installation of a VMware hypervisor. As we illustrated in the diagrams, a cloud DCN may have at least 11 Cat-6 cables connected to switch networks. In other words, two connection lines in a network topology schematic will end up with more than 11 cables. Therefore, cable management is always an issue for a cloud data center. That is why we briefly touched on the topic of different scenarios of rack management, such as ToR, EoR, and MoR arrangements.

13.7 REVIEW QUESTIONS

1. What is the principle of a switch forwarding a data packet?
2. What are the major differences between a switch and router in processing data traffic?
3. Why is switch not a technical term?
4. If the application requires processing layer 4 or above data traffic, which network device should be selected?
5. Can you list at least three major vendors of network vendors who have more than 10% market share?
6. When you make a purchasing decision or a selection of vendor for network switch and router equipment, what are your key criteria?
7. If the business requires building a portable small data center, what is the right topology to recommend?
8. If a $DCell_0$ has five nodes, what is the total number of nodes at $DCell_3$?
9. If the switch has eight ports, how many switches do I need to support a level 2 BCube DCN and how many nodes can the level 2 BCube support?
10. If I have many priority business applications, can I adopt the VL2 topology? Explain the reasons why or why not.
11. What is the key difference between a conventional DCN and cloud DCN?
12. In a topology diagram, there are two lines connected to a switch network. In reality, how many Cat-6 links should I have at least?
13. Please list the pros and cons of the fat tree topology and Al-Fares fat tree fabricated with COTS switches.

CLOUD COMPUTING COST MODELS AND FRAMEWORK IV

Part IV presents one of the three foundational elements to support cloud data center cost modeling for a decision maker. It consists of three chapters. Each chapter will have three sections. Chapter 14 is informative; the goal is to define the concept of cost models. Then it will clearly define the purpose of cost model, answering the question of why we need them. Lastly, it will point out challenges of cost modeling.

In Chapter 15, we will review four different categories of cost models in detail. This is the literature review chapter. We will review numerous works from over the last 50 years. Based on the 50-year literature review, we will classify numerous models into four different categories, business, finance, operation, and technology, to derive a cost framework. Following the cost framework, selected models will be described in detail.

Chapter 16 or the last chapter of Part IV shows readers how to use the right model to calculate costs correctly. The example mainly focuses on TCO/ROI. It is the practical (or hands-on) chapter for cost model calculation.

Overall, these three chapters or nine sections provide the basic cost framework for a simple cost calculation, in order summarize various capital, pre-operation and operational expenditures (or capex, pre-opex and opex) items. The ultimate goal of these chapters is to capture all cost items and frame them into the right structure, and then follow the proper process to calculate these items.

In this part, what the topic will be touched on is a micro view of cost model, which the cost model can be categorised at the tactical level. In the following part or Part V, we will talk about the macro cost model and adopt different methodologies to make macro predications or forecasts. Of course, not all decisions require a macro level of cost modeling. We will analyze the circumstances in Part V. We illustrate the overall cost modeling structure in Figure 14.1.

COST MODELING: TERMS AND DEFINITIONS

This chapter will unfold the content in the following order. First, a number of common terms or concepts will be defined and clarified, and these terms, such as cost analysis, cost model, cost methodology, and cost framework, will be applied in the following discussion extensively, because very often, many people use these terms or words interchangeably. It is often very confusing. We try to give functional definitions of all these terms so readers will not have any confusion. Second, we will provide a simple formula for the cost model and then we spell out the ultimate goal of cost modeling. Third, in order to reach the final goal, there are many challenges. We will clearly identify these challenges.

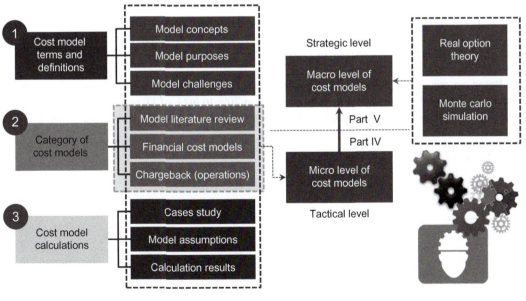

FIGURE 14.1

Part IV structure.

14.1 CONCEPT OF COST MODEL

The concept of a cost model is to define all basic elements needed to construct a cost framework for a cloud computing data center. It consists of costs, benefits, risks, cost model metrics, time, and a framework.

14.1.1 DEFINITION OF COST

In order to understand cost modeling, we should understand two key words: "cost" and "model" as well as the term "cost model." What is cost and what is a model? The Oxford English Dictionary (OED) provides the lexical definition of cost as "the amount that has to be paid or spent to buy or obtain something" or "require the payment of a specified sum of money before it can be acquired or done." It originally came from Latin word, "Constare" meaning price. In other words, the cost means the price that should be paid for acquiring, producing, or maintaining something, usually measured in a type of resource unit, such as money, time, energy, expense, or expenditure. From a resource perspective, a functional definition of cost means one type of resource consumption.

There are two types of resources. One is the tangible resource, and most tangible resources of cloud computing are physical and semi-physical IT infrastructure, such as software, middleware, CPU, memory, storage, network, data center facility, etc. Another type of resource is an intangible one, such as information, files, knowledge, wisdom, virtual infrastructures, brand names, customer databases, and so on. With an intangible resource, people can't see it, touch it, feel it, smell it, or taste it. It is invisible but it certainly exists in our universe and of course, it also exists in our cost model. And yet, these resources quite often ignored during the cost modeling process because they are quite difficult to measured and calculate because they are very often subjective. A cost modeling analyst or a decision maker may face an infinite number of variables to select from. This selection process is very often subjective.

Based on our experience, the most difficult activity in cost modeling is to quantify intangible resources. However, the intangible cost may make up 70% to 80% of IT project cost. Unfortunately, many organizations fail to pay attention or even consider the intangible resource costs due to a number of reasons, such as:

- Difficult to define
- Hard to quantify
- Complicated to measure
- Always changing
- Uncertainty
- Very tedious

It is difficult to find a clear benchmark or methodology to calculate these intangible IT resources. If you do find something, you may be very disappointed because many results or conclusions are very subjective. It seems to be quite challenging to use a scientific or probabilistic method to define them. Does the problem have a solution? The answer is "Yes." This is the intention of this book, in which we try to offer a combination approach to resolve the cloud cost modeling problem. In the following three chapters, we will unveil this approach step by step.

14.1.1.1 Tangible costs

Tangible costs are physical cost items; they could be either visible or invisible cost items. Most tangible cost items are three-dimensional objects, such as computer hardware (including physical servers, storage, memory, and other peripheral devices), data center facility equipment, space or buildings, and network devices. The invisible cost items are things that we are unable to see and normally are not included in the purchase price for computer equipment or systems, such as training, upgrading, maintenance, repair, and warranty costs. These items are still considered tangible cost items because when a system is broken down, you need a spare part to replace it. Maintaining or managing spare part stock is not free, but all these cost items are invisible from a purchasing perspective. Perhaps this is why sometimes we call this hidden costs or operation costs or operational expenditures.

In essence, the tangible cost is closely associated with the tangible benefits that may contribute to a company and increase a company's business value. These benefits can be easily delivered in a tangible format, such as cash flow, expansion of customer base, growing market share, and quick return on investment. Tangible costs and benefits can be considered to be at a tactical level. Very often, the investors or sponsors or stakeholders want to see some justifications or results within a relative short time period, such as 12 months or less. If it is a long-term investment project, investors want to see some clear milestones that are measurable; they must be quantifiable.

14.1.1.2 Intangible costs

In contrast to tangible costs, there are many intangible costs, where the purchasing occurs without a physical substance exchanging hands, such as advertising costs, branding costs, the cost expenditure to improve customer satisfaction rate or loyalty, market research costs, strategy and legal consultant fees (excluding those costs associated with project delivery), and training costs to improve employee morale and innovation capability. Again, all these costs are in conjunction with many intangible benefits that are quite challenging to measure, such as brand names, customer satisfaction rate, and employee morale. Often, the benefits of these cost items cannot be directly measured. For example, employee morale may be measured by employee productivity and staff churn rate. This measure may take a long time to realize, typically more than 12 months or 24 months.

These cost items are considered strategic costs or at a strategic level. These costs might not deliver benefits immediately. The results of some projects or programs may even become worse before they get better because these projects may disrupt the current operations, such as an IT transformation program. Now, the question is, how can we measure or justify these cost items at a strategic level? The popular approach is to adopt a method that is similar to tangible cost measurement and then add many educated guesses or assumptions. Unfortunately, education guesses and assumptions are very subjective. Most of these assumptions are based on individual opinion, intuition, and experiences. They are not very reliable, especially for long-term assumptions. How can we quantify these cost items? Before we dive into these cost items in detail, we first clarify three basic parameters to measure these cost items.

14.1.1.3 Cost parameters

The cost parameters consist of three basic elements:

- Quantity
- Unit price
- time

Actually, these are the three fundamental metrics to measure a cost model. Quantity is also sometimes called volume. The higher the volume is, the higher the total cost. The traditional management practice is often to leverage the scale of the volume, eliminating operation silos to drive the overall cost down. Many IT vendors or suppliers will provide a volume discount, such as 5%, 10%, or even 30% if the purchased volume exceeds a certain threshold.

Unit price is also called unit cost. It represents the cost of a single product or service unit. For example, the unit price of a general physical server may cost $2,000, but for a virtual machine or a virtual hosting server, it costs only $0.10 per hour. The virtual server adopts a different way to calculate unit cost. It is a service-based calculation. The typical example is the IT professional labor rate, which may be calculated at $150 per hour or $1,500 per day for a special IT service rate, such as fixing a bug or testing a software application.

When an IT producer or an entrepreneur marks the unit cost for his/her product or service, it should include all fixed costs (hardware, manufacturing equipment, and facility) and all variable costs (labor, materials, power, and other consumable goods). If the unit cost is the selling price from an IT vendor, then a profit margin has to be added on. Traditionally, the calculation of unit cost is equal to all fixed costs plus all variable costs and a desirable profit margin divided by the total volume produced or provided (see Figures 14.2 and 14.3).

If the selling price is from a retailer or a distributer, the marked unit price should also include the selling cost. From a producer's perspective, it may also include a certain percentage wholesale discount to the retailer. In other words, the producer should either add the cost to the product or reduce its profit margin. Although we call some items fixed costs, the concept of "fixed" is a relative term. It has a time stamp on it. It is subject to change at any time. From this perspective, the unit cost is always a variable even if we ignore all variable costs.

You may hear the famous slogan, "time is money." But how much is it? Based on microeconomic theory, it is the opportunity cost. In simple terms, it is the cost of giving up the opportunities

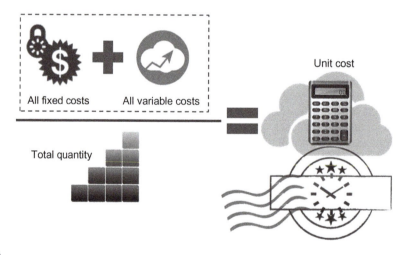

FIGURE 14.2

Unit cost.

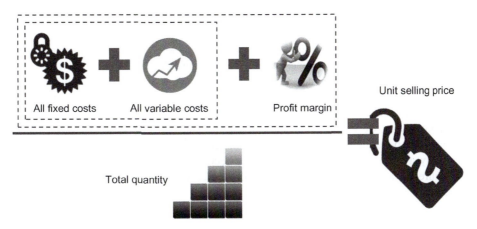

FIGURE 14.3

Unit selling price from a vendor.

to do other things. For example, if you decided to become an IT consultant, you have given up the opportunity to become an IT executive, for which the pay may be far better. Time is not a retrievable thing. The opportunity cost is an either/or relationship rather than "and." In this sense, an economist is always looking at future cost rather than sunk cost. In the IT world, IT asset value has a unique meaning, as we have Moore's law, which can be used in determining depreciation in value over a certain period of time (for example, every 18 months).

14.1.1.4 Sunk cost

Sunk cost represents the cost that already occurred or happened in the past. The characteristics of sunk cost are similar to one of the three cost elements, time, which is an unrecoverable or historical cost. For example, if one company has paid $2 million dollars for three years of hardware service warranty, it is unrecoverable.

From an economist's perspective, sunk cost has another meaning in terms of a decision making fallacy for an investment, in which the costs and benefits have no correlation. In other words, the costs that you have already paid will be irrelevant to the benefits that you would expect.

Considering the following example. Suppose you spent $1,000 and bought a laptop PC just about 12 months ago and the warranty has just expired. Unfortunately, the laptop starts bothering you due to many small issues, such as slower processing speed, frozen screens, and an intermittent wireless connection. The common way of thinking is that although I cannot get my money back, it is still running. You can get away with it by rebooting your laptop frequently. I should keep it until the laptop is totally broken down or at least 2 years later, which is after the asset has fully depreciated.

Surely, you wouldn't get your two-thirds of $1,000 (or $666) back if you keep it. The money that you have spent has been sunk. It doesn't have any relationship with your decision whether you want keep it or not. The primary criteria that you should consider are whether the laptop would impact your future earnings or opportunity cost. Imagine how much valuable time has been lost on your existing laptop due to rebooting and the slow access speed. You can use that time and the additional opportunities to earn more than what you are using the existing laptop if you can replace it with a new laptop.

In essence, when you think about whether you should keep the existing laptop or not, you shouldn't take previous cost into consideration because the decision that you will make is only going to impact on your future, not your past. Sunk cost is a very important concept in the decision-making process, especially when making decisions on life cycles. We will give more details on how this relates to cost modeling later.

In the above case, we pay for the laptop up front. The purchase cost to acquire the laptop is called a capital expenditure (or capex in short). Instead of buying it outright, I can also lease the laptop and pay a monthly fee. Now, the cost has become an operational expenditure (or opex). If this cost is directly associated with my product or service volume, it is called a direct variable cost (or DVC).

14.1.1.5 Direct Variable Cost (DVC)

Direct variable cost means the costs are changing with the volume of product that you may produce. When we define cost parameters, the unit cost is equal to all fixed costs plus all variable costs and then divided by the total volume that has been produced (see Figure 14.1).

The concept of DVC is related to the volume of sales. The amount of DVC depends on the volume of products that have been sold. Cloud computing has provided an opportunity for many cloud consumers to shift their budget allocation from capex to opex. One of cloud computing's characteristics is "pay as you go" (PAYG). This is a revolutionary method that changes the way the customer consumes the computer resource. Actually, the idea of PAYG is not new. It is similar to the management approaches known as just in time (JIT), which was initiated by Toyota.

In theory, this new approach of computer resource consumption has shifted the financial risks from computer consumers to cloud service providers. For example, if a business plan or forecast requires 30 hosting servers to hosting web contents, a customer database and account payments, a traditional way of budgeting is to allocate $135 k capex up front to buy, install, provision, and deliver 30 physical hosting servers and software licenses and get them up and running (assume each server would cost $4,500). This is the capital expenditure. The issue is that this business forecast or market demand is not 100% certain. The business may need more if the market is growing very quickly. Of course, it may take three years to fill up the capacity of 30 hosting servers. For many large enterprises, the forecast capacity is always too high because the time to deliver the additional computer capacity is extended due to the need to walk through an approval process. Clearly, there is capacity waste. If the average utilization rate is 25% in 3 years, then the real capital utilization rate for the capex would only be $33,750 (to simplify our example, we exclude other cost items and assume the maximum utilization rate of all servers is 100% in this case). This means that approximately $100 k capex has been wasted because these servers have to be recycled after three years according to Moore's law.

With cloud computing, the company doesn't have to allocate $135 k capex up front. What the consumer has to do is to pay an hourly rate or flat rate for PAYG. When the market is up, you buy more computer capacity; when the market is down, you just simply switch off the number of virtual machines (VMs) and reduce your computer capacity. The cost of buying VM capacity has become a DVC. Ideally, this model is quite efficient for small and some medium companies.

14.1.1.6 Capital Expenditure (Capex)

Capital expenditure is the money expended for purchasing new assets, new facilities, and the capability to deliver new products and provide extra production. This type of cost consists of both tangible and intangible costs. For example, if a company wants to host a different new mobile website and the existing server capacity and access speed is not enough to cope with the new content customers, the cost of purchasing, installation, and provisioning new physical servers is the capital expenditure (or capex).

In addition, the spending on research and development for a new product or service should also be considered capex. Clearly, this kind of capital spending is seeking new revenue sources and profits.

Spending on purchasing assets such as new physical servers, storage equipment, and data center facilities would be tangible costs. Spending on assets such as copyrights, brand names, patents, trademarks, goodwill and any research project for substantially improving existing products, process, systems and services are examples of intangible costs.

Very often, the purpose of artificially classifying an expenditure into two different categories (capex and opex) is to measure a company's financial performance against the industry benchmark. Normally, if a company diverts its resources into new products, new services, and expansion of existing production capability, it means the company has potential for growth. The business is focusing on future growth opportunities for profits or benefits.

14.1.1.7 Operational Cost or Operational Expenditure (Opex)

In contrast to capex, another type of cost expenditure is the operational cost or operating expenses or revenue expenditures (or opex in short). The typical types of opex would be employees' salary, day-to-day expenditures, maintenance costs, utility consumption, repair costs, rental fees, and selling, general & administrative expenses (SG&A).

Taking the above example, the opex is the money spent for IT administrators or professionals to operate these hosting servers for mobile web content or to serve many web content consumers. The operating activities may include regular software upgrades, patches, bug fixing, facility maintenance, and support. In essence, the money has been spent to turn inventory into products or services. This is opex. The business is normally under normal operational circumstances.

In general, many companies or businesses are pursuing opex reduction without any impact on their operational capability to produce quality products or services. Of course, opex reduction could be a double-edged sword. For example, laying some research and development staff off might not have an immediate impact on the current business but the company might suffer long-term consequences, such as competitiveness and capability to innovate.

14.1.2 CAPEX AND OPEX SHIFT IN A CLOUD ENVIRONMENT

As we indicated in Chapter 1 , the cloud business model has enabled many cloud consumers to shift capex to opex because the way of consuming IT resources has been moving from "build" to "buy" and from "buy" to "lease." Once IT resource consumption has been categorized as opex, it becomes a day-to-day expense or turning inventory into products. It becomes a category of SG&A or an overhead type of cost (see Figure 14.4).

Connotations of capex ⟶ *Connotations of opex*

- Prosperity
- Future growth
- New products & services
- Innovation & new ideas
- Capacity expansion

- Maintenance
- Repair
- Legacy
- Overhead
- Administrative cost

Paradigm shift

FIGURE 14.4

Financial meaning of shifting budget allocation from capex to opex.

The financial connotation of this paradigm shift may be quite devastating to the IT department of any company. Logically, if all IT infrastructures have been shifted to the cloud or "the Big Switch" [7] has occurred, it doesn't make sense to keep any IT people around. There is no IT system to be built or updated or maintained. Now, the question is, is it true that "IT doesn't matter" any more [10]?

Well, it really depends on who you are. The cloud technology or business model may also enable you to move your budget from opex to capex, which is the opposite direction.

If you an individual consumer or even a small business owner (who has less than a dozen employees), surely "IT doesn't matter" in comparison with your core business because:

1. Your IT workload may be fluctuate from time to time.
2. You cannot afford to have a dedicated IT professional.
3. After all, once your capex is shifted to opex, you can claim all your expenses back on your taxes.

In general, flying to a cloud is better than in-house computation for individual or small business. However, if you are a large enterprise or a publicly listed corporation, you might have to look at this from different angles:

1. Remember the first of Joe Wienman's 10 Cloudonmoics laws [253]: "An on-demand service provider typical charges a utility premium." It is common sense that "buy" is always cheaper than "lease." For example, Amazon EC2 has the rates in Table 14.1 for general purposes in the Asia Pacific (Sydney) region.

We can simply calculate the cost for one vCPU cost for one or three years, which would be $1,384.08/year and $4,152.24/three years, respectively. However, if you buy one HP server, for example, an HP DL385p-G8, that costs $2,185 (refer to Table 11.7). If we just ignore other cost items, such as space, power, and cooling, the price of the Amazon service seems to be nearly double than what you can buy. Of course, we have not taken into account of network equipment and other operating costs. Likewise, the vCPU is not equal to one CPU socket or even a CPU core.

Table 14.1 Amazon EC2 Prices for Asia Pacific (Sydney) Region

VM Configuration	vCPU	ECU	Memory (GB)	Instance Storage (GB)	Linux/Unix Usage
M3.medium	1	3	3.75	1X4SSD	$0.158/hour
M3.large	2	6.5	7.5	1X32SSD	0.315/hour
M3.xlarge	4	13	15	2X40SSD	$0.63/hour
M3.2xlarge	8	26	30	2X80SSD	$1.26/hour

Amazon only provides the EC2 Computer Unit (ECU) number. One ECU may be equivalent to the CPU capacity of a 1.0–1.2 GHz 2007 AMD Opteron or 2007 Intel Xeon processor. In comparison, the HP DL385-G8 is equipped with an AMD 6200 series processor. If the physical node is configured with a 6284SE, it has 16 cores and each core's speed is 2.7 GHz. This means that the equivalent cost of "buy" capacity has much more power than the "lease" one.

Some cloud service providers may offer free cloud storage or computer services (see Appendix E). However, they only provide very limited capacity. No large enterprises or publicly listed companies can run their business based on free cloud services. One of the core six economic principles is "there is no such thing of free lunch."

2. IT doesn't only mean information and technology but also innovation and creation if a company utilizes the IT resources effectively. In comparison with other utilities, such as water, sewage, electricity, gas, public transport, parking, even telecom, IT is far more complex because it not only has hardware, but also software. It would be quite challenging to draw a simple line between capex and opex in the reality. For example, your company has decided to migrate all computer capacity into the cloud, and a cloud service provider will provide all computer resources that you need. Your company may sign a service contract with this cloud service provider. The cloud service provider will charge a fee based on your usage time with a particular configured instance or PAYG. You have completed the so-called "paradigm shift" from capex to opex. However, the cloud service provider doesn't know what your purpose is. If you are going to host a server for market research of new products or services, this should be classified as capex in theory but all your computer resources belong to a opex lump sum. It would be unwise to build another standalone physical server for R&D purposes. The most efficient method is to fire up a VM instance from your existing cloud service provider for R&D purposes. The question is, how do you differentiate the cost? The simple answer is to keep the time and category. This is the purpose of a chargeback or showback, which we are going to discuss in the following chapter.

3. Once you make the big switch, all your IT professional expertise will go with it. We are in the information age. IT talent or knowledgeable workers will be critical for many companies to compete long-term [249]. After all, an ordinary utility application is much simpler than a computer application. Cloud migration may have a butterfly effect and unintended consequences. For some large enterprises, the capex shifting may lead to many unintended consequences. In essence, the surface value of capex savings may just be one side of the story. We might have to check both sides.

On the opposite side of cloud consumers, you may be able to move part of the IT budget allocation from opex to capex (in the opposite direction) by leveraging the virtualized infrastructure if you are one of the cloud service providers. What this means is that you do not have to pay any money on break/fix costs for IT hardware, such as server maintenance or warranty cost. All you have to do is to add new server capacity into a hosting server cluster or farm if one server fails (assuming the server model has backward compatibility).

For example, VMware High Availability (HA) can handle failed physical nodes and recover VMs. The principle of VMware HA is to use a software agent along with network and datastore heartbeats to detect any offline host. Once it finds a host off the air, it can automatically restart VMs that belong to this failed physical node on other physical nodes in the cluster. The implication of this virtualized feature is that break-/fix for physical servers becomes unnecessary (see Figure 14.5). What you have to do is just to take out the faulty physical node and add another backward compatible node into the cluster. The implication of these hypervisor features is that you can shift your opex into capex. In other words, the virtual files or VMs that are sitting on the top of a physical cluster are just like a vehicle and you can roll over over faulty physical nodes. It has transferred a maintenance and support (or break/fix) problem into a server cluster capacity issue.

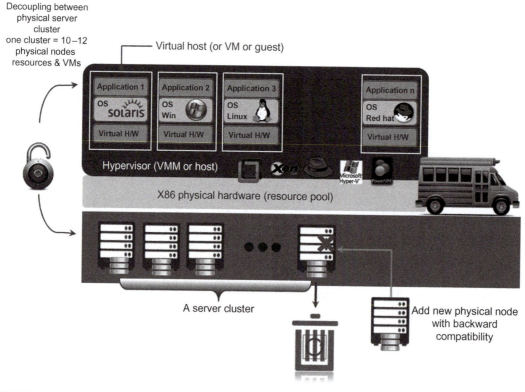

FIGURE 14.5

Implication of VMW are High Availability (HA) and Fault Tolerance (FT) features.

14.1.3 **BENEFITS**

A benefit means a company gains profits due to product and service sales or gains advantages due to opex minimization or optimization. Benefits can be tangible and intangible. The common tangible benefits would be cash flow, cash income, and cost reduction. In essence, it is the net profit gain for a running business. The intangible benefits would include raising customer satisfaction rate, improved employee motivation, growing market share, and better reputation for a company's brand. In the IT industry, the intangible benefits are important, especially for many startup companies. There are many methods to measure intangible benefits, such as multiobjective, multicriteria modes, value analysis, critical success factors, and etc. As we have indicated before, many strategic or long-term benefits are intangible measurements and they are quite difficult to measured or quantify because they are subjective and predictive in nature. We will discuss these topics in later chapters.

14.1.4 **RISKS AND OPPORTUNITY**

If a business has the opportunity to gain profits and advantages, the business will also have the risk of losing the profits and advantages. The term "risk" means a business has the potential to lose profits or values. Any investment decision will have risks. Risk is pervasive. Our life is full of risks. You cannot find a business that has no risks at all. The opposite side of risk is opportunity. Risks and opportunities coexist in this world. Normally, the higher the risk of the business, the higher the benefit or profit that could be achieved.

From this perspective, "risk" is a probability of negative consequence for an uncertain future event. In contrast, "opportunity" would normally mean the possibility of a desirable outcome under uncertain circumstances in the near future. The nature of the future is uncertain and unknown because there is a lack of information about future events. There are two levels of meaning for "unknown":

1. Unknown because we do not have enough information about the future event
2. Unknown because we do not know what we do not know

The common expression of risk can be presented in the following formula:

$$Risk = Probability \times Negative\ Outcomes$$

Likewise, opportunity can be expressed in a similar formula:

$$Opportunity = Probability \times Positive\ Outcomes$$

Here, we have two variables: probability and outcomes in term of risks and opportunities. If the probability is equal to 0, it means that you can either ignore risks or opportunities. However, if the probability is equal to 1, then the future event or expected value will become certain or inevitable. Risk will become loss and opportunity can turn out to be profit. In the real world, a zero probability is highly unlikely for a future investment decision. Likewise, nothing is 100% certain.

Opportunities are always accompanied by risks. Very often, an opportunity resides in a risk. One investment decision for an investment project may involve many risks and opportunities. The overall expected result is equal to the sum of risks and opportunities:

$$Overall\ Expected\ Value = \sum_{i=1}^{n} Risk_i \times P_r + \sum_{l}^{m} Opportunity_l \times P_o$$

If the overall expected value is negative, then it is a highly risky project. Otherwise, it is an opportunity.

14.1.5 DEFINITION OF MODEL

The original meaning of model is "a three-dimensional representation of a person or thing or of a proposed structure, typically on a smaller scale than the real object" based on the OED. The typical example is an airplane model. This is the physical definition of a model. The second aspect of the definition is "a thing used as an example to follow or imitate." One example is when one person's behavior or style of resolving issues or problems becomes a typical example that other people can follow, such as a business model. The third aspect of the definition represents an abstract concept; it states that a model is "a simplified description, especially a mathematical description of a system or a process or a relationship between certain inputs and certain outputs, to assist the calculations and predictions." It is a logical or abstract way of thinking to describe the nature of the real world (see Figure 14.6).

If we look from a scientific perspective, modeling is just one way of analyzing or analogizing the real world. There are six different ways of analyzing the real world:

1. Model (such as an airplane model; it could be full scale)
2. Prototype (an early version of a product or sample to test a concept; it might not have to be full scale)
3. Mockup (it looks like a real object but is doesn't have the guts)
4. Simulation (it doesn't have the real or physical object or environment, it is not real)
5. Virtual reality (closer to a fancy reality)
6. Tele-presence (a hologram, just a 3D image)

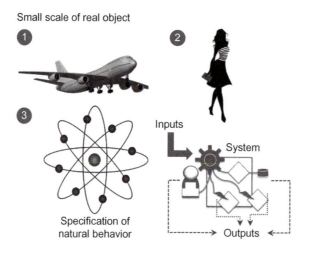

FIGURE 14.6

Definition of model.

We will discuss more details about simulation with real option theory in later chapters but in this chapter, we will concentrate on cost modeling.

The meaning of model or cost model in this book is actually a price analysis, with analogizing and reasoning for any pre-implementation project related to cloud computing. It is a part of the strategic planning exercise or decision-making process, especially for a multimillion-dollar investment project. Most companies will decide on a multimillion-dollar project after doing a cost model because from a cloud service provider's perspective, the cloud computing market is competitive and customers are always asking for more for less. Taking one of the cloud computing or IaaS pioneer companies, Amazon, as an example, the on-demand service instance is based on the hourly rate of a "pay as you go" (PAYG) cost model. This competitive business model has put a lot of cost pressure on many other hosting business competitors in this market.

As a cloud service consumer, although you may take some advantage of IaaS, you need to know the impact on your business if cloud security or availability becomes an issue. You have to have a comparison cost model to decide whether you should move to the public cloud or continue to use a local data center.

In a very competitive environment, a decision maker needs a very precise cost model to decide on business outcomes, whether you are a cloud service provider or a consumer. Without the cost model, it would be challenging to make rational investment decisions in this fast-changing world.

People might argue some that "good" decision makers may be able to make the right investment decision based on their instinct, intuition, cumulative experience, and insight rather than a cost model. This may explain why many shareholders or investors pay those high-flying executives bucket-oads of money to steer a large enterprise based on their successful track records. However, the thing we do not see is that personal instinct or intuition or cumulative experience also cretes a mental model. Precisely, it is a pattern or a process of pattern recognition. The issue with instinct or intuition is that they can never be quantified or made transparent. Many people believe that an intuitive decision is purely based on luck. It is not reliable or repeatable. Very often, these high-flying executives make terrible decisions. There have been so many giant enterprises such as Enron, Lehman Brothers, Primus Telecom, and Global Crossing destroyed by many bad decisions.

In today's world, even if you are an experienced decision maker, without a correct cost model, making a correct investment decision could become mission impossible. The risk can be enormously high. For a small project, you can afford to take some risks, but for a multimillion-dollar investment, the consequence of the investment failure could be devastating.

A cost model can help a decision maker to quantify and visualize the problems and possible scenarios. It is a kind of analysis tool for making rational decisions. Our mind does not always make rational decisions. Based on Daniel Kahneman's theory, our intuitive decisions are always faster than our rational ones.

Based on the above definition of model, it is not too difficult to see that a cost model or models are important analysis and decision support tools in the context of the competitive cloud computing market. With the help of cost models, it is possible to calculate the marginal cost of cloud computing products or services.

Cloud computing cost models are dependent on a mathematical representation of a set of business and technical assumptions associated with a cloud computing market. In this sense, a cost model is quantified by many assumptions, which include different ICT technologies, system operation, cloud architecture, business profile, financial situation, and market environment.

In essence, a model (or a cost model) is one of the approaches to define the behavior of an object or thing that may happen or has occurred in the real world. What we emphasize here is the third aspect of the model definition that discusses a mathematical formula to describe the relationship between the number of inputs and outputs (see Figure 14.6).

All models are involved in making assumptions. The model can only approximate the real world. It can never describe it exactly, because many assumptions that we made about the model might be highly subjective and uncertain. For example, consider if I made an assumption of 16 VMs per particular physical server or node (or virtual machine density), such as for a HP DL385 G8, and each physical node costs $2,185. If the business needs 250 hosting servers, how many physical nodes should I have or how much should I spend for physical nodes?

$$N_{PN} = \frac{N_{VM}}{VM_D} = \frac{250}{16} = 15.625$$

where N_{PN} = number of physical nodes, N_{VM} = number of virtual machines, VM_D = VM density.

The cost to purchase physical nodes would be equal to $16 \times \$2,185 = \$34,960$. In other words, I have to spend around $35 k capex to purchase an HP DL385 G8. As we can see in this cost model, the key assumption is the VM density being 16. This is really an arbitrary number. It can be 15, 18, or even 20. It would be dependent on the business or application requirements, which mean the workload running on each physical node. Figure 14.7 shows a typical server cluster's workload (a cluster has 10 physical nodes).

Based on the above Figure 14.7, the average CPU utilization rate is below 20% and memory usage is below 50%. It illustrates that the original assumption, 16 VMs per physical node, is overshooting or too conservative for the true business workload. Unfortunately, no one can make 100% accurate assumptions and there will be always a gap between the real workload measurements and

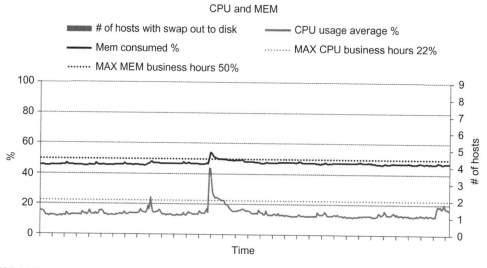

FIGURE 14.7

Example of a server cluster's workload.

assumptions. Most of time overshooting would be better than undershooting. The only question is by how much. If the gap is below 25%, it will be considered a good assumption.

14.1.5.1 Objective cost model

As we have mentioned above, a cost model can help a decision maker make the right decision. This means that the cost model is often built before the decision is made. You may say, why should we establish a cost model after a decision has been made? It is actually called a subjective cost model if a model is built after a decision has been made. But for now, let's discuss the objective cost model.

The objective cost model means the model is built from the bottom to the top according to the objective evidence or factors. Normally, the assumptions of cost models are based on historical data, some industry benchmarks, consulting advice and vendor suggestions.

In essence, the decision is made after the cost model's conclusions have been made. It is objective and has less subjective influence from some key decision makers. The process of building a cost model is based upon the standard business analysis and it is transparent. For example, one of the model assumptions of average VM density is 12 per physical node according to historic data. Of course, the real data shows the figure varies from time to time. One day it may be 9 or 11 and another day it may move up to 13 or 15. The average VM density is 12 with a standard deviation of ± 2.58.

If you are one of the business analysts for cloud computing, the processing steps for objective cost modeling are the following:

1. Understand the business problem and collect the data associated with costs.
2. Select the right cost modeling method or methods, such as TCO/ROI or cost/benefit ratio or breakeven based on business requirements, especially the strategic goal.
3. Define all transparent assumptions.
4. Build or establish a cost model or models.
5. Run analysis for all data (marketing, technology, business applications, and operations).
6. Draw a conclusion from analysis and optional solutions including pros and cons.
7. Make recommendations.

The above cost modeling process is similar to the process that we presented in Chapter 2, which was for business problem analysis. The key difference between these two processes is the cost modeling process builds a cost framework to simulate a real world scenario and the business problem analysis identifies the real issue and tries to solve it. Actually, we can consider cost modeling as a subprocess of the business problem solving process. In other words, cost modeling is a child process and business problem solving is a parent process.

A decision maker or group of decision makers will make their own decision based on the cost modeling analysis, conclusion, and recommendations. This kind of linear way of cost modeling goes from bottom to top. It isn't affected by any decision maker's personal influence or subjective instruction. Of course, if the model builder and the decision maker are the same person, then it would be quite challenging to keep the model as objective as possible. One way of doing so is to keep all counterarguments for every favorable conclusion. In short, you should try to be as dialectic or objective as possible, and not be dogmatic or prejudiced during the cost modeling process.

There is another similar term to objective cost modelling, so-called "ex-ante" analysis. "Ex-ante" is a Latin word meaning "beforehand" or "before the event." It is a typical financial or economic term that stands for comparing options or alternatives prior to a decision or a selection.

Ex-ante analysis will generate the expected values (either profits or loss) in advance of a decision. Of course, the expected values are not certain as future events have not occurred yet. The key difference between objective cost modeling and "ex-ante" analysis is that objective cost modeling emphases dialectic, impartial, and unprejudiced, while "ex-ante" analysis focuses on the time of decision.

14.1.5.2 Subjective cost model

Subjective cost modeling does not mean that the cost model is constructed based on a personal favor or preference. It is still built up on the truth, facts, and logic. The key difference between objective and subjective cost modeling is the time of cost modeling. If the model is established before decision making, it is an objective cost modeling. If it is established in the aftermath, it is subjective cost modeling. The purpose of subjective cost modeling is to check a decision maker's initiation or gut feeling.

You may wonder why people need aftermath cost modeling. A decision maker may want to check his/her intuition after a decision has been made. Under many circumstances, there might not be enough time for a decision maker to make a decision based on a proper cost model. After all, the cost modeling process needs time.

As Mortimer J. Adler said, "The essence of tragedy is time, or rather the lack of it. There is no problem in any Greek tragedy that could not have been solved if there had been enough time, but there is never enough. Decisions, choices have to be made in a moment, there is no time to think and weigh the consequences. It is easy for us see what should have been done, but would we have been able to see in time?" [89]. In other words, when we are building a cost model, we should never forget the fourth dimension—time. Although the investment decision has been made even if the result of cost modeling is contradictory to the decision that has been made, there is still space to revise it for some investment projects.

In contrast to the above "ex-ante" process, there is another Latin word that represents the opposite—"ex-post." It means after the event, when all the dust has settled. All uncertainty values have become crystal clear. "Ex-post" is an aftermath decision analysis or post-decision evaluation. The purpose of "ex-post" is to see if an IT investment met with the expected values or not. It can be considered historical data analysis to assist in future decision making (see Figure 14.8).

In comparison with ex-post, subjective cost modeling emphasizes decision time and the purposes of modeling. The main goal of subjective cost modeling is to verify the decision's assumptions and expected values. It is not to dig into the historical data. From this perspective, this kind of modeling is subjective.

In essence, subjective cost modeling is trying to rationalize a decision maker's decision that has already been made. Arguably, this kind of cost modeling can be highly controversial or self-serving. From a pattern recognition perspective, it can be interpreted as verifying a decision maker's hidden pattern or implicit gut feeling (see Figure 14.9).

Therefore, subjective cost modeling can be a tool or a process for a decision maker to bring a complex idea from implicit to explicit or to crystalize one's thinking or gather supporting evidence and facts for the decision.

It may be also a communication tool for a decision maker to persuade others to accept his/her decision. One of the typical examples was that Lee Iacocca used a cost model to convince Henry

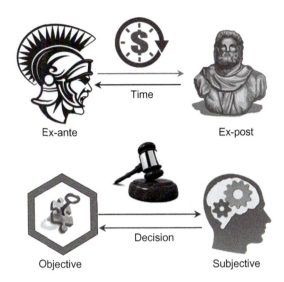

FIGURE 14.8

Ex-ante and Ex-post vs. objective and subjective cost modeling.

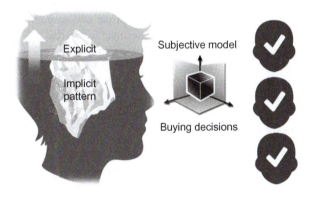

FIGURE 14.9

Subjective cost modeling For decision rationalization.

Ford II about the investment decision that he had already made for his idea for the Ford Mustang (see Figure 14.10).

14.1.6 MODEL MEASUREMENT OR METRICS

It doesn't matter whether it is an objective or subjective model. The critical issue is how good it is. This issue leads to the following question: how can we measure a cost model or what are the metrics for a cost model?

FIGURE 14.10

Example of subjective cost modeling for decision making.

The ultimate goal of a cost model is to help a decision maker solve a problem. If it can't, the model has no value whatsoever. It would totally waste time and resources. Therefore, the purpose of cost modeling is not the development of the model itself. The real purpose of cost modeling is to find the best solution for business problems. For example, the cost modeling of a cloud computing investment project appears to be just the process of developing a model, but the real aim of the cost modeling is to help a decision maker to find the right solution at the right time with the right amount of computer resources for the right business application. In Chapter 3, we raised the issue of how to develop a cloud cost model to resolve the life-cycle problem of E25K server fleet.

Therefore, the criteria for cost model metrics are:

1. Usefulness or value of a model from a decision maker's perspective. In short, the goal of a cost model is to see what a decision maker wants, for example, a clear strategic roadmap for cloud computing investment strategy for the next three years. The model will give a clear answer for how much capital should be invested each year for the next three years and if the cloud market conditions change, the model can justify the investment capital in order to maximize the return on investment (ROI) and minimize the investment risks.

2. How good is the model? As we have indicated before, all models are approximated. The value that a model can calculate or predict has a certain degree of error. A good model should have error within an expected level, such as $\pm 5 \sim 10\%$ variation.

3. How many constraints can the model work with? This is the scope of the model or limitation of analysis. It represents how adaptable the model is. All models have their boundary conditions. Beyond these constraints or conditions, the model will not work well. A good model should be very adaptive and flexible with different conditions.

4. A good model should be an effective persuasive tool for a decision maker to convince others to support his/her decision. In this sense, it should be a good strategic tool to articulate the

decision maker's vision and make an implicit idea explicit. For example, a simple mathematical formula, $y = kx$, can represent a linear proportional relationship between cost input (x) and profit output (y).

5. The cost of modeling itself. This is measured by two elements: time and cost. The common benchmark of cost modeling is that it should represent less than $2\% \sim 5\%$ of the total cloud project cost. The time should be between four weeks to three months. This is dependent on the complexity of an object. The details of length of time and value of cost modeling can be decided by a list of requirements, such as complexity, functions, modeling methods, and model criteria.

In summary, the metrics of a cost model can be classified into two categories: soft metrics and hard metrics. The soft metrics would include:

- Usefulness
- Adaptability and constraints
- Clarity

The hard metric measurements for a cost model may consist of:

- Cost
- Variation or accuracy
- Length of time to establish

All these above metrics can be quantified using dollar terms.

14.1.7 ANALYSIS

We have mentioned "analysis" many times above. The term "analysis" is very pervasive. It means detailed examination of the elements or structure of something. There are different types of analysis, such as value analysis, cost/benefit analysis, mathematical analysis, psychological analysis, etc. The meaning of the word is quite obvious, but difficult to fully understand. A few of the closer synonyms of analysis are "exploration," "investigation," "evaluation," and "interpretation." The purpose of defining analysis here is not to discuss the lexical meaning of analysis but rather to lay out the foundation of cost modeling.

As we have stated before, cloud cost modeling could be a very complex process that involves many variables and crosses many disciplines, such as finance, marketing, product or service design, procurement, and utilities. IT analysis alone cannot provide a satisfactory answer. A cloud data center investment decision should be a multicriteria decision analysis (MCDA).

Therefore, our definition of cost model is just one degree of analysis at the micro level. The total solution for cloud cost modeling should include not only many micro levels of analysis but also a macro level of investigation or evaluation as a good cost model should be able to:

- Cope with an ever-changing environment
- Provide insight or wisdom power to a decision maker
- Clarify interaction of multiple variables
- Highlight the dominant influencing factors at the macro level
- Create an explicit assumptions boundary

- Generate manageable choices or options
- Explain the reasons behind each solution
- Recommend a smart solution
- Be easy to understand or grasped
- Be a good communication tool to convince majority stakeholders

14.1.8 FRAMEWORK AND METHODOLOGY

In the previous sections, we introduced two terms: "cost" and "model," as well as many definitions associated with these two important terms. If we can borrow Timothy J. Kehoe's [166] phrase **"Every analysis is a model"** then the model can be narrowly interpreted as "every analysis." In this sense, only one model is capable of describing or capturing a complex phenomenon, such as cloud computing. This is why we often achieve an inaccurate result with one model or a single analysis, such as breakeven. This cost model may ignore growth potential and other intangible benefits over the long term.

If one model cannot resolve a complex problem, how about a set of models? Would that work? As Aminul Haque et al. [167] stated in their paper: "Due to the limitation of a single model to satisfy a large scale cooperation problem, multiple models can add value."

This leads to another term of our discussion, which is "framework." The term "framework" means "an essential supporting structure of a building, vehicle or object." It is a backbone or foundation of many objects. From a decision-making perspective, it is a set of principles, assumptions, constraints, and even complex ideas that we use when we are forming our decisions and judgments. In other words, a "framework is a system of rules, ideas or beliefs that is used to plan or decide something or a supporting structure around which something can be built."

The framework articulates a big picture. It is strategically oriented and focused on multiple criteria and impacts, looking at interactions among different variables across many different disciplines. A physical model is a visible and physical entity and a virtual model is a descriptive relationship between inputs and outputs, often a mathematical formula.

Of course, not every model can be calculated. If a model cannot be formulated, we will call it a "methodology." The concept of a methodology is similar to a framework, and means "a system of broad principles or rules from which a specific method or procedures may be derived to interpret or solve different problems within the scope of a particular discipline. Unlike an algorithm, a methodology is not a formula but a set of practices" [168]. From a cloud computing and IT investment perspective, the lines blur among cost analysis, cost model, cost framework, and investigation methodology. Many people often use them interchangeably. They have some common points or characteristics but we should also understand they are different (see Figure 14.11).

Because an investment methodology is unlike an algorithm, "there are no single, simple methodologies that will give a consistent reliable and optimal solution to manager facing an IT investment decision" [169].

In essence, a framework is a strategically oriented structure to support a backbone or foundation of many objects or concepts while a cost model is a tactical analysis for one or many aspects of single object. If a model cannot be described in a mathematical formula, we call it a methodology. We will adopt not only cost modeling and a cost framework but also different methodologies to describe cloud computing cost relationships and phenomena.

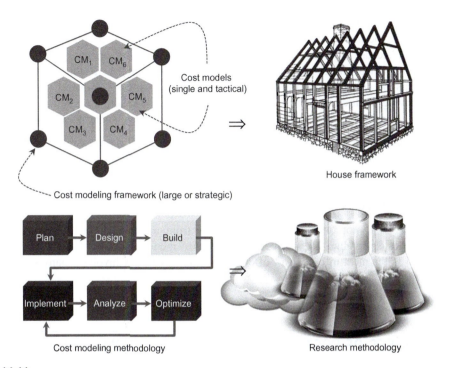

FIGURE 14.11

Framework and methodology.

14.1.9 FORMULATING A COST MODEL

Once we understand the above definitions and terms, including cost, model, cost model, analysis, framework, methodology, and their relationship, then we will possibly be able to formulate a general cost model. As we have indicated in the above, the very short definition of cost model is "a set of mathematical equations that can convert certain amount of resources inputs into cost data or outputs." This is a very simple and common definition. The comprehensive definition of cost model is defined by ITIL, and can be classified as the service type of cost model: "In order to calculate the costs of providing services it is necessary to design and build a framework in which all costs can be recorded and allocated or apportioned to specific customers or other activities. Such 'Cost Models' can be developed to show, for example, the cost of each service, the cost for each customer or the cost for each location" [170].

For the purposes of this book, our definition of cost model is a functional/stipulative definition, where the formula of the cost model can be presented as follows:

$$Cost\ Framework\ (TA_i, SA_k) = \sum_{i=1}^{n} TA_i + \sum_{k=1}^{m} SA_k$$

Here, $TA_i = $ *tactical analysis*, which includes operational analysis, technology analysis, and financial analysis. These are objective analysis with tangible values. Normally, they are quite simple or very straightforward.

SA_k = *strategic analysis*, which includes all additional analysis, such as economic forecasts and business analysis. The methods for this kind of analysis will include real option theory and Monte Carlo simulation because these are probability analyses with intangible or strategic values.

The objective part of the cost model equation is easier to establish. It consists of all physical cost components of cloud computing that we can physically measure, quantify, and calculate. Based on reviewing the literature about cost modelling, we can see there are a few important ingredients that are missing in many cost analyses or models. The reasons behind these issues are:

- It is too difficult to quantify a strategic or intangible value, such as forecasting the value of cloud computing growth.
- People are not aware of the components that have a significant impact on the outcome of the cost model.
- The cost items cannot be presented or articulated clearly.

Therefore, we will not only analyze cloud costs from a conventional perspective but also emphasize the strategic value. The strategic value of cost modeling is a probability plus a simulation analysis. It is the most difficult part of cost modeling because it involves many subjective and rational assumptions.

14.2 PURPOSES OF COST MODELING FOR CLOUD COMPUTING

Cost modeling is closely associated with a business strategy, which is an implementation plan for a company (either a cloud service provider or service consumer) to generate its business revenue or profit and to predict the operational cost or capital investment for the business. It can be either very simple or very complex. It is really dependent on the type and size of business.

The cost modeling analysis basically utilizes different types of information and data, and then articulates a concise formula so a decision maker can make the right decision at the right time based on a set of assumptions. The purpose of having a cost model or models and a cost framework are:

- Visualize abstract structure of the complex world
- Organize our concepts, thoughts, and ideas
- Communicate and convince other people

14.2.1 VISUALIZE ABSTRACT STRUCTURE OF THE COMPLEX WORLD

"Visualize abstract structure of the complex world" means the model establishes the concept of cloud computing costs and illustrates the structure of an abstract subject in a visible form to enable a decision maker to comprehend the scope and process of the cloud business.

Normally, it is quite challenging to visualize an abstract structure because an abstract concept or idea isn't easy to represent in a three-dimensional world. One of the purposes of cost modeling is to simplify the complex world around us and describe it with a concise model (see Figure 14.12).

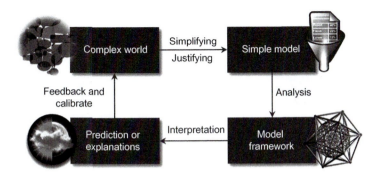

FIGURE 14.12

A simple process for cost modeling.

FIGURE 14.13

Organize thoughts and ideas.

A cost model has the key characteristics of the complex world or object that the model is describing. It brings an abstract concept or idea to a concrete and visible model that can be defined as a simple relationship between inputs and outputs.

14.2.2 ORGANIZE CONCEPTS, THOUGHTS, AND IDEAS

"Organize our concepts, thoughts, and ideas" means the cost modeling tool not only describes the business concept but also lays out the details of thoughts and ideas so a decision maker can utilize this model to make the right decision.

The purpose of organizing concepts, thoughts, and ideas is often related to subjective cost modeling, where a decision maker might have a gut feeling for the investment decision, but the gut feeling is fuzzy and foggy. If you hear a decision maker say, "I know what it is, but I do not know how to explain it" it means he/she needs a cost model to organize his/her thoughts and ideas (see Figure 14.13).

In other words, one of the purposes of cost modeling is as a mental exercise to clear one's mind. It is one of the good tools for articulating an issue for problem solving or decision making. If we introduce a time component into our calculation for a cost model, such as net present value (NPV),

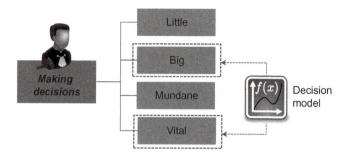

FIGURE 14.14

Decision and decision outcomes.

it would be impossible to make the right decision for the future value of a present estimation just based on personal intuition. Of course, not all decisions need cost modeling. Only the decisions that are vital, big, and have a long-term impact, such as a multimillion-dollar investment for a cloud computing project, must have a cost model to assist decision makers (see Figure 14.14).

In short, one of purposes of cost modeling is to leverage logical reasoning for clear thinking.

14.2.3 COMMUNICATE WITH OTHER PEOPLE

This has two aspects. (1) We can use the cost model as a reference model to make sure all people involved are on the same page. For a very large cloud computing project, the conversation between the line of business and IT professionals can be very confusing without proper orientation or a common reference. There may be a risk of comparing apples with oranges and wasting much valuable project time. (2) Once the decision is made, all people should understand what the project goal is and what criteria will be used to measure the project goals (see Figure 14.15).

An efficient cost model is not only very helpful for project delivery but also can make sure the project will be delivered on time and within the budget. Looking ahead, cloud cost modeling will become one of enterprise planning tools for many enterprises to forecast IT expenses or budget.

14.3 CHALLENGES OF CLOUD COST MODELING

Before moving on to the next topic of cloud cost modeling, it is very important for us to fully understand the challenges of cost modeling because it is a very complicated process involving many variables and uncertainty factors. Sometimes, it is almost impossible for people to define and measure the cloud. Different people have been trying to use different rules (or models) to measure the "sky." However, none of the cost models is quite compelling. One of the obvious reasons is that cloud computing is virtual and evolving rather than physical and static. Taking a hosting server as an example, the unit cost is a virtual machine (VM), which is literally a software file rather than a physical object. You can see it via a virtual machine monitor (VMM) but you cannot feel, touch, and grab it.

FIGURE 14.15

Purpose of cost model as a communication tool.

Table 14.2 P2V Relationship	
Physical vs. Virtual	**Description of Physical to Virtual (P2V) Relationship**
1-to-1	One physical server is equivalent to one virtual machine
1-to-Many	One physical server equals many virtual machines
Many-to-1	Many physical servers equal one virtual machine
Many-to-Many	Many physical servers host many virtual machines

From an architecture perspective, once a physical server or a node has been virtualized, the old one-to-one relationship between one physical node and one operating system has gone. The relationship between a VM and a physical node can be configured to either one-to-many or many-to-one or many-to-many (see Table 14.2).

This nature of a dynamic changing environment will be very challenging for cost modeling because the application workload and server resources do not hold a one-to-one relationship. In one minute, one physical server might be diverted to many workloads or instances. In another minute, many physical servers or nodes might be dedicated to one workload.

In short, making workload assumptions for each physical node is an uncertain process. You might be able to figure out the average workload for the entire cluster (for example, typically 10 or 12 physical nodes, see Figure 14.5) after the cloud cluster has been implemented and in operation but it would be difficult to find out the workload for an individual physical node if the cluster environment is very dynamic. Some VMs have to be been suspended, resumed, and migrated from one physical node to another or even from one cluster to another with variations in requirements.

From sever virtualization technology perspective, an administrator can temporarily freeze or suspend a VM or deploy memory overcommitment technology to implement a swap to disk, balloon driver, and memory compression. These technologies make the cost model of cloud computing even more complex.

As illustrated in Figure 14.7, the average memory consumption rate of a cluster is normally higher than CPU usage. In this case, memory consumption is about four times more than CPU usage (memory 50% vs. CPU 13%). This phenomenon is why some hypervisors develop the technology to reclaim some idle memory resources from a virtual host. VMware calls it a memory balloon driver; with it the hypervisor can ask the guest VM to release some idle memory that has been allocated. It is also called memory overcommitment. It is good for a cloud consumer to maximize the usage of physical node resources, but it certainly creates an issue when making assumptions about the unit cost for each physical node.

From a human perceptive, the cost model of cloud computing can be either subjective or objective. Most of us are risk averse but many entrepreneurs prefer to take risks. For example, if a business application prefers to set the maximum ceiling of CPU usage to 55%, but your experiences tell you that when the maximum utilization rate has reached 75%, the performance of the application is good, would you take a risk or just set up the utilization ceiling based on the application requirement? If the CPU usage ceiling is set over 55%, then a cloud service provider will take risks in terms of the VM's performance. If the CPU usage ceiling is set below 55%, the unit cost of the VM will be increased. If you are a decision maker, would you take the risk to increase the CPU usage ceiling? You might have to check the overall SLA metrics of the IaaS and balance the expected risk and cost.

Overall, the cost models of cloud computing are mental frameworks that we employ to articulate our understanding of the complex world around us and to ensure that we can reach the right strategic conclusion based on many abstract and mental processes of thinking (see Figure 14.16).

As we can see in Figure 14.16, the mental framework include some factors (represented as symbols F_1, F_2 ... F_i) and excludes other factors. It is dependent on how the assumptions have been made. This mental framework of cost models is sometimes also called the boundary condition. It can decide how the model is applied.

You might notice that there is another small frame within a big frame. If you consider the big frame as a strategic view, then the smaller frame is a tactical module. Many smaller tactical modules form a large strategic frame. It is similar to a city having many suburbs, a suburb having many building blocks, a building block having many houses and apartments, a house having many rooms, a room having a few windows, and a window having a few frames. The list can go on and on. This approach can be referred to as a divide and conquer technique. The critical issue is how to decide on the boundary and how to draw the boundary conditions. It is normally dependent on the time and resources of the cost modeling.

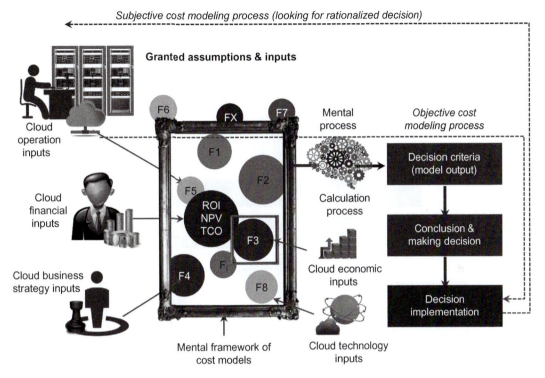

FIGURE 14.16

Mental framework of cost modeling.

Within a cost framework, we may have cost models or smaller frames that analyze price structures from different perspectives, such as finance, operations, technology, data center facility, server, storage, and network. In order to organize and visualize various cost components in ever-changing environments, we have to adopt different analytic tools of cost modeling and cost methodologies to articulate the cost framework. And then we use this framework to support our cloud business strategy (see Figure 14.17). We will give more details in the next chapter.

From an end-to-end perspective of cloud cost modeling, we will have two levels of analysis:

1. Tactical or tangible or concrete analysis
2. Strategic or intangible or abstract analysis

The tactical or tangible analysis is relatively easier than the strategic or intangible one. Most calculations for tangible analysis are quite simple, and involve either summing or subtracting the value of benefits or costs. It may also be considered a stack layer model. The fundamental challenging issue is how to include or exclude these factors or inputs and how to establish the framework boundary at the tactical level. Obviously, one factor may have more influence than others at the strategic level. The popular solution is to adopt the sensibility test for different assumptions at the strategic level.

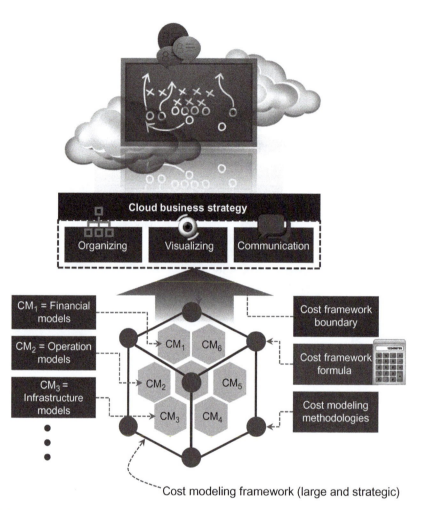

FIGURE 14.17

Cost framework, modeling, analysis, and methodologies.

When we move the cost model analysis to the strategic level, the main challenge is how to interpret the intangible or strategic value or even subjective imagination into tangible values or concrete measureable units. Overall, we should understand the limitations of cost modeling.

14.3.1 NOT ALL FACTORS ARE WITHIN THE FRAMEWORK

We should understand that the framework is a simplified prototype for a complex world. First, there are many facts (such as F_6, F_7, F_8, and F_X) that have been excluded from this framework because some facts are more important than others in term of the decision conclusion. It is impossible to

| Flexibility | Size of frame | Limited mental capacity | Time stamp |

FIGURE 14.18

Limitations of cost modelling.

include everything in a model or a framework. If it does include everything, it will not be a model but rather the real world. Moreover, the modeling process will lose its purpose of framing and simplification.

14.3.2 LIMITATION OF FRAMEWORK SIZE

The size of this framework can be big or small. It depends on many factors including project time and resources, individual experience, knowledge, and scope of a job (see Figure 14.18). Ultimately, the size of the framework will be decided by its goal, time, and resources.

Time and resources are limited. The issue is how to come up with the best cost model or framework with limited time and resources. This is the skill involved in cost modeling.

14.3.3 OBJECTIVE OR SUBJECTIVE PROCESS OF COST MODELING

The process of the cost model can be either objective or subjective. If it is objective, it means that that the process is fairly linear and opened. The conclusion will be made after data collection and multiple modeling stages. The decision will be made or selected among many recommended conclusions or options. In contrast, the subjective process may start from the opposite direction, in which the conclusion has already been reached and the action has already been taken. The purpose of subjective cost modeling is for a decision maker to check his/her intuition or to verify the decision and see whether the decision can be supported by analysis or fit within the reality or not. In addition, subjective cost modeling is used to establish a communication tool and persuade others to get on board.

14.3.4 LIMITATION OF INDIVIDUAL KNOWLEDGE AND EXPERIENCE

We can use different cost models with different size frameworks to analogize to reality. Obviously, the selection of the type of cost model and framework size is based on an individual's experience and expertise, knowledge, insight, and wisdom. Perhaps it is based on a person's gut feeling. From this perspective, it is subjective.

14.3.5 A TIME STAMP ON THE MODEL

Any cost model and conclusion is temporary and subject to revision because the world we are living in today is so dynamic and always changing. Therefore, some facts may be influential today, but they might not be that dominant tomorrow. Vice versa, some not so important facts that we have excluded in the current model may become critical or too important to be ignored.

The framework often involves many granted assumptions during our mental processes and these assumptions will define how things work in the dynamic and ever-changing environment. However an assumption is an assumption. It is not a fact. Unfortunately, we have seen many people take assumptions as fact during a modeling process. It may lead to either an overshooting or undershooting scenario during the period of decision making. Subsequently, this may cause a company to lose many valuable resources. It is not only money but also business opportunities.

Furthermore, how we frame a cost model can often shape the decision that a decision maker makes. If we consider prospect theory, different frameworks of a cost model for the same thing will reach different conclusions.

In essence, the challenge at the tactical level is how to make assumptions and include and exclude many boundary conditions. When the cost model is elevated into the strategic level, the issue is how to interpret intangible values and abstract ideas into tangible measurements.

14.4 SUMMARY

We introduced terms and definitions of cost modeling for cloud computing. This is the foundation for us to build up cost models and a cost framework for the decision maker to make the right investment decision.

A cost model is actually one type of price analysis. In order to provide a strategic solution under an ever-changing environment, you might need more than one model to describe a complex cost problem, in which case we build a cost framework.

When we articulate a cost framework, we will face at least four different challenges: how to set a framework boundary; how to decide on the framework size; how to be objective or dialectic; and how to understand the limitations of the framework and particular model or models.

The critical point that we have developed is to classify the analysis into two levels:

1. Tactical level
2. Strategic level

Each level has its function with respect the big picture so that we will not confuse a model and framework's purpose and application. In essence, it would be impossible to draw a conclusion for a multimillion-dollar cloud project based on a single cost analysis. We will have to look at problem from different perspectives and draw a rational solution from multiple disciplines "because all the wisdom of the world is not found in one little academic department."[1]

---

[1]Charlie Munger, Warren Buffett's business partner.

14.5 **REVIEW QUESTIONS**

1. What is a cost model?
2. What is a cost framework?
3. What are the differences between a cost model and framework?
4. Why do we need a cost model?
5. If I do not have a cost model, can I make the right decision?
6. What are the risks for me if I do not have a cost model?
7. Why have there been so many cost models for IT investment?
8. Name various categories of cost models.
9. What is the most important cost model from a financial and business perspective?

COST MODEL CATEGORIES

15

Following the description of the concept of cost modeling in Chapter 14, we will begin with a literature review first in this chapter. It will cover different literature sources, such as research papers, books, and industrial whitepapers regarding cost models over the last 50 years of IT history. We will differentiate these models using different categories that across the finance, IT operations, and computer science disciplines. Ultimately, we will provide a practical approach to draw a cost framework for the decision maker in terms of rolling out a cloud project. From a practical process perspective, we will mainly concentrate on the set of financial and IT operations cost models as well as the relationship among these models.

When we unveil the process of these financial cost models for cloud cost modeling, we will particularly highlight many popular financial terms, such as sales revenue, capital expenditure (or capex), operational expenditure (or opex), asset value, profit margin, return on investment (ROI), and total cost of ownership (TCO) because these terms form the cornerstone of IT performance metrics or key performance indicators (KPIs) for any cloud project. In essence, this chapter will present two basic components (see Figure 15.1):

- Cost model literature review
- Financial cost models

15.1 REVIEW OF COST MODELS

Since the 1960s, there have been literally millions of cost models or methodologies created regarding IT investment or evaluation based on T.J.W. Renkema and E.W. Berghout's [171] research in 1997. They stated that new methods were published almost daily. Obviously, the IT industry is a highly dynamic and fast changing industry. Each cost analysis will come from different perspectives with different interests. As a result, a particular model or method must be established to evaluate the particular IT investment project. If each cost model analyst wants to emphasize their own environment (namely, technology, people, time, and resources), it is inevitable that millions of cost models will be generated. As we indicated in the last chapter, if we see each cost model as one analysis, the result of millions of cost models should not be surprising. The question is, how can we categorize these models and how doe we leverage the experience of these models for today's cloud environment, rather than reinventing a wheel? Dutch researchers T.J.W. Renkema et al. [172] summarized 65 popular evaluation methodologies (or cost models) for cost modeling (see Appendix F). Although new methods or techniques or models have been created almost every

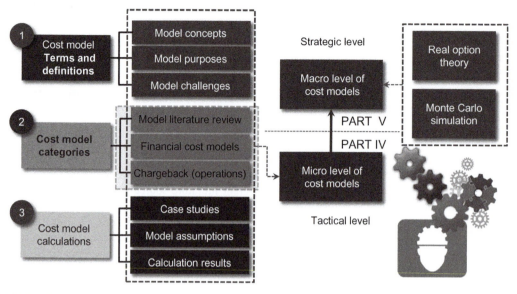

FIGURE 15.1

Moving to next topic in cost modeling.

day, these new models are very often "building on the extensive body of knowledge that is already incorporated in the available methods."

The common problem of cost modeling since the 1960s has always been how to decide which models are designed for which circumstances. In other words, every model is just one snapshot of a particular case. It is just momentarily true, which means the majority of models can not be generalized. In order to resolve this issue, the authors tried to provide an open solution to classify all cost models into four different approaches:

- Financial approach
- Multicriteria approach
- Rational approach
- Portfolio approach

The authors believed that each generic model should possess certain aspects or basic criteria or requirements. These requirements are:

- The model should be well documented and accessible for further analysis.
- The model should be well structured. This implies that a method consisting of mere guidelines is insufficient.
- The model should be characteristic of the approach reviewed or be often used in practice.

Moreover, the paper presented a comparison table for 10 different models classified by four approaches against the following four basic criteria (see Appendix D for more details):

- Objectives
- Evaluation criteria

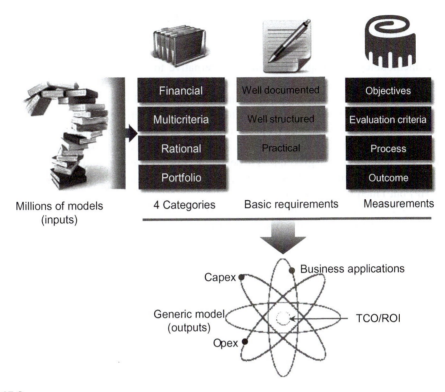

FIGURE 15.2

Categories of cost models.

- Support for evaluation process
- Type of outcome

We summarize the paper in Figure 15.2.
The authors summarized the purposes of building a model with four basic questions:

1. Does the model give new insight (business insight)?
2. Does the model give complete results?
3. Is the model easy to use?
4. Does the model give control over the decision-making process?

These questions or measurements are very valuable materials for our cost modeling process. Following Renkema and Berghout's paper in the 1990s, Marc J. Schniederjans et al. simplified 65 models into three large categories and downsized to 47 different models [173]:

- Financial IT investment
- Multicriteria IT decision making
- Other IT investment

By reviewing the literature from 1987 to 2003, Schniederjans et al. concluded that "there are no single, simple methodologies that will give a consistent, reliable and optimal solution to mangers facing an IT investment decision. One type of investment methodology can suggest one alternative and another methodology a completely different alternative to an IT investment decision choice." This leads to the old modeling problem of garbage in, garbage out. Therefore, Schniederjans et al. proposed their alternative solution, which is summarized in Table 15.1.

These methods were a good starting point to investigate different IT investment cost models. We will select a few models from this table for our cloud computing cost modeling process in later chapters. The issue with Marc J. Schniederjans et al.'s approach is that these models appear to be too general. The authors didn't give enough detail on how to use these methodologies or model with a particular investment case. For example, the authors had described an analytical hierarchy process (AHP) but failed to give further details.

In order to understand the cost modeling process from a historical perspective, we will begin with examining the cost model for the first Intel CPU.

Table 15.1 IT Investment Decision Methodology

Methodologies (or Models)	Type	Description
Analytical hierarchy process	Multicriteria	Calculate the overall score of decision-makers' pairwise comparisons
Balanced scorecard	Other	Evaluate investment from the user, business value, efficiency, and innovation/learning perspectives
Critical success factors	Other	Obtain, compare, and rank factors critical to business success and based on these rankings, deduce investment priorities
Decision theory	Multicriteria	Calculate the expected value of investing in alternative investments
Accounting rate of return	Financial	Compare the average after-tax profits with initial investment cost
Delphi method	Other	Obtain consensus of experts' opinion concerning the best alternative investment
Satisfaction & priority survey	Other	Survey and compare user and MIS professionals' opinions on the effectiveness and importance of installed systems
Game theory	Other	Calculate payoff of investment based on actions of the competition, mathematics, and economic theory
Payback period	Financial	Calculate time required to recoup initial cost
Information economics	Financial	Calculate the overall value of an investment based on enhanced ROI, business domain, and technology domain criteria

15.1.1 **THE COST MODEL OF THE FIRST CPU**

Based on information from the Computer History Museum, if the first x86 CPU was the Intel CPU 4004, then the earliest cost model could be traced back to in early 1970s. It was a highly business-oriented cost model that was established by both Intel and Nippon Calculating Machine (NCM). The model was specified by the contract [174] and signed between two parties. Basically, it was a volume-driven cost model and emphasized delivery time. Of course, NCM had the exclusive commercial rights for the 4004 chip that was dedicated to NCM desktop calculators (see Figures 15.3 and 15.4).

In today's terms, the cost model is 1-to-1 relationship. The contract stated the NCM has the exclusive rights to the 4004 Intel chip. If Intel sold the 4004 CPU to other parties within three years, it would be penalized by NCM, but the penalty value would be deprecated in each month until the end of the three-year contract.

Although the agreement between Intel and NCM was a commercially oriented contract, it did reflect the cost component of computing for each desktop calculator. This cost model was quite simple, direct, and straightforward because there was no resource sharing. In other words, all costs of CPU would be diverted to the NCM desktop calculator project. From the NCM perspective, it might also be considered a project-based cost model.

Later, Federico Faggin who was both the Busicom project manager and the designer of the 4004 CPU, convinced Intel management that the 4004 chip couldn't only be applied to Busicom's desktop calculator but also could adopted by other applications. Actually, this chip had been

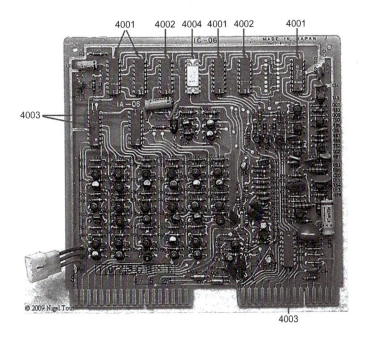

FIGURE 15.3

NCM desktop calculator's printed circuit board equipped with first CPU, the Intel 4004 [175].

FIGURE 15.4

NCM desktop calculators [175].

sold for many applications, such as bank teller terminals, blood analyzer (for Demark), pinball machines, cash registers, and inventory control for petrol stations and breeding cows. This was the first prototype of a shared cost model computing history. It was also the beginning of the 1-to-many cost model.

Although the 4004 microprocessor (4 bit) chip might have only sold about one million in volume, it had laid out the foundation for later x86 CPU models, such as the Z80 (8 bit), 8080 (8 bit), 80286 (16 bit), 80386 (32 bit), 80486 (32 bit), Pentium (32 bit), Xeon (64 bit)...

Since 2008, cloud computing has been taking off. Many IT consumers or enterprise users are considering whether they should move their IT applications to a cloud environment or not. Although there are academic papers on cloud computing cost models, Intel's example provides an easier methodology for building a cloud cost model, where a detailed cost structure is built at a tactical level and there is shared cost at a strategic level (see Figure 15.5).

15.1.2 RECENT CLOUD COMPUTING COST MODELS

By reviewing a lot of recent literature on cloud cost modeling, we will derive an interactive cost framework between the tactical level and strategic level. Let's begin with walking through some of the latest developments regarding cost modeling for cloud computing.

In both 2009 and 2010, Edward Walker [176] published two articles for calculating NPV values to measure the unit cost of CPUs and storage. The comparison of NPV values is the baseline of an investment decision of whether a business should "lease" or "purchase" computer resources. Walker's cost model had 10 parameters to calculate. These calculations are for both the lease and buy solutions. He concluded that if NPV (purchase) is greater than NPV (lease), then the investment decision should be "buy"; vice versa, if the NPV (lease) is higher than NPV (purchase), the

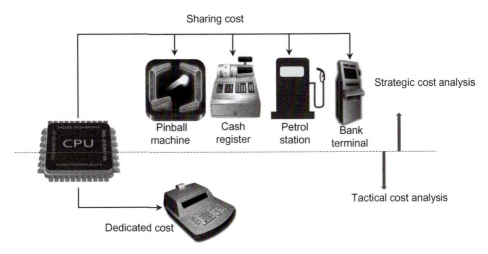

Sharing cost

Pinball machine
Cash register
Petrol station
Bank terminal

CPU

Strategic cost analysis

Tactical cost analysis

Dedicated cost

FIGURE 15.5

Idea from first CPU cost modeling solution.

investment decision should be "lease" (refer to the following four equations). Although it may appear to be an oversimplified cost model, it is a good starting point to enlighten other people to build other much more realistic models:

$$NPV = C_0 + \sum_{T=1}^{Y} \frac{C_T - A}{(1+k)^T}$$

$$R(purchase) = NPV/NPC = \frac{\left(1 - \frac{1}{\sqrt{2}}\right) \times \sum_{T=0}^{Y-1} \frac{C_T}{(1+k)^T}}{\left(1 - \frac{1}{\sqrt{2}}\right)^Y \times TC}$$

$$R(lease) = NPV/NPC = \frac{\sum_{T=0}^{Y-1} \frac{C_T}{(1+k)^T}}{Y \times TC}$$

where C_0 = initial capital cost, C_T = annualized cash flow (=profit−cost), T = time, A = the server cluster's original purchase cost, k = capital cost or interest rate, Y = number of years to be calculated, NPC = net present capacity over an operational life span of Y years, and TC = total useful capacity, which represents the expected CPU hours users consume $TC = TCPU \times H \times \mu$ (where TCPU = the total CPU cores the server cluster has, H = expected number of operational hours the server provides annually, and μ = expected server utilization).

The author provides very direct cost comparisons with his results and Amazon's Elastic Computer Cloud (EC2) prices. The key assumptions made were the following: (1) fully populated 44 1 RU computer blade rack where each unit costs $2,000; (2) power consumption 20 kW; (3) utilization rate is between a high of 90% and low of 40%; and (4) the utility cost (HVAC) is between $0.07/kWh and $0.4/kWh. The conclusion was that if the life cycle time is between 6 and 7 years, the "stay in house" (or purchase) option is preferred; otherwise, the lease option would be desirable.

If the depreciation assumption of CPU assets is between 3 and 4 years, (or about two generations of CPU according to Moore's law) then the purchasing option should not be considered in the first place. Actually, a common financial practice for many large enterprises and organizations is to write off their computer or IT assets after three years. This means that the computer assets' value will be equal to zero after three years.

In the paper, the author used Amazon's EC2 prices as the benchmark for the decision whether to lease or buy. As we know, Amazon's IaaS or Amazon Web Services (AWS) not only provides EC2 services, but also Simple Storage Service (S3). One year later, the same author published another paper on disk storage cost modeling [177]. The decision model was similar to the CPU one but with a slight modification that we summarize in the following:

$$\Delta\text{NPV} = \sum_{T=0}^{N} \frac{C_T - E_T + L_T}{(1+I_F)^T} + \frac{S}{(1+I_F)^N} - C$$

$$S = \gamma * \Omega * \lceil V_T \rceil_\Omega * K * e^{-0.438T}$$

$$C_T = -\rho * H_T - (365 * 24) * \delta * (P_C + P_D * \lceil V_T \rceil_\Omega)$$

$$E_T = (1.03 * \lceil V_T \rceil_\Omega - \lceil V_{T-1} \rceil_\Omega) * \Omega * K * e^{-0.438T}$$

where S, C_T, and E_T represents the expected end of life disk salvage value, the operation cost in year T, L_T = lease payment at year T, C = initial capital cost, I_F = Interest rate for financing (see Table 15.2). The calculation example that the author provided showed that the threshold level of the decision to buy or lease was four years. The author concluded that if the expected lifespan of disk storage is more than four years, the buy decision would be preferred; otherwise the lease option would be a better value for the business. The author made a few major assumptions for the cost model, such as the unit cost declining with increasing storage volume; also, the technology of the disk driver interface or block-oriented storage protocol was SATA (refer to Section 12.4.2.2 for more details).

However, the author indicated that the purpose of the paper was just to "stimulate discussion, debate and future work in quantitative modeling of the cloud computing industry." This is a good stepping stone to build a cost model from a financial perspective (NPV). However, the cost model appears to be only focusing on part of thecloud infrastructure. The article lacked consideration for other cost components, such as data center facility, power, space, cooling, cloud migration (or physical to virtual, P2V, migration), system reliability, service performance, availability, scalability, maintainability, adaptability, usability, security, multitenancy, auto-orchestration, system integration, and supportability.

15.1.2.1 Hybrid solution for cloud computing cost model

In 2010, Stamatia Bigi et al. [178] addressed the issue from a different angle, and examined the following primary question: Is the migration to the cloud the most profitable option for every business? They tried to identify all relevant costs for a business to deploy applications on either cloud

Table 15.2 Symbols for Storage Cost Model	
Term	**Description**
δ	Cost of electric utility ($/kW hour)
Ω	Size of purchased disk drives (Gbytes)
ρ	Proportional difference between human effort in maintaining a purchased versus a leased storage infrastructure
γ	Used disk depreciation factor on salvage
C	Disk controller unit cost ($)
H_T	Annual human operation salary ($)
I_F	Risk-free interest rate (%)
K	Current per-Gbyte storage price ($/Gbyte)
L_T	Expected annual per-G byte lease payment ($/Gbyte/year)
P_C	Disk controller power consumption (kW)
P_D	Disk drive power consumption (kW)
V_T	Expected storage requirement in year T (Gbytes)
T	Number of year (Year)
ΔNPV	Net Present Value Difference ($) between purchased NPV and leased NPV

computing or on-premises infrastructure. They proposed a three-step decision model (see Figure 15.6) for evaluating the two alternatives (fly in the cloud and stay in house).

In addition, the authors provided six driving forces for their cost models:

- Operation drivers
- Business premises drivers
- Product drivers
- Process drivers
- Software process drivers
- Cultural and experience drivers

If we use the authors' terms, it seems to be a methodology rather than a cost model. In the conclusion, the authors summarized that neither extreme options (cloud and on-premises) would be appreciated for a particular business. The final pervasive model would be dominated by hybrid solutions for both cloud computing and in-house infrastructure. The conclusion may be correct, but the authors did not provide enough quantified evidence to support their claims. If this is the case, the conclusion seems to be more like a prediction than the scientific fact.

In contrast, Ali Khajeh-Hosseini et al. provided some kind of comparison of cost among three public cloud providers (see Tables 15.3 and 15.4). This comparison is supported by two cost modeling tools.

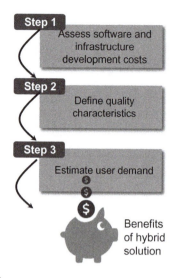

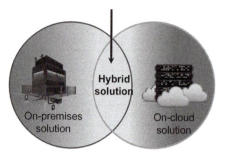

Step 1
Assess software and infrastructure development costs

Step 2
Define quality characteristics

Step 3
Estimate user demand

Benefits of hybrid solution

An optimised solution for a business

Hybrid solution

On-premises solution

On-cloud solution

Decision model criteria for IT manager
- Cost of migration
- Cost of QoS for cloud
- Cost of software development
- Number of users

FIGURE 15.6

Three-step approach and hybrid solution.

Table 15.3 Cost of Different Cloud Providers [181]			
Cost ($)	AWS US-East	FlexiScale	Rackspace
First month	$18,980	$5,060	$6,550
Monthly average	$1,916	$5,151	$6,732
Total for 3 years	$85,950	$185,345	$242,170
Difference with AWS		+2X	+3X

Table 15.4 Cost of Different Deployment Options on AWS-EU			
Cost ($)	Nonelastic	Elastic	Elastic, small instances
First month	$67,350	$65,430	$75,260
Monthly average	$6,259	$4,334	$4,175
Total for 3 years	$286,415	$217,470	$221,385

The first tool is to estimate the cost of a public cloud for IaaS usage. The cost components included cloud migration, data center equipment, IT infrastructure, data center facility site, software licenses, system engineering, software changes, IT professionals, and resource usage patterns. The author particularly highlighted Amazon example based on the EC2 cost comparison spreadsheet [179], which was presented by Amazon in 2009 and revised in February 2010.

Table 15.5 Amazon EC2 Cost Comparison Calculator					
Price Model	Amazon EC2 (On-Demand)	Amazon EC2 (1 Year Reserved)	Amazon (3 Year Reserved)	Co-Location	On-Site (On-Premises)
Annual TCO	$229,675	$189,817	$156,567	$1,470,070	$2,572,634
Price Ratio of Comparison	1.5	1.2	1	9.4	16.4

In the example, Amazon's cost comparison calculator gave three comparison scenarios:

- Amazon EC2 (7 assumptions)
- Co-location (19 assumptions)
- On-site (24 assumptions)

But the final calculation results exhibited by Amazon were five comparison cases and three of them were Amazon's AWS products. It should not be surprising that the most favorable TCO price was the EC2 three-year contract (the longest service contract locked in with Amazon) (see Table 15.5).

As we can see, the price ratio in the five-case comparison demonstrated that the co-location price was 9.4 times more than the three-year EC2 contract and on-site would be 16.4 times more than the three-year EC2 case. One of the key assumptions of these cases was that 1,000 EC2 standard small instances would be equal to 1,000 physical servers or nodes and the unit cost of each server was only equal to $363. This assumption doesn't appear to match reality.

The author indicated that Amazon's spreadsheet for the cloud utility billing model has three uncertainty issues:

1. The actual resources consumed by a system, which are determined by its load
2. The deployment options used by a system, which can affect its costs as things like data transfer is more expensive between clouds compared to data transfer within clouds
3. Cloud providers' prices, which can change on short notice

It is right that the actual resource consumption is not based on an arbitrary number, such as 1,000 instances, but rather a workload pattern. It is also true that the cost of data transfer between clouds is much higher than the price to move the data within a cloud data center. The third issue seems to be less significant because both the "co-location" and "on-site" prices were well above the EC2 cost. It is highly unlikely that the EC2 cost would increase 10 times within three years.

The second tool is an assessment of risks against benefits for a decision maker. For the risk/benefits assessment tool, the paper identified a total of 10 benefits from three perspectives (technical = 5, financial = 2 and organization = 3). However, the number of risks appears to be two times more than the benefits; they are given from five perspectives (organization = 6, legal = 5, technical = 4, security = 3, and financial = 2) (see Figure 15.7).

This method is similar as Hubbert Smith's method [128] of comparing HDD and SSD. Again, these tools are more like a methodology. As the paper summarized in the section on literature review, there are not many cost modeling tools available to support an enterprise decision maker for consideration of either migrating a IT system to a cloud or staying in-house. However, there are

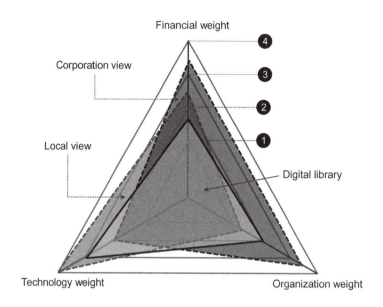

FIGURE 15.7

The weighted average risk and benefit assessment for cloud migration.

numerous whitepapers supported by cloud providers that offer a lot of advice. IT consultancies might also give many frameworks and assessment tools but "such tools are either marketing tools or they are not widely available as they are based on closed proprietary technologies that are often accompanied by expensive consultancy contracts." Therefore, the paper just concentrates on describing and evaluating these two "important" tools rather than real cost modeling.

In the conclusion, the paper summarized a few limitations. First, it only discusses IaaS for the public cloud. Second, the cost model does not consider project management in terms of cloud migration. Third, the risk/benefit assessment is just a starting point for analysis. Two case studies represented two extreme cases (one is a small company and the other is a large enterprise). Due to many identified higher risks, the author concluded that public IaaS would be better for special IT functions, such as off-site backup and disaster recovery. This conclusion may be true, but the authors didn't have enough convincing evidence to support their conclusion.

15.1.2.2 Cloud service provider's cost model

Instead of analyzing the costs from NPV, public IaaS cloud, and cloud consumer perspectives, Albert Greenberg et al. [183] from Microsoft research described the cloud computing cost components of a data center to support a cloud. The paper addresses the issues from a cloud provider perspective. The cost model was based on 50,000 servers and associated data center infrastructure. The assumption for money growth is 5%, which represents the interest that money would earn if the capital is not invested in a cloud data center project, but deposited into a bank. The authors presented a rough guide of the amortized cost ratio for a data center to provide cloud services (see Tables 15.6 and 15.7). However, these cost ratios appear to be too loose or imprecise. Many major cost items do not seem to be included, such as provisioning, P2V, space, software, etc. However, the data does provide a direction for other people to do future studies.

Table 15.6 Guide to Where Costs Go in a Data Center

Amortized Cost	Components	Subcomponents
~45%	Server	CPU, memory, storage systems
~25%	Infrastructure	Power distribution and cooling
~15%	Power	Electrical utility costs
~15%	Network	Links, transit, equipment

Table 15.7 Admin IT Staff to Server Ratio

Data Center Type	IT Staff to Server Ratio
Typical cloud	1:100
Well-run cloud	1:1,000
Large cloud	1:1000,000

The paper concluded that underutilization of a cloud data center is the major cost for a cloud service provider. The reasons for underutilization are:

- Uneven application
- Uncertainty in demand forecasts
- Long provisioning time scales
- Risk management
- Virtualization shortfalls

Based on the authors' view, there are four approaches to solving underutilization issues:

1. Increase internal data center network agility
2. Provide appreciated incentives to shape cloud resource consumption
3. Improve geo-diversification of data centers.
4. New systems to manage the geo-distribution of state

15.1.2.3 Optimizing cost models

Many cloud service providers claim many benefits for people that migrate their IT systems to the cloud. The "on-demand" consumption model [181] presented by Amazon argues that a cloud consumer can consume computing resources as they need them, which is the so-called pay-as-you-go (PAYG) model. However, Chew-Yean Yam et al. from Hewlett Packard Lab raised the following question in their paper: "If the cloud is so good then why aren't companies using it more?" [180].

The paper explained the reasons behind the above question and listed 11 hurdles or obstacles for a company to overcome before considering a cloud solution:

1. Business processes are heavily integrated with both IT infrastructure and standard applications
2. Considerable custom applications

3. Client and third-party vendor supporting systems and network
4. Middleware support system for business applications (such as identity, messaging, and database)
5. Security concerns
6. A long process of negotiation with a cloud provider for a service contract
7. Existing in-house IT infrastructure life-cycle term
8. Data or information control
9. For any large organization, existence of multiple internal stakeholders with different preferences and priorities
10. Limited set of business level services in a cloud
11. Cloud is still an emerging technology

In summary, the above 11 hurdles can be probably categorized into three large groups:

- Business applications (2, 9, 10)
- Process (1, 3, 4, 6, 7, 8)
- Technology (5, 11)

And then, the authors presented a possible solution, the so-called real option theory. The cost model of the optimum threshold value that is expressed in the following equation is used to decide whether an IT system should be migrated to a cloud or not:

$$V_y^* = \frac{\beta_+}{\beta_+ - 1} \left(C_y + P_x + \frac{V_x}{r} \right)$$

where β = coefficient that represents a combination of the discount rate, dividend yield, and uncertainty factors:

$$\beta = \frac{1}{2} - \frac{(r - \delta)}{\sigma^2} + \sqrt{\left(\frac{(r - \delta)}{\sigma^2} - \frac{1}{2} \right)^2 + \frac{2r}{\sigma^2}} > 1$$

V_y = optimum threshold value for migrating to a cloud, V_x = net value provided by the cloud, C_y = initial capex, P_x = penalty for existing IT, γ = discount rate, δ = uncertainty range from $0 \sim 1$, and δ = dividend yield.

Because there is so much uncertainty around cloud services, the paper recommended that a decision maker should consider cloud migration as a multiphase investment project rather than a once-off event. Strategically, real option theory can help a decision maker to establish the right strategy in term of optimizing cost, adopting emerging technology, competing in the market landscape, and fulfilling regulatory requirements.

Regarding this model (Real Option theory) assumptions the authors assumed the higher cost is the low benefits will be, the higher uncertainty is the medium cost should be, and the high benefits is, the low cost will occur. This assumption may appear to be arbitrary. Moreover, the paper only gave a relative definition of "real option" in comparison with the definition of financial option but it failed to define the true meaning of real option theory and its practical methodology. We will discuss the real option theory in Chapter 18.

Table 15.8 Variable Costs for Cloud Computing

Variable Cost Items	Percentage of Cost
Administration cost	37%
Depreciation cost	23%
Idle time cost	18%
Occupancy cost	17%
Network infrastructure	5%

15.1.2.4 Cost model using the method of traditional economic mapping

Werner Mach and Erich Schikuta [235] from the University of Vienna presented a cloud cost model for both consumer and provider that focuses on variable cost. They covered the traditional economic scopes for the foundation of cost modeling:

- Operating production factors
- Production
- Sales theory
- Investment and finance

Then, the paper shifts gears and switches to the infrastructure of cloud computing. When the authors demonstrated a calculation example, their fixed capital cost narrowed down to three major infrastructure components:

- Server
- Storage devices
- Network devices

The unit cost assumption for a virtual machine (VM) was based on Java Virtual Machine. The power consumption data originated from the SPECpower_ssj2008 benchmark. For the overall variable cost, the authors provide an overview (see Table 15.8 and Figure 15.8) of variable costs.

Unfortunately, the authors didn't explain how they achieved this result or provide evidences to support this cost overview.

The calculation of the fixed cost was very straightforward. The cost calculation appears to be a linear model based on three cost components plus server power consumption. The model seems to be oversimplified because many cost components have been excluded, such as life cycle, security, operating system, middleware, delivery, provisioning, disaster recovery (DR), high availability (HA), data center facility infrastructure (or HVAC), maintenance support, etc.

15.1.2.5 Cost model oriented by service level agreement (SLA)

We can find many IT whitepapers and research papers that address the issue of cloud infrastructure cost, but there are few papers that discuss the cloud cost associated with Service Level Agreements (SLAs). Amazon's public cloud can only provide SLA = 99.95% (http://aws.amazon.com/ec2-sla/). It means the monthly downtime would be 21.9 minutes. This means that a cloud provider can

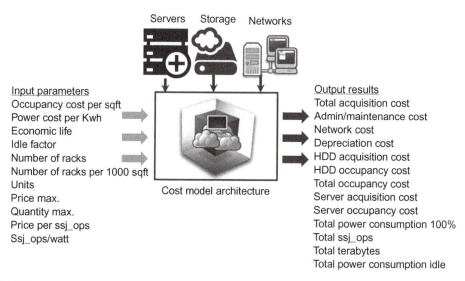

Servers   Storage   Networks

Input parameters
Occupancy cost per sqft
Power cost per Kwh
Economic life
Idle factor
Number of racks
Number of racks per 1000 sqft
Units
Price max.
Quantity max.
Price per ssj_ops
Ssj_ops/watt

Cost model architecture

Output results
Total acquisition cost
Admin/maintenance cost
Network cost
Depreciation cost
HDD acquisition cost
HDD occupancy cost
Total occupancy cost
Server acquisition cost
Server occupancy cost
Total power consumption 100%
Total ssj_ops
Total terabytes
Total power consumption idle

FIGURE 15.8

Cost model architecture based on SPEC benchmark methodology.

support 99.95% SLA with one-minute downtime every business day. Would that be acceptable for the particular business application? What if a business application needs 99.999% (or five 9s)? What if the business application is mission critical during business hours but can be relaxed after business hours? How much does it cost for 99.99% or 99.999% of SLA? How can we translate each nine digit to a dollar value in terms of cloud infrastructure? Chapter 4 (refer to Table 4.6) and Chapter 12 (refer to Table 12.9) have given somewhat of an answer from a data center UPS and storage reliability perspective. We can probably use the data as a reference point.

Further, the above SLA is only represented in the quality domain. What about the quantity domain of the SLA? For example, consider a cloud customer in a small- or medium-size business that is running one particular application in a cloud environment. If the application might only impact on a certain number of customers (or 50 end users) but not all end users (or 2,000 end users), how can we calculate SLA performance? Therefore, the questions for the SLA would be:

1. What kind of SLA or how many nines does my business require?
2. Is the SLA for end-to-end service delivery or just for infrastructure (or IaaS)?
3. How many impacted customers will be acceptable for a specified SLA?
4. Does my business need a different SLA for different days or different times of day?
5. Does my business or application need 24 × 7 support?
6. What is the acceptable mean time to repair (MTTR)?
7. What is the acceptable mean time to failure (MTTF) for my application?

In 2007, Rajkumar Buyya et al. proposed the concept of SLA-oriented management of a container within the Web Service Resource Framework (WSRF) grid-computing environment to self-manage resources and meet specified SLA requirements. [236] This SLA is derived from quality of

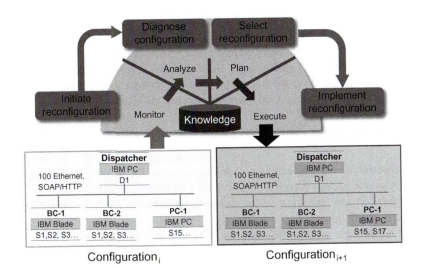

FIGURE 15.9

Auto-computing model for self-reconfiguration.

service (QoS) and health metrics (H-metrics). This self-management definition is similar to today's concept of "cloud orchestration" or "auto-orchestration," which consists of four elements:

- Self-configuration
- Self-optimization
- Self-healing
- Self-adapting

The container is similar to the current version of a virtual machine. The authors presented the migration algorithms if the specified SLA had been violated or degraded.

Earlier Li et al. developed a self-configurable service based system with a similar approach [237]. They implemented an automatic computing mechanism for configuration and reconfiguration, a self-configuration service-based system to satisfy an SLA with minimal resource consumption.

The article proposed an autonomic computing model for self-reconfiguration, which includes monitoring, analyzing, planning, and executing four steps corresponding to four configuration steps: "initiate reconfiguration," "diagnose configuration," "select reconfiguration," and "implement reconfiguration" (see Figure 15.9).

The above reconfiguration process is trigged by:

- SLA violation
- Performance degradation
- Resource overconsumption or overcommitment
- Resource underutilization

Rajkumar Buyya et al. proposed an SLA-orientated resource management architecture in order to cope with the rapidly and frequently changing requirements of cloud computing [238].

The architecture supports integrated market-based resource policies for flexible resource provisioning and allocation.

The paper reviewed four traditional resource management methods, including Condor Resource Management Systems (RMS), LoadLeveler, Load Sharing Facility (LSF), and Portable Batch System (PBS) and indicated these methods would not be able to support today's cloud computing needs because those methods cannot differentiate service priority and are unable to deliver SLA-oriented services to end users.

Many recent cloud resource management packages provide different levels of SLA-driven functions such as:

- Dynamic provisioning and computing resource reservation for diverse applications within a data center (open source packages such as Eucalyptus, OpenStack, Apache VCL)
- Auto-configuration and managing an abstraction layer between a physical node and operating system (Citrix Essentials)
- Web-based solution for users to fully control life cycle of VMs (Enomaly Elastic Computing Platform)
- Building IaaS and providing a common interface with AWS EC2 API with third-party modular extensions (Eucalyptus framework)
- Global framework compatible with AWS EC2 front-end API (Nimbus toolkit)
- Dynamic resource allocation feature via Haizea lease scheduler (OpenNebula)

The authors proposed another alternative open source solution by using Aneka as a cloud middleware, a platform for building and deploying distributed applications on both private and public clouds with SLA orientation. The basic idea of the resource allocation is based on the following SLA-oriented resource management architecture (see Figure 15.10).

With a similar approach, Nicolas Bonvin et al. [239] made some progress on automatic SLA-driven provisioning for cloud applications in contrast to "best effort" resource deployment and static resource allocation, which either overprovisions or underallocates computing infrastructure resources.

The paper proposed the concept of components and a middleware called "Scarce" (Scattered Autonomic Resources) to manage the cloud infrastructure with six major functions in order to achieve automatic SLA-driven provisioning of cloud infrastructure resources:

- Adaptive adjustment of cloud resource allocation in order to statistically satisfy response time or availability SLA requirements (adaptive adjustment for SLA requirements).
- Cost-effective resource allocation and component placement for minimizing the operational costs of the cloud application (cost-effective resource allocation).
- Detection and removal or replacement of stale cloud resources (monitoring & actions).
- Component replication and migration for accommodating load variations and for supple load balancing (load balancing).
- Decentralized self-management of the cloud resources for the application (decentralized).
- Geographically diverse placement of clone component instances (geographic diversity).

The auto SLA-driven provisioning logic is handled by a few algorithms (see Figure 15.11).

One year later, Artur Andrzejak et al. [240] suggested a "decision model for Cloud Computing under SLA constraints." This decision model assumed a AWS EC2 public cloud environment with a spot instance resource bidding scenario. The spot instance was introduced by Amazon in 2009.

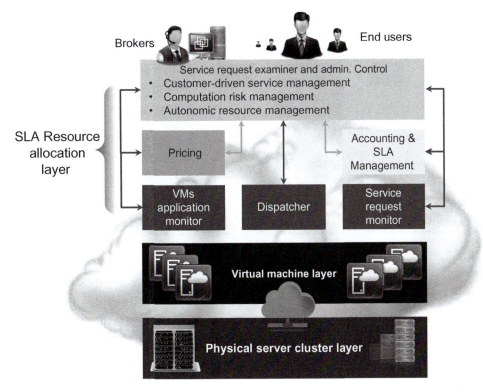

FIGURE 15.10

High-level system architectural framework.

Since then, AWS has a total of $42 + 6 = 48$ price categories. The proposed probabilistic model tried to find an optimized value between the minimized bidding price and specified SLA requirements. This SLA included sufficient resource availability within the desired time period.

However, the authors did not clearly define the SLA type. Based on the context of the article, the meaning of SLA is not the conventional meaning of SLA but rather a specified time length to execute or perform certain computing tasks for the lowest bidding price. Therefore, the decision model is fit for scientific purposes rather than business applications.

15.1.2.6 Cost model from a TCO perspective

In Apr 2008, Xinhui Li et al. [241] published a paper and discussed different methods and tools of cost analysis (or models) for cloud computing. The paper created a framework to calculate cloud total cost of ownership (TCO) and utilization cost. They developed their cost model (see Figure 15.12) into a web tool to calculate cost distribution and utilization factors based on IBM China Research lab's internal virtualized cloud environment (data center facility infrastructure). This model provided a foundation for establishing cost optimization indicators and evaluating cloud economic efficiency.

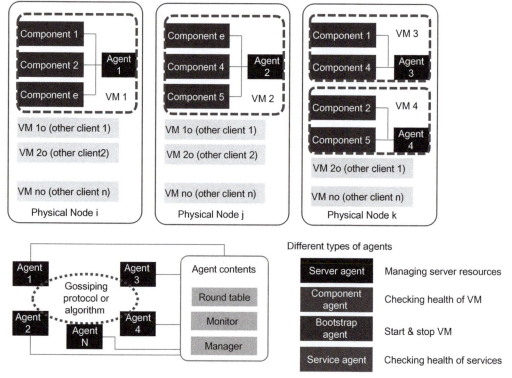

FIGURE 15.11

Auto-SLA-driven cloud resource provisioning.

The paper calculated the TCO as the sum of all eight costs components presented in eight equations. In terms of VM density, the authors left it to a cloud provider or a cost model analyst to decide the real figure because the relationship among physical servers (physical server number = N_S), VMs (number of VM = N_{VM}), and VM density (VM $_{density}$) can be expressed as follows:

$$N_s = \frac{N_{VM}}{VM_{density}}$$

However, the article did give an example and calculated the maximum number of VMs by using IBM's Processor Value Unit (PVU) calculation methodology to estimate the maximum number of VMs on the physical host server [242].

In addition, the authors introduced a bin-packing algorithm to minimize the number of 42RU racks for different types of physical server or node combinations. The paper didn't provide detailed

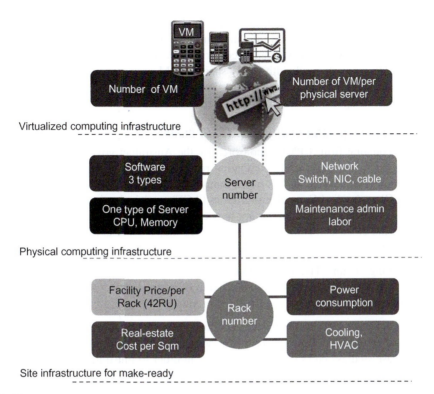

FIGURE 15.12

Eight elements of cost model.

examples how to use bin-packing algorithm for the cost modeling process outside of the following generalized equation shown as following:

$$Minimise \ B = \sum_{i=1}^{n} y_i$$

$$subject \ to \ \sum_{j=1}^{n} a_i x_{ij} \leq V y_i, \ \forall_i \in \{1, \ldots, n\}$$

$$\sum_{i=1}^{n} x_{ij} = 1, \ \forall_j \in \{1, \ldots, n\}$$

$$y_i \in \{0, 1\}, \ \forall_i \in \{1, \ldots, n\}, \ x_{ij} \in \{0, 1\}, \ \forall_i \in \{1, \ldots, n\} \forall_j \{1, \ldots, n\}$$

where B = number of rack, V = standard 42 RU size, a_j = particular size of physical server, and n = number of physical servers with different sizes. x is a variable for physical server and y is a variable for racks.

Finally, the paper proposed the concept of a cloud balance factor for eight defined metrics, which would be used to optimize cloud infrastructure cost in data centers. The authors argued that one element increasing in capacity will not necessarily expand cloud capacity. This is a valid argument, especially for network bandwidth, CPU speed, RAM capacity, and even IT professionals' skill set. The article shows there is no one-to-one linear relationship between overall cloud capacity and one of the eight components.

15.1.2.7 Computable general equilibrium (CEG) model

In April 2012 accounting firm, KPMG, sponsored by the Australian government, telco companies, and IT heavyweights presented a cloud computing report [243] to investigate the economic impact of cloud computing across different Australian industries. KPMG adopted the Computable General Equilibrium (CEG) or Applied General Equilibrium (AGE) model to estimate or quantify the macro economic benefits in term of cloud computing impact over a 10-year period.

It argues that the cloud computing will deliver three major benefits for adopters or consumers. These benefits are:

- Direct cost saving (assume IT cost savings)
- Productivity improvement (increase output per unit of cost)
- Innovation (ability to deliver new and evolving products)

As the report indicated, its key information sources were derived from two consulting firms, OVUM [244] and Booz/Allen/Hamilton [245]. In addition to CEG model analysis, the report also provided seven case studies across different industries in order to illustrate the benefits of the cloud and future outlook.

It appears that the report did not differentiate among ICT, IT, and cloud computing. All these terms become interchangeable in the report. Overall, the report appears to just reiterate the few benefits that have been already identified by some of US consulting companies, but fails to provide valuable information for our cost modeling purposes.

15.2 CLOUD COMPUTING ISSUES, IMPACTS, THE RIGHT QUESTIONS FOR THE COST MODEL

Before KPMG, another accounting firm, Ernst & Young [246], provided a similar report to address issues and economic impacts. It consisted of 10 topics related to cloud computing:

- Price and business models
- Vendor management & strategic sourcing
- Availability and interoperability
- Security and privacy
- Standards and risk management
- Government role
- Accounting
- Cross-border taxation of Cloud Service Provider (CSP) arrangements
- Regulatory compliance
- Outlook

The report raised four questions for cloud consumers and five questions for cloud service providers regarding cost models.

15.2.1 CLOUD SERVICE CONSUMERS

- Does my CSP charge a premium for consumption that exceeds agreed-upon levels?
- Should I risk increasing CSP "lock-in" by optimizing my software design to take advantage of my infrastructure or platform CSP's particular pricing approach?
- How much customization does my application require, and how does my CSP charge for it?
- Are there any relatively obscure software functions that my organization nonetheless depends on?

15.2.2 CLOUD SERVICE PROVIDERS

- What is the economically justifiable price point for my service, and how will it change over time?
- How can I structure a pricing program that helps to smooth out consumption of my infrastructure?
- What is the best model for deploying new functionality to my customers? Is an "open source" model an option?
- Does it make sense to expose discrete elements of functionality for separate purchase by customers?
- How often should we reevaluate our pricing model to grow revenue?

In summary, the report provided a list of important issues and impacts regarding cloud pricing and business models (refer to Table 15.9).

15.3 COST MODELS OVER THE LAST 50 YEARS

Up to now, we have briefly reviewed 10 different cost models based on different perspectives. These models can be considered as taking a horizontal view. In order to have a big picture of the cost framework at the strategic level, we can review models from a historical perspective. The historical view of a cost model can be considered a vertical view. Basically we can classify these horizontal models into four different categories:

- Economic cost framework
- Financial cost models
- Operations cost models
- Technology/infrastructure cost models

They address four different cost aspects to support a decision maker in making the right decision for cloud computing investment projects. Tables 15.10 and 15.11 and Figure 1.3 present a high level picture of cost model evolution based on a chronological basis.

We will begin with investigating 11 financial cost models first because these financial models are the baseline models from the last 50 years or so. The financial category of cost modeling is universal. It is "generalpurpose" cost modeling. Any commercial entity has to have a financial cost model for its operations. As we can see from the above literature review, many cost models of cloud computing are derived from different financial cost models, such as NPV. Any public

Table 15.9 Cloud Computing Price and Business Model Issues and Impact

Issues	Impacts
Maximizing asset utilization	Pricing programs must encourage customer behavior that helps smooth consumption peaks and valleys
Granularly detailed service pricing	Enables customers to optimize service cost via their software design, but could increase vendor lock-in
Capital expenditure	Corporate preference to use traditional return on investment (ROI) measures in making capital expenditure decisions could apply downward pressure to cloud pricing
SaaS customization	Because it requires nonstandard, negotiated pricing, customization reduces the potential economic benefit of cloud models
Functionality "menu"	If providers make all functions available from a configuration menu, the possibility of differentiation via IT is diminished or eliminated
Funding innovation relevant to customer subsets	Given shared infrastructure, the economic model is unclear for innovation that benefits only a few customers; clearinghouses or application exchanges may evolve to fill the need
National regulation, particularly of data location, security and privacy	Creates obstacles to optimal asset utilization of cloud infrastructure

Table 15.10 Cost Model Evolution

	1960–1980	1981–2000	2001–Present
Financial	Capex, Pre-opex & opex	Fragmented capex & opex	Opex
Economic	Make	Buy	Rent
Operation	Isolation, Centralize	Decentralisation	Network centralization
Technology	Special technology	IT application technology	General purpose technology

company has to report to the market its financial results twice a year. A financial model is vital for any company whether it is cloud services provider or consumer.

Most financial cost models are designed to be effective for tangible measurements, but they normally cannot capture many intangible and indirect benefits, especially for some of the large enterprises that have a shared IT infrastructure.

In order to address some intangible issues, we will work a high-level economic perspective. This leads to the economic metrics. The economic metrics can help a decision maker to formulate the right business strategies in the competitive cloud computing environment and develop the decision maker's capability to make an effective assessment for the business application.

These economic metrics are derived from six basic economic principles and three core concepts:

1. People respond to incentives.
2. There is no such thing as a free lunch.

Table 15.11 Four Levels of 50 Cost Models

Economic Models	Financial Models	Operation Models	Technology/Infrastructure Models
Zero-Based Budgeting	Accounting Rate of Return (ARR)	No Cost Allocation	Below the Floor (Data Center Facility)
Critical Success Factors	Breakeven Point (BEP)	Non-IT-Based Cost Allocation (3 models)	Above the Floor Infrastructure, CPU, Memory, Storage, Network
Decision Bayesian Analysis	Cost Benefits Ration (CBR)	IT Domain-Based Cost Allocation (7 models)	Hypervisors & Operation System
Balanced Scorecard	Cost Revenue (CR)	Fee-Based Cost Allocation	Middleware
Analytical Hierarchy Process	Internal Rate of Return (IRR)	Negotiated Flat Rate	Project Planning & Delivery
Decision Theory	Net Present Value (NPV)	Tiered Flat Rate	Bin Packaging
Delphi Method	Simple Payback Period (SPP)	Transaction Ratio-Based Cost	Cobb-Douglass
Game Theory	Discount Payback Period (DPP)	Activity-Based Cost	x86 Platform
Satisfaction & Priority Survey	Profitability Index (PI)	SLA Performance-Based Cost	RISC Platform
Benefits–Risks Portfolio	Return on Investment (ROI)	Business-Based Cost Allocation	Open Source
Application Benchmark Technique	Total Cost of Ownership (TCO)	Fixed Revenue-Based Cost	Proprietary
Bedell's Method	TCO/ROI	Fixed Revenue with Predefined Range	Dedicated/Utility Hosting
CGE (AGE)		Profile Oriented Cost	
Real Option Theory		Capacity Reservation Cost	
Monte Carlo Simulation		Bidding Instance*	

3. There are always at least two sides to every interaction.
4. The law of unanticipated influences (chaos theory, called the butterfly effect).
5. The law of unintended consequences (multiple consequences).
6. No one is, and no one ever can be, in complete control.

In addition to these six principles, there are also three core analytic concepts for economic models:

- Rationality
- Marginal
- Optimization

From an economic sense, a human being is fundamentally rational in his/her behavior. People will decide strategically rather than accidently. This means people will make a rational decision with four simple steps.

1. Clarify the objective.
2. Identify all possible alternative paths to achieve the objective.
3. Evaluate carefully the payoffs from each of those alternatives.
4. Select the best option and implement the finalized decision.

The assumption of rationality means a decision maker will always choose the option with the highest net payoff. The proposition of rationality has two aspects: one is to help with the prediction and description of model behavior and the other is to present a process to evaluate based on the facts and draw conclusions in term of values.

The concept of "marginal" is to analyze carefully sequences of small variation made on the margin. The reason for conducting marginal analysis is that the world is not made with only two extremes or two colors: black and white. Therefore, our decision should not be "all" or "nothing" but rather involve marginal trade-offs. In other words, one model may be a little bit more or less than another in terms of marginal value. It is a relative or comparison value. The concept of "marginal" also means that a rational decision maker will adjust on the margin if the marginal value fluctuates from time to time or place to place.

The last core metric of the economic model presents the idea of making the best attempt with limited resources or given a set of constraints. The optimal solution is to find the balance between maximum achievement and the limited resources.

An economic cost model implies a decision maker is aware of existing incentives but most importantly that he/she will find these surrounding incentives. It also means anticipating what's strategically rational for them and how that will affect a decision maker's options. It is focusing on the margin, on trade-offs, and on adjustments to reach the optimal balance.

Due to the limited space of this book, we will not be able to cover all the models but we will focus on the most important financial models.

15.4 COMMON FINANCIAL COST MODELS

From Table 15.9, we notice that many models are not able to provide a clear dollar value or quantitative measurements. As we indicated in the above literature review, many cost models may only exist in theory because they are not practical to implement. In contrast, the financial cost models are very good tools that provide us with concrete and quantitative measurements. They are much more tangible and easier to grasp. Many other types of models are either too complex or intangible or hard to use as a communication tool. We should always remember that one of the purposes of cost modeling is to communicate with others or convince others. Therefore, we should have a clear understanding of these financial models. Now let's focus on these 11 financial cost models, which are listed in Table 15.12.

In the last two rows of the above table, we see the "return on investment" (ROI) and the total cost of ownership (TCO) model. We can also combine these two models to measure the financial performance (TCO/ROI). Actually, the combination TCO/ROI metric is one of the

Table 15.12 Financial Cost Model for IT Investment Decision Making

No.	Type of model	Description
1	Account rate of return (ARR)	Compare the average after-tax profit with initial investment cost
2	Breakeven	Compare the present value of costs with the present value of benefits
3	Cost benefit	Compare cost with benefits that can be directly and indirect attributed to the model
4	Cost Benefit ratio	Calculate the ratio of costs of an IT investment to its benefits measured in monetary terms and compare to a threshold ratio
5	Cost revenue	Compare costs with benefits that can be directly attributed to the cloud computing project
6	Internal rate of return (IRR)	Calculate the return that equates the net present value of an investment to zero
7	Net present value (NPV)	Discount cash inflows and compare them to cash outflows
8	Payback period	Calculate the time required to recoup initial cost
9	Profitability index	Calculate the per dollar contribution of an investment
10	Return on investment (ROI)	Calculate the return of an investment
11	Total cost of ownership (TCO)	Calculate the lifetime ownership cost of investment

KPI metrics for many enterprises. Although there may be more than 11 models, the most important and popular models are IRR, NPV, payback period, ROI, and TCO. These models are the cost modeling pillars that support the annual budgeting for different project for many enterprises or organizations or government agencies, such as cloud computing. Let's examine these financial models in detail.

15.4.1 ACCOUNTING RATE OF RETURN (ARR)

The accounting rate of return (ARR) is a ratio to measure the average accounting net profit or return from a particular project. This average accounting net return is calculated on a yearly basis. People often use ARR to compare a company's internal hurdle rate to an investment decision purpose. The formula for ARR is as follows:

$$ARR = \frac{P_{Ave\_net}}{C_0}$$

Here, P_{ave_net} = average annual net profit or income from a cloud computing project and C_0 = initial investment capital.

For example, a cloud-computing proposal requires a $60,000 hardware investment. The life cycle of the server asset is normally three years and the average cash flow income is $35 k for year 1, $50 k for year 2 and $65 k for year 3, respectively (see Table 15.13).

Table 15.13 ARR Model

Item/Time	Year 1	Year 2	Year 3
Cash flow income	$35,000	$50,000	$65,000
Hardware depreciation	$20,000	$20,000	$20,000
Net profit	$15,000	$30,000	$45,000

Table 15.14 BEP Model

Cost Items	Initial Capex (C1)	Fixed Cost (C2)	Sales Price per VM	Direct Cost per VM
Cost per unit	$50,000	$70,000	$800	$200

The average annual net profit $= (\$15\,k + \$30\,k + \$45\,k)/3 = \$30\,k$. Therefore, the ARR $= \$30\,k/\$60\,k = 50\%$.

ARR is quite simple in comparison with other financial models. It is quite easy for nonfinancial professional people to understand. However, it doesn't take account of the time value of money. It can be calculated in different ways, which are really dependent on inaccurate assumptions, such as cash flow income and asset depreciation rate from every year. Because ARR is based on average annual net profit, if the business or project has a maintenance cost cycle time longer than one year, then the result of ARR may become inconsistent.

15.4.2 BREAKEVEN POINT (BEP)

In very simple terms, the breakeven point (BEP) means that the total revenue generated by a business or project equals its total costs. The equation for BEP is based on a cost-volume-profit model. The unit for BEP can be either the number of units to be sold or the total dollar value of sales. Normally, it is preferable to use the number of units to be sold for a business or a project. The equation for BEP is:

$$BEP(x) = \frac{\sum_{i=0}^{n} C_i}{P_{perunit} - DC_{perunit}} \dots \text{ or simply stated,}$$

Breakeven Point (Sales Revenue) $=$ Fixed **Cost** (Capex) $+$ Variable **Cost** (Opex)

Here $\sum_{i=0}^{n} C_i =$ the total fixed cost of the business or project, $i =$ each cost item, $P_{per\ unit} =$ price of sale for each unit and $DC_{per\ unit} =$ direct cost for each unit to be sold.

For example, if we assume the set of parameters in Table 15.14 for a cloud computing project or business (assume a cloud computing service provider), we have:

$$BEP(x) = \frac{\$50,000 + \$70,000}{\$800 - \$200} = 200(VM)$$

The total sales revenue for a cloud service provider company to break even would be $160,000. This is the cutoff point for the company to make profit after 200 virtual machines (VM) have been sold.

This model is very good for estimating the sales volume to recover the investment cost. However, there are a few issues when adopt BEP that could make it difficult to calculate a very precise result:

- It is quite difficult to quantify the unit cost for each virtual machine (VM), especially if the cloud-computing infrastructure has legacy hardware or is shared among different businesses or projects. The standard deviation of average unit cost may vary considerably.
- If the unit of sales price is not fixed (for example the sales price has a volume discount) then the BEP might not fit.
- We assume all units of direct cost (DC) are unchanged. In reality, it would be impossible to make this assumption.

15.4.3 COST/BENEFIT AND COST/BENEFIT RATIO

Cost/benefit is also referred to cost/benefit analysis (CBA). It is a model where all costs and benefits, whether they are tangible or intangible or direct or indirect, are taken into consideration. Very often, we use the cost/benefit ratio formula to represent the CBA model:

$$CBA(\$) = \frac{\sum_{i=1}^{n} (B_d + B_{id})_i}{\sum_{l=1}^{n} (C_d + C_{id})_i}$$

Here B_d = direct benefit, B_{id} = indirect benefits, C_d = direct cost, C_{id} = indirect cost, i & l & n = different benefit and cost items, and CBA = cost/benefit ratio. We use the example in Table 15.15 to illustrate the CBA model.

$$CBA(\$) = \frac{\$500,000 + \$400,000}{\$50,000 + \$10,000} = \$15$$

The calculated result equals $15 dollars. This means that for every dollar of investment capital, the project will get $15 dollars in benefits back. However, all indirect benefits and costs would be quite difficult to define or quantify, such as opportunity costs or brand name benefits. Indirect or intangible cost and benefits will be always subjective.

Table 15.15 CBA Model

Cost & Benefit Items	Direct Benefit	Indirect Benefit	Direct Cost	Indirect Cost
Value ($)	$500,000	$400,000	$50,000	$10,000

15.4.4 COST OF REVENUE MODEL

Cost of revenue analysis (CRA) can be considered as a special case of CBA. If we take away all indirect or intangible revenue and costs of the CBA shown in the above equation and Table 15.15, we will obtain a cost of revenue result. The CRA model is often applied for service industries:

$$CRA(\$) = \frac{\$500,000}{\$50,000} = \$10$$

This information for cost of revenue can be found in any public company's income statement. It only reflects the direct cost of goods and services that have been sold. It means that the cost components are to directly produce goods and services. These components include labor, material, and supplies. If the cost expenditures are independent of the level of production, such as capex to improve production efficiency or overhead salary costs, then these cost components are indirect costs.

From an account perspective, a cloud-computing consumer can leverage cloud computing services (XaaS) to significantly reduce its indirect costs. In other words, cloud computing can help many companies to transfer their indirect costs to direct costs. We will have further discussion on this in the following chapters.

15.4.5 INTERNAL RATE OF RETURN (IRR)

The standard definition of the IRR formula is that the sum of all values equal zero, where we are talking about the net present value of all the cash flows (it doesn't matter whether the cash flow is positive or negative) from a cloud computing business or investment projects. From this formula, we can get the result for IRR. We then use this IRR against the company's internal hurdle rate.

IRR measures or evaluates the preferences of an investment project. If the IRR of a new investment project exceeds a company's required rate of return (sometimes called as a hurdle rate; it is dependent on whether the project is a higher or lower risk one), it should be approved. However, if the IRR falls below the required rate of return (or an internal hurdle rate), the project should be rejected.

The formula for *IRR* is:

$$P_0 + \frac{P_1}{1 + IRR} + \frac{P_2}{(1+IRR)^2} + \frac{P_3}{(1+IRR)^3} + \ldots + \frac{P_n}{(1+IRR)^n} = 0$$

Here, P_0, P_1, ..., P_n equals the cash flows in a certain period (normally one year), 1, 2, ..., n, respectively; and IRR equals the project's internal rate of return.

In order to clarify the IRR definition, let's have a look at the following example.

Assume a cloud computing service provider has the following estimates of initial investment capital and cash flow revenue in next three-year period (refer to Table 15.16), What is the IRR?

Table 15.16 Capex and Three-Year Cash Flows				
	Year 0 (Capex)	Revenue Year 1	Revenue Year 2	Revenue Year 3
Cash Flow	−$210,000	$60,000	$120,000	$130,000

From the above table, we can find that the IRR = 19.61. If we replace IRR with 19.61, we can achieve a result by setting the above formula equal to zero:

$$-\$210,00 + \frac{\$60,000}{1+19.61} + \frac{\$120,000_2}{(1+19.61)^2} + \frac{\$130,000_3}{(1+19.61)^3} = 0$$

Assume the company's internal hurdle rate is 12.5% for a lower risk project and 19.5% for a higher risk project; the 19.61% IRR result would be approved by the investment criteria.

15.4.5.1 *What are the pros and cons of IRR?*

A decision maker uses IRR to prioritize or weight different projects by their overall rate of return rather than the net present value (NPV). Normally, the higher the IRR, the better the project is. However, there are some cons or limitations of adopting the IRR to evaluate different investment projects. For example, IRR is only suitable for a project that has continuous cash flow revenue.

Furthermore, IRR will not give you the absolute size of the investment. This means that IRR can only focus on a higher rate of return even if the overall size of investment or the return is very small. For example, IRR will favor a project that has a $1 investment with returning $5 rather than another project that has a $1 million investment with a $3 million return. Another con is that IRR cannot be applied if the investment generates interim cash flows. Finally, IRR does not consider the cost of capital and cannot compare projects with different durations.

15.4.6 NET PRESENT VALUE (NPV)

One of most popular financial cost models or measurement is net present value (NPV). The formula for net present value looks similar to IRR but it includes the time value of money. It compares the value of money today to the value of that same amount of money in the future because of inflation rate, capital cost, etc. We often use NPV for capital budgeting, where we estimate the investment profitability for a cloud project within a certain period of time. It discounts the future cash flow income or revenue with a specified interest rate. Normally, this rate is the capital cost or borrowing cost, such as 4% or 5%:

$$NPV = \sum_{t=1}^{T} \frac{CF_t}{(1+r)^t} - I_c$$

Here, CF_t is the net cash flow at the time or "t." It also means the future value. The capital letter "T" is the unit of time. Normally it is an integer number, such as one year or six months or three months. I_C is the initial investment capital and r is the interest rate, which is the capital cost.

For instance, if one cloud computing proposal suggests that the cloud business would have the cash flow revenue in Table 15.17 and an initial capital requirement, the question which a decision maker faces is whether he/she should make this investment or not. The answer is based on the NPV value. If it is negative, the investment should be rejected; otherwise, the investment proposal should be approved.

Table 15.17 NPV of Proposed Cloud Computing Investment Project							
I_C	CF_1	CF_2	CF_3	CF_4	CF_5	Interest Rate	NPV
Initial Investment	Year 1	Year 2	Year 3	Year 4	Year 5		
−$350,000	$56,000	$115,000	$210,000	$180,200	$156,000	5.5%	$237,537

15.4.6.1 What are the pros and cons of the NPV model?

Pros:

NPV calculates the time value of money. In comparison with other cost models, such as simple payback period (SPP) and accounting rate of return (ARR), it is more reliable and accurate. In addition, it is quite straightforward to calculate.

Cons:

The future revenue income or cash flow is basically based on a simple estimation or gut feeling. The longer the period is, the less accurate of the future predicated revenue would be. In addition, the revenue prediction is basically a single linear assumption. We will have further discussion about real option theory (or model) and Monte Carlo simulation (ROT + MS) to overcome these NPV disadvantages in later chapters.

15.4.7 SIMPLE PAYBACK PERIOD (SPP)

The concept of a payback period is similar to breakeven. The model is very simple, and involves calculating the required time or period to recover the initial investment capital for a cloud project. Typically, the longer the payback period is, the more undesirable the project.

The formula of the payback period is as follows:

$$SPL(Payback\_Period) = \frac{C_0(initial\_capital)}{C_t(Annual\_cashflow\_in\_average)}$$

Here, SPL = the length of simple payback period, C_0 = initial investment capital, and C_t = annual cash inflow on average.

For example, assume a cloud project requires an $80,000 capex investment and the estimated annual cash inflow from this project is $20,000 on average. Therefore, the payback period would be four years:

$$SPL = \frac{\$80,000}{\$20,000/year} = 4$$

This cost model has two major issues:

1. It doesn't take into consideration any benefits that occur after a payback period. As a result, it does not calculate the profitability of the project.
2. It ignores the time value of money, which is a capital cost.

For these reasons, net present value (NPV), internal rate of return (IRR), or discounted cash flow models are generally preferred for project assessment.

Table 15.18 DPP							
Items	Year 0	Year 1	Year 2	Year 3	Year 4	Year 5	Year 6
Cash Flow	−$80,000	$20,000	$20,000	$20,000	$20,000	$20,000	$20,000
Rate	12%						
PVF		0.8929	0.7972	0.7118	0.6355	0.5674	0.5066
DCF		$17,857	$15,944	$14,236	$12,710	$11,349	$10,133
NPV		−$62,143	−$46,199	−$31,963	−$19,253	−$7,904	$2,228

15.4.8 DISCOUNTED PAYBACK PERIOD

The above formula (SPL) only presents the face value of investment capital or money but does not take into consideration the time value of money. Any capital has to include its borrowing cost (or capital cost), such as the certain interest rate.

Therefore, the discounted payback period (DPP) is more accurate at reflecting the real payback period. The formula of the above equation should include the present value factor (PVF):

$$PVF = \frac{1}{(1 + i)^n}$$

The DPP formula would be:

$$DPP = Y_n + \left| \frac{C_n}{C_p} \right|$$

- Y_n = the last year of discounted cumulative cash flow with negative value
- C_n = absolute value of discounted cumulative cash flow in the last year with negative value
- C_p = the present value (PV) after the last year of negative cash flow (absolute cumulative cash flow)

We can borrow the above simple payback length (SPL) example for our DPP explanation (see Table 15.18).

$$DPP = 5 + \left| \frac{-\$7,904}{\$10,133} \right| = 5.78$$

Instead of a four-year payback period, if we take into consideration a 12% interest rate or discount rate, the real payback period or discount payback period would be almost six years.

15.4.9 PROFITABILITY INDEX

The profitability index (PI) is another way of representing the net present value (NPV) model. The difference is that the NPV measures the absolute value, but the PI shows a relative value in a ratio

Table 15.19 Example of Profitability Index

Value Items	Initial Capital Year 0	Year 1 Revenue	Year 2 Revenue	Year 3 Revenue	Interest Rate
Cash flow	−$150,000	+$50,000	+$80,000	+$100,000	6%
Present value		$47,170	$71,200	$83,962	
NPV	$52,331				
PI	1.349				

format. The PI is calculated by dividing the present value of future income of a project or business by the initial investment capital of the project as follows:

$$PI = \frac{NPV_{future}}{C_i} = 1 + \frac{NPV}{C_i}$$

Here, PI = profitability index, NPV (future) = present value of future income or cash flow, and C_i = initial investment capital. We use the data in Table 15.19 to demonstrate the example for this model.

Both PI and cost/benefit analysis (CBA) are ratio metrics but CBA does not consider the time value of money. If the PI value is greater than 1, then the project is worthwhile for inclusion on a decision maker's radar screen (see Table 15.18).

15.4.10 RETURN ON INVESTMENT (ROI) MODEL

Return on investment (ROI) is one of the financial performance measurements that we use to evaluate the efficiency of a capital investment and operation or compare the efficiency of different investment projects. It is quite simple to calculate ROI; the benefit (investment return) is divided by the cost of the investment. The result is shown as a percentage or a ratio:

$$ROI(\%) = \frac{P_i - C_0}{C_0}$$

Here, ROI represents "return on investment" in percentage. P_i = gain from investment or business revenue and C_0 = cost of investment or investment capital or all expenditures.

ROI is a very popular financial metric because it is comprehensive and concise. From a decision maker's perspective, if a cloud investment project has a negative ROI, or if there are other alternative projects with a higher ROI, then the lower ROI project should be banned.

However, when we use this formula, we should keep in mind that the definition of "gain from investment or business" and cost of investment is not very precise or restrictive. It depends on the particular circumstances and how you include or select elements of the return on investment and associated costs. It is how you measure the return (or benefits) and costs. Therefore, there is no single right calculation. From this sense, this metric could be subjective.

For example, a product analyst may compare two different products by dividing the gross profit that each product has generated based on the respective production expenses. A financial analyst, on the other hand, may compare the same two products using a totally different ROI calculation with different sets of assumptions, perhaps by dividing the net profits of an investment by the total value of all resources that have been applied to produce and sell the product.

The downside of ROI calculation is that it can be easily manipulated to suit the subjective purposes, and the result can be expressed in many different ways. Therefore, when we use this model, we have to make sure that a decision maker understands what input assumptions are being employed.

There are many IT business books [247] and articles that address the topic of ROI. Based on the research of Roulstone et al. [248], the ROI model has been redefined over the last 25 years and thousands of studies are developed every year. The ROI methodology has been adopted by hundreds of organizations across manufacturing, service, nonprofit organizations, government agencies, and technology sectors. Several hundred case studies have been published on the ROI topic. Almost 5,000 individuals have been certified to implement the ROI methodology (or model) in their organizations and many organizations across 50 countries have adopted the ROI methodology. Two dozen books have been developed to support the process. The professional ROI network, with hundreds of members, shares information. The implementation of the ROI model may cost 4% to 5% of the IT project budget.

15.4.11 TOTAL COST OF OWNERSHIP

The total cost of ownership (TCO) measures all the cost components during the lifetime of a business. It does not just include one-off asset purposing costs (such as hardware and software costs for a cloud computing project) but also consists of operations and asset decommissioning costs. In other words, when a decision maker is making a purchasing decision, he/she doesn't only examine the short-term costs (such as purchase cost and training expenditure) but also ongoing costs associated with this purchase. If we sum up all short- and long-term costs, this is the total cost of ownership. It is better to reflect a business or a project cost during its lifetime. The lower the TCO value, the better the business is to run:

$$TCO = C_i + C_{bf} + C_{bc} + C_{tu} + C_t + C_f + C_d + C_m + \ldots + C_{os}$$

Here

C_i = cost of initial investments for a cloud project or business
C_{bf} = cost of hardware break/fix or maintenance and support
C_{bc} = cost of business continuity or disaster recovery
C_{tu} = cost of technology upgrade or refresh
C_t = cost of staff training and education
C_f = cost of data center facility (such as HVAC)
C_d = cost of decommissioning or exit
C_m = cost of application migration
C_{os} = cost of other shared components

15.4.12 TCO/ROI MODEL

In order to avoid some of the pitfalls of either the TCO or ROI calculation model, some prefer to combine both TCO and ROI (or TCO/ROI) to evaluate the financial performance or metrics for an investment project.

As we observed, ROI doesn't not restrict whether both return and cost are direct or indirect. It depends on an individual's preference, knowledge, experience, or particular circumstances. Subsequently, different calculations of ROI could be far apart. With TCO, the model only calculates the expenses or investment cost rather than profit or gain from a project. Therefore, either TCO or ROI alone would not be able to paint the full picture.

It is better to employ TCO/ROI with other financial toolkits or models, such as NPV, IRR, and payback period to precisely estimate return on investment through the lifetime of a project. We will give an example of TCO/ROI calculation in a later chapter to illustrate this cost model.

Financial cost model types measure the efficiency of investments for both capex and opex (sometime including pre-opex). There are so many metrics to be measured. As we can see from the above formulas, they are basically direct measurements or metrics.

In summary, there is no single cost model that can measure all aspects of a particular business application. If we would like to obtain the full picture of cloud cost, we should understand what the business goal is and how can we measure the business gains. And then, we should be able to achieve a realistic cost model for a particular project. Overall, the most widely deployed cost models are NPV and TCO/ROI. Actually, many virtualization technology vendors [EMC VMware, Microsoft Hyper-V, Oracle (LDoM or VM Manager), IBM PowerVM, and Citrix Xen] along with Amazon provide free TCO/ROI calculation tool for cloud computing (IaaS) consumers to evaluate their business cases or cloud projects. One of typical business cases is physical to virtual (P2V) migration.

15.5 SUMMARY

This chapter is divided into two major parts: the first part is a literature review of cost models from the first x86 CPU or 4004 chip to the latest cloud cost models. The second part is all financial cost models, where profits and losses can directly be translated into a dollar value. Based on the Schniederjans et al. classification, we divided the 50 most popular IT cost models into four big categories:

- Economic models
- Financial models
- Operation models
- Technology/infrastructure models

The logic behind this classification is based on different strategic orientations. Some models do not have a price relationship between inputs and outputs. These models are more like methodologies, rather than cost models, such as Delphi, critical success factors, satisfaction, and priority. We can use these models for making assumptions at a strategic level.

In contrast, nearly all financial models have a definable relationship between inputs and outputs. Actually, these financial models existed before the emergence of the cloud computing paradigm. The financial cost models are not only designed for cloud computing investment projects, but also for ordinary corporation or enterprise investment projects. NVP, IRR, and TCO/ROI are not only the most valuable cost models because they take into consideration the time value of money, and they are also very concise models for communication.

That is why we spent a lot of space to describe individual financial cost models. Furthermore, we didn't only give an example for each financial model but also summarized pros and cons.

15.6 **REVIEW QUESTIONS**

1. How many cost models are there?
2. Why are there so many cost models?
3. What do you believe is the the best way to classify different cost models and why?
4. What is difference between a methodology and cost modeling?
5. Do you think the price model for the first x86 CPU (4004) was the right cost model?
6. Do you think AWS is a good cloud solution (cost model) for backup and disaster recovery?
7. Do you think the % of amortized cost for data center cost components provided by Albert Greenberg et al. (refer to Table 15.5) is adequate?
8. In general, how many common financial cost models are there?
9. What are the issues with the ARR model?
10. If the initial investment capex = $54 k, and the average annual net profit = $36 k, what is the ARR? Assume the IT asset depreciation time = three years.
11. If I use the BEP model, which issues should I pay attention to?
12. You have been directed to adopt CBA model; if Bd = $40 k, Bid = $200 k, Cd = $45 k and Cid = $22 k, what is the CBA?
13. What is the difference between CBA and CRA?
14. Why do we need an IRR model and what is another name for IRR?
15. In what ways is NPV better than IRR?
16. What are the pros and cons of NPV?
17. What is TCO/ROI?
18. What are the reasons for combining TCO and ROI during the cost modeling process?

CHARGEBACK

Building on our earlier discussion, this chapter reintroduces the concept of chargeback or show-back. Historically, there are five cost allocation models in terms of cloud opex. In this chapter, we will detail each model. The purpose of establishing a cloud opex model is to make sure that the cloud cost is transparent so that we can make good assumptions for cloud opex items. It will assist us in building a better cloud cost model or overall framework.

16.1 INTRODUCTION TO CHARGEBACKS

The term "operation" has quite a broad range of meaning. It can often be interpreted as an active process, an organized activity among a number of people, a mathematical process, or performing a surgical process. The connotation of operation is dependent on the real circumstances. Sometimes, operating, managing, and organizing are interchangeable. It may be even more confusing when we are trying to figure out the cost associated with IT operations. In order identify the operating costs, let's explore the details of IT operations.

The general meaning of IT operations for IT activities is the organizational structure that describes how we operate, manage, and process the IT workload to meet the production and customer requirements. There have been various IT operating models or frameworks since the 1980s. The following common operating models have been developed during different time periods with different focuses (see Figure 16.1):

1. Information Technology Infrastructure Library (ITIL v2 & v3)
2. Enhanced Telecom Operation Map (eTOM)
3. Control Objectives for Information and Related Technology (Cobit)
4. Capability Maturity Model Integration (CMMI)
5. IT Capability Maturity Framework (IT-CMF)
6. IT Service Management Forum (IT-SMF, BSI5000)
7. IBM John Zachman Model
8. IBM Rational Unified Process (IBM RUP)
9. Agile
10. Six Sigma
11. Application Service Library (ASL)
12. Business Information Service Library (BiSL)
13. Master Data File (MDF)

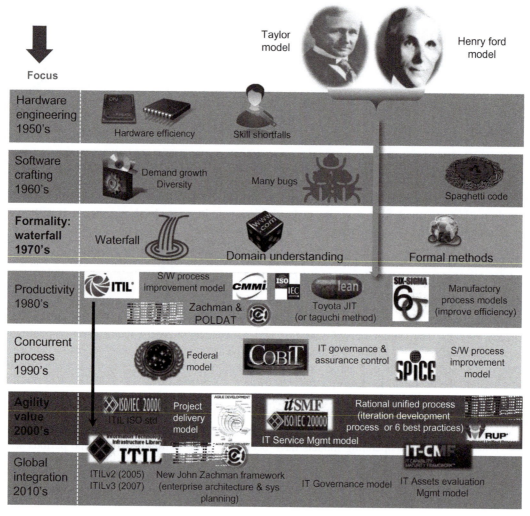

FIGURE 16.1

Evolution of operatng models and standards.

Different models may have different purposes; for example Agile is mainly designed for IT service delivery, ITIL targets overall operations improvements and Six Sigma is mainly focused on IT system maintenance and support. Many big enterprises or government agencies have applied these operating models from time to time. It is really dependent on the leadership's preferences. However, the results were not very significant in comparison with efforts and resources that companies have sunk into. As Rob Addy [251] indicated there are "enough of the management fads, marketing hype and analyst bluster..."

Of course, this doesn't mean that these operating models or procedures are not good or wrong. It indicates that the success of the IT operation is not only dependent on the IT operating model itself but also the business that IT supports. In order to make the business successful, the cost of IT operations must be transparent. One of the critical reasons for many LoBs having many negative impressions of IT operations is that the IT cost has never been transparent to the business in many large organizations. Now that the cloud is coming to play, the cost transparency issue has increasingly become critical for cloud projects because of the nature of the shared resource pool for cloud infrastructure.

16.1.1 UNDERSTANDING ENTERPRISE IT OPERATIONS

In order to build a rational cloud cost model in term of opex, we can leverage these models to make operating costs transparent. Before resolving this, let's have a look at what the IT group operates. For many large enterprises, the internal IT group is mainly responsible for maintaining and upgrading many customized enterprise IT applications such as:

- Enterprise resource planning (ERP)
- Finance resource management (FRM)
- Supply chain management (SCM)
- Human resource management (HRM)
- Customer relationship management (CRM)
- Point of sale (POS)
- Production development management (PDM)

The ERP applications operate the business, manage enterprise resources (both material and labor), and organize the relationships of the business in terms of business to shareholders or stakeholders (B2S), business to customers (B2C), business to employee (B2E), business to business (B2B), business to partners (B2P), and business to government (B2G) (see Figure 16.2).

Of course, many software vendors provide ERP applications. Based on Wikipedia [250] there are at least 20 open source applications, such as payroll, accounts receivable, procurement, inventory management, finance, business intelligence and more than 63 proprietary software packages for different market segments from low end to high end.

One of the CRM software companies, Salesforce.com, found that traditional IT operations were very inefficient because the customer has to buy an ERP license, and maintain and upgrade this software. They offer different approaches for customers, which is called Software as a Service (SaaS) or End of Software or No Software. Salesforce started to sell a subscription-based CRM application in 1999 [252] in competition with Siebel. Over the last 14 years or so, the company has been growing dramatically. In 2013, the company reported it had 32% growth and the revenue hit the $3b mark. (In comparison, in 2003 the company only had $50.99m in revenue.) The share price of the company has increased almost tenfold since it was listed on NYSE (see Figure 16.3).

IDC estimated that the SaaS market will reach $150.1b in 2013 and that there are more 1,000 worldwide SaaS providers with over $33b spent in investments globally. The Salesforce.com phenomenon has indicated that:

1. There is a growing market demand for SaaS.
2. The traditional operating model is not very efficient.
3. Salesforce.com has provided alternatives for a company that would like to outsource its ERP.

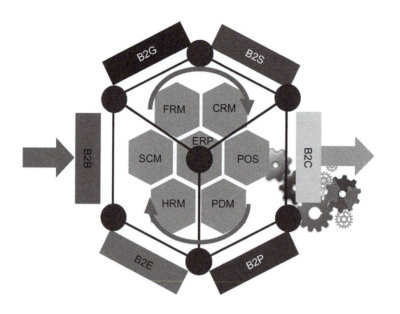

FIGURE 16.2

Typical enterprise IT applications or software.

FIGURE 16.3

History of Salesforce.com, Inc. share prices.

4. It provides opportunities for an enterprise to integrate and consolidate both external and internal IT resources and achieve the economies of scale.
5. The operating model of SaaS will provide cost savings for customers.
6. If CRM alone can provide such cost-savings potential, the cost savings for the entire ERP suite will be enormous.

Traditionally, there has always been issue with IT cost being transparent in large organizations because the IT metrics are difficult to share or too general. As John Baschab and Jon Piot [254] indicated, "the CIO is evaluated on the level of output from the IT department compared to the input required to produce the results. In this case, the output is effective technology that drives productivity, profits, user satisfaction, competitive advantage, and new revenue streams. The input is the capital in terms of labor and dollars." Unfortunately, the outputs of both business and operating values cannot be measured very clearly, even if an IT group has gone through one IT process frameworks or another (see Figure 16.4).

In other words, there is no a direct cost linkage between IT inputs and outputs, which we often call "cost transparency" (see Figure 16.5). This issue has become increasingly challenging when IT infrastructures are virtualized. One of the proposed solutions to resolve this issue is chargeback or

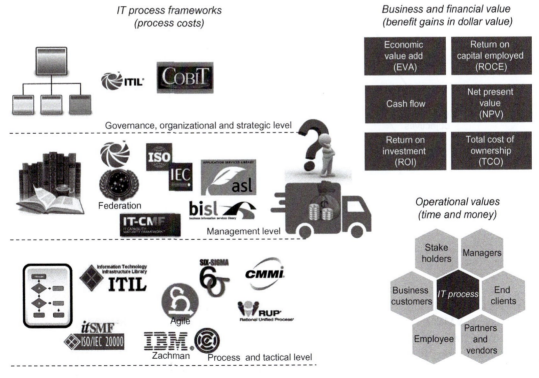

FIGURE 16.4

Value proposition of IT operating process frameworks.

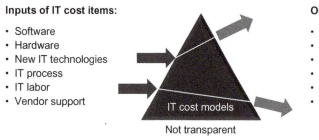

Inputs of IT cost items:

- Software
- Hardware
- New IT technologies
- IT process
- IT labor
- Vendor support

IT cost models

Not transparent

Outputs delivered to LoB units

- Productivity
- Profits
- Customer experiences or satisfaction
- Competitive advantages
- New revenue streams
- Effective technologies

FIGURE 16.5

Cost transparency issues.

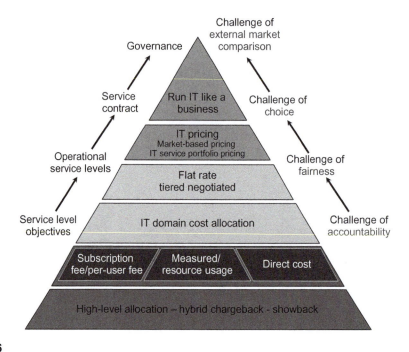

FIGURE 16.6

Hierarchy cost-allocation evolution from Gartner (Kurt Potter).

showback. The solution is to build an account engine that is embedded in a VM management system, such as VMWare's vCenter, Microsoft's System Center, or Citrix's XenApp.

Back in 2007, one of Gartner's senior analysts in IT business management, Kurt Potter, advised companies to bring back the IT chargeback system. He wrote a paper and claimed that the chargeback methodology can balance the conflicting priorities of simplicity, fairness, predictability, and controllability. It is a good tool for IT competitiveness and effectiveness [255] (see Figure 16.6). Ironically, in 2010, another Gartner analyst, David Coyle [256] asserted that chargeback was fine

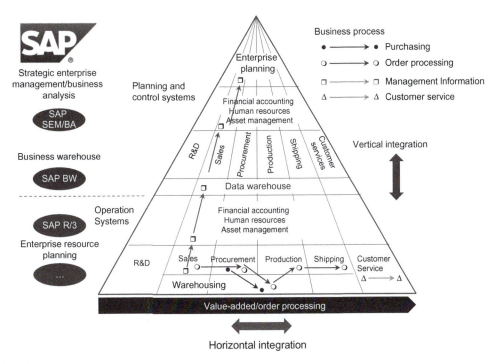

FIGURE 16.7

Classification of Business Information Systems triangle [276].

in theory but was not an effective tool in the quest to optimize IT operations. I do not know whether people should laugh or cry after they have bought a chargeback license and implemented this methodology and then hear Gartner's conflicting messages.

Anyway, the basic idea of this method is a cost allocation hierarchy with different maturity levels. It is not new. If we push further back in time, we can find this kind of cost allocation hierarchy is actually similar to Merten's [257] Classification of Business Information Systems triangle [276] proposed by SAP in 2005 (see Figure 16.7).

A few corporations tried this chargeback model, but it was not very successful. Perhaps, Kurt Potter might be right: "Chargeback is 20% reporting and 80% politics."

It might be 80% political but it would be unwise to throw out the baby with the bathwater. Actually, chargeback or showback could be a good tool to verify many operational assumptions in a bottom-up direction during the cost modeling process.

After reviewing the literature and whitepapers as well as many different chargeback or showback schemes for cost allocation, such as VMware, IBM, Cisco, and BMC, we list six cost allocation layers with 21 different cost allocation components (see Figure 16.8).

As Kurt Potter indicated in his paper, the original purpose of the cost allocation hierarchy was for showback within a large enterprise, which helps management to identify how to achieve better efficiency for the IT infrastructure. It is a reporting system for "responsibility accounting."

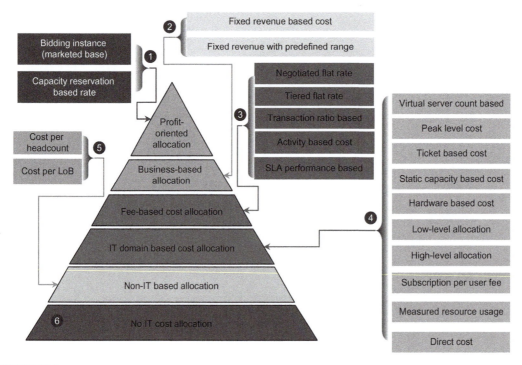

FIGURE 16.8

Cloud cost allocation with different dimensions.

We use this hierarchy to analyze or evaluate cloud costs from an IT resources consumption perspective. For both the cloud service provider and consumers, we can verify the operational cost assumptions for both the cloud infrastructure and applications. It is the linkage between IT costs and business benefits.

We will investigate the operation cost models in the sequence from bottom to top shown in Figure 16.8. Further, we will lay out the details of the total 21 operating cost models in six categories plus pros and cons of each cost model. The bottom line of operating cost models is looking for efficiency (utilization rate) impacts on the overall cost framework.

16.2 NO IT COST ALLOCATION

With no IT cost allocation, the IT resource consumers, normally a corporation's internal users, have no accountability and responsibility for IT expenses. They consider the internal IT resources free. They do not understand and do not want to know the cost of IT resources that they are consuming. The IT group will pay for all expenditures, capex, and opex within the IT budget bucket.

If there is no IT cost allocation to the IT users, it means the cost is not transparent. It leads to two serious issues in terms of very low IT resource utilization rate:

1. Because the IT resources appear to be free, the users will allocate IT resources as much as possible for either their production development or operations with the highest SLA. We have to understand that IT usage capacity and allocation capacity are two different concepts. Normally, IT capacity means allocation resources. Subsequently, the real usage of IT capacity is very low. For some mobile hosting applications, the server utilization rate is as low as below 1%.
2. In order to be competitive in the marketplace, the line of business (LoB), especially production groups, will continue to develop a series of new products to test the market. In other words, the R&D group needs very dynamic IT resources, and the group will create virtual machines (or virtual servers) very often if the IT infrastructure has been virtualized. If IT resources are free, people who are from the LoB group will not care about switching off the VM. If the IT infrastructure has not been virtualized, the physical server will not be switched off or decommissioned on time. The asset record may show the asset is still utilized but in reality, the asset is idle.

As we likely know, the IT department is highly dynamic group. The average staff turnover rate is around two to three years. It is very common that there is more contract labor than full-time employees in many organizations. That is why many people in the IT industry often say that CIO stands for "Career Is Over." As a result, if the asset cannot be switched off or decommissioned on time, you might have to spend double the amount of efforts to do it because:

- It is difficult to trace back the asset owner and users.
- We lose setup and configuration data for the asset.
- When you need to figure out the maintenance and support service level with your service vendors, you might sign the wrong SLA for a particular asset.

The only advantage of no IT cost allocation is that you do not have to spend a lot of time or effort to track, monitor, and report the current status of IT assets. It may save you time and effort to manage the IT assets because the status of an IT asset is relative simple, as all assets are in active status unless they are faulty.

You might use the IT industry benchmark to allocate IT cost or budgeting. The typical benchmark would be the ratio of IT expenses (or IT budget) vs. sales revenue. The lower end of the ratio is below 2%. However, for an IT or software or telco company, the ratio may be around 4% or higher and the average ratio is 3.5%, according to PwC data in 2005 (Table 16.1) [286].

When we use the benchmark to allocate the IT budget, we should understand the issues with the benchmark for IT expenses:

1. The benchmark figure is always historic data. It does not reflect the current market.
2. The benchmark is always generalized. It has a disappointing way of being too general. The more general the benchmark, the more remote it is from the intricacies of the actual situation when you

Table 16.1 IT Expenses as Revenue Percentage

	Industry Other Than High Tech	High Tech and IT Industries	Average Percentage
IT expenses as % of revenue	<2%	>4%	3.5%

try to follow it. In other words, you may allocate a large IT fund for a particular initiative or project. Because your IT expenditure has reached the benchmark celling, your business case will not be approved. Likewise, based on the benchmark, the IT budget might allocate too much capex or opex in the particular financial year. If you do not spend it, you might not be able to roll it into the next financial year. In addition, you may also face budget cuts in the next year.

Although there are many organizations still using this approach to allocate IT cost or budget, it is a very inefficient way to allocate IT resources.

In essence, the "no IT cost allocation" or the industry benchmark method offers no benefits for our cost modeling. The only valuable information is that the industry benchmark can be the initial reference point of the assumptions when we start to build a cost model.

16.3 NON-IT-BASED COST ALLOCATION

The term "non-IT-based cost allocation" means the IT cost allocation has nothing to do with actual IT resource consumption. The IT cost is dependent on a standard formula for different line of business units. It could be based on headcount or a percentage of revenue or budget of the LoB. It does not measure the IT resources that are consumed by each LoB unit. This non-IT-based cost allocation is similar to the above no IT cost allocation. The only difference is that the former one bases the IT budget allocation on the company's general revenue percentage and the latter one is dependent on the LoB unit.

It may appear that the budget allocation has been narrowed down to an individual line of business unit, but it basically doesn't resolve any of the issues we have stated above. An example of non-IT-based cost allocation is shown in Table 16.2.

The non-IT-based cost model focuses on accountability issues rather than real IT resource consumption. This is not a valuable method to pin out the exact IT resource consumption for the cost modeling process.

16.4 IT DOMAIN–BASED COST ALLOCATION

This cost allocation uses IT metrics to measure usage or resource consumption, such as CPU, disk read and write, memory, network transmissions, network data received, storage, and so on. The advantage for this type of cost allocation is that it correlates to both hardware and software resources (and infrastructure services). In comparison with the previous two types of cost allocation, this approach has many advantages but it has some disadvantages as well:

- It appears too difficult to have accurate measurements.
- It may be too costly to implement.
- It can be quite difficult for users to correlate their business activities with the IT infrastructure.

Table 16.2 IT Cost Allocation Based on Line of Business Unit

Benchmark	Finance	Production	HR	Operation	Procurement	Marketing	Sales
IT cost% to LoB	8%	15%	5%	35%	5%	7%	20%

- Even if the business activities can be loosely correlated with IT infrastructure or resources, the IT infrastructure configuration has to be frequently changed when the business activities are changed.
- If update and reconfiguration process is manual, the amount of efforts or human resources that are consumed may be too high in comparison with the output.

Overall, this IT domain–based cost allocation method is heading in the right direction. In order to align with users' business activities, IT domain–based cost allocation can be classified with 10 different approaches (or cost models). We will give details of each approach in the following sections.

The following series of cost models resolve the issue of fairness.

16.4.1 DIRECT COST

The direct cost approach allocates all cost to the business unit or users who "own" the IT infrastructure, such as hardware, software, maintenance, and IT support costs. This is normally applied in a dedicated hosting cost model. In other words, the IT infrastructure or service is not shared with other business units or users. This kind of cost model can be considered a project-based cost. It is the traditional and silo way of cost modeling. It is very simple to implement. However, it would be very costly to the business. If a project doesn't have enough funding, it wouldn't be possible to utilize some good software applications. It may eliminate further opportunities for the business to win big market share.

It is quite good for application development and dedicated project circumstances. Actually, this is a typical one-to-one relationship style of cost modeling. It is reasonably effective for dedicated service. Early IT cost modeling, such as for the Intel 4004 CPU, was based on this model.

16.4.2 MEASURED RESOURCE USAGE

This approach is strictly based on IT infrastructure service consumption or usage. This is a very common way for many retail cloud infrastructure service providers, such as Amazon and Rackspace, to charge their customers. It is a resources-based charge to determine equitable cost allocations for the distributed system.

Normally, it has a series of metrics that measures different operating systems and applications, but also captures or tracks data usage to determine the cost of a particular IT environment such as hosting web servers, file servers, and database servers.

For example, one user may operate a VM to host a web server, which consumes very little resources, while another user may operate a VM for a SQL server that consumes almost all of the host server's available CPU, cache, and memory resources. The cloud service provider can differentiate these two particular resource consumption instances with different charges because one user consumes more resources than others, such as one measuring the vCPU or vMemory usage and the other measuring the number of VM instances.

This is a static or preconfigured method of resource allocation. It cannot measure how a user consumes the physical IT resources. If a consumer cannot predict or estimate the workload, then the only way is a trial and error method to figure out the right amount of IT capacity.

Table 16.3 An Example of Resource Usage Configuration by VMware Chargeback

Base Rate	Unit	Initial Configured ($)
vCPU	GHz/hour	0.045
Disk read & write	Hour	0.100
Disk read	Hour	0.060
Disk write	Hour	0.060
Memory	GB/hour	0.035
Network received & transmitted	GB/hour	0.100
Network received	GB/hour	0.100
Network transmitted	GB/hour	0.100
Storage	GB/hour	0.150
vCPU	Count	1
Other Costs		
High availability (HA)	Month	3,000
Fault tolerance (FT)	Month	1,200
VM creation	Once-off	20
VM delete	Once-off	10
Fixed Costs		
Infrastructure build cost	Once-off	100
New provision	Once-off	4000
Deprovisioning	Once-off	1800
OSI management fee		
Unmanaged	Once-off	50
Frozen	Once-off	50

One advantage of resource usage–based cost allocation is that it can control the excessive demands or resource allocations for certain LoB units. It can also drive or influence user's behavior in how they consume IT infrastructure resources, as you only "pay for what you consume." It is quite fair to all customers. For many large organizations, this model treats internal users as external consumers.

The disadvantages of this approach are that is quite labor intensive for IT admins to keep track of resources. It also can be less transparent since it is derived from multiple resource factors. In addition, it may take quite a while for IT admins to utilize the right configurations for measurements because of the lack of historical data (see Table 16.3).

As we can see in Table 16.3, it is quite challenging to fairly configure the right dollar amounts for resource consumption. This kind of cost allocation is fit for storage, email, and telecom type of services. However, this is the first step to initiate the chargeback mechanism and later the cost configuration can be fine-tuned based on the feedback and calibration.

16.4.3 SUBSCRIPTION-BASED COST ALLOCATION

This cost allocation is on a fixed basis. It disregards IT resource consumption. It is the "pay-per-user" cost model. The operating costs of IT infrastructure resources are calculated and amortized across a subscription period (for example, yearly or a three-year term) and then divided among all users of IT services. The typical example that uses this charge method is Salesforce.com.

The advantage of this method is that is very simple to implement and calculate. The cloud service provider will have regular, predictable, and sustainable revenue or booked cost.

For example, assume that if a large enterprise has finance, procurement, production, marketing, and operations, or five LoB units, the total cost of purchasing, training, upgrading, installation, configuration, and support for an ERP application software would be around $1,200,000. If the estimated life cycle is around five years, the annual cost of this application is $240,000 and the monthly cost would be $20,000. The subscription cost for each LoB unit is equal to $4,000 per month per LoB (or per user).

The disadvantage of this method is that it doesn't differentiate amongst different users. It assumes that all users or LoB units will use this service at the same level on a constant basis. Users or LoBs that have excessive usage and peak time usage do not have to worry about penalties or costs.

This kind of cost allocation is better for a cloud service provider who has a large infrastructure resource pool. From the cloud consumer's perspective, it is better applied for customers who are not very sensitive to the subscription fee or when the subscription fee is not very expensive anyway in comparison with the business revenue. In addition, it is useful if the usage is unpredictable but the service is required to be "always on."

16.4.4 HIGH-LEVEL ALLOCATION

This method only allocates large cost items that are related to LoB units or users, such as a cloud data center infrastructure (HVAC), server cluster, large memory, core network, expensive application software package, IT labor, professional services, and ongoing power consumption. The minor cost items can be omitted, such as once-off training costs or once-off change request costs.

The advantage of high-level cost allocation is that it simplifies cost calculations. It would be quicker to calculate the cost in comparison with comprehensive or a low-level cost allocation calculation model.

The disadvantage lies in how to control what is omitted. It is difficult to decide which cost component should be omitted and which one should be included. This kind of decision would be based on personal experience and an individual's intuition. The better way to decide on an omitted object is to run sensitivity analysis. It may be even more complicated than a comprehensive cost model.

It is normally applied at the high-level strategic planning stage or during annual IT budget allocation. Basically, it is for a strategic decision maker who is above or at the level of C-class executives, such as CEO, COO, CIO, CFO, CTO, or the director of a company board. The decision will have an impact for a three- to five-year term or an even longer period.

16.4.5 LOW-LEVEL ALLOCATION

In contrast with "high-level allocation," this drills down the detail of each cloud cost element. The advantages and disadvantages are the opposite of high-level cost allocation. It is normally applied for detailed project planning, cost estimation, or cloud business case approval.

The cost decision will have an impact in the very short term, such as three or six months. Very often, this cost allocation method is used at a project or program manager level.

16.4.6 HARDWARE-BASED COST

The user or LoB pays for their own hardware, such as the HDD, hosting server, or type of memory with a particular specification. For example, a customer may need 300GB storage with an FC-RAID-1 configuration for the HDD and speed = 15,000 rpm.

The advantage of hardware-based cost is very straightforward and the cost allocation is a self-explanatory model because the user or the customer pays for the cost. However, a large corporation will not allow any kind of hardware to be installed in its system. There is a policy or guidelines for IT hardware installation and support.

Therefore, the disadvantage of hardware-based cost is figuring how to set up the policy or guidelines as to what can be installed on the storage LUN or on a server cluster or an extra access firewall. For example, some companies have a security policy prohibiting an Internet-facing VM from being installed on the same host server as backend virtual servers. Or, some organizations do not use a RAID-1 storage HDD configuration while others don't have the maintenance support for a particular storage application such as SAN. For example, if the company only has NAS storage hardware that is supported by NetApp for its maintenance, it would take a lot of effort to negotiate another support contract with EMC for a particular high-level SAN storage application.

In addition, every hardware device needs backup or disaster recovery (DR) support. The IT group has to allocate a certain amount of opex for each hardware component that is purchased by different LoB units. As as result, the IT group's opex may be out of control.

16.4.7 STATIC CAPACITY–BASED COST

This kind of cost allocation means a consumer pays for a fixed capacity regardless of its consumption status. It is best to implement as capacity "slices." Slices can be aggregated from a large resource pool or more granular (individual VMs). For example, a customer may need 1TB raw storage capacity with an IP SAN connection. However, this customer didn't know what the kinds of HDD are; what access speed is; how redundancy is configured; etc.

It is relatively easy to meter or measure customer usage and it is simple for a customer to understand the bill for allocation of these slices that they consume.

This model may be less transparent than other cost allocation methods, such as hardware-based cost.

16.4.8 TICKET-BASED COST

In this category, a user basically consumes IT resources based on an e-ticket that can be used in a validated period, such as a number of hours specified in a restricted time range or particular day or even week or month. It is more like a voucher.

An IT admin can issue e-ticket quantities and prices based on the workload pattern of a cloud cluster system and the time. The cloud service provider can adjust or fine-tune the workload and help eliminate usage peaks, ensuring business continuity.

It is quite simple to implement. All that a cloud service provider has to do is monitor ticket pricing, cloud workloads, and response time, which makes sure there is low latency for web portal services.

This cost allocation can be the strongest cost justification model. Both the cloud service provider and consumer can monitor a specific ticket, and both sides can monitor the exact usage for the particular application level.

Customers can design their usage pattern to optimize price and avoid peak usage time if the workload is not very urgent.

The cloud service provider can offer customers under the ticket-based cost model three price levels:

- Network access bandwidth (8 Mbps, 10 Mbps, or 100Mbps)
- Service level guarantees (such as Platinum, Gold, Silver, and Bronze)
- Peak usage capacity allocation

The only disadvantage is e-ticket hoarding or accumulation, which can prevent the e-ticket-based model from operating effectively. In order to avoid this issue, the e-ticket must be issued by the "use-by" date on the e-ticket.

16.4.9 PEAK LEVEL—BASED COST

Peak level cost allocation uses the workload pattern to price the resource cost. Cloud consumers will be billed according to their peak and off-peak usage time, not average usage. This model is similar to utility charging models, such as for electricity.

The advantage of this cost allocation is very simple. It's similar to metering the usage. There are only two metering levels, peak and off-peak. The IT administrators only monitor and record the peak usage resources. It is easier to show consumers when they are using more than a certain threshold of resources.

The disadvantage is that the cloud service provider may penalize consumers if the peak and off-peak time has been shifted or even if during the specified peak time, there is not a lot of traffic, such as during special holidays or big events.

16.4.10 VIRTUAL SERVER— OR VM ACCOUNT—BASED COST

This cost allocation is based on the number of VMs on a particular physical node. A large physical hosting server or a server cluster can vary from 10 VMs to 100 VMs per physical node. If one physical server has been configured with 10 VMs and a "Client A" consumed three VMs, then Client A will be billed for 30% of this physical server's overall capex + opex. Normally, the cloud service provider can use a standard VM template to price the service. For example, Amazon Web Service has a "High-Memory Instance" VM template (see Table 16.4).

The advantage of VM-based charges is that they are easy to measure and bill. However, it is not absolutely fair because not all VMs consume the same amount of hardware resources.

Table 16.4 AWS High Memory Instance (VM) configuration Template

High–Memory Instance	Template Configuration
Memory	17.1 GB
CPU	6.5 EC2 computer units (2 virtual cores with 3.25/per EC2 compute units
Storage	420 GB
Platform	64-bit
I/O performance	Moderate
EBS-optimized available	No
API name	M2.xlarge

In summary, all the above 1- cost allocation methods are based on IT terminology. It doesn't matter whether it is high- or low-level cost allocation. It either charges for physical resource consumption or bills on virtual resources. This has provided a stepping stone for sophisticated cost allocation methods. To some degree, these are still not very cost transparent for the business.

16.5 FEE-BASED COST ALLOCATION

If a cloud service provider is charging its customers based on an annual fee or yearly usage, we call it a fee-based cost charge model. For an internal IT group, this method can be considered the classic annual "budgeting approach". The main focus of this cost allocation method is to focus on fairness. We can classify this fee-based chargeback method with four different approaches;

- Negotiated flat rate
- Tiered flat rate
- Transaction ratio–based fee
- SLA performance–based rate

Let's investigate all these cost allocation methods in detail.

16.5.1 NEGOTIATED FLAT RATE

The negotiated flat rate means the price will be discussed and settled between a cloud service provider and a cloud service consumer based on a flat rate for each physical node or server cluster because some VMs may consume more resources than others. It is highly recommended that both parties use two different flat rates, one basic flat rate and one high-capacity flat rate.

The advantage of a negotiated flat rate is that it doesn't force inexperienced cloud consumers to use complex and time-consuming methods for determine each monthly bill. It is easier for the cloud service consumer to stay on budget. However, the disadvantage is lack of usage transparency.

This will work best for a virtual data center scenario.

Table 16.5 Tiered Flat Rate Price for Hosting Storage

Tiered Level	Platinum	Gold	Silver	Bronze	Archive	Avg.
Units	(primary GB)	(primary GB)	(primary GB)	(primary GB)		Ave Cost/ SAN Port
SAN ports ($/port/month)	$55	$35	$25	$20	$5	$29.00
Director port ($/port/ month)	$90	$80	$70	$60	$50	$70.00
SAN port management ($/port/month)	$50	$40	$30	$20	$10	$30.00
Software power path ($/port/month)	$45	$$35	$25	$15	$10	$26.00
Usable capacity ($/GB/ month)	1.52	0.88	0.64	0.23	0.25	$0.70
Capacity management ($/GB/month)	1.60	1.52	0.96	0.52	0.30	
Total	$3.12	$2.40	$1.60	$0.75	$0.55	$155.70

16.5.2 TIERED FLAT RATE

This cost allocation works according to service level differentiation (e.g., Platinum, Gold, Silver, Bronze, Basic, or Best Effort). It can also be divided into two levels: base level service flat fee (such as a service template) and above base level service fee. The customers can move their service levels up and down based on current needs.

The typical example of a tiered flat rate is for hosting storage products, such as the following example for enterprise hosting storage products (see Table 16.5). This table is similar to Table 12.10 but the following table has project-oriented pricing.

The advantages and disadvantages of a tiered flat rate are similar to those for negotiated flat rates.

16.5.3 TRANSACTION RATIO–BASED COST

This cost allocation model is similar to "virtual server" based cost allocation. It is based on hosts' transactions against the shared services among different tiered hosts. For example, assume there are two virtual host servers located on two different tiers (one on tier 1 and the other on tier 2) and each is transmitting workload on two different transmission lines; one is on Transmission System 1 (or T1, at 1.554Mbits) and the other is on T2 (6.312Mbits). If tier 1 hosts 25,000 transactions against the shared infrastructure, and tier 2 hosts 50,000 transactions, then tier 1 would account for 33.3% of the total shared infrastructure cost. This is normally applied for a shared infrastructure network. In other words, you can show back the cost of the 33.3% workload for tier 1 and 67.7% for tier 2. The workload transaction ratio for tier 1 and tier 2 is 1/3 (see Table 16.6 and Figure 16.9).

Table 16.6 Transaction Ratio–Based Cost

Service Tiers	Transaction Volume	Network Type	Cost	Transaction Ratio
Tier 1	25,000	T2 (6.312Mbits)	$2,000	
Tier 2	50,000	T1 (1.554Mbits)	$2,000	1:3
Total	75,000		$4,000	

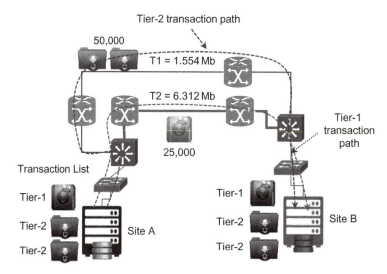

FIGURE 16.9

Transaction ratio–based cost.

Of course, you can differentiate the price between T1 and T2 in terms of bandwidth or network speed on top of the service tiers. You can also add other service features onto tier 1 transactions. In this case, the cost model can to control the transaction ratio (1:3) along with the cost ratio (1:1).

The advantage of this cost structure is that it is a usage-based cost. It is quite transparent to the business or consumers. They know what they pay for. The problem with this cost model is that it is time-consuming and complex. The cloud service provider has to keep track of each transaction.

16.5.4 ACTIVITY-BASED COST

This is a good way to allocate usage cost. The issue is how to define the activity. If both the cloud service provider and consumer can perfectly understand the definition of the activity and price model, then it makes the cost allocation fair, transparent, and predicable. It is easier for he cloud consumer to understand the invoice. It is similar to a "pay as you consume" cost model.

The advantages are as follows. (1) It increases fairness for clients who use the shared infrastructure. (2) It can help the LoB unit or customer understand what their usage and costs are. (3) It can also help a cloud service provider to understand what the customers want and continuously improve their service standards and efficiency. Ultimately, the cloud service provider can reduce the cost of service to be competitive in the marketplace. (4) From a cloud service consumer perspective, this cost model is fair to every consumer. (5) Price is only based on volume of transactions (i.e., service usage). (6) From a cloud service provider's perspective, it can establish a business-oriented operation structure and cut out many inefficient activities. (7) The transaction data would be quite easy to collect. (8) The cloud service provider can supply sufficient details for bills to allow customers to influence consuming behavior (usage) and to reduce the cost. (9) The service information is easier to trace.

The only disadvantage is for the cloud service provider, as the cloud service revenue could fluctuate according to consumer demand. This requires the cloud service provider to increase its resource pool and operate the services on using economics of scale.

16.5.5 SLA PERFORMANCE METRICS

The SLA performance metrics approach means that the cost allocation is based on service level plus mean time to repair (MTTR) or inherent availability = MTTF/(MTTF + MTTR) and number of customers impacted. From an end-to-end perspective, the availability would be equal to the multiplication of the availability of all network components if the network devices are connected in series. If the network is connected in parallel and series, then the E2E availability has to be calculated inversely; this is unavailability or $1 -$ availability (see Figure 16.10):

$$A_{\text{com}} = [1 - (1 - A_{s1} \times A_{s2} \times A_{s3}) \times (1 - A_{p1} \times A_{p2} \times A_{p3})] = 0.99983$$

$$A_{e2e} = A_1 \times A_2 \times A_3 \times A_{\text{com}} \times A_4 \times A_5 \times A_6 = 0.9999^6 \times 0.99983 = 0.999384$$

From a cloud service consumer's perspective, the price of the maintenance plus the support contract can be based on resources or the number of customers in operation (or service in operation, SIO) or a certain percentage of the project cost.

The resource-based contract means that a cloud client will pay the number of full time equivalent (FTE) professionals necessary to maintain the specified SLA. For example, to maintain five 9s SLA (24×7), the cloud service provider needs at least seven professional FTE staff (such as IT admins, software engineers, project managers, data center operators, etc.) for a certain number of physical servers. In addition, it might need a disaster recovery (DR) facility to support the committed services.

A customer- or SIO-based support contract means the cloud service provider will charge the fee based on the number of cloud consumer (here, a cloud consumer means a company that runs a business), such as $5 dollars per SIO.

Some cloud service providers might charge support costs based on the proportion of project cost. This project cost means the cloud infrastructure cost. For example, the project would roll out 10 racks of physical servers. If the rack life-cycle cost is $120,000 per rack, then the total capex cost of the project is equal to $1.2m. The maintenance and support contract cost would be calculated as between 10% ~ 12% of the total of the project cost, which is $120k ~ $144k per annum. Along with capex, the opex will be charged based on SLA metrics (see Table 12.9).

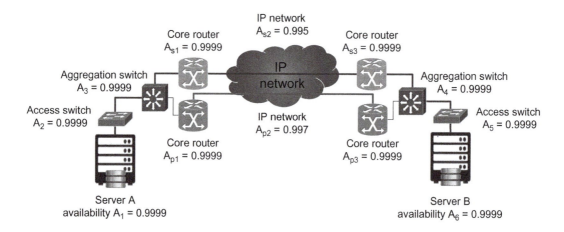

FIGURE 16.10

E2E network availability.

Here 13x5 means 7:00 to 20:00, five days per week. It excludes weekends and public holidays. The higher the SLA, the higher the contract cost would be. Some cloud service providers support basic SLA plus on-call. This would be cheaper than 24×7 support cost. However, the MTTR would be longer than Gold, Platinum, and Business Critical (BC) offerings.

The advantage of this cost model is that it is closely related to the business operation or business application. The disadvantage is that it is not very transparent in terms of cost allocation. It may be a fit within a big enterprise between an IT group and the other LoB units.

16.6 BUSINESS-BASED COST ALLOCATION

Business-based cost allocation is where the cloud service provider will charge based on a cloud user's business activity or revenue. For example, the cloud service provider may charge a customer $3 per transaction or $5 per VM creation or $8 per vSwtich migration among different clusters.

The advantages of this cost model are similar to those we discussed with virtual server–based cost allocation. However, the disadvantage of this cost model is that it may be too complicated or tedious. The price model could be unfair to a customer who uses a particular application function that only has a small customer base.

16.6.1 FIXED REVENUE-BASED COST

Fixed revenue cost allocation means a cloud service client will provide fixed compensation for the service resources, for example 5%–10% of business revenue or gross profit. The advantage is that customers have greater predictability of shared service costs, but the disadvantage is that they could be exposed to risk due to the transaction volume increasing dramatically. If the business growth is quite difficult to be forecaste, this is not the right model. This model is similar to DVC.

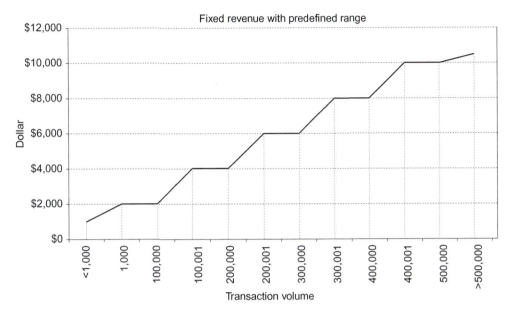

FIGURE 16.11

Fixed revenue with predefined range.

16.6.2 FIXED REVENUE WITH PREDEFINED RANGE

A cloud service consumer will provide fixed payment for services, as long as resource utilization or transaction volumes stay within a predefined range of activity. If the activity goes above or below the range, the price will be adjusted accordingly (see Figure 16.11).

The advantage of this cost model is that it is favorable for the cloud service provider if it has cost advantages and the cloud client may perceive it to be fair, as the price model is based on the volume of transactions or usage and only a cloud service provider will be exposed to the potential risks due to uncontrollable or unpredictable market size. In addition, the cloud service consumer doesn't have to pay a fixed cost if the transaction volume is below a predefined range.

The only disadvantage is that the customer may perceive that cost savings or efficiency improvements are not passed on because normally the cloud service provider will charge a premium for the services.

16.6.3 PROFIT-ORIENTED COST MODEL

This is a market base or competitive cost model. This approach treats IT and business units or cloud service consumers as one entity to generate profits. Therefore both parties will share the risk of exposure to uncontrollable factors.

The advantage is that both the internal IT group and external cloud service providers are on equal footing. However, the disadvantage is that immature strategic decision making can lead organizations to outsource the core functions and suffer the long term consequences.

It is a quite sophisticated cost model, which it is to challenge the external market rate that is offered by other cloud service providers. We can consider this is a profit oriented cost model, which we can further classify into two sub-models.

- Capacity reservation–based rate
- Bidding instance

16.6.3.1 Capacity reservation–based rate

A cloud service provider would like to have some kind of certainty and ask a customer to commit to a reserved capacity; above the capacity reservation, the cloud service provider will share risk with the cloud service clients. Therefore, the cloud service provider can reduce the risks of the initial cloud infrastructure investment.

This is normally applied to a mature business, where the cloud service consumer has a preditable customer base.

The advantage is that the cloud service provider will have assurances for its initial investment. The disadvantage is the cloud service client will take more risk. However, if the business is very mature, the baseline cost is quite certain. Therefore, this is one of the good cost models for a mature business.

16.6.3.2 Bidding instance (market base rate)

If cloud service providers have extra capacity for cloud infrastructure during a particular time period, they can put their additional capacity up an auction. Whoever bids the highest price will own the particular time slot for IT resources or cloud computing power.

Aminul Haque et al. [288] in their paper suggested the five most widely proposed auction models, which are:

- English Auction Interaction (EA)
- Continuous Double Auction (CDA)
- Commodity Market Model (CMM)
- Tender/Contract-Net-Protocol (CNP)
- Bargaining Protocol (BAR)

The advantage of the auction model is that the cloud service providers can fully utilize their extra capacity. Theoretically speaking, if the market is mature enough, no cloud resources should be wasted. However, in reality, the market is not so sophisticated and transparent. The auction models are too complicated to understand. It is not quite transparent to a cloud service user. Subsequently, the consumer may pay a higher price than the capacity reservation cost. In addition, cloud service providers will not guarantee resource capacity for a user's application requirements. The cloud consumers have to take the risk.

16.7 SUMMARY

Up to now, we have reviewed and explained 21 different operational models. We have spelled out both the advantages and disadvantages (pros and cons) for each operating model. Clearly, no model is perfect for both cloud service providers and consumers. The decision maker can select a model based on his own business strategy and circumstances.

Overall, the chargeback mechanism is divided into six layers. The bottom two or three layers (non-IT based, IT based) are focused on accountability issues and oriented toward IT hardware or domains. The fee-based layer is oriented toward service levels or operational activities. It is driven by fairness between the cloud service provider and cloud consumers. The next layer up is oriented toward the business. It has a direct link between IT services and business revenue. The last layer is oriented toward the market. It is directly making comparisons between the internal and external efficiency of the IT operation.

The main purposes of presenting these models are:

- Presenting a line of thinking on how to recover the IT investment cost (or capex & opex)
- Aligning or making a connection between IT expenses and line of business units
- Making IT costs transparent
- Ultimately, making the cost model assumptions much more realistic

These models can be applied for any IT resource user but the original goal of the chargeback mechanism was for cost transparency between IT groups and internal LoB units in a large corporation. Based on many practical experiences, this is fine in theory but it is quite challenging to implement because it can potentially eliminate a lot of politics and finger pointing. Ironically, if you want to implement it properly, you need a lot of political skills.

The ultimate goal of this chapter is to establish the assumption foundation for our cost framework. As we stated before, many assumptions that we made are very subjective. The cloud model is relative new. In order to build a realistic cost model, we need to verify many subjective assumptions. Chargeback is one of the good mechanisms to make IT cost transparent at a tactical level.

In the following chapters, we will give a detailed example to demonstrate how to establish and calculate cloud costs.

16.8 REVIEW QUESTIONS

1. Is a chargeback really useful? Explain why?
2. What is the fairest cost model among the IT domain–based cost models and why?
3. What is the issue with ticket-based cost modeling?
4. Is there any problem with VM account–based cost modeling?
5. If so, what is the right solution to resolve it?
6. What is the real purpose of leveraging the chargeback mechanism?
7. Why do people say that chargeback is 20% reporting and 80% politics?
8. Why is the chargeback mechanism good in theory but not in practice?
9. If you are asked to implement a chargeback project in order to verify the cost assumptions of capex and opex, what do you do?

CLOUD STRATEGY AND CRITICAL DECISION MAKING

Part V is the last part of this book. It only consists of two chapters. The main focus of this part is to address macro issues of cost. When we are building a cost model we often pay too much attention to the trees but miss the forest. This is why Part V discusses the topic of cost modeling at a strategic level.

If we see cost modeling as a vertical process, then the first study case shown in Chapter 3 is a bottom-up process to establish a cost model. It is often applied to the scenario of operating cost rationalization in a mature business environment. In both Chapters 17 and 18, we will focus on a top-down process to build up a cost model. It is normally dealt with in a new business environment, in which the business revenue or forecast is uncertain. It can be considered revenue-driven cost modeling.

Of course, these two approaches to cost modeling do not exclude each other but rather are complementary. We can probably use both approaches for cross-checking purposes if the modeling data is available. The ultimate goal is to construct a realistic cost model so a decision maker can make the right decision.

COST MODEL CALCULATION

In this chapter, we will unveil a case study that shows how to calculate the cost details based on the theory of cost models. In other words, we will combine both "bottom-up" (or tactical level) and "top-down" (or strategic level) approaches for this case study. It will be divided into three main logical parts:

- Introduction of case study
- Model assumptions
- Calculation process and calculation results

The calculation in this chapter is basically a financial cost model using NPV (net present value) that we described in Chapter 15. The benefit of an NPV calculation is that it takes into consideration the time value of the money. This type of calculation is what we call it a tactical detail. In the next chapter, we will use this case and sort out the strategic calculation based on real option theory and Monte Carlo simulation (see Figure 17.1).

17.1 CASE STUDY
17.1.1 COMPANY HISTORY

The case study that we are going to focus on is one of leading web portal companies; it mainly does advertising for both residential and commercial properties. The aim of this web portal company are to deliver effective online advertising solutions through its website to help real estate agents with their businesses, including property sales and rent. The company only deals with real estate agents rather than individual property owners. This means the business model of this portal company is business to business (or B2B). Any individual property owner has to deal with a particular local real estate agent.

Looking back to its history, the portal company was founded in 1995 and publically listed in December 1999 or during the dot-com boom period. The company started to have a net profit cash flow in 2004 and has awarded dividends since 2009. It has 46.24% average revenue growth rate during the last 10 years or so (see Table 17.1 and Figures 17.1 and 17.2).

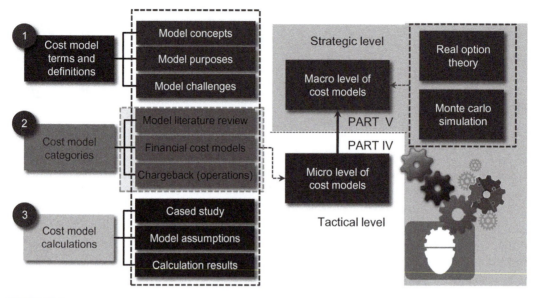

FIGURE 17.1

Macro view of cost modeling.

As of 2013, the company operates 13 websites around the world. Its multinational portfolio websites can attract more than 11 million[1] unique browsers per month. The company has about 600 full-time equivalent (FTE) employees. From Figures 17.2 and 17.3, we can see that the company still maintained two-digit growth even during the 2008 and 2009 financial crisis.

17.1.2 BASIC BUSINESS PROFILE

Once we have a brief view of the company's history, the next step is to review the business profile, where we identify what the business needs or estimate the required IT capacity. In Chapter 2, we have already described the five phases of the process flowchart for business problem solving. This is the preparation phase of cost modeling. It can also be considered as part of the RDD and BRD process.

Based Table 17.1, it is quite clear that the primary requirement for this web portal company is to work with all real estate agents or clients and upload all the adverting materials to the company's website within the specified time period. This is the primary product or service provided by this portal company. It is also the key revenue source for the portal company to grow and make profit. From a market perspective, this business should be quite competitive in terms of price and service quality. Currently, the business assumptions are:

- The number of new listed properties for sale advertised = 1800−2700 per week.
- The number of new listed properties for rent advertised = 700−1,000 per week.

---

[1]Nielsen Online, Market Intelligence, Total Traffic for Audited Sites, http://www.nielsen.com/au/en.html.

Table 17.1 A Web Portal Company's Business Briefing

Year	2003	2004	2005	2006	2007	2008	2009	2010	2011	2012	2013
Revenue $000	9,540	19,145	33,624	60,872	107,293	155,633	167,795	194,355	238,401	277,613	336,460
Net Profit after Tax	−1,539	2,477	8,092	8,222	15,064	25,488	28,703	49,366	67,505	86,782	109,748
FTE	60	106	159	294	479	667	600*	600*	600*	600*	600*
Employee Expenses	3,714	6,741	12,155	23,329	40,598	49,373	59,841	63,372	67,363	74,013	85,108
Consultant & Contract	240	143	367	881	3,266	5,543	7,857	8,368	10,285	8,838	9,682
Marketing Expenses	941	3,913	7,077	10,465	15,800	14,715	15,327	16,665	25,415	32,315	41,372
Technology Expenses	240	337	862	1,664	2,981	3,662	5,317	8,875	8,924	10,132	8,742
Depreciation Amortization Expenses	2,689	369	1,051	2,297	4,973	6,404	7,348	7,088	10,489	15,184	18,670
Operation Expenses	8,343	16,278	26,951	38,910	59,286	87,438	105,304	116,348	135,220	140,482	163,574
Profit Growth Rate		260.9%	226.7%	1.6%	83.2%	69.2%	12.6%	72.0%	36.7%	28.6%	26.0%
Revenue Growth Rate	61%	100.7%	75.6%	81.0%	76.3%	45.1%	7.8%	15.8%	22.7%	16.4%	21.0%

Note: All expenses and revenue units are $000.
*Note: Since 2010, the annual report has not stopped to provide FTE details. We assume this number has not been changed since 2010.

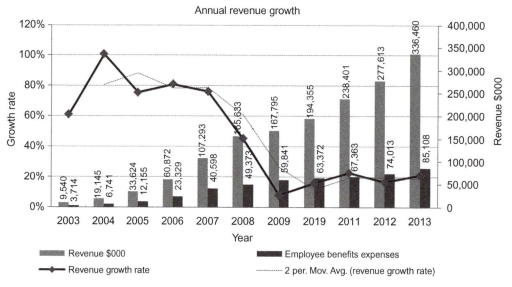

FIGURE 17.2

A web portal company's revenue and growth rate.

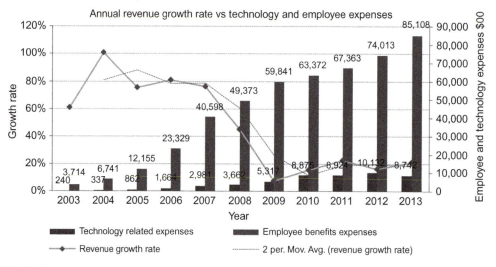

FIGURE 17.3

Annual revenue growth rate vs. technology and employee expenses.

- Each property file will be on the portal for a 6 to 8 week (average) campaign.
- Each standard advertising file = 2−5MB; if the adverting file includes a video file the file size = 25−30MB. The rule of thumb is that 5% of service will require the video feature.
- For each property, a standard ad file will receive 2,000 to 4,000 hits during the period of the advertising campaign. In theory, the more features the ad has, the more web browsers will hit it. Of course, the portal company will charge more. We assume the business has four different advertising products in the product portfolio:
  1. Standard ad (2,000−4,000 hits): 20% of the total ads
  2. Feature ad (6,000−12,000 hits):40% of the total ads
  3. Highlight ad (16,000−32,000 hits): 35% of the total ads
  4. Premiere ad (30,000−60,000 hits): 5% of the total ads

Based on this business portfolio, it shouldn't be so difficult to identify IT capacity.

17.1.3 CURRENT IT ASSETS AND OPERATION

Now, before moving to the next analysis step, let's review the existing IT assets this portal company has to cope with the current business demands. In order to accommodate the existing workloads, the company has the following IT infrastructure:

1. It has more than 400 physical server nodes that are located in three local data centers that are provided by three different data center service providers. This is the co-location scenario. The company's strategic plan is to consolidate the three data centers or co-lo sites into one.
2. These physical nodes are mixed with both x86 and RISC servers and supported by different major vendors (HP, Dell, IBM, and Oracle/Sun).
3. The company has adopted a hybrid cloud solution, where more than 80 physical nodes have been virtualized. But it only has about 90 virtual machines (VMs) in operation. In other words, the P2V ratio is only 1:1.125.
4. Currently, the company uses Citrix Xen as the hypervisor for its virtualized infrastructure. It is planning to drop Citrix Xen and replaced it with VMWare vSphere 5
5. It also uses Amazon EC2 as its disaster recovery (DR) site.
6. The main applications and operation systems running on these servers are: Microsoft SQL, Apache, .Net, Linux, Tomcat, Citrix Xen, VMware, and Apple iOS.
7. The company's IT strategy is to virtualize all dedicated nodes. The decision on whether they should move all workloads into the cloud or not has not been made yet.

17.1.4 STRATEGIC IT INVESTMENT DECISION OPTIONS

Given the current IT conditions and prediction of business growth (20−30% growth), the question is, how can the decision maker make the right and strategic IT investment decision to support the company's growing business needs over the next five years or so? There are many strategic options. Actually, the number of options can be infinite based on decision theory. However, in order to build a concise cost framework, we can roughly simplify the infinite number of IT investment options into three basic options (see Figure 17.4).

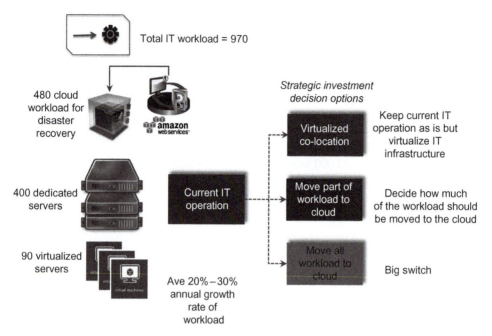

Total IT workload = 970

480 cloud workload for disaster recovery

400 dedicated servers

Current IT operation

90 virtualized servers

Ave 20%–30% annual growth rate of workload

Strategic investment decision options

Virtualized co-location — Keep current IT operation as is but virtualize IT infrastructure

Move part of workload to cloud — Decide how much of the workload should be moved to the cloud

Move all workload to cloud — Big switch

FIGURE 17.4

Strategic IT investment decision options.

The first strategic option is "Virtualized Co-location" (assume that the company doesn't own the data center facility because its core business is web hosting or web advertising). The reason to virtualize the existing infrastructure is to find the opportunity to reduce IT infrastructure cost, both capex and opex.

The second decision option is to move part of or a proportion of the workload into the cloud and reduce the footprint of the existing co-location infrastructure. This option is a strategy to move capex into opex. The reason to select this strategy is because the cloud business model is not very mature. It may need more time to be understood. Another critical reason is to avoid lock up with particular vendor or a cloud service provider.

The third option is to totally embrace the cloud, moving all IT workload from three co-lo sites to the cloud or to a cloud service provider. This means that the portal company doesn't need to allocate IT capex budget and all IT expenditure will become opex. From a sourcing perspective, this option is more like an outsourcing solution.

This process may appear to be a strategic planning process but it is really a cost modeling issue. We will establish the cost framework around these IT investment decision options.

In the following sections, we will first build a simple cost model of stack layers, including all the necessary cost components for a web portal company to operate its portal business.

17.1.4.1 Data center facility capex

- Space
- Racks and cabling
- Power: UPS & PDU

- Air conditioning
- Site security and fire suppression

17.1.4.2 IT hardware expenses

- Server equipment
- Memory
- Storage SAN and NAS
- Network, access and aggregation switches, core routers and load balancers
- Firewall and security

17.1.4.3 Software licenses

- Hypervisors
- Operating system
- Middleware
- Network management and monitoring
- Applications

17.1.4.4 Other implementation costs

On top of all the purchasing cost components, there are many implementation cost items such as:

- Project planning
- Project management
- Design, build, and test
- Project delivery and integration
- Operation, management, and optimization
- Exit and life cycle

All these cost components may belong to IT project costs, such as IT consultant and professional costs. Figure 17.5 is one example of cost assumptions for project delivery. We call this project-oriented cost modeling.

Figure 17.4 shows a typical example of making cost assumptions regarding an IT project. The first block is for capacity planning and implementation and includes a Requirement Definition Document (RDD) or Business Requirements Document (BRD), Key Decision Document (KDD), and Solution Architecture Design (SAD). It is the first phase of project. The second block is shows the operation from a life-cycle perspective. It includes ongoing opex, training, and exit costs.

17.1.4.5 Building an E2E cost framework

Of course, the project-oriented cost modeling will not give us the full picture of the cost framework. In order to find a full and clear picture of the cost framework, we can compile all cost items that we have described in earlier chapters into a two-dimensional 4×4 block matrix that consists of four stacks of components layers and four delivery stages. However, if we add the equipment life cycle or technology exit stage, the cost framework would become five stages (see Figure 17.6).

As we can see, the example in Figure 17.6 has a lot of detail. This is an example of a cost framework for one company's ×86 virtualization program. Actually, this cost framework can be considered a 13×6 or 13×7 matrix. You can build as many as you like. However, if it becomes

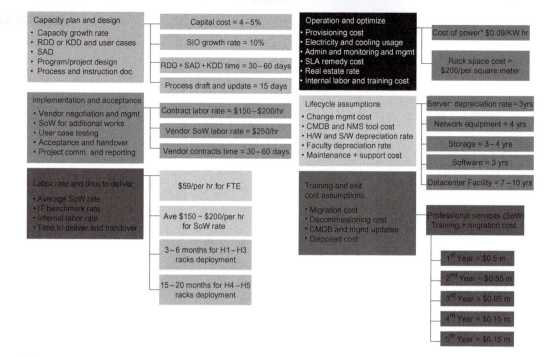

FIGURE 17.5

Example of cost assumptions for IT project delivery.

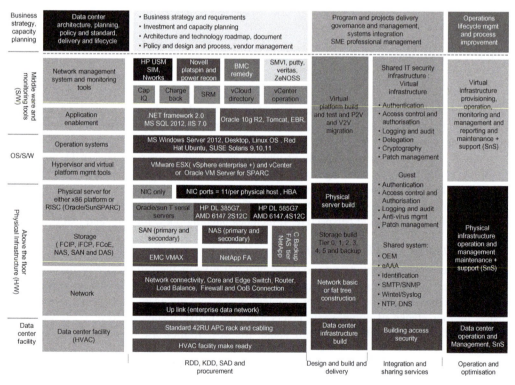

FIGURE 17.6

Example of E2E cost stack-based framework.

Infrastructure layers

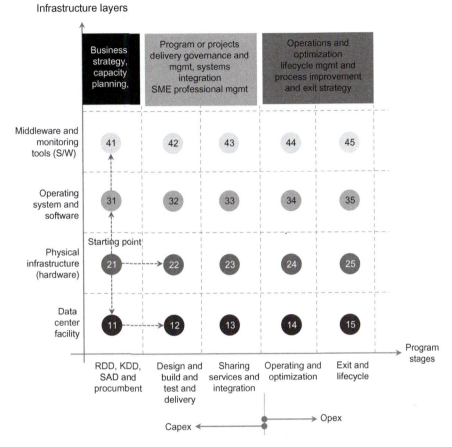

FIGURE 17.7

Generalized 4×5 matrix cost framework.

too complicated, you cannot use it as a communication tool. Remember, one of the cost modeling purposes is to communicate with other people and ultimately to convince the decision maker and stakeholders to make the right decision.

Therefore, we can simplify the above example just into a concise 4x5 matrix (see Figure 17.7). It consists of four infrastructure stack layers and four or five phases in terms of IT evolution. Many cost frameworks will exclude the technology exit or life-cycle phase. However, it becomes increasingly critical for an IT infrastructure due to Moore's law. Therefore, we include the life-cycle phase into the cost framework.

You might ask, "Where is the starting point to calculate the cost?" This is a good question. We can begin from the left side at the bottom point, "11," which is the data center facility, but based on our experience, the better starting point would be "21" or servers because you can start from this point to figure out the workload. Of course, the matrix "21" consists of 12 elements or more (see Figure 17.5). The reason to select a physical server as the starting point is that the server is the computer system's brain. Without it, the entire system will fail.

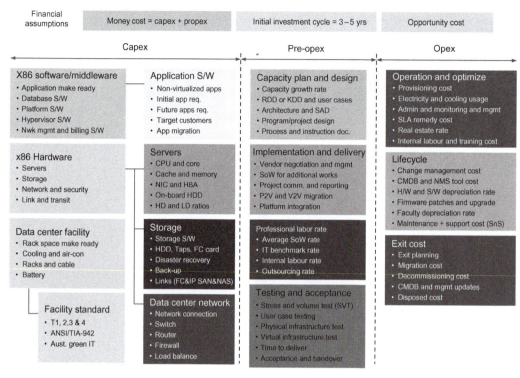

FIGURE 17.8

Financially oriented cost modeling.

Referring to Section 15.1.2.2 or Albert Greenberg et al.'s [183] proposition, the server may cost as much as 45% of total infrastructure cost. Their conclusion might be too extravagant, but it emphasized one important point: the server is one of the highest cost components for a cloud infrastructure.

You may notice that there is differentiation between capex and opex for different technology phases or stages in Figure 17.7. Actually, this is another way of cost modeling from financial perspective (see Figure 17.8).

For financial budgeting purposes, we must have financially oriented cost modeling. The model should include:

- Capital expenditure (Capex)
- Pre-operational expenditure (Propex)
- Operational expenditure (Opex)

Most of the pre-opex items can be capitalized. It is just another name to differentiate the purchasing cost. Basically, it is the program or project costs, for example a trial to test an idea or to prove a concept. It can be categorized as the operational part of research and development (R&D) costs. It can also be considered an implementation cost item. Different companies may have different cost booking practices.

17.1.5 MODEL ASSUMPTION DETAILS

17.1.5.1 Server workload assumptions

Based on the workload of this web portal company, we can make the following assumptions for iserver needs:

- Nonvirtualized servers or nodes = 400 (one-to-one relationship)
- Virtualized physical servers or nodes = 90
- Cloud environment host servers or VMS = 480 (for disaster recovery purposes)

All together, the portal company has a total IT workload = $400 + 480 + 90 = 970$.

Also, according to history data, the following assumptions can be made. The average growth rate for 11 years = 46.24%, but the standard deviation = 32.6%. However, if we exclude the financial crisis impact in 2008, the average growth would be 18.98% and standard deviation = 3.4% during the last four years (from 2010 to 2013). Therefore, we have reasonable confidence to predict future IT workload in next few years by using these figures.

17.1.5.2 Server cost assumptions and vendor selection decision

In this case, we use a low-end HP server as an example. Readers can select any major vendor, such as Dell, Cisco, IBM, Lenovo, Huawei, Fujitsu, or Oracle. Normally, Lenovo, Huawei, and Dell are the major vendors for the low-end x86 server market. HP and Fujitsu occupy the middle level or even high end of the server market. IBM and Oracle normally charge a premium price at the high end of the server market.

Cisco is one of the dominant vendors in the network equipment market. Since 2009, Cisco has gotten into the x86-server market, and especially stepped into the x86 blade server market. The brand name of its blade server is Universal Computer Server (UCS). If the business has expanded very rapidly and the data center facility can accommodate high-density racks, the Cisco UCS blade server could be one of the solutions and Cisco could be a potential vendor.

HP, IBM, and Oracle (formerly Sun Microsystems) are three major vendors providing RSIC servers, but the Oracle/Sun RISC server, namely the Sun SPARC server is very popular and it has a big market share. Although Oracle now provides x86 servers, it specializes in RISC servers. Oracle could be one of the competitive RISC server vendors if the business is using Sun Solaris operating system because one of the cost considerations is that Oracle will not charge a Solaris license fee when adopting Oracle's hardware. Of course, if the operating system is Open Solaris, then the OS cost is not an issue.

In Table 17.2, we highlight the details of physical server configurations and assumptions for the portal company and we assume that the life cycle is three years. It is really dependent on each individual company's policy. Some companies may extend the life cycle time to four years. Others may start the clock time from when the system is in operation, and they will exclude delivery or pre-operation time. This means that the life cycle is longer than four years.

Moreover, it is important to pay attention to the warranty period and cost. HP may ask its customers to pay for the three-year compulsory warranty. Based on the rule of thumb, the warranty cost may be around 10−12% of the hardware purchasing cost.

Regarding operating server delivery and operating costs, we can either refer to Uptime Institute's whitepaper [112] or leverage the existing chargeback meter to allocate the operating costs.

Table 17.2 Physical Node or Server Cost Assumptions

Cost Items	Unit	Value & Quantity	Assumption Comments
Traditional servers per unit	$	$2,000	Refers to HP DL G3 or G4 or G5 1RU server model
No. of sockets per server	Each	1	Starting price with minimal configuration
No. of cores per socket	Each	2	Intel Core i3 or dual core
RAM	GB	32	Starting price with minimal configuration
Server amortization	Months	36	Life cycle based on Moore's law
DAS	GB	100	
NAS	GB	100	
New servers per unit	$	$10,000	Referring to HP DL G8 1RU or 2RU server model
No. of sockets per server	Each	1	Middle range server, up to 2 sockets
No. of cores per socket	Each	6	It can be 4, 6, or 8 cores
RAM	GB	128	Up to 768GB
IP SAN	GB	100	
Server amortization	Months	36	Life cycle based on Moore's law
VM per core	Each	1	VMWare suggestion

17.1.5.3 Network cost assumptions

If we adopt the Cisco recommended network architecture or a basic tree topology, the network equipment costs should include access, aggregation switches, and core routers (refer to Chapter 13, Section 13.4.1). Of course, Cisco and Juniper hardware is just an example. You can select other vendors' products.

Based on the previous information from Chapter 13, other vendors' products may be much cheaper; Huawei's access switch may be approximately up to 50% cheaper than Cisco's, and has similar or equivalent functionality. Generally speaking, Huawei's product is 20–30% cheaper than its competitors. However, Cisco may offer a certain percentage discount, such as a 10–30% discount for its loyal customers or strategic partners who make a large volume purchase order. Surely, each vendor may provide certain % discount. It is really dependent on the price negotiation.

In addition, there is an uplink cost for the portal company to maintain the connectivity of the Internet. We assume two different prices: one is for normal business and the other is for backup or redundancy (see Table 17.3).

17.1.5.4 Storage cost assumptions

The storage cost assumptions are basically based on the business requirements and they should cover the peak workload demand. If we assume that the upper limit of business demand is 102GB, the IT people have to allocate at least the same amount of storage capacity to meet the business demand. On the other side of the equation, the minimum storage requirement for the business is around 70GB. In other words, the IT storage capacity should maintain 70 to 102GB storage space

Table 17.3 Network Equipment Cost

Cost Items	Unit	Value & Quantity	Assumption Comments
Access or ToR Switch	Each	$3,000	Cisco Catalyst 4948, 48 ports or Cisco 3560
Aggregation Switch	Each	$10,000	Cisco Nexus
Core Router	Each	72,500	Cisco 7600 series or Juniper EX 8208, 128 ports
Load Balancer	Each	$16,000	F5
Firewall Hardware	Each	$35,000	Juniper NetScreen
Network Amortization	Months	48	Based on Moore's law
Primary Uplink	Per month	$990	Fibre Ethernet excluding installation cost, $3,000
Redundancy Uplink	Per month	$650	Fibre Ethernet broadband

at any given time for web content servers. Assuming these are first priority storage files, which are tier-0 and tier-1 files and 102GB contents have to be kept for between 15 and 26 weeks on the portal, referring to Table 12.7, we can roughly estimatied the cost for the total Capex investment budget at ~$24,000–$41,000 (HDD only) with a 48-months life cycle. Of course, the exact purchase price will depend on the unit cost of each HDD at the particular time.

Currently, the IT storage industry is undergoing a major transformation, as the price of SSDs is approaching equivalence with HDDs. The cost modeling for storage cost assumptions might have to be reviewed again in 6 months' time.

We have to be aware that we did not include other cost items in the above estimation, such as software licenses, implementation, maintenance, and other cost items. In other words, the total capex cost investment budget is just the pure HDD cost.

If we try to achieve a very realistic cost estimate, we not only include the tier-0 and tier-1 storage but also add tier-2, tier-3, and tier-5 (or archive storage). In Table 17.4, we will give an estimated result, where tier-1 may be allocated for email, the operating system, applications, and other file storage, tier-2 for daily backup storage, tier-3 for other miscellaneous files, and tier-5 (or archive storage) diverted to long-term backup storage.

Again, Table 17.4 is also a rough estimation because we did not calculate the business performance requirements, such as IOPS, and read and write speed. If a reader would like to get more a accurate estimate, you can drill down further by referring to Chapter 12. This is one level of calculation for the cost of HDDs item from business demand. However, we must also consider another cost component, which is the storage network type, such as DAS, NAS, and SAN. If the existing storage connection is dominated by DAS and NAS solutions, the virtualized storage will be transferred to mainly IP SAN solutions plus a certain storage capacity using NAS to support the above business operations. We assume that the each nonvirtualized or physical server will need 200GB local storage capacity (100GB DAS and 100GB NAS requirement) and the virtualized server only needs an average of 100GB per physical node. This means the virtualized server can save at least 50% in storage capacity. Other cost items will include NIC or iSCSI cards. These cards might be included in a server package when the server is purchased. But the HBA card that costs $1,250 per card will not be included. Moreover, the associated SAN switch cost would be added in the cost bill for an additional $6,000 each.

Table 17.4 Storage Cost Assumptions

Business Requirements	Unit	%	Storage Capacity (GB)	Comments
Residential Sale Business				
1800–2700 files per wk	2Mb per file	20%	1.08	Standard Ad
1800–2700 files per wk	3Mb per file	40%	3.240	Feature Ad
1800–2700 files per wk	5Mb per file	35%	4.725	Highlight Ad
1800–2700 files per wk	30Mb per file	5%	4.050	Premiere Ad
Total Storage for Sales			13.095	
6 Week Ad Campaign			78.570	Cumulative Ad Quantity
Residential Rental Business				
700–1,000 per week	2Mb per file	60%	1.200	Standard Ad
700–1,000 per week	3Mb per file	20%	0.6	Feature Ad
700–1,000 per week	5Mb per file	15%	0.75	Highlight Ad
700–1,000 per week	30Mb per file	5%	1.5	Premiere Ad
Total Storage for Rentals			4.5	
Keep 6 Week Ad Campaign			24.3	Cumulative Ad Quantity
Storage required for tier-0	$1.43/GB/month		103	$7,070
Storage required for tier-1	$0.32/GB/month		1,000	$15,360
Storage required for tier-2	$0.20/GB/month		5,000	$48,000
Storage required for tier-3	$0.13/GB/month		10,000	$62,400
Archived = tier-5	$0.03/GB/month		40,000	$72,000
Total Cost			66,103	$204,830

17.1.5.5 Data center facility cost assumptions

There are two different ways to calculate data center facility costs: one is to just simply add all cost items together and divide by the volume of hosting servers. The other is to adopt the rack-based cost model. Many major rack vendors, such as APC, Emerson or Rittal, provide the cost structure for the TCO of a rack.

We have laid out all the details of a data center facility from site selection to physical site security and fire suppression. In this case, the business would not have an interest in building their own data center facility because the capital cost is too high and its core business is real estate web content. The better solution for the data center facility infrastructure would be either a co-location solution or IaaS or Data Center as a Service that is provided by one of cloud service providers.

As a result, the rack-based model would be better fit for this case. Based on APC's data [258], we can see that each rack would cost $80k to $150k for the TCO if the life cycle of a rack is 10 years (see Figure 17.9).

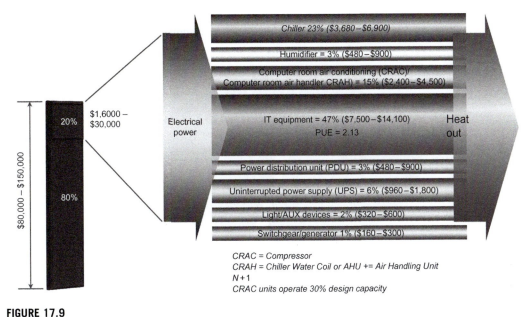

Chiller 23% ($3,680–$6,900)

Humidifier = 3% ($480–$900)

Computer room air conditioning (CRAC)/
Computer room air handler CRAH) = 15% ($2,400–$4,500)

IT equipment = 47% ($7,500–$14,100)
PUE = 2.13

Power distribution unit (PDU) = 3% ($480–$900)

Uninterrupted power supply (UPS) = 6% ($960–$1,800)

Light/AUX devices = 2% ($320–$600)

Switchgear/generator 1% ($160–$300)

20% $1,6000 –
       $30,000

80%

$80,000 – $150,000

Electrical
power

Heat
out

CRAC = Compressor
CRAH = Chiller Water Coil or AHU += Air Handling Unit
N + 1
CRAC units operate 30% design capacity

FIGURE 17.9

Traditional data center faculty cost benchmark per rack.

This suggests that the main opex component, power consumption, is around $30k. In other words, the annual fee for power consumption is $3k per annum or $250 per month. The other proportional costs will be equal to $120k. If we break the cost item down further, we find there are nine cost components for this 2N redundancy rack (see Figure 17.10). For all these nine cost items, 50% of the cost is capex equal to $60k and the other 50% of the cost is opex.

However, if we compare TCO cost percentage of a rack under a traditional data center system, many cost items just have a slight difference except for the power equipment, which is double the amount of the modern data center rack (36% vs. 18%) (see Figure 17.11). Wendy Torell's data [259] claimed that the power equipment cost being double that of the modern data center rack is partly due to a substantial oversizing factor (roughly 30%).

APC Schneider provides a TCO calculator tool. It shows how to calculate or to estimate TCO and compare between a new build and upgrading the existing co-location (see Figure 17.12). However, this TCO calculation tool only support lower heat density racks, where the average power of rack that is below 5kW.

17.1.5.6 VMware hypervisor license cost assumptions

The VMware hypervisor or vSphere and vCenter license fees may vary from time to time. Not all VMware software components will be included in one vSphere license. VMware will have additional licensing fee for different software components that are added on. For example, VMWare will charge a separate license fee for Cap IQ and Chargeback, vCenter Site Recovery Manager (SRM), vCenter Operations vCloud Director, and vFabric 5. Since September 2010, VMware has begun to charge for these software licenses on a per VM basis (see Table 17.5).

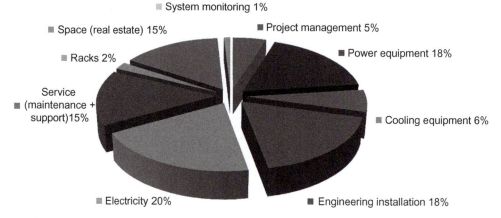

FIGURE 17.10

Modern rack cost breakdown of TCO per rack.

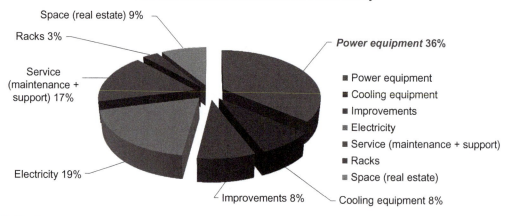

FIGURE 17.11

Traditional rack TCO cost breakdown.

There are many options for a VMware license. Here, we just highlight some features of vSphere and associated cost items. The precise way of identifying all cost items is to check the Solution Architecture Document (SAD) for the details. VMware also provides its TCO/ROI calculator tool for any customer to calculate the cost [261]. You can use a trial to check the default assumptions that VMware has suggested. Similarly, Microsoft Hyper-V provides an integrated Virtualization ROI tool [262] to calculate the virtualization cost. Actually, many major hypervisor and server

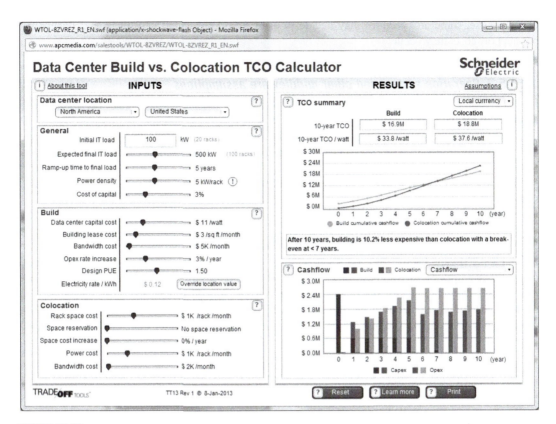

FIGURE 17.12

APC Schneider data build vs. colocation TCO calculator [260].

Table 17.5 VMware vSphere License Cost				
Cost Items	**Unit Cost**	**Vol.**	**Subtotal Cost**	**Assumption Comments**
vSphere per CPU socket per year	$400.49	15	$6,007.35	Based on vSphere version 5
Acceleration Kit per 6 CPU socket	$4,742.81	3	$14,228.43	
Storage application	$615.66	1	$615.66	
vCenter Server	$799.52	1	$799.52	
Total			$21,650.96	

vendors, such as IBM, Oracle, HP, and Cisco provide a TCO/ROI calculator or advisor and argue that their products are better for TCO and ROI. It is not about the calculation results. It is about the assumptions you make. It is similar to a frame of a screen to select a particular view. And it may be just a moment of truth.

Of course, some architectures may decide to use Citrix Xen, which doesn't have a license fee, but support costs may occur.

17.1.5.7 Operation system and other middleware assumptions

In this example, we only select Red Hat Enterprise Linux (RHEL) as the operating system. The assumption for the RHEL license fee and support cost is $3,998 per annum.

The other middleware manages workload from physical to virtual or P2V. Novell's Platespin can work with VMware, Hyper-V and Citrix XenServer to create VM instances from a physical server or node.

We assume the license fee of Platespin is $456,383 for a once-off capex and five-year opex support.

17.1.5.8 Amazon EC2 and S3 cost assumptions

Similar to VMware license fees or vSphere functionalities, Amazon EC2 and S3 also provides many service options for the customer. We just show one of the options in the service location Asia Pacific (Sydney). The name of this instance type is "m3. Medium" and it is configured with the Red Hat Enterprise Linux operating system and offers "Reserved Effective Hour Cost." There are six types of operating systems. Three of them are Linux OS and other three are Windows:

- Linux
- Red Hat Enterprise Linux
- Suse Linux Enterprise Server
- Windows
- Windows and Web SQL Server
- Windows and Standard SQL Server

In addition these types of OS, Amazon also provides the Elastic Block Store (EBS) option which supports persistent block level storage volumes. It doesn't only offer high availability and fault tolerance but also supports low latency.

Altogether, Amazon EC2 has about 222 price options or cost models for different operating systems and different cloud service features. It would be quite challenging for any new customer to understand or to decide which price model is the right one for his/her business. Of course, if the particular OS has been decided, the options can be narrowed down to 37.

Table 17.6 Amazon EC2 and S3 Cost Assumptions*

Cost Items	Unit Cost	Vol.	Subtotal	Assumption Comments
Up-front cost of a medium reserved instance	$500	1	$500	EC2 Disaster Recovery
Cost of medium reserved instance per hour	$0.116	8760 hours	$1033.68	EC2 Disaster Recovery
Transfer out per instance (GB) up to 10TB/month	$0.19	135GB	$25.65	S3 Disaster Recovery

*Please note that AWS unit cost is subjected to change anytime. The price shown in this table is just an indication. For further details, please refer to http://aws.amazon.com/ec2/pricing/.

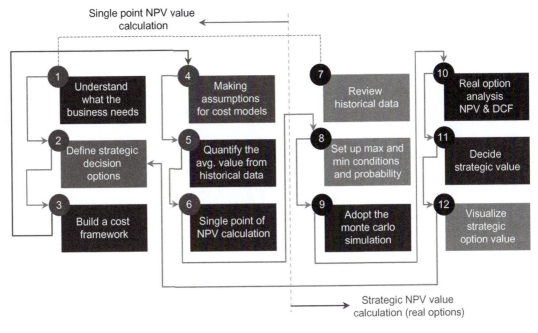

FIGURE 17.13

Calculation processing steps.

Furthermore, the customer can decide on the billing options. There are seven different billing options. Amazon's price model is to encourage the customer to select a reserved price model so that the cloud service provider will have business revenue certainty.

17.2 CALCULATION STEPS AND RESULTS

Up to now, we have made all assumptions for the costs of four stack layers based on the cost framework represented as a 4×5 matrix. This is the most tedious and important step for the cost modeling process. Once the assumption process is finalized, the next step is to calculate the single point of NPV or discount cash flow (DCF) values for the business using the average workload for the next five years. This process utilizes the historical data and then predicts the future investment capex budget; we stated this concept in Chapter 2, Section 2.3.5 as "looking forwards, reasoning backwards" (see Figure 17.13).

In Chapter 13 when discussing the data center network (DCN), we mentioned the term "single point of failure" with regard to DCN reliability. The term is self-explanatory. In this chapter, we introduce the term "single point of value" (SPoV), which has a financial connotation. The value can be either NPV or DCF or any forecasted value for future capex budget.

Similar to the concept of single point of failure, single point of value means the predicted figure or number that is fixed at a certain point of quantity or volume. It doesn't have any variation

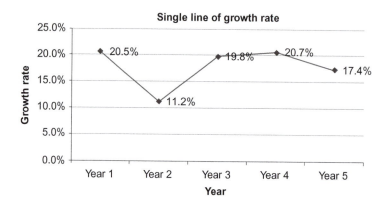

FIGURE 17.14

Single point of value forecast.

or deviation. For example, if a market research report predicts that an IT company's business will have 5% growth in the next year, this 5% is the single point of value because the report doesn't give any probability or variation of this 5%. It is a fixed value. Furthermore, if the forecast is to predict business growth in the next 5 years, the connection of each single point in each year will become a line of SPoV (see Figure 17.14).

The question is, "Would this be possible in the real world?" The answer would be quite obvious. It is impossible. If so, how can we handle the variation of forecasts? All these questions will be answered in the next chapter, but now we will focus on the linear SPoV first.

In Chapter 15, we gave a brief introduction to 11 popular financial cost models. The question is, "Why should we select the NPV model to calculate investment capex?" The reasons to adopt the NPV as a financial cost model for our analysis are:

1. The purpose of this cost calculation is to decide whether we should make an investment or not. It is a cost and profit forecast for the next five years. This is the business goal or business need for this case study. TheNPV model takes into consideration the time value of money or capital cost and all cash flows. In other words, the present money is more valuable than future money because you can take today's money to make future money. In addition, there is the factor of inflation rate or money deprecation. It can also be considered as earning interest if the money is deposited in a bank. If the opportunity cost is excluded, the NPV is one of the fairest cost models to evaluate many cloud investment projects.
2. It is a common practice for many corporations or organizations to measure and evaluate the value of different projects when a decision maker is making an investment decision.
3. With this model, it is easy to visualize and communicate the exponential component, namely interest rate. Human beings are very good at understanding linear relationships intuitively, but have difficulty in digesting the exponential or percentage relationship.
4. It is a good communication tool to discuss with different stakeholders.
5. If the interest rate is decided, the NPV calculation will become objective and very straightforward.
6. It is widely applied for capex budgeting.

17.2.1 **CALCULATE GROWTH RATE**

In order to calculate the single point of value (SPoV) of the NPV, we have to calculate or decide the growth rate in the next five years. There are four ways to estimate the future growth rate:

1. Extract it from historical data.
2. Take the estimated value from a market research report.
3. Ask the decision maker or experts or consultants. This is quite subjective.
4. Refer to the industry benchmark value.

In order to be objective, the future market demand will be presented in two sets of values: one is maximum demand or growth and the other is the minimum growth rate. We will first assign 50% of the probability to the maximum growth and 50% to the minimum one. Later, in the next chapter, we will use Monte Carlo simulation to estimate the probability of revenue income or cash flows.

There are many forecasting techniques used to make a prediction for future business growth. Basically, these techniques can be classified into three big categories or methods:

- Quantitive (statistical models)
- Qualitative (nonstatistical models, intuitive judgment, Delphi)
- Technological

Under the category of statistical models, we can also adopt different statistical techniques that can calculate various error and deviations, such as:

- Mean absolute deviation (MAD)
- Mean square error (MSE)
- Mean absolute percentage error (MAPE)
- Mean percentage error (MPE)
- Root mean square (RMS)

In order to simply the calculation process, we will just adopt Microsoft Excel's "Growth" function to predict the future growth based on the existing historical data in this case. The MS "Growth" function is basically and exponential growth formula that can be represented as the following formula:

$$y = bm^x$$

For the highest and lowest demand calculation, we add the standard deviation onto the result of the growth function for the high demand and subtract the standard deviation from the result for the low demand.

Please note that the standard deviation that we use is not over an 11-year period, but only five years; the financial crisis impact has been excluded, otherwise the variation or standard deviation of data is too high (see Table 17.7).

If the standard deviation between 2009 and 2013 was 5.8%, then we will have the high and low demand data in Table 17.8 in next five years. (The existing workload number is 970.).

Once we have the high- and low-demand volume of the IT workload, we can calculate the expected value of the workload, which is equal to high demand multiplied by 50% + low demand multiplied by 50% (see Table 17.9):

$$\text{Exp Value of Workload} = \text{High Demand} \times 50\% + \text{Low Demand} \times 50\%$$

Table 17.7 Recapping the Historical Data between 2008 and 2013

Year	2008	2009	2010	2011	2012	2013
Revenue $000	155,633	167,795	194,355	238,401	277,613	336,460
Net Profit after Tax $000	25,488	28,703	49,366	67,505	86,782	109,748
FTE	667	600	600*	600*	600*	600*
Employee Expenses $000	49,373	59,841	63,372	67,363	74,013	85,108
Consultant & Contract $000	5,543	7,857	8,368	10,285	8,838	9,682
Marketing Expenses $000	14,715	15,327	16,665	25,415	32,315	41,372
Technology Expenses $000	3,662	5,317	8,875	8,924	10,132	8,742
Depreciation Amortization Expenses $000	6,404	7,348	7,088	10,489	15,184	18,670
Operation Expenses $000	87,438	105,304	116,348	135,220	140,482	163,574
Profit Growth Rate	69.20%	12.60%	72.00%	36.70%	28.60%	26.00%
Revenue Growth Rate	45.10%	7.80%	15.80%	22.70%	16.40%	21.00%

Note: After 2009, the annual report did not give Full Time Equivalent (FTE) staff number. We assume this number has not been changed since 2009.

Table 17.8 Predicated Growth Rate with High- and Low-Demand Workload

Year	2014	2015	2016	2017	2018
Predicated Growth Rate (by Growth Function)	20.47%	11.21%	19.83%	20.69%	17.37%
High Demand Rate + 5.8%	26.27%	17.02%	25.63%	26.49%	23.17%
Workload with High Demand	1,225	1,433	1,801	2,277	2,805
Low Demand Rate − 5.8%	14.67%	5.41%	14.03%	14.89%	11.57%
Workload with Low Demand	1,112	1,173	1,337	1,536	1,714

Table 17.9 Expected Value of Workload

Year	2014	2015	2016	2017	2018
Workload with High Demand	1,225	1,433	1,801	2,277	2,805
Probability of High Demand	50%	50%	50%	50%	50%
Workload with Low Demand	1,112	1,173	1,337	1,536	1,714
Probability of Low Demand	50%	50%	50%	50%	50%
Expected Demand Volume	1,169	1,303	1,569	1,907	2,259
Expected Growth Rate	20.47%	11.49%	20.41%	21.54%	18.50%

Table 17.10 Planning of % Both Dedicated and Virtualized Workload in Next Five Years

Year	2013	2014	2015	2016	2017	2018
% Dedicated Workload	41.2%	27.5%	13.7%	0.0%	0.0%	0.0%
% Virtualized Workload	9.3%	22.9%	36.4%	50.0%	50.0%	50.0%
% Amazon EC2 Workload (IaaS) for DR	49.5%	49.7%	49.8%	50.0%	50.0%	50.0%
Total	100.0%	100.0%	100.0%	100.0%	100.0%	100.0%

Table 17.11 Workload over Next 5 Years

Year	2013	2014	2015	2016	2017	2018
Dedicated Workload Number	400	321	179	—	—	—
Virtualized Workload Number	90	267	475	784	953	1,130
Amazon EC2 Workload (IaaS) for DR	480	580	649	784	953	1,130
Total	970	1,169	1,303	1,568	1,906	2,260
Expected Revenue Forecast Growth $000	$336.46	$405.34	$451.93	$544.15	$661.38	$783.73
Normalized Growth Rate		20.5%	11.5%	20.4%	21.5%	18.5%

We have assumed the probability of both high and low demand is 50%. The probability is an arbitrary value. The probability of high and low demand can also be set to 40% and 60% or even 30% and 70%. It is dependent on the market research or sales target. The decision on the probability value can be quite subjective. However, you can adopt different forecasting methodologies to decide this value, such as the Delphi method that we mentioned above. That topic is beyond the subject of this book.

17.2.2 CALCULATE DEDICATED AND VIRTUALIZED WORKLOAD

If the virtualized co-lo project needs three years to be completed, we will have the following table for the percentage of virtualized and dedicated workload over the next three years (see Table 17.10). This means that the same percentage (13.6%) of the dedicated workload will be transformed into a virtualized infrastructure. Of course, the total amount of growth IT workload will remain the same as the expected value (see Table 17.9) in every year (see Table 17.11).

In the next step, we will work out the capital cost to support the predicted growth plan. We will start with physical server nodes, storage, network, software, middleware, and the project implementation costs based on the above process and assumptions.

Referring to the above assumptions, it is important to note that each dedicated server ($2,000k per server) can only correspond to one workload but the new physical node ($10,000 per server) can accommodate up to six workloads (or VMs per physical server). Therefore, we will have the quantity of the total physical nodes for the next five years (see Table 17.12).

Table 17.12 The Number of Virtualized and Dedicated Servers in the Next 5 years

Year	2013	2014	2015	2016	2017	2018
Dedicated Workload Server Number	400	321	179	–	–	–
Virtualized Workload Number	90	267	475	784	953	1,130
Virtualized Physical Nodes	15	45	80	131	159	189
No. of Virtualized Servers for Hypervisor[1]	2	2	2	2	2	2
New Virtualized Servers for Capex	17	30	35	51	$28 + 17^2 = 45$	$30 + 47 = 77$
Total Number of Virtualized + Dedicated Servers	417	368	261	133	161	191

[1]Here, the virtualized server for the hypervisor is assumed to be separated from the workload.
[2]After three years, the old virtualized physical servers have to be decommissioned and replaced by new servers.

Table 17.12 illustrates a transformation process from dedicated servers to virtualized servers (or nodes). It is important to notice that the old one-to-one dedicated relationship will be replaced by a one-to-many relationship in terms of physical to virtual (P2V). It is easy to understand the dedicated or nonvirtualized server has one workload corresponding to one physical server but with a virtualized server, this relationship doesn't exist. Based on our previous assumption, the relationship of P2V is 6 to 1, which means six workloads will be loaded on one virtualized physical server. In addition, the IT capacity also has to accommodate the new workloads due to business growth. The logical assumption is that all new workloads will be on virtualized servers or the cloud infrastructure and not on the dedicated server.

Similarly, we will have storage, network, and switch equipment. Overall, we will have what is listed in Table 17.13, which summarizes all the cost components (cost analysis). These figures are quite subjective. They can be altered from time to time. You can have your own configurations and assumptions to construct your own cost models.

The key assumptions for the both capex and opex are:

- Workload capacity planning or workload transformation (P2V)
- Asset depreciation rate (normally, it is decided by a company's financial policy)
- P2V ratio for each physical node
- Unit price of server, storage, and network components
- The volume of physical servers to be cycled and the cost every year
- IT project delivery costs (or implementation cost)
- Software and middleware license fees

In order to simplify the calculation, the total IT investment capex doesn't include other cost items such as data center facilities, firewall, decommissioning, capacity planning, SAD, KDD, SVT, and RDD.

The IT investment capex is just purchasing cost components. Normally, the IT labor costs are very high. Based on previous cost modeling experiences, the implementation cost components may be around three or four times higher than purchasing components, especially for many developed

Table 17.13 Summary of IT Capex Forecast for Next Five Years					
Year	2014	2015	2016	2017	2018
Physical Server Cost ($000)	$300	$350	$510	$450	$770
Storage Cost ($000)	$192	$333	$501	$744	$883
Network Cost ($000)	$93	$100	$100	$57	$57
Software Cost ($000)	$1,526	$626	$526	$272	$422
Middleware Cost ($000)	$22	$22	$22	$22	$22
Total IT Purchasing Capex ($000)	−$2,133	−$1,431	−$1,659	−$1,545	−$2,154
Total IT Implementation Capex ($000)	−$4,266	−$2,862	−$3,318	−$3,090	−$4,308
Purchasing + Implementation IT Capex	−$6,399	−$4,293	−$4,977	−$4,635	−$6,462
Predicted Technology Capex ($000)	−$90,868	−$9,345	−$9,597	−$8,755	−$9,275

Note:
1. Purchasing IT capex = all hardware + software purchase costs.
2. Implementation IT capex = IT delivery costs, installation, configuration, cabling, and planning costs.

countries. It is really dependent on the IT project delivery efficiency of each individual company. If we assume the IT project delivery cost is roughly two times the purchasing cost components, then we will have a total number for IT capex cost forecasting for the next five years (see Table 17.13).

In Table 17.13, we use the growth function to predicte the technology capex based on the previous five years' expenditure. As we can see there is a gap between IT capex and total technology capex. It might be due to web content and other application development costs.

In addition to capex, we will have opex, which is shown in Table 17.14. One thing should that should be mentioned is that once the virtualization project has been delivered, the maintenance cost, especially for the warranty cost items of server and storage, should be significantly lower than than before the virtualizing project. We might still have to maintain a warranty for some network hardware components. Assuming that the virtualized project has been delivered according to three-year plan, Table 17.14 doesn't include maintenance and support costs for hardware from 2017 to 2018.

17.2.3 CALCULATE STATIC NET PRESENT VALUE (NPV)

Up to this point, we have completed all the preparation steps for the NPV calculation. In Chapter 15, we have mentioned that the ultimate purpose of the cost modeling is to evaluate the IT investment decision and grasp the business insight. One of the key business or financial metrics is to make sure that the money invested now will generate enough discount cash flow in the predicted period. This discount cash flow means the time value of the money. In other words, the capital cost or borrowing cost or simply the interest rate should be taken into consideration for the cost modeling.

Table 17.14 Summary of Opex Cost Forecast for Next Five Years

Year	2014	2015	2016	2017	2018
Maintenance Break/Fix ($000)	$394	$424	$446	–	–
Software Support Costs ($000)	$183	$258	$321	$354	$404
Amazon EC2 DR Cost ($000)	$575	$728	$854	$1,073	$1,361
Total Predicted IT Opex ($000)	$1,152	$1,410	$1,621	$1,427	$1,765
Predicated Total Opex ($000)	$117,616	$143,898	$145,967	$144,791	$124,976

Note: Please note that the total predicated IT opex might not include maintenance and warranty costs, but the total opex should consist of other operational cost items, such as sales and marketing. It is the normalized operation cost. Again, the calculation of the predicated opex is based on the growth function.

Table 17.15 PV and NPV Values of IT Capex in 5 Years

Year	2014	2015	2016	2017	2018
Expected Total Revenue Forecast ($m)	$405	$452	$544	$661	$784
Normalized Growth Rate	20.5%	11.5%	20.4%	21.5%	18.5%
Net Expected Growth Revenue (CF_t) ($m)	$69	$47	$92	$117	$122
35% Proportional Revenue Contribution by IT ($m)	$24.15	$16.45	$32.20	$40.95	$42.70
Total Technology Capex ($m) in 5 Years ($m)	−$72.8				
If r = 25%, T = 5					
PV ($m)	$19.32	$10.53	$16.49	$16.77	$13.99
NPV ($m)	$4.30				

According to Section 15.4.6, we should have the following NPV formula:

$$NPV = \sum_{t=1}^{T} \frac{CF_t}{(1+r)^t} - I_c$$

Based on this formula and predicted revenues and the total IT capex or technology capex in next five years, we can calculate the NPV value (Table 17.15).

All above NPV values are relative to assumptions that we have made before. If we change the assumptions, the NPV will also be changed. Therefore, we should list all the following assumptions for the above NPV calculation:

1. Although we have five years of revenue forecasting, the calculation only uses three years of cash flow because IT assets only have a three-year lifetime.
2. The assumption for internal interest rate or hurdle rate is 25%. It is a very high IRR. Normally, the IRR would be 12% for a lower risk project.

3. If the interest rate is greater than 27.5%, the NPV value will become negative. It is quite obvious that the interest rate will not reach as high as 10% in next three years under the current financial circumstances.

4. The expected next year's net cash flow is the difference between next year's revenue and this year's revenue. For example, the net expected growth of 2014 is equal to the expected forecast revenue ($405.34 million in 2014) minus this year's revenue ($336.46 million in 2013) = $68.88 million or $69 million.

5. The growth revenue forecast is based on the simple MS Excel "growth" function.

6. Notice that not all growth revenue will be contributed by IT or technology. Some of the revenue will be generated by marketing, sales, production, etc. However, we assume 35% of revenue will be generated by IT- or technology-related capex because this is a web portal company. It would be quite challenging to differentiate the revenue contribution from different projects' capex because today's IT infrastructure is deeply shared.

7. The total initial capex is $72.8m but it will not be paid in a lump sum up front. It will be a yearly capex budget that is between $13m and $15m per year. However, in order to simplify the calculation, here we assume $72.8m as a lump sum payment up front. Subsequently, the actual NPV should be higher than what we have calculated.

8. In addition, our IT capex isn't only to meet the growth demand but also to migrate the existing IT workload from the old IT infrastructure (or to virtualize the existing IT infrastructure) to new or virtualized servers. Based on the previous definition, this kind of expenditure may be a part of opex, but this is not a simple replacement. The virtualized IT infrastructure enables new functions and features, such as fault tolerance, high availability, Transparent Internet Lot of Links (TRILL), etc. Therefore, all IT expenditures for the virtualization transformation should be considered IT capex.

17.3 CONCLUSION OF CASE STUDY

The result of this NPV calculation exercise has indicated that IT or technology capex will have a positive NPV impact for the company. If the proposed IT capex supports workload growth, a decision maker should approve it based on the above NPV calculation. However, when the interest rate is above 27.5%, the decision maker should be very careful on the decision of any proposed IT capex budget.

On the other hand, if the revenue forecast is dropped by 6% every year, the 2015 NPV will start to become negative. The 6% revenue decline could be one of the indicators or the threshold level for a decision maker to have a close look at the IT or technology expenditure proposal or capex budgeting.

In other words, if the growth rate is around 12%−14% and the interest or hurdle rate is below 27.5%, the IT investment decision should always go ahead.

This case study is based on a mature business model. It has almost 20 years' history. The revenue stream is relatively stable and easier to predict. However, for a startup company, the revenue stream or cash flow would be quite challenging to estimate. There will be no historic capital expenditures or IT capex data. The initial capex has to be built from the ground up for budgeting

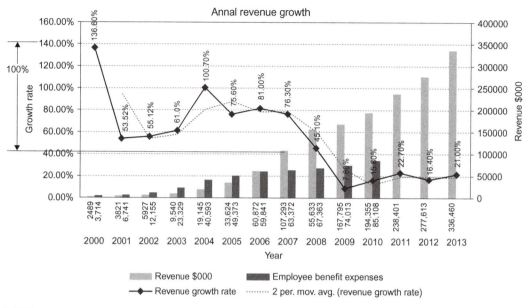

FIGURE 17.15

History of annual growth rate.

purposes. However, the good news is that the new startup business doesn't have legacy IT equipment, so we can exclude life-cycle costs.

If we check the history of this company, we can find the revenue of this company was very volatile during the early years. Even after 5 years' operation, the variation of the revenue growth rate was around 100% between 1999 and 2008 (see Figure 17.15).

This has raised the question, "How can a decision maker decide the capex budget for a startup company or for a project that has no historic data?"

To present this question in another way, if one company's decision maker is facing many different IT project proposals, unfortunately none of them has the sufficient historic data to predict the future revenue or cash flow and none of the projects can cross the hurdle rate just based on the static NPV calculation. How can a decision maker make the right investment decision or select the right investment project? Obviously, the decision maker may have a few options:

1. Select one of the projects based on personal intuition (experiences).
2. Wait or hold the proposal until the forecast revenue has a positive contribution to NPV (environment changes).
3. Dismiss all the proposals and ask for new proposals (dismiss altogether).

Of course, there may be many other options available, such as asking a consultant or expert's options or handing the decision power to someone else or just simply closing down the business. Here, if we just restrict ourselves to the above options, what is the right choice?

For option 1, it will highly depend on personal experiences and insight. A decision based on personal intuition is not bad thing. It is actually an approach based on pattern recognition, but it could be very unreliable because humans have many cognition biases. To some degree, it is kind of luck. We will discuss this later.

For option 2, it may be one of the good options, but it could be a bad decision because many investment opportunities may be lost. In addition, if the NPV value is just below the hurdle rate or even, is the decision still OK?

For option 3, again, it could be one of the good options. However, if there is no time for a business analyst to do redo the work or there is no good valuable project available, how can a decision maker make the right decision?

The answer should be the strategic value of the project. Many proposed projects are just stopped at the static NPV calculation. In many circumstances, the static NPV value of many projects will not cover the initial investment capex. It seems to be very risky, but it doesn't mean that these projects are bad or worthless. It actually means that sometimes, the strategic value of some good projects have not been discovered.

The true value of any project should be the sum of the static value of NPV plus the strategic value of NPV. How can we decide the strategic value of NPV? The answer is real option theory plus Monte Carlo simulation. It is a valuable tool to measure a project with very volatile revenue, such as cloud projects, because these projects have high strategic values.

In the next chapter, we discuss real option theory and Monte Carlo simulation to decide on the strategic value of a project.

17.4 SUMMARY

This chapter focused on four major parts:

- Understanding the business portfolio and strategic decision options
- Making assumptions
- Building cost models and the framework
- Calculating the NPV results

Understanding the business portfolio is actually finding out the business revenue and growth profile. This is the key influence for the NPV value. Of course, without business growth, it wouldn't make any sense to spend capex. So, the first thing is to understand the business that the IT supports. For a mature business, it would be quite easy to figure out the business. Based on statistics theory, the more data points there are, the more accurate the prediction is. However, if the business was very volatile during the early stages, these early data points might have to be excluded.

If the company is a startup, there will be many uncertainty factors influencing the business revenue. Therefore, the static NPV calculation is not fit. We have to adopt the real option theory and Monte Carlo simulation to resolve a highly volatile business circumstance.

Assumptions can be divided into two parts:

- Purchasing cost assumptions
- Implementation cost assumptions

Purchasing assumptions are relatively easier to make. If we adopt the 4x5 matrix for the cost framework, four big cost components (server, storage, network, and facility) are on the left side of the cost framework. We can start from the server cost and then work out other costs. The physical server capacity is based on the business workload. This is why we need to know the business profile first for the cost modeling calculation exercise. The other purchasing cost items would include many different types of software and middleware license fees, such as operating system, application software, middleware or hypervisor, and monitoring systems, as well as P2V management tools. If one of the decision options is to build youf own cloud infrastructure, some software license fees would be quite high. This is just the capex. If we consider total cost of ownership (TCO), the purchasing cost should include warranty and maintenance and support (M&S) costs for hardware and support and subscription (SnS) for software as well as operatiion management costs.

Making implementation assumptions is not as easy as making purchasing cost assumptions because these assumptions are highly subjective and vary from one company to another. They are mainly IT delivery cost, capacity planning, configuration, integration and optimization costs. One of the effective approaches is to adopt the benchmark or the ratio of the total of purchasing costs. However, this is not very accurate either. Sometimes, it could be misleading. Therefore, we should be very careful when making implementation assumptions according to a benchmark or a ratio approach.

As we mentioned in Chapter 14, the cost framework can be built with two levels of structure: tactical level and strategic level. In this chapter, we focus on the calculation at the tactical level, which is the single point of value (SPoV) or static value of revenue estimation or discount cash flow income for the NPV calculation.

Once initial capex and future revenue have been decided, the process of calculation is relatively easy and quite straightforward.

Because many assumptions are subjective, it is important to test the boundary conditions by changing the hurdle rate and making different revenue assumptions. Subsequently, the corresponding NPV value might be changed from positive to negative or vice versa.

In essence, the primary purpose of cost modeling is to support a decision maker in making the right investment decision. One of the key metrics to making the right decision is whether the proposed project can make profit within the specified period for the investment that is made now. In other words, the profit should be greater than the cost. From a decision maker's perspective, only three elements have to be examined very carefully: investment capital, the revenue that the capital can generate, and the time value of money. This leads to the calculation of static NPV if we just need a figure of fixed revenue or profits.

However, the real world is not fixed or static. The future is quite difficult to be predict. Everything is changing or evolving. Therefore, some kind of adjustment should be made for the static NPV value, which is the so-called expanded NPV value or eNPV. It is a static NPV value plus an option value based on real option theory.

17.5 **REVIEW QUESTIONS**

1. Why should we use the revenue-driven or top-down cost modeling approach for this case?
2. Will the bottom-up approach work for this case?
3. Based on the historical data, this portal company's revenue growth rate is very volatile. If we assume this volatility will continue, what is the right approach to establish a cost model?
4. As a BA, do you think cloud computing fits for this business? If yes, why? If not, why not?
5. If you were the decision maker for this business, would you consider the cloud as your only IT infrastructure or as a complementary solution for your existing IT infrastructure?
6. If you are were the IT infrastructure manager, how do you manage the life-cycle program for this IT infrastructure?
7. Do you think the cost reduction is achievable? If so, what percentage reduction can you achieve?

REAL OPTION THEORY AND MONTE CARLO SIMULATION

18

In the last chapter, we raised many questions about the traditional approaches of calculation for NPV and TCO/ROI. The result of these approaches is linear, static, and presents a single point of value. For an emerging market or dynamic business, these approaches to calculation do not reflect the real world scenario. In this chapter, we will propose a new approach of calculation to predicte NPV and TCO/ROI, namely, Monte Carlo simulation plus real option theory.

We will divide this chapter into seven sections:

- Overview of real option theory (ROT)
- Basic concept of the real option theory approach
- Types of real options and their applications
- Concept of Monte Carlo simulation (MCS)
- Details of MCS process
- Process details of MCS plus ROT analysis
- Pros and cons of MCS and ROT

Overall, this chapter only has three main topics: real option theory, Monte Carlo simulation, and the combination of two approaches for cloud project investment decision making analysis. We will begin with real option theory (ROT).

18.1 OVERVIEW OF REAL OPTION THEORY

As we have already touched on the term of real option in the last chapter, you may ask: "What does real option really mean?" "Why should we adopt this theory for a decision making process for cloud investment projects?" To answer these questions, we should go back and review the issues with the traditional NPV or static NPV calculation. This issue leads to the point of assumptions for the NPV formula.

In the previous case study, when we were trying to calculate the NPV result, we had to make some reasonable assumptions to forecast the cash flow or incoming revenue for the next five years based on the existing business operation information, research capabilities, and current understanding of the market. Not only are the assumptions of forecasting very subjective, but they are also fixed or static. The principle of the traditional NPV approach is to assume this world is relatively stable or in very slow motion. It would be relatively accurate if we could wind back our clock a half century.

However, we have moved into the information age. The world has not only become very flat but also very dynamic. Moore's law has profoundly changed the way that people are estimating or predicting future values. Today, many digital equipment or consumer electronic devices only last few years, not a lifetime, such as digital cameras, mobile handsets, LCD TV, laptop PC, tablets, etc. Today's unattainable products (due to being too expensive) will become tomorrow's throw-away items.

The rapidly changing pace of technology has led to the traditional way of predicting the future business revenue through the NPV calculation becoming inadequate or simply not enough. As a matter of the fact, "The simple NPV rule is not just wrong; it is often very wrong" [263]. If this is so, how can we overcome the issues with the traditional method of estimating future business revenue? This question leads to the topic of real option theory.

18.2 HISTORY OF REAL OPTIONS

In order to sort out the concept of "real options," we have to understand the meaning of option. From a financial perspective, the simple meaning of option is the reserved right for a person to either purchase or sell the real underlying asset at a particular price by a particular date in a financial market, such as a future clearinghouse. This reserved right is written into a contract where the particular date and price is specified. In the financial vocabulary, the price to be dealt is also called the exercise or strike price and the date is labeled as the expiration or maturity date.

This reserved right to purchase or buy the real asset is named a "call" option. In contrast, the reserved right to sell is named the "put" option.

In term of option categories, we often hear there are two types of option categories: one is the "European" option and other is "American" option. The European one is where the option can only be exercised (purchased) at the expiration date but the American option can be exercised at any time up to the maturity date.

The original meaning of option can be traced back to a Bible story or 1700 BC. It was actually a future contract between Jacob and his father-in-law. The modern sense of future contract started from Thales, who reserved olive presses ahead of time and only rented them out at a higher price when the demand for olive presses hit the peak. Of course, Thales' reason for doing this was not for him to earn the profit but rather to convince other people that his philosophy could be beneficial.

The most significant event in the history of the futures market occurred in 1848; from this point the Chicago Board of Trade has developed as a major center for the trading of futures commodities. In the mid-1800s, New York financier Russell Sage provided synthetic loans to customers by leveraging the principle of put-call parity (see Figure 18.1). The interest rate of the synthetic loans was significantly higher than the usury laws permitted.

In the spring of 1973, Fisher Black and Myron Scholes [264] published their paper and discovered the famous Black-Scholes formula to illustrate the relationship among options price, underlying stock, maturity of the option, and the interest rate. In essence, the formula demonstrated how to "create a hedged position by going short two options and long one stock." Such a position will be

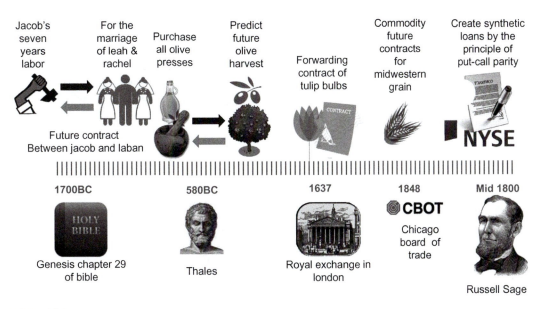

FIGURE 18.1

History of options or future contract.

close to riskless. Of course, many people now believe that the Black-Scholes formula does not work for the pricing of derivative financial products. We will not discuss this topic because it is beyond the main topic of this book.

By working off this financial concept, Stewart Myers [265] created a strategic decision concept, where he indicated that many corporate investment decisions can be regarded as "financial options"; for example, growth investment opportunities are similar to "call options." Myers called the values of these investment opportunities "real options" in contrast to a "financial option that does not buy the real asset."

After nearly 20 years, real options theory has become a practical method for many practitioners. In 1993, Angelien G.Z. Kemna [266] published a paper and demonstrated seven case studies for a number of Shell operating companies with regard to capital budgeting decisions. In 1996, Lenos Trigeorgis [267] published his famous book and consolidated the real options theory, bringing it from the academic world to the corporate arena (see Figure 18.2).

Strictly speaking, the history of real option theory is very short (see Figure 18.3) and shorter than NPV methodology. Even in the academic world, it is still relatively new. In 2011, James Mills [268] estimated there would be only about 15 universities that were teaching real options courses in the US. In essence, although real option theory is a much better approach in comparison with the traditional capital budgeting method, it is not widespread in the corporate world yet. The previous experience [269] of adopting the NPV methodology may indicate that the real option theory may take years to become popular in the industrial world (see Figure 18.4).

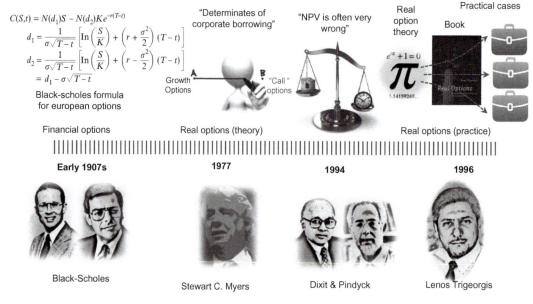

FIGURE 18.2

Major contributors to real option theory.

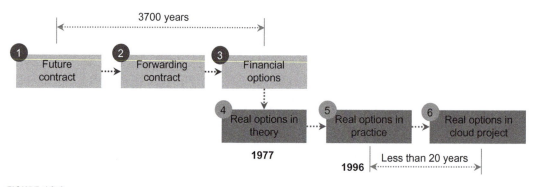

FIGURE 18.3

The root of real options theory.

18.3 WHAT ARE REAL OPTIONS?

Based on the brief history of real option theory, you may have some basic idea of what a real option is. In very simple terms, real option theory is the derivative concept that borrows from the financial option. It estimates an investment project that is dependent on real assets to support a firm's decision process or capital budget planning.

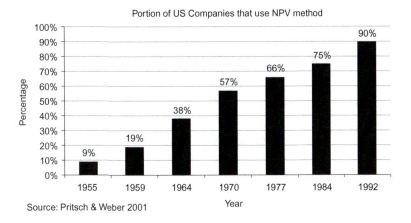

Portion of US Companies that use NPV method

Source: Pritsch & Weber 2001

FIGURE 18.4

It took 37 years for US companies to adopt the NPV method [269].

In the traditional or static NPV evaluation we demonstrated in the last chapter, all assumptions regarding the project's revenue stream or cash flow income and the initial investment capital are predecided or fixed. The project will be implemented based on the static and fixed data. It assumes that people will stick with the original plan or not deviate from their original plan. However, in the real world, especially in the IT industry, many IT projects will be altered or changed in term of scope, size, and time during the lifetime of IT project. Actually, IT professionals will learn from the project and make many changes along the way in order to respond to many unexpected change requirements. For a software development project, the buzzword is to be "agile" or "flexible."

Similarly, real option theory is trying to discover the flexibility of a project investment and see whether this project has a strategic value that can contribute to the total value of the project from a financial perspective or not.

In comparison with many traditional investment decision processes, the superiority of real option theory is that it asks some very simple and fundamental questions for some investment projects during a decision process than the traditional methods don't:

- Does an investment project have enough flexibility or other opportunities?
- Does a project have other choices or options?
- If a project does have options, when and how will they arrive or under what kind of circumstances they will arrive?
- What is the nature of these choices? Or what are the characteristics of these choices?
- How can we maximize the payoff of these options?

These may sound like strategic questions. Actually, real options analysis searches for the strategic value of a project. Strategy is all about choices or alternatives. For a cloud business strategy, the choice is to decide whether we should seek or explore certain markets or products or customers at different periods of time.

Most of us like certainty and don't like frequent change or uncertainty. It's human nature. However, real option theory sees the world from a dynamic and strategic perspective. It is a different way of thinking. It reframes the world from a strategic level to form or create different choices or options for a decision maker.

Surely, it is quite challenging to frame these choices or options because the real option is not only a science but also an art. What is the "art"? It means the practice of real option theory. It is how to translate the theory into strategic insight or wisdom for a real cloud investment project. It is also how to convert academic theory to corporate benefits. This the most challenging part of the real option theory.

"The underlying logic of the real options framework is based on the realization that future investment opportunities are contingent on prior investment commitments" [270] Referring to Chapter 14, real option theory can also be considered as ex-ante (before the event) analysis from a cost modeling perspective.

18.3.1 EQUATIONS OF REAL OPTION THEORY

In order to calculate the real option values, equations for real options have been developed. It is a combination of the traditional NPV method plus many option values or choices. To some degree, the real option value is the expanded net present values (or eNPV). Therefore, the statement made by Dixit & Pindyck [263] is not 100% accurate. The traditional NPV is not very wrong but rather incomplete or inaccurate from an end-to-end (E2E) lifetime perspective of an investment project.

If we use a mathematical formula to represent the real option concept, it is equal to the traditional NPV value plus other option values:

$$Real\ Options\ Values = eNPV = NPV + Options\ Values$$

If you still remember our approach to defining the term "cloud computing" in Chapter 1 and Section 1.3, this formula is perfectly aligned with the method of functional definitions. The common way of defining the term "cloud computing," real option theory and critical decision making can build a solid foundation for us to analyze the cost framework of cloud computing for decision making.

18.3.2 CRITERIA OF REAL OPTIONS FROM A PROJECT PERSPECTIVE

Real option theory sounds superior. Can the real option theory be applied for any project under any investment circumstance? The simple answer would be "no." Martha Amram and Nalin Kulatilaka [271] provided five different scenarios when real option theory can be applied:

- When a project needs updates and mid-course strategy corrections.
- When the NPV value should be captured by the possibility of future growth options.
- When the outlook is so uncertain and it is sensible to wait for more information so that a decision maker can avoid regret for an irreversible investment decision that must be made now.
- When uncertainty is large enough to make flexibility a consideration. Only the real option approach can correctly value investment flexibility.
- When there is a contingent investment decision. No other approach can correctly estimate this type of opportunity.

The first scenario is fairly self-explanatory. As we have indicated before, a strategy is all about choices. Strategy corrections mean selecting different choices. If a project needs to be upgraded during its lifetime, real option analysis would be a useful tool to analyze the strategic value for a project. This scenario to apply the real options is where a decision maker has already understood the project will be altered before it starts.

The second scenario means the value of future growth opportunities is larger than the current cash flow. In other words, the future growth value is better than today's benefits. Again, this is to focus on future or strategic values for a specified period of time. Real option analysis can quantify these future or strategic values.

The third circumstance is focusing on waiting for more information on a favorable situation. If there is not enough information to quantify the future beneficial values now, real option analysis will suggest the "waiting" option is better than regretting an irreversible investment decision.

The fourth scenario is to say that the uncertainty is too large to be ignored and the real option analysis can provide the correct value for the investment flexibility of a project.

The last scenario is that a project needs a contingency plan to make a change and no other analysis would be better than real option analysis to identify future opportunity values.

In essence, these five scenarios for applying real options analysis can basically be summarized into three basic criteria (see Figure 18.5).

- Know there will be changes for an investment project
- Not enough information for future values
- Uncertainty is too large

In contrast to Martha Amram and Nalin Kulatilaka's application criteria for real option theory, Ron Adner and Daniel A Levinthal [270] argued that if the choice or option set evolves as a consequence of prior actions, the real option framework is less applicable.

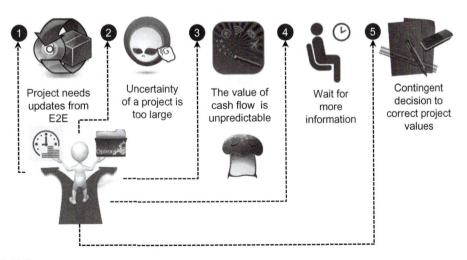

FIGURE 18.5

Criteria for real option analysis.

18.3.3 REAL OPTIONS FOR INVESTMENT DECISION

The above proposition leads to the question of what types of investment strategies or decisions are fit for real option theory analysis. Again, Martha Amram and Nalin Kulatilaka argued six types of investment strategies are satisfactory for real option theory analysis (see Figure 18.6):

1. Learning investment strategy
2. Modular or discrete investment strategy
3. Insurance investment strategy
4. Irreversible investment strategy
5. Flexible investment strategy
6. Platform investment strategy

18.3.3.1 *Learning option*

This is a trial- and-error type of investment strategy or proof of concept (PoC). The scale of the investment project is normally very small because one of the final options or choices may be abandoned. The purpose of the learning investment strategy is to test the water and gain valuable information that is unavailable now. The project can adopt a simulation method or make a prototype model. This investment strategy is to focus on gaining the unavailable information.

18.3.3.2 *Modular or discrete option*

The investment project can be broken into different modules that are independent from each other. For instance, a software system supported by federation architecture can be built independently with a number of specified interfaces to be connected with other software modules. Taking VMware as example, the vSphere platform (or a system) can be independent with other VMware

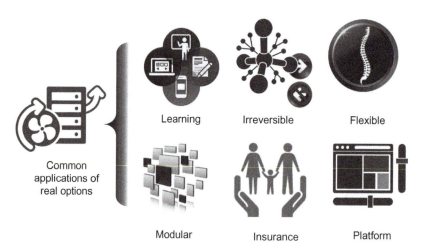

FIGURE 18.6

Types of investment strategy for real options.

products or software components, such as Chargeback, CapIQ, vCloud directory, Site Recover Manager (SRM), vCenter Operation and VMware Fusion (see Figure 18.7).

From VMware's business perspective, each module can be considered as one option of an extra revenue source. Of course, vSphere (the flagship product of VMWare) can be built as an integrated software system with all other functions. However, it may be too risky in terms of cost.

18.3.3.3 Insurance option

The purpose of the insurance investment strategy is to reduce future risks due to uncertainties. The typical example is to abandon or to stop further investment in a project. In financial terms, it is the "put" option.

18.3.3.4 Irreversible option

The term "irreversible" means the investment project can't be turned back or even stopped because it is too costly to do so. In other words, the value of reversing the project would be greater than the value of the associated choices considered by the traditional analyzing tools. However, real option analysis can identify these irreversible options and truncate the further loss.

18.3.3.5 Flexible option

With the traditional analysis method or tools, such as NPV, it is impossible to identify the flexibility of the strategic choices in the original plan. However, real option theory can build flexibility into the strategic plan in the initial stage.

18.3.3.6 Platform option

Traditional analysis methods fail to recognize research and development (R&D) as an investment platform for potential opportunities in the near future. The value of such platform investment will lead to marketable products and potential new business revenue streams. Traditional analysis tools

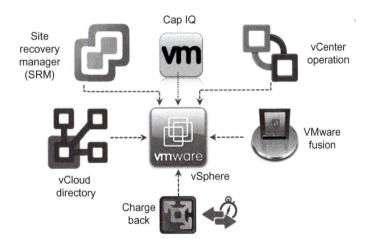

FIGURE 18.7

VMWare hypervisor.

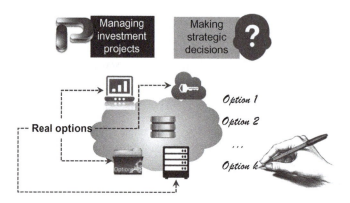

FIGURE 18.8

Criteria of real options.

would substantially undervalue these platform investments. In contrast, real option theory would be an ideal tool to identify these platform investment values.

In summary, this addresses the criteria of real option theory from two different angles (see Figure 18.8):

- Managing investment projects
- Making strategic investment decisions

18.4 POSSIBLE REAL OPTIONS

The next logical question is, "How many real options are there from the perspective of managing an investment project and making a strategic decision?" Lenos Trigeorgis [267] summarized real options into seven different types that are very commonly applied for different applications:

1. Options to expand or future growth options
2. Options to be built in phases or time-to-build options (phase-based investment project)
3. Options to interact or multiple interacting options
4. Option to switch
5. Option to defer (or to delay)
6. Option to alter the operation scale
7. Option to abandon (put option, insurance)

18.4.1 GROWTH OR EXPANSION OR LEVERAGING OPTION

A growth option means that the project that has been already implemented could not generate sufficient revenue to justify its capex, but it might create other expected or unexpected lucrative business opportunities to bring in multiple cash flows in the future. For instance, a cloud service company launched a cloud storage service. The service might not be able to generate enough revenue to cover the capex of establishing its storage infrastructure in seven years, but the cloud storage service will generate other revenue streams, such as online advertising, content management, broadband connections, and even mobile service revenues that are other unexpected opportunities for business growth.

In essence, it is using one investment project to leverage other growth options or opportunities. Another typical example is developing the right portfolio for R&D investment projects. Actually, it shouldn't be called a growth or expansion option, but rather a leveraging or portfolio option.

18.4.2 TIME-TO-BUILD OR OPEN OPTION

The time-to-build option is a type of phase-based investment or an investment project that can be divided into multiple phases. Each phase can be considered as one of the options. When newly arriving information, such as market conditions or financial circumstances, is negative or unfavorable to the overall investment strategy, the particular project will be abandoned. Likewise, if the newly arriving information is good, then a decision maker can select the growth or expansion or switch option.

For example, a cloud investment project can be divided into pilot, small-scale, and large-scale phases. If the new market information (such as too many cutthroat competitors) appears to be against the cloud investment project during the pilot phase, the investment project can be abandoned to cut further losses or deferred until the market conditions have become favorable to the investment project.

This is a type of "wait to see" option via a step-by-step approach until the future investment conditions have become clear.

18.4.3 MULTIPLE INTERACTING OPTIONS

The term "multiple interacting options" means to combine various options that occur during an investment project's lifetime. It indicates an investment project may include many different options. One option might have a negative impact on the project at a particular time but other options might have a positive impact on the project. However, the combination of different options will generate a favorable outcome or good results for the investment project.

18.4.4 OPTION TO SWITCH

This is one of the typical options that any strategic decision maker often adopts. It reflects the flexibility of choice in the strategic decision-making process. This option is to respond to any changes because of investment environment shifts or movements. Any investment project should consist of various inputs and outputs. If input conditions (such as market conditions) have changed, we should also make corresponding changes to achieve favorable outcomes. The available alternatives when making this change are the options to switch.

18.4.5 OPTION TO DEFER

This is the option to hold or postpone further investment for a project until the market conditions are favorable to the investment project. For example, the continuously declining cash flow income of the project has become obvious or a sharp interest rate rise has hit the threshold level at which the NPV generates negative values, but the future of the project still seems to be quite bright. The option to defer would be a good strategic move to maximize the overall benefit of the project.

18.4.6 OPTION TO ALTER THE OPERATING SCALE

This option is similar to option to defer or switch. It's also in response to environmental changes for a project but the change is not to stop or switch, but rather to change the scale or scope of the project. It can be either scaled up or down. If the option is to scale up, this would be the option to expand or grow. If the option is to scale down, it should be the option to contract.

18.4.7 OPTION TO ABANDON (PUT OPTION)

The option to abandon is similar the financial term "put option." It means that a decision maker has decided to sell the remaining value (or salvage value) of an investment project. This option might revise the initial calculation result of the NPV value.

18.4.8 DIFFERENT TERMS FOR REAL OPTIONS

There are other researchers that use different terms to describe the same concepts of these real options. One typical example is Johnathan Mun's [273] classification. He expanded the number of real options to 12 different categories:

1. Option to grow
2. Option to wait and see or to open
3. Option to delay (similar to defer)
4. Option to expand (similar to growth)
5. Option to contract (similar to scale down)
6. Option to choose (similar to switch)
7. Option to put
8. Option to switch resources
9. Sequential compound option
10. Compound option
11. Changing strike option (similar as switch)
12. Changing volatility option (similar as switch)

This classification of real options is more closely associated with the financial meaning of option. Actually, the underlying contents of these terms are sometimes very similar. This is why both option theories sometimes share many common words and terms.

18.5 REAL OPTIONS VERSUS FINANCIAL OPTIONS

Because the concept of real options is derived from financial terms, it is not surprising that ROT may adopt many common words to outline the investment opportunities for the real assets. There have been many research papers that use many of the common terms and assumptions of financial options, such as defer, put, call, and strike. This may lead to some confusion for people in implementing the real option calculation process. Although both option theories are similar, there are many differences. In order to differentiate the two option theories, Johnathan Mun highlighted nine common differentiating points between them (see Table 18.1).

For example, a real option's value is based on the NPV of incoming or forecasted cash flow of an investment project or other business variables, but the financial option is valued according to the current stock price. We can draw certain analogies between the two options, but the fundamental methods for evaluating the options is different. Another key difference is that the financial option can be traded in the financial market, but there is no market to trade real options.

Table 18.1 Real Options versus Financial Options [297]

	Real Options	Financial Options
1	Longer maturity, usually in years.	Short maturity, usually in months.
2	Underlying variables are revenue stream or free cash flows, which in turn are driven by market competition, demand, and management.	Underlying variable driving its value is equity price or price of a financial asset or stock price.
3	The option values can add strategic value to a project through management decisions and flexibility.	It can't control option values by manipulating stock prices.
4	The option value may be worth more than a million or even billion dollars.	The option values are usually small.
5	It is the market competition that drives the option value at a strategic level.	The option value is normally isolated from market competitive effects. The option price is irrelevant to the competition.
6	The history is relatively short, only less than 40 years when Stewart C. Myer used the term "real option" in 1977. However, it took until 1996 for Lenos Trigeorgis to build the bridge between Myer's theory and the corporation's capital budgeting practice	It has been traded since the middle of the 1800s.
7	It is usually solved using closed-form equations and binomial lattices with simulation of the underlying variables, not on the option analysis.	It is often solved using closed-form partial differential equations and simulation/variance reduction techniques for exotic options.
8	It is not for proprietary trading in nature, with no comparable market.	It is a marketable and traded security with comparable pricing information.
9	Management assumptions and actions drive the value of a real option.	Management assumptions and actions have no bearing on valuation.

Table 18.2 Analogy between Real and Financial Options

	Real Options	Financial Options
S	Underlying value of option is the NPV of incoming cash flow of investment project	Underlying value of the option is the stock price
X	Amount of money to be invested or received in launching (exercising) the action (option)	Exercise (strike) price
T	Time is based on when the decision must be made	Time is until the option expires
σ	The value of option varies with time and usually is very volatile	The value is normally quite stable
R	Risk-free discount rate	Risk-free rate of interest
D	Payoff will be the cash inflows of the investment project during the lifetime	Payoff will be the underlying assets or stock dividends.

Moreover, Tero Haahtela [272] reviewed many classic research papers and comprehensively listed 37 difference points between real and financial options from both theoretical and practical perspectives in 2012. By highlighting these differences, the author tried to argue that new practical approaches to evaluate real options are required. In contrast, many academic formulas, such as complicated or difficult mathematical models, should be kept out of the practical world. After all, the goal of real option theory is to help a decision maker make the right decision at the right time rather than a theoretically correct one. It is just one of the tools for the decision process.

Similarly, we had an equivalent conclusion in Chapter 14, where one of main purposes for cost modeling was to communicate and persuade other people to accept one of the particular options among many choices. If the model has become too complicated or too difficult to understand, it would jeopardize its practical value.

From this perspective, this book will only focus on a few practical methods for real option analysis, such as the binomial lattice tree, to illustrate how the ROT approach can provide valuable insight for cloud investment decision making; we will come back on this topic in a moment.

In addition to the many differences, Tero Haahtela also listed some of the key analogous features between real and financial options (see Table 18.2), which not only helps many practitioners to understand the ROT in the right way but also helps in evaluating the strategic options.

Actually, it doesn't matter how we can classify and differentiate both real and financial options, the fundamental issue is, "How can we understand some important features of real option theory?" This question leads to the inquiry of, "How can we estimate the true value of these features (six) in a practical way?"

18.6 REAL OPTIONS VERSUS TRADITIONAL APPROACHES

As we indicated in Chapter 1, cloud computing is not really a new technology but rather a new business model. The model has many uncertainties and the cloud environment is very volatile. The traditional capital budgeting tools, such as NPV, will be insufficient to assist a decision maker in

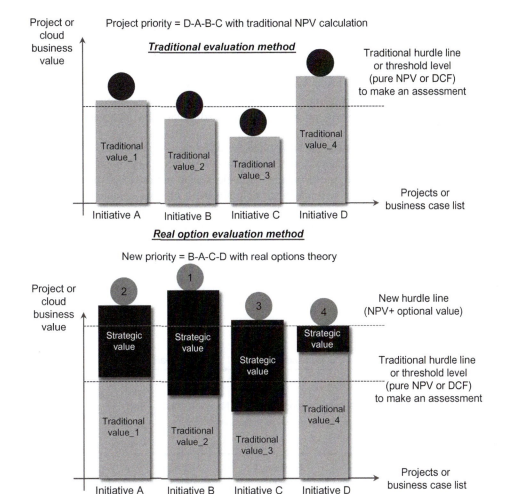

FIGURE 18.9

Traditional method versus real option.

making the right decision at the right time because traditional analysis tools can only provide a static or fixed value of NPV in term of costs and benefits for cloud investment projects. Real option theory does not only elevate the cloud cost modeling from a tactical level to strategic level, but also unfolds a series of dynamic and flexible NPV values.

To illustrate that ROT can add strategic value, suppose we have four cloud investment projects. According to the traditional NPV approach, the decision priority for these four investment projects should be D first followed by, A, B, and C according to the calculated static NPVs (see Figure 18.9).

However, if we use real option theory and reestimate each project's potential cash flow and overall benefits, we find that the investment priority should been changed to B first followed by A, C, and D. The initiative "C" or project "C" that used to be listed last now has become the third option. It is possible that a project that has the lowest static NPV value may potentially have the highest strategic value overall. This is how real option theory or analysis can add strategic value for a process of strategic investment decision making. It provides many new strategic options and can reprioritize investment projects in ways that the traditional NPV approach is incapable to discovering.

Overall, different approaches should be applied for different circumstances. As Johnathan Mun emphasized, "Traditional approaches are more relevant for shorter time frames that are somewhat deterministic. In a longer time frame where strategic opportunities arise, a more appropriate approach incorporates new advanced analytics, including Real Options, Monte Carlo Simulations, and Portfolio Optimization" (see Figure 18.10).

What do the traditional approaches mean to Johnathan Mun? The author indicated there are three mainstream evaluation approaches that are considered as traditional methods to define business values. These approaches are typically applied for property and business assets:

- Market approach
- Income approach
- Cost approach

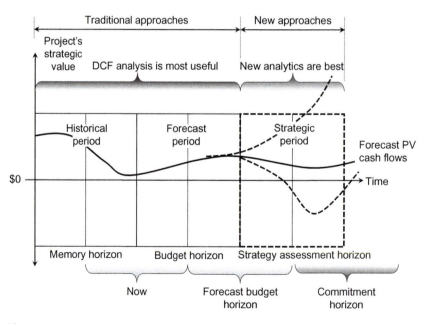

FIGURE 18.10

Adopting different approaches to analzse project value [273].

The market approach is to compare the asset values in the marketplace. In other words, the asset's value is determined by the selling price of an asset on the market. It assumes that the market price is a fair market value. However, the market is very often irrational. The typical example would be a property asset that is sold on the property market. The approach to estimate the property may have a certain evaluation criteria but there are no particular scientific rules to reflect the true value of the asset. Normally, the price of the asset follows the rule of supply and demand.

The income approach focuses on the future potential profit or free cash flow generation potential. This cash flow will be discounted by these net free cash flows to a present value. In essence, this approach is closely associated with three major elements, namely cash flow, capital, and interest rate.

The cost approach defines the cost that would occur if the assets were created or produced. Again, this asset evaluation approach is normally applied for a property, especially for a new one. For example, the cost approach can define that the value of a new property should be equal to the land cost plus the building cost. This evaluation approach is much accurate than the market one.

Although these traditional approaches are fundamentally sound by the financial theories, they can't provide strategic flexibility values for a decision maker. In contrast to these common traditional approaches, Johnathan Mun listed three new approaches:

- Real option theory (eNPV)
- Monte Carlo simulation
- Portfolio optimization

The key difference between the traditional and new approach is that new approaches not only provide flexible values or strategic options, but also explore the value-added insight for those projects that were undervalued based on those traditional approaches. Furthermore, the author framed these analytical approaches into a 2x2 matrix from a type of analysis and analytic direction perspective (see Figure 18.11).

This matrix has shown some of the relationship between traditional and new analytic approaches, but the author didn't give a detailed explanation of how some of the new terms, such as scenario and premium value analysis, are associated with traditional approaches. Based on the book context, it appears discounted cash flow (DCF) may correspond to the "income, "premium value is related to "cost," and scenario reflects the meaning of "market." The decision process underpins all traditional and new approaches.

This figure indicates that the real option theory and Monte Carlo simulation approaches are the new quantitative analysis. These analysis approaches quantify cost details from bottom to top. They have many unique features. As we can see, many strategic values can't be clearly identified by many traditional approaches except DCF. (Actually, DCF is a special case of real option theory. We will touch on this issue just in a moment.) These values can only be recognized by gut feeling or personal experience.

The elegance of real options theory and Monte Carlo simulation is that many strategic values can be quantified or identified from the bottom to the top. As never before, many implicit ideas, fuzzy perceptions, and flexible choices can be explicitly made transparent for a decision maker. The new analytic approaches are not only theoretically true but also are practically doable on two

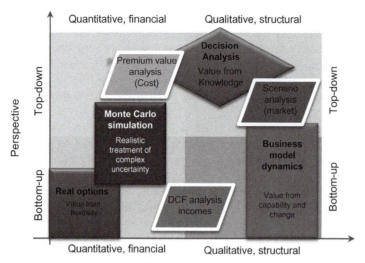

FIGURE 18.11

2 x 2 Classification matrix of new and traditional analytic approaches [273].

conditions: one is that they work; the other is that their working leads us to the right end, an end we desire.

This is the most significant point of real option theory and Monte Carlo simulation. This is why these new approaches are important and applied to cloud cost modeling.

Up to this point, we have unveiled the details of real option theory. You might wonder what Monte Carlo simulation is. Before we move to the process of real option calculation, we will now explain the Monte Carlo simulation method or approach.

18.7 WHAT IS MONTE CARLO SIMULATION (MCS)?

There have been many definitions of Monte Carlo simulation. People describe the concept of MCS from different perspectives. We can classify these definitions into four big categories (see Figure 18.12):

- Process
- Technique
- Principle
- Applications

An example of a process definition is "Monte Carlo simulation is a method of analysis based on artificially recreating a chance process (usually with a computer), running it many times, and directly observing the results." [274]. It emphasizes the artificial process by a computer to generate the result.

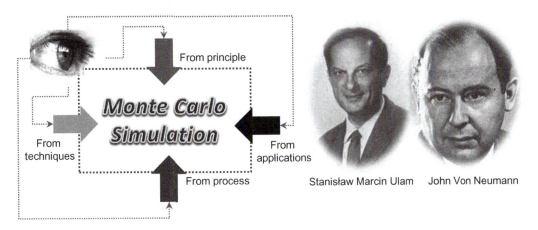

FIGURE 18.12

Defining Monte Carlo simulation from four perspectives.

A technique definition has more details than the process one. For instance:

Monte Carlo methods are based on the analogy between probability and volume. The mathematics of measure formalizes the intuitive notion of probability, associating an event with a set of outcomes and defining the probability of the event to be its volume or measure relative to that of a universe of possible outcomes. Monte Carlo uses this identity in reverse, calculating the volume of a set by interpreting the volume as a probability. In the simplest case, this means sampling randomly from a universe of possible outcomes and taking the fraction of random draws that fall in a given set as an estimate of the set's volume. The law of large numbers ensures that this estimate converges to the correct value as the number of draws increases. The central limit theorem provides information about the likely magnitude of the error in the estimate after a finite number of draws" [275].

The key information of this technical definition is that the "estimate converges to the correct value as the number of draws increases."

On the other hand, one of the concise definitions from the principle perspective is, "The Monte Carlo method is a numerical method of solving mathematical problems by the simulation of random variables" [276]. It emphasizes two points: numerical method and the simulation of random variables.

Since Monte Carlo simulation was invented by both Stanisław Marcin Ulam and John Von Neumann in 1940s, the method has been widely spread to many fields, especially in physics and finance. People use this method to explore the probability of phenomena at a macro level, which is difficult to determine using many traditional analysis methods. As Malvin Kalos et al. indicated, "The essence of the method is the invention of games of chance whose behaviour and outcome can be used to study some interesting phenomena" [277].

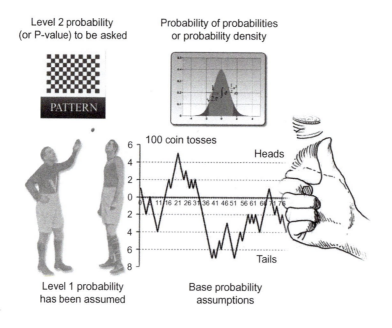

FIGURE 18.13

Probability of probability or probability density.

In essence, if we condense or boil all above definitions down to their very basic meanings, we can find the concept of Monte Carlo simulation has two underlying philosophical ideas:

1. Probability of probability (Monte Carlo tests) or probability density
2. Analogy to the real world through many random chances (simulation process)

Let's use two examples to illustrate these two ideas behind the Monte Carlo method.

18.7.1 PROBABILITY OF PROBABILITY (MONTE CARLO TESTS)

What does probability of probability mean? In very simple terms, it is a probability density or probability distribution or pattern (see Figure 18.13). We can use the following example to illustrate the meaning of probability of probability.

Assume that I toss a coin 100 times. I find that the first result of 100 flips has a probability of 20% for heads and 80% for taisl. The question is, how likely will this 20-80 ratio be if I make another 100 flips? The answer will be "I'm not sure." Suppose I make another 100 tosses, but I achieve 48 heads and 52 tails (or a 48/52 ratio) the second time. Now, the question is, what is the most likely scenario is if I toss a coin 100,000 times?

This is the Monte Carlo question. Let's reframe this problem in another way, in which we can consider each 100 flips as an event. If I run this event 100 times, what is the most likely probability that I will have 20−80 or 48−52 (Figure 18.14)? We can consider 20−80 or 48−52 as a special event.

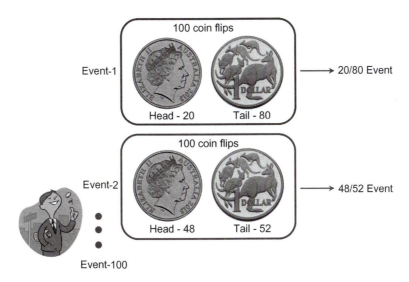

FIGURE 18.14

Tossing a coin 100,000 times.

The answer of this question is quite obviously the 20−80 ratio (or probability) will be very tiny in comparison with the 48−52 probability. Actually, the 48−52 probability will be greater than 40% if the tossing number is large enough. It will be quite easy to use MS Excel to calculate this result by generating a random number via the "RAND()" function. This example has demonstrated that the Monte Carlo method can examine complex aggregations from simple actions.

18.7.2 SIMULATION PROCESS

The second key point of the Monte Carlo method is the simulation process. The typical example is to estimate an irrational number: π. Image you have two guns and try to shoot a target that is a quarter circle in one 1 x 1 square (see Figure 18.15).

Clearly, if the shooting process is completely random, then some of the shots will hit the target (or be within the circle) and others may miss out (or be outside of the circle). In order to get an intuitive experience, you can use MS Excel to have a trial. What you can do is to replace two guns with two random number generators, $X = $ RAND() and $Y = $ RAND() (see Table 18.3).

Remember that MS Excel's random number is always than less 1 so that the square of two numbers would be either greater than "1" or less than "1." If we assign the bullets hit outside as "0" $= x^2 + y^2 \geq 1$ and inside as "1" $= x^2 + y^2 \leq 1$ and I shoot 1,000 times (1,000 of X and 1,000 of Y), then we will have the following ratio:

$$Ratio = \frac{I}{Total\ number\ of\ shots} = \frac{I(X^2 + Y^2 < 1)}{Total\ number\ of\ shots} = \frac{777}{10000} = 0.777$$

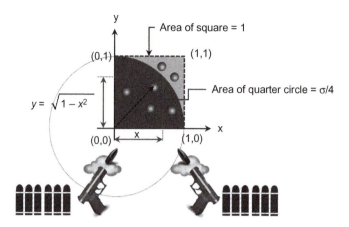

FIGURE 18.15

Process of estimating π.

Table 18.3 Monte Carlo Simulation of Estimating π			
Gun X	**Gun Y**	**If within the circle[1]**	**If outside the circle**
X = RAND()	Y = RAND()	"1" = I = $X^2 + Y^2 < 1$	"0" = O = $X^2 + Y^2 \geq 1$
[1]The equation of a circle can be represented as $x^2 + y^2 = R^2$; because $R = 1$, $x^2 + y^2 = 1$.			

Remember this is only a quarter of a circle. If we multiple this ratio by 4, we will have 3.108:

$$Estimating\ \pi = Ratio \times 4 = 0.777 \times 4 = 3.108$$

Because both "X" and "Y" are equal to completely random numbers, the numbers "I" and "O" will be changed if "X" and "Y" change. However, the number "I" will be around 750 and 800. Again, we can easily use MS Excel to replicate this example.

If we increase the number of shots from 1,000 to 1,500, the estimated number will be equal to 3.1387 [(1177/1500) x 4], which is very close to the number $\pi = 3.141516\ldots$ Of course, we can also use a definite integral to get this surface area (or the result of "π"):

$$S_{\frac{\pi}{4}} = \int_0^1 \int_0^{\sqrt{1-X^2}} dxdy = 0.785398$$

Here, we just try to demonstrate that we can use the above equation (or another method) to find the irrational number "π" in order to prove the point that Monte Carlo simulation is not a very efficient way to calculate the number unless other methods have all been exhausted.

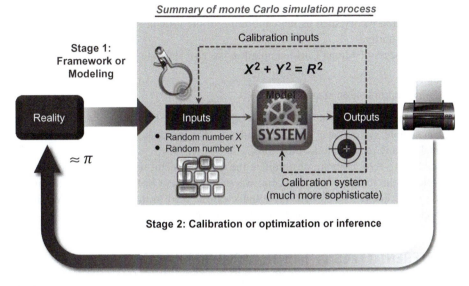

FIGURE 18.16

Mechanism of Monte Carlo simulation system for estimating π.

The example of estimating "pi" has demonstrated the following points:

1. The principle of Monte Carlo simulation (here, we emphasize the simulation process) can formulate the world as many little steps and each step or iteration involves realization of the world if the number of little steps is large enough.
2. In order to run a Monte Carlo simulation, we must have the right system or model. In the above example, the system or model system is the circle equation:

$$X^2 + Y^2 = R^2$$

3. Without this system, the random numbers will not eventually converge to a desirable result or outcome (see Figure 18.16), which is π in this case.

Similarly, the model system of tossing a coin is to multiply a random number (function "RAND()" in Microsoft Excel) by the number 2 and round the result of the multiplied number down to the near the nearest integer [in MS Excel it would be INT (RAND()*2)]; we will then have either "1" or "0." If we assign "1" to head and "0" to tails, we will have a very simple tossing model system for Monte Carlo simulation.

In Figure 18.16, we have two types of calibration. We can either calibrate inputs or the system if the output results do not fit reality or the desired outcome. Input calibration is relatively easier than system calibration. In other words, a system calibration needs much more sophisticated skills than input calibration because the results of system calibration are much more volatile than changing the inputs. Taking the above estimation of the irrational number "π" case, if the estimated result is far from the expected number, 3.14, we can increase the volume of inputs, for example from 1,000 to 1,500.

The reason to highlight the issue of calibration is there will be many applications of input calibration for real option theory such as the calibration of the growth rate probabilities. We will touch on this issue very shortly.

Overall, the process of Monte Carlo simulation has two separate stages:

1. Modeling stage
2. Calibration or optimization stage

The stage of modeling (or making a framework) means to take a frame from reality and then fit it into a manageable system that can be calculated. The process of this stage is to simplify the world and make many reasonable assumptions.

The second stage is to calibrate or optimize the model system; this takes the simulation result to infer the world or the reality. One thing that we should always keep in mind is that just having a good model system doesn't mean that the outputs will be a fit to the real world. We should understand which circumstances are a fit for Monte Carlo simulation and which are not.

18.7.3 DIFFERENT TYPES OF MONTE CARLO SIMULATION

Normally, we can classify Monte Carlo simulation (MCS) systems or models into two big categories or four different types:

- Single-stage MCS
- Multiple-stage MCS
- Mixture MCS
- Markov chain MC (or MCMC) simulation

18.7.3.1 Linear MCS

Linear MCS consists of single-stage and multiple-stage MCS models (see the left side of Figure 18.17). As we can see, the relationship between the starting stage R and the resulting stages X, Y, and Z are linear and direct, and they will have a probabilities of occurring P_x, P_y, and P_z from the starting point of R.

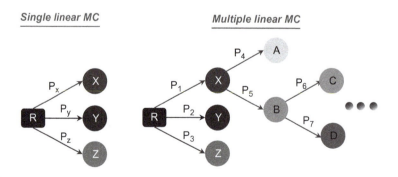

FIGURE 18.17

Linear Monte Carlo simulation systems.

A more sophisticated MCS model is to extend the single-stage MCS model further to multiple stages (see the right side of Figure 18.17), where the MCS model is expanded from R to X, Y, Z and then to A, B and from B to C, D. The number of stages can be infinite.

18.7.3.2 Nonlinear MCS

In contrast to linear MCS models, we can have mixture MCS models (see the left side of Figure 18.18), in which the probability of itself is a probability. In other words, the subpopulation of probability is within the total population of probability, and the subpopulations are associated with mixture distributions or functional distributions.

To implement mixture MCS modeling, you have to make postulates and identify the subpopulation first. There will be different probability patterns from stage R to other stages M, N, and L.

The most sophisticated MCS model is the Markov chain Monte Carlo simulation (MCMC), in which the current state will be based on the previous stages. In other words, the state of M occurring will influence the transactions of state N, L, and O. It is a recursive model.

In essence, the linear MCS models should be sufficient to handle most of the problems. They are easier to understand. The results of MCS can be validated directly. In contrast to nonlinear MCS models, they are the black boxes. It will be quite challenging to see how the inputs and outputs interact with each other and lead to the desired results.

Subsequently, unless you have been fully convinced that the results of linear MCS models might go nowhere and you have full confidence that nonlinear MCS can bring some extra insight for your problem solving, it is not recommended to explore the nonlinear MCS model for your problem. In short, you should be very careful in adopting the nonlinear MCS model.

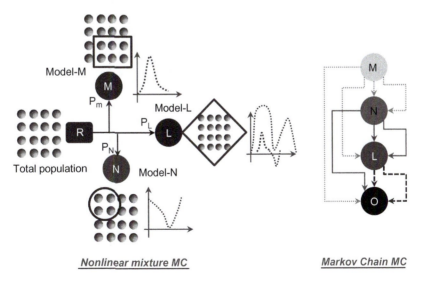

Nonlinear mixture MC   *Markov Chain MC*

FIGURE 18.18

Nonlinear Monte Carlo simulation systems.

18.7.4 PROS AND CONS OF MONTE CARLO SIMULATION (MCS)

Up to now, we have explained the concept of Monte Carlo simulation from different perspectives. We have also illustrated two typical examples of MCS applications, the model system behind the simulation, and the significant points of this method. You might have a better idea of how MCS works.

However, you may have more questions from an application perspective, namely how to apply the MCS in real world scenarios and the pros and cons of applying MCS.

18.7.4.1 What is MCS good at? (Pros)

If a problem has very simple actions or steps to formulate an event but the aggregation of these events becomes very complex, MCS is very good at predicting or resolving this kind of problem, such as dropping sand into the existing pile of sand if we know the process of dropping (see Figure 18.19).

Another good MCS application is when the analyzed problem has many uncertainties. For example, consider an investment project that isn't sure of the certainty of future cash flow due to market growth.

MCS is also very useful to investigate some hidden drivers or potential influences or unexpected contributors that may dominate the outputs or results.

The other problem that can be resolved by the MCS method is to simplify complex systems. For example, a telco company has a very complex network infrastructure, which consists of an Enterprise Data Network (EDN), Fibre Channel over Ethernet (FCoE), Fibre Channel (FC) network, and IP network. If we want to understand the likelihood of breakage of a simple component or how much data traffic can flow through it, MCS is very good at simplifying these results and aggregating the key piece of information for a decision maker (see Figure 18.20).

18.7.4.2 What is MCS not good at? (Cons)

In order to implement the MCS method in the right way, we should be fully aware of the fact that MCS is not good for some applications. For example, it will not be good for application to the

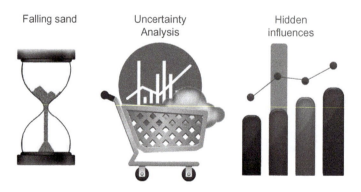

Falling sand   Uncertainty Analysis   Hidden influences

FIGURE 18.19

Modeling of dropping sand.

investigation of a simple action due to complex aggregations. The typical example is understanding how the customer composition of a particular popular consumer product is distributed on different age groups. There are many underlying drivers for customer to buy a certain brand product. MCS is not good at finding the underlying drivers that create this result.

MCS is only good at approximation, not exactness. As we know, MCS will take simple inputs through the model system and reach the output. How realistic this result is will be dependent on your own interpretation. MCS can't give the exact answer. In order to get a reasonable result, we have to use calibration and system adjustment and make the result more realistic, such as in the above example of estimating "π."

Often, MCS is quite difficult to communicate to people who are not familiar with the MCS model. Because of this barrier, a good result from MCS calculation may have little influence on some key decision makers.

If you have a certain amount of MCS calculation experience, you might find that MCS is very sensitive to inputs and parameters of the model system. In other words, even if you make some slight and reasonable adjustments of the input value, the outputs will be totally different from the inferred result. In essence, the robustness of MCS is an issue fin application.

In the example of estimating "π," we already mentioned that MCS is not very efficient. Often it is very slow in getting the result in comparison with other methods. This means that if the decision maker would like to get an immediate answer, this is not a good tool to get such a quick answer.

18.7.4.3 Good applications for MCS

Here, we listed some of the good applications for MCS:

- Financial growth
- Insurance or risk analysis
- Cloud network

In our application of a cloud project investment, we understand all the details at a tactical level, but we are not sure of the overall picture at a strategic level. If the simulation model system is converging, we can adopt MCS to analyze the cloud investment project because MCS is good for our converging process.

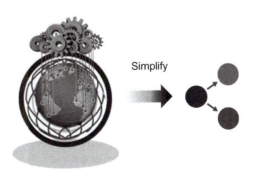

FIGURE 18.20

Simplify complex systems.

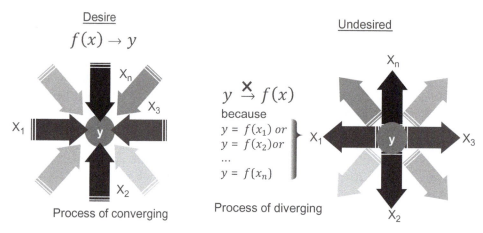

FIGURE 18.21

Preference to go from complex to simple.

18.7.4.4 Bad applications for MCS

In contrast to converging processes, MCS is not good for these applications:

- Market prices
- Weather patterns
- Biological systems

This is because we can't have a complete picture of all actions at a detailed level and have to infer from the aggregated result. This means that it is impossible to obtain all possibilities from one single point. It doesn't matter how good the system is. The process of simulation is diverging.

In mathematic terms, we want infer from a complex system to a simple value and we don't want the other way around (see Figure 18.21) because from f(x) to Y is only one possibility. It is converging. However, if we go from Y to f(x), there will be infinite possibilities.

If we look from a model evolution perspective, we can find the original f(x) was actually a static single point, such as a traditional NPV. However, as Sheldon M. Ross indicated, "Any realistic model of a real world phenomenon must take into account the possibility of randomness" [278]. Therefore, the MCS process replaces single points of inputs with realistic probability distributions (see Figure 18.22).

As a result of this replacement, we will obtain the probability of probability, where we have the defined probabilities at level 1 as inputs to be processed into a probability at level 2 as an output by a simulation process. This is the essence of the MCS process and the heart of this simulation process is theoretically random. We use the word "theoretically" because when we implement MCS, we can't have absolutely random numbers, but rather pseudorandom numbers.

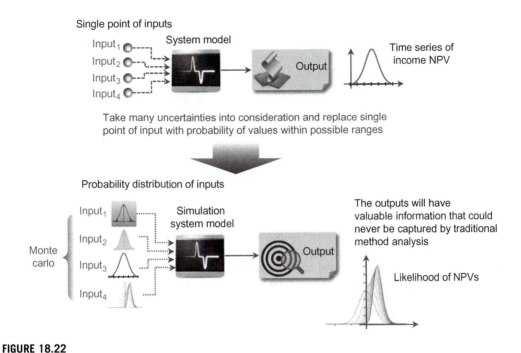

FIGURE 18.22

Replacing single points of inputs with probabilities.

18.8 RANDOM NUMBERS AND BROWNIAN MOTION

Let's examine the concept of random and pseudorandom random numbers as well as Brownian motion, because these concepts will underpin the practical process of real option theory and Monte Carlo simulation:

- Pseudorandom versus random numbers
- Brownian motion

18.8.1 PSEUDORANDOM VERSUS RANDOM NUMBERS

From the above two practical examples, we have seen that at the core of the MCS process is a random number generator. For many ordinary practitioners, Microsoft Excel is often a practical and handy tool to generate MCS results. We often use its random number generator function [or "RAND()"]. We hope the function "RAND()" can generate enough random numbers for us to implement the MCS process. In other words, we expect the generator [RAND()] should produce an infinite stream of random variables that are totally independent based on a uniform probability distribution between 0 and 1 (see Figure 18.23).

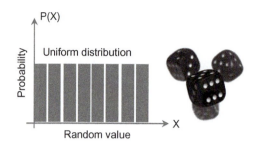

FIGURE 18.23

Uniform distribution.

Derrick Emma Lehmer [279] (famous mathematicians, Berkeley) defined the random number as follows: "a random sequence is a vague notion embodying the idea of a sequence in which each term is unpredictable to the uninitiated and whose digits pass a certain number of tests, traditional with statisticians and depending somewhat on the uses to which the sequence is to be put." However, in reality, the RAND() function is not a pure random generator but rather a pseudorandom number generator (PRGN). The PRGN has algorithms that can automatically generate a long string of unpredictable numbers with quite good random properties. However, the sequence of this long-run number string will eventually repeat itself in terms of friction or a pattern. In short, the pseudorandom number generator will have a repeating cycle that is too large to notice for a practical application. Gerard M. Verschuuren [280] highlighted one of the most common pseudorandom number generators, the linear congruenital generator:

$$X_{n+1} = (aX_n + b)mod\ m$$

In contrast, a real random number will never repeat itself, but it only exists in the natural world. This means that practically, we have no other alternative than adopting pseudorandom numbers that are generated by the RAND() function.

18.8.2 BROWNIAN MOTION (BM) AND GEOMETRIC BM

18.8.2.1 Brownian motion

The Brownian motion phenomenon was first described by German biologist Wilhelm Friedrich von Gleichen-Rußwurm (1717–1783) in the 18the century and published by Scottish botanist Robert Brown (1773–1858) in 1828 in the *Philosophical Magazine and Annuals of Philosophy*. The title of the article was "The discoverer of the motions of the particles of the Pollen." The phenomenon can be observed under a microscope when plant pollen is dropped into water and generates an incessant and irregular movement of the pollen particle.

What Brown found was that the motion of a particle is caused by constant bombardment by water molecules (see Figure 18.24). This irregular motion of a suspended particle (or grain) is named Brownian motion.

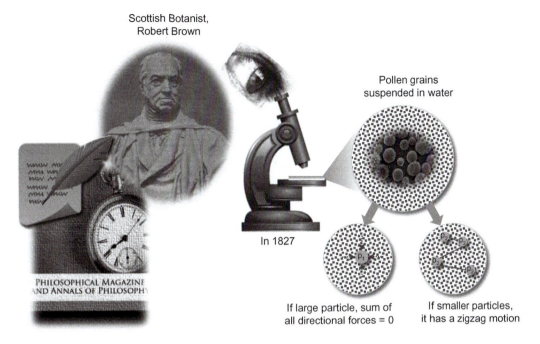

FIGURE 18.24

Normal Brownian motion.

If the particle is quite large, the surrounding water molecules will hit this large particle from all sides. On average, the impact of all directional forces will be naturally cancelled out. Subsequently, the result of all directional forces on this large particle will be zero.

On the other hand, if many particles are quite small they will be hit by a mass number of water molecules from all directions. Furthermore, the forces from all directions do not even hit the smaller particle. This will generate a new force. The new force will change the direction of this smaller particle. When it moves around, it creates a zigzag motion (see Figure 18.24).

In order to describe Brownian motion in mathematical terms, we assume a particle or grain in d spatial dimensions. The particle has the following characteristics:

1. It has continuous movement.
2. The motion of the particle is absolutely random.
3. The motion is unaffected by changing the origin of time.

The normal Brownian motion defines the particle movement in "d" spatial dimensions and is donated as R^d (real number set). The variables of the particles' new forces are the Gaussian random vectors. (We will define the principle of Gaussian random vectors in a moment.)

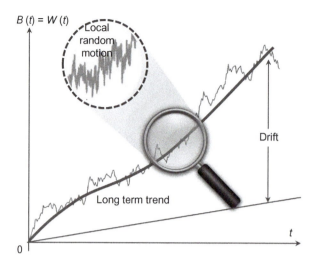

FIGURE 18.25

Wiener process or standard Brownian motion.

18.8.2.2 Wiener process or standard brownian motion

If there is only one dimension of Brownian motion = B(t), it begins at $B_0(t = 0) = 0$ (or the origin) and follows a stochastic process based on stationary and independent increments mixing with the local random motion (or Gaussian process); we call it asWiener process [W(t)] or standard Brownian motion. Actually, this process can be considered as a combination of both local random motion and a long-term trend (see Figure 18.25).

The Wiener process is a continuous stochastic movement in which the random variation in a logarithm scale follows along a long-term trend with drift. In essence, the Wiener process has the following three basic components:

1. Long-term trend (or Levy process)
2. Local motion (or Gaussian distribution)
3. Drift from mean

18.8.2.2.1 Levy Processes

A stochastic process with stationary independent increments is called a Levy process, in honor of the French mathematician Paul Levy (1886−1971). Moreover, Levy processes include not only the Wiener process but also a compound Poisson process (see Figure 18.26).

However, we will only focus on Brownian motion in this book for the purposes of real option theory. In Figure 18.25, we only showed one Wiener process (half of a symmetric random walk). If we include many Wiener processes and stop at any time t_1, t_2, and t_3, we can see the evolution of the Gaussian distribution.

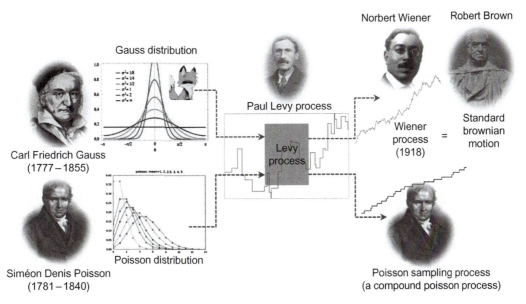

FIGURE 18.26

Relationship of Levy process with other processes and distributions.

18.8.2.2.2 Mathematical Terms of Standard Brownian Motion

As we have stated above, standard Brownian motion is a stochastic process that can be defined in mathematical terms, with four main properties:

1. $W(0) = 0$,[1] when $t = 0$.
2. The function $t \rightarrow W(t)$ is continuous in t with probability $= 1$.
3. The Wiener process has a set of $W(t)$ values (or $\{W(t)\}_{t>0}$). These values are stationary and independent increments.
4. The increment $W(t + s) - W(s)$ has the normal or Gaussian $(0,t)$ distribution (see Figure 18.27).

For any $t > 0$ the random variable $W(t) = W(t) - W(0)$, in the increment in $[0,t]$, is the normal distribution with 0 mean and variance t; the density function can be represented as:

$$f(t, x) = \frac{1}{\sqrt{2\pi t}} e^{-x^2/2t}$$

From the theory of a normal distribution with μ mean and σ variance, the density function should be:

$$f(x) = \frac{1}{\sqrt{2\pi}\sigma} e^{-\frac{(x-\mu)^2}{2\sigma^2}}$$

---

[1] W(t) means Wiener process or standard Brownian motion.

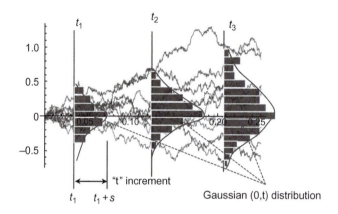

FIGURE 18.27

Normal distributions of Brownian motion.

The implication of standard Brownian motion is that the random walk has a limitation, which is that the percentage of volatility $\sigma = 1$ and $\mu = 0$ because the normal distribution is the standard normal distribution. It is the special case of a Brownian motion B(t).

For p $\in$ [0, 1] the pth percentile of W(t) is $F^{-1}(p)\sqrt{t}$ F^{-1} is the functional integration of the density function of the normal distribution:

$$F(x) = \frac{1}{\sqrt{2\pi}} \int_{-\infty}^{x} e^{-u^2/2} du$$

18.8.2.2.3 Brownian Motion with Drift

Brownian motion with drift should be satisfied with a stochastic differential equation (SDE). If BM with drift has constant drift and diffusion coefficients, we should have:

$$dB(t) = \mu dt + \sigma dW(t)$$

If the initial value B(t) = x_0, we should have the following integration result:

$$B(t) = x_0 + \mu t + \sigma W(t)$$

Here, B(t) is the Brownian motion and is normally distributed with mean value = $x_0 + \mu t$ and variance $\sigma^2 t$. The density function of this BM with drift is:

$$f(t,x) = \frac{1}{\sigma\sqrt{2\pi t}} e^{-\frac{(x-x_0-\mu t)^2}{2\sigma^2 t}}$$

And the functional integration of the above density function is:

$$F(x) = \frac{1}{\sigma\sqrt{2\pi}} \int_{-\infty}^{x} e^{-\frac{[u-x_0-\mu]^2}{2\sigma^2}} du$$

18.8.2.2.4 Geometric Brownian motion

A geometric Brownian motion B(t) can also be presented as the solution of a stochastic differential equation (SDE), but it has linear drift and diffusion coefficients:

$$dB(t) = \mu B(t)dt + \sigma B(t)dW(t) \ or \ \frac{dB(t)}{B(t)} = \mu dt + \sigma dW(t)$$

If the initial value of Brownian motion is equal to $B(t) = x_0$ and the calculation $\sigma B(t)dW(t)$ can be applied with Ito's lemma [to $F(X) = \log(X)$]:

$$B(t) = e^{\log x_0 + \hat{\mu}t + \sigma W(t)} = x_0 e^{\hat{\mu}t + \sigma W(t)} \ where \ \hat{\mu} = \mu - \frac{1}{2}\sigma^2$$

Here, W(t) is log normally distributed, with:

$$Mean = E[B(t)] = x_0 e^{\mu t}$$

$$Variance = Var[B(t)] = x_0^2 e^{2\mu t}(e^{\sigma^2 t} - 1)$$

The density is:

$$f(t, x) = \frac{1}{\sigma\sqrt{2\pi t}} e^{-(\log x - \log x_0 - \hat{\mu}t)^2 / 2\sigma^2 t}$$

In summary, the ultimate goal of describing the details of Brownian motion and other associated processes is to use this concept for real option theory application. The graphical representation of all these different Brownian motions is shown in Figure 18.28.

The key distinguishing point among different Brownian motions is the different types of drift. If the drift is 0, it is standard BM. If the drift is constant, it is BM with constant drift. If the drift is linear, it is geometric BM.

18.9 MCS AND ROT PROCESS

Once we have cleared away all the theoretical issues of real option theory (ROT), Monte Carlo simulation (MCS), and geometric Brownian motion (GBM), we can drill down to the next phase of cost modeling analysis, namely, the process steps for ROT and MCS calculation. We basically leverage these mathematical tools for calculation of different real options from a cloud investment perspective.

18.9.1 CALCULATION PROCESS

Again, the detail of the calculation process steps can be divided into two levels:

1. Tactical level
2. Strategic level

Each level of the analysis process consists of five steps. Altogether, there are 10 processing steps from an end-to-end perspective. Actually, the tactical level of analysis is basically the traditional analysis process plus Monte Carlo simulation (MCS), but it begins with a strategic view or

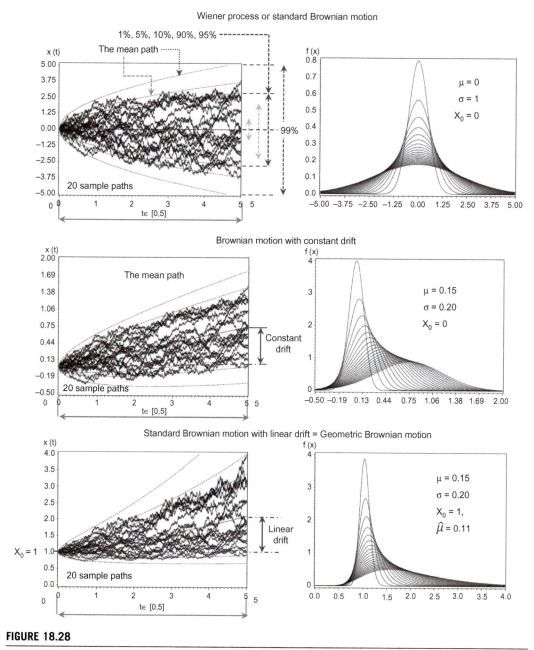

FIGURE 18.28

Graphical representations of different Brownian motions [281].

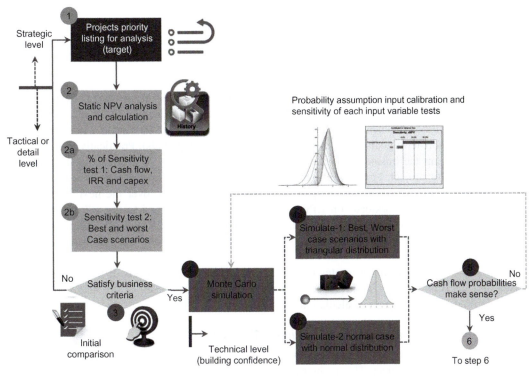

FIGURE 18.29

Tactical level of ROT and MCS analysis process.

management intuition. However, it is mainly focused on the profitability of each individual project. We can consider this process as a top to bottom approach. It is a detailed analysis for each individual project (see Figure 18.29).

18.9.2 TACTICAL LEVEL OF ANALYSIS

If we refer to Chapter 17, we understand that we have already implemented some steps of the tactical level of analysis. There is only one part of the process that has not been touched, which is Monte Carlo simulation. Now, let's walk through and complete the tactical level of the process.

18.9.2.1 Project prioritization and listing target projects for analysis

The first step of the tactical level of the process is to decide onthe target projects to be analyz ed. For example, one IT company has the following project list from different line of business (LoB) units for next year's capital budget process:

- Customer-orientated cloud projects
- Upgrade existing data center for current workload expansion

- X86 server virtualization
- Migration of part of workload to a cloud
- Life-cycle existing RISC server platform (server, storage, and network)
- Build new data center facility
- Build disaster recovery infrastructure

To quantify priority is a very complex task. A company's executive team, stakeholders, and key decision maker should give the guidance for the initial project prioritization list based on the company's vision, mission, business strategy, and technology capabilities; the market environment; and long-term and short-term goals (such as growth and cost efficiency goals). Practically, the executive team should set up the business criteria or IT infrastructure strategy or a threshold level for any capital program or project. For example, the CIO can set up an IT infrastructure strategy that decides to adopt the x86 server as the company's default server platform over the next 3 years. This means that all existing workloads on RISC servers have to be migrated to the x86 platform. The threshold level would be something like "Internal Rate of Return (IRR) = 12%." Business criteria may include revenue growth rate, return on investment period, profit margin, risks, and other assumptions.

This step is looking from the strategic level to prioritize a list of projects. It is a subjective step based on a decision maker's intuition and experience. However, the result of this step will be eventually verified by later objective calculations.

18.9.2.2 Static NPV calculation (Traditional Analysis)

Based on the listed priority of all projects, we can use the traditional NPV formula to calculate the present value for each project. This is the traditional analysis process. The calculation itself is quite simple and straightforward, and will be based on the above business criteria and key assumptions: IRR, initial investment capital, period of time for each project, and forecasted cash flow or revenue income each year. This is a single point of analysis.

Ultimately, this step checks a decision maker's intuition. It is a reality check to see whether the listed project meets the specified business criteria or not. It is the step of moving from strategic intuition down to a tactical or detail level.

18.9.2.3 Verifying business criteria

This step is to compare the result of static NPV with the business criteria that has been set up by the decision makers. This is an initial comparison for the first static NPV calculation based on many preliminary assumptions. However, we should be very careful with this initial comparison. The lower static NPV value might not mean that the overall value of the project is lower. If we refer to Figure 18.9, we find that the total value of a project is equal to a static NPV value plus a strategic value. Therefore, unless there are some obvious findings, such as a large amount of negative revenue contributions in the next few years and a gloomy strategic outlook, then we should go back to review either the revenue assumptions or the internal hurdle rate or the initial investment capital.

18.9.2.4 Monte carlo simulation for revenue forecasting

The goal of this step is to replace a single point of estimation with a probability distribution for future revenue growth or cash flow income. This is why we select the MCS method to predict the future business growth. The key point of the MCS methodology is to let nature to decide the future. As we spelle out at the beginning of this chapter, however, the first step may be subjective. All key assumptions and judgments are based on personal experience or an individual's intuition or perception. They may be true or facts, but they are often false because no one is perfect so no one's decision is perfect. Human beings often have many cognition biases. This is why we need many scientific tools, such as MCS, to check our intuition.

MCS can make revenue forecasts and decision assumptions much more realistic for the selected probabilities' inputs. It adds more objective characteristics into subjective assumptions.

In essence, the MCS process is objective, but the input to the MCS process model is subjective. You have to make subjective assumptions to define the MCS input model. From this perspective, you can't have an 100% objective model, only a relatively objective one.

18.9.2.5 Checking that everything makes sense and MCS input calibration

This step is actually the process of MCS calibration if we refer to Figure 18.16. There are two types of calibration: input calibration and model system (or system) calibration, which is the Monte Carlo system. We will normally focus on input calibration because the common MCS model is linear and simpler. As we have emphasized above, the calibration of the model system requires sophisticated skills and confidence in the MCS system.

The goal of MCS input calibration is to make sure that the result of the MCS process makes sense, so that the result of the MCS is aligned with reality and the company's capabilities. If the result doesn't make sense, input adjustments should be made.

Even if the initial output result does make sense, it is also a good idea to change the probabilities or probability distribution inputs and examine the sensitivity of the MCS system. Generally, there are seven types of common probability distributions that we often adopt for MCS input models(see Figure 18.30):

- Normal distribution
- Lognormal distribution
- Triangular distribution
- Uniform distribution
- Poisson distribution
- Exponential distribution
- Geometric distribution

Remember that an MCS system is very sensitive to the input parameters. By changing different inputs, you will understand the limitations of your MCS model. This process can be considered scenario tests. Normally, we can have three different types of scenarios for to check that everything makes sense:

- Best case scenario
- Normal case scenario
- Worst case scenario

The result of this step is that we should have a rationalized mean value "μ" and variation value "σ."

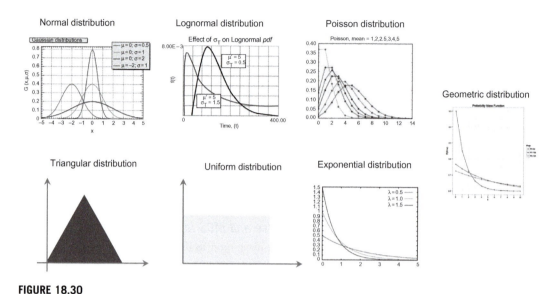

FIGURE 18.30

Different probability distribution inputs.

18.9.3 STRATEGIC LEVEL OF ANALYSIS

The strategic level of analysis is the real option theory (ROT) process. This process elevates all the details of tactical analysis to the strategic level. This part of the process is working from the bottom to the top (see Figure 18.31). There are also five (or seven) steps.

18.9.3.1 Strategic level of real options problem

This first step is to identify the overall problem at the strategic level, such as the problem of gaining market share, increasing profit margin, lifting the revenue growth rate, or even exiting a certain market and redirecting a certain percentage of IT resources to the company's core business. It is how to frame the number of real options at a strategic level.

We have to analyze a number of options for one portfolio of many projects. The analysis will not only focus on the profit gain of one individual project but also leverage some projects for overall strategic gains. As a result, the ROT process will lead to a set of decision options for different projects including "expand," "abandon," "switch," "defer," etc.

18.9.3.2 Real option modeling

ROT analysis has a number of methodologies to calculate option value; most of them are derived from financial option analysis approaches, such as:

- Black-Scholes model
- Closed-form models
- Partial differential equations
- Multinomial, trinomial, quadrinomial, and binomial lattice approaches

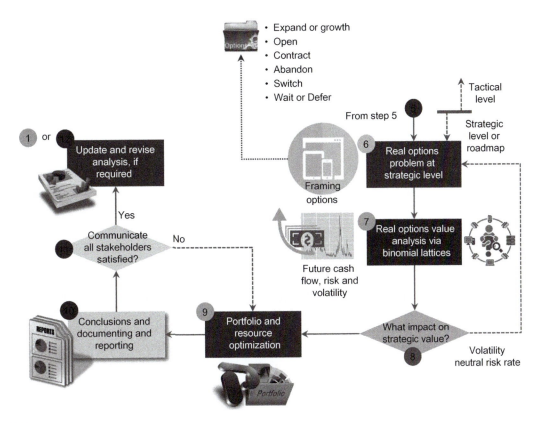

FIGURE 18.31

Strategic level of ROT and MCS analysis process.

In this book, we will focus on the binomial lattice approach only. The reason to adopt this model is that it is easier to visualize, understand and communicate with project sponsors, customers, and many stakeholders. The real option value analysis is the time series–based calculation. The volatility of the future cash flow is basically measured by standard deviation of the logarithmic value on the future revenue stream. However, the initial value or the starting point of ROT analysis is the static NPV (or sNPV) calibrated by Monte Carlo simulation. Overall, it is a three-dimensional calculation of the NPV result, namely time, probability, and optional value (see Figure 18.32).

18.9.3.3 Portfolio and resource optimization

If it is just a single project exercise, this step can be ignored. However if there are multiple projects under one program umbrella, this is a critical step. It coordinates all other projects and makes sure all projects will aim at the common goal. For example, a cloud service provider has set a certain date to launch the new cloud services. It has to upgrade its existing data center facility and IT

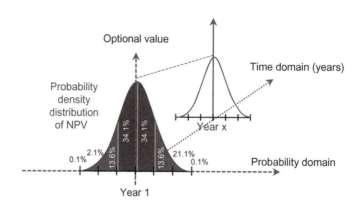

FIGURE 18.32

Real option analysis values.

infrastructure (server, storage, and network) because the expected workload will be increased rapidly in the next few years.

Assume you are a program manager for IaaS (or data center as a service). You might have at least seven cloud infrastructure projects that can bring a strong cash flow stream to your company in the next few years. These projects are:

- Data center facility (space, power, and cooling)
- Service installation and server virtualization
- Storage (NAS and SAN)
- Network
- Cloud application
- Cloud service management
- Leverage other existing cloud service provider's resources

Each project will provide different static and strategic NPV values because of different service prices. It is so important to coordinate all the projects properly when you add different elements of cloud infrastructure capacity via a modular manner (or a federation model). You certainly don't want to see that the network capacity is greater than the ability of the servers or that the provisioning of data center power (PDU and UPS) is behind the server installations in 12 months.

18.9.3.4 Documenting conclusions and recommendations

The result of real option theory calculation and Monte Carlo simulation has to be documented and the final conclusions and recommendations should be provided. It is unacceptable to give ambiguous conclusions or asking for further resources to study unless the business strategy has been changed.

As an IT business analyst or strategic capacity planner, you should provide explicit conclusions and recommendations for a decision maker or decision committee. Most importantly, you have to lay out your assumptions, methodologies, models, and overall framework for your conclusions and recommendations. Without it, no decision maker will take your results seriously.

In order to convince your stakeholders and decision makers, you have to prepare an effective communication plan for your calculation results and conclusions. The concept of MCS is not very straightforward and real option theory is relatively new. There are not many people understand these concepts. Therefore, the calculation of ROT and MCS value is one thing; convincing your stakeholders and decision makers is another thing. Based on previous experience, we believe in the following important points when you make your recommendations as well as documenting your results and conclusion:

- Understand your audience
- Use language that your audience can understand
- Ask and answer the questions that your audience or stakeholders care about the most
- Replace complex mathematical jargon with common terms
- Keep it as simple as possible [or "Keep it simple, stupid" (KISS)]
- Spell out the critical assumptions and cost framework
- Highlight the key conclusions and recommendations (if there more than three bullet points, group them into three)

18.9.3.5 Update and revise

Once the analysis or report has been completed, it doesn't mean it is the end of story. Actually, it is just a starting point. Today, nothing stands still. Everything is evolving. Although we have adopted very sophisticated tools and methodologies to predict future cash flow, they are always subject to upgrade if new information or data becomes available. Subsequently, the calculation results and analysis report as a whole should be periodically reviewed or revised to make sure the overall projects or program are aligned with a company's strategic direction. The recommended period would be between three to six months. It is an iterative process.

18.10 SUMMARY OF MCS AND ROT CONCEPTS

The above process may appear to be quite complex. Actually, it is quite straightforward. If we boil down all 12 steps into very basic elements, we can see there are actually four levels and four feedback loops of the process for MCS + ROT analysis (see Figure 18.33).

- Strategic and subjective
- Strategic and objective
- Tactical and objective
- Traditional and objective

The first step begins at strategic level using many subjective judgments, such as project portfolio selection. There will be many initial decisions and assumptions that are made based on personal experience and intuition. However, if there is enough historic data, the initial decisions and assumptions can refer to the historic data. For example, we can use "Growth," "Forecast," and "Logest" in MS Excel to predict the future cash flow.

Once the key parameters have been decided, the process is moved to the traditional and objective level, which is basically calculating the static or single point of NPV. It is the process of moving from art to science or from top to the bottom. In other words, it is the starting point of checking the decision maker's intuition.

Step 3 has a feedback process mechanism. This means that if the result is too far apart from reality, the inputs of static NPV calculation should be revised. From step 3, the process is moving to the tactical and objective level. This part of the process is basically the Monte Carlo simulation, which is where we replace single point of inputs with probability distribution. At this level, there is also a feedback mechanism to calibrate the inputs of MCS.

The next level of the process is the real option theory analysis. It consists of five steps from steps 6 to 10. This part of the process is to review the dynamic NPV values from a time domain perspective. Actually, it should consist of two components:

- Real option process
- Optimization process

In this book, we will recommend the binomial lattice model for real option theory analysis because it is closely aligned with a decision tree model. The process of this analysis model can be visualized very clearly.

The final part of ROT + MCS is the communication and upgrading process. Overall, the entire process of analysis is moving from the strategic to tactical level and then moving from the tactical level back to the strategic level. It is a "U" processing shape.

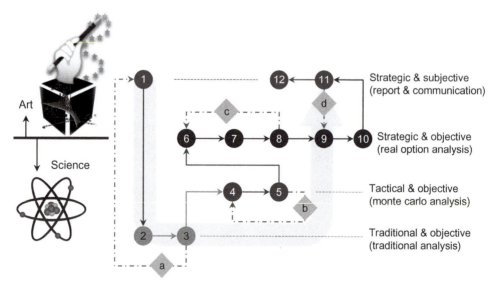

FIGURE 18.33

Summary of MCS + ROT analysis.

18.11 MCS ANALYSIS PROCESS DETAILS

Now, we can use the example in Chapter 17 to calculate both the ROT and MCS value. Based on the last static NPV (sNPV) calculation (see Table 17.15), we should have the results in Table 18.4 for the sNPV result. This is a summary of Table 17.15.

18.11.1 SENSITIVITY ANALYSIS WITH DCF (FIVE-YEAR REVENUE)

We have marked the above NPV value as static NPV or sNPV. This means that it assumes that the future will be fixed. We know this is not true. In order to have a much more realistic assumption in the decision-making process, we have to use a sensitivity analysis. This simply means testing the variation of each variable in the NPV equation during the specified time period. If the period of time (five-year investment term in this case) is fixed, then we will be able to test the variation of future cash flow (or discount cash flow, DCF), interest rate, and initial capex.

In the above case, if we examine these three variables (expected revenue or DCF, interest rate, and initial capex) with $\pm 10\%$ variation for the above base case, we should have Tables 18.5−18.7.

Table 18.4 Base Case Scenario

Year	2014	2015	2016	2017	2018
Expected Revenue ($m)	$24.15	$16.45	$32.20	$40.95	$42.70
Capex ($m) in 5 years ($m)	−$72.8				
If r = 25%, T = 5,					
PV ($m)	$19.32	$10.53	$16.49	$16.77	$13.99
NPV ($m)	$4.30				

Table 18.5 DCF or Future Cash Revenue Sensitivity Test

Year	2014	2015	2016	2017	2018
	$24.15	$16.45	$32.20	$40.95	$42.70
+10%	$2.415	$1.645	$3.22	$4.095	$4.27
Total +10% DCF Increase ($m)	$26.57	$18.10	$35.42	$45.05	$46.97
+10% NPV ($m)	$12.01				
−10%	−$2.415	−$1.645	−$3.22	−$4.095	−$4.27
Total −10% DCF Decrease ($m)	$21.74	$14.81	$28.98	$36.86	$38.43
−10% NPV ($m)	−$3.41				

Table 18.6 Initial Capex Sensitivity Test

Year	2014	2015	2016	2017	2018
Expected Revenue ($m)	$24.15	$16.45	$32.20	$40.95	$42.70
NPV ($m) of +10% Capex −$80.08	−$2.98				
NPV ($m) of −10% Capex −$65.52	$11.58				

Table 18.7 Interest Rate or Internal Return Rate (IRR) Sensitivity Test

Year	2014	2015	2016	2017	2018
Expected Revenue ($m)	$24.15	$16.45	$32.20	$40.95	$42.70
NPV ($m) +10% of IRR = 27.5%	−$0.04				
NPV ($m) of +10% IRR = 22.5%	$9.06				

18.11.1.1 *Change Discount Cash Flow (DCF)* ± *10%*

As we can see, if the future cash flow decreases 10% every year and other variables are not changed, the NPV will be negative (see Table 18.5).

18.11.1.2 *Change initial capex* ± *10%*

The initial capex is one of the controllable items. Later, we will use Monte Carlo simulation to compare the sensitivity of all three variables and see which variable is most sensitive to NPV value. Based on Table 18.6, we find that if the initial Capex is increased 10%, the NPV value will become negative with a result of −$2.98 million.

18.11.1.3 *Change interest rate* ± *10%*

Table 18.7 demonstrates that if the IRR reaches 27.5% or we have a 10% increase, the NPV value will also become negative.

Now, we can summarize all above tables into one table and see the overall picture of the impact of the three variables (see Table 18.8).

Table 18.8 demonstrates that if we vary (10% in this case) one of three variables at any given time and hold the other two variables unchanged, the most sensitive variable is the initial capex value, which has the biggest swing range. This is a good sign or indication because the initial capex is one of the controllable items when we roll out cloud projects.

18.11.2 SENSITIVITY ANALYSIS WITH DIFFERENT SCENARIOS

Scenario analysis tests the NPV value under different circumstances. Here, we just investigate NPV values under the worst, best, and normal scenarios. It holds IRR and initial capex unchanged and investigates the variation of the future revenue income or future cash flow. It is not a minor

Table 18.8 Summary of Sensitivity Test

	Input Values			NPV Calculation Results		
Sensitivity Variable Items	+10%	−10%	Base Case	+10%	−10%	Variation
Initial Capex	−$80.08	−$65.52	−$72.80	−$2.98	$11.58	$14.56
Internal Return Rate (IRR)	27.50%	22.50%	25%	−$0.04	$9.06	$9.09
Future DCF Year 1	$26.57	$21.74	$24.15	$6.24	$2.37	$3.87
Future DCF Year 4	$45.05	$36.86	$40.95	$5.98	$2.62	$3.36
Future DCF Year 3	$35.42	$28.98	$32.20	$5.95	$2.65	$3.30
Future DCF Year 5	$46.97	$38.43	$42.70	$5.70	$2.90	$2.80
Future DCF Year 2	$18.10	$14.81	$16.45	$5.36	$3.25	$2.11

Table 18.9 Scenario Sensitivity Test

Year	2014	2015	2016	2017	2018
Normal Case ($m)	$24.15	$16.45	$32.20	$40.95	$42.70
Worst Case ($m) −50%	$12.08	$8.23	$16.10	$20.48	$21.35
Best Case ($m) +50%	$36.23	$24.68	$48.30	$61.43	$64.05
	NPV	Probability			
Normal NPV ($m)	$4.30	50%			
Worst NPV ($m)	−$34.25	30%			
Best NPV ($m)	$42.85	20%			

adjustment but rather a radical change of the future DCF, such as −50% or +50%. This analysis will provide a subjective evaluation; different probabilities may occur (see Table 18.9).

If we assign different probabilities (50% for normal, 30% for worst, and 20% for best) to each scenario, we will achieve a so-called expected value:

$$\text{Expected NPV} = 4.3 \times 50\% + (-34.25) \times 30\% + \$42.85 \times 20\% = \textbf{\$0.44 million}$$

Of course, we can assign any value of probabilities (10%, 25%, or 65% …) to different scenarios. It is subject to personal intuition or experience. If you don't have enough experience for a particular market, such as the cloud service market, you adopt a trial and error method to verify and make sure the expected value makes sense for the MCS analysis.

Now, the issue we face is that all probabilities are decided subjectively. Which NPV is the right one, $4.3 million or $0.44 million? In order to resolve this issue, we can probably borrow the tool of Monte Carlo simulation (MCS). Of course, there are other methods available to solve the same problem, but based on our discussion in the Section 18.7.4.1 about what MCS is good for, the MCS tool is best fit for this issue.

18.11.3 MONTE CARLO SIMULATION (MCS) ANALYSIS

How can we run MCS? Based on the sensitivity analysis, we can have two types of MCS analysis:

- Scenario MCS (radical sensitivity)
- Normal case MCS (general sensitivity)

Actually, each type of MCS will have different model systems (see Figure 18.16). The first type simulates the NPV under a radically changing environment, simulate the sensitivity of radical assumption changes. The second one simulates the NPV value under a small range of variation (or general sensitivity). In our case, the standard deviation is only 10%. In the following example, we will first simulate the radical sensitivity or scenario case of MCS, looking at the best, normal, and worst case scenarios.

18.11.3.1 Scenario MCS (Radical Sensitivity)

The model system for scenario MCS is to adopt a triangular distribution with worst, normal, and best case scenarios as input parameters into the simulation model. We can design our own Monte Carlo Simulation system with MS Excel (generate samples) or the R program.

In order to save time on coding, we just use the existing proprietary software package, Crystal Ball. It is provided by Oracle. Of course, it has to be used in conjunction with MS Excel. People can download a free trial version from the Oracle website [282] for 15 days. Crystal Ball is one of the most common and popular software packages among many enterprises and government agencies. It is a good tool for capital budgeting and the decision-making process.

Once you are familiar with this application software, it is quite easiy to generate an MCS result. The process steps are:

- First, we define the assumptions (MCS probability distribution model = Triangular, Worst = −34.25, Normal = 4.3 and Best = 42.85) (see Table 18.9).
- Second, we define the forecast (income revenue or cash flow in the next five years).
- Third, we run the simulation with a certain number of trials (in this case = 10,000).

From Figure 18.34, we can see that the simulation result of the NPV value range ($53.42m from −22.56 to 30.86) is quite large with 90% certainty. In other words, if you want a 90% confidence level of NPV value, the possible NPV will vary from −22.56 to + 30.86. From such a large range of NPV values, it would be impossible for a decision maker to make the right decision. However, Figure 18.35 does provide some kind of certainty, with an almost 60% chance that the NPV will be greater than zero. In order to obtain a desirable certainty for decision making, we have to use the second model system of MCS or normal case MCS.

18.11.3.2 Normal case MCS (General Sensitivity)

The second model system of MCS focuses on two components of the MCS model system:

- Initial capex
- Internal return rate (IRR)

We assume both IRR and initial capex have 10% standard deviation. In other words, the variation of initial capex will be between $80.08m and $65.52m and IRR will be between 22.50% and

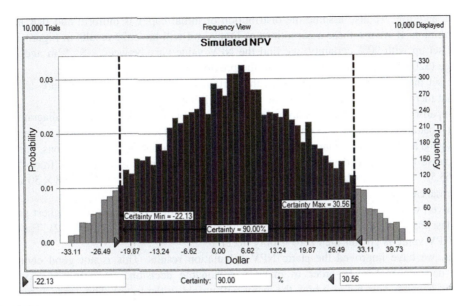

FIGURE 18.34

Simulate NPV with triangular distributed model system (90% certainty).

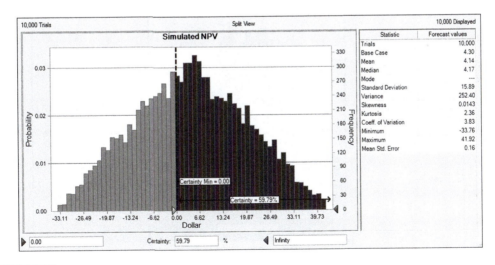

FIGURE 18.35

MCS NPV greater than 0: certainty = 59.82%.

27.5%. In addition, we also assume the distribution of initial capex is uniform and IRR has a normal distribution. If we use these assumptions as inputs, we will have the results in Figure 18.36.

If we set up with 90% certainty, we find the NPV value vary between −$5.52m and $14.69m. This range ($20.21m) is much narrower than the previous one ($53.42m).

If we set the minimum NPV value = 0, the certainty will be 75.23% (see Figure 18.37). This means that there is a75.23% chance that the project will have a positive NPV.

In comparison with Table 18.8, the normal case MCS cannot only build a visualized diagram for communication but also provide clear certainty for a decision maker. However, we must be aware that MCS is only as good as its assumption inputs. Again, it comes back to the subjective assumptions. For example, if we increase the standard deviation of the initial capex range from 10% to 50% (from " −$80.08 and −$65.52" to "−$109.2m (= 72.8 + 72.8 × 50%) and −$36.4m (= 72.8 − 72.8 × 50%)" in the above normal case, we can see the certainty will be decreased (see Figure 18.38).

Moreover, we find the expected NPV distribution value will become flat (the highest probability value is less than 0.03 and the max and min variation is $100.81 rather than $42.32). The certainty that the NPV value is greater than zero is only 56.21%.

So far, we have improved the static NPV calculation results. This is not good enough for a strategic decision maker. In order to make a reasonable decision, we will not only want to know what happens now but also how the event will unfold in the future. This leads to real options theory (ROT).

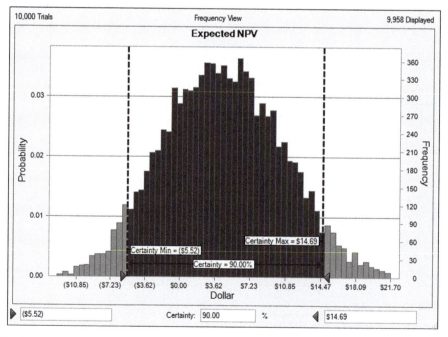

FIGURE 18.36

Normal case MCS NPV with 90% certainty.

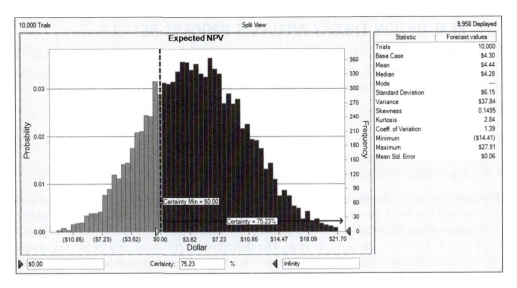

FIGURE 18.37

Normal case MCS (capex variation $\pm 10\%$) for NPV > 0.

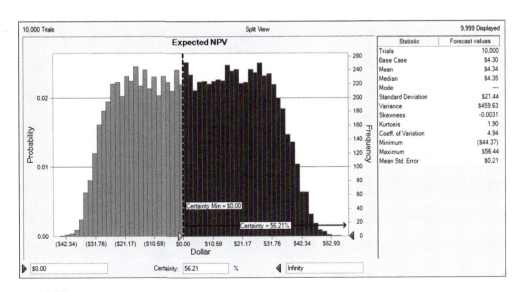

FIGURE 18.38

Normal case MCS with increased initial capex variation = $\pm 50\%$ for NPV > 0.

18.12 REAL OPTION THEORY ANALYSIS PROCESS DETAILS

In Section 18.10.2.2, we briefly mentioned four different approaches to analyze an option value, but these approaches are very special in nature and difficult to explain or communicate. In contrast, binomial lattices are easy to be calculate, process, and communicate. The key advantages of binomial lattices are:

- Visible
- Highly flexible
- Aligned with decision tree model
- Fit with geometric or exponential Brownian motion model

However, one of the disadvantages of binomial lattices is that the technique will require considerable time and computer power to calculate the result if there are many time steps. Fortunately, if the calculation of the binomial lattice only needs a few time steps, such as three or five time steps or years, it will become a manageable task. The definition of binomial lattices is very simple. It consists of a number of events in a lattice. For example, a three time-step binomial lattice has a total of 10 nodes (see Figure 18.39).

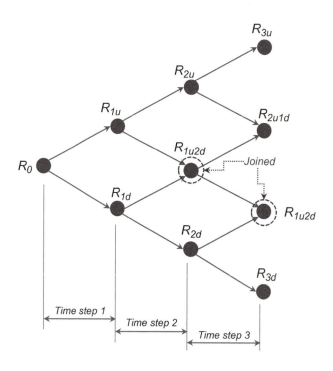

FIGURE 18.39

Three-time-step binomial lattice with joined nodes.

As we can see, R_0 is the starting point of the real option value at time 0. R_{1u} stands for one real option value up at time step 1 and R_{1d} means one real option value down at time step 1. It is quite easy to infer the rest of the values in the binomial lattice. Also, the model should create two option values for each node until the end of the lattice (starts from R_0). By the binomial lattice theory, each node can also not be joined (see Figure 18.40). This model is only applied for two or more stochastic underlying variables.

In this book, we will only focus on a real option analysis process using the approach of a binomial lattice with joined nodes (see Figure 18.38). Before moving onto the details of the real option analysis process, let's clarify the basic tool of this approach, namely the binomial lattice or binomial tree.

18.13 REAL OPTION THEORY PROCESS EQUATIONS

In comparison with geometric Brownian motion (GBM), a binomial lattice is a simplified and discrete model. It was initially developed by Cox et al. [283] in order to simplify the Black-Scholes partial differential equation (PDE) model to evaluate derivatives. It doesn't require calculus. It converges to GBM or exponential Brownian motion (EBM) when the time step (Δt) tends to zero.

The essence of the Cox model has three basic components or equations:

1. Up option value: $u = e^{\sigma\sqrt{\Delta t}}$
2. Down option value: $d = \frac{1}{u} = e^{-\sigma\sqrt{\Delta t}}$
3. Risk neutral transitional probability: $p = \frac{e^{r\Delta t} - d}{u - d}$

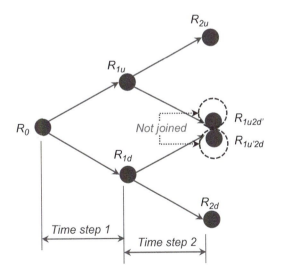

FIGURE 18.40

Two-time-step binomial lattice with nonjoined nodes.

Here, the term "risk neutral transitional probability" mean the "r" (or interest rate) is supposed to be a constant or unchanged. If the rate does change, the probability will compensate for it.

Furthermore, the letter "σ" stands for volatility or standard deviation and Δt means the time step. The unit of time step is normally one year. You can also assume six months. It is dependent on your ROT assumptions.

If we use a diagram to illustrate Cox's binomial lattice model, we get Figure 18.41.

Remember that real option theory (ROT) was derived from financial option theory. Therefore, many books or papers use the symbol "S" to stand for stock option. This book adopts the letter "R" meaning real option. In addition, there are two points that we have to emphasize for the above three equations:

1. The volatility (σ) is the key. If σ is equal to zero (σ = 0), then there will be no real option values. It will become a static NPV value (see Figure 18.42). In other words, the model will collapse and become a one line a linear model. Notice that the R_0 value is based on R_{1u}, R_{1d}, and probability. This implicates the backwards calculation process.
2. From the GBM or EBM equation $\frac{dR}{R} = e^{\mu\sqrt{\Delta t}+\sigma\sqrt{\Delta t}}$, we know that the differential equation has two components: the first component, $e^{\mu(\Delta t)}$, will determine the slope or growth rate and the second component, $e^{\sigma\sqrt{\Delta t}}$, will simulate the local motion of the binomial lattice "u" (up) and "d" (down) (see Figure 18.43).

18.13.1 IMPLEMENT THE REAL OPTION VALUE CALCULATION PROCESS

Once we understand all the ROT processing equations shown above, we should be able to implement the real option value calculation process. Let's use the above example to calculate the real option result.

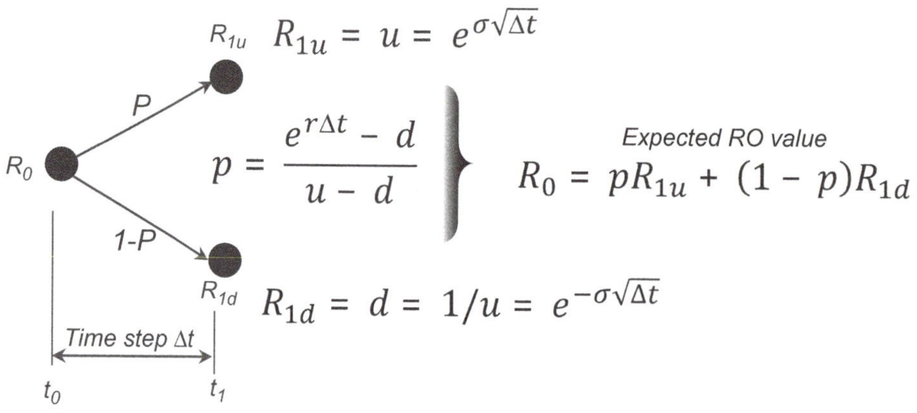

$$R_{1u}\ R_{1u} = u = e^{\sigma\sqrt{\Delta t}}$$

$$p = \frac{e^{r\Delta t} - d}{u - d}$$

Expected RO value

$$R_0 = pR_{1u} + (1 - p)R_{1d}$$

$$R_{1d}\ R_{1d} = d = 1/u = e^{-\sigma\sqrt{\Delta t}}$$

Time step Δt

t_0 t_1

FIGURE 18.41

Cox's binomial lattice model.

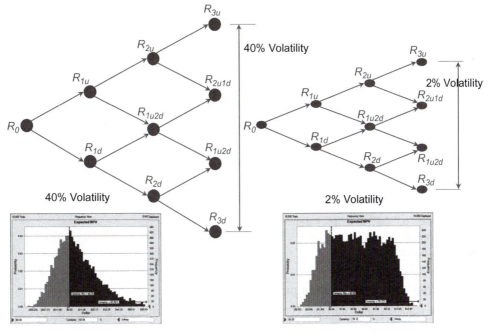

FIGURE 18.42

Volatility of binomial lattice model.

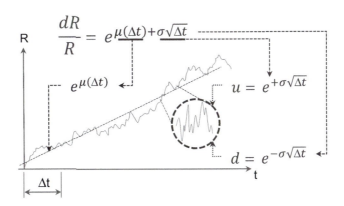

FIGURE 18.43

Implication of GBM or EBM equation.

Assume the web portal company in Chapter 17 is trying to decide on strategic options to predict its IT investment projects. Particularly, it has three strategic options:

- Expanding its current operations
- Contracting its overseas operation
- Abandoning part of its capex program or one of its projects

Before the calculation process, we need to know some initial data or assumptions for this web portal company. Based on the above sNPV calculation, we should have the initial optimistic value (or best scenario) of sNPV, $R_0 = \$42.85m$ (see table 18.9). The risk neutral rate $r = 0.05$ or 5%, and the forecast volatility of future revenue income is 20%. The time span is five years. Subsequently we should have a "u" and "d" value based on the Cox binomial lattice model:

The calculation process can be divided into three steps:

1. Calculate the "u," "d," and "p" values
2. Forward process
3. Backward induction process

18.13.1.1 Step 1: Binomial lattice process

For step 1, we calculate the "up" and "down" coefficient values due to the GBM or Cox's model volatility and then calculate the probability value. The calculation itself is very simple. We should have the following results for "u," "d," and "p":

$$u = e^{\sigma\sqrt{\Delta t}} = 1.221403 \text{ and } d = e^{-\sigma\sqrt{\Delta t}} = 0.818731 \text{ and } p = \frac{e^{r(\Delta t)} - d}{u - d} = 0.577493$$

Here, $\sigma = 20\%$, $\Delta t = 1$ and $r = 0.05$.

18.13.1.2 Step 2: forward process

Step two involves deciding on the transitional option value at each node (see Figure 18.44). This step is also quite straightforward, as we directly multiply the "up" or "down" optional coefficient value and the sNPV or R_0. The number of times to multiply the coefficient value is dependent on the position of the node in the binomial lattice or time stes. For example, R_{5u} means the node has five time steps and we should multiply the up coefficient five times (power of 5). If the node is R_{3u1d}, we should multiply 3 "up" coefficients and 1 "down" coefficient because the node is at time step 4. Remember the number of "ups" plus the number of "downs" is equal to the total number of time steps.

18.13.1.3 Step 3: backward induction process

Step 3 is the final step in calculating the final real option value. This is the expected real option value that has taken into consideration the risk neutral rate. We start from the final time step of the node and calculate the expected value for the previous time step (see Figure 18.45). Although the calculation process is very tedious, it is very simple.

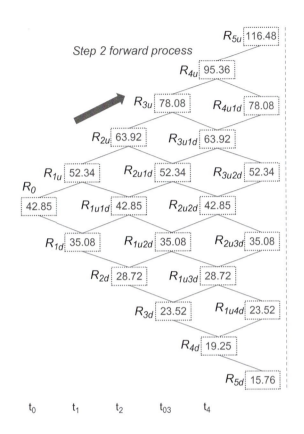

Step 2 forward process

R_{5u} 116.48

R_{4u} 95.36

R_{3u} 78.08 R_{4u1d} 78.08

R_{2u} 63.92 R_{3u1d} 63.92

R_{1u} 52.34 R_{2u1d} 52.34 R_{3u2d} 52.34

R_0

42.85 R_{1u1d} 42.85 R_{2u2d} 42.85

R_{1d} 35.08 R_{1u2d} 35.08 R_{2u3d} 35.08

R_{2d} 28.72 R_{1u3d} 28.72

R_{3d} 23.52 R_{1u4d} 23.52

R_{4d} 19.25

R_{5d} 15.76

t_0 t_1 t_2 t_{03} t_4

FIGURE 18.44

Binomial lattice forward process (step 2).

As we can see in Figure 18.45, the R_0 value has been increased from $42.85m to $55.02m. In comparison with the initial sNPV or the R_0 value, this is an extra added value of $12.17m. This is the strategic real option value, which is due to future volatility and uncertainty. Based on this calculation of the real option result, a decision maker will have the following decision options

- If the real option value is above $40m, the project or business should be opened.
- If the real option value is greater than $60m, the project or business should be expanded by 50% and the expansion cost will be $10m (either via acquisition or a capex program)
- If the real option value is above $30m but below $40m, it should be contracted by 50% and the cost savings for the contraction is $20m.
- If the real option value is below $30m, the project or business should be abandoned and sold to other companies that are managing their business.

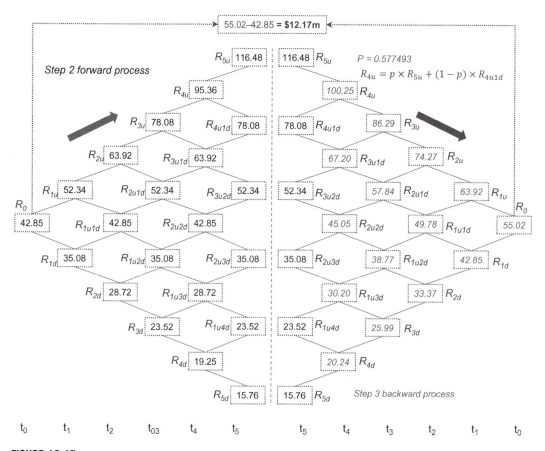

FIGURE 18.45

Binomial lattices backward process (step 3).

For the R_{5u} node, the recalculated expanded real option value is equal to R_{5u} (expanded 50%) $= 1.5 \times 116.48 - 20 = \$154.72$. If the real option value of a node is greater than \$40 but less than \$60, the node will be kept open. If the real option value is less than \$40 but greater than \$30, the option value should be contracted. Taking R_{2u3d} as an example: R_{2u3d} (Contract) $= 35.08 \times 0.5 + 20 = \$37.54$. As the real option value is less than 30, the option is abandoned. The recalculation of each node is quite easy (see Figure 18.46).

This example has illustrated that real option analysis is a good tool for project investment planning, especially for a cloud computing project because the cloud investment environment is very volatile. This volatility has created a strategic value for a cloud investment project.

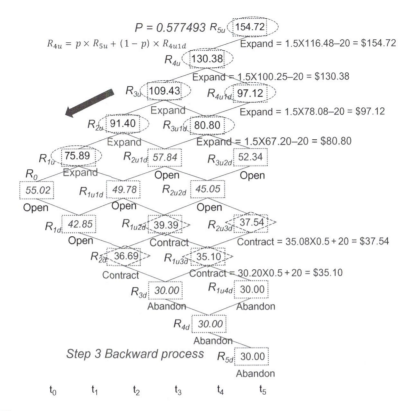

$$P = 0.577493 \quad R_{5u} \boxed{154.72}$$
$$R_{4u} = p \times R_{5u} + (1-p) \times R_{4u1d}$$
Expand = 1.5X116.48–20 = \$154.72
$$R_{4u} \boxed{130.38}$$
Expand = 1.5X100.25–20 = \$130.38
$$R_{3u} \boxed{109.43} \quad R_{4u1d} \boxed{97.12}$$
Expand
Expand = 1.5X78.08–20 = \$97.12
$$R_{2u} \boxed{91.40} \quad R_{3u1d} \boxed{80.80}$$
Expand
Expand = 1.5X67.20–20 = \$80.80
$$R_{1u} \boxed{75.89} \quad R_{2u1d} \boxed{57.84} \quad R_{3u2d} \boxed{52.34}$$
Expand   Open   Open
$$R_0$$
$$\boxed{55.02} \quad R_{1u1d} \boxed{49.78} \quad R_{2u2d} \boxed{45.05}$$
Open   Open   Open
$$R_{1d} \boxed{42.85} \quad R_{1u2d} \boxed{39.39} \quad R_{2u3d} \boxed{37.54}$$
Open   Contract   Contract = 35.08X0.5 + 20 = \$37.54
$$R_{2d} \boxed{36.69} \quad R_{1u3d} \boxed{35.10}$$
Contract   Contract = 30.20X0.5 + 20 = \$35.10
$$R_{3d} \boxed{30.00} \quad R_{1u4d} \boxed{30.00}$$
Abandon   Abandon
$$R_{4d} \boxed{30.00}$$
Abandon
Step 3 Backward process $$R_{5d} \boxed{30.00}$$
Abandon

$t_0 \qquad t_1 \qquad t_2 \qquad t_3 \qquad t_4 \qquad t_5$

FIGURE 18.46

Strategic choices based on real option values.

However, there are many assumptions that have to be made during the process of ROT analysis, such as volatility value, thresholds of different real option values, etc. These assumptions are subject to time of project delivery, technology development, cloud market climate, management skill, and other uncertainties. Again, the real option approach is a combination of subjective assumptions and objective mathematic calculation. In essence, real options analysis can only add in value in the following situations:

- When the project is uncertain.
- The project environment is very volatile. Actually, the more volatile the environment, the greater the value of the real option (or strategic value) is.
- The decision maker must be flexible and prepare for changes.
- Management should have a strategic view and be willing to execute rational strategies.

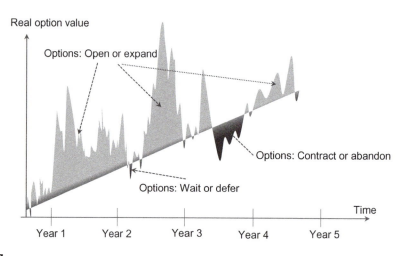

FIGURE 18.47

Example of overall picture for project environment over five years.

Real option analysis doesn't only provide calculable, flexible, and strategic NPV values for a decision maker, but also illustrates the overall picture or project environment when a certain strategy is executed. It gives an opportunity for a decision maker to optimize the strategic choices or options and respond to the real world and the ever-changing environment (see Figure 18.47).

"To create a good analogy, real option analysis is a strategic road map that can direct a decision maker through unfamiliar territory" [284].

Of course, we can't trust ROT and MCS blindly. As we have indicated before, ROT and MCS analysis is only as good as its inputs and its assumptions. For example, if the model system is not good enough, the MCS result will be useless. Likewise, if the threshold level of the option value is inadequate, the decision to "expand," "open," "contract," "switch," or "abandon" may result in bad consequences. That is why people often say real option analysis is part science and part art.

Here, we have only tried the binomial lattice approach. There are many other models or approaches to calculate real option values, such as partial different equations (PDE) and closed-form solutions, which are also very popular. Readers can adopt these models and run a trial for the ROT calculation process.

At the beginning of this book, we raised the questions "How can we measure the sky?" and "Why is this so important?" Throughout this book, we have basically answered these questions. The bottom line of the first question is building a cost model or framework for the cloud computing business and the essence of the second question is how to apply the cloud cost model to the decision-making process.

The methods of measuring the sky can be classified into two different approaches or two different levels based on different circumstances:

1. The tactical level of cost modeling, where we build a cloud cost model with multiple layers.
   Normally, this is suitable for the purpose of IT opex cost reduction. For many large organizations,

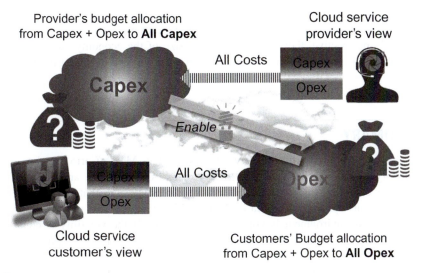

FIGURE 18.48

Significance of cloud computing.

IT infrastructure is often shared by many internal line of business (LoB) units. The IT expenditures (both capex and opex) have no direct relationship with the business revenues contributed by each LoB unit. The method of IT budget allocation (or cost modeling) has no other alternative other than adopting the industry benchmark across all LoB units. As a result, the cost model is built up from the bottom and layer by layer. It can be considered a tactical level of cost modeling. From a cloud service consumers' perspective, cloud cost modeling can help them understand that the cloud environment can shift IT capex to opex. Vice versa, from the cloud service providers' perspective, cloud cost modeling can shift IT opex to capex.

2. Strategic level of cost modeling, which consists of both MCS and ROT modeling. Actually, MCS checks subjective assumptions or personal intuition. It replaces a single point of NPV with a certain probability distribution. ROT is the extension of static NPV. The strategic value of ROT analysis is built up on future volatility or risk. The higher the volatility is, the higher strategic value we can achieve. As a matter of fact, the static NPV is a special case of ROT model when the volatility value "σ" is equal to zero. We often use MCS + ROT to analyze revenue-based cloud projects or project portfolios during the investment decision process.

Of course, we can also combine both tactical and strategic cost modeling for any cloud (business) environment, to measure the sky. The result of this cost modeling can assist decision makers in making the right cloud investment decision at the right time.

The significant point of cloud computing is that a cloud environment can enable a cloud services consumer's budget allocation to be shifted from capex + opex to almost all opex. Vice versa, it can also enable the cloud services provider's budget allocation to be moved from capex + opex to almost all capex (see Figure 18.48).

From a cloud service consumer's perspective, they shift the risks of inefficient or idle IT infrastructure capacity to the cloud service providers via the cloud mechanism of PAYG. From a cloud service provider's perspective, they can leverage the size of the economy and their knowledge of cloud computing and run the cloud infrastructure with a very competitive cost model.

18.14 SUMMARY

Within this chapter, we mainly discussed two topics, namely Monte Carlo simulation (MCS) and real option theory (ROT). We began with a history of real option theory and laid out the different real options. The essence of ROT is that it has the strategic value that the traditional NPV (or sNPV) calculation can't provide. The reason behind this strategic value creation is that the nature of the future business environment is volatile and uncertain. If the volatility is equal to zero, the real option or strategic value will collapse to zero. In other words, the real option value should be equal to the static NPV value.

From a geometric Brownian motion (GBM) or EBM equation perspective, we can see that real option analysis or the second component of the equation $e^{\pm\sigma\sqrt{\Delta t}}$ mainly resolves the issue of "local motion." It will not change the final result of the strategic option value or disproportionally add extra value to NPV. In other words, the second component of $e^{\pm\sigma\sqrt{\Delta t}}$ or the volatility variation will have no impact on the final strategic NPV value R_0, but it adds a proportional amount of sNPV to the final strategic NPV. However, we have to indicate that this component or volatility variation will change the optiol value of R_{ud} within the binomial lattice.

The main driver behind the final strategic real option value is the neutral risk rate. Referring to Figure 18.9, we have four projects, A, B, C, and D. If we assume the traditional NPV values, volatility, and neutral risk rate of each project are as shown in Table 18.10, we should have the results seen in Figures 18.49 and 18.50.

It makes sense that the higher the risk is, the more reward you will get. However, we have to be aware that the extra strategic value can also go south or downwards. Remember that Brownian motion is symmetric. That is why the extra strategic value is closely related to neutral risk rate rather than volatility. The extra strategic value can be considered a long-term trend. It has been resolved by MCS.

Table 18.10 The Main Drivers behind the Final Strategic NPV

Project ID	sNPV ($m)	Volatility	U	D	P	Neutral Risk Rate	Final Strategic NPV R_0	Extra Value ($m)
Project A	90	20%	1.22	0.82	0.58	0.05	115.6	25.6
Project B	60	40%	1.49	0.67	0.60	0.15	127.0	67.0
Project C	50	50%	1.65	0.61	0.53	0.15	105.9	55.9
Project D	100	10%	1.11	0.90	0.53	0.01	105.1	5.1

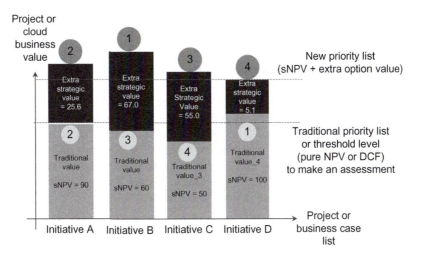

FIGURE 18.49

Project priority reshuffle with extra strategic option values.

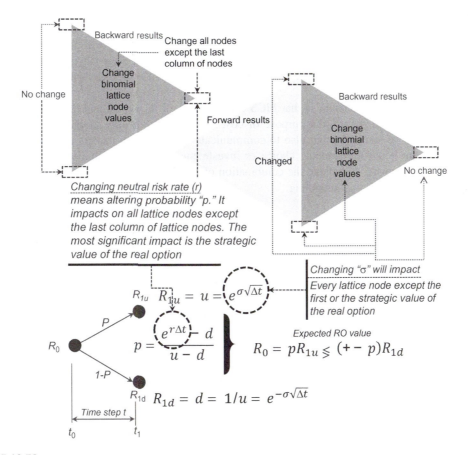

FIGURE 18.50

Consequence of changing "r" and "σ".

On the topic of MCS, we first discussed the history and concept of MCS and then gave two typical examples that demonstrated how to run a MCS process. Moreover, we highlighted the pros and cons of different types of MCS. The essence of MCS is the model system.

After all the foundational work, we provided a process flow chat to show how to calculate the real option value by combining both MCS and ROT. Of course, MCS can be independently implemented. In the example, we provided two different types of MCS or two different types of model systems. In order to save programming time, we adopted the Oracle Crystal Ball software package in conjunction with MS Excel to run MCS. With Oracle Crystal Ball, two different types of model system inputs mean two different sets of defined assumptions:

1. The first simulation simulates the worst, normal, and best case scenarios. The defined assumption or MCS model system is triangular.
2. The second simulation simulates the normal case with an assumed standard deviation. The defined assumption or MCS model system is normal distribution.

The MCS method provides the most likely or possible scenario at a point of time based on sNPV value. It only provides the possibility for a certain threshold level, such as the likelihood or probability of the event that the sNPV is greater than zero. It is not an overall picture or a strategic roadmap for a decision maker if the external conditions have been changed. In order to have a strategic roadmap, we have to use the ROT process. Therefore, MCS outputs will become the inputs to the ROT process. In comparison with the sNPV process, MCS replaces a single point with probability distributions or model systems and lets nature decide the result rather than artificial selection or assumptions.

One of the biggest advantages is that MCS can simulate all the inputs and demonstrate a visual result. As we indicated before, the purpose of cost modeling is not only to check an individual's intuition or to prove some idea but also to communicate with decision makers or stakeholders and to convince them about the strategic choice or investment. Of course, binomial lattices also have this feature. That is why we believe the combination of MCS and ROT (binomial lattices) is one of the better tools for cloud cost modeling.

18.15 REVIEW QUESTIONS

1. Why do we say that a traditional finance capital budgeting tool, such as sNPV, is insufficient for a cloud investment project or program?
2. What are the key factors that will impact on MCS results?
3. What are the pros and cons of the MCS method?
4. When should I avoid adopting the MCS method?
5. Does the MS Excel RAND() function generate real random numbers? If not, why?
6. If one cloud investment project predicts future cash flow, IRR, and initial capex as shown in Table 18.11 and if the standard deviation for both IRR and initial capex is 40%, what is the certainty that the NPV is greater than zero? (Answer: 78.34%, the MCS result. See Figure 18.51. Hint: Use uniform distribution for capex and normal distribution for IRR.)

Table 18.11 MCS Process Problem

	T = 0 (Initial Capex)	T = 1	T = 2	T = 3	T = 4	T = 5
Forecast Revenue and Initial Capex	−$100	25	40	35	30	70
IRR	20%					
sNPV	$11.46					

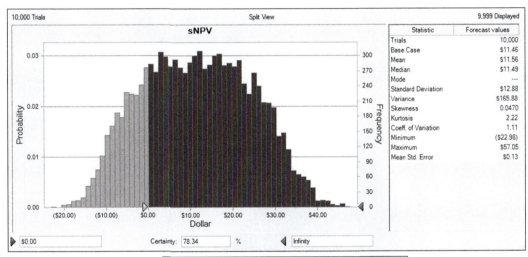

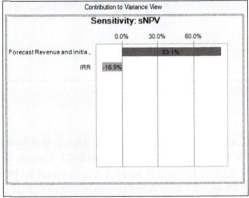

FIGURE 18.51

Sensitivity for volatility of 40% initial capex.

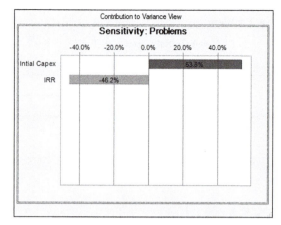

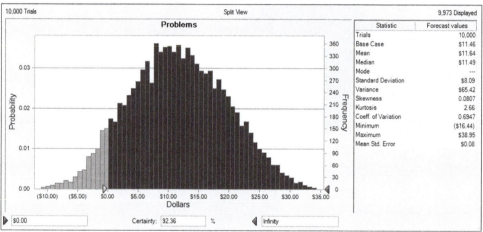

FIGURE 18.52

Sensitivity and MCS result for initial capex volatility = 20%.

7. Based on problem 6, with sNPV value = $11.46, what is the final strategic value and extra added value for sNPV via the binomial lattice method? Assume the risk neutral rate = 5%. (Answer: $14.71 and $3.25.) If the risk neutral rate is equal to 10%, what is the final strategic value? (Answer: $18.89 and $7.43.) What is sensitivity of initial capex and IRR? (Answer: initial capex = +83.6% and IRR = 16.4%; see Figure 18.51.) If the volatility of initial capex is reduced to 20%, what is the sensitivity of initial capex and IRR? (Answer: initial capex = 53.8% and IRR = −46.2%; see Figure 18.52.)

APPENDICES

APPENDIX A CATALOGUE OF MAJOR IT PROJECT CATASTROPHE

	Year	Company	Outcome (Costs in US$)	Value
1	1992	Budget Rent-A-Car, Hilton Hotels, Marriott International and AMR(American Airlines)	Travel reservation system cancelled after $165million is spent	$165
2	1993	Greyhound Lines Inc.	Bus reservation system crashes repeatedly upon introduction, contributing to revenue loss of $16 million	$61
3	1993	London Ambulance Service [UK]	Dispatch system cancelled in 1990 at $11.25 million, second attempt abandoned after deployment, costing $15 million	$26
4	1993	Allstate Insurance Co.	Office automation system abandoned after deployment, cost $130 million	$130
5	1993	London Stock Exchange [UK]	Taurus stock settlement system cancelled after $600 million is spent	$600
6	1994	Chemical Bank	Software error causes a total of $15 million to be deducted from 100,000 customer accounts	$15
7	1994	State of California	DMV system cancelled after $44 million is spent	$44
8	1994	U.S. Federal Aviation Administration	Advanced automation system cancelled after $2.6 billion is spent	$2,600
9	1995	Toronto Stock Exchange [Canada]	Electronic trading system cancelled after $25.5 million is spend	$26
10	1996	FoxMeyer Drug Co.	$40 million ERP system abandoned after deployment, forcing company into bankruptcy	$40,000
11	1996	Arianespace[France]	Software specification and design errors cause $350 million Ariane 5 rocket to explode	$350
12	1997	Oxford Health Plans Inc.	Billing and claims system problems contribute to quarterly loss; stock plummets, leading to $3.4 billion loss in corporate value	$3,400
13	1997	State of Washington	Department of Motor Vehicle (DMV) system cancelled after $40 million is spent	$40
14	1997	U.S. Internal Revenue Service	Tax modernization effort cancelled after $4 billion is spent	$4,000

(Continued)

Continued

	Year	Company	Outcome (Costs in US$)	Value
15	1998	Snap-on Inc.	Problem with order-entry system contribute to revenue loss of $50 million	$50
16	1999	Hershey Foods Corp	Problems with ERP system contribute to $151 million loss	$151
17	1999	State of Mississippi	Tax system cancelled after $11.2 million is spent; state receives $185 million damages	$196
18	1999	United Way	Administrative processing system cancelled after $12 million is spent	$12
19	2000	Washington, D.C.	City payroll system abandoned after deployment costing $25 million	$25
20	1997– 2000	Millennium Experience and the Millennium Dome – UK	Public exhibition, The Millennium Dome in London, UK	$978
21	2001	Kmart Corp.	Supply-chain management system cancelled after $130 million is spent	$130
22	2001	Nike Inc.	Problems with supply-chain management system contribute to $100 million loss	$100
23	2002	CIGNA Corp.	Problems with CRM system contribute to $445 million loss	$445
24	2002	Sydney Water Corp. [Australia]	Billing system cancelled after $33.2 million is spent	$61
25	2002	McDonald's Corp.	The Innovative information-purchasing system cancelled after $170 million is spent	$170
26	2003– 04	AT&T Wireless	Customer relations management (CRM) upgrade problem leads to revenue loss of $100 million	$100
27	2004	Hewlett-Packard Co.	Problems with ERP system contribute to $160 million loss	$160
28	2004	J Sainsbury PLC [UK]	Supply-chain management system cancelled after deployment costing $527 million	$527
29	2004	Ford Motor Co.	Purchasing system abandoned after deployment costing approximately $400 million	$400
30	2004	Avis Europe PLC [UK]	Enterprise resource planning (ERP) system cancelled after $54.5 million is spent	$55
31	2004– 05	UK Inland Revenue	Software error contributes to $3.45 billion tax credit overpayment	$3,450
32	2005	Hudson Bay Co. [Canada]	Problems with inventory system contribute to $33.3 million loss	$33
33	2005		Virtual Case File – Project Trilogy	$170

Continued

	Year	Company	Outcome (Costs in US$)	Value
		Federal Bureau of Investigations (FBI) – USA		
34	2005–2008	Denver Airport Baggage System Case Study	Denver International Airport Baggage Handling System case study	$560
35	2006	Department of Homeland Security – Emerge2 Project – USA	Plans for the Emerge2 system (Electronically Managing Enterprise Resources for Government Efficiency and Effectiveness)	$20
36	2000–2007	Airbus SAS – France	Commercial aircraft development A380	$6,100
37	2006	Canadian Federal Government – Canada	Firearms Registry, Canadian Firearms program	$1,000
38	2006	University of Wisconsin	Payroll and benefits system project is abandoned after 5 years of effort.	$28
39	2006	Department of Defence – Australia	Seasprite Helicopters, Australian Navy first grounds (May 2006) and then scraps (Mar 2008)	$1,000
40	2006	Department for Environment, Food and Rural Affairs (DEFRA) – UK	Single Payment Scheme. Following a European Union agreement to standardize subsidy payments to farmers, DEFRA develops systems to enable payments to UK farms.	$610
41	2007	New South Wales Government – Australia	TCARD, Smart card transit project to allow single ticket across train, ferry and bus transit cancelled after years of delays and cost overruns.	$465
42	2007	Service Personnel and Veterans Agency – UK	JPA (Joint Payroll Administration), new system to unify Army	$100
43	2007	Lufthansa Systems – Germany	FACE (Future Airline Core Environment), new airline passenger reservation system cancelled after 2 years of work.	Undisclosed
44	2007	Social Insurance Agency – Japan	Japanese government admits they can no longer identify the true owners of 50,000,000 pension accounts.	Undisclosed
45	2007	Medical Training Application System – UK	Junior doctors forced to reapply directly to hospitals after a new centralized system for matching doctors and postings disintegrates.	$12
46	2007	American LaFrance – USA	ERP (counting, purchasing, inventory, production, payroll, and finance services), bankruptcy.	Undisclosed
47	2007	Registry Office System – UK	New system to register births, marriages, and deaths across the UK	$12

(Continued)

	Year	Company	Outcome (Costs in US$)	Value
			purchased from a US company and adapted for use in the UK.	
48	2007	State of Wisconsin	EnABLES (Enhanced Automated Benefits Legal Enterprise Services), replacement for a 1970s system used for tracking unemployment claims cancelled after only 1 of 7 phases is successfully completed.	$23
49	2007	Centrica PLC – UK (British Gas)	Jupiter, efforts to combine billing systems for electrical and gas supply into a single system dissolve into a shambles.	$687
50	2007	Los Angeles Unified School District (LAUSD) – USA	New payroll system goes seriously wrong. Some teachers are paid $10,000 for one month's work while others receive just 20¢ for the same job.	$95
51	2007	West Jet – Canada	New passenger reservations system, efforts to implement a new customized reservations system cancelled amid delays and quality concerns.	$34
52	2002– 2007	Government of British Columbia – Canada	Fast ferries, design, build, and deploy high speed ferries	$460
53	2008	Dept. Homeland Security	Railhead, efforts to upgrade existing anti-terror tracking systems run into serious architectural and quality flaws.	$500
54	2008	Edinburgh Fringe Festival (World's largest arts festival)	Implementation of a new online ticketing tool fails the day after production release.	Undisclosed
55	2008	HM Revenue and Customs – UK	Errors in the software and the processes used for handling data result in overpayment of billions of dollars worth of tax credits for parents with children in the United Kingdom.	$5,600
56	2008	Rate Collection Agency – Northern Island	Abbacus, problems with local property tax ("property rates") collection system result in $260M worth of payments going uncollected.	$260
57	2008	Ministry of Defence – UK	Chinook helicopter upgrade, Problems with cockpit software leave 8 Chinook helicopters intended for "specials ops" grounded after 7 years of effort. Maintained in special air-conditioned hangers, the aircraft have never seen operational use.	$1,000
58	2008	Justice Department – Australia	Lack of planning and underestimation cited as a primary contributors to a 9-year delay in the full deployment of the Criminal Justice Enhancement Program	$54

Continued

	Year	Company	Outcome (Costs in US$)	Value
			(CJEP) for use by the Australian Justice department. Costs balloon by 400%.	
59	2008	Transit Ticketing Authority – Melbourne Australia	MYKI, smart card system to allow bus, rail, and tram travel on a single ticket delayed by as much as 5 years and over budget by between $200M and $350M depending on press reports.	$1,500
60	2008	Department for Transport – UK	Program to improve efficiency in the UK's Department of Transport ends up costing more than it saves. By sharing hardware and software services across the department the project was intended to save the organization $114M.	$160
61	2008	US Census Bureau – Field Data Collection Automation (FDCA)	Requiring up to 1 million temporary workers to be hired, trained, deployed, and managed, the US decennial census is one of the world's grandest administrative tasks.	$10,000
62	2008	British Airways – UK	Move of operations into Heathrow Terminal 5 Opening of Heathrow Terminal 5 labeled a fiasco after 28,000 bags get lost and hundreds of flights are cancelled.	$32
63	2008	Waste Management Inc – USA	Enterprise Resource Planning system implementation fails to meet needs.	$100
64	2008	Qantas – Australian airline	"Jetsmart" engineering parts management system is renamed "Dumbjet" by aircraft engineers because the system is so difficult to use.	$40
65	2009	Sydney Water – Australia	Customer Management System, project to modernize and consolidate Sydney Water's Customer Management Systems runs into trouble.	$70
66	2009	Canadian Payments Association – Canada	Truncation and Electronic Cheque Presentment (TECP)	$300
67	2009	London Stock Exchange – UK	After four years of development, but just two years of use, the London Stock Exchange's flagship trading platform (TradElect) is to be decommissioned and replaced.	$68
68	2009	Veterans Affairs – USA	After seven years of development the Veterans Affairs (VA) Replacement Scheduling Application (RSA) is scrapped.	$41
69	2009	The foundation for student life (Oslo) – Norway	As part of a move to SAP the Oslo-based Foundation for Student Life elected to tie the laundry facilities in the	$14

(Continued)

	Year	Company	Outcome (Costs in US$)	Value
			student village into their accounting systems.	
70	2009	US Navy	Marine One, to allow for rapid and safe transport of the President and other VIPs, the US Government maintains a fleet of VIP transport helicopters.	$13,000
71	2009	National Offender Management Service – UK	Integrated offender management system, C-NOMIS, efforts to integrate prison and probation systems from different local authorities into one national system fail.	$375
72	2009	MI5–MI6 – UK	Intelligence sharing system, Scope, reported to be tens of millions of pounds.	$50
73	2009	City of Vancouver – Canada	While we do not often touch on construction projects in this database, a construction project is still a form of technology project.	$250
74	2009	Air Canada	Following more than 3 years of development effort, Air Canada suspends its efforts to implement a next-generation air reservation and departure control system.	$67
75	2010	British Sky Broadcasting (BSkyB)	Customer Relations Management system, Sky CRM Project.	$265
76	2010	City of New York – USA	CityTime, employee time recording, city's new time recording system for employees goes 10 times over budget and is delivered 6 month late.	$540
77	2010	Fire Services – UK	Centralize control over fire dispatch functions, FiReControl	$650
78	2010	Queensland Health – Government of Queensland – Australia	Payroll (ERP) Shared Services Initiative – LATTICE replacement, for 8 years, in an effort to save costs, the Queensland Government initiated a "shared services" program in 2003.	$1,265
79	2010	Dept. Homeland Security – USA	Secure Border Initiative Network, virtual border control system.	$1,000
80	2010	Microsoft – USA	Microsoft's "Kin" phones (Kin one and Kin two) are withdrawn from the market after just two months.	$1,000
81	2010	Dept. of Primary Industries – Governement of Victoria – Australia	Smart meters, costs to deploy smart electrical meters to all households and small businesses in Victoria, Australia balloon from $800M to $2.25B.	$2,250
82	2010	National Health Service – UK	NHS Care Records Service (world's largest civil IT project) Rollout of the Care Records Service component of the UK's National Program for IT grinds to	$24,000

Continued

	Year	Company	Outcome (Costs in US$)	Value
			a halt after pilot sites report significant problems.	
83	2011	Victoria Police Department – Australia	LINK, Law enforcement assistance program, project aimed at implementing a new Law Enforcement Assistance Program to replace an 18 year old system are suspended for 6 months due to technical and cost related issues.	$100
84	2011	J.P. Morgan Chase & Co.	Financial risk analysis tool New Synthetic Credit VaR (Value at Risk) Model, sometimes the mightiest of the mighty is humbled by the meekest of the meek.	$6,000
85	2011	Department of Defence – Australia	Design and development of naval vessels, Australian Defence Minister scraps a $40M project to build 6 new landing craft for use by the Australian Navy.	$40
86	2012	Northern Rock Asset Management UK	Sometimes, the devil really is in the details! With a history dating back to the 1850s, Northern Rock Bank became part of an international news story when in late 2007 the company was engulfed in the subprime mortgage debacle.	$400
87	2012	US Department of Defence – U.S. Air Force	Integrated supply chain and logistics system, Expeditionary Combat Support System (ECSS), deploy and maintain 5,400 high-tech aircraft plus coordinate 330,000 active personnel.	$1,000
88	2012	Project Orca – 2012 US Presidential Campaign	Orca, political campaign – operations management system.	Undisclosed
89	2012	Department of Transport – UK	West Coast Rail Franchise Competition, tendering process for operations of passenger rail system, operated by private companies; the British rail system is divided into a number of distinct regions.	$225
90	2012	Knight Capital – USA	Share trading system. In a story that reminds us of the need for proper testing standards, a software "glitch" at Knight Capital resulted in a $400M loss in just 30 minutes!	$400
91	2012	Sanctuary of Mercy Church – Borja, Spain	Granted, this is the smallest project in the catalog, but it is a good illustration of one of the most basic building blocks	Unknown

(Continued)

	Year	Company	Outcome (Costs in US$)	Value
			of a successful project: the need for people with the right knowledge.	
92	2012	G4S Security Services – UK	Provision of security personnel for the 2012 London Olympic games, 3,500 British military personnel are called in at the last minute to plug gaps.	$60
93	2012	Department of Health – Victoria – Australia	Health SMART, e-health records, efforts to integrate patient health records with functions for financial management, patient management, resource management, and medical image archiving are stopped after the project exceeds its original cost estimates by $240M.	$566
94	2012	US Army – Army Uniforms	Design and deploy new uniforms, Universal Camouflage Pattern (UCP).	$5,000
95	2012	British Home Office – UK	Mobile computing implementation, Mobile Information Programme (MIP), equipping 41,000 British Police Officers with Blackberry devises was intended to cut down on paperwork.	$103
96	2012	Department of Homeland Security – USA	Integrated security system, Project Shield. A project aimed at providing live camera links from police cars and other fixed locations to a central command location fails to achieve the desired results.	$45
97	2012	British Rail – UK	Advanced Passenger Train (APT), design and development of high speed trains.	$150
98	2012	Bristol Aeroplane Company – UK	Bristol Brabazon, aircraft design and development	$350
99	2013	Avon Products – Canada	Product sales and ordering system, the "Promise" project, Ding-dong – Avon calling.	$125
100	2013	Department of Health and Human Services – USA	e-Commerce marketplace, The Affordable Care Act.	Unknown
101	2013	British Broadcasting Corporation – UK	Digital archive, the Digital Media Initiative. Having started operations in 1922, the British Broadcasting Corporation (BBC) is one of the world's oldest and most respected media production and broadcasting organizations.	$100

Continued

	Year	Company	Outcome (Costs in US$)	Value
102	2013	J.C. Penney	Nationwide merchandise pricing strategy, fair and square.	$1,000
103	2013	New Zealand Ministry of Education	Payroll system, Novopay. A 2010 report by accounting firm KPMG shone a spotlight on ineffective project management practices in New Zealand, reporting that a shocking 70% of organizations included in the survey had experienced a failed project over a 12-month period.	$30
104	2013	State of California	Payroll and benefits system, 21st Century Project (MyCalPAYS). As with many large organizations, the state of California has over the years built up a complex interconnected set of IT systems to support their daily operations. Managing multiple systems can however be costly.	$254
105	2013	Marin County	Enterprise Resource Planning system — Accounting package, MERIT (Marin Enterprise Resource Integrated Technology), Marin County (Marin).	$33
106	2013	Boeing Commercial Aeroplanes — USA	Project Name 787 Dreamliner, Project type: Chimerical aircraft development, Time: Between Jan 2003 and Jan 2013.	$23,000
107	2013	State of Minnesota	e-Commerce marketplace, The Affordable Care Act - Mnsure, In Oct 2013, President Obama's Healthcare.gov website caused a stir by becoming the year's biggest troubled IT project story.	$150
108	2013	Australian Federal Government	Personally Controlled Electronic Health Records (PCEHR).	$467
109	2013	Royal Bank of Scotland	30,000 people did not receive social welfare payments.	unknown
110	2013	Deloitte Unemployment System	Project Name: The Department of Unemployment Assistant Project Time: 2007 to 2013.	$114
		Total		$1,740,038m

Continued

APPENDIX B AN EXAMPLE OF BRD TEMPLATE

Business Requirements Document

Project Sponsor_____

Project No:_____

Priority:_____

Target Date: _____

Approved By: _____   Date_____
            Name, Line of Business Unit

Approved By: _____   Date_____
            Name, Line of Business Unit

Prepared By: _____   Date_____

Version No:_____

B.1 BUSINESS REQUIREMENTS DOCUMENT TABLE OF CONTENTS

1. Version Control
   - Revision History
   - Responsible, Accountable, Consulted, and Informated (RACI) or BRD Process Chart
2. External References
3. Glossary
4. Executive Summary
   - Overview
   - Background
   - Objectives
   - Requirements
   - Proposed Strategy
5. Product/Solution Scope
   - Included in Scope
   - Excluded from Scope
   - Constraints
6. Business Case
7. Business Services and Processes
   - Impact of Proposed Changes on Business Services and Processes
   - Business Service and Process Overview Diagrams
   - Business Process Workflow Requirements
   - Business Service Level (Nonfunctional) Requirements
8. Roles and Responsibilities
   - All Parties
   - Business Owners or Sponsors
   - Other Systems
   - Role Map
9. Business Rules
10. State Diagrams
11. Cloud Resource Requirements
    - User Requirements
    - User Task Overview Diagram
    - User Task Descriptions
    - Cloud Service Level (Nonfunctional) Requirements
    - System State Requirements
    - Testing State
    - Disabled State
    - Static Model
    - Static Model: Diagrams
    - Multiplicity Rules Table
    - Entity Documentation

12. Test Plan
    - Quality Assurance Responsibilities
    - QA Standards and Guidelines
    - Review and Audit Plan
    - Quality Records
    - Tools, Techniques, and Methodologies
    - Testing Activities
    - Preparatory Activities
    - White-Box Testing
    - "Fit for Purpose" Testing
    - Nonfunctional Testing
    - User-Acceptance Testing
13. Deployment Plan
    - Training
    - Conversion
    - Scheduling of Jobs
    - Rollout
14. End-User Procedures
15. Post-Implementation Follow-Up
16. Other Issues
17. Sign-Off

APPENDIX C GLOBAL DATA CENTER MAP (100 COUNTRIES AND 3236 DATA CENTERS FOR COLOCATION IN 2014 BASED ON DATACENTERMAP.COM)

Country Name	No.	Country Name	No.	Country Name	No.	Country Name	No.
Angola	1	Finland	12	Lebanon	1	Qatar	3
Argentina	8	France	130	Libya	1	Romania	34
Australia	88	Germany	167	Liechtenstein	3	Russia	38
Austria	17	Gibraltar	3	Lithuania	6	Saudi Arabia	18
Azerbaijan	1	Greece	10	Luxembourg	12	Serbia	2
Bahrain	1	Greenland	1	Macedonia	1	Singapore	20
Bangladesh	1	Guatemala	1	Malaysia	28	Slovakia	14
Belarus	2	Guernsey	3	Malta	8	Slovenia	7
Belgium	29	Guernsey	3	Mauritius	7	South Africa	19
Bolivia	1	Hong Kong	40	Mexico	9	South Korea	4
Brazil	29	Hungary	8	Moldova	1	Spain	49
Bulgaria	20	Iceland	4	Montenegro	1	Sweden	34
Cambodia	3	India	97	Morocco	4	Switzerland	59
Canada	107	Indonesia	32	Nepal	1	Taiwan	4
Cayman Islands	2	Iran	8	Netherlands	1	Thailand	10
Chile	5	Ireland	18	New Zealand	16	The Bahamas	2
China	54	Isle Of Man	2	Nigeria	2	The Netherlands	80
Colombia	4	Israel	4	Norway	17	Turkey	31
Costa Rica	6	Italy	40	Pakistan	10	Ukraine	24
Croatia	2	Japan	38	Palestine	1	United Arab Emirates	7
Cyprus	9	Jersey	5	Panama	3	United Kingdom	210
Czech Republic	17	Jordan	4	Philippines	2	Uruguay	4
Denmark	29	Kenya	2	Poland	27	USA	1266
Egypt	9	Kuwait	1	Portugal	24	Venezuela	1
Estonia	7	Latvia	19	Puerto Rico	1	Vietnam	5

APPENDIX D COMPARISON OF DIFFERENT COST MODELS

	Financial			Multicriteria		Ratio		Portfolio		
	Payback Period	IRR	NPV	Info Economics	SIESTA	Return on Mgmt	IT Assessment	Bedell		Investment Portfolio
Investment Mapping										
Objects of the method	IS proj.	IS proj.	IS proj.	IS proj.	IS proj.	Org. level	IS proj. & org. level	IS proj. & org. level	IS proj.	IS proj. & org. level
Type	All	All	All	IS	IS	ALL	IS	IS	IS	IS
Financial evaluation criteria	Return	Return	Return	Return	unknown	New unit of measure	Profitability	No preference	Return (NPV)	Return (IRR)
Nonfinancial	None	None	None	4 bus., 1 tech. criteria	7 bus., 6 tech criteria	Not clear	Different bus criteria	Quality and importance	Only bus. & IT domain	3 benefits & 3 investment orientation
Risks	Deduction from expectation	Deduction from expectation	Deduction from expectation	1 bus., 3 tech. risks	4 bus., 8 tech. risks	None	None	None		Deduction from expectation
Spread of benefits & sacrifices										
Support evaluation process prescription for use	None	None	None	Discuss example, mention disciplines responsibilities, mention discipline	None	None	None	Evaluation once a yr., mentions discipline more	Discuss	
End of use	Easy	Easy	Easy	Easy & flexible	More difficult	Quite easy, data not for public use	Quite easy, data not for public use	More difficult	Quite easy	Quite easy
Type of outcome	Interval	Interval	Interval	Ordinal	Ordinal	Interval	Several scales	Interval	Ordinal & nominal	Interval

APPENDIX E NINETEEN FREE CLOUD STORAGE OPTIONS (2013 DATA)

Cloud Providers*	Free Cloud Storage Size (GB)	Size 1 (GB)	Price for Size 1	Size 2 (GB)	Price for Size 2	Size 3 (GB)	Price for Size 3	Size 4 (GB)	Price for Size 4	Size 5 (GB)	Price for Size 5
Amazon Cloud Drive (Per Year)	5	20	$10	50	$25	100	$50	200	$100	1,000	$500
Apple iCloud (Per Year)	5	10	$20	50	$100						
Box (per Month)	5	25	$9.99	20	$9.99	1 User	$15	3~500	$Quote	1,000	
Dropbox (per month)	2	100	$9.99	100	$99/y	500	$49.99	500	$499/y	1,000	$795/y
Google Drive (per month)	5	25	$2.49	100	$4.99	200	$9.99	1,000	$49.99	16,000	$799.99
Media Fire (per month)	15	250	$4.5	1,000	$49						
Sky Drive (per Year)	7	20	$10	50	$25	100	$50				
Mimedia (per month)	10	100	$4.99	500	$20	500	$199/y	1,000	$35	1,000	$325/y
Spider Oak (per Month)	2	100	$10	100	$100/y			1,000	$100	1,000	$1,000/y
Sugar Sync (per Month)	5	30	$4.99	30	$49.99/y	60	$9.99	60	$99,99y	500	$39.99
Symform (largest free storage)	10	2,000									
Syncplicity (per Month) By EMC	10	50	$15	Unlimited	$45						
Mega Cloud (per month)	16	100	$9.99	200	$19.99						
Box (per month)	5	1,000	$15	unlimited	Quote						
CX.COM (per month)	10	25	$4.99	50	$9.99	175	$24.99				
Ubuntu One (per month)	5	20	$2.99	20	$29.99/y						
Wuala (per month)	5	20	€2.99	50	€5.99	100	€9.99	200	€19.99	500	€49.99

*Note: A cloud service provider will change its free cloud storage configuration at any time.

APPENDIX F LIST OF DIFFERENT COST MODEL ANALYSIS

No.	Methods	References
1	Accounting Rate of Return	Bacon
2	Analytic Hierarchy Process	Saaty in Carter
3	Application Benchmark Technique	Powell
4	Application Transfer Team	Lincoln
5	Automatic Value Points	Lincoln
6	Balanced Scorecard	Kaplan and Norton
7	Bayesian analysis	Kleijinen
8	Bedell's	Bedell van Reeken
9	Buss's	Buss
10	Benefit/Risk Portfolio	McFarlan and McKenney
11	Benefits assessment grid	Huigen and Jansen
12	Breakeven	Sassone
13	Boundary Value	Farbey
14	Cost/Benefit Analysis	King and Schremes
15	Cost/Benefit Ratio	Yan Tam
16	Cost Displacement/Avoidance	Sassone
17	Cost Effectiveness Analysis	Sassone
18	Cost Value Technique	Joslin
19	Cost Revenue Analysis	Farbey
20	Critical Success Factors	Rockart
21	Customer Resource Lifecycle	Ives and Learmonth
22	Decision Analysis	Sassone Powell
23	Delphi Evidence	Powell
24	Executive Planning for Data Processing	Lincoln
25	Functional Analysis of Office Requirements	Schaeffer
26	Game Playing	Farbey
27	Hedonic Wage Model	Sassone
28	Information Economics	Parker
29	Internal Rate of Return	Breakey and Myers
30	Investment Mapping	Peters
31	Investment Portfolio	Berghout and Meertens
32	Information System Investment Strategies	Lincoln
33	Multiobjective, Multicriteria Methods	Farbey
34	Net Present Value	Brealey and Myers
35	Option Theory	Dos Santos Kambil
36	Payback Time	Brealey and Myers
37	Potential Problem Analysis	Powell
38	Profitability index	Bacon
39	Process Quality Management	Lincoln

Continued		
No.	**Methods**	**References**
40	Quality Engineering	Hochstrasser
41	Return on Investment	Brealey and Myers
42	Return on Management	Strassmann van Nievelt
43	Requirements-Costing Technique	Joslin
44	Schumann's Method	Swinkel and von Irsel
45	SESAME	Lincoln Shorrock
46	Seven Milestone Approach	Silk
47	SIESTA	Irsel
48	Strategic Application Search	Lincoln
49	Strategic Option Generator	Wiseman
50	Systems Investment Methodology	Lincoln
51	Simulation	Kleijnen Farbey Powell
52	Sociotechnical Project Selection	Udo and Guimaraes
53	Satisfaction and Priority Survey	Lincoln
54	Structural Models	Sassone
55	System Dynamics Analysis	Wolstenhome
56	Systems Measurement	Spraque en Carlson Powell
57	Time Savings Times Salary	Sassone
58	User Utility Function Assessment Technique	Powell
59	Value Analysis	Keen
60	Wisesma's Method	Wissema
61	Zero-Based Budgeting	Zmud

APPENDIX G SERVER PRODUCTS PROVIDED BY MAJOR SERVER DIFFERENT VENDORS

G.1 IBM RACK-MOUNTED SERVER

Configurations/Models	IBM System × 3250 M5	IBM System × 3750 M4	IBM Zystem 3850 × 5
No. of CPU Sockets	1 (Intel Core i3)	4 (Xeon E5-4600)	2-4 Xen 2.4GHz
No of Cores	2 or 4	4 or 6 or 8	10
Cache Size	8 MB	200 MB	30MB
Max RAM Size	32 GB	1.5TB	3.0TB
Memory Slots	4	48	64
I/O Slot	2 PCIe 3.0	2 ports of 1GbE & dual 10GbE	10Gbps FC, 10Gbpse
Warranty	3 (9 × 5)	3 (9 × 5)	3 (9 × 5)
Physical Size	1RU	2RU	4RU
Max. Internal Storage	12TB	16TB	4.8TB
Starting Price	$885	$5,375	$7,465

G.2 DELL RACK-MOUNTED SERVER

Configurations/Models	PowerEdge R210 II	PowerEdge R820	PowerEdge R910
No. of CPU Sockets	1 (Xeon, Celeron or Core i3)	4 (Xeon E5-4600)	4 (Xeon 7500)
No. of Cores	2 or 4 core	4, 6, or 8	8 or 10 core
Cache Size	8 MB	2.5MB/per core (Max 20MB)	30 MB
Max RAM Size	16GB	1.5TB	2TB
Memory Slots	4	48	64
I/O Slot	1PCIe 2.0 one × 16	7 PCIe slots	10 PCIe 2.0 + 1 storage slot
Warranty	To be Decided	To be Decided	To be decide
Physical Size	1RU	2RU	4RU
Max. Internal Storage	4 TB	16TB	16TB
Starting Price	$865 ($609)	$6908 ($5,179)	$7,486 ($5,609)

G.3 LENOVO RACK-MOUNTED SERVER

Configurations/Models	Lenovo RD330	Lenovo RD430	Lenovo RD640
No. of CPU Sockets	2 (Xeon E5-2400)	2 (Xeon E5-2400)	2 (Xeon E5-2600)
No of Cores	16	16	24
Cache Size	10 MB L3	15 MB L3	?
Max RAM Size	192GB	192GB	320GB
Memory Slots	12	12	20
I/O Slot	2 PCIe 3.0 1 × 8 & 1 × 16	4 PCIe 3.0	5 PCIe 3.0
Warranty	3 Year (24 × 7)	3 Year	3 Year
Physical Size	1RU	2RU	2RU
Max. Internal Storage	12TB	36TB	32TB
Starting Price	$1,129	$1,729	$1,599

G.4 HUAWEI RACK-MOUNTED SERVER

Configurations/Models	Huawei RH1285	Huawei RH2285	Huawei RH5485
No. of CPU Sockets	1 or 2 (Xeon 5500/5600)	2 (Xeon E5-2400)	4 (Xeon E7 4800)
No. of Cores	2,4 or 6 per socket	4, 6, or 8 per socket	10 per socket
Cache Size	12MB L3	20 MB L3	24MB L3
Max RAM Size	96GB	384 GB	1 TB
Memory Slots	12	12	64

Continued			
Configurations/Models	**Huawei RH1285**	**Huawei RH2285**	**Huawei RH5485**
I/O Slot	One PCIe , ×8	4 PCIe slots	7 PCIe 2.0 10GE, FC HBA
Warranty	To be decided	To be decided	To be decided
Physical Size	1RU	2RU	4 RU
Max. Internal Storage	4TB	38TB	On demand
Starting Price	To be decided	To be decided	To be decided

G.5 ORACLE/SUN ×86 RACK-MOUNTED SERVER

Configurations/ Models	Oracle/Sun X3-2	Oracle/Sun X3-2L	Oracle/Sun X2-8
No. of CPU Sockets	1-2 (Xeon E5-2600)	1-2 (Xeon E5-2600)	2-4 (Xeon E7-8800)
No. of Cores	8 cores per socket	8 cores per socket	8 or 10 cores per socket
Cache Size	32KB L1/256KB L2/20MB L3	32KB L1/256KB L2/20MB L3	128 MB
Max RAM Size	512GB	512GB	4TB
Memory Slots	16	16	32
I/O Slot	4 PCIe 3.0	6 PCIe 3.0	8 PCIe 2.0
Warranty	One year	One year	One year
Physical Size	1 RU	2RU	4 RU
Max. Internal Storage	12 TB	37TB	SSD 4.8TB
Starting Price	$5,296	$6,418	$40,277

G.6 FUJITSU RACK-MOUNTED SERVER

Configurations/ Models	Fujitsu Primergy RX100	Fujitsu Primergy RX300	Fujitsu Primergy RX500
No. of CPU Sockets	1 (Core i3)	2 (Xeon E5-2600)	2 or 4 (Xeon E5-2600)
No of Cores	2 or 4 core	6 cores per socket	4 or 6 or 8 core per socket
Cache Size	8MB	12MB	20 MB
Max RAM Size	32GB	8GB − 1536GB	8 GB − 1536 GB
Memory Slots	4	8	48
I/O Slot	3 PCIe 3.0	7 PCIe 3.0 (5 × 8 & 2 × 16)	9 PCIe 3.0 × 8 + 2 PCIe 3.0 × 16
Warranty	One year	3 year	3 year
Physical Size	1 RU	2 RU	4 RU
Max. Internal Storage	4 TB	18TB	To be decided
Starting Price	To be decided	To be decided	To be decided

G.7 CISCO RACK-MOUNTED SERVER

Configurations/ Models	Cisco UCS c22M3	Cisco UCS c420 M3	Cisco UCS c460 M2
No. of CPU Sockets	1 or 2 (Xeon E5-2400)	4 (Xeon E5-4600)	(Xeon E7-4800)
No. of Cores	4, 6 or 8 per socket	4,6 or 8 per socket	6, 8 or 10 per socket
Cache Size	10, 15 or 20 MB	20 MB	30MB
Max RAM Size	32GB	1.5TB	2TB
Memory Slots	12	48	64
I/O Slot	2 PCIe 3.0	7 PCIe 3.0	10 PCIe 3.0
Warranty	3 year parts	3 year parts	3 year parts
Physical Size	1 RU	2RU	4RU
Max. Internal Storage	1,168GB (8x146GB) 8 HDD	2,336 (16X146GB) 16 HDD	12 HDD
Starting Price	$1,349	$7,837	$8,519

APPENDIX H TIA-942 TELECOMMUNICATION INFRASTRUCTURE STANDARD FOR DATA CENTER TIER

Attributes/ Statistics	Tier 1	Tier 2	Tier 3	Tier 4
Power & Cooling Delivery Paths	1 active	1 active	1 active + 1 passive	2 active
Redundant Components	N	N + 1	N + 1	2 (N + 1)
Support Space to Raised Floor Ratio	20%	30%	$80 \sim 90\%$	100%
Initial Watts/ Square Foot	$20 \sim 30$	$40 \sim 50$	$46 \sim 60$	$50 \sim 80$
Ultimate Watts/Square	$20 \sim 30$	$40 \sim 50$	$100 \sim 150$	150+
Raised Floor Height	12" (307mm)	18"(457m)	$30 \sim 36$" $(762 \sim 914mm)$	$30 \sim 36$"
Floor Loading Pounds/ Square Foot	85(5.98 kg/cm)	100 (7.03 kg/cm)	150 (10.55 kg/cm)	150+
Utility Voltage	208,480	208,480	$12 \sim 15kV$	$12 \sim 15kV$

Continued

Attributes/ Statistics	Tier 1	Tier 2	Tier 3	Tier 4
Utility Entrance	Single feed	Single feed	Dual feed	Dual feed from different substations
Equipment Power Cords	Single cord with 100% capacity	Dual cord with 100% capacity on each cord	Dual cord with 100% capacity on each cord	Dual cord with 100% capacity on each cord
Generator Fuel Capacity	8 hrs. but no generator required if UPS backup time is more than 8 mins	24 hours	72 hours	96 hours
Months to Implement	3	3~6	15~20	15~20
Year First Deployed	1965	1970	1985	1995
Construction $/Square Foot	$450/Square Foot	$600/Square Foot	$900/Square Foot	$1,100 + /Square Foot
	$5,000/Square Meter	$6,520/Square Meter	$9,687/Square Meter	$11,840/Square Meter
Annual IT Downtime Due to Site	28.8 hrs.	22.0 hrs.	1.6 hrs.	0.4 hrs.
Operation Center	Not Required	Not Required	Required	Required
Gaseous Fire Suppression system	Not Required	Not Required	Approved System	Approved System
Site Availability	99.671%	99.749%	99.982%	99.995%

References

[1] Benioff M. Behind the cloud: The untold story of how salesforce.com went from idea to Billion-Dollar Company — and revolutionized an industry. Jossey-Bass; 2009. pp. 2, 10, 136.

[2] Isaacson W. Steve Jobs: The exclusive biography. Little Brown Book Group; 2011. p. 47.

[3] Zairi M. Theory of benchmarking. Butterworth-Heinemann; 2003. p. 12.

[4] Chou T. Cloud: Seven clear business models. Active Book Press, LLC; 2010.

[5] Akerlof G. The market for lemons: Quality uncertainty and the market mechanism. Q. J. Econ. 1970;84 (3):488−500.

[6] Friedman TL. The world is flat: A brief history of the twenty-first century. Farrar, Straus and Giroux; 2006.

[7] Good News in Digital Age. <http://e-vangelie.blogspot.com.au/>.

[8] Gartner's 2013 Hype Cycle for Emerging Technologies Maps Out Evolving Relationship Between Humans and Machines.<http://www.gartner.com/newsroom/id/2575515>.

[9] Carr N. The big switch: Rewriting the world, from edison to google, January. W.W. Norton & Company; 2008.

[10] Carr N. IT doesn't matter, Harvard Business Review, May 2003.

[11] Carr N. Does IT matter, Harvard Business Review Press, April 2004.

[12] Moore GA. Crossing the chasm, marketing and selling high-tech products to mainstream customers, revised edition; 1999. p. 47.

[13] Vaquero LM, Rodero-Merino L, Caceres J, Lindner M. A break in the clouds: Towards a cloud definition, ACM SIGCOMM computer. Commun Rev 2009;39(1):50−5.

[14] Kuhn TS. The structure of scientific revolutions. 2nd ed. The Enlarged, University of Chicago Press; 1970. 1962, p. 66.

[15] Grove AS. Only the paranoid survive. Crown Business; 1999.

[16] Rensin DK. Building a windows IT infrastructure in the cloud. O'Reilly; 2012.

[17] Chorafas DN. Cloud computing strategies. CRC Press; 2011.

[18] Buyya R, et al. Cloud computing and emerging IT platforms: Vision, hype, and reality for delivering computing as the 5th utility. Future Generation Computer System June 2009;25(6):599−616.

[19] Marks EA, Lozano B. Executive's guide to cloud computing. John Wiley & Sons, Inc.; 2010. pp. 28, 78−81.

[20] Define The Cloud. <http://www.definethecloud.net/>.

[21] The NIST Definition of Cloud Computing. <http://csrc.nist.gov/publications/nistpubs/800-145/SP800-145.pdf>.

[22] Chellappa R. Intermediaries in cloud-computing: A new computing paradigm. INFORMS Dallas 1997 cluster: Electronic commerce. Texas, Dallas; 1997.

[23] Goldworm B, Skamarock A. Blade servers and virtualization transforming enterprise computing while cutting costs. Wiley Publishing; 2007. p. 28.

[24] Foster I, Kesselman C. The grid: Blueprint for a new computing infrastructure. Elsevier Inc.; 1998.

[25] Buyya R, Venugopal S. A gentle introduction to grid computing and technologies, CSI communications. Mumbai. India: Computer Society of India (CSI); 2005;29(1).

[26] Berman F, Fox G, He T. Grid computing: making the global infrastructure a reality. John Wiley & Sons; 2003. p. 15.

[27] Realizing the information future: The internet and beyond. National Academy Press; 1994. p. 53.

[28] Padua D, editor. Encyclopaedia of parallel computing. Springer; 2011. pp. 1409−16.

[29] Blair-Chappell S, Stokes A. Parallel programming with intel parallel studio XE. John Wiley & Sons, Inc.; 2012. p. 4.

[30] Gebali F. Algorithms and parallel computing. John Wiley & Sons, Inc.; 2011. pp. 2–14.

[31] McCool M, et al. Structured parallel programming patterns for efficient computation. Morgan Kaufmann; 2012. p. 60.

[32] De Roure D, Baker MA, Jennings NR, Shadbolt NR. The evolution of the grid. 2003. pp. 1–37.

[33] Padua D, editor. Encyclopedia of parallel computing. Springer; 2011. p. 574.

[34] Ricky Kwok Y-K. Peer-to-peer computing kwok applications, architecture, protocols, and challenges. CRC Press; 2012.

[35] Magoules F. Fundamentals of grid computing theory, algorithms and technologies. CRC Press; 2010. p. 2.

[36] Garfinkel S. In: Abelson H, editor. Architects of the information society, thirty-five years of the laboratory for computer science at MIT. MIT Press; 1999.

[37] Brown R. Business essentials for utility engineers. CRC Press; 2010. p. 30.

[38] Bunker G, Thomson D. Delivering utility computing business-driven IT optimization. John Wiley & Sons Ltd; 2006. p. 11.

[39] Carr NG. The end of corporate computing. MIT Sloan Management Review Spring 2005;46(3):66–74.

[40] Collection of Internet maps. <http://scjsin.websandboxes.com/tag/internet-backbone/>.

[41] Almond C, Chiquito PC, Fachim CH, Kim S, Okajima M, Rämö P. Multitenant utility computing on IBM power systems running AIX. IBM Press; 2009. pp. 3–5.

[42] Mell P, Grance T. The NIST definition of cloud computing, recommendations of NIST. NIST special publication 800-145; 2011. p. 2.

[43] Armbrust M, Fox A, Griffith R, Joseph AD, Katz RH, Konwinski A, et al. Above the clouds: A Berkeley view of cloud computing, electrical engineering and computer sciences. University of California at Berkeley; 2009 Technical Report No. UCB/EECS-2009-28.

[44] Williams Dr. MI. A quick start guide to cloud computing: moving your business into the cloud. Kogan Page Limited; 2010. p. 17.

[45] Kondo D, Javadi B, Malecot P, Cappello F, Anderson DP. Cost-benefit analysis of cloud computing versus desktop grids, Parallel & distributed processing, 2009. IPDPS 2009. IEEE International Symposium, pp. 1–12.

[46] Alford T, Morton G. The economics of cloud computing: addressing the benefits of infrastructure in the cloud. Booz Allen Hamilton; 2009.

[47] West DM. Saving money through cloud computing. Brookings; 2010. pp. 1–14.

[48] Etro F. The economics of cloud computing. IUP J Managerial Econ 2011;IX(2):1–16.

[49] Howard P. The economics of cloud managed integration. Bloor Research; 2012. pp. 1–4.

[50] Harms R, Yamartino M. The economics of the cloud. Microsoft; 2010. pp. 1–22.

[51] Kepes B, Cloudonomics the economics of cloud computing, Diversity Limited, sponsored by Rackspace Hosting. 2012, pp. 1–16.

[52] Forrest W. Clearing the air on cloud computing. Mckinsey and Company; 2009. pp. 1–34.

[53] Zells L. Managing software projects: Selecting and using PC-based project management system. Tarquim Publications; 1990.

[54] Dinsmore PC, Cabnis-Brewin J., The AMA handbook of project management. 2nd ed. AMA; 2006. p. 445.

[55] The Standish Group, Chaos Manifesto 2013, Think Big, Act Small. 2013.

[56] Why Software Fails. <http://spectrum.ieee.org/computing/software/why-software-fails>.

[57] Why Do Projects Fail? <http://calleam.com/WTPF/?cat = 4>.

[58] The worst IT project disasters of 2013. <http://www.cio.com.au/article/533907/worst_it_project_disasters_2013/>.

[59] Sydney Water Doesn't Seem to Learn Prior IT Lessons Well. <http://spectrum.ieee.org/riskfactor/computing/it/sydney-water-doesnt-seem-to-learn-prior-it-lessons-well>.

[60] Dobelli R. The art of thinking clearly. Hodder Stoughton; 2013. p. 19.

[61] Saaty TL, Vargas LG. Decision making with the analytic network process: Economic, political, social and technological applications with benefits, opportunities, costs and risks. 2nd ed. Springer Science Business Media; 2013. p. 120.

[62] Blais SP. Business analysis: best practices for success. John Wiley & Sons, Inc; 2012. pp. 3−12.

[63] Open Data Center Alliance Usage Model. <http://www.opendatacenteralliance.org/>

[64] Anderson DR, et al. An introduction to management science quantitative approaches to decision making, revised thirteenth edition. South-Western, a part of Cengage Learning; 2012. pp. 5−16.

[65] Weese S, Wagner T. CBAP/CCBA certified business analysis study guide. Wiley Publishing, Inc; 2011. pp. 3−32.

[66] Hugos M, Hulitzky D. Business in the cloud: What every business needs to know about cloud computing. John Wiley & Sons, Inc.; 2011. p. 101.

[67] Jansch I. PHP/Architect's guide to enterprise PHP development. Marco Tabini & Associates, Inc.; 2008. p. 50.

[68] DeMarco T, Lister T. Peopleware productive projects and teams. 2nd ed. Dorest House Publishing Co.; 1999. p. 116.

[69] Weese S, et al. CBAP/CCBA certified business analysis study guide. Wiley Publishing Inc.; 2011. p. 124.

[70] Posamentier AS, et al. The art of problem solving: a resource for the mathematics teacher. Crowin Press, Inc; 1996. pp. 1−82.

[71] Schwartz B. The paradox of choice. Australia: Harper Collins Publishers; 2007. p. 47−75.

[72] Wiegers KE. Software requirements. 2nd ed. Microsoft Press; 2003. p. 106.

[73] Sobel D. Longitude: The true story of a lone genius who solved the greatest scientific problem of his time. Walker Publishing Company, Inc.; 1995.

[74] Kahneman D. Thinking, fast and slow. Farrar, Straus and Giroux; 2011. p. 16.

[75] System Requirements and Supported Platforms for Siebel Business Applications. <http://docs.oracle.com/cd/E11886_01/siebel/srsphomepage.html>.

[76] About Events and Event Logging. <http://docs.oracle.com/cd/E14004_01/books/SysDiag/SysDiagEvntLogAdmin3.html#wp1004867>.

[77] Ramo JC. The age of the unthinkable: Why the new global order constantly supervises us and what to do about it. Little, Brown and Company; 2009.

[78] Data Centre Inefficiencies Drive Telstra Rethink. <http://www.computerworld.com.au/article/376530/data_centre_inefficiencies_drive_telstra_rethink/#closeme>.

[79] Telstra Struggles to Keep Data Centres Operating. <http://www.itwire.com/data-management/45112-telstra-struggles-to-keep-data-centres-operating>.

[80] Turner JR. The handbook of project-based management: Leading strategic change in organizations. 3rd ed. The McGraw-Hill Companies, Inc.; 2009.

[81] Dow W, et al. Project management communications bible. Wiley Publishing, Inc.; 2008.

[82] Kolb RW. Encyclopedia of business ethics and society. SAGE Reference Publication; 2008. p. 276.

[83] Rosas-Guyon III L. Nearly free IT: How the cloud can dramatically reduce your technology costs. Heretic Cow Publishing; 2009.

[84] Online Backup Feature Comparison. <http://www.thetop10bestonlinebackup.com/online-backup-comparison>.

[85] Bauer E, Adams R. Reliability and availability of cloud computing. IEEE Press; 2012. pp. 8−15.

[86] Arregoces M, Portolani M. Data center fundamentals. Cisco Press; 2004. p. 5.

[87] Allspaw J. The art of capacity planning. O'Reilly; 2008. p. 11.

[88] Barker A. 30 Minutes . . . to brainstorm great ideas. Kogan Page; 1997. p. 8.

[89] Adler MJ, Van Doren C. How to read a book, simon & schuster. A Touchstone book; 1972. pp. 147−148.

[90] Gigerenzer G, Selten R. Bounded rationality: The adaptive toolbox. The MIT Press; 2001. pp. 13−37.

[91] Fox A, Patterson D. Engineering long-lasting software: An agile approach using saas and cloud computing beta edition, 0.9.0. Strawberry Canyon LLC; 2012. Chapter 5.2.

[92] Data Centres. <http://agict.gov.au/policy-guides-procurement/data-centres>.

[93] Colocation Data Centers. <http://www.datacentermap.com/datacenters.html>.

[94] Rath J. Data Center Site Selection, Datacenterlinks.com, 2007, pp. 1–37.

[95] Rauscher KF, Krock RE, Runyon JP. Eight ingredients of communications infrastructure: A systematic and comprehensive framework for enhancing network reliability and security. Bell Labs Tech J 2006;11(3):73–81.

[96] EMC, IDC digital universe study: Big Data, Bigger Digital Shadows and Biggest Growth in the Far East, p. 4. <www.whizpr.be/.../Media_Presentation_2012_DigiUniverseFINAL1.pdf>.

[97] Total Number of Websites. <http://www.internetlivestats.com/total-number-of-websites/>.

[98] Priest Rapids Hydroelectric Project Relicensing. <http://www.hdrinc.com/portfolio/priest-rapids-hydro-electric-project-relicensing>.

[99] Updated Airside Free Cooling Maps The Impact of ASHRAE 2011 Allowable Ranges. <http://www.thegreengrid.org/~/media/WhitePapers/WP46UpdatedAirsideFreeCoolingMapsTheImpactofASHRAE2011-AllowableRanges.pdf?lang=en>.

[100] Quincy, WA – Big Data Centers Leverage Abundant, Inexpensive Renewable Energy. <www.coloand-cloud.com/editorial/quincy-wa-big-data-centers-leverage-abundant-inexpensive-renewable-energy/>.

[101] Andrzejak A, Arlitt M, Rolia J. Bounding the resource savings of utility computing models, HP, 2002.

[102] Cockcroft A, Walker B. Capacity planning for internet services: Quick planning techniques for high growth rates. Sun Microsystems, Inc.; 2000. p. 2.

[103] EAAC, Electricity prices in Australia: An international comparison, A report to the energy users association of Australia, March 2012. p. 11, <http://www.euaa.com.au/>.

[104] The Green Grid, White Paper #16, Quantitative efficiency analysis of power distribution configurations for data center, December 2008. p. 3.

[105] Koutitas G, Demestichas P. Challenges for energy efficiency in local and regional data centers. Journal of Green Engineering; 2010. p. 12.

[106] Council Bluffs, Iowa. <http://www.google.com.au/about/datacenters/inside/locations/council-bluffs/>.

[107] Google's Data Center Hovering Above the Floor in Council Bluffs, Iowa. <http://www.google.com.au/about/datacenters/gallery/#/tech/3>.

[108] Google's data centers use color-coded pipes to indicate what they're used for.<http://www.google.com.au/about/datacenters/gallery/#/tech/9>.

[109] Alger D. The art of the data center. Pearson Education Inc.; 2013. p. 64.

[110] Kahr J, Thomsett MC. Real estate market valuation and analysis. John Wiley & Sons, Inc; 2005. p. 49.

[111] Data Center Definition and Solutions. <http://www.cio.com/article/499671/Data_Center_Definition_and_Solutions>.

[112] Koomey J PhD. White paper, A Simple Model for Determining True Total Cost of Ownership for Data Centers, Version 2.1, March 31, 2008, Uptime Institute, p. 7.

[113] Shapiro E, Mackmin D, Sams G. Modern methods of valuation. 11th ed. Routledge; 2013. pp. 12–14.

[114] Gartner Says Energy-Related Costs Account for Approximately 12 Percent of Overall Data Center Expenditures. <http://www.gartner.com/newsroom/id/1442113>.

[115] A Simple Model for Determining True Total Cost of Ownership for Data Centers. <http://www.missioncritical-magazine.com/ext/resources/MC/Home/Files/PDFs/%28TUI3011B%29SimpleModelDetermingTrueTCO.pdf>.

[116] Greenberg A, Hamilton J, Maltz DA, Patel P. The cost of cloud research problems in data center networks, published by Microsoft Research Redmond WA, USA, published by ACM SIGCOMM Computer Communication Review, January 2009; 39(1): 68–73.

[117] Fairfax S, et al. La. Reliability Analysis of the APC InfraStruXure® Power System, White Paper 111, Revision 1, M Technology, Inc.

[118] The Data Center Journal. <http://www.datacenterjournal.com/>.

[119] Emerson Network Power, Ponemon Institute Study Quantifies Cost of Data Center Downtime. <http://emersonnetworkpower.com/en-US//About/NewsRoom/NewsReleases/Pages/EmersonNetworkPower,Ponem-onInstituteStudyQuantifiesCostofDataCenterDowntime.aspx>.

[120] Meta Group, IT performance engineering and measurement strategies: Quantifying performance and loss, Fibre Channel Industry Association.

[121] UPS Topologies Large Critical Power Systems. <http://www.ge-spark.com/spark/resources/white-papers/UPS_Topologies_Large_Critical_Power_Systems.pdf>.

[122] McCluer S. Battery technology for data centers and network rooms: Lead-acid battery options, White paper 30, Revision 12, APC, p. 2.

[123] Rumsey Engineers Inc. Data center energy benchmarking study, February 2003. pp. 4–5.

[124] Data Processing and Communications Facilities. <http://www.meengineering.com/data-processing-and-communications-facilities>.

[125] Calculating Total Power Requirements for Data Centers. <http://www.gocsc.com/uploads/white_papers/1c360f8416e4436c86b8c0874e65be5e.pdf>.

[126] Energy Logic: Reducing Data Center Energy Consumption by Creating Savings that Cascade Across Systems. <https://www.cisco.com/web/partners/downloads/765/other/Energy_Logic_Reducing_Data_Center_Energy_Consumption.pdf>.

[127] Schulz G. The green and virtual data center. CRC Press; 2009. pp. 137, 259.

[128] Smith H. Data center storage cost-effective strategies, implementation, and management. CRC Press Taylor & Francis Group; 2011. p. 29.

[129] A white paper from the experts in business-critical continuity, precision versus comfort cooling choosing a cooling system to support business-critical IT environments, Emerson Network Power, 2010. p. 1.

[130] Whitman WC, Johnson WM, Tomczyk JA, Silberstein E. Refrigeration and air conditioning technology. 6th ed. Cengage Learning; 2009. p. 2.

[131] Stoecker WF, Jones JW. Refrigeration and air conditioning. 2nd ed. McGraw-Hill; 1987. p. 14.

[132] Trott AR, Welch T. Refrigeration and air-condition. 3rd ed. Butterworth-Heinemann; 2000. p. 232.

[133] Air – Water Vapor Mixtures. <http://www.ohio.edu/mechanical/thermo/Applied/Chapt.7_11/Chapter10b.html>.

[134] Data-Center Uptime and Energy Efficiency. <http://hpac.com/iaq-amp-ventilation/data-center-uptime-energy-efficiency>.

[135] Hundy GF, Trott AR, Welch TC. Refrigeration and air-conditioning. 4th ed. Butterworth-Heinemann; 2008. p. 287.

[136] Rasmussen N. The different types of air distribution for IT environments, ACP White paper 55, 2012, p. 3.

[137] Green IT: Data Centre Design. <http://www.oucs.ox.ac.uk/greenit/oxford-central-machine-room-design.xml?ID = body.1_div.6>.

[138] APC, White Papers. <http://www.apc.com/prod_docs/results.cfm?DocType=White + Paper&Query_Type=10>.

[139] The Different Technologies for Cooling Data Centers. <http://www.apcmedia.com/salestools/VAVR-5UDTU5/VAVR-5UDTU5_R2_EN.pdf>.

[140] STULZ, White Papers. <http://au.stulz.com/downloads/white-papers/>.

[141] Sawyer RL, Making large UPS systems more efficient, APC Whitepaper, 2012, p. 5.

[142] Optimizing Your Infrastructure for Cloud Computing. <http://www.bomoro.com/powerware/wp_cloud_computing.htm>.

[143] Dunckel W, Rongere FX. A practical method to reduce HVAC energy in data centers, pacific gas and electric company. ACEEE Summer Study on Energy Efficiency in Industry; 2009. pp. 1–65.

[144] McGuckin P. Cool more with less in your data center. Gartner; 2008.

[145] Kennedy D. Cold aisle containment for improved data center cooling efficiency, Rittal White Paper 506, 2012, p. 21.

[146] Focused cooling using cold aisle containment, A white paper from the experts in business-critical continuity, Emerson Network Power, Liebert, 2009.

[147] Goren B. Cold aisle containment system performance simulation, data center white paper, Eaton, 2011.

[148] Niemann J. Hot aisle vs. cold aisle containment, APC White Paper Number 135, 2008.

[149] Selecting the Optimal Data Center Cooling Solution. <http://www.ptsdcs.com/Selecting-the-Optimal-Data-Center-Cooling-Solution.asp>.

[150] T Systems, White Paper. <http://www.t-systems.com/prepage-whitepaper/whitepaper-download/1016440?ts_refBeanId=827836>.

[151] Rasmussen N, Standley B. Cooling strategies for IT wiring closets and small rooms, Whitepaper 68, APC, 2001, p. 9.

[152] Dunlap K, Rasmussen N. Choosing between room, row, and rack-based cooling for data centers, White Paper 130 Revision 2, 2012, p. 8.

[153] Google: Raise Your Data Center Temperature. <http://www.datacenterknowledge.com/archives/2008/10/14/google-raise-your-data-center-temperature/>.

[154] Nosayba El-Sayed Ioan Stefanovici George Amvrosiadis Andy A. Hwang, Bianca Schroeder, Temperature Management in Data Centers: Why Some (Might) Like It Hot, SIGMETRICS'12, June 11−15, 2012.

[155] HP Proliant DL 380 G8 Server User Guide. 2011, p. 82. <ww1.hp.com/products/quickspecs/14212_div/14212_div.pdf>.

[156] Harvey T, et al. Update air-side free cooling maps: the impact of ASHRAE 2011 Allowable Ranges, White paper#46, The Green Grid, p. 4.

[157] Shehabi A, Horvath A, Nazaroff W. Energy implications of economizer use in California data centers. ACEEE Summer Study on Energy Efficiency in Buildings; 2008. pp. 3-319−3-330.

[158] Sujatha DC, Abimannan S. Energy efficient free cooling system for data centers, 2011, 2011 Third IEEE International Conference on Cloud Computing Technology and Science, pp. 646−651.

[159] The Green Grid. <http://www.thegreengrid.org/>.

[160] Free-Cooling Estimated Savings. <http://cooling.thegreengrid.org/namerica/WEB_APP/calc_index.html>.

[161] Carboy R. How to choose a fire suppression system for your server room, data center or NOC. Peripheral Manufacturing, Inc.; 2007. p. 3.

[162] Halon Alternatives Research Corporation. <http://www.harc.org/>.

[163] Montreal Protocol. <www.worldbank.org/montrealprotocol>.

[164] Jayaswal K. Administering data centers: servers, storage, and voice over IP. Wiley Publishing, Inc.; 2006. pp. 8, 28.

[165] Morris I. Why the west rules − for now: The patterns of history and what they reveal about the future, October 25. Picador; 2011.

[166] Kehoe TJ, Srinivasan TN, Whalley J. Frontiers in applied general equilibrium modelling in honor of herbert scarf. Cambridge University Press; 2005. p. 16.

[167] Haque A, Alhashmi SM, Parthiban R. An inspiration for solving grid resource management problems using multiple economic models, part of economics of grids, clouds, systems, and services. In: Vanmechelen K, Altmann J, Rana OF, editors. 8th International Workshop, GECON 2011 Paphos, Cyprus, December 5, 2011 Revised Selected Papers, Springer, p. 26.

[168] BusinessDictionary. <http://www.businessdictionary.com/>.

[169] Schniederjans MJ, Hamaker JL, Schniederjans AM. Information technology investment decision-making methodology. World Scientific Publishing Co. Re. Ltd.; 2004.

[170] Cost Model. <http://www.knowledgetransfer.net/dictionary/ITIL/en/Cost_Model.htm>.

[171] Renkema TJW, Berghout EW. Methodologies for information systems investment evaluation at the proposal stage: A comparative review Elsevier. Inf Softw Technol 1997;39:1−13.

[172] Strictly speaking, the meaning of Information System (IS) is broader than Information Technology (IT) because it normally consists of three components: People, process, and IT. But today, most people in the IT profession do not make a distinction. The terms IS and IT becomes interchangeable.

[173] Schniederjans MJ, Hamaker JL, Schniederjans AM. Information technology investment: Decision-making methodology. Singapore: World Scientific; 2010.

[174] Photos of the original document can be found in the following address. <http://www.hi-ho.ne.jp/busicom/intel1.html>.

[175] The Busicom 141-PF Calculator and the Intel 4004 Microprocessor. <http://www.vintagecalculators.com/html/busicom_141-pf_and_intel_4004.html>.

[176] Walker E. The Real Cost of a CPU Hour, published by IEEE computer Magazine Apr-09, pp. 35–41.

[177] Walker E. To Lease or Not to Lease from Storage Clouds. IEEE Computer Magazine Apr-10, pp. 44–50.

[178] Bibi S, Katsaros D, Bozanis P. Application Development: Fly to the Clouds or Stay in-House? 2010 Workshop on Enabling Technologies: Infrastructure for Collaborative Enterprise. IEEE Computer Society; 2010. pp. 60–65.

[179] Khajeh-Hosseini A, Sommerville I, Bogaerts J, Teregowda P. Decision support tools for cloud migration in the enterprise. 2011 IEEE 4th International Conference on Cloud Computing, pp. 541–8.

[180] Yam C-Y, Baldwin A, Shiu S. Migration to cloud as real option investment decision under uncertainty, by Security Analytics, Cloud & Security Lab, HP Bristol UK. 2011 International Joint Conference of IEEE Trust Com-11/IEEE-ICESS-11/FCST-11, 2011, pp. 940–949.

[181] Authors used Amazon's spreadsheet for cost comparison.

[182] The $15.3 Billion Server Market – Surprisingly Buoyant In Q1 2012. <http://www.itcandor.com/server-q112/>.

[183] Greenberg A, Hamilton J, Maltz DA, Patel P. The cost of cloud research problems in data center networks, published by microsoft research redmond WA, USA. ACM SIGCOMM Computer Communication Review, Jan. 2009;39 (1):68–73.

[184] ISC Domain Survey. <https://www.isc.org/services/survey/>.

[185] Energy Savings via Virtualization. <http://www.gartner.com/id = 796212>.

[186] Intel 4004. <http://en.wikipedia.org/wiki/Intel_4004>.

[187] Guthrie F, Lowe S. VMware vSphere Design. 2nd ed. John Wiley & Son; 2013. p. 110.

[188] Chapter in the History of Blade Computing Closed. <http://hippster.com/pages/history.html>.

[189] egenera, Board of Directors. <http://www.egenera.com/board-investors-board-bio.htm>.

[190] Bryant RE, O'Hallaron DR. Computer systems: A programmer's perspective. Prentice Hall; 2011. pp. 342–343.

[191] ExtremeTech. <http://extremetech.com>.

[192] ARM's Stiff Upper Lip Trembles at Chipzilla's Medfield. <http://www.extremetech.com/mobile/114149-arm-stiff-upper-lip-trembles-at-intel-medfield/3>.

[193] Logical Domains 1.2 Administration Guide. <http://docs.oracle.com/cd/E19227-01/820-7253/usingterminaltool/index.html>.

[194] Cease Fire in HDD Vs. SSD Price War – PriceG2. <http://www.storagenewsletter.com/rubriques/market-reportsresearch/cease-fire-in-hdd-vs-ssd-price-war-priceg2/>.

[195] Kasavajhala V. Solid state drive vs. hard disk drive price and performance study, A Dell Technical White Paper, 2011.

[196] About RAID levels and ClearCase. <http://www-01.ibm.com/support/docview.wss?uid=swg21149421>.

[197] Future Compute Memory Non Volatile Memory (NVM) in Compute. <http://www.stanford.edu/class/ee380/Abstracts/081112-Fazio-slides.pdf>.

[198] When Will SSD Have Same Price as HDD. <http://www.storagenewsletter.com/rubriques/market-reportsresearch/when-will-ssd-have-same-price-as-hdd-priceg2/>.

[199] Micheloni R, Marelli A, Eshghi K. Inside solid state drives (SSDs). Springer Science + Business Media Dordrecht; 2013. pp. 6, 10.

[200] RAM SSDs versus Flash SSDs. <http://www.storagesearch.com/ssd-ram-v-flash.html>.

[201] Validating the Reliability of Intel® Solid-State Drives. <http://www.intel.com.au/content/dam/doc/technology-brief/intel-it-validating-reliability-of-intel-solid-state-drives-brief.pdf>.

[202] Total Cost of Solid State Storage Ownership. <http://www.snia.org/sites/default/files/SNIA_TCOCALC_Workpaper_Final_0.pdf>.

[203] iSCSI and FCoE: A Comparison. <http://www.cisco.com/en/US/prod/collateral/switches/ps9441/ps9670/white_paper_c11-495142.html>.

[204] Schulz G. Cloud and virtual data storage networking: Your journey to efficient and effective information services. CRC Press; 2012. p. 40.

[205] Jackson M. SAS storage architecture (Revision 1.1). Mindshare Press; 2005. p. 43.

[206] Troppens U, Muller-Friedt W, Wolafka R, Erkens R, Haustein N. Storage networks explained basics and application of fibre channel SAN, NAS, iSCSI, InfiniBand and FCoE. 2nd ed. John Wiley and Sons, Ltd; 2009. p. 449.

[207] Tiered Storage Takes Center Stage. <http://www.oracle.com/us/corporate/analystreports/corporate/horison-tiered-storage-197857.pdf>.

[208] VMware vSphere 5.5 Documentation. <http://pubs.vmware.com/vsphere-55/index.jsp?topic=%2Fcom.vmware.vsphere.networking.doc%2FGUID-0D1EF5B4-7581-480B-B99D-5714B42CD7A9.html>.

[209] 8.0% Y/Y Growth for WW External Disk Storage Systems in 2Q12 for IDC. <http://www.storagenewsletter.com/rubriques/market-reportsresearch/idc-ww-system-disk-2q12/>.

[210] Carrier Router/Switch Market Roars Back in 2Q13; Europe Gains, Too. <http://www.infonetics.com/pr/2013/2Q13-Service-Provider-Routers-Switches-Market-Highlights.asp>.

[211] Kachris C, Bergman K, Tomkos I. Optical interconnects for future data center networks. New York: Springer Science + Business Media; 2013. p. 71.

[212] Villar JA, Andujar FJ, Sanchez JL, Alfaro FJ, Duato J. C-switches: Increasing switch radix with current integration scale, 2011 IEEE International Conference on High Performance Computing and Communications, pp. 40–49.

[213] Dally WJ, Towles B. Principles and practice of interconnection networks. Morgan Kaufmann; 2004. p. 30.

[214] Newman P. Fast packet switching for integrated services: A dissertation submitted for the Degree of PhD, December 1988, Wolfson College University of Cambridge; p. 42.

[215] Liu Y, Muppala JK, Veeraraghavan M, Lin D, Hamdi M. Data center networks, topologies, architectures and fault-tolerance characteristics. Springer; 2013. p. 16.

[216] Zhang Y, Su A-J, Jiang G. Understanding data center network architectures in virtualized environments: a view from multi-tier applications. Elsevier; 2011. pp. 2196–208.

[217] Popa L, Ratnasamy S, Iannaccone G, Krishnamurthy A, Stoica I. A cost comparison of data center network architectures, November 30. ACM CoNEXT; 2010.

[218] Duato J, Yalamanchili S, Ni LM. Interconnection networks: an engineering approach, Revised Printing. Morgan Kaufmann Publishers; 2003. pp. 8, 27.

[219] Ni LM. Issues in designing truly scalable interconnection networks, IEEE, 1996 International Conference on Parallel Processing Workshop, pp. 74–83.

[220] Wu K, Xiao J, Ni LM. Rethinking the architecture design of data center networks. Springer-Verlag Berlin Heidelberg; 2012. pp. 1–9.

[221] Al-Fares M, Loukissas A, Vahdat A. A scalable, commodity data center network architecture, SIGCOMM'08, August 17–22, 2008, pp. 63–74.

[222] Cisco: Cisco data center infrastructure 2.5 design guide, p. 2-1, <http://www.cisco.com/en/US/docs/solutions/Enterprise/Data_Center/DC_Infra2_5/DCInfra_2a.html>.

[223] Guo C, Wu H, Tan K, Shiy L, Zhang Y, Lu S. DCell: A scalable and fault-tolerant network structure for data centers, SIGCOMM'08, August 17–22, 2008.

[224] Guo D, Chen T, Li D, Li M, Liu YH, Chen G. Expandable and cost-effective network structures for data centers using dual-port servers. IEEE Trans Comput 2013;62(7).

[225] Guo C, Lu G, Li D, Wu H, Zhang X, Shi Y, et al. BCube: A high performance, server-centric network architecture for modular data centers, SIGCOMM'09, August 17−21, 2009.

[226] Greenberg A, Hamilton JR, Jain N, Kandula S, Kim C, Lahiri P, et al. VL2: A scalable and flexible data center network, SIGCOMM'09, August 17−21, 2009, pp. 51−62.

[227] Kim J, Dally WJ, Abts D. Flattened butterfly: A cost-efficient topology for high-radix networks. ISCA'07, June 9−13, 2007.

[228] Thamarakuzhi A, Chandy JA. Design and implementation of a nonblocking 2-dilated flattened butterfly switching network, Communications (LATINCOM), 2010 IEEE Latin-American Conference, pp. 1−6.

[229] NetFPGA. <http://netfpga.org/index.html>.

[230] Kim J, Dally WJ, Scott S, Abts D. Technology-driven, highly-scalable dragonfly topology, international symposium on computer architecture. IEEE Computer Society; 2008. pp. 77−88.

[231] Kim J, Dally WJ, Scott S, Abts D. Cost-efficient dragonfly topology for large-scale systems, January/February. Micro; 2009. pp. 2−9.

[232] Maksic N, Smiljani A. Improving utilization of data center networks, November. IEEE Communication Magazine; 2013. pp. 32−38.

[233] Liao Y, Yin D, Gao L. DPillar: Scalable dual-port server interconnection for data center networks, IEEE International Conference on Computer Communications and Networks (ICCN), 2010, pp. 1−6.

[234] Abts D, Kim J. High performance data center networks architectures, algorithms, and opportunity. Morgan & Claypool; 2011. p. 20.

[235] Mach W, Schikuta E. A consumer-provider cloud cost model considering variable cost, 2011 Ninth IEEE International Conference on Dependable, Autonomic and Secure Computing, pp. 628−35.

[236] Reich C, Bubendorfer K, Banholzer M, Buyya R. A SLA-oriented management of containers for hosting stateful web services. In: Proceedings of the IEEE Conference on e-Science and Grid Computing, Washington, DC, USA; 2007.

[237] Li Y, Sun K, Qiu J, Chen Y. Self-reconfiguration of service-based systems: A case study for service level agreements and resource optimization. In: ICWS'05: Proceedings of the IEEE International Conference on Web Services (ICWS'05), Washington, DC, USA; 2005. IEEE Computer Society, pp. 266−273.

[238] Buyya R, Garg SK, Calheiros RN. SLA-oriented resource provisioning for Cloud Computing: Challenges, architecture, and solutions. International Conference on Cloud and Service Computing. pp. 1−10.

[239] Bonvin N, Papaioannou TG, Aberer K. Autonomic SLA-driven provisioning for cloud applications, cluster, cloud and grid computing (CCGrid), 2011 11th IEEE/ACM International Symposium; 23−26 May 2011. pp. 434−43.

[240] Andrzejak A, Kondo D. Decision model for cloud computing under SLA constraints, modeling, analysis & simulation of computer and telecommunication systems (MASCOTS), 2010 IEEE International Symposium on August 2010, pp. 257−66.

[241] Li X, Li Y, Liu T, Qiu J, Wang F. The method and tool of cost analysis for cloud computing, cloud computing. CLOUD'09. IEEE International Conference; 21−25 September 2009, pp. 93−100.

[242] Processor Value Unit Calculator. <https://www-112.ibm.com/software/howtobuy/passportadvantage/valueunitcalculator/vucalc.wss>.

[243] Modelling the Economic Impact of Cloud Computing. <https://www.kpmg.com/AU/en/IssuesAndInsights/ArticlesPublications/Documents/modelling-economic-impact-cloud-computing.pdf>.

[244] Ovum. <http://ovum.com/section/home/>.

[245] Cloud Computing. <http://www.boozallen.com/consulting/technology/cloud-computing>.

[246] EY Cloud Computing. <http://www.ey.com/GL/en/Industries/Technology/EY-Cloud-computing>.

[247] Hermann DS. Complete guide to security & privacy metrics: Measuring regulatory compliance, operational resilience & ROI. Auerbach; 2007.

[248] Roulstone DB, Phillips JJ. ROI for technology projects: measuring and delivering value. Butterworth-Heinemann; 2008. p. 9.

[249] Rothwell WJ. Invaluable knowledge securing your company's technical expertise. AMA; 2011. p. 150.

[250] Comparison of Accounting Software. <http://en.wikipedia.org/wiki/Comparison_of_accounting_software>.

[251] Addy R. Effective IT service management to ITIL and beyond! Springer; 2007. p. 33.

[252] Benioff MR, Adler C, Chairman & CEO of salesforce.com. Behind the Cloud: The untold story of how salesforce.com went from idea to billion-dollar company—and revolutionized an industry. Jossey-Bass, 2009, p. 11.

[253] The 10 Laws of Cloudonomics. <http://gigaom.com/2008/09/07/the-10-laws-of-cloudonomics/>.

[254] Baschab J, Piot J. The executive's guide to information technology. John Wiley & Sons, Inc.; 2007. p. 44.

[255] Potter K. Chargeback methods that will change IT competitiveness and effectiveness, 23 June. Gartner; 2010.

[256] Analyst: Chargeback too Complex for Most IT Shops. <http://www.itnews.com.au/News/170507,analyst-chargeback-too-complex-for-most-it-shops.aspx/0>.

[257] Wigand RT, Mertens P, Bodendorf F, Konig W, Picot Dr. A, Schumann M. Introduction to business information systems. Springer; 2003. p. 7.

[258] Rasmussen N. Determining total cost of ownership for data center and network room infrastructure White Paper 6, Revision 4, APC, p. 4.

[259] Torell W. Data center physical infrastructure: optimizing business value, white paper 117, APC, p. 10.

[260] Data Center Capital Cost Calculator. <http://www.apcc.com/tools/isx/tco>.

[261] VMWare ROI TCO Calculator. <http://roitco.vmware.com/vmw/>.

[262] Microsoft Datacenter TCO Analysis Tool. <http://www.datacentertcotool.com/>.

[263] Dixit A, Pindyck R. Investment under uncertainty. Princeton University Press; 1993. p. 136.

[264] Black F, Scholes M. The pricing of options and corporate liabilities. J Polit Econ 1973;81(3):637−54.

[265] Myers SC. Determinants of corporate borrowing, Sloan School MIT, Cambridge, revised version July 1977, pp. 147−75.

[266] Kemna AGZ. Case studies on real options, Financ Manage 22(3): 259−70.

[267] Trigeorgis L. Real options. The MIT Press; 1996.

[268] James Mills. <http://www.cgu.edu/pages/6046.asp>.

[269] Schulmerich M. Real options valuation, the importance of interest rate modelling in theory and practice, 2nd ed., Springer, p. 28.

[270] Adner R, Levinthal DA. What is not a real option: Considering boundaries for the application of real options to business strategy. Acad Manage Rev 2004;29(1):74−85.

[271] Amram M, Kulatilaka N. Real options: Managing strategic investment in an uncertain world. Harvard Business School Press; 1999. pp. 24−27.

[272] Haahtela T. Differences between financial options and real options, Lecture Notes in Management Science. 4th International Conference on Applied Operational Research, Proceedings, 2012; vol. 4, pp. 169−178.

[273] Mun J. Real options analysis tools and techniques for valuing strategic investment and decisions. John Wiley & Sons; 2002. p. 84.

[274] Barreto H, Howland FM. Introductory econometrics: Using monte carlo simulation with microsoft excel. Cambridge University Press; 2006. p. 216.

[275] Glasserman P. Monte Carlos methods in financial engineering. Springer; 2003. p. 1.

[276] Sobol IM. A primer for the Monte Carlo method. CRC Press; 1994. p. 1.

[277] Kalos MH, Whitlock PA. Monte Carlo methods. Wiley-VCH Verlag GmbH & Co. KGaA; 2004. p. 1.

[278] Ross SM. Introduction to probability models. 9th ed. Elsevier Inc.; 2007. p. 1.

[279] On the Adequacy of Psuedo-Random Number Generators. <http://ecommons.cornell.edu/bitstream/1813/8548/1/TR000664.pdf>.

[280] Verschuuren GM. Excel simulations. Holy Macro! 2014. p. 109.

[281] Pacati C. Brownian motion and geometic brownian motion, 2011. pp. 1−7.

[282] Oracle Crystal Ball. <http://www.oracle.com/us/products/applications/crystalball/overview/index.html>.

[283] Cox JC, Ross SA. Mark Rubinstein, option pricing: a simplified approach. J Financ Econ. September 1979;229−63.

[284] Brach MA. Real options in practice. John Wiley and Sons; 2003.

[285] Meier M, Sinzig W, Mertens P. Enterprise Mgmt with SAP SEM/Business analytics. 2nd ed. Springer; 2005. p. 3.

[286] Price waterhouse coopers, Why isn't IT spending creating more value? 2007.

[287] Why isn't IT spending creating more value? <https://www.pwc.com/en_US/us/increasing-it-effectiveness/assets/it_spending_creating_value.pdf>.

[288] Haque A, Alhashmi SM, Parthiban R. An inspiration for solving grid resource management problems using multiple economic models, economics of grids, clouds, systems, and services 8th International Workshop, GECON 2011 Paphos, Cyprus, December 5, 2011, Revised Selected Papers, Springer, 2011, pp. 1−16.

[289] Bowman Jr. RH. Business continuity planning for data centers and systems: A strategic implementation guide. John Wiley & Sons, Inc; 2008. p. 120.

[290] Rouse WB. Enterprise transformation: understanding and enabling fundamental change. John Wiley & Sons, Inc; 2006. pp. 39−68.

[291] Barroso LA, Hölzle U. The data center as a computer: An introduction to the design of warehouse-scale machines. Google Inc., Morgan & Claypool; 2009. p. 71.

[292] Vellani KH. Strategic security management: a risk assessment guide for decision makers. Elsevier Inc.; 2007. pp. 6, 247, 248.

[293] Porter ME. Competitive advantage creating and sustaining superior performance. The Free Press; 1985. pp. 4−37.

[294] Porter ME. Competitive strategy techniques for analyzing industry and competitors. The Free Press; 1998.

[295] Treacy M, Wiersema F. Customer intimacy and other value discipline, January-February. Harvard Business Review; 1993. pp. 84−93.

[296] Aven T. Misconceptions of risk. John Wiley and Sons; 2010. p. 3.

[297] Mun J. Modeling risk applying monte carlo risk simulation, strategic real options, stochastic forecasting, and portfolio optimization. 2nd ed. John Wiley & Sons, Inc.; 2010. pp. 16, 100.

[298] Reduce IT Costs and Increase Control. <http://www.vmware.com/solutions/consolidation/consolidate.html>.

[299] O'Regan G. A brief history of computing. Springer-Verlag London Limited; 2012. p. 22.

[300] Vail Farr J. Systems life cycle costing economic analysis, estimation, and management. CRC Press; 2011.

[301] Remenyi D, Remenyi B. How to prepare business cases: A practical guide for accountants. Elsevier Ltd.; 2010. p. 131.

[302] Worldwide PC Market. <http://www.etforecasts.com/products/ES_pcww1203.htm>.

[303] Computer Sales Statistics. <http://www.statisticbrain.com/computer-sales-statistics/>.

[304] Wang JX. What every engineer should know about business communication. CRC Press; 2008.

[305] Chambers HE. Effective communication skills for scientific and technical professionals. Perseus Publishing; 2001.

[306] Dow W, PMP, Taylor B. Project management communications bible. Wiley Publishing, Inc; 2008.

[307] Wolvin AD. Listening and human communication in the 21st century. John Wiley & Sons, Ltd.; 2010.

[308] Albers MJ. Communication of complex information user goals and information needs for dynamic web information. Lawrence Erlbaum Associates; 2005.

[309] Caunt J. Organise yourself. 3rd ed. Kogan Page; 2010. p. 22.

[310] Palmer S, Cooper C. How to deal with stress. 2nd ed. Kogan Page Limited; 2010.

[311] Rothman J. Manage your project portfolio: Increase your capacity and finish more projects. The Pragmatic Bookshelf; 2009.

[312] Forsyth P. 100 great time management ideas. Marshall Cavendish International; 2009.

[313] Hoover J. Best practices: Time management set priorities to get the right things done. Harper Collins Publishers; 2007.

[314] Dittmer RE. 151 quick ideas to manage your time. The Career Press; 2006.

[315] Raiffa H, Richardson J, Metcalfe D. Negotiation analysis: The science and art of collaborative decision making. Harvard University Press; 2007. p. 191.

[316] Lyons C. I win you win: The essential guide to principle negotiation. A&C Black Publishers Ltd; p. 206.

[317] Kenny DA. Interpersonal perception: A social relations analysis. The Guilford Press; 1994. p. 26.

[318] Schelling TC. The strategy of conflict. Harvard University Press; 1981. p. 81.

[319] Josyula V, Orr M, Page G. Cloud Computing: Automating the virtualized data center. Cisco Press; 2012. p. 140.

[320] Nokia and TietoEnator, OSS/BSS reference architecture and its implementation scenario for fulfillment, Whitepaper, p. 4.

[321] Morgan MG, et al. Uncertainty: A guide to dealing with uncertainty in quantitative risk and policy analysis. Cambridge University Press; 1990. p. 13.

[322] Huynh V-N, et al. Integrated uncertainty management and applications: advances in intelligent and soft computing. Springer; 2010. pp. 357−69.

[323] Jordan I. Decisions under uncertainty probabilistic analysis for engineering decisions. Cambridge University Press; 2005.

[324] Alessandri TM, et al. Managing risk and uncertainty in complex capital projects Elsevier. Q Rev Econ Finance 2004;44:751−67.

[325] Wysocki RK. Adaptive project framework, managing complexity in the face of uncertainty. Addison-Wesley, Education Inc.; 2010.

[326] Kane WS. The truth about thriving change, life is 10% of what happens to you and 90% of how you react...". Person Education Inc.; 2008. p. 2−4.

[327] Wash M. 54 approaches to managing change at work. Dorrance Publishing; 2010. p. 121.

[328] Carnall C. Managing change in organizations. 5th ed. Pearson Education Ltd; 2007. pp. 254−94.

[329] Delong TJ. Flying without a net: turn fear of change into fuel for success. Harvard Business Review Press; 2011.

[330] Carnall CA. Managing change in organizations. 5th ed. Pearson Education Ltd; 2007.

[331] Fadem T. The art of asking: ask better questions, get better answers. FT Press; 2008. pp. 91−118.

[332] Key Facts. <http://www.innovation.gov.au/SmallBusiness/KeyFacts/Pages/default.aspx>.

[333] Neil Browne M, Keeley SM. Asking the right questions: A guide to critical thinking. Pearson Education; 2007. p. 25−33.

[334] Podeswa H. The business analyst's handbook. Course Technology, a part of Cengage Learning; 2009. p. 246.

[335] Fournier G. Essential software testing: a use-case approach. CRC Press; 2009. pp. 95−124.

[336] Antonopoulos N, Gillam L. Cloud computing principles, systems and applications. Springer; 2010. p. 350.

[337] McKinsey Report Highlights Failure of Large Projects: Why It is Better to be Small, Particularly in IT. <http://blogs.gartner.com/mark_mcdonald/2012/10/29/mckinsey-report-highlights-failure-of-large-projects-why-it-is-better-to-be-small-particularly-in-it/>.

[338] Delivering Large-Scale IT Projects on Time, on Budget, and on Value. <http://www.mckinsey.com/insights/business_technology/delivering_large-scale_it_projects_on_time_on_budget_and_on_value>.

[339] Risk Factor. <http://spectrum.ieee.org/blog/riskfactor>.

[340] The Complete Data Center Build vs. Buy Calculator. <http://www.thecloudcalculator.com/calculators/build-vs-buy.html>.

Index

Note: Page numbers followed by "*f*" and "*t*" refer to figures and tables, respectively.

Fujitsu rack-mounted server, 791
Functional definitions (FD), 9
Functional rooms, of data center, 185–188
    computing functions, 187–188
        computer rooms, 187–188
        entrance rooms, 187
        telecommunication rooms, 188
    operational functions, 188
        common area, 188
        general office space, 188
        network operation rooms, 188
    utility support functions, 186
        electrical rooms, 186
        mechanical rooms, 186
        staging area, 186

G

Gartner's hype cycle, 13, 13f
    of cloud computing, 15f
    and Moore's Technology Adoption Life
        Cycle, 14f
Gas laws, 263
Gateway, 515–516
Gay-Lussac's law, 264
General office space, 188
Generators, 202–206
Geological disaster, 164
Geometric Brownian motion, 741
Global data center map, 785
Global warming potential (GWP), 350
Glycol-cooled system, 279, 282t
Google data center, 168, 170f
Government policy, 168
Green Grid organization, 330
Grid computing, 25–27
Gustafson-Barsis' Law, 20

H

Halocarbons, 350
Halon, 349–350
Hard disk drive (HDD), 425–433, 445–446
    evolution, 430–433
    physical metrics, 427–430
    versus solid state disk, 450
Hard floors
    flooded approach for, 286–287
    fully ducted for both supply and return air
        with, 289
    fully ducted/contained approach for, 287–288
    locally ducted for supply air with, 288

targeted/locally ducted approach for, 287
Hardware parallelism, 17–18
    memory parallelism, 17–18
    processor parallelism, 17
Hardware-based cost, in IT infrastructure, 662
Heat, 252
    airflow and airflow rate, 262–264
        Boyle's law, 263
        Charles' law, 264
        gas laws, 263
        Gay-Lussac's law, 264
    fan types and fan laws, 264–266
        axial and propeller fans, 265
        centrifugal and radial fans, 266
        fan laws, 266
    heat transfer equation, temperature changes based on,
        276–277
    humidity, 254–255
        absolute humidity, 255
        humidity ratio, 255
        psychometric chart, 257–258
        refrigeration, 258–262
        relative humidity, 255
        and temperature, 255–257
    removal, technologies for, 277–281
        air-cooled DX system, 277, 282t
        air-cooled self-contained system, 278, 282t
        ceiling mounted cooling system, 279, 282t
        chilled water system, 280–281, 282t
        glycol-cooled system, 279, 282t
        water-cooled system, 279–280, 282t
    temperature, 253–254
        dew-Point Temperature (DPT), 254
        dry-Bulb Temperature (DBT), 253
        and humidity, 255–257
        wet-bulb temperature (WBT), 254
Hidden requirements, identifying in business, 141
High-level allocation, in IT infrastructure, 661
High-Performance Computing (HPC), 9–10
Historic event analysis, 84
Horizontal distribution area (HDA), 187
Host Bus Adaptor (HBA) devices, 562
Hot aisle containment, 311–312, 312f, 314t, 324
HP, 685
HP BL460c G7, 568, 572f
HP DL385 G7, 568, 569f
    back panel configuration, 569f
    Configuration of, 570f, 571f
HP Integrated-Light-Out (ILO), 560
HP ProLiant Series Rack Servers, 393t
Huawei rack-mounted server, 790–791
Hub, 499–502, 500f